Publisher's Letter

Graham Jones, President

It is official, after over a year in lockdown, people are overwhelmingly seeking to explore and fill their time with memorable experiences, from boating to camping to space travel. In our industry, boating has surpassed milestones never before seen. Recreational boating is seeing record sales numbers, inventory shortages and unprecedented demand. All of this means there is a large influx of new customers entering our waterways and industry.

With a lot of boaters just learning their new vessel or taking to the water on an unknown adventure, it means we will all likely have an encounter with someone just learning the ropes. I encourage everyone who loves boating to think about your first steps on a boat, or the first few months (or even years) when entering this lifestyle. There is a learning curve, mistakes are made and you likely needed help from someone with more experience than you. As boaters, we know it is our job to help one another and I want to reinforce that in today's environment.

At Waterway Guide we are doing our part by focusing on the customer experience through safe and informed boating. We want to keep these new boaters in their boats for a long time, taking them from a hobby to a lifestyle. W... along 75 years' worth of local knowledge on hundreds of destinations, channel information and ports across our waterways is as valuable as it gets, especially for a new boater. Information can instill confidence in any boater to take that trip they never felt was possible, enhance the voyage and hopefully keep a lot of these new boaters around for a while.

The data also shows that many of these new boaters are younger and less experienced. While a positive sign for the future of our industry, Waterway Guide's challenge in today's environment is digital delivery of our content across many devices and platforms. So we continue to innovate. In March of 2021 we launched the new Waterway Guide mobile app for iOS. This is an effort to optimize our planning tools for mobile devices and provide an easy way for boaters to consume our content and interact with it in the same place. The result is a culmination of our popular cruising guides mixed with our expansive map-based planning tool, Waterway Explorer (waterwayguide.com). Please give it a download and let us know your thoughts.

As more boaters splash their boats into our beautiful waterways, our team is standing by and committed to help making the experience of planning and traveling by boat easier, safer and more enjoyable.

Thank you for playing your part in this and we look forward to seeing you on the water!

Graham Jones, President

THE CRUISING AUTHORITY FOR 75 YEARS

WATERWAY GUIDE OFFICES
Corporate/Production Office
16273 General Puller Hwy.
P.O. Box 1125
Deltaville, VA 23043
804-776-8999
804-776-6111 (fax)
www.waterwayguide.com

BOOK SALES
waterwayguide.com/shipstore
800-233-3359

Waterway Guide Media, LLC , the publisher of Waterway Guide (Guide), makes reasonable efforts to ensure the accuracy of the information in this Guide. However, Waterway Guide must rely on others over which it has no control for certain information. In addition, no book or guide is a substitute for good judgment, experience and firsthand knowledge. Therefore, Waterway Guide hereby gives notice that the charts, descriptions, and illustrations in this Guide are not to be used for navigation. The use of any navigational reference or description contained in the Guide is at the user's own risk. Inclusion in the Waterway Guide of marine facilities, services, restaurants and other information is for informational purposes only; no guarantee is provided as to the accuracy or current status of this information, nor does Waterway Guide Media, LLC endorse any of the facilities or services described herein.

Because Waterway Guide Media Group, LLC cannot and does not guarantee or warrant that the information in the Guide is complete or current, Waterway Guide Media Group, LLC disclaims all warranties, express or implied, relating to the information in any manner, including, without limitation, implied warranties of merchantability and fitness for a particular purpose.

Waterway Guide Media Group, LLC shall not be liable to the purchaser or any third party for any loss or injury allegedly caused, in whole or in part, by Waterway Guide Media Group, LLC and/or Waterway Guide (or the information contained therein) or for consequential, exemplary, incidental or special damages. Furthermore, in any event, Waterway Guide Media Group, LLC's liability, if any, shall never exceed the amount paid by the original purchaser for the directory.

To provide the most complete and accurate information, all facilities have been contacted within the past year. Although facility operators supplied this data, we cannot guarantee accuracy or assume responsibility for errors. Entrance and dockside soundings tend to fluctuate. Always approach marinas carefully. Reference numbers on spotting charts indicate marina locations. Aerial photos are for general overview only and are not to be used for navigation.

WATERWAY GUIDE THE CRUISING AUTHORITY

FOUNDED IN 1947

Publisher	**JEFF JONES** jjones@waterwayguide.com
President	**GRAHAM JONES** graham@waterwayguide.com
Editor-in-Chief	**ED TILLETT** etillett@waterwayguide.com
Managing Editor	**JANI PARKER** jparker@waterwayguide.com
Graphic Design/ Production Manager	**SCOTT MCCONNELL** scott@waterwayguide.com
Operations Manager	**HEATHER SADEG** heather@waterwayguide.com
Marketing & Advertising Traffic Manager	**ETHAN JETT** ethan@waterwayguide.com
Book Sales Manager	**LINDA JERNIGAN** linda@waterwayguide.com
Sales & Marketing Manager	**KELLY CROCKETT** kelly@waterwayguide.com
Senior Advisor/ Skipper Bob Editor	**TED STEHLE** tstehle@waterwayguide.com
News Editor	**LISA SUHAY** lisa@waterwayguide.com
Web Master	**MIKE SCHWEFLER**
Office Assistant	**LEON HOLZMAN**

NATIONAL SALES

GRAHAM JONES graham@waterwayguide.com

REGIONAL MARKETING REPRESENTATIVES

KELLY CROCKETT kelly@waterwayguide.com
PETE HUNGERFORD pete@waterwayguide.com
RAY CLARK ray@waterwayguide.com

REGIONAL CRUISING EDITORS

MARK BAKER
SCOTT RICHARD BERG
MICHAEL CAMERATA
MATT & LUCY CLAIBORNE
CAPT. GEORGE & PAT HOSPODAR
MICHAEL O'REILLY & ANN PHILLIPS
MARY & THERON RODRIGUEZ
BOB SHERER (CONTRIBUTING EDITOR)

CUBA CRUISING EDITORS

ADDISON CHAN
NIGEL CALDER (CONTRIBUTING EDITOR)

@Waterway Guide @waterway_guide

Printed in Canada

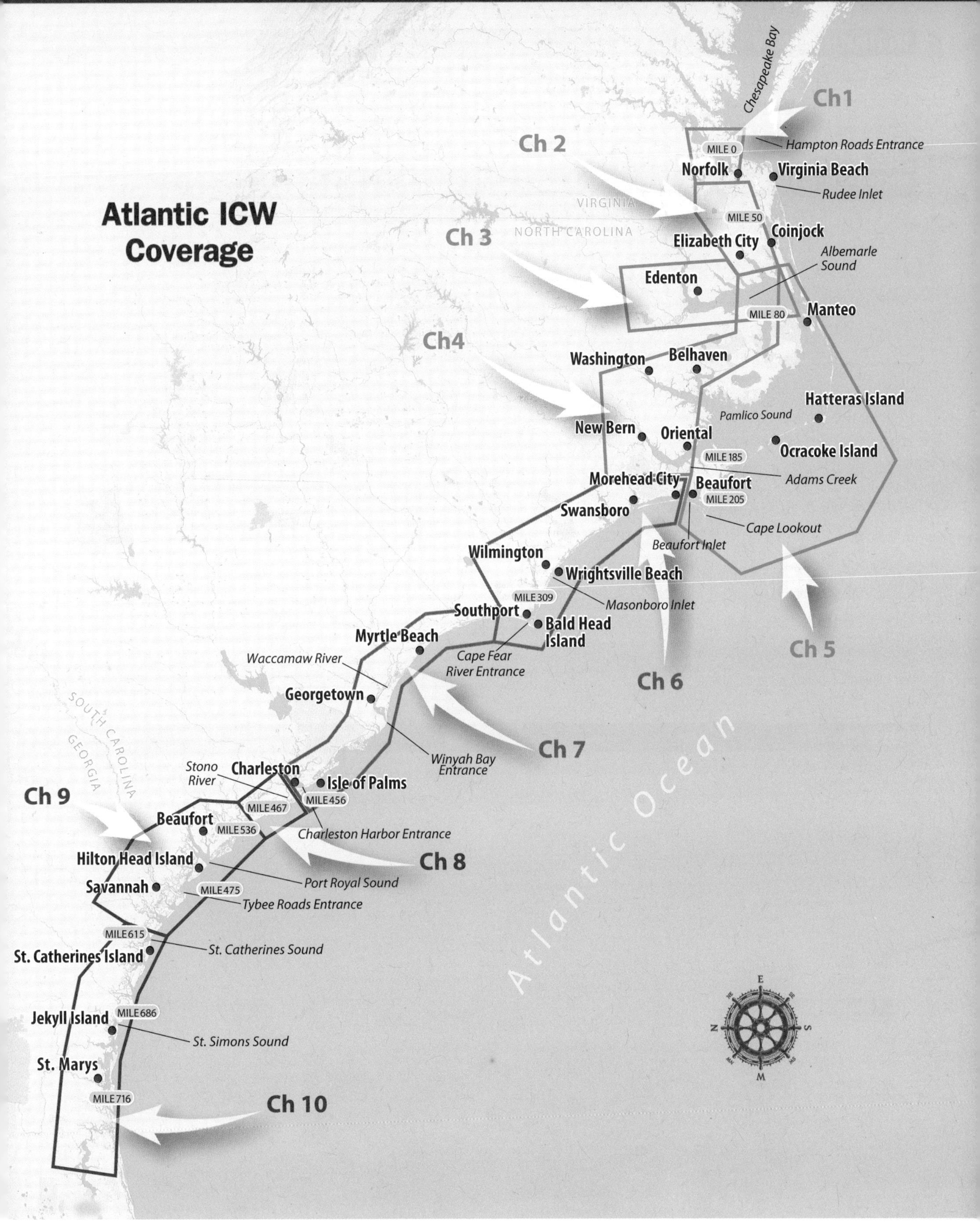

Atlantic ICW Coverage
Chesapeake Bay
Ch1
Ch 2
MILE 0
Hampton Roads Entrance
Norfolk
Virginia Beach
Rudee Inlet
VIRGINIA
NORTH CAROLINA
Ch 3
MILE 50
Coinjock
Elizabeth City
Albemarle Sound
Edenton
MILE 80
Manteo
Ch4
Washington
Belhaven
Hatteras Island
Pamlico Sound
New Bern
Oriental
Ocracoke Island
MILE 185
Morehead City
Beaufort
Adams Creek
MILE 205
Swansboro
Cape Lookout
Beaufort Inlet
Wilmington
Wrightsville Beach
Masonboro Inlet
MILE 309
Southport
Bald Head Island
Myrtle Beach
Cape Fear River Entrance
Ch 5
Ch 6
Waccamaw River
Georgetown
SOUTH CAROLINA
GEORGIA
Ch 7
Winyah Bay Entrance
Stono River
Charleston
Isle of Palms
Ch 9
MILE 467
MILE 456
Beaufort
MILE 536
Charleston Harbor Entrance
Hilton Head Island
Ch 8
Port Royal Sound
Savannah
MILE 475
Tybee Roads Entrance
MILE 615
St. Catherines Island
St. Catherines Sound
Atlantic Ocean
Jekyll Island
MILE 686
St. Simons Sound
St. Marys
MILE 716
Ch 10

INTRODUCTION

SKIPPER'S HANDBOOK

INLETS

Murrells Inlet, SC

HAMPTON ROADS, VA TO THE NEUSE RIVER, NC

Before you can begin your journey down the ICW, you must traverse the 10-mile stretch through the Hampton Roads area. This is the home to the world's largest naval base and is one of the busiest harbors on the ICW. The "official" beginning of the ICW is at Mile Zero in Norfolk, VA. At Mile 7.3 you must choose one of two very different routes south: the Albemarle-Chesapeake Canal or the Dismal Swamp Canal. The two routes converge on the southern side of the Albemarle Sound. North Carolina's sounds (Inner Banks) and the Outer Banks are rewarding side trips and are unlike any other regions along the Mid-Atlantic coast. The barrier islands extend in a crescent from the Virginia state line, then swing back at Cape Hatteras.

BEAUFORT, NC TO ISLE OF PALMS, SC

After passing through the sister cities of Beaufort and Morehead City (Mile 205), the ICW follows the open Bogue Sound and New and Cape Fear Rivers to an area known as "The Ditch." The dredged channel cuts through low marshy islets, across several small rivers and finally through a long land cut that ends in Charleston Harbor. This is where the Cooper and Ashley Rivers meet and is a favorite destination for cruisers.

CHARLESTON, SC TO ST. MARYS, GA

It's 244 miles along the ICW from Charleston to Florida's state line. During this stretch of the ICW, you will wend your way across wide river mouths, through a series of sounds and past numerous coastal inlets. The banks are lined with woods, moss-covered live oaks and marshland. You may even glimpse the ocean. When you leave Georgia, you will notice a change from open sounds and rivers to creeks connected by narrow land cuts.

INDEXES

Meet Our Cruising Editors

Waterway Guide's on-the-water Cruising Editors bring us firsthand information about the navigation, news and trends along the waterways we cover. In addition to contributing to the annual guide, they provide daily updates on the Waterway Explorer at www.waterwayguide.com. We are pleased to introduce you to our crew.

Mark Baker and his partner, Ann, have been avid "part-time liveaboards" since purchasing their 37-foot, shoal-draft, racer/cruiser 12 years ago. Since that time they have put over 10,000 nautical miles under the keel and have personally made all repairs and upgrades to their sailboat. Favorite sailing grounds include Penobscot Bay, ME; Narragansett Bay, RI; The Florida Keys; The Bahamas; and beautiful Florida Bay and The Everglades. They enjoy meeting new folks in the towns and cities along the way and also seeking out secluded spots to enjoy the natural world and to experience some good ol' gunkholing. Ann is a talented birdwatcher and Mark enjoys underwater photography and the study of geology. As former teachers, both are practitioners of lifelong learning.

Scott Richard Berg is a lifelong boater and full-time cruiser with five decades of experience on a range of vessels from el Toro prams to a 135-foot Baltic Trader. He operated CHARDONNAY BOATWORKS, a full service marine repair company, for many years from a series of cruising sailboats (all named *CHARDONNAY*). A full-time delivery captain, Scott holds a 100-ton Masters License, is a past president of the Seven Seas Cruising Association, an ABYC Certified Master Technician and holds an Amateur Extra Class radio license. Scott is once again cruising the east coast of the U.S. after spending several years at the Capital Yacht Club in Washington, DC.

Michael Camarata started sailing in the early 1970s when he bought a car-top sailboat with his future wife, Carol Zipke. Within a few years they had a sailing dinghy and had TWO sails to deal with! Boats got larger and more complicated in the following decades. They now live aboard a 44-foot catamaran, *Infinite Improbability*, which is likely their last upgrade. Originally they cruised Long Island Sound out to Nantucket and north of the Cape Cod Canal but now, having sold all their "dirt-based" property, cruise from southern New England to the Florida Keys with the seasons, mostly via the ICW. They moor near the Mystic, CT, area in the summer and Marathon, FL, in the winter.

Capts. Matt & Lucy Claiborne are full-time cruising sailors and storytellers. After college, Matt and Lucy lived on a 32-foot sailboat in the Florida Keys. Even while working in the "real-world" as professors at a university, they continued cruising and camping with a trailerable 21-foot cuddy cabin. In 2014, they cast off on a full-time sailing adventure on a 38-foot Lagoon catamaran. Both Matt and Lucy have USCG Master and FAA pilot licenses. They are full-time digital nomads who work from their boat. Their favorite offices are quiet anchorages; their favorite coworkers are dolphins and pelicans. Matt and Lucy are passionate about education and helping new boaters fulfill their cruising dreams. In 2019, they purchased their "forever dream boat"–a Cabo Rico 38 named *Dulcinea*. After a year outfitting for off-the-grid living and long-distance cruising, you'll now find them cruising Chesapeake Bay, the ICW, Bahamas and beyond with their adventure dog, Chelsea.

Capt. George & Patricia Hospodar have been boaters for over 45 years and have cruised more than 50,000 miles together aboard two sailboats and their 48-foot Symbol motor yacht, *Reflection*. George has been a 100-ton licensed U.S. Coast Guard Captain for 30 years. He and Pat are proud Platinum Loopers, lifetime members of the America's Great Loop Cruisers' Association and New Jersey Harbor Hosts. Together they have authored two popular boating books: "Reflection on America's Great Loop" and "The Great Loop Experience from Concept to Completion" as well as serving as Cruising Editors for Waterway Guide publications. They have also been featured speakers at many boat shows, TrawlerFests and other nautical events.

Michael O'Reilly & Ann Phillips came to sailing by first messing about with canoes and kayaks while living on the Canadian shore of Lake Superior. Sailing replaced the smaller boats and over the last 15-plus years they have enjoyed many extended summer cruises. After completing a cruise through four of the five Great Lakes, they spent a few years exploring Lake Ontario and the Thousand Islands. One season was spent traveling the St. Lawrence River all the way to Newfoundland, which is the current "home" for their boat. Mike is a long-time freelance journalist, writing mostly about the sciences. With the transition to this new watery life, Mike now spends most of his work time writing about traveling, destinations and cruising. Ann is an accomplished photographer. Together they are chronicling their life afloat.

Mary & Tharon Rodriguez are Cruising Editors for the fresh waters of Lake Michigan and Lake Huron. They have been sailing for under a decade but have sailed Michigan to the Bahamas and everything in between. Their sailing vessel is *Tipsy Gypsy*, a 36-foot Nonsuch docked in their home port of Muskegon, MI. They are both digital nomads, working and cruising on a regular basis. They are based back in Michigan after multiple years of living aboard on the east coast. If you see them around, be sure to say hi! They are fun-loving, adventure-seeking, mid-westerners with a whole lot to offer our team. Learn more about these young cruisers at www.maryandtharon.com

Bob & Ann Sherer started sailing in 1985 with charters in Maine, Florida and the Caribbean followed by their first sailboat in 1986 which then lead to a 38-foot Ericson, followed by their present boat, a 42-foot Beneteau 423 in 2004. They started their yearly cruises on the ICW from New York to Key West in 2010 and Bob became known as Bob423, the person to follow for advice navigating through the many shoals of the ICW. He published his first *ICW Cruising Guide* in 2015 and has published an updated edition every year. The guide not only includes charts to avoid groundings but also tips learned from years of boating and a review of basic and advanced topics covering the ICW and is available on Amazon.com in paperback and eBook formats.

In 2018, Bob joined Waterway Guide as an on-the-water Editor, specializing in the Atlantic ICW and maintaining the Waterway Guide alerts for the ICW. That same year, Bob started the ICW Cruising Guide Facebook page, which has grown to over 13,500 members. His most recent efforts include the publishing of Bob423 Tracks in GPX format for free downloading, which follow the deep-water path around the shoals of the ICW to enable a less stressful cruise in staying out of the mud. He is routinely consulted by NOAA, the USACE, and the Coast Guard on matters affecting the boating public. Bob and Ann reside 9 months of the year aboard their latest boat, a 42-foot Beneteau 423 sailboat, with their fearless dog, Hoolie, a Brittany.

Addison Chan is an experienced software entrepreneur, a world traveler and a committed sailing cruiser. He is the founder of Land and Sea Software Corp. which has engineered a revolutionary platform to produce mobile friendly, piracy-resistant, interactive content for traditional publishers. Waterway Guide Media is using the platform to provide its users with an enhanced digital experience that always delivers the most currently available information to mobile devices.

Addison and his wife, Pat, have traveled extensively through Cuba, Mexico and the Bahamas on their 42-foot Catalina sailboat, acquiring deep local knowledge over the years. The depth of his local knowledge and understanding of local culture is evident in his work as the coauthor of *Waterway Guide Cuba,* which is the gold standard of cruising guides for Cuba. His latest project has the working title of "A Handbook for Comfortable Cruising in The Bahamas" which will be representative of a new breed of interactive cruising guides. He is active within the cruising community and maintains the popular Cuba, Land and Sea and Bahamas Land and Sea groups on Facebook.

Other Contributors

Waterway Guide gathers information and photos from a variety of sources, including boaters, marinas, communities and tourism divisions. We would like to thank everyone who contributed to this edition.

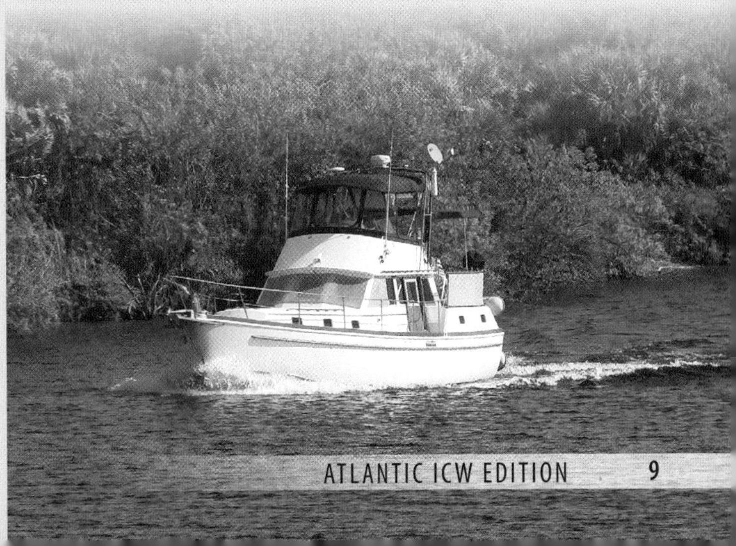

About Our NOAA Chart Extracts

The U.S. Department of Commerce National Oceanic and Atmospheric Administration (NOAA) has advanced its plan of phasing out the updating and printing of nautical charts effective February 2021. Under the new practice NOAA will revise and refresh vector data that will be available to Electronic Navigational Charts (ENC) platforms only. The standardized data can be used by chart plotters and other map applications for creating visual displays of depths, aids to navigation (ATONS), points of interest and extensive details related to navigation, tides, shorelines, hazards and more. Updating of paper charts by NOAA will conclude in 2025, as will chart number references. For those who want printed outputs of nautical charts at various scales for specific geographical areas, the charts may still be obtained using several methods and suppliers. Visit www.noaa.gov for details.

Waterway Guide's objective is to offer the most up-to-date information available through use of NOAA's data superimposed on appropriate base maps. Because the printed charts from NOAA that have served us over the years are no longer supported, and have been supplanted by a new method of management and distribution of information, the chart extracts in this publication have been designed to address our distinctive editorial objectives.

Waterway Guide participated in workshops and seminars to develop a working relationship with NOAA and arrived at solutions for displaying acceptable levels of navigation and situational awareness in our various media platforms. Using NOAA-supplied vector data superimposed on geographically accurate base maps that were generated and supplied by Aqua Map, our publications now contain uncomplicated extracts of the geographical areas described in the accompanying text and tables throughout our guidebooks. The chartlets, as we identify them, contain shorelines, ATONS, water depths, landmarks, street and city names when available, and locations of marinas, all at sufficient levels of detail and scale for ease of interpretation. The chartlets are provided for reference only and not to be used for navigation.

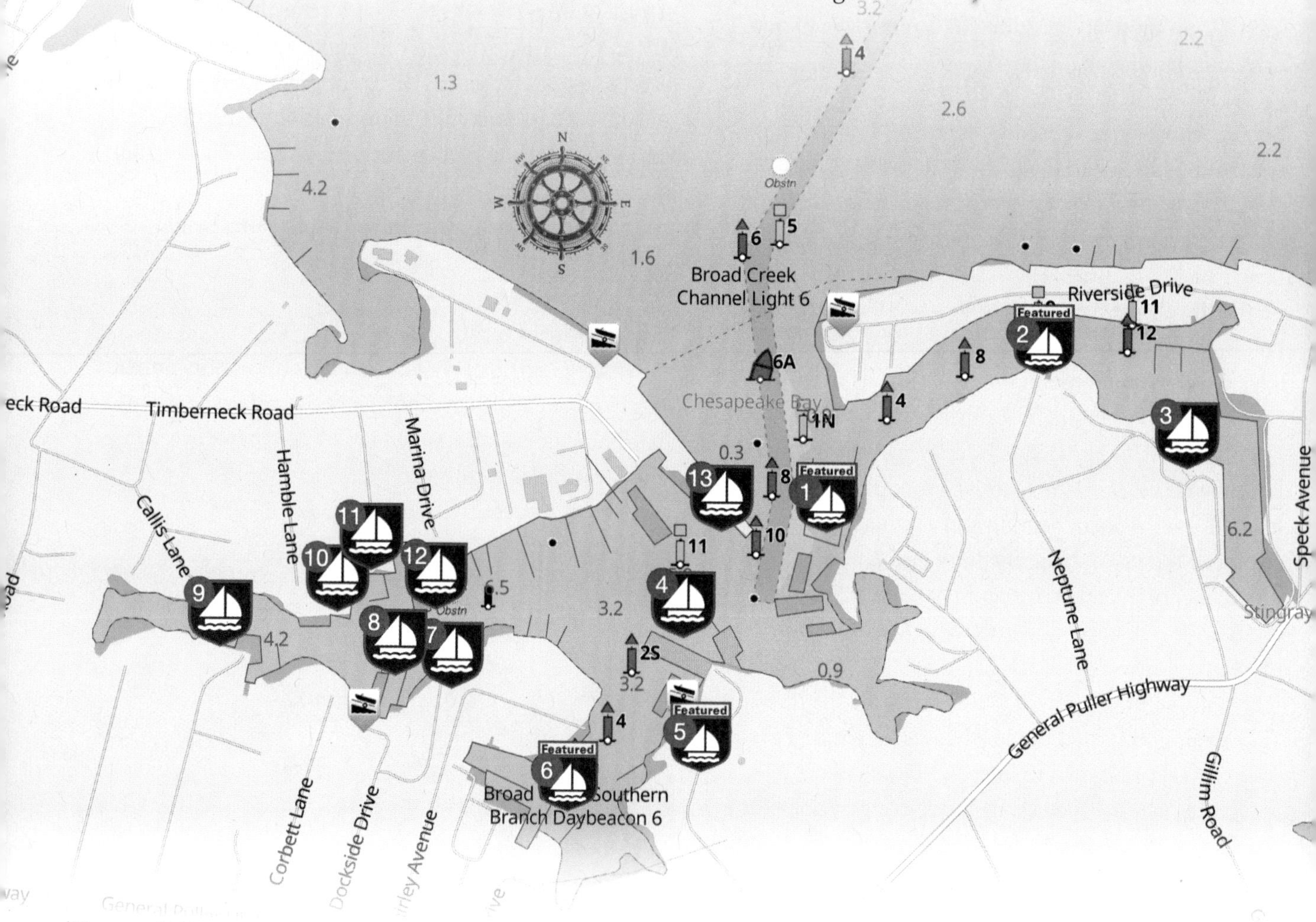

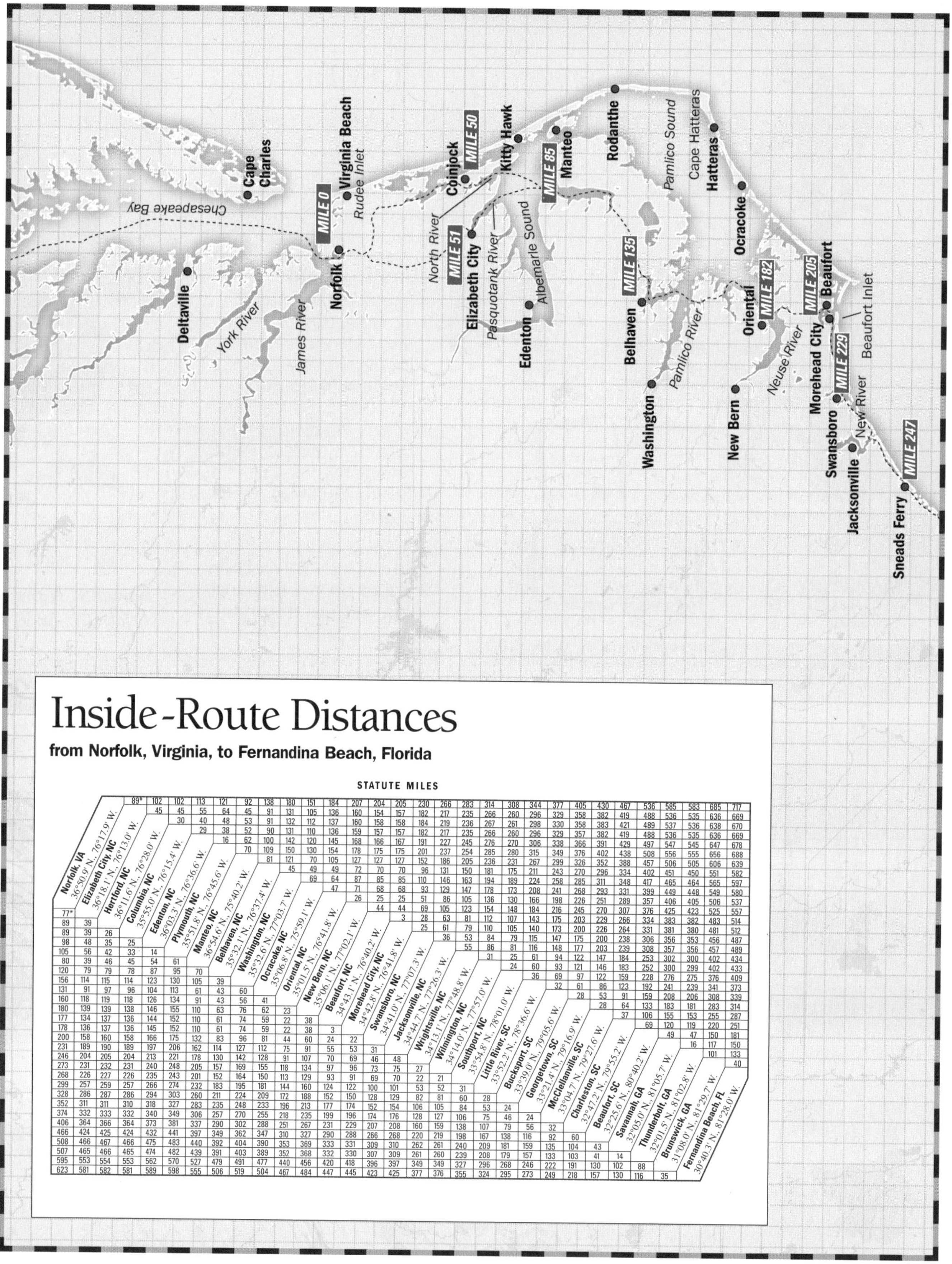

Inside-Route Distances

from Norfolk, Virginia, to Fernandina Beach, Florida

STATUTE MILES

	Elizabeth City, NC	Hertford, NC	Columbia, NC	Edenton, NC	Plymouth, NC	Manteo, NC	Belhaven, NC	Washington, NC	Ocracoke, NC	Oriental, NC	New Bern, NC	Beaufort, NC	Morehead City, NC	Swansboro, NC	Jacksonville, NC	Wrightsville, NC	Wilmington, NC	Southport, NC	Little River, SC	Bucksport, SC	Georgetown, SC	McClellanville, SC	Charleston, SC	Beaufort, SC	Savannah, GA	Thunderbolt, GA	Brunswick, GA	Fernandina Beach, FL
Norfolk, VA 36°50.9' N., 76°17.9' W.	89*	102	102	113	121	92	138	180	151	184	207	204	205	230	266	283	314	308	344	377	405	430	467	536	585	583	685	717
Elizabeth City, NC 36°18.1' N., 76°13.0' W.		45	45	55	64	45	91	131	105	136	160	154	157	182	217	235	266	260	296	329	358	382	419	488	536	535	636	669
Hertford, NC 36°11.6' N., 76°28.0' W.			30	40	48	53	91	132	112	137	160	158	158	184	219	236	267	261	298	330	358	383	421	489	537	536	638	670
Columbia, NC 35°55.0' N., 76°15.4' W.				29	38	52	90	131	110	136	159	157	157	182	217	235	266	260	296	329	357	382	419	488	536	535	636	669
Edenton, NC 36°03.3' N., 76°36.6' W.					16	62	100	142	120	145	168	166	167	191	227	245	276	270	306	338	366	391	429	497	547	545	647	678
Plymouth, NC 35°51.8' N., 76°45.6' W.						70	109	150	130	154	178	175	175	201	237	254	285	280	315	349	376	402	438	508	556	555	656	688
Manteo, NC 36°54.6' N., 75°40.2' W.							81	121	70	105	127	127	127	152	186	205	236	231	267	299	326	352	388	457	506	505	606	639
Belhaven, NC 35°32.1' N., 76°37.4' W.								45	49	49	72	70	70	96	131	150	181	175	211	243	270	296	334	402	451	450	551	582
Washington, NC 35°32.6' N., 77°03.7' W.									69	64	87	85	85	110	146	163	194	189	224	258	285	311	348	417	465	464	565	597
Ocracoke, NC 35°06.8' N., 75°59.1' W.										47	71	68	68	93	129	147	178	173	208	241	268	293	331	399	449	448	549	580
Oriental, NC 35°01.5' N., 76°41.8' W.											26	25	25	51	86	105	136	130	166	198	226	251	289	357	406	405	506	537
New Bern, NC 35°06.1' N., 77°02.1' W.												44	44	69	105	123	154	148	184	216	245	270	307	376	425	423	525	557
Beaufort, NC 34°43.1' N., 76°40.2' W.													3	28	63	81	112	107	143	175	203	229	266	334	383	382	483	514
Morehead City, NC 34°42.8' N., 76°41.8' W.														25	61	79	110	105	140	173	200	226	264	331	381	380	481	512
Swansboro, NC 34°41.0' N., 77°07.3' W.															36	53	84	79	115	147	175	200	238	306	356	353	456	487
Jacksonville, NC 34°44.7' N., 77°26.3' W.																55	86	81	116	148	177	203	239	308	357	356	457	489
Wrightsville, NC 34°13.1' N., 77°48.8' W.																	31	25	61	94	122	147	184	253	302	300	402	434
Wilmington, NC 34°14.0' N., 77°57.0' W.																		24	60	93	121	146	183	252	300	299	402	433
Southport, NC 33°54.8' N., 78°01.0' W.																			36	69	97	122	159	228	276	275	376	409
Little River, SC 33°52.2' N., 78°36.6' W.																				32	61	86	123	192	241	239	341	373
Bucksport, SC 33°39.0' N., 79°05.6' W.																					28	53	91	159	208	206	308	339
Georgetown, SC 33°21.4' N., 79°16.9' W.																						28	64	133	183	181	283	314
McClellanville, SC 33°04.7' N., 79°27.6' W.																							37	106	155	153	255	287
Charleston, SC 32°47.2' N., 79°55.2' W.																								69	120	119	220	251
Beaufort, SC 32°25.6' N., 80°40.2' W.																									49	47	150	181
Savannah, GA 32°05.0' N., 81°05.7' W.																										16	117	150
Thunderbolt, GA 32°01.5' N., 81°02.8' W.																											101	133
Brunswick, GA 31°08.0' N., 81°29.7' W.																												40

	Norfolk, VA	Elizabeth City, NC	Hertford, NC	Columbia, NC	Edenton, NC	Plymouth, NC	Manteo, NC	Belhaven, NC	Washington, NC	Ocracoke, NC	Oriental, NC	New Bern, NC	Beaufort, NC	Morehead City, NC	Swansboro, NC	Jacksonville, NC	Wrightsville, NC	Wilmington, NC	Southport, NC	Little River, SC	Bucksport, SC	Georgetown, SC	McClellanville, SC	Charleston, SC	Beaufort, SC	Savannah, GA	Thunderbolt, GA	Brunswick, GA
Elizabeth City, NC	77*																											
Hertford, NC	89	39																										
Columbia, NC	89	39	26																									
Edenton, NC	98	48	35	25																								
Plymouth, NC	105	56	42	33	14																							
Manteo, NC	80	39	46	45	54	61																						
Belhaven, NC	120	79	79	78	87	95	70																					
Washington, NC	156	114	115	114	123	130	105	39																				
Ocracoke, NC	131	91	97	96	104	113	61	43	60																			
Oriental, NC	160	118	119	118	126	134	91	43	56	41																		
New Bern, NC	180	139	139	138	146	155	110	63	76	62	23																	
Beaufort, NC	177	134	137	136	144	152	110	61	74	59	22	38																
Morehead City, NC	178	136	137	136	145	152	110	61	74	59	22	38	3															
Swansboro, NC	200	158	160	158	166	175	132	83	96	81	44	60	24	22														
Jacksonville, NC	231	189	190	189	197	206	162	114	127	112	75	91	55	53	31													
Wrightsville, NC	246	204	205	204	213	221	178	130	142	128	91	107	70	69	46	48												
Wilmington, NC	273	231	232	231	240	248	205	157	169	155	118	134	97	96	73	75	27											
Southport, NC	268	226	227	226	235	243	201	152	164	150	113	129	93	91	69	70	22	21										
Little River, SC	299	257	259	257	266	274	232	183	195	181	144	160	124	122	100	101	53	52	31									
Bucksport, SC	328	286	287	286	294	303	260	211	224	209	172	188	152	150	128	129	82	81	60	28								
Georgetown, SC	352	311	311	310	318	327	283	235	248	233	196	213	177	174	152	154	106	105	84	53	24							
McClellanville, SC	374	332	333	332	340	349	306	257	270	255	218	235	199	196	174	176	128	127	106	75	46	24						
Charleston, SC	406	364	366	364	373	381	337	290	302	288	251	267	231	229	207	208	160	159	138	107	79	56	32					
Beaufort, SC	466	424	425	424	432	441	397	349	362	347	310	327	290	288	266	268	220	219	198	167	138	116	92	60				
Savannah, GA	508	466	467	466	475	483	440	392	404	390	353	369	333	331	309	310	262	261	240	209	181	159	135	104	43			
Thunderbolt, GA	507	465	466	465	474	482	439	391	403	389	352	368	332	330	307	309	261	260	239	208	179	157	133	103	41	14		
Brunswick, GA	595	553	554	553	562	570	527	479	491	477	440	456	420	418	396	397	349	349	327	296	268	246	222	191	130	102	88	
Fernandina Beach, FL 30°40.3' N., 81°28.0' W.	623	581	582	581	589	598	555	506	519	504	467	484	447	445	423	425	377	376	355	324	295	273	249	218	157	130	116	35

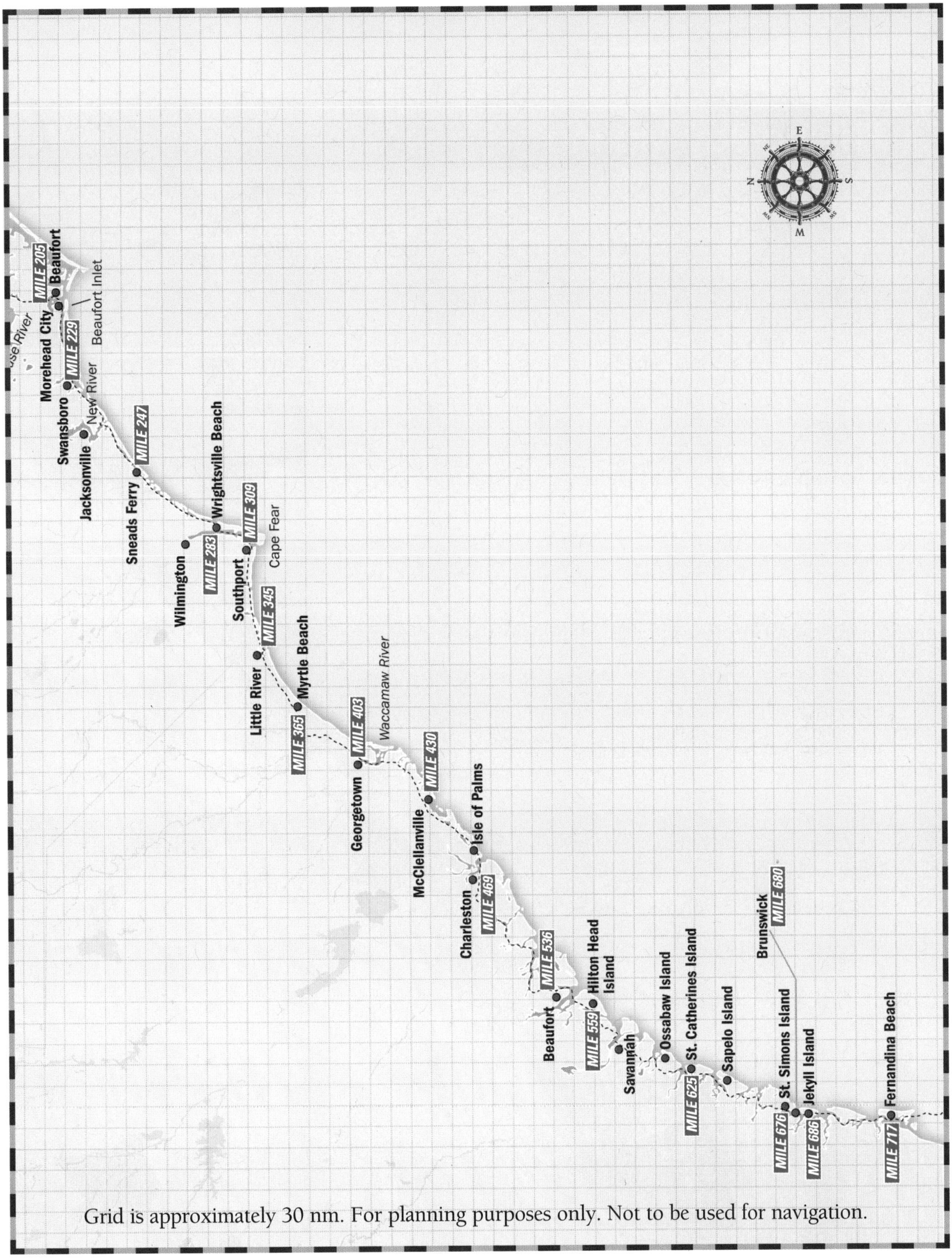

Grid is approximately 30 nm. For planning purposes only. Not to be used for navigation.

Fishing Bay Marina

DELTAVILLE, VIRGINIA

519 Deagle
Deltaville, VA 23
Phone: (804) 776-6
Fax: (804) 776-8
info@fishingbay.c

On the beautiful deep waters of Fishing Bay at the mouth of the Piankatank River, Fishing Bay Marina is located in Deltaville, Virginia. The marina offers slip holders and transients a secure, comfortable and amenity-filled facility, with easy access to the Chesapeake Bay and the Piankatank River. It is nicely sheltered by Stove Point Neck.

- Transient Slips accommodating vessels larger than 200ft.
- Approach/Dockside Depth: 18 / 15 ft.
- Tide Range: 1.5 ft.
- Fuel Dock with ValvTect Marine Fuel – gas and diesel (including high-speed)
- Pump-out and water services
- Virginia Clean Marina
- Olympic size swimming pool
- Clean, air-conditioned bathhouses
- Laundry washer and dryer
- Captain's Lounge
- Ice, Grills, and Bicycles
- FREE WiFi High-Speed Internet
- Courtesy Car
- Horseshoe Pits & Volleyball Court
- Close proximity to town

VIRGINIA CLEAN MARINA

804-776-6800 • www.fishingbay.com

SKIPPER'S HANDBOOK

Port Security

The U.S. Coast Guard and Customs and Border Patrol–both components of the Department of Homeland Security–handle port security in the United States. Local law enforcement agencies and the FBI also have a role in port security at the local and regional level. Each year more than 11 million maritime containers arrive at our seaports. At land borders, another 11 million arrive by truck and 2.7 million by rail. Homeland Security is responsible for knowing what is inside those containers, whether it poses a risk to the American people and ensuring that all proper revenues are collected.

As an example, one in five food items is now imported. American consumers demand fresh limes and blueberries all year round and, as a result, during the winter months in the U.S. nearly 80 percent of the fresh fruits and vegetables on our tables come from other countries. With the ever-increasing amount of trade, the agricultural risks to the United States grow. The threat to crops and livestock is real.

In response to this threat and others, the U.S. Coast Guard has established "protection zones" around all U.S. Navy vessels, tank vessels and large-capacity cruise vessels, even when underway. U.S. Navy bases, U.S. Coast Guard bases and some shoreside facilities such as nuclear power plants are also in protection zones. Non-military vessels (this means YOU) are not allowed within 100 yards of these protection zones. To do so can rack up serious civil penalties and even imprisonment.

These protection zones vary from port to port and from facility to facility but ignorance of the protection zones is not a viable excuse. Having said that, law-abiding boaters sometimes find themselves unable to comply with the letter of the law without hitting a jetty, for example. In such cases, common sense and good communication should prevail.

America's Waterway Watch Program

Government officials view the recreational boating community as an ally. We can do our part (and perhaps stave off more stringent regulations and surveillance measures) by becoming familiar with the Coast Guard's America's Waterway Watch program. Think of it as a neighborhood watch program for the waterways.

It is not the intent of America's Waterway Watch to spread paranoia or to encourage spying on one another and it is not a surveillance program; it is instead a simple deterrent to potential terrorist activity. The purpose of the program is to allow boaters and others who spend time along the water to help the authorities counter crime and terrorism. To report suspicious behavior, call the National Response Center at 877-249-2824 (877-24WATCH). For immediate danger to life or property, call 911 or contact the U.S. Coast Guard on Marine VHF Channel 16.

Staying safe and responsible requires a little forethought and vigilance on your part. Following the steps outlined below will help ensure a trouble-free journey and keep you and your crew out of the headlines.

Be Prepared

- Before you leave, check the current charts for the area in which you will be traveling and identify any security areas. Security zones are highlighted and outlined in magenta with special notes regarding the specific regulations pertaining to that area.
- Check the latest *Local Notice to Mariners* (available online at www.navcen.uscg and posted at some marinas) and identify any potential security areas that may not be shown on the chart.
- Prior to your departure, listen to VHF Channel 16 for any Sécurité alerts from the Coast Guard (departing cruise ships, U.S. Navy vessels, fuel tankers, etc.) for the area you will be cruising.
- Talk to other boaters in your anchorage or marina about the areas where you will be traveling. They may have tips and suggestions on potential security zones or special areas they may have encountered along the way.

Stay Alert While Underway

- Mind the outlined magenta security areas noted on your charts.
- Look for vessels with blue or red warning lights in port areas and, if approached, listen carefully and strictly obey all instructions given to you.
- Keep your VHF radio switched to VHF Channel 16 and keep your ears tuned for bulletins, updates and possible requests for communication.
- Avoid commercial port operation areas, especially those that involve military, cruise line or petroleum facilities. Observe and avoid other restricted areas near power plants, national monuments, etc.
- If you need to pass within 100 yards of a U.S. Navy vessel for safe passage, you must contact the U.S. Navy vessel or the Coast Guard escort vessel on VHF Channel 16 to let them know your intentions.
- We advise that if government security or the U.S. Coast Guard hails you, do exactly what they say, regardless of whether or not you feel their instructions have merit.

Additional Resources
Atlantic Intracoastal Waterway Association: www.atlanticintracoastal.org.
America's Waterway Watch: www.americaswaterwaywatch.org
Department of Homeland Security: www.dhs.gov
U.S. Customs and Border Protection: www.cbp.gov

Customs Reporting Procedures

Operators of small pleasure vessels, arriving in the U.S. from a foreign port are required to report their arrival to Customs and Border Patrol (CBP) immediately. The master of the vessel reports their arrival at the nearest Customs facility or other designated location. These reports are tracked in the Pleasure Boat Reporting System. An application to lawfully enter the U.S. must be made in person to a CBP officer at a U.S. port-of-entry when the port is open for inspection.

CBP has designated specific reporting locations within the Field Offices that are staffed during boating season for pleasure boats to report their arrival and be inspected by CBP. The master of the boat must report to CBP telephonically and be directed to the nearest Port of Entry to satisfy the face-to-face requirement, or report to the nearest designated reporting location, along with the boat's passengers for inspection.

You may be required to rent a car or take a cab to the nearest airport or federal office several miles away for the inspection. These offices are often closed on weekends. If your arrival is after working hours, you are required to stay on board and clear in the next morning. You must, however, clear in within 24 hours of your arrival. Everyone on board, regardless of nationality, has to report in person. U.S. nationals must take their passports or passport cards. All non-U.S. Nationals should take their passports with valid visas and a Green Card, if held. Take your boat papers, either U.S. documentation or state registration with state decal number. You should also present a list of firearms and ammunition on board.

Clearing In with the ROAM App

Travelers arriving by boat into many popular U.S. ports can check into the country on their phones or tablets. The Reporting Offsite Arrival–Mobile (ROAM) app is the official replacement for the Local Boater Option (LBO) and Small Vessel Reporting System (SVRS) programs that have been used over the years. These programs required an initial interview to get in but usually resulted in a quick phone call instead of a face-to-face meeting to re-enter the U.S.

If you have a www.Login.gov account, you can log into the app immediately. If you need a password, the app directs you to the website. Then it walks you through the steps, including entering the specifics for each person on board and for your vessel. Once you've entered all of the details and submitted it for a review, an officer may initiate a video call to discuss the trip or to ask any necessary questions. All of this happens directly inside the app. Of course, there are still instances where in-person reporting is required. If you require an I-94, need to pay customs fees or duties, or need to obtain a cruising permit, you will still need to check in in-person. Boaters are still required to have a current fee decal onboard.

Now that the app has been implemented on a larger scale, travelers entering by boat in the Great Lakes; most of the East Coast (Delaware to Florida); Texas and San Diego, CA; and the U.S. territories in the Caribbean can use the app. New locations are continually being added, and because the program is new, it's probably a good idea to call your port of arrival to ensure they are using the ROAM app.

To download the ROAM app, just search the Apple App Store or the Google Play Store on your device. For more information, visit the CBP website or contact the CBP office at your port of arrival.

Additional Resources
U.S. Customs and Border Control: www.cbp.gov/travel/pleasure-boats-private-flyers
Designated Port of Entry (Key West): 301 Simonton St., Ste. 20, 305-296-5411

Picking an Anchorage (excerpt)

We all know that unless it is an emergency, in addition to being verboten, it's just plain common sense and courteous to avoid encroaching on or anchoring in a marked channel, or in a location that inhibits a boat's access to or from a slip, mooring, boatyard, or marina, or that interferes with another anchored vessel. Otherwise, just about any other location is fair game, but there are a few prerequisites that should be met in order to qualify it as an acceptable anchorage.

First, there's a minimum acceptable depth of water, which is determined by your boat's draft, plus any additional distance the tide will drop, plus another foot or two–just in case. In dam controlled waterways, the height of the water level above normal pool should also be considered, as the elevated pool level can be lowered back to normal pool without notice, often quickly–think hours.

Also, the wind, depending on its direction can blow water out, anywhere from a few feet in gale force conditions, to ten feet or more in storms or hurricane force winds. Water levels can also become lower than normal when:: the moon is in perigee, or during seiches, spring tides, and winter solstice. Neglecting these influences could leave the boat bottoming out, aground, or with too little water to get over a bar.

The amount of rode that you can deploy establishes the maximum depth in which you can anchor. If you're anchoring to 5:1 scope, then one fifth the length of your rode is the maximum depth where you can set your anchor; however, in demanding conditions you may need to use 10:1 scope; if so, one tenth the length of your rode would be the maximum depth where you'd want to set your anchor.

Fetch–the distance that the wind can blow over the water without obstruction–can also be a factor when choosing an anchorage, as it can affect comfort. The greater the fetch, the bigger the seas or waves, the more uncomfortable the boat's motion. Our goal is to try to anchor where the fetch is less than a few hundred yards, as beyond this, wave action becomes livelier.

It's prudent to enter unfamiliar anchorages slowly, remaining alert to potential hazards, not just below the surface, but overhead, too–you want enough clearance to prevent snagging bridges, tree limbs, or other dangers, and with power lines, to prevent arcing.

If obstructions are a concern or soundings reveal questionable depths, not only where the boat will initially be anchored, but later where the boat might swing if wind or current shifts direction or strength, then relocate the anchor, or set out an additional anchor or two in a manner that would keep the boat away from any danger.

And keep in mind that your anchor must be compatible with the type of seabed in which you will be anchoring, as well as sized for the wind speed and seas that you will encounter.

Cruising guides are a great resource for identifying anchorages, but if you keep the above guidelines in mind, you just might discover many others, perhaps some that are picturesque, others offering solitude... maybe both.

Rudy and Jill Sechez are the authors of "ANCHORING–A Ground Tackler's Apprentice." To read more, order a copy at www.waterwayguide.com or call 800-233-3359. Rudy and Jill are Trawler Training and Anchoring Consultants, providing one-on-one onboard sessions, consultations, and group seminars. They are also available to talk to groups and clubs. To arrange to have them speak to your organization, contact them at rudyandjill@yahoo.com.

VHF Communications

Skippers traveling the U.S. inland waterways use their VHF radios almost every day to contact other vessels and bridgetenders, make reservations at marinas, arrange to pass other vessels safely and conduct other business. Waterway Guide has put together the following information to help remove any confusion as to what frequency should be dialed in to call bridges, marinas, commercial ships or your friend anchored down the creek.

Remember to use low power (1 watt) for your radio transmission whenever possible. If you are within a couple of miles of the responding station (bridge, marina or other craft), there is no need to broadcast at 25 watts and disturb the transmissions of others 25 miles away.

Channel Usage Tips

- VHF Channel 16 (156.8 MHz) is by far the most important frequency on the VHF-FM band. VHF Channel 16 is the international distress, safety and calling frequency.
- If you have a VHF radio on your boat, Federal Communications Commission (FCC) regulations require that you maintain a watch on either VHF Channel 09 or 16 whenever you are underway and the radio is not being used to communicate on another channel. Since the Coast Guard does not have the capability of announcing an urgent marine information broadcast or weather warning on VHF Channel 09, it recommends that boaters remain tuned to and use VHF Channel 16.
- Recreational craft typically communicate on VHF Channels 68, 69, 71, 72 or 78A. Whenever possible, avoid calling on VHF Channel 16 altogether by prearranging initial contact directly on one of these channels. No transmissions should last longer than 3 minutes.
- The Coast Guard's main working VHF Channel is 22A and both emergency and non-emergency calls generally are switched there to keep VHF Channel 16 clear. Calling the Coast Guard for a radio check on VHF Channel 16 is prohibited.
- Radio-equipped bridges on the Atlantic ICW use VHF Channel 09 with a few exceptions.
- The Bridge-to-Bridge Radio Telephone Act requires many commercial vessels, including dredges and tugboats, to monitor VHF Channel 13. VHF Channel 13 is also the frequency used by bridges in several states.

Distress Calls

MAYDAY: The distress signal "MAYDAY" is used to indicate that a vessel is threatened by grave and imminent danger and requests immediate assistance.

PAN PAN: The urgency signal "PAN PAN" is used when the safety of the ship or person is in jeopardy.

SÉCURITÉ: The safety signal "SÉCURITÉ" is used for messages about the safety of navigation or important weather warnings.

VHF Channel 16 is the distress call frequency. The codeword "MAYDAY" is the international alert signal of a life-threatening situation at sea. After a MAYDAY message is broadcast, VHF Channel 16 must be kept free of all traffic, other than those directly involved in the rescue situation, until the rescue has been completed.

If you hear a MAYDAY message and no one else is responding, it is your duty to step in to answer the call, relay it to the nearest rescue organization and get to the scene to help. Remember, a MAYDAY distress call can only be used when life is threatened. For example, if you have run on the rocks but no one is going to lose their life, that is NOT a MAYDAY situation.

Note: The Coast Guard has asked the FCC to eliminate provisions for using VHF Channel 09 as an alternative calling frequency to VHF Channel 16 when it eliminates watch-keeping on VHF Channel 16 by compulsory-equipped vessels. Stay tuned for updates.

How to Make a Distress Call

MAYDAY! MAYDAY! MAYDAY!

This is: Give your vessel name and call sign.

Our position is: Read it off the GPS or give it as something like "2 miles southwest of Royal Island." (Your rescuers must be able to find you!)

We are: Describe what's happening (e.g., on fire/hit a reef/sinking).

We have: Report how many people are on board.

At this time we are: Say what you're doing about the crisis (e.g., standing by/abandoning ship).

For identification we are: Describe your boat type, length, color, etc. (so your rescuers can more readily identify you).

We have: List safety equipment you have (e.g., flares/smoke/ocean dye markers/EPIRB).

We will keep watch on Channel 16 as long as we can.

VHF Channels	
09	Used for radio checks and hailing other stations (boats, shoreside operations). Also used to communicate with drawbridges in Florida.
13	Used to contact and communicate with commercial vessels, military ships and drawbridges. Bridges in several states monitor VHF Channel 13.
16	***Emergency use only.*** May be used to hail other vessels, but once contact is made, conversation should be immediately switched to a working (68, 69, 71, 72, 78A) VHF channel.
22	Used for U.S. Coast Guard safety, navigation and Sécurité communications.
68 **69** **71** **72** **78A**	Used primarily for recreational ship-to-ship and ship-to-shore communications.

Rules of the Road

Anyone planning to cruise U.S. waterways should be familiar with the rules of the road. *Chapman Piloting: Seamanship and Small Boat Handling* and *The Annapolis Book of Seamanship* are both excellent on-the-water references with plentiful information on navigation rules. For those with a penchant for the exact regulatory language, the U.S. Coast Guard publication *Navigation Rules: International–Inland* covers both international and U.S. inland rules. (Boats over 39.4 feet are required to carry a copy of the U.S. Inland Rules at all times.)

Following is a list of common situations you may likely encounter on the waterways. Make yourself familiar with them, and if there is ever a question as to which of you has the right-of-way, let the other vessel go first.

Sailors need to remember that a boat under sail with its engine running is considered a motorboat.

Passing or Being Passed:

- If you intend to pass a slower vessel, try to hail them on your VHF radio to let them know you are coming.
- In close quarters, BOTH vessels should slow down, which normally allows the faster vessel to pass quickly without throwing a large wake onto the slower boat.
- Slower boats being passed have the right-of-way and passing vessels must keep clear of these slower vessels.

- As you pass a slower boat, take a look back to see how they were affected by your wake. Remember: YOU are responsible for your wake. It is the law to slow down and it is common courtesy.

At Opening Bridges:

- During an opening, boats traveling with the current go first and generally have the right-of-way.
- Boats constrained by their draft, size or maneuverability (e.g., dredges, tugs and barges) take priority.
- Standard rules of the road apply while circling or waiting for a bridge opening.

Tugs, Freighters, Dredges & Naval Vessels:

- These vessels are usually constrained by draft or their inability to easily maneuver. For this reason, you will almost always need to give them the right-of-way and keep out of their path.
- You must keep at least 100 yards away from any Navy vessel. If you cannot safely navigate without coming closer than this, you must notify the ship of your intentions over VHF Channel 16.
- Keep a close watch for freighters, tugs with tows and other large vessels while offshore or in crowded ports. They often come up very quickly, despite their large size.
- It is always a good practice to radio larger vessels (VHF Channel 13 or 16) to notify them of your location and your intentions. The skippers of these boats are generally appreciative of efforts to communicate with them. This is especially true with dredge boats on all the waterways.

Additional Resources
U.S. Coast Guard Boating Safety Division: www.uscgboating.org
U.S. Coast Guard Navigation Center: www.navcen.uscg.gov

In a Crossing Situation:

- When two vessels under power are crossing and a risk of collision exists, the vessel that has the other on her starboard side must keep clear and avoid crossing ahead of the other vessel.
- When a vessel under sail and a vessel under power are crossing, the boat under power is usually burdened and must keep clear. The same exceptions apply as per head-on meetings.
- On the Great Lakes and western rivers (e.g., the Mississippi River system), a power-driven vessel crossing a river shall keep clear of a power-driven vessel ascending or descending the river.

Power Vessels Meeting Any Other Vessel:

- When two vessels under power (either sailboats or powerboats) meet "head-to-head," both are obliged to alter course to starboard.
- Generally, when a vessel under power meets a vessel under sail (i.e., not using any mechanical power), the powered vessel must alter course accordingly.
- Exceptions are vessels not under command, vessels restricted in ability to maneuver, vessels engaged in commercial fishing or those under International Rules such as a vessel constrained by draft.

Two sailboats meeting under sail:

- When each has the wind on a different side, the boat with the wind on the port side must keep clear of the boat with the wind on the starboard side.
- When both have the wind on the same side, the vessel closest to the wind (windward) will keep clear of the leeward boat.
- A vessel with wind to port that sees a vessel to windward but cannot determine whether the windward vessel has wind to port or starboard will assume that windward vessel is on starboard tack and keep clear.

Keep Watch for Crab Pots!

While crab pots with marker buoys are not intentionally placed inside navigational channels, they sometimes break loose and find their way there. The terms "pot" refers to the enclosed traps (usually a framework of wire) used to catch crabs in shallow waters. The attached retrieval markers can range from colorful buoys to empty milk jugs (or anything else that floats). Most buoys are painted in a color that contrasts the water surface but some are black or even dark blue, which are especially difficult to see in the best of conditions. You do NOT want to get a line wrapped around your prop so it is advisable to have a spotter on the foredeck when traversing fields of pots.

Coast Guard Requirements

The U.S. Coast Guard stands watch at all times to aid vessels of all sizes and the persons on board. In some areas, you can quickly reach the Coast Guard by dialing *CG on a cellular phone. If you have a question of a non-emergency nature, the Coast Guard prefers that you telephone the nearest station. As always, if there is an emergency, initiate a "MAYDAY" call on VHF Channel 16.

In addition to aiding boaters in distress, the Coast Guard also enforces maritime law and conducts safety inspections. While a Coast Guard boarding can be unnerving, if you are responsible and prepared, it will only take 15 to 30 minutes and will be a non-event. First, have your boat in order. This includes having your vessel documentation, registration and insurance documents on hand, as well as your passport. Organize this in a binder and keep it in the nav station so you don't have to fumble around looking for documents and paperwork. You will need to acknowledge the location of any weapons on board and show a permit (when required by state law). The officers will likely focus on areas with the largest safety concerns including the following.

Note that state and local requirements are also considered. If there is a minor violation, they may give you a written warning explaining what needs to be fixed to be in compliance. If you are found with a small violation and correct it quickly, then this will merely be a chance to interact with those whose goal is to keep you as safe as possible on the water.

Life Jackets: One Type I, II, II or V per person plus one Type IV throwable device is required. PFDs must be U.S. Coast Guard-approved, wearable by the intended user and readily accessible. The Type IV throwable device must be located so that it is immediately available.

Visual Distress Signals: All vessels 16 feet and over must be equipped with minimum of 3 day-use and 3 night-use or 3 day/night combination pyrotechnic devices. Non-pyrotechnic substitutes are orange flag (for day use) and electric S-O-S signal light (for night use). Flares must be up to date (e.g., not expired).

Sound Producing Devices: A whistle, horn, siren, etc. capable of a 4-second blast audible for 0.5 mile must be on board for use during periods of reduced visibility. Boats 65 feet and over must have a bell and one whistle or horn required to signal intentions.

Navigation Lights: All powered vessels under 12 meters (39.4 feet) must have working navigational lights and an independent all-around anchor light. Sailboats under power are considered powerboats and must follow "power" rules.

Fire Extinguisher: U.S. Coast Guard-approved, marine-type fire extinguishers are required on any boat with enclosed fuel or engine spaces, enclosed living spaces or permanent (not movable by one person) fuel tanks. They must be in good working condition and readily accessible. (Number of units required depends on vessel length.)

Ventilation: Boats built after August 1, 1980, with enclosed gasoline engines must have a powered ventilation system with one or more exhaust blowers.

Backfire Flame Arrester: All gasoline-powered inboard/outboard or inboard motor boats must be equipped with an approved backfire flame arrester.

Pollution Placard: It is illegal to discharge oil or oily waste into any navigable waters of the U.S. Boats over 26 feet must display a durable oily waste pollution placard of at least 5 by 8 inches in a prominent location.

MARPOL Trash Placard: It is illegal to dump plastic trash anywhere in the ocean or navigable waters of the U.S. Boats over 26 feet must display a durable trash placard at least 4 by 9 inches in a prominent location.

Navigation Rules: Boats 39.4 feet and over must have a copy of current Navigation Rules on board. You can download a copy at www.uscgboating org.

Marine Sanitation Devices: The discharge of treated sewage is allowed within 3 nm of shore except in designated "No Discharge Zone" areas. The Coast Guard will check that overboard discharge outlets can be sealed (and remain sealed if within 3 nm of shore).

Reference Materials

U.S. Coast Guard Local Notice to Mariners

The U.S. Coast Guard provides timely marine safety information for the correction of all U.S. Government navigation charts and publications from a wide variety of sources, both foreign and domestic via the *Local Notice to Mariners*. These are divided by district, updated weekly and available as a PDF at www.navcen.uscg.gov. (Select LNMs tab at top of page.)

Cruising Guides

- *ICW Cruising Guide (by Bob423)*, Robert A. Sherer
- *Skipper Bob Cruising Guides*, Ted Stehle (editor)

Navigation

- *A Boater's Guide to Federal Requirements for Recreational Boaters.* Covers equipment requirements, navigation rules and aids to navigation, a sample float plan and safety and survival tips. Can be downloaded as a PDF at www.uscgboating.org/images/420.PDF.
- *NAVIGATION RULES, INTERNATIONAL—INLAND*, U.S. Dept. of Homeland Security. The U.S. Coast Guard requires all vessels over 39 feet carry this book of the national and international rules of the road. Can be downloaded as a PDF at www.navcen.uscg.gov.
- *U.S. Coast Pilot (1-5)*, NOAA. Includes piloting information for coasts, bays, creeks and harbors. Also includes tide tables and highlights restricted areas. Updated weekly and can be downloaded as a PDF at www.nauticalcharts.noaa.gov/publications/coast-pilot/index.html.
- *U.S. Chart No 1. (Chart Symbols)*. Describes the symbols, abbreviations and terms used on NOAA nautical charts. Available online at www.nauticalcharts.noaa.gov/publications/us-chart-1.html.
- *U.S. Aids to Navigation System* is a downloadable guide from the U.S. Coast Guard with basic information on the recognition of U.S. Aids to Navigation System (ATONS). Find it at www.uscgboating.org/images/486.PDF.

Maintenance

- *Boatowner's Mechanical & Electrical Manual* (4th Edition), Nigel Calder
- *Boatowner's Illustrated Electrical Handbook*, Charlie Wing
- *Boat Mechanical Systems Handbook*, David Gerr

Seamanship

- *Anchoring: A Ground Tackler's Apprentice*, Rudy and Jill Sechez
- *Boater's Pocket Reference*, Thomas McEwen
- *Chapman Piloting & Seamanship* (68th Edition), Charles B. Husick
- *Eldridge Tide and Pilot Book* (Annual), Robert E. and Linda White
- *Heavy Weather Sailing* (7th Edition), Peter Bruce
- *Nigel Calder's Cruising Handbook*, Nigel Calder
- *Offshore Cruising Encyclopedia*, Steve & Linda Dashew
- *The Annapolis Book of Seamanship* (4th Edition), John Rousmaniere
- *The Art of Seamanship*, Ralph Naranjo
- *World Cruising Essentials*, Jimmy Cornell

First Aid & Medical

- *Advanced First Aid Afloat* (5th Edition), Dr. Peter F. Eastman
- *DAN Pocket Guide to First Aid for Scuba Diving*, Dan Orr & Bill Clendenden
- *First Aid at Sea*, Douglas Justin and Colin Berry
- *Marine Medicine: A Comprehensive Guide* (2nd Edition), Eric Weiss and Michael Jacobs
- *On-Board Medical Emergency Handbook: First Aid at Sea*, Spike Briggs and Campbell Mackenzie

About the Weather

Every day on the water can't have balmy breezes, abundant sunshine and consistently warm weather; however, staying out of bad weather is relatively easy if you plan ahead. The National Weather Service (NWS) provides mariners with continuous broadcasts of weather warnings, forecasts, radar reports and buoy reports over VHF-FM and Single Side Band (SSB) radio. There are almost no areas on the Atlantic ICW where a good quality, fixed-mount VHF cannot pick up one or more coastal VHF broadcasts. Also, there is no substitute for simply looking at the sky, and either stay put or seek shelter if you don't like what you see.

Reading the Skies

Water and metal are excellent conductors of electricity, making boating in a thunderstorm a risky prospect. While the odds of a given boat being hit are small, the consequences are severe and deadly. Do not try and play the odds! The best advice if you are out on the water and skies are threatening is get back to land and seek safe shelter, but that's not always practical for cruisers who live aboard or are not near land.

Thunderstorms occur when air masses of different temperatures meet over inland or coastal waters. An example of this would be when air with a high humidity that is warm near the ground rises and meets cooler air, which condenses and creates water droplets. This releases energy, which charges the atmosphere and creates lightning. This is why thunderstorms are a daily occurrence between March and October near southern waterways.

A tell-tale sign of a thunderstorm is cumulonimbus clouds: those tall clouds with an anvil-shaped (flat) top. Thunderstorms can also precede even a minor cold front. Keep in mind that thunderstorms generally move in an easterly direction so if you see a storm to the south or southwest of you, start preparing.

Don't Wait Until It's Too Late!

Almost all lightning will occur within 10 miles of its parent thunderstorm, but it can strike much farther than that. Also, the current from a single flash will easily travel for long distances. Because of this, if you see lightning or hear thunder, you CAN get struck!

Weather Apps (Free)
Boat Weather
Buoycast: NOAA Marine Forecast
National Hurricane Center Tracker
NOAA Marine Weather Radar
NOAA Weather
PredictWind
Wind Alert
Windfinder
Windy
Weather Online
Accuweather (www.accuweather.com)
BoatUS Hurricane Tracking & Resource Center (www.boatus.com/hurricanes/tracking)
Buoy Weather (www.buoyweather.com)
Coastal Marine Forecast (www.weather.gov/marine)
National Hurricane Center (www.nhc.noaa.gov)
National Weather Service (www.weather.gov)
Passage Weather (www.passageweather.com)
Predict Wind (www.predictwind.com)
Sailflow (www.sailflow.com)
The Weather Channel (www.weather.com)
Windfinder (www.windfinder.com)

The ability to see lightning will depend on the time of day, weather conditions and obstructions, but on a clear night it is possible to see a strike more than 10 miles away. Thunder can also be heard for about 10 miles, provided there is no background noise such as traffic, wind or rain.

If you see lightning, you can determine the distance by timing how long it takes before you hear thunder. The old rule that every 5 seconds of time equals 1 mile of distance works well. So if it takes 20 seconds to hear thunder after you see lighting, then the storm is 4 miles away. Time to drop anchor and "hunker down"!

Lightning Safety Tips

Lightning tends to strike the tallest object and boats on the open water fit this profile. The lightning will try to take the most direct path to the water, which is usually down the mast on a sailboat or the VHF antenna on a powerboat. However, both sailboats and powerboats with cabins–especially those with lightning protection systems properly installed–are relatively safe, provided you keep a few things in mind:

- Before the storm strikes, lower, remove or tie down all antennas, fishing rods and flag poles.
- Stay down below and in the center of the cabin. Avoid keel-stepped masts and chain plates (on sailboats) and large metal appliances such as microwaves or TVs. Remove any metal jewelry.
- Disconnect the power and antenna leads to all electronics including radios. Do not use the VHF radio unless absolutely necessary.
- If you are stuck on deck, stay away from metal railings, the wheel, the mast and stays (on sailboats) or other metal fittings. Do not stand between the mast and stays as lightning can "side-flash" from one to the other.
- Stay out of the water and don't fish or dangle your feet overboard. Salt water conducts electricity, which means that it can easily travel through the water toward you.
- Don't think rubber-soled deck shoes will save you; while rubber is an electric insulator, it's only effective to a certain point. The average lightning bolt carries about 30,000 amps of charge, has 100 million volts of electric potential and is about 50,000°F.

If You Are Struck:

1. **Check people first. Many individuals struck by lightning or exposed to excessive electrical current can be saved with prompt and proper cardiopulmonary resuscitation (CPR). Contrary to popular belief, there is no danger in touching persons after they have been struck by lightning.**
2. **Check the bilge as strikes can rupture through-hull fittings and punch holes in hulls. Props and rudders are natural exit points on boats.**
3. **Check electronics and the compasses. Typically everything in the path of the lightning is destroyed on the way down to the water including instruments, computers and stereos.**
4. **Consider a short haul to check the bottom thoroughly. Lightning strikes sometimes leave traces of damage that may only be seen when the boat is out of the water.**

Don't Rush Back Out

Because electrical charges can linger in clouds after a thunderstorm has passed, experts agree that you should wait at least 30 minutes after a storm before resuming activities. And remember: If you can hear thunder, you can still be struck by lightning!

Natural Seasickness Remedies

- *Take slow, deep breaths.* This helps soothe upset stomach and dizziness.
- *Focus on the horizon.* Keep your body still and head facing forward and watch a stationary object. Taking the helm always helps.
- *Ginger can help.* Eat ginger snaps, drink ginger tea or ginger ale or digest in capsule form ahead of time.
- *Peppermint works too.* Sucking on a peppermint candy, drinking peppermint tea or breathing in peppermint oil dabbed on a cloth can help with stomach issues.
- *Try acupuncture wristbands.* Apply pressure to specific points on your wrist to reduce nausea.

Float Plan

BoatU.S.

1. Phone Numbers

Coast Guard: ____________

Marine Police: ____________

Local TowBoatU.S. Company: ____________

2. Description of the Boat

Boat Name: ________ Hailing Port: ________

Type: ________ Model Year: ________

Make: ______ Length: ______ Beam: ______ Draft: ______

Color, Hull: ______ Cabin: ______ Deck: ______ Trim: ______ Dodger: ______

Other Colors: ________ # of Masts: ________

Distinguishing Features: ____________

Registration No: ________ Sail No: ________

Engine(s) Type: ______ Horsepower: ______ Cruising Speed: ______

Fuel Capacity, Gallons: ________ Cruising Range: ________

Electronics/Safety Equipment Aboard

VHF Radio: ______ Cell Phone: ______ CB: ______ SSB: ______

Frequency Monitored: ______ Loran: ______ SatNav: ______

Depth Sounder: ______ Radar: ______ GPS: ______

Raft: ______ Dinghy: ______ EPIRB: ______ A/B/C/406M (Indicate Type)

3. Trip Details

Owner/Skipper (Filing Report): ____________

Phone: ________ Age: ______

Address: ____________

Additional Persons Aboard, Total: ______

Name: ________ Age: ______

Address: ________ Phone: ______

Boating Experience: ____________

Name: ________ Age: ______

Address: ________ Phone: ______

Boating Experience: ____________

Name: ________ Age: ______

Address: ________ Phone: ______

Boating Experience: ____________

Name: ________ Age: ______

Address: ________ Phone: ______

Boating Experience: ____________

Name: ________ Age: ______

Address: ________ Phone: ______

Boating Experience: ____________

Departure Date/Time: ______ Return No Later Than: ______

Depart From: ____________

Marina (Home Port): ________ Phone: ______

Auto Parked At: ____________

Model/color: ________ Lic. # ______

Destination Port: ____________

________ ETA: ______ No Later Than: ______

Phone: ____________

Anticipated Stopover Ports: ____________

________ ETA: ______ No Later Than: ______

Phone: ____________

________ ETA: ______ No Later Than: ______

Phone: ____________

________ ETA: ______ No Later Than: ______

Phone: ____________

________ ETA: ______ No Later Than: ______

Phone: ____________

________ ETA: ______ No Later Than: ______

Phone: ____________

Plan Filed With: ____________

Name: ________ Phone: ______

Get in the habit of filing a Float Plan. It can assure quicker rescue in the event of a breakdown, stranding or weather delay. Fill out the permanent data in Sections 1 and 2. Then, make enough copies to last for the season. If you file a Float Plan with someone not at your home, such as a harbormaster or boating friend, be sure to notify them as soon as you return. Don't burden friends or authorities with unnecessary worry and responsibility if you are safe.

Check your *BoatU.S. Towing Guide*. Some listed companies will accept a verbal Float Plan via telephone or VHF.

Ditch Bag Checklist

Rescue Items

- [ ] Functioning, registered EPIRB
- [ ] Handheld VHF radio (waterproof or in sealed pouch with extra batteries)
- [ ] Sea anchor, drogue and line
- [ ] Manual inflation pump
- [ ] Selection of flares (parachute and handheld) and smoke signals
- [ ] Strobe light (may be present in inflatable PFD)
- [ ] Flashlight & batteries (headlamp is ideal)
- [ ] Whistle (may be present in inflatable PFD)
- [ ] Signal mirror
- [ ] Handheld GPS or compass (for position)
- [ ] Small pair of binoculars (to confirm a boat or plane spotting before using flares)

Survival Items

- [ ] Sponges and bailer (with handle)
- [ ] Patch kit for inflatable dinghy or life raft (or emergency clamps)
- [ ] Water (individually sealed or in collapsible containers)–at least 2 gallons per person
- [ ] Emergency food rations and can opener (if needed)
- [ ] Power Bars
- [ ] Prescription medications
- [ ] Seasickness medications/remedies
- [ ] First aid kit
- [ ] Multipurpose tool or sailor's knife
- [ ] Waterproof matches

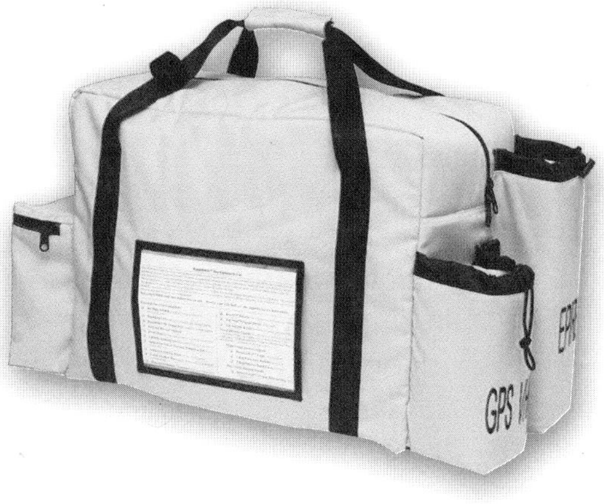

Other Items

- [ ] Solar blanket
- [ ] Heavy-duty coated gloves
- [ ] Duct tape
- [ ] Sewing kit
- [ ] Simple fishing gear (line, jigs, hooks, etc.)
- [ ] Polypropylene line
- [ ] Waterproof sunscreen and zinc oxide
- [ ] Bug repellent
- [ ] Ziploc bags (gallon size)
- [ ] Paper and pen in Ziploc bag
- [ ] Spare prescription glasses and sunglasses (polarized to reduce glare)
- [ ] Laminated copies of passports or license
- [ ] Cash ($50 in small bills)
- [ ] Copy of the yacht's papers (including insurance)

Tropical Weather & Hurricanes

While all coastal areas of the country are vulnerable to the effects of a hurricane (especially from June through November), the Gulf Coast, Southern and Mid-Atlantic states typically have been the hardest hit. But northern locales aren't immune; several destructive hurricanes have dealt a blow to areas in New England over the last 100 years including Hurricane Sandy in 2012 and Matthew in 2016. While hurricanes can create vast swaths of devastation, ample preparation can help increase your boat's chances of surviving the storm.

According to the National Weather Service, a mature hurricane may be 10 miles high with a great spiral several hundred miles in diameter. Winds are often well above the 74 mph required to classify as hurricane strength, especially during gusts. Hurricane damage is produced by four elements: tidal surge, wind, wave action and rain.

Distance from Eye	Force Level	Wind Speed
150 miles	Force 8	34–40 knots
100 miles	Force 11	56–63 knots
75 miles	Force 12	over 64 knots

- Tidal surge is an increase in ocean depth prior to the storm. This effect, amplified in coastal areas, may cause tidal heights in excess of 15 to 20 feet above normal. Additionally, hurricanes can produce a significant negative tidal effect as water rushes out of the waterways after a storm.
- Wind gusts can exceed reported sustained winds by 25 to 50 percent. For example, a storm with winds of 150 mph might have gusts of more than 200 mph, according to the National Weather Service.
- Wave action is usually the most damaging element of a hurricane for boaters. The wind speed, water depth and the amount of open water determine the amount of wave action created. Storm surges can transform narrow bodies of water into larger, deeper waters capable of generating extreme wave action.
- Rainfall varies but hurricanes can generate anywhere from 5 to 20 inches or more of rain.

Hurricane Categorization

CATEGORY	PRESSURE	WIND SPEED	SURGE
1	Above 980 mb (Above 28.91 in.)	64–82 knots (74–95 mph)	4–5 ft. (1–1.5 m)
Visibility much reduced. Maneuvering under engines just possible. Open anchorages untenable. Danger of poorly secured boats torn loose in protected anchorages.			
2	965-979 mb (28.50-28.91 in.)	83-95 knots (96-110 mph)	6-8 ft. (1.5-2.5 m)
Visibility close to zero. Boats in protected anchorages at risk, particularly from boats torn loose. Severe damage to unprotected boats and boats poorly secured and prepared.			
3	945-964 mb (27.91-28.50 in.)	96-113 knots (111-130 mph)	9-12 ft. (2.5-3.5 m)
Deck fittings at risk and may tear loose, anchor links can fail and unprotected lines will chafe through. Extensive severe damage.			
4	920-944 mb (27.17-27.91 in.)	114-135 knots (131-155 mph)	13-18 ft. (3.5-5.4 m)
Very severe damage and loss of life.			
5	Below 920 mb (Below 27.17 in.)	Above 135 knots (131-155 mph)	Above 18 ft. (Above 5.4 m)
Catastrophic conditions with catastrophic damage.			

If your boat is in a slip, you have three options: Leave it where it is (if it is in a safe place); move it to a refuge area; or haul it and put it on a trailer or cradle. Some marinas require mandatory evacuations during hurricane alerts. Check your lease agreement and talk to your dockmaster before a hurricane if you are uncertain. Keep in mind that many municipalities close public mooring fields in advance of the storm. In some localities, boaters may be held liable for any damage that their boat inflicts to marina piers or property; check locally for details. Because of this, rivers, canals, coves and other areas away from large stretches of open water are best selected as refuges.

Consult your insurance agent if you have questions about coverage. Many insurance agencies have restricted or canceled policies for boats that travel or are berthed in certain hurricane-prone areas. Review your policy and check your coverage as many insurance companies will not cover boats in hurricane-prone areas during the June through November hurricane season. Riders for this type of coverage are notoriously expensive.

Preparing Your Boat

- Have a hurricane plan made up ahead of time to maximize what you can get done in the amount of time you will have to prepare (no more than 12 hours in some cases). Plan how to tie up the boat or where to anchor before a hurricane is barreling down on you. Make these decisions in advance!
- Buy hurricane gear well in advance. When word of a hurricane spreads, local ship stores run out of storm supplies (anchors and line, especially) very quickly.
- Strip everything that isn't bolted down off the deck of the boat (e.g., canvas, sails, antennas, bimini tops, dodgers, dinghies, dinghy motors, cushions, unneeded control lines on sailboats) as this will help reduce windage and damage to your boat. Remove electronics and valuables and move them ashore.
- Any potentially leaky ports or hatches should be taped up. Dorades (cowls) should be removed and sealed with deck caps.
- Make sure all systems on board are in tip-top shape in case you have to move quickly. Fuel and water tanks should be filled, bilge pumps should be in top operating condition and batteries should be fully charged.
- You will need many lengths of line to secure the boat; make certain it is good stretchy nylon (not Dacron). It is not unusual to string 600 to 800 feet of dock line on a 40-foot-long boat in preparation for a hurricane. If you can, double up your lines (two for each cleat) as lines can break during a strong storm. Have fenders and fender boards out and make sure all of your lines are protected from chafing.
- If you are anchored out, use multiple large anchors; there is no such thing as an anchor that is too large. If you can, tie to trees with a good root system such as mangroves or live oaks. Mangroves are particularly good because their canopy can have a cushioning effect. Be sure mooring lines include ample scope to compensate for tides 10 to 20 feet above normal.
- Lastly, do not stay aboard to weather out the storm. Many people have been seriously injured (or worse) trying to save their boats during a hurricane. Take photos of the condition in which you left your boat and take your insurance papers with you.

Returning Safely After the Storm

- Before hitting the road, make sure the roads back to your boat are open and safe for travel. Beware of dangling wires, weakened docks, bulkheads, bridges and other structures.
- Check your boat thoroughly before attempting to move it. If returning to your home slip, watch the waters for debris and obstructions. Navigate carefully as markers may be misplaced or missing.
- If your boat should sink, arrange for engine repairs before floating it but only if it is not impeding traffic. Otherwise, you will need to remove it immediately. Contact your insurance company right away to make a claim.

Additional Resources
National Hurricane Center: www.nhc.noaa.gov
BoatUS Hurricane Tracking & Resource Center: www.boatus.com/hurricanes

Dealing With Onboard Waste

Up until the late 1980s, many boaters simply discharged their untreated sewage overboard into the water. After a revision to the Clean Water Act was passed in 1987, the discharge of untreated sewage into U.S. waters within the 3-mile limit was prohibited. Shortly thereafter, pump-out stations became a regular feature at marinas and fuel docks throughout the U.S. waterways.

Simply stated, if you have a marine head installed on your vessel and are operating in coastal waters within the U.S. 3-mile limit (basically all of the waters covered in the guide you are now holding), you need to have a holding tank and you will obviously need to arrange to have that tank pumped out from time to time.

Government regulation aside, properly disposing of your waste is good environmental stewardship. While your overboard contribution to the waterways may seem small in the grand scheme of things, similar attitudes among fellow boaters can quickly produce unsavory conditions in anchorages and small creeks. The widespread availability of holding tank gear and shoreside pump-out facilities leaves few excuses for not doing the right thing.

No-Discharge Zones

- No-Discharge means exactly what the name suggests: No waste, even waste treated by an onboard Type I marine sanitation device (MSD), may be discharged overboard. All waste must be collected in a holding tank and pumped out at an appropriate facility.

- Keep in mind that there are some areas that forbid overboard discharge of any waste including gray water from showers or sinks. Familiarize yourself with local regulations before entering new areas to ensure you don't get hit with a fine.

The Law

- If you have a marine head onboard and are operating on coastal waters within the U.S. 3-mile limit (basically all of the waters covered in this guide), you need to have an approved holding tank or Type I MSD. In a No-Discharge area even a Type I MSD system must have a holding tank.

- All valves connected to your holding tank or marine head that lead to the outside (both Y-valves AND seacocks) must be wire-tied, padlocked or absent of the valve handle and in the closed position. Simply having them closed without the (non-releasable) wire ties will not save you from a fine if you are boarded.

- You may discharge waste overboard from a Type I MSD in all areas except those designated as No-Discharge Zones. A Type I MSD treats waste by reducing bacteria and visible solids to an acceptable level before discharge overboard.

- While small and inconvenient for most cruisers, "Port-A-Potties" meet all the requirements for a Type III MSD as the holding tank is incorporated into the toilet itself.

Pump-Out and Holding Tank Basics

- Some marinas are equipped with pump-out facilities, normally located at the marina's fuel dock. Note that some marinas charge a fee for the service.

- Several municipalities and local governments have purchased and staffed pump-out boats that are equipped to visit boats on request, especially those at anchor. Radio the local harbormaster to see if this service is available in the area you are visiting. There is normally a small fee involved.

- You will want to keep an eye out on your holding tank level while you are cruising, especially if you are getting ready to enter an area where you many not have access to proper pump-out services for a few days. Plan a fuel stop or marina stay to top off the fuel and water tanks and empty the other tank before you set out into the wild.

Marine Sanitation Devices

- Type I MSD: Treats sewage before discharging it into the water using maceration. The treated discharge must not show any visible floating solids and must meet specified standards for bacteria content. Raritan's Electro Scan and Groco's Thermopure systems are examples of Type I MSDs. Not permitted in No-Discharge Zones.
- Type II MSD: Type II MSDs provide a higher level of waste treatment than Type I units and are larger as a result. They employ biological treatment and disinfection. These units are usually found on larger vessels due to their higher power requirements. These may not be discharged in No-Discharge Zones.
- Type III MSD: Regular holding tanks store sewage until the holding tank can either be pumped out to an onshore facility or at sea beyond the U.S. boundary waters (i.e., 3 miles offshore).

Penalties and Fines

- Misuse or failure to equip a vessel with a Marine Sanitation Device may result in a non-criminal infraction with a $56 penalty.
- Illegal dumping/discharge of a Marine Sanitation Device may result in a non-criminal infraction with a $250 penalty.

Additional Resources

BoatU.S. Guide to Overboard Discharge:
www.boatus.com/foundation/guide/environment_7.html

EPA Listing of No-Discharge Zones:
www.epa.gov/vessels-marinas-and-ports/no-discharge-zones-ndzs-state

Distances: Inside (ICW) Route–Norfolk, VA to Fernandina Beach, FL

Inside Route Distances - Norfolk, Virgina to Fernandina Beach, Florida (nautical and statute miles)

	Fernandina Beach, FL	Brunswick, GA	Thunderbolt, GA	Savannah, GA	Beaufort, SC	Charleston, SC	McClellanville, SC	Georgetown, SC	Bucksport, SC	Little River, SC	Southport, NC	Wilmington, NC	Wrightsville, NC	Jacksonville, NC	Swansboro, NC	Morehead City, NC	Beaufort, NC	New Bern, NC	Oriental, NC	Ocracoke, NC	Washington, NC	Belhaven, NC	Manteo, NC	Plymouth, NC	Edenton, NC	Columbia, NC	Hertford, NC	Elizabeth City, NC	Norfolk, VA
Norfolk, VA	623	595	507	508	466	406	374	352	328	299	268	273	248	231	20	178	177	180	160	131	156	120	80	105	98	89	89	77*	•
Elizabeth City, NC	581	553	465	466	424	364	332	311	286	257	226	231	204	189	158	136	134	139	118	91	114	79	39	56	48	39	39	•	89
Hertford, NC	582	554	466	467	425	366	333	311	287	259	227	232	205	190	160	137	137	139	119	97	115	79	46	42	35	26	•	45	102
Columbia, NC	581	553	465	466	424	364	332	310	286	257	226	231	204	189	158	136	136	138	118	96	114	78	45	33	25	•	30	45	102
Edenton, NC	589	562	474	475	432	373	340	318	294	266	235	240	213	197	166	145	144	146	126	104	123	87	54	14	•	29	40	55	113
Plymouth, NC	596	570	482	483	441	381	349	327	303	274	243	248	221	206	175	152	152	155	134	113	130	95	61	•	16	38	48	64	121
Manteo, NC	555	527	439	440	397	337	306	283	260	232	201	205	178	162	132	110	110	110	91	61	105	70	•	70	62	52	53	45	92
Belhaven, NC	506	479	391	392	349	290	257	235	211	183	152	157	130	114	83	61	61	63	43	43	39	•	81	109	100	90	91	91	138
Washington, NC	519	491	403	404	362	302	270	248	224	195	164	169	142	127	96	74	74	76	56	60	•	45	121	150	142	131	132	131	180
Ocracoke, NC	504	477	389	390	347	288	255	233	209	181	150	155	128	112	81	59	59	62	41	•	69	49	70	130	120	110	112	105	151
Oriental, NC	467	440	352	353	310	251	218	196	172	144	113	118	91	75	44	22	22	23	•	47	64	49	105	154	145	136	137	136	184
New Bern, NC	484	456	368	369	327	267	235	213	188	160	129	134	107	91	60	38	38	•	26	71	87	72	127	178	168	159	160	160	207
Beaufort, NC	447	420	332	333	290	231	199	177	152	124	93	97	70	55	24	3	•	44	25	68	85	70	127	175	166	157	158	154	204
Morehead City, NC	445	418	330	331	288	229	196	174	150	122	91	96	69	53	22	•	3	44	25	68	85	70	127	175	167	157	158	157	205
Swansboro, NC	423	396	307	309	266	207	174	152	128	100	69	73	46	31	•	25	28	69	51	93	110	96	152	201	191	182	184	182	230
Jacksonville, NC	425	397	309	310	268	208	176	154	129	101	70	75	48	•	36	61	63	105	86	129	146	131	186	237	227	217	219	217	266
Wrightsville, NC	377	349	261	262	220	160	128	106	82	53	22	27	•	55	53	79	81	123	105	147	163	150	205	254	245	235	236	235	283
Wilmington, NC	376	349	260	261	219	159	127	105	81	52	21	•	31	86	84	110	112	154	136	178	194	181	236	285	276	266	267	266	314
Southport, NC	355	327	239	240	198	138	106	84	60	31	•	24	25	81	79	105	107	148	130	173	189	175	231	280	270	260	261	260	308
Little River, SC	324	296	208	209	167	107	75	53	28	•	36	60	61	116	115	140	143	184	166	208	224	211	267	315	306	296	298	296	344
Bucksport, SC	295	268	179	181	138	79	46	24	•	32	69	93	94	148	147	173	175	216	198	241	258	243	299	349	338	329	330	329	377
Georgetown, SC	273	246	157	159	116	56	24	•	28	61	97	121	122	177	175	200	203	245	226	268	285	270	326	376	366	357	358	358	405
McClellanville, SC	249	222	133	135	92	32	•	28	53	86	122	146	147	203	200	226	229	270	251	293	311	296	352	402	391	382	383	382	430
Charleston, SC	218	191	103	104	60	•	37	64	91	123	159	183	184	239	238	264	266	307	289	331	348	334	388	438	429	419	421	419	467
Beaufort, SC	157	130	41	43	•	69	106	133	159	192	228	252	253	308	306	331	334	376	357	399	417	402	457	508	497	488	489	488	536
Savannah, GA	130	102	14	•	49	120	155	183	208	241	276	300	302	357	356	381	383	425	406	449	465	451	506	556	547	536	537	536	585
Thunderbolt, GA	116	88	•	16	47	119	153	181	206	239	275	299	300	356	353	380	382	423	405	448	464	450	505	555	545	535	536	535	583
Brunswick, GA	35	•	101	117	150	220	255	283	308	341	376	402	402	457	456	481	483	525	506	549	565	551	606	656	647	636	638	636	685
Fernandina Beach, FL	•	40	133	150	181	251	287	314	339	373	409	433	434	489	487	512	514	557	537	580	597	582	639	688	678	669	670	669	717

Distances: Outside (Coastwise) Route–Norfolk, VA to Key West, FL

Coastwise Distances – Norfolk, Virginia to Key West, Florida
(nautical miles)

	Straits of Florida	Key West, FL	Miami, FL	Port Everglades, FL	Port of Palm Beach, FL	Stuart, FL	Fort Pierce, FL	Cape Canaveral, FL	St. Augustine, FL	Jacksonville, FL	Fernandina Beach, FL	Brunswick, GA	Savannah, GA	Port Royal, SC	Charleston, SC	Georgetown, SC	Wilmington, NC	Southport, NC	Morehead City, NC	Diamond Shoals, NC	Norfolk, VA	Chesapeake Bay Entrance
Chesapeake Bay Entrance 36°56.3'N., 75°58.6'W.	942	881	743	720	678	666	647	612	557	560	533	527	476	465	402	365	336	315	222	117	27	-
Norfolk, VA 46°50.9'N., 76°17.9'W.	969	908	770	747	705	693	674	639	584	587	560	554	503	492	429	392	363	342	249	144	-	
Diamond Shoals, NC 35°08.0'N., 75°15.0'W.	825	764	626	603	561	549	530	495	440	443	416	410	359	348	285	248	219	198	105	-		
Morehead City, NC 34°42.8'N., 76°41.8'W.	772	711	573	550	509	497	476	438	377	379	352	346	295	284	220	184	154	133	-			
Southport, NC 33°54.8'N., 78°01.0'W.	707	646	508	485	443	423	407	367	296	294	265	260	206	191	130	87	21	-				
Wilmington, NC 34°14.0'N., 77°57.0'W.	728	667	529	506	464	444	428	388	317	315	286	281	227	212	151	108	-					
Georgetown, SC 33°21.4'N., 79°16.9'W.	671	610	472	449	407	391	368	324	246	247	216	210	154	141	79	-						
Charleston, SC 32°47.2'N., 79°55.2'W.	633	572	434	411	369	353	329	283	199	197	166	156	102	90	-							
Port Royal, SC 32°22.3'N., 80°41.6'W.	605	544	406	383	341	324	298	251	157	152	120	110	51	-								
Savannah,GA 32°05.0'N., 81°05.7'W.	604	543	405	382	340	324	298	251	152	145	115	104	-									
Brunswick,GA 31°08.0'N., 81°29.7'W.	549	488	350	327	285	268	242	195	90	82	50	-										
Fernandina Beach, FL 30°40.3'N., 81°28.0'W.	526	465	327	304	262	242	216	169	61	53	-											
Jacksonville, FL 30°19.2'N., 81°39.0'W.	523	462	324	301	256	240	214	167	56	-												
St. Augustine, FL 29°53.6'N., 81°18.5'W.	475	414	276	253	211	192	167	120	-													
Cape Canaveral, FL 28°24.6'N., 80°36.5'W.	374	313	175	152	110	91	69	-														
Fort Pierce, FL 27°27.5'N., 80°19.3'W.	316	255	117	94	52	32	-															
Stuart, FL 27°12.2'N., 80°15.6'W.	300	239	101	78	36	-																
Port of Palm Beach, FL 26°46.1'N., 80°03.0'W.	267	207	68	46	-																	
Port Everglades, FL 26°05.6'N., 80°07.0'W.	226	165	27	-																		
Miami, FL 25°47.0'N., 80°11.0'W.	211	151	-																			
Key West, FL 24°33.7'N., 81°48.5'W.	73	-																				
Straits of Florida 24°25.0'N., 83°00.0'W.	-																					

GPS Waypoints

The following list provides selected waypoints for the waters covered in this book. The latitude/longitude readings are taken from government light lists and must be checked against the appropriate chart and light list for accuracy. Some waypoints listed here are lighthouses and should not be approached too closely as they may be on land, in shallow water or on top of a reef. Many buoys must be approached with caution, as they are often located near shallows or obstructions. The positions of every aid to navigation should be updated using the Coast Guard's *Local Notice to Mariners* (www.navcen.uscg.gov/lnm).

The U.S. Coast Guard will continue to provide Differential GPS (DGPS) correction signals for those who need accuracy of 10 meters or less, even though most GPS receivers now come with an internal capability for receiving differential signals.

Prudent mariners will not rely solely on these waypoints to navigate. Every available navigational tool should be used at all times to determine your vessel's position.

Hampton Roads to Rudee Inlet

LOCATION	LATITUDE	LONGITUDE
Little Creek Entrance Lighted Buoy 1LC	N 36° 58.083'	W 076° 10.067'
Lynnhaven Roads Fishing Pier Light	N 36° 55.000'	W 076° 04.717'
Cape Henry Light	N 36° 55.583'	W 076° 00.433'
Rudee Inlet Lighted Whistle Buoy RI	N 36° 49.783'	W 075° 56.950'

Albemarle Sound to Neuse River

LOCATION	LATITUDE	LONGITUDE
Albemarle Sound Entrance Light AS	N 36° 03.733'	W 075° 56.133'
Albemarle Sound North Light N	N 36° 06.100'	W 075° 54.750'
Albemarle Sound South Light S	N 36° 01.083'	W 075° 57.617'
Pasquotank River Entrance Light PR	N 36° 09.367'	W 075° 58.650'
Pungo River Junction Light PR	N 35° 22.667'	W 076° 33.583'
Goose Creek Light 1	N 35° 20.400'	W 076° 35.750'
Bay Point Light	N 35° 10.350'	W 076° 30.317'
Bay River Light 1	N 35° 09.800'	W 076° 32.017'
Neuse River Junction Light	N 35° 08.783'	W 076° 30.183'
Whittaker Creek Light 2	N 35° 01.383'	W 076° 41.150'
Smith Creek (Oriental) Channel Light 1	N 35° 00.900'	W 076° 41.467'
Adams Creek Light 1AC	N 34° 58.500'	W 076° 41.767'

Oregon Inlet to Cape Lookout

LOCATION	LATITUDE	LONGITUDE
Oregon Inlet Jetty Light	N 35° 46.433'	W 075° 31.500'
Hatteras Inlet Light	N 35° 11.867'	W 075° 43.933'
Diamond Shoal Lighted Buoy 12	N 35° 09.083'	W 075° 17.550'
Ocracoke Light	N 35° 06.533'	W 075° 59.167'

Beaufort Inlet to Florida Border

LOCATION	LATITUDE	LONGITUDE
Beaufort Inlet *(NOTE: This is not the location of a particular buoy.)*	N 34° 38.000'	W 077° 41.000'
Masonboro Inlet *(NOTE: This is not the location of a particular buoy.)*	N 34° 10.000'	W 077° 47.000'
Frying Pan Shoals Lighted Buoy 16	N 33° 28.783'	W 077° 35.083'
Cape Fear R. Ent. Lighted Whistle Buoy CF	N 33° 46.283'	W 078° 03.033'
Oak Island Light	N 33° 53.567'	W 078° 02.100'
Little River Inlet Lighted Whistle Buoy LR	N 33° 49.817'	W 078° 32.450'
Winyah Bay Lighted Whistle Buoy WB	N 33° 11.617'	W 079° 05.183'
Charleston Ent. Lighted Buoy C	N 32° 37.083'	W 079° 35.500'
North Edisto Rvr. Ent. Lig. Whistle Buoy 2NE	N 32° 31.350'	W 080° 06.850'

Beaufort Inlet to Florida Border (cont.)

LOCATION	LATITUDE	LONGITUDE
South Edisto Rvr. Approach Lig. Buoy A	N 32° 24.717'	W 080° 17.700'
St. Helena Sound Entrance Buoy 1	N 32° 21.667'	W 080° 18.450'
Port Royal Sound Lighted Whistle Buoy P	N 32° 05.133'	W 080° 35.033'
Calibogue Sound Entrance Daybeacon 1	N 32° 02.850'	W 080° 50.533'
Tybee Lighted Buoy T	N 31° 57.883'	W 080° 43.167'
Wassaw Sound Lighted Buoy 2W	N 31° 51.550'	W 080° 53.017'
Ossabaw Sound Ent. Lighted Buoy OS	N 31° 47.800'	W 080° 56.200'
St. Catherines Sound Lighted Buoy STC	N 31° 40.217'	W 081° 00.200'
Sapelo Sound Buoy S	N 31° 31.200'	W 081° 03.900'
Doboy Sound Lighted Buoy D	N 31° 21.233'	W 081° 11.400'
Altamaha Sound Shoal Light	N 31° 18.867'	W 081° 15.333'
St. Simons Sound Lig. Buoy STS	N 31° 02.817'	W 081° 14.417'
St. Andrew Sound Outer Ent. Buoy STA	N 30° 55.550'	W 081° 18.967'
St. Marys Rvr. Approach Lighted Buoy STM	N 30° 42.900'	W 081° 14.650'

Bridge Basics

Bridges have to be factored in when planning a trip. Depending on where you cruise, you may be dependent on bridge openings; a particular bridge's schedule can often decide where you tie up for the evening or when you wake up and get underway the next day. While many are high (over 65 feet) and some usually remain open (such as railroad bridges), others are restricted for different hours in specific months, closed during rush hours and/or open on the quarter-hour, half-hour or even at 20 minutes and 40 minutes past the hour.

To add to the confusion, the restrictions are constantly changing. Just because a bridge opened on a certain schedule last season does not mean it is still on that same schedule. Changes are posted in the Coast Guard's *Local Notice to Mariners* reports, which can be found online at www.navcen.uscg.gov/lnm. It is also a good idea to check locally to verify bridge schedules before your transit.

Calling a Bridge

Most bridges monitor VHF Channel 09, designated by the Federal Communications Commission as the "bridgetender channel." Bridges in NC and VA still answer on VHF Channel 13, as do the locks in the Okeechobee.

In any waters, it is a good idea to monitor both the bridge channel and VHF Channel 16–one on your ship's radio and one on a handheld radio, if your main set doesn't have a dual-watch capability–to monitor oncoming commercial traffic and communications with the bridgetender.

When using VHF, always call bridges by name and identify your vessel by name and type (such as sailing vessel or trawler) and whether you are traveling north or south. If you are unable to raise the bridge using VHF radio, use a horn signal.

If the gates do not come down and the bridge does not open after repeated use of the radio and the horn, call the Coast Guard and ask them to call the bridgetender on the land telephone line, or you may be able to call the bridge directly. Phone numbers for many bridges are given in the following Bridges & Locks section, although some of the numbers are not for the actual bridgetender, but for a central office that manages that bridge. Some bridges are not required to open in high winds. If you encounter a bridge that won't open, it is prudent to drop the hook in a safe spot until the situation is resolved.

Swing bridges have an opening section that pivots horizontally on a central hub, allowing boats to pass on one side or the other when it is open.

Lift bridges normally have two towers on each end of the opening section that are equipped with cables that lift the road or railway vertically into the air.

Most bridges carry a tide board to register vertical clearance at the center of the span. (Note that in Florida waters the tide board figure–and the one noted on the chart–is generally for a point that is 5 feet toward the channel from the bridge fender.) In the case of arched bridges, center channel clearance is frequently higher than the tide gauge registers. So check your chart and the tide boards and, unless it specifically notes that vertical clearance is given "at center," you may be able to count on a little extra height at mid-channel under the arch of the bridge. Some bridges may bear signs noting extra height at center in feet.

Because many bridges restrict their openings during morning and evening rush hours to minimize inconvenience to vehicular traffic, you may need to plan an early start or late stop to avoid getting stuck waiting for a bridge opening.

Pontoon bridges consists of an opening section that must be floated out of the way with a cable to allow boats to pass. Do not proceed until the cables have had time to sink to the bottom.

Bascule bridges are the most common type of opening bridge you will encounter. The opening section has one or two leaves that tilt vertically on a hinge, like doors being opened skyward.

Bridge Procedures:

- First, decide if it is necessary to have the drawbridge opened. You will need to know your boat's clearance height above the waterline before you start. Drawbridges have "clearance gauges" that show the closed vertical clearance with changing water level but a bascule bridge typically has 3 to 5 feet more clearance than what is indicated on the gauge at the center of its arch at mean low tide. Bridge clearances are also shown on NOAA charts.

- Contact the bridgetender well in advance (even if you can't see the bridge around the bend) by VHF radio or phone. Alternatively, the proper horn signal for a bridge opening is one prolonged blast (four to six seconds) and one short blast (approximately one second). Bridge operators sound this signal when ready to open the bridge, and then usually the danger signal–five short blasts–when they are closing the bridge. The operator of each vessel is required by law to signal the bridgetender for an opening, even if another vessel has already signaled. Tugs with tows and U.S. government vessels may go through bridges at any time, usually signaling with five short blasts. A restricted bridge may open in an emergency with the same signal. Keep in mind bridgetenders will not know your intentions unless you tell them.

- If two or more vessels are in sight of one another, the bridgetender may elect to delay opening the bridge until all boats can go through together.

- Approach at slow speed and be prepared to wait as the bridge cannot open until the traffic gates are closed. Many ICW bridges, for example, are more than 40 years old and the aged machinery functions slowly.

- Once the bridge is open, proceed at no-wake speed. Keep a safe distance between you and other craft as currents and turbulence around bridge supports can be tricky.

- There is technically no legal right-of-way (except on the Mississippi and some other inland rivers) but boats running with the current should always be given the right-of-way out of courtesy. As always, if you are not sure, let the other boat go first.

- When making the same opening as a commercial craft, it is a good idea to contact the vessel's captain (usually on VHF Channel 13), ascertain his intentions and state yours to avoid any misunderstanding in tight quarters.

- After passing through the bridge, maintain a no-wake speed until you are well clear and then resume normal speed.

Locks & Locking Through

Many rivers in North America are a series of pools created by dams. When the dams also include locks, navigation is possible beyond the dam. Locks are watertight chambers with gates at each end. They raise and lower boats from one water level to the next. Many cruisers find locking through a pleasant experience and part of the adventure of boating.

Lock Types

- Conventional lift locks are single chambers that raise and lower boats.
- Flight locks are a series of conventional lift locks.
- Hydraulic lift locks have water-filled chambers supported by rams or pistons that move in opposite directions. The movement of one chamber forces the movement of the other via a connected valve. The chamber in the upper position adds sufficient water to cause it to drop, forcing the lower chamber to rise. The chambers have hinged gates fore and aft that contain the water and allow boats to enter or leave.
- Marine railways convey boats over obstacles, usually a landmass, by containing boats in a gantry crane that moves over the land and deposits the boat on the other side of the obstruction.

River locks are usually conventional lift locks. The dam deepens water around shoals and the lock allows vessels to bypass the dam. Conventional lift locks work by gravity alone. Water passively flows into or out of the lock. When the lock is filling, the valve at the upper end of the lock is opened and water flows in. The downstream lock gate is closed, preventing the escape of the water. This is the time of greatest turbulence in the locks and the time of greatest vigilance for boaters. When the upper water level is reached, the upper lock gate opens to allow boats to exit or enter.

When the lock empties, both lock doors are closed, a valve on the lower end of the lock is opened and water exits. This creates a surge of water outside the lock but inside the lock, the water recedes like water in a tub. When the water level in the lock is the same as the lower river level, the lower lock gate opens and vessels leave.

Locking Protocol

Call ahead on VHF Channel 13 (or sound three blasts) for permission to lock through. Indicate whether you are northbound (upbound) or southbound (downbound). Your presence and communication indicate to the locktender your desire to lock through.

Wait a safe distance from the lock or find an anchorage nearby and within sight of the lock.

Prepare for locking by placing large fenders fore and aft and having lines ready. Fender boards are useful because they protect your fenders and provide a skid plate against the dirt and algae on the lock wall.

When approaching the lock, stay back to allow outbound vessels to clear the lock. Do not enter until signaled to do so. Signals vary. Look for a telephone/pull rope at the lock wall; listen for a whistle blast–one long and one short blast or three blasts; look for a "traffic" light–green, yellow or red. Follow directions given by the locktender. The order of priority is:

1. U.S. Military
2. Mail boats
3. Commercial passenger boats
4. Commercial tows
5. Commercial fishermen
6. Pleasure Craft

When the locktender turns on the green light or calls for you to enter, enter in the order that boats arrived at the lock. The longest waiting boat goes first, unless directed by the locktender, who may call boats in according to size and the configuration of the lock. Do not jump the line, do not scoot in front of others and defer to faster boats so you do not have them behind you after you leave the lock.

When entering the lock, leave no wake, heed instruction and respect other boaters. If they are having trouble and appear unsettled, stand by until they are secure. Listen to the directives of the locktenders. Some lock systems require all line handlers to wear personal flotation devices (PFDs). Crew members on the bow should wear PFDs.

You will be directed by the locktender to a place along the lock wall. You will find an inset mooring pin (floating bollard), vertical cable or a rope.

- If there is a floating bollard, secure the boat to the pin via a center cleat by wrapping the line around the pin then back to the boat cleat.
- If there is a vertical cable, wrap the line around the cable and bring it back to the boat; the loop will ride up or down the cable.
- If there is a drop-down line, bring the line around a cleat and hold it. DO NOT TIE THE LINES! If you are asked to provide a line, throw it to the locktender. After the locktender has secured it, take the bitter end and wrap–but do not tie–around a cleat. Attend the bow and the stern, and adjust the line(s) as the boat rises or falls in the lock chamber.

In crowded locks, move forward as far as you can to make room for others coming in behind you. Small boats may raft to bigger boats. Set adequate fenders for fending off another vessel.

Inside the lock chamber, turn off engines when secure. Exhaust fumes contained in the lock chamber are an irritant to people in small, open boats. Attend the lines at all times. Be prepared for turbulence when the lock fills. Never use hands or feet to fend a boat off a lock wall. Stay alert to other boats. Be prepared to quickly cut a line if needed.

When the lock reaches its determined depth/height, the locktender will loosen the line and drop it to you if you are using a line attached at the top of the lock. After receiving a whistle blast by the locktender, recover any lines used, and prepare to exit. Leave the lock in the same order as entering. Do not rush ahead of those in front of you.

Bridge & Lock Schedules

KEY:	**Statute Miles from ICW Mile 0** / **Vertical Clearance**
	Drawbridge clearances are vertical, in feet, when closed and at Mean High Water in tidal areas. Bridge schedules are subject to schedule changes due to repairs, maintenance, events, etc. Check Waterway Explorer at www.waterwayguide.com for the latest schedules or call ahead.

East Coast ICW

VA BRIDGES MONITOR VHF CHANNEL 13

Mile	Clearance	Bridge
2.6	6'	**Belt Line Railroad Bridge:** Usually open. Remote operation. When the bridge closes for any reason, the controller will announce 30 min. in advance, 15 min. in advance, and immediately proceeding the actual lowering over VHF Channel 13. 757-271-1741
2.8	145'	**Jordan Bridge:** Fixed
3.6	10'	**Norfolk & Western Railroad Bridge:** Usually open. Clearance of 9 feet or less has been reported. 757-494-7371
5.8	35'	**Gilmerton Bridge:** Opens on signal, except from 6:30 a.m. to 8:30 a.m. and 3:30 p.m. to 5:30 p.m., Mon. through Fri. (except federal holidays), when the draw need not open. Draw will not open if adjacent railroad bridge is closed. 757-485-5488/-5567
5.8	7'	**Norfolk Southern #7 Railroad Bridge:** Usually open. Remote operation. 757-924-5320
7.1	65'	**I-64 Bridge:** The draw will open on signal if at least 24-hour notice is given.
8.9	95'	**Veterans Bridge:** Fixed
11.3		**Great Bridge Lock:** Opens on signal but coordinates with Battlefield Blvd. Bridge. 757-547-3311
12.0	8'	**SR 168 (Battlefield Blvd.) Bridge:** Opens on signal, except 6:00 a.m. to 7:00 p.m. daily, when the draw need only open on the hour. The drawtender may delay the hourly opening up to 10 min. past the hour for approaching vessels. Timed to open with Great Bridge Lock. 757-482-8250
13.0	65'	**Chesapeake Expressway (VA 168 Bypass) Bridge:** Fixed
13.9	7'	**Albemarle & Chesapeake Railroad Bridge:** Usually open.
15.2	4'	**Centerville Turnpike (SR 170) Bridge:** Opens on hour and half-hour, except Mon. through Fri. from 6:30 a.m. to 8:30 a.m. and 4:00 p.m. to 6:00 p.m. (except federal holidays and weekends), when the draw need not open. The drawtender may delay the hourly opening up to 10 min. past the hour for approaching vessels. 757-547-3631/-3632
20.2	6'	**SR 165 (North Landing) Bridge:** Opens on signal, except from 6:00 a.m. to 7:00 p.m., when the draw need only open on the hour and half-hour. 757-482-3081
28.3	65'	**Pungo Ferry (SR 726) Bridge:** Fixed
49.9	65'	**Coinjock (U.S. 158) Bridge:** Fixed

Dismal Swamp Canal

VA & NC BRIDGES MONITOR VHF CHANNEL 13

Mile	Clearance	Bridge
10.5		**Deep Creek Lock:** Opens at 8:30 a.m., 11:00 a.m., 1:30 p.m. and 3:30 p.m. 757-487-0831
11.1	4'	**Deep Creek Bridge:** Openings coordinated with lock operation. 757-487-0831
28.0	0'	**Dismal Swamp Canal Visitor Center Foot Bridge:** Usually open. This is a floating pontoon bridge. 252-771-6593
31.5	65'	**U.S. 17 Hwy. Bridge:** Fixed
32.6	4'	**South Mills Bridge:** Openings coordinated with lock operation. 252-771-5906
32.7		**South Mills Lock:** Opens at 8:30 a.m., 11:00 a.m., 1:30 p.m. and 3:30 p.m. 252-771-5906
47.7	3'	**Norfolk Southern Railroad Bridge:** Usually open. (Note: Bridge is hand operated.) 866-527-3499 (for emergencies only)
50.7	2'	**U.S. 158 Hwy. Bridge:** Opens on signal, except from 7:00 a.m. to 9:00 a.m. and 4:00 p.m. to 6:00 p.m., Mon. through Fri., when the draw need only open at 7:30 a.m., 8:30 a.m., 4:30 p.m. and 5:30 p.m. if vessels are waiting to pass. 252-331-4772

East Coast ICW (cont.)

NC BRIDGES MONITOR VHF CHANNEL 13

84.2
14'
Alligator River (U.S. 64) Bridge: Opens on signal. (Note: Bridge may not open if wind speed exceeds 34 knots.) 252-796-7261

113.9
65'
Fairfield (NC 94) Bridge: Fixed

125.9
64'
Wilkerson (U.S. 264) Bridge: Fixed. (Also known as the Walter B. Jones Bridge.) (Note: This bridge is lower than the authorized 65-foot fixed vertical clearance.)

157.2
65'
Hobucken (NC 33/304) Bridge: Fixed

195.8
65'
Core Creek (NC 101) Bridge: Fixed

203.8
65'
Beaufort Channel (U.S. 70) Bridge: Fixed

203.8
4'
Beaufort Channel Railroad Bridge: Usually open.

206.7
65'
Atlantic Beach Bridge: Fixed. (Note: Clearance may be closer to 63 feet.)

226.0
65'
B. Cameron Langston Bridge: Fixed. (Also known as the Emerald Isle Bridge.)

240.7
12'
Onslow Beach Swing Bridge: (Use northwest draw.) Opens on signal, except from 7:00 a.m. to 7:00 p.m., when the draw need only open on the hour and half hour. You MUST signal, even though the operator may see you waiting. 910-440-7376

252.3
64'
NC 210 Hwy. Bridge: Fixed. (Note: This bridge is lower than the authorized 65-foot fixed vertical clearance.)

260.7
65'
Surf City (NC 50) Bridge: Fixed

278.1
20'
Figure Eight Island Swing Bridge: Opens on the hour and half-hour. (Note: Bridge may not open if wind speed exceeds 30 mph.) 910-686-2018

283.1
20'
SR 74 Bridge: Opens on the hour 7:00 a.m. to 7:00 p.m. Schedule may change during special events. (Also known as Wrightsville Beach Bridge.) (Note: Actual clearance is lower than charted. May be as low as 14 feet.) 910-256-2886

295.7
65'
Snows Cut (U.S. 421) Bridge: Fixed

311.8
65'
Oak Island (NC 133) Bridge: Fixed

316.8
67'
Middleton Street Bridge: Fixed

323.6
65'
Holden Beach (NC 130) Bridge: Fixed

333.7
65'
Ocean Isle (NC 904) Bridge: Fixed

337.9
65'
Mannon C. Gore (Sunset Beach) Bridge: Fixed

SC BRIDGES MONITOR VHF CHANNEL 09

347.2
65'
Nixon Crossroads Bridge: Fixed

347.3
7'
Captain Archie Neil "Poo" McLauchlin (Little River) Swing Bridge: Opens on signal. 843-280-5919

349.1
65'
Robert Edge Parkway Bridge: Fixed. (Also called the **North Myrtle Beach Connector Bridge**.)

353.3
31'
Barefoot Landing Swing Bridge: Opens on signal. 843-361-3291

355.5
65'
Conway Bypass (SC 22) Twin Bridges: Fixed

357.5
65'
Grande Dunes Bridge: Fixed

360.5
65'
Grissom Parkway Bridge: Fixed

365.4
16'
SCL Railroad Bridge: Usually open. (Referred to with adjacent railroad bridge as **Combination Bridges**.)

365.4
65'
U.S. 501 Bridge: Fixed

366.4
65'
Fantasy Harbor Bridge: Fixed

371.0
11'
Socastee Swing Bridge: (Use southeast draw.) Opens on signal. 843-347-3525

Mile	Clearance	Bridge
371.3	65'	**Socastee (SC 544) Hwy. Bridge:** Fixed. (Note: Clearance as low as 61 feet has been observed.)
372	65'	**Carolina Bays Parkway (SC 31) Bridge:** Fixed
402.1	65'	**Ocean Hwy. (U.S. 17) Bridge:** Fixed
411.5	0'	**Estherville-Minim Canal Bridge:** Usually open, except when a vehicle needs to cross (infrequent). Watch for flashing yellow lights on sign. This is a floating swing bridge. The bridge rests against the east bank of the river when in the open position.
458.9	65'	**Isle of Palms Connector Bridge:** Fixed (Note: Clearance may be lower than charted.)
462.2	31'	**Ben Sawyer Memorial (SC 703) Bridge:** Opens on signal, except from 7:00 a.m. to 9:00 a.m. and from 4:00 p.m. to 6:00 p.m., Mon. through Fri. (except federal holidays), when the draw need not open. On Sat., Sun. and federal holidays from 9:00 a.m. to 7:00 p.m. the draw need open only on the hour. Use the west span. 843-883-3581
469.9	67'	**James Island Expressway Bridge:** Fixed
470.8	33'	**Wappoo Creek (SC 171) Bridge:** Opens on signal, except from 6:00 a.m. to 9:29 a.m. and 3:31 p.m. to 7:00 p.m., Monday through Friday, (except federal holidays), when the draw need not open. Between 9:30 a.m. and 3:30 p.m., Monday through Friday (except federal holidays), when the draw need only once an hour on the half hour. 843-852-4157
479.3	65'	**John F. Limehouse Hwy. Bridge:** Fixed
501.3	65'	**McKinley Washington Jr. (SR 174) Bridge:** Fixed)
536.0	30'	**Lady's Island (Woods Memorial) Bridge:** Opens on signal, except from 6:30 a.m. to 9:00 a.m. and 3:00 p.m. to 6:00 p.m., Mon. through Fri. (except federal holidays), when the draw need not open to navigation; and from 9:00 a.m. to 3:00 p.m., when the draw need open only on the hour. During the months of Apr., May, Oct. and Nov., Mon. through Fri. (except federal holidays), the draw will open on signal except from 7:00 a.m. to 9:00 a.m. and from 4:00 p.m. to 6:00 p.m., when the draw need not open to navigation; and from 9:00 a.m. to 4:00 p.m., when the draw need open only on the hour and half-hour. 843-521-2111
539.7	65'	**McTeer Memorial Twin Bridges:** Fixed
557.5	65'	**Wilton J. Graves (U.S. 278) Hwy. Bridge:** Fixed

GA BRIDGES MONITOR VHF CHANNEL 09

Mile	Clearance	Bridge
579.9	21'	**Causton Bluff (Sam Varnedoe/SR 26) Bridge:** Opens on signal, except 6:30 a.m. to 9:00 a.m. and 4:30 p.m. to 6:30 p.m., Mon. through Fri. (except federal holidays), when the draw need only open at 7:00 a.m., 8:00 a.m. and 5:30 p.m. (Note: Clearance may be higher than charted.) 912-897-2511
582.8	65'	**State of Georgia Memorial (U.S. 80) Bridge:** Fixed (Also called **Thunderbolt Bridge**.)
592.9	65'	**Diamond Causeway (Skidaway) Bridge:** Fixed
674.5	65'	**F.J. Torras Causeway Bridge:** Fixed
684.4	65'	**Jekyll Island (SR 520) Bridge:** Fixed

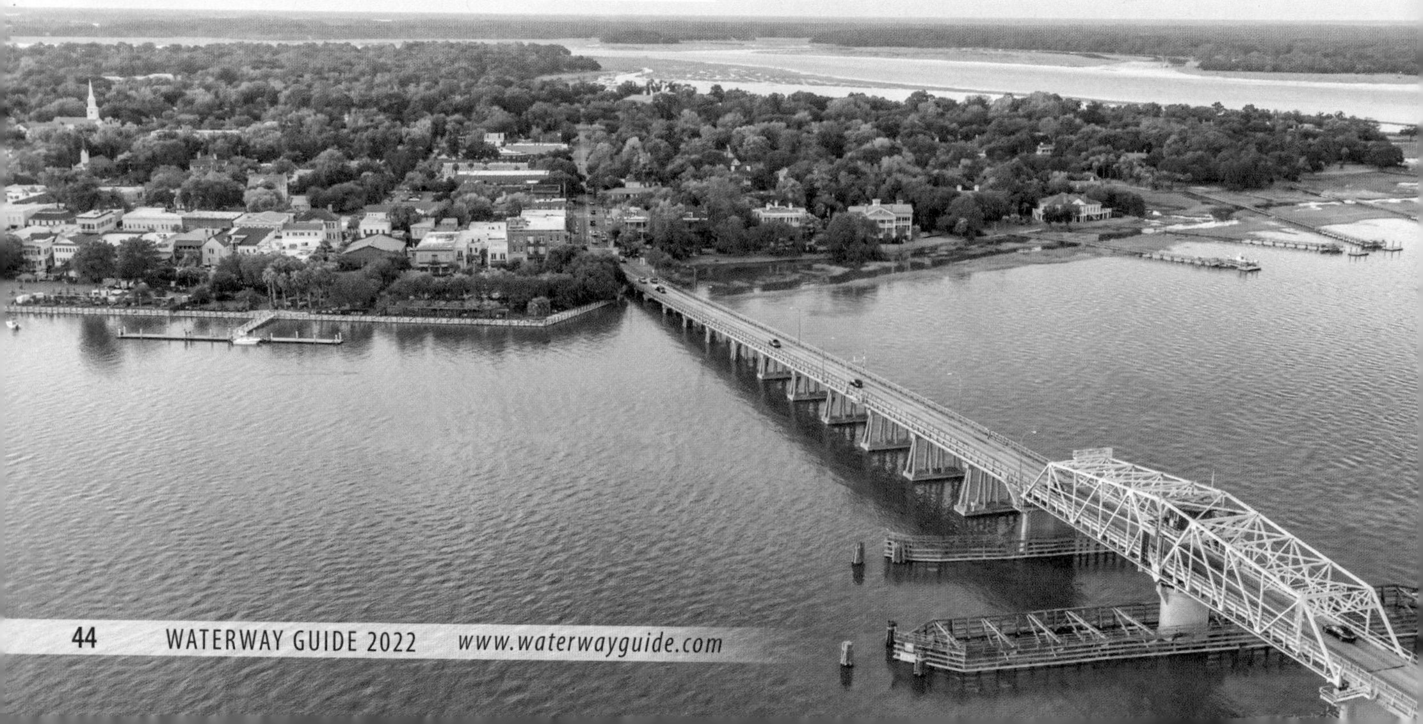

Inlets: Norfolk, VA to St. Marys, GA

Cruising the "inside waterway" (the ICW) is a bit like driving down I-95. There are areas where every amenity and convenience you need is but an exit away (especially in FL), and then there are stretches with only marsh and woods as far as the eye can see (mostly in SC and GA). And like I-95 there is constant construction, many speed-restricted areas and several bridges to pass under. (The lowest bridge clearance on the ICW is the Julia Tuttle Causeway at Mile 1087.1 in Miami, which is 56 feet.) The main difference between the highway and the waterway is the "road maintenance." With federal funding for dredging being scarce, shoaling has been more commonplace on the ICW and the "projected depths" on the NOAA charts can no longer be considered valid. This, alone, will drive (pun intended) some vessels to take the offshore (Atlantic Ocean) route.

Offshore Runs: Some boaters choose the offshore run to save time or to get a break from the bridge openings and speed restrictions. Many sailboats will take this option to turn off the engine and unfurl the sails. You may be forced to take the offshore route due to vessel draft or vertical clearance. Regardless of your reasons for exiting the ICW, there are numerous inlets along the coast that will allow you to duck in or back out should the weather turn. Keep in mind that not all inlets are navigable and some are treacherous under certain conditions. This section will assist you in recognizing those but it is still important to study the charts, pay attention to the weather and seek current local knowledge before proceeding on an offshore run.

Overall Mileage: Heading north or south, many skippers mistakenly assume that they will shorten their trips by going out to sea and running down the coast. The distances shown here–both inside (ICW) and outside (from inlet to inlet)–demonstrate that this is not necessarily true. Keep in mind that even if outside distances from sea buoy to sea buoy are virtually the same as the ICW distances, the mileage in and out to the buoys adds to the total coastwise figure.

Cautions and Warnings: Before you begin an offshore passage, take an honest accounting of your vessel, your crew and yourself. Is each of you up to the task? Is the vessel properly outfitted? Do you have the necessary safety equipment, charts, long distance communications gear such as single sideband radio (SSB), an Emergency Position Indicating Radio Beacon (EPIRB) and life raft? Do you and your crew have adequate experience in boating and navigation to attempt an offshore coastal passage?

Check the weather using as many sources as possible. If you have access to weather routing services, they are a good option, particularly for longer offshore passages. You are seeking a weather window with enough space on each side to get you safely out and back in, with room for unexpected contingencies.

Of course, always file a float plan with a reliable person. A sample float plan is provided in this guide. You might also look into the free app BoatSafe Free, which allows you to create a float plan and email it to participants or emergency contacts.

Entering & Exiting: Plan your trip so that you enter in daylight, with the tide, particularly if your boat is slow or underpowered. Remember that wind against tide can create short, steep waves in an inlet that can quickly make even a ship channel impassable for slower boats. If conditions are bad when you reach the sea buoy for an inlet, you may find yourself being driven ashore by wind or waves and unable to find the inlet buoys. It may be better to remain well offshore in rough conditions, possibly continuing to a better inlet.

Be advised that the markers at some inlets are moved on a regular basis and the buoys should be honored. Should you find yourself at an inlet and needing direction, a call on VHF Channel 16 for local knowledge is likely to bring you a response. Sea Tow and TowBoatU.S. are two other knowledgeable sources. The Coast Guard may also be able to assist you, but only if it is indeed an emergency.

Resources: Prior to your voyage, there are a number of online sources that can familiarize you with the inlets, including the following:

- **Waterway Explorer** (www.waterwayguide.com)–Website provides chart and satellite views of the inlets plus cruising details from local boaters.
- **United States Coast Pilot** (www.nauticalcharts.noaa.gov)–Nine-volume annual publication distributed by the Office of Coast Survey (NOAA) to supplement nautical charts.
- ***Local Notice to Mariners*** (www.navcen.uscg.gov, then select the LNMs tab)–Weekly updates provided by The U.S. Coast Guard to provide corrections to navigational publications and nautical charts.
- **Tide Tables** (www.tidesandcurrents.noaa.gov)–Provided by NOAA to provide tidal predictions (highs and lows) for specific areas.

Norfolk, VA to St. Marys, GA Entrances & Inlets

Recommended (big ship) inlets in this section are denoted with this symbol:

Inside vs. Outside Mileage

Entrance & Inlet Distances

Hampton Roads to Beaufort Inlet:
222 nm (outside)/204 sm (ICW)

Beaufort Inlet to Cape Fear River Entrance:
115 nm (outside)/105 sm (ICW)

Cape Fear River Entrance to Winyah Bay Entrance:
65 nm (outside)/97 sm (ICW)

Winyah Bay Entrance to Charleston Harbor Entrance:
46 nm (outside)/58 sm (ICW)

Charleston Harbor Entrance to Port Royal Sound Entrance:
57 nm (outside)/85 sm (ICW)

Port Royal Sound Entrance to Tybee Roads Entrance:
10 nm (outside)/27 sm (ICW)

Tybee Roads Entrance to St. Simons Sound Entrance:
62 nm (outside)/102 sm (ICW)

St. Simons Sound Entrance to St. Marys River Entrance:
21 nm (outside)/36 sm (ICW)

Note: In keeping with standard NOAA conventions, outside (ocean) distances are measured in nautical miles (nm), while ICW distances are measured in statute miles (sm):

1nm = 1.15 sm

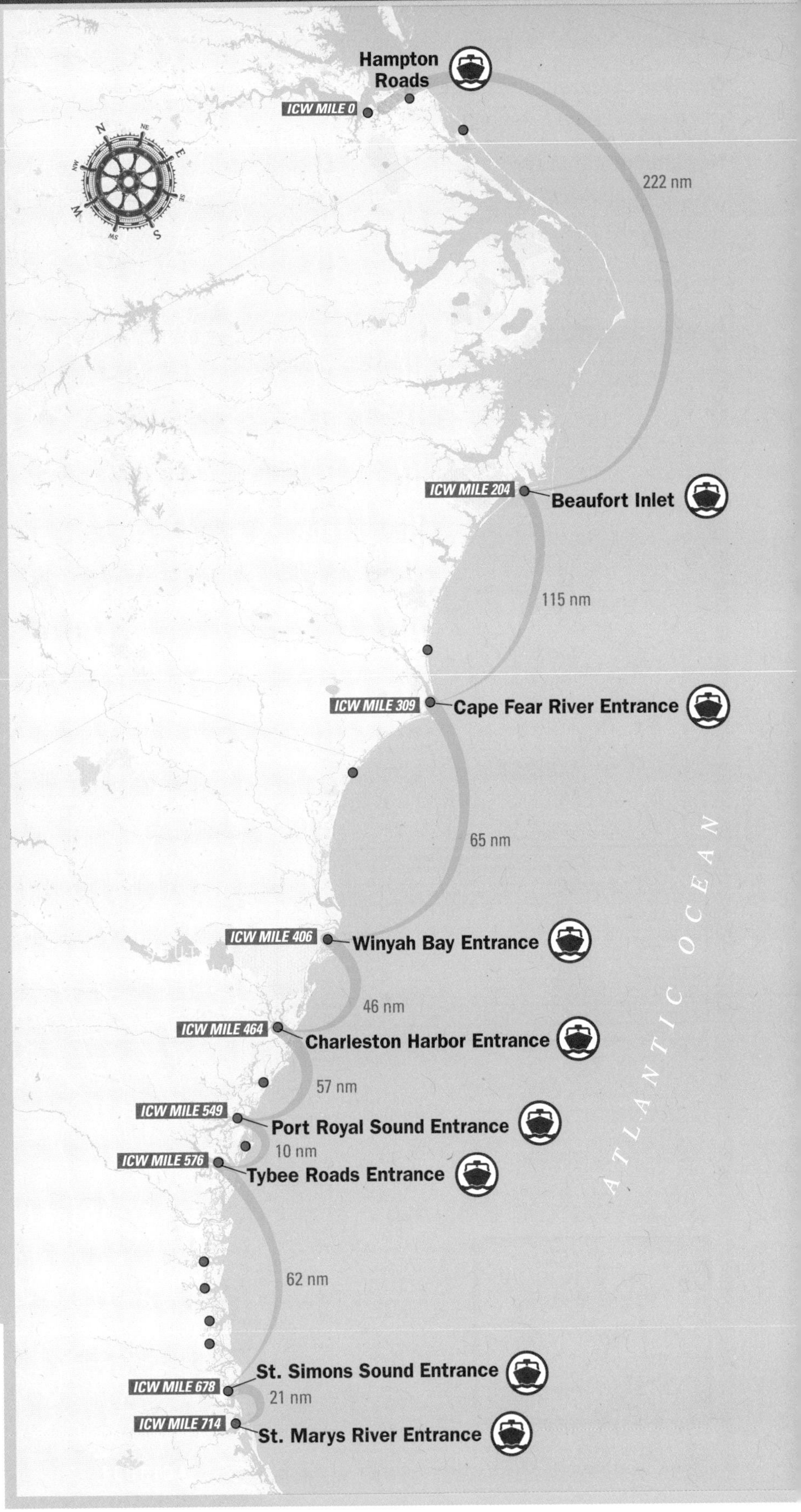

Sea Buoy: None. Use waypoint N 36° 58.113'/W 76° 19.980'.

Overview: Strategically situated at Mile Zero, the "official" beginning of the ICW, Norfolk offers nearly every type of marine service and equipment.

Navigation: From the waypoint, follow the well-marked Thimble Shoal Channel east and south to flashing red "2C" off Cape Henry, where the mouth of the Chesapeake Bay meets the Atlantic Ocean. Along this stretch, you will pass through or over the 17-mile-long Chesapeake Bay Bridge-Tunnel.

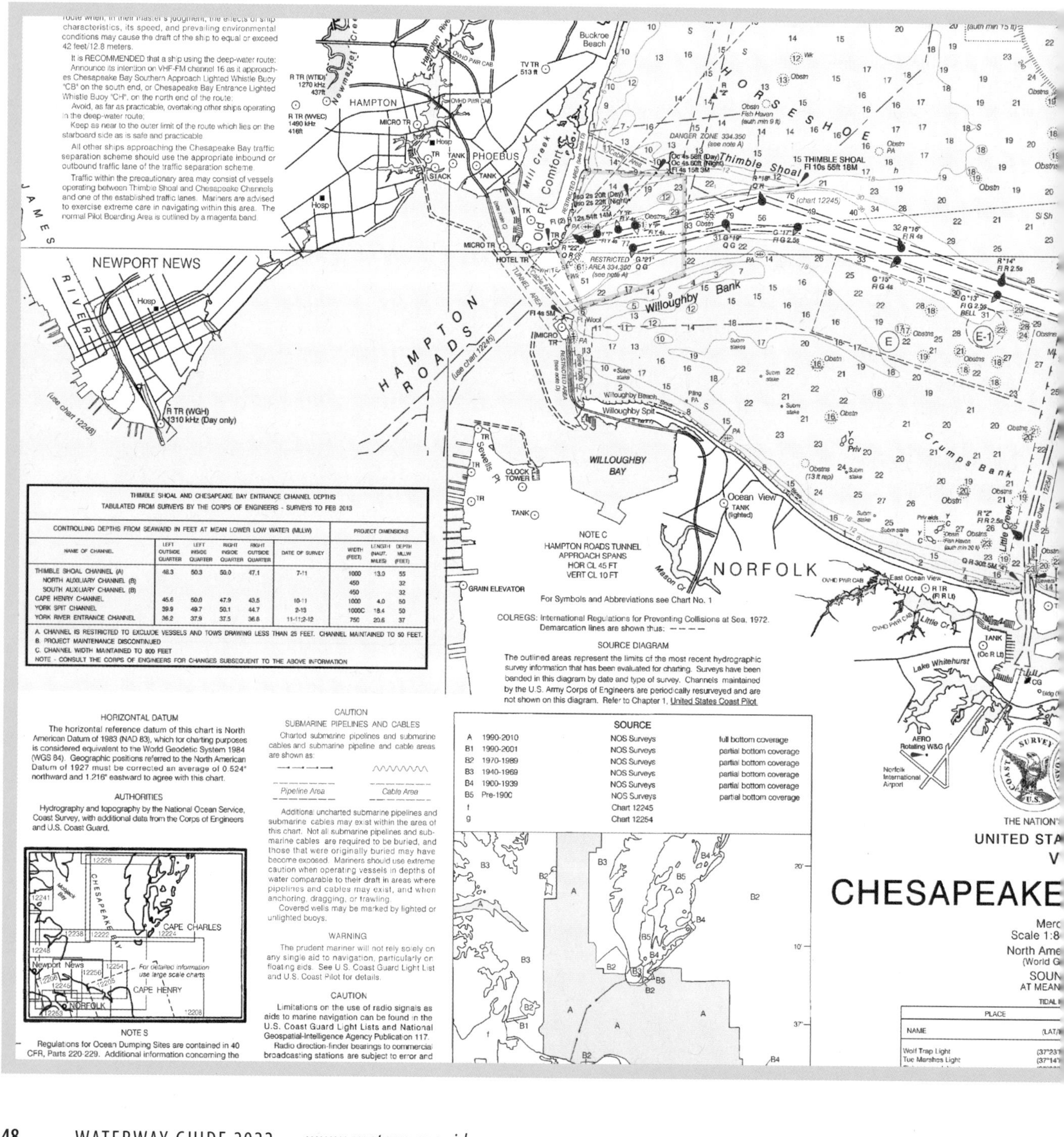

Cautions & Hazards: This is a busy port. Naval Station Norfolk, the largest naval installation in the world, is homeport for the U.S. Navy's Atlantic Fleet, encompassing aircraft carriers, cruisers, destroyers, frigates, support ships, nuclear submarines and admiral's barges. The world's merchant fleet loads and unloads cargo at the Hampton Roads as well.

Depth: See interactive charts on Waterway Explorer at www.waterwayguide.com.

ICW Connection: Norfolk is located at Mile Zero (the beginning) of the ICW.

Nearest Recommended Inlet: The next big ship inlet is Beaufort Inlet, NC, which is 222 nm.

Use Chart 12221

Sea Buoy: No sea buoy here. Use waypoint N 36° 55.350'/W 76° 05.370'.

Overview: Provides easy and fast access to the Atlantic Ocean, Chesapeake Bay or the ICW. Marinas catering to sportfishermen abound. Located just southeast of the Chesapeake Bay Bridge Tunnel, inside Cape Henry. This is not a jettied inlet like many others.

Navigation: From the waypoint, proceed 0.25 nm on a heading of 196° M to green "IL." Follow the markers in just past red nun "6" where you will encounter the fixed Lesner Bridge with a vertical clearance of 45 feet. Note that there are fixed bridges with 20- to 36-foot clearances to negotiate to the south, which eventually leads to Broad Bay. There are anchoring possibilities in Broad Bay.

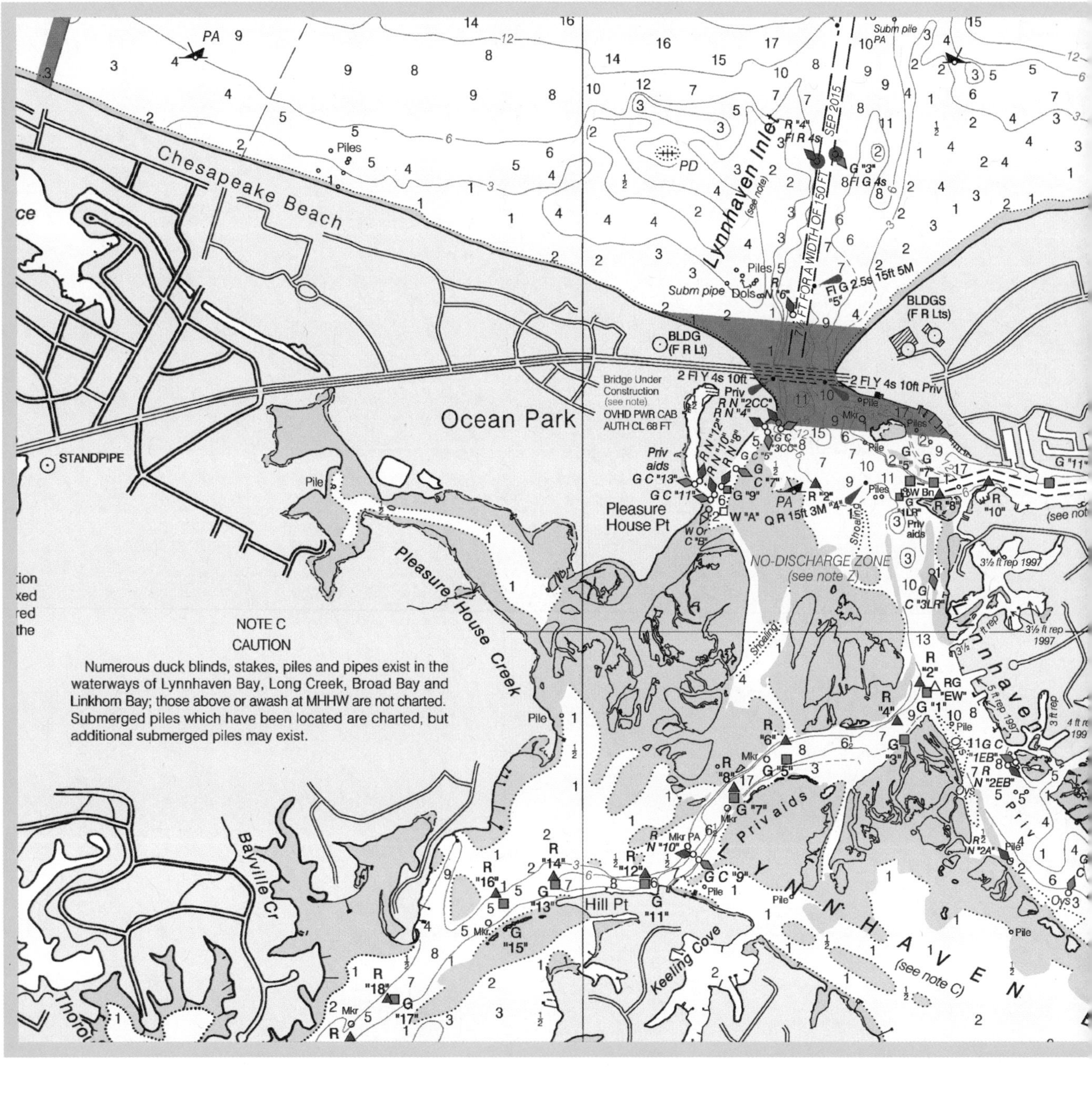

Cautions & Hazards: The straight, dredged entrance channel runs through a series of fixed and floating markers before passing under the 45-foot vertical clearance fixed bridge. Other than the height restriction, there are no other hazards, except a fairly strong current through the bridge.

Depth: The area was last dredeged in spring 2019. See interactive charts on Waterway Explorer at www.waterwayguide.com.

ICW Connection: None.

Nearest Recommended Inlet: If you cannot clear the bridges in Lynnhaven, you can proceed to Hampton Roads, 13 nm to the west, or proceed out and around Cape Henry to the south for about 14 nm to Rudee Inlet. Note that Rudee Inlet also does not connect with the ICW.

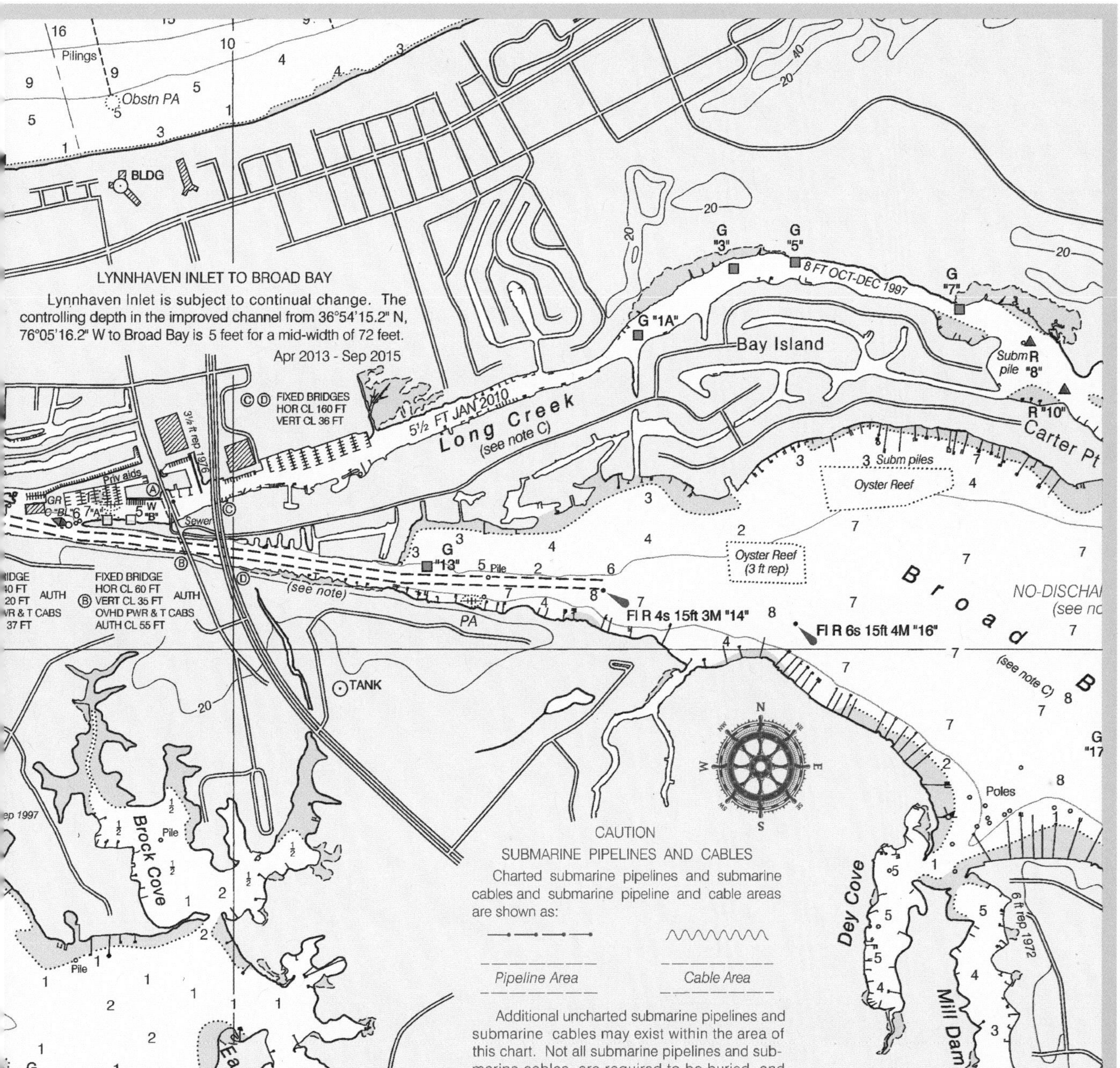

Use Chart 12254

Rudee Inlet, VA

Sea Buoy: Lighted red and white Morse (A) whistle buoy "RI" located at N 36° 49.790'/W 75° 56.950' (1 nm east-northeast of the jetties).

Overview: Two jetties protect the inlet, which offers easy access to the Atlantic. Quick access to the Atlantic Ocean ha made Rudee Inlet a haven for sportfishing boats.

Navigation: Dredged channel leads between the jetties to a basin just inside, then westward to a safety area about 0.2 nm above the entrance. Lake Rudee is to the north and Lake Wesley to the south. Two fixed highway bridges with a vertical clearance of 28 feet cross the arm of the inlet leading to Lake Rudee. Several overhead power and telephone cables with charted vertical clearances of 54 feet cross east of the bridge. The depths at the inlet and in the lakes can b 7 feet at MLW. Vessels that cannot get under the bridge can dock at Lake Wesley to the south.

Cautions & Hazards: Dredged frequently but shoals quickly across the south side of the channel, starting from the outer edge to the centerline, beginning approximately 40 feet east of the east end of the South Jetty and extending out eastward approximately 230 feet. Deeper draft vessels should seek local knowledge before attempting to enter.

Depth: See interactive charts on Waterway Explorer at www.waterwayguide.com.

ICW Connection: None.

Nearest Recommended Inlet: About 66 nm to the south is Oregon Inlet, NC, recommended only in good weather and calm seas. Cape Henry is 5.5 nm north at the entrance to the Chesapeake Bay.

Nearby facilities: Berths, electricity, gasoline, diesel fuel, water, ice and marine supplies are available.

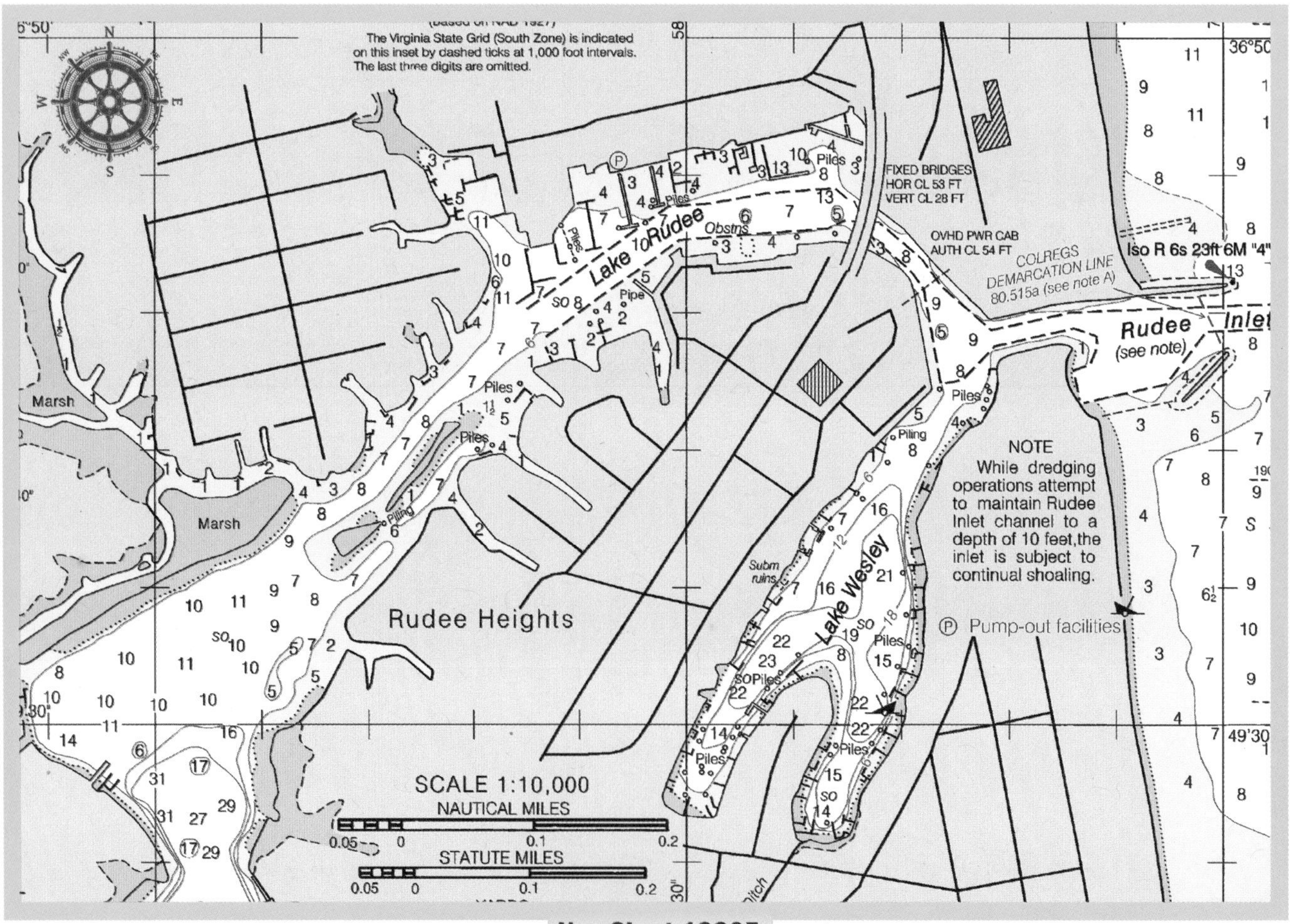

Use Chart 12205

Sea Buoy: Lighted red and white Morse (A) (RACON) whistle buoy "BM" located at N 34° 34.830'/ W 76° 41.550' (5 nm out).

Overview: Wide, deep and very well marked. Farthest "northerly" inlet recommended for transient recreational boaters. To the north lie the Outer Banks; rounding them entails a long passage in Atlantic Ocean waters.

Cautions & Hazards: Areas of shoaling have been identified throughout the Beaufort Inlet and Harbor; however, dredging in 2019 should alleviate some of those issues. Current runs 2 knots on the flood. Mariners are urged to use extreme caution when transiting the area.

Navigation: As this is a big ship entrance, you can forgo the sea buoy, which is more than 5 nm out, and start your approach from flashing green buoy "9" and flashing red bell buoy "10," which are just southwest of N 34° 40.000'/W 76° 40.000'. From here, follow the markers and stay in the center on a course slightly east of north to quick flashing red buoy "16" on Shackleford Point, then bear west of north. Shoaling was reported at quick flashing red buoy "16."

If you are headed for Beaufort itself, take the channel leading to the east side of Radio Island, taking care to round quick flashing red buoy "2." Don't cut flashing red buoy "20" short; it is very shallow out of the channel. If your destination is Morehead City, bear to port at flashing green buoy "21," and then continue to follow the big ship markers under the bridge.

Depth: This area was last dredged in spring 2019. See interactive charts on Waterway Explorer at www.waterwayguide.com.

ICW Connection: Proceed to the turning basin (ICW Mile 204) and bear to port if you are heading south on the ICW. If heading north, continue through the Beaufort Channel Railroad Bridge (4-foot closed vertical clearance, usually open), followed by the fixed Beaufort Channel Bridge (65-foot vertical clearance) immediately ahead of you.

Nearest Recommended Inlet: Barden Inlet is about 6 nm to the east at Cape Lookout, and even though it is no longer considered navigable for cruising vessels, a sheltered anchorage can be found behind Cape Lookout. Bogue Inlet is 20 nm to the southwest. Masonboro Inlet at Wrightsville Beach, a popular passage choice in settled weather, is about 65 nm distant.

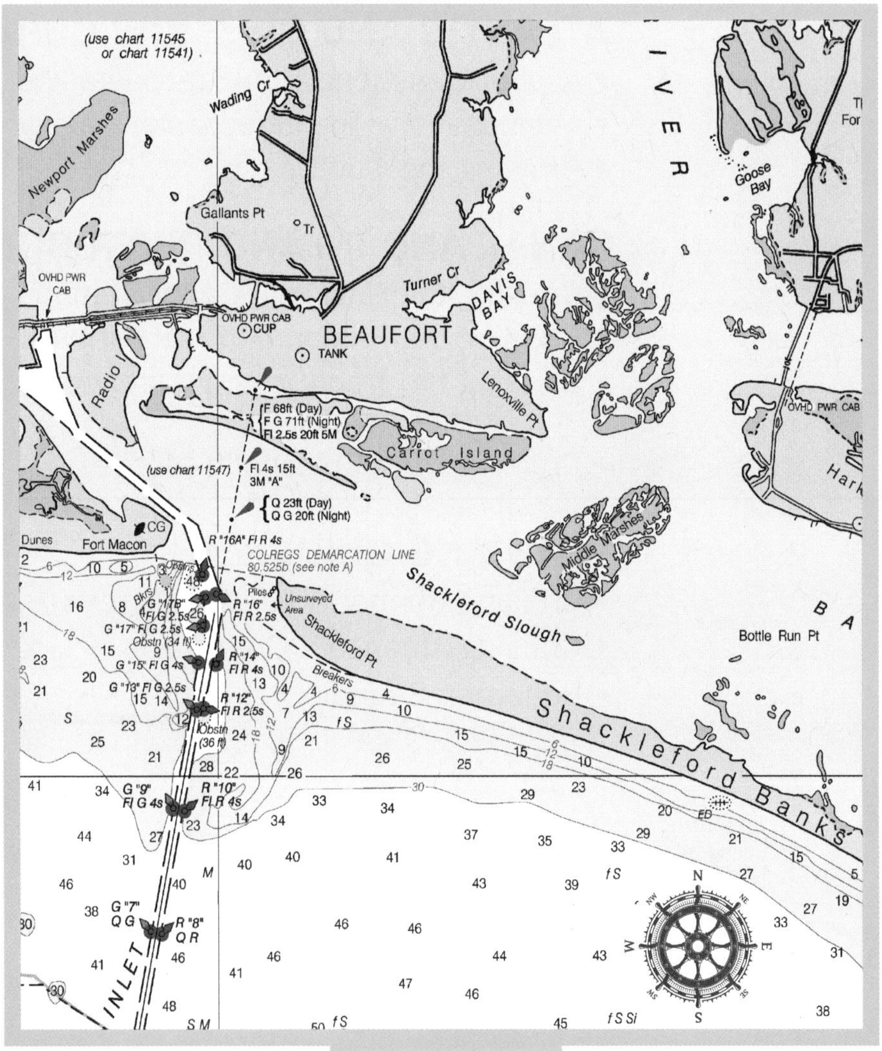

Use Chart 11544

Masonboro Inlet, NC

Sea Buoy: Lighted red and white Morse (A) whistle buoy "A" at N 34° 10.600'/ W 77° 47.870'.

Overview: Uncomplicated entrance protected by jetties on both sides and with good depths within. Popular with sportfishermen. Coast Guard Station Wrightsville Beach is just past red daybeacon "10."

Navigation: From the sea buoy, jetties lie to the northwest and are unmarked. Once inside, if you are headed to Wrightsville Beach, bear to starboard at green and red daybeacon "WC" and then turn to port at Motts Channel a bit farther up. If Masonboro is your destination, continue straight ahead.

Cautions & Hazards: There are no particular difficulties with this inlet, although a southeasterly wind can cause difficult conditions for smaller boats.

Depth: See interactive charts on Waterway Explorer at www.waterwayguide.com.

ICW Connection: ICW Mile 285 lies straight ahead past Shinn Creek.

Nearest Recommended Inlet: This is a good inlet for faster boats or for early-rising sailors or trawler skippers wanting to get off the ICW to or from Beaufort, NC, which is just under 65 nm to the northeast. Some slow-boat skippers make this an overnight passage, arriving at either end shortly after sunrise. Carolina Beach Inlet is 6 nm to the south, but a wiser and quicker course is to continue on the ICW from Masonboro, enter the Cape Fear River through Snows Cut, catch the outgoing tide and proceed to Southport (or detour upriver to visit Wilmington).

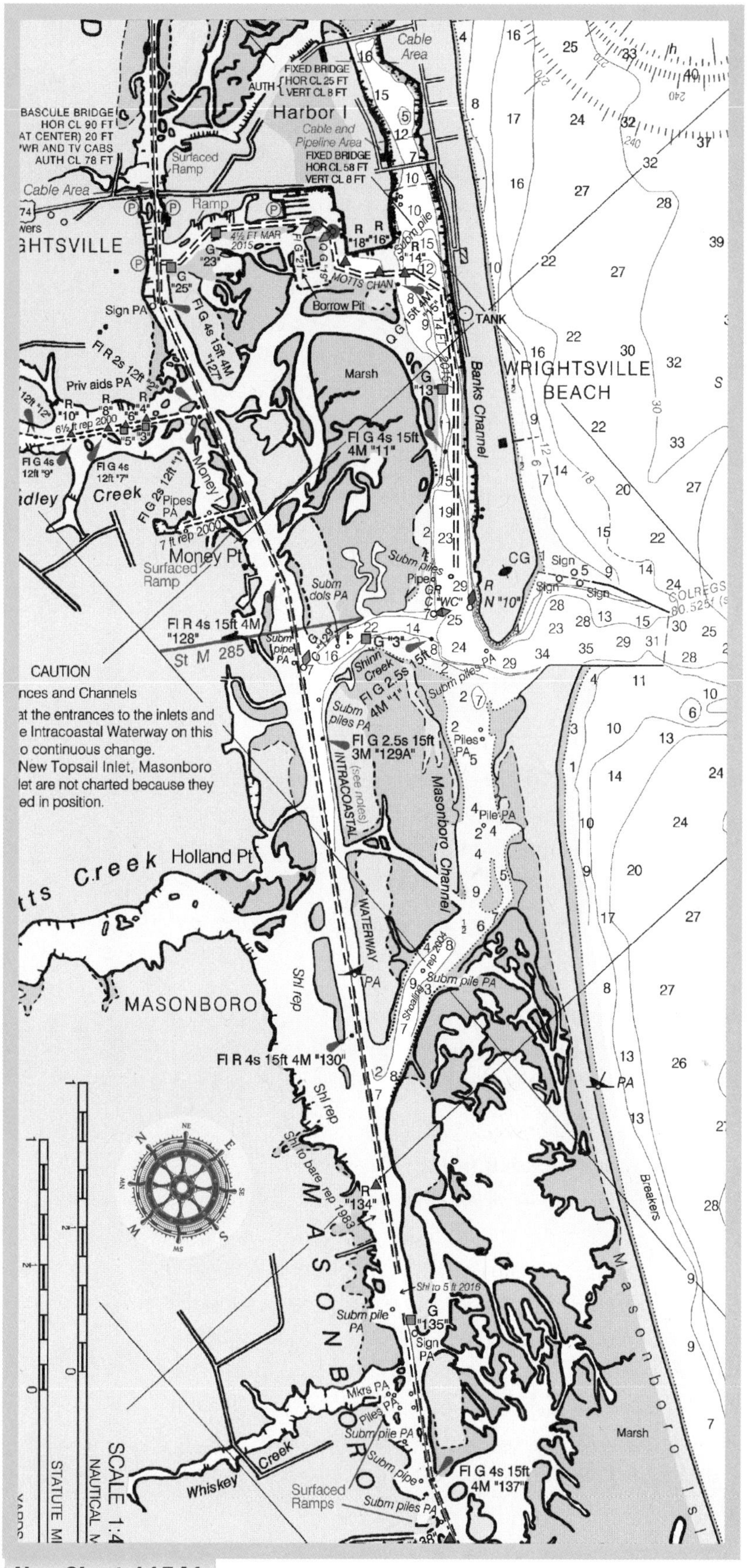

Use Chart 11541

Sea Buoy: Lighted red and white Morse (A) (RACON) whistle buoy "CF" at N 33° 46.280'/W 78° 03.020' (5 nm out).

Overview: Well-marked big ship channel protected from the north and an easy entrance day or night.

Navigation: Cruisers can approach using the waypoint N 33° 50.370'/W 78° 01.780', which is close to red buoy "8" where the surrounding waters begin to shallow. From flashing red buoy "8," proceed slightly east of north to quick flashing red buoy "10" and then to quick flashing red buoy "12,"(flashing green "11" may be missing) where you can pick up the Bald Head Shoal Range. For those headed north, we advise you stay on the ICW here to avoid a significant detour around Frying Pan Shoals, which extend 30 nm out into the Atlantic.

Cautions & Hazards: Daytime entrances are straightforward. As this is a busy inlet, keep a constant watch posted for big ships. The current is very strong; time your entrance to take advantage of the tides. Northbound in slower boats would be well-advised to check the tides before attempting the Cape Fear River's strong currents.

Depth: See interactive charts on Waterway Explorer at www.waterwayguide.com.

ICW Connection: Connects with the ICW at Mile 308.5. Heading north, the ICW follows the big ship channel toward Wilmington. To head south on the ICW, bear to port at Southport.

Nearest Recommended Inlet: Little River Inlet, SC, is about 24 nm to the west-southwest and takes you past the Lockwood's Folly and Shallotte Inlets, which are known for severe shoaling. The best option is Winyah Bay, SC (65 nm to the sea buoy), with its well-marked shipping channel. The drawback is that rejoining the ICW to continue south involves coming back north over 8 miles into the inlet, or 15 miles if Georgetown is your destination. Any northbound coastal passage requires rounding Frying Pan Shoals. The most prudent path is to continue northward on the ICW and use Masonboro Inlet at Wrightsville Beach, NC, as your jumping-off point to go offshore to Beaufort, NC.

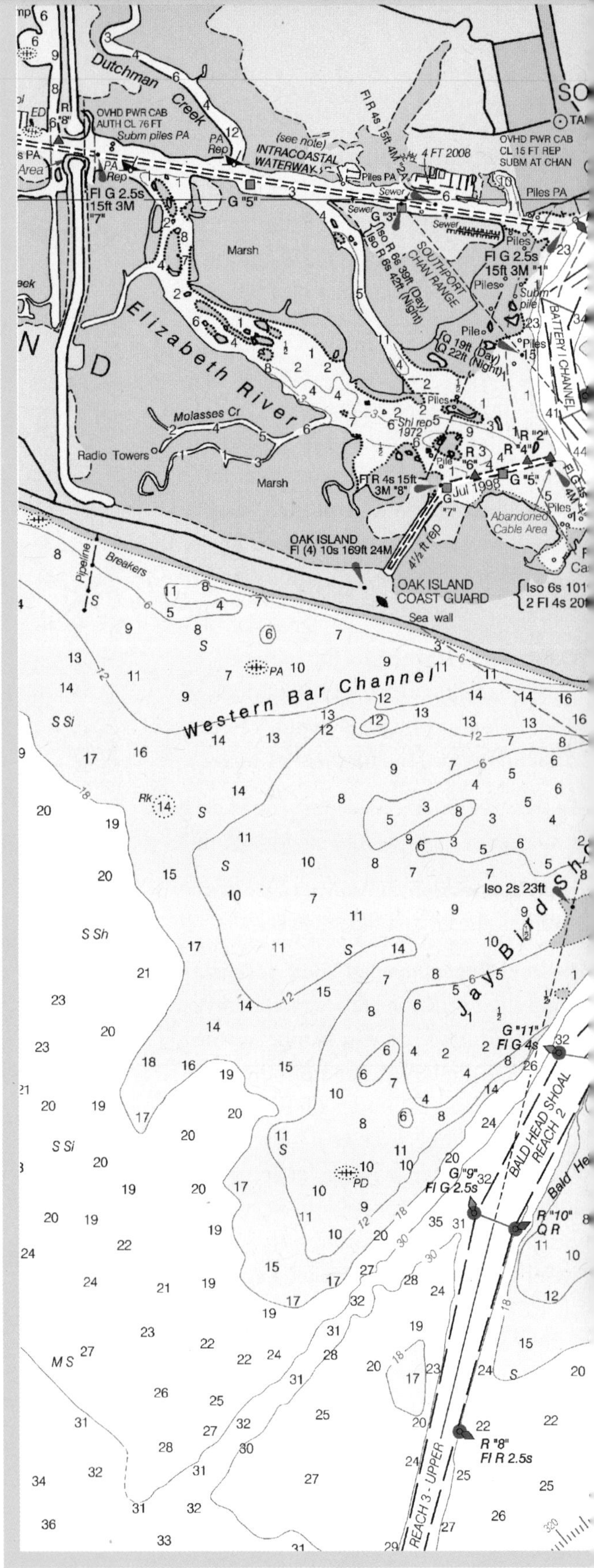

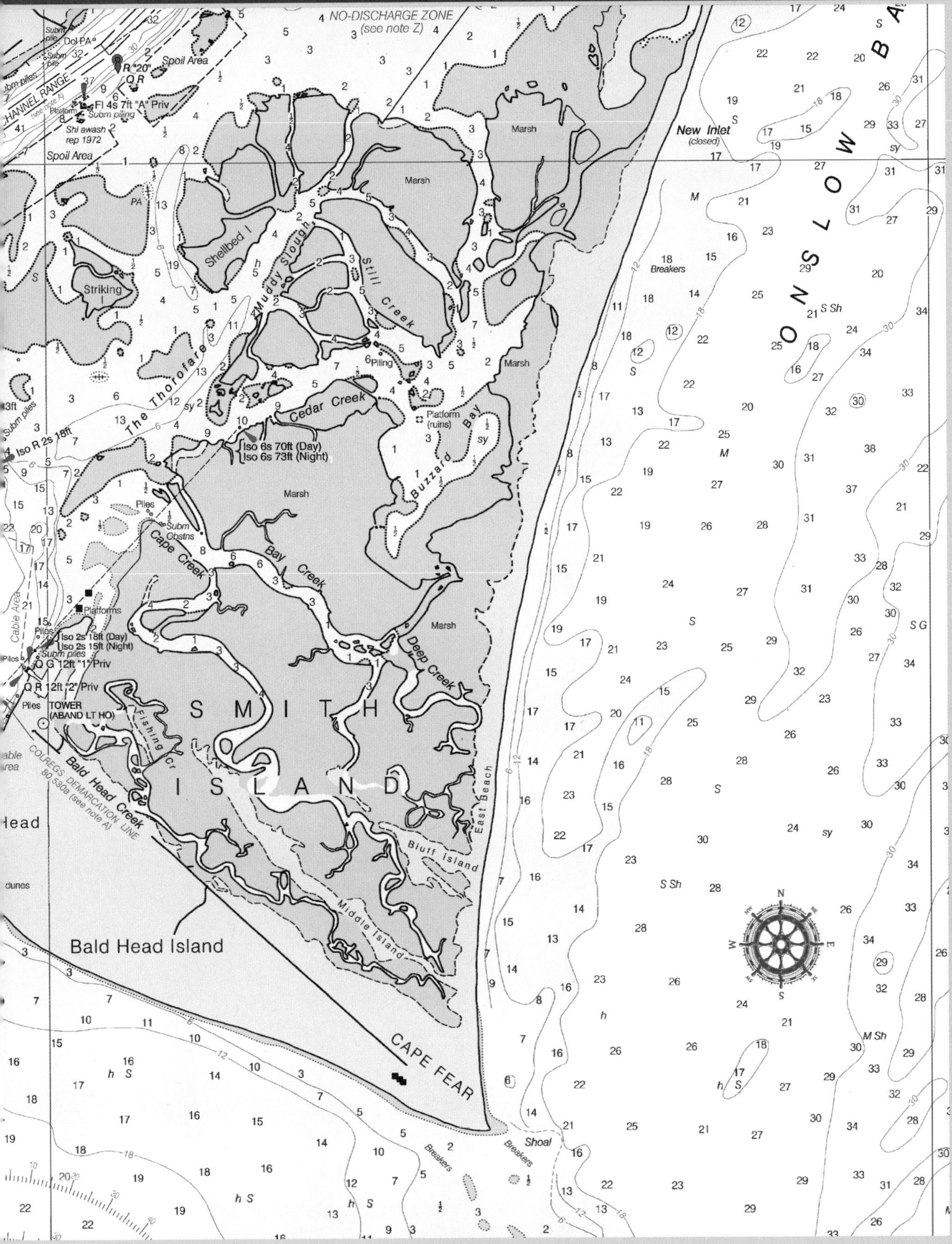

Use Chart 11537

Sea Buoy: Lighted red and white Morse (A) whistle buoy "LR" in position N 33° 49.890'/W 78° 32.430'.

Overview: Deep, wide and busy, with a steady flow of tourist and fishing boats. Presents little difficulty in most conditions.

Navigation: From the sea buoy, proceed to the entrance markers on the ends of the twin breakwaters, keeping clear of the shoal to your northeast. The inlet then sweeps west. The channel is well marked with a controlling depth of 10 feet MLW and should present no difficulties.

Cautions & Hazards: There is a 5-foot shoal just off the east jetty (starboard on entry) that is awash with breaking waves in the right conditions. The chart shows three submerged wrecks near the entrance.

Depth: See interactive charts on Waterway Explorer at www.waterwayguide.com.

ICW Connection: Connects to the ICW a little more than 1 nm to the north at Mile 343.

Nearest Recommended Inlet: The sea buoy for Winyah Bay lies 47 nm to the southwest. The Cape Fear River entrance is 24 nm to the east. Both are well marked and deep. Remember that all ICW markers have either a yellow square or a yellow triangle on them.

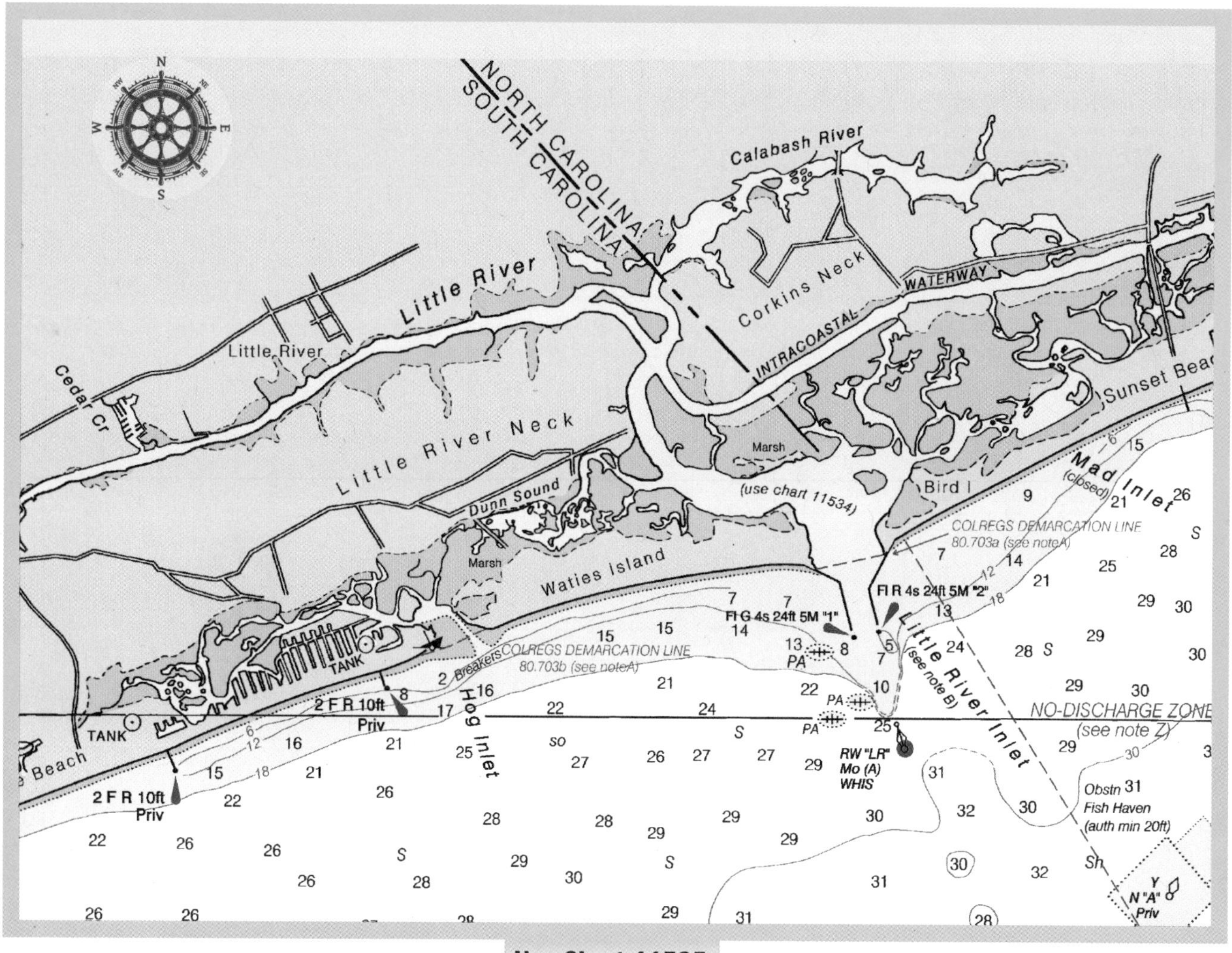

Use Chart 11535

Winyah Bay Entrance, SC

Sea Buoy: Lighted red and white Morse (A) whistle buoy "WB" in position N 33° 11.620'/W 79° 05.180'.

Overview: Well marked and deep. Presents a challenge for underpowered vessels with its strong currents. It pays to watch the tide here and enter or leave with the current. Nighttime entry is feasible due to well-marked ranges.

Navigation: Georgetown Light, 85 feet above the water, shines from a white cylindrical tower on the north side of Winyah Bay entrance. Smoke from one or another of the stacks in Georgetown can often be seen from well offshore. The sea buoy is well out; recreational vessels can safely approach waypoint N 33° 11.570'/W 79° 07.040', which is just east of red buoy "4." From the waypoint, entry is straightforward on a heading of due west, turning to northwest at red buoy "8" and north-northwest after that.

Cautions & Hazards: Conditions can be particularly bad at the ends of the jetties when tide opposes wind. Also, much of the south jetty is visible only at low water. Northbound vessels need to be aware of the shoals to the south and west of the channel and not stray west of the waypoint. Anything under 20 feet MLW indicates you are too far west on your approach.

Depth: See interactive charts on Waterway Explorer at www.waterwayguide.com.

ICW Connection: Connects to the ICW at Mile 406 (9 nm). Southbound traffic coming from offshore will want to leave the main shipping channel sooner, veering to port at flashing green buoy "17" to enter the ICW via the Western Channel.

Nearest Recommended Inlet: Murrells Inlet, a good secondary inlet with no connection to the ICW, is 19 nm to the north. The entrance to Cape Fear is 65 nm to the northeast. The entrance to Charleston is 46 nm to the southwest. The latter two are big-ship channels.

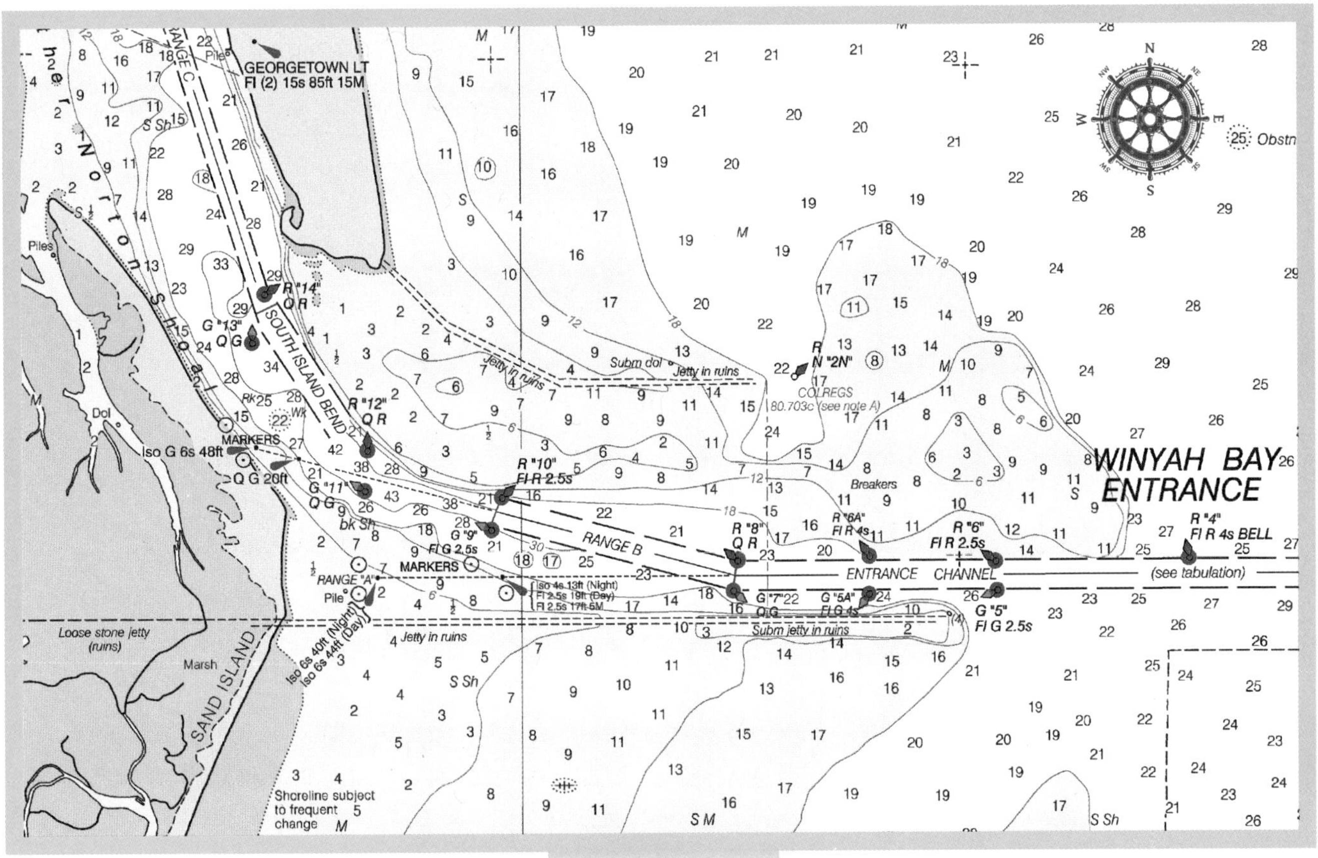

Use Chart 11532

Sea Buoy: Lighted red and white Morse (A) (RACON) whistle buoy "C" located at N 32° 37.070'/W 79° 35.490'.

Overview: Heavily used ship channel with a great deal of commercial traffic day and night.

Navigation: This is a Class A inlet for big ships with lots of deep water all about. The sea buoy is 10 nm farther out than necessary for recreational craft. A waypoint at N 32° 42.86'/W 79° 47.550' between green buoy "15" and red buoy "16" saves considerable time although southbound vessels need to be aware of the shoaling to the north and guide their course appropriately, coming in on a southwesterly heading. Several lighted buoys are missing or off station in this inlet. Follow the existing markers in, and if continuing south on the ICW, bear to the west on the South Channel Range. Those northbound or heading for the Cooper River continue, using the Mount Pleasant Range and following it out of the channel, watching for flashing red buoy "1" about 0.25 mile to the east marking the entrance to the northbound ICW.

Cautions & Hazards: Smaller vessels are advised to stay to the edge of the channel until reaching the inlet jetties. There is a ship anchorage to the north of the channel farther out, but it is not a place for smaller vessels. Be aware

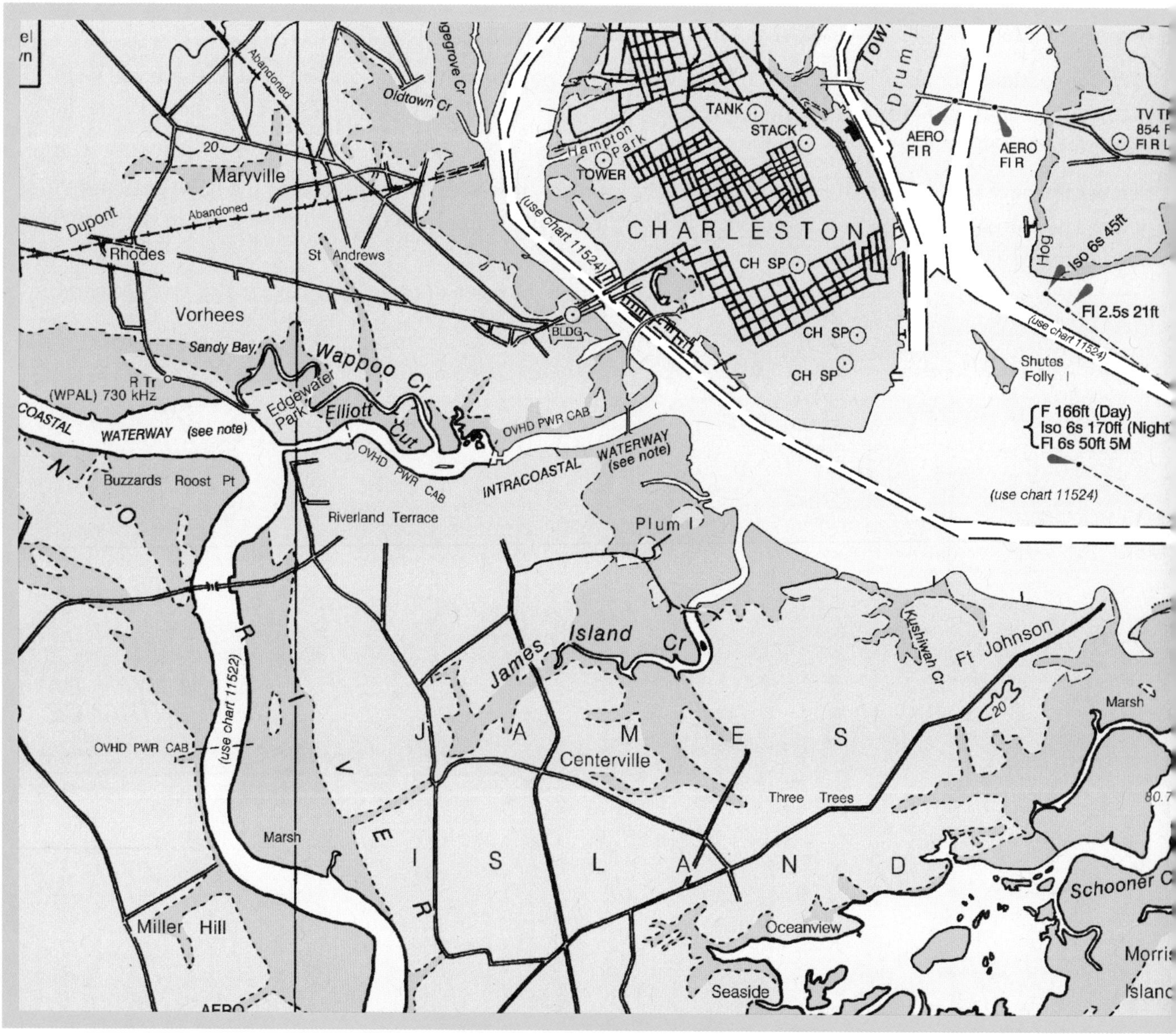

of the partially submerged jetties north and south of the channel at quick flashing green buoy "17" and quick flashing red buoy "18." After clearing the jetties, do not proceed onto the charted Middle Ground without a harbor chart (NOAA Chart 11524) that provides expanded coverage. This inlet can be very confusing for nighttime entries due to the many lights both on the water and land, and the considerable traffic you'll encounter at all hours.

Depth: See interactive charts on Waterway Explorer at www.waterwayguide.com.

ICW Connection: Southbound ICW intersects at Mile 464.1.

Nearest Recommended Inlet: The Winyah Bay entrance is 46 nm to the northeast. For the southbound cruiser, North Edisto is a fair weather-only inlet 21 nm to the southeast. Port Royal Sound, 57 nm to the southeast, is deep and well marked but has a great disadvantage for slow moving craft: The entrance channel begins 9 nm offshore as a cut through shallow banks.

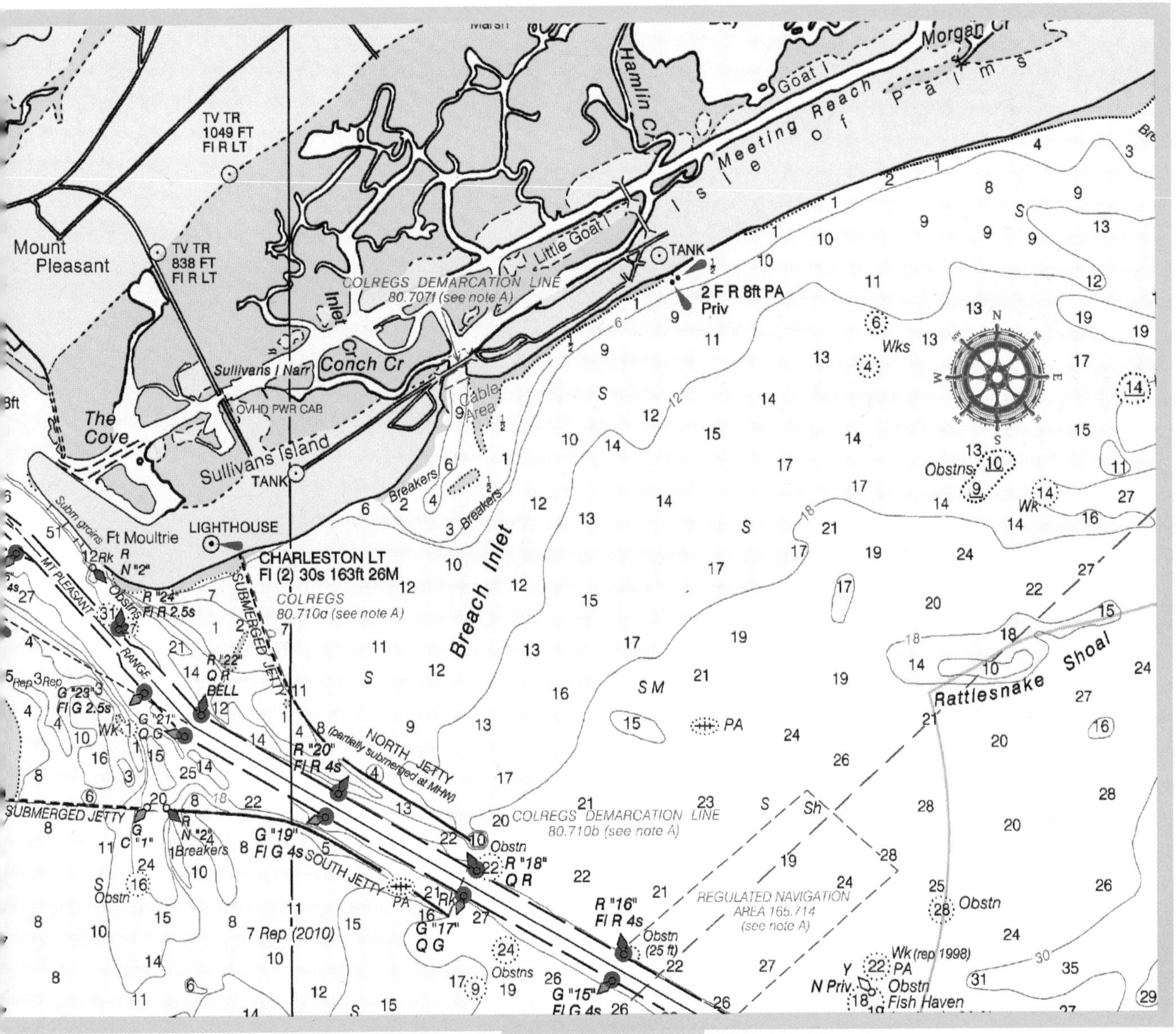

Use Chart 11521

Sea Buoy: Flashing red whistle buoy "2NE" located at N 32° 31.360'/W 80° 06.850'.

Overview: Entrance is a straight shot, with shoals to the west and breakers to the northeast.

Navigation: Proceed on a course of 286° M, leaving flashing red buoy "6" to starboard (red nun buoy "4" is close by), turning to 325° M, picking up green can buoy "7" before lining up with the charted range that leads you close alongside flashing green buoy "9."

Cautions & Hazards: The chart shows a 5-foot-deep section near flashing red buoy "6," which will not be a problem provided you keep the marker to starboard on entering.

ICW Connection: Connects to the ICW approximately 7.5 nm from the inlet at White Point (Mile 496.7).

Depth: See interactive charts on Waterway Explorer at www.waterwayguide.com.

Nearest Recommended Inlet: The entrance to Charleston Harbor is 21 nm to the northeast. For southbound vessels, the entrance to Port Royal Sound is 35 nm to the southwest; Tybee Roads, GA and the Savannah River are 46 nm away.

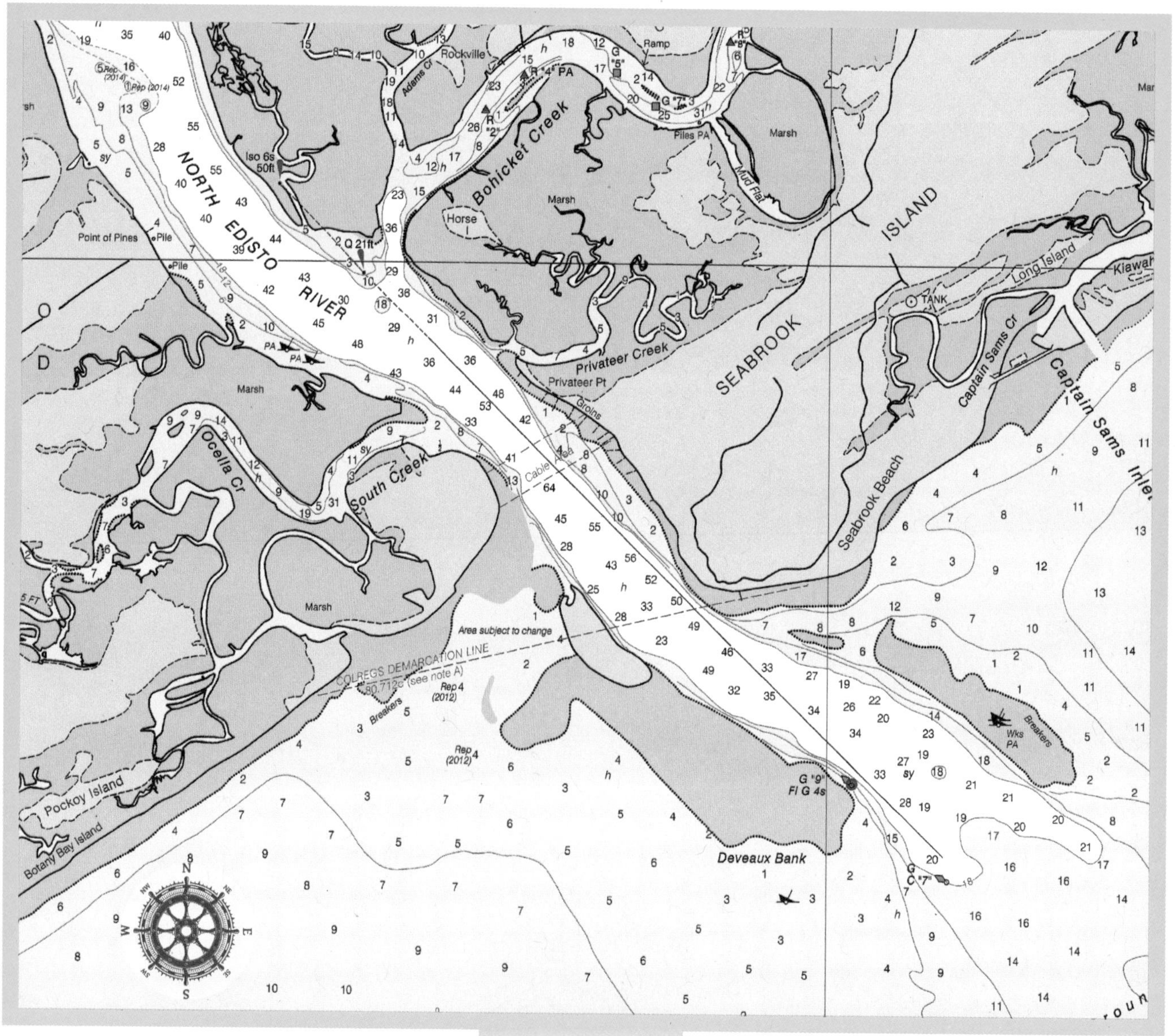

Use Chart 11521

Port Royal Sound Entrance, SC

Sea Buoy: Lighted red and white Morse (A) whistle buoy "P" located at N 32° 05.140'/W 80° 34.960'.

Overview: Wide, deep and very long. If headed south offshore, this is not the best option as a point of entry, as you will backtrack some distance to re-enter the ocean.

Navigation: From the sea buoy, head north and follow the range to flashing red buoy "14," then veer to the west to quick flashing green buoy "25," where you can head west as noted to the southbound ICW and Hilton Head Island, or north to Beaufort, SC. There are ranges northbound to quick flashing green buoy "37" on the Beaufort River.

Cautions & Hazards: If you are going northbound after dark, there are land-based lights that can confuse even the best navigator. Also, if there is any sort of wind against tide, or you are bucking the current, things are likely to get a bit rough.

Depth: See interactive charts on Waterway Explorer at www.waterwayguide.com.

ICW Connection: Connects to the ICW after quick flashing green buoy "25" at approximately Mile 548.6.

Nearest Recommended Inlet: To the northeast, about 21 nm away, begins the channel into St. Helena Sound. The North Edisto entrance is 36 nm away and Charleston, SC, 57 nm. Southbound, the Tybee Roads, GA, entrance to the Savannah River and Hilton Head, SC, is about 10 nm away on a southerly course.

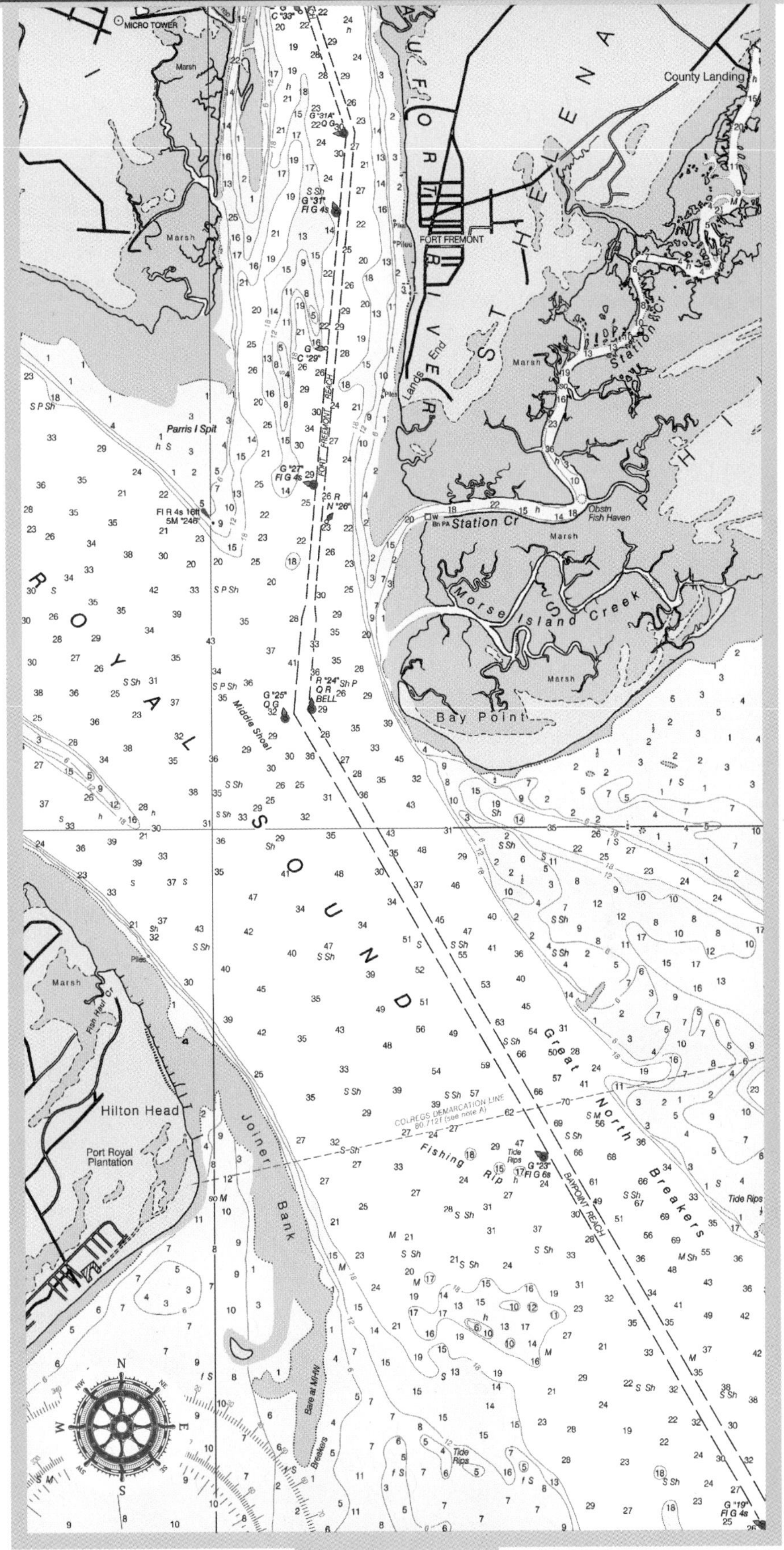

Use Chart 11516

Sea Buoy: Use the sea buoy for Tybee Roads, lighted red and white Morse (A) (RACON) buoy "T" located at N 31° 57.700'/W 80° 43.100'.

Overview: Alternative to Tybee Roads, this entrance leads to Calibogue Sound and Hilton Head Island.

Navigation: For South Hilton Head Island via Calibogue Sound, use the sailing directions for entering the Savannah River but stay on Bloody Point Range after flashing red buoy "14," passing the lower range light and leaving green daybeacon "1" well to port. Next, keep clear of the 5- to 6-foot deep shoal at the back Bloody Point Range, and then turn north toward quick flashing green buoy "3." Depths will briefly fall to 8 to 10 feet MLW from 14 feet, then rise again as you pass quick flashing green buoy "3." At quick flashing green buoy "3," turn due north, and proceed to flashing green buoy "5," where you can then follow the remaining channel markers into Calibogue Sound.

Cautions & Hazards: Coming from the north, mariners need to be aware of Gaskin Banks, an extensive shoal area extending nearly 8 nm out from Hilton Head Island. There is also a submerged breakwater north of the Tybee Roads channel that is roughly parallel to flashing red buoys "12" and "14," which must be avoided if one is heading toward Calibogue Sound. Entering this inlet needs your full attention when transiting.

Depth: See interactive charts on Waterway Explorer at www.waterwayguide.com.

ICW Connection: Connects to the ICW at the Cooper River (Mile 564).

Nearest Recommended Inlet: At night or in heavy seas, forgo Calibogue Sound and continue on Tybee Roads to the Savannah River entrance. Port Royal Sound is 10 nm to the northeast.

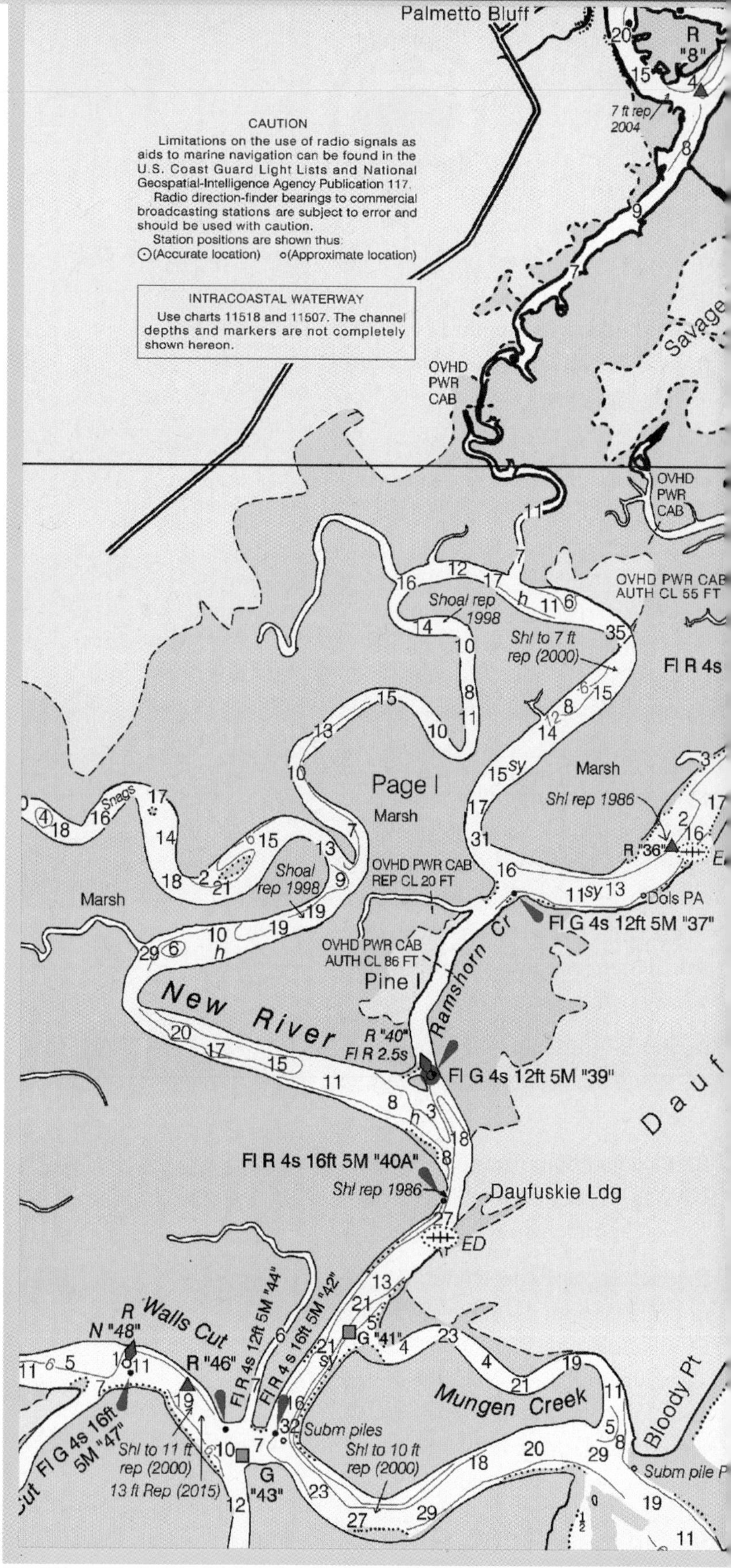

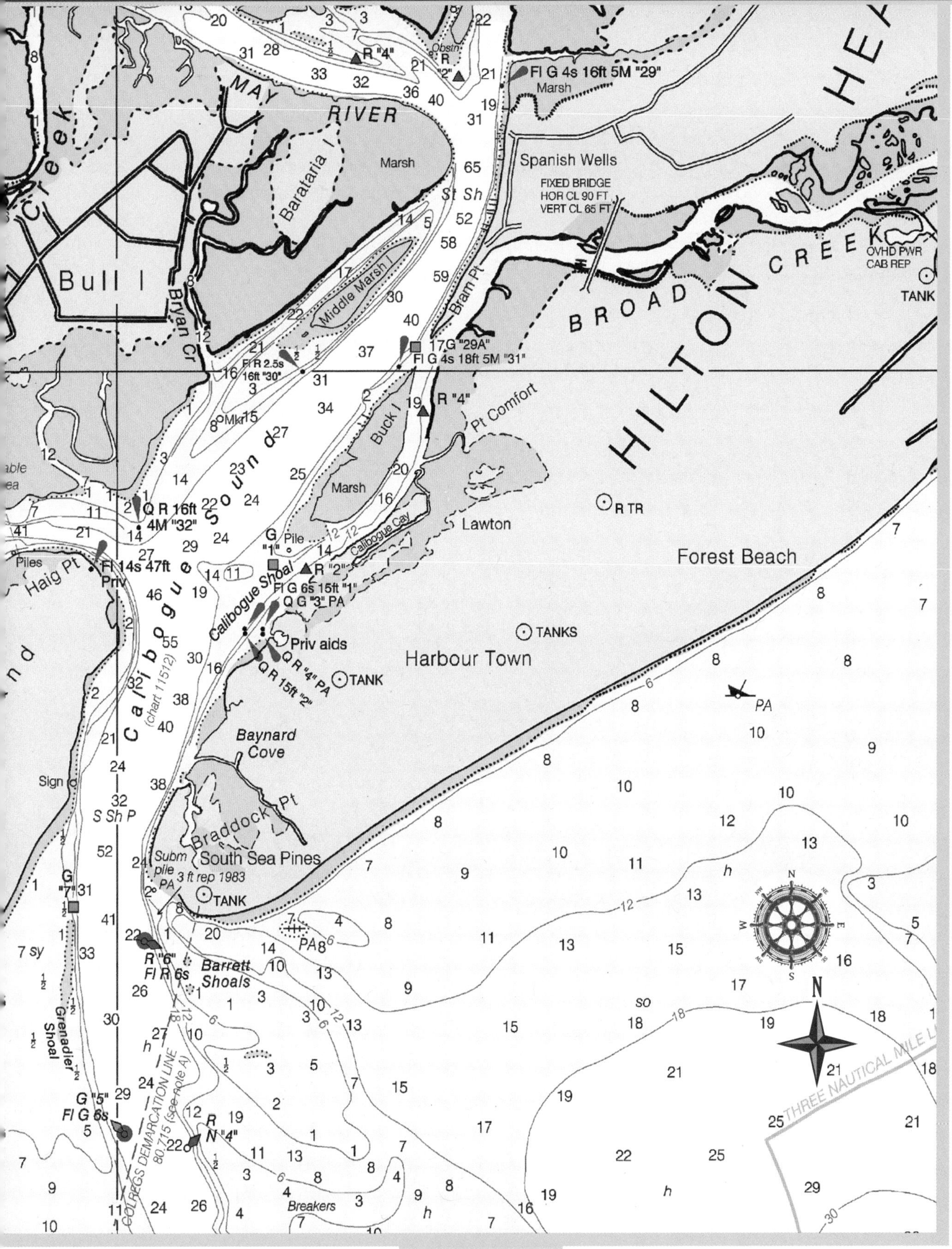

Use Chart 11513

Sea Buoy: Lighted red and white Morse (A) (RACON) buoy "T" located at N 31° 57.700'/W 80° 43.100'.

Overview: Big ship entrance, offering entry to Savannah via the Savannah River.

Navigation: Entering the channel from the sea buoy, follow the Tybee range to quick flashing red bell buoy "8," turning north to follow the Bloody Point Range to flashing red "14." Turning to port here, follow the Jones Island Range to flashing red buoy "18," and then turn slightly southwest and continue in on Tybee Knoll Cut Range to flashing red buoy "24." Here, you will have Oyster Bed Island to your north and Cockspur Island to the south. Pick up New Channel Range and follow the channel markers. Note the partially submerged breakwater that begins just past flashing red buoy "18," which is marked by a flashing white light, noted as "Fl 4s 16ft 5M" on your chart.

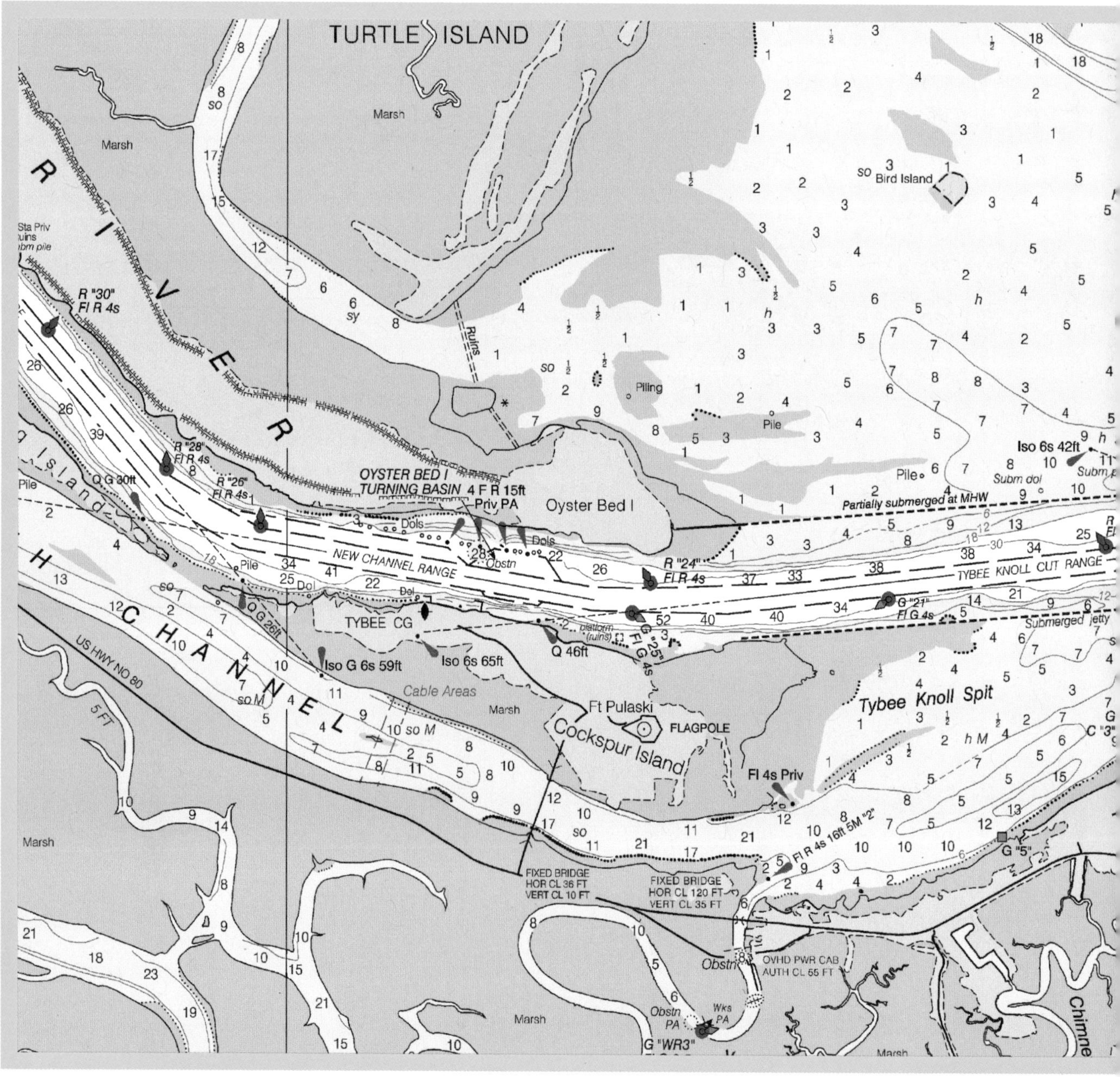

Cautions & Hazards: Coming from the north, mariners need to be aware of Gaskin Banks, an extensive shoal area extending nearly 8 nm out from Hilton Head. Also to be avoided is a submerged breakwater north of and roughly parallel to flashing red buoy "12" and flashing red buoy "14."

Depth: See interactive charts on Waterway Explorer at www.waterwayguide.com.

ICW Connection: Savannah River crosses ICW at Fields Cut (Mile 575.7), directly opposite flashing green buoy "35."

Nearest Recommended Inlet: Northbound cruisers heading for Hilton Head may detour from Tybee Roads to make Calibogue Sound, with an entrance that is usable by day and in settled weather. From Tybee Roads, the sea buoy for Port Royal Sound is 10 nm to the northeast. If southbound, Wassaw Sound, 10 nm to the southwest, is another strictly fair-weather, daylight entrance. Ditto for St. Catherines Sound, 22 nm away.

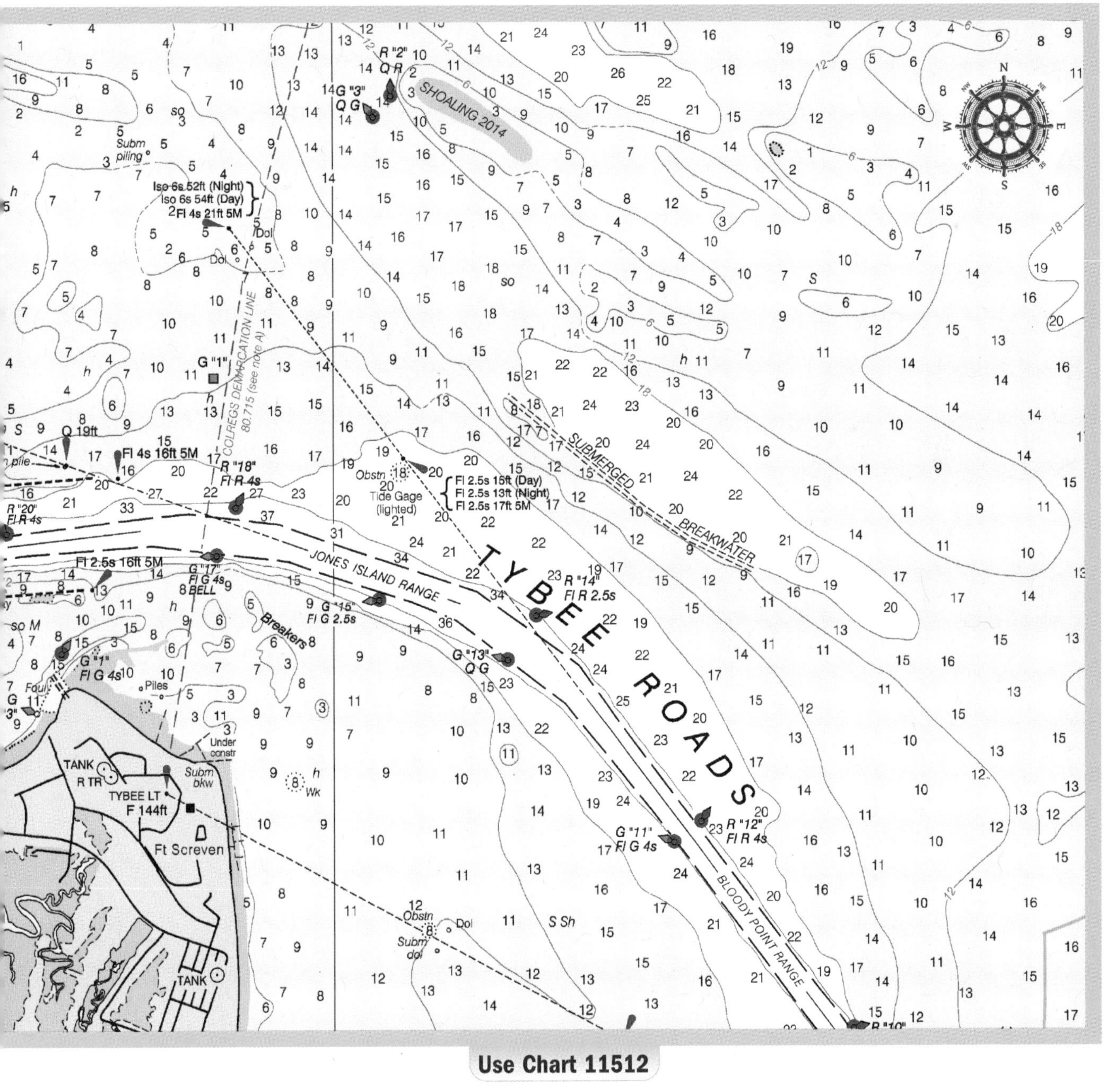

Use Chart 11512

Wassaw Sound Entrance, GA

Sea Buoy: Flashing red buoy "2W" located at N 31° 51.560'/W 80° 53.000'.

Overview: Popular local inlet, but not one for dark and stormy arrivals without local knowledge, as it is poorly marked and surrounded by shoals nearly 5 nm out from the entrance.

Navigation: Current and trustworthy local knowledge required. The entrance to Wassaw Sound changes continually, so red buoys "4," "6" and "8" are not charted. Before beginning this inlet, mark a boundary line on your chart running due south from flashing red buoy "10." From flashing red buoy "2W," head west-northwest and curve to the north around the shoal to starboard until you reach the above noted line from flashing red buoy "10." Head due north to green can buoy "9" and turn northwest to follow the markers; depths will be 20 feet MLW or better. Stay to the center of Wilmington River until you turn to the north after flashing red "22" and then stay to the east side of the river for deep water.

Cautions & Hazards: The 2 nm from the sea buoy to the first markers are tricky, with shoals on both sides, breakers and no markers. Just east of green can "9" and flashing red can "10" there is extensive shoaling. If you draw more than 5 feet, think twice before entering this inlet. The inlet has no lighted markers until you are inside, and it would be foolhardy to enter at night.

Depth: See interactive charts on Waterway Explorer at www.waterwayguide.com.

ICW Connection: Wilmington River meets the ICW at Skidaway Narrows (Mile 585.5), about 3.5 nm north of flashing red buoy "20" at the river's entrance.

Nearest Recommended Inlet: The deep water entrance to the Savannah River at Tybee Roads, GA is 10 nm to the northeast. Southbound, fair-weather inlets include St. Catherines at 12.5 nm away and Sapelo Sound at 22 nm.

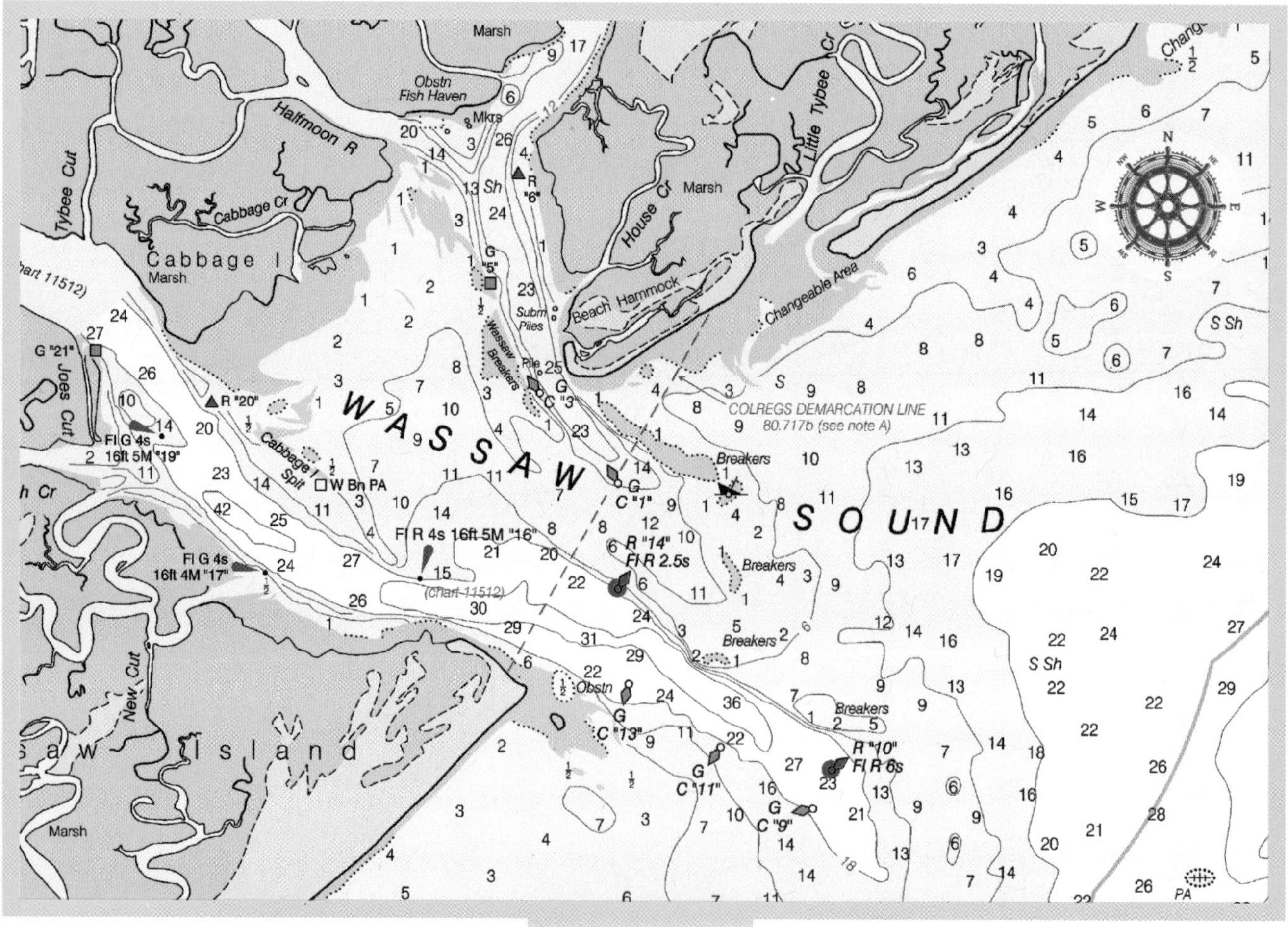

Use Chart 11509

Sea Buoy: Lighted red and white Morse (A) (RACON) buoy "STC" located at N 31° 40.198'/W 81° 00.235'.

Overview: Wide, uncomplicated entrance with good depths within.

Navigation: Heading west from the sea buoy, turn in between green can "1" and flashing red "2" and head north to flashing green "5" in no less than 12 feet at MLW. (Or head straight from RW "STC" to flashing green "5" where you may see 9-foot MLW depths.) The channel turns west toward green can "7."

Cautions & Hazards: The charted Middle Ground Shoal is to the southwest of green can "7." Be sure to stay well off to the north.

Depth: See interactive charts on Waterway Explorer at www.waterwayguide.com.

ICW Connection: St. Catherines Sound Entrance intersects the ICW at Mile 618, about 3nm from flashing green "5" at the entrance.

Nearest Recommended Inlet: The Wassaw Sound Entrance is 12 nm to the north, while the Sapelo Sound Entrance is 9.5 nm to the south.

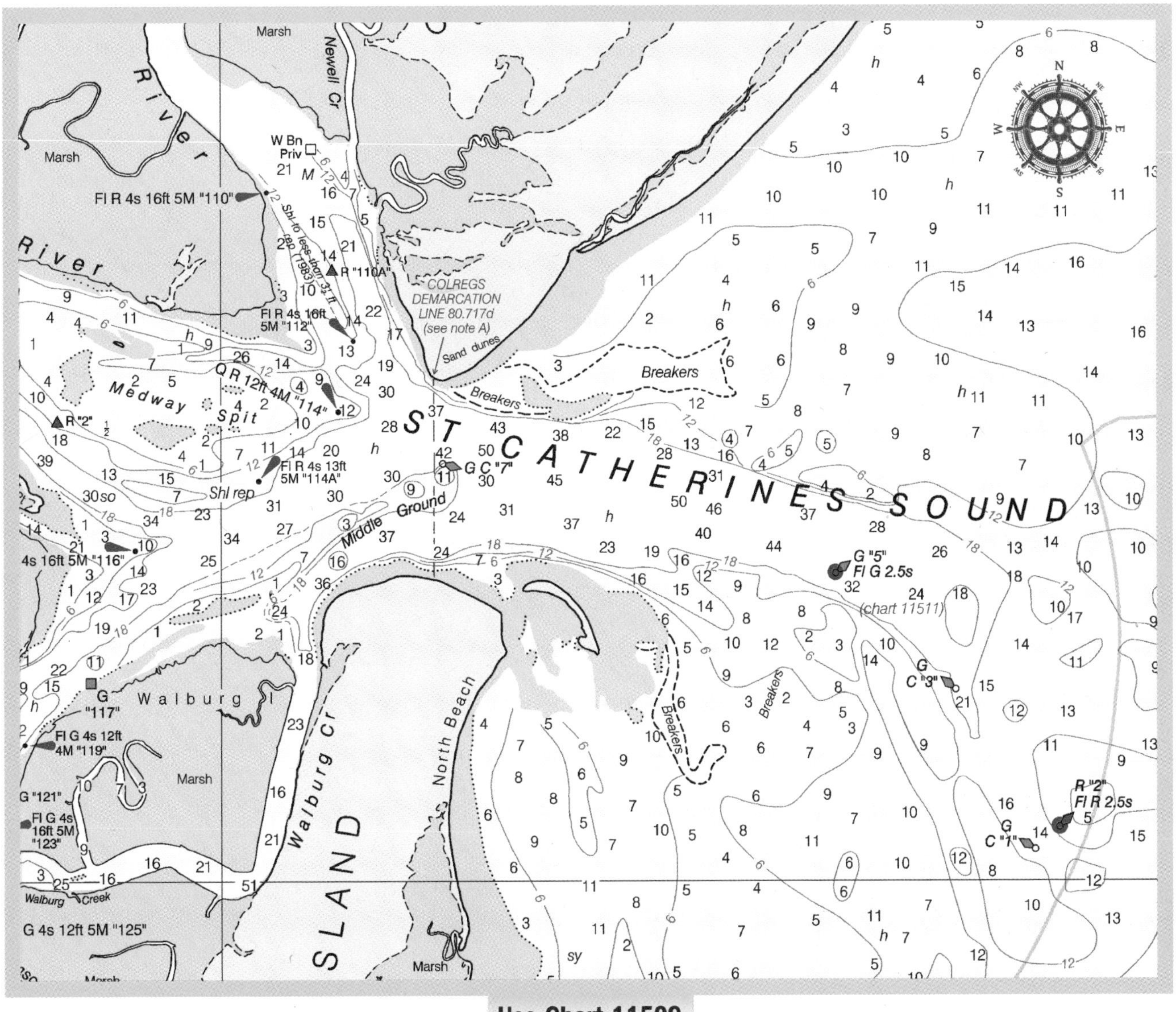

Use Chart 11509

Sapelo Sound Entrance, GA

Sea Buoy: Red and white can buoy "S" located at N 31° 31.210'/W 81° 03.890'.

Overview: Used by fishermen and shrimpers, not to mention legendary pirate Edward Teach ("Blackbeard"). (You will pass just north of Blackbeard Island and Blackbeard Creek while transiting this inlet.) Southbound cruisers hoping to avoid the Georgia ICW rarely use the inlet, preferring to jump offshore through the big ship channels at Charleston, Port Royal or Savannah.

Navigation: Current and trustworthy local knowledge required. From the sea buoy, proceed first to red nun buoy "2" and then head slightly south of west to green can buoy "3." Depths will drop from more than 20 feet down to 12 feet MLW along the way. If you see 10-foot MLW depths, you are in trouble and need to reverse course. At green can buoy "5," you will see 20-plus-foot MLW depths return, and it is a simple matter of following the red buoys in until you meet up with the ICW past red nun buoy "10."

Cautions & Hazards: Not the best inlet in rougher weather, due to extensive shoals to the north and south of the inlet. Sound is quite wide and the aids to navigation are unlighted, making it unfavorable for nighttime passage except by the well experienced. Depths between green can buoy "3" and green can buoy "5" drop to 12 feet MLW in places, and there are breaking shoals to the north of the channel; otherwise, depths typically run to over 20 feet MLW. Do not be tempted to cut corners. Once in the sound, be aware of the shoal by green daybeacon "143" and stay at least 100 feet off.

Depth: See interactive charts on Waterway Explorer at www.waterwayguide.com.

ICW Connection: Junction of Sapelo Sound and ICW is at Mile 632.

Nearest Recommended Inlet: Northbound, you should bypass St. Catherines Sound (9.5 nm) and continue to Wassaw Sound (22 nm) if conditions are calm or, best yet, go on to Tybee Roads to the Savannah River (31 nm). Southbound, the ship channel at St. Simons Sound is 29.5 nm away.

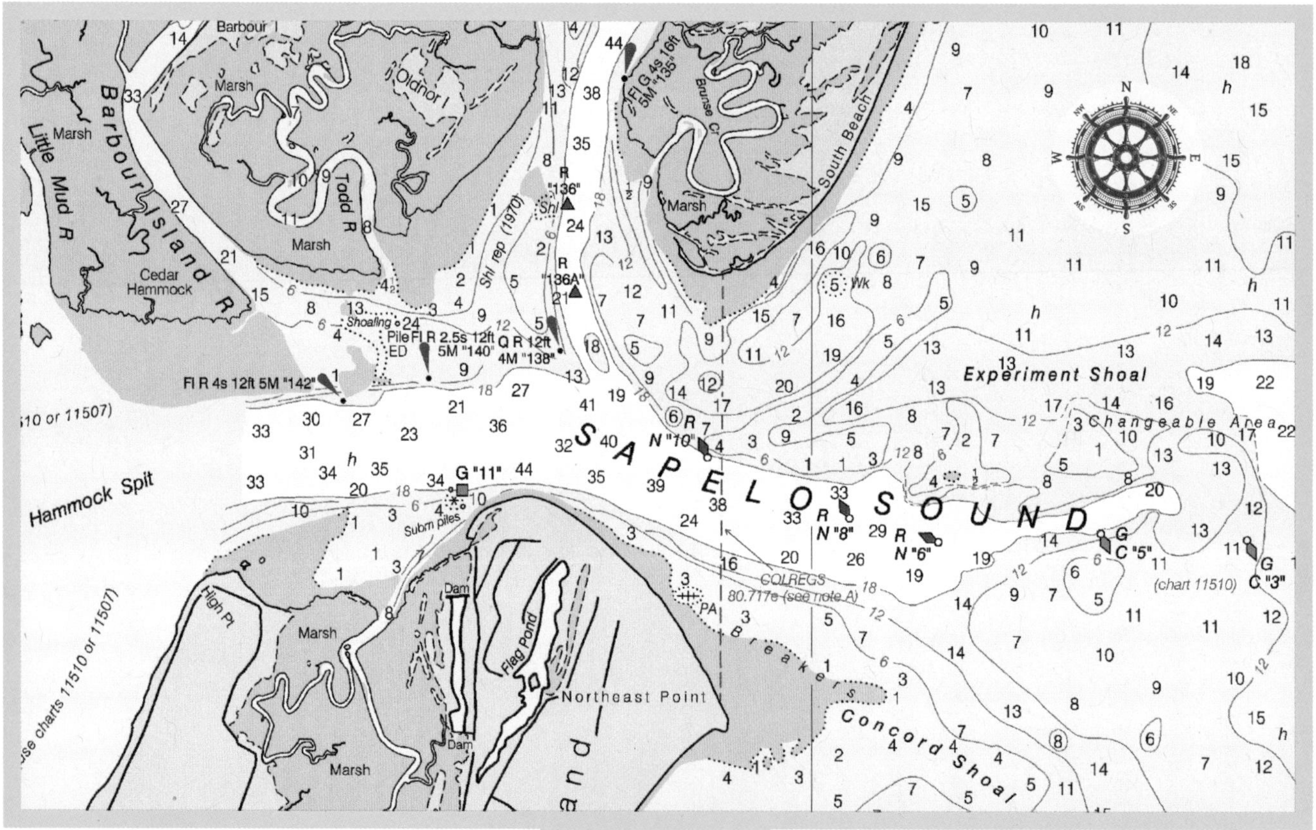

Use Chart 11509

Doboy Sound Entrance, GA

Sea Buoy: Lighted red and white Morse (A) buoy "D" located at N 31° 21.230'/W 81° 11.390'.

Overview: Uncomplicated and breakwaters may give some protection from south-setting waves.

Navigation: Heading slightly north of west from the sea buoy, continue in past the breakwaters to the north of red nun buoy "4." The channel shoals to 7 feet MLW approaching green can "3," then deepens again. Continue to red nun "8" on the northerly point of land in 20- to 40-foot depths. Once in the sound, keep an eye out for shoaling.

Cautions & Hazards: Breakwaters to the north and a long easterly shoal on the south side are the main hazards here. Aside from the sea buoy and flashing red "8," all of the aids to navigation in this inlet are unlighted, making it a difficult, if not dangerous, nighttime passage.

Depth: See interactive charts on Waterway Explorer at www.waterwayguide.com.

ICW Connection: About 2.5 nm from the inlet proper, Doboy Sound intersects the ICW just above Commodore and Doboy Islands at Mile 649. The ICW runs around the north and west sides of Doboy Island.

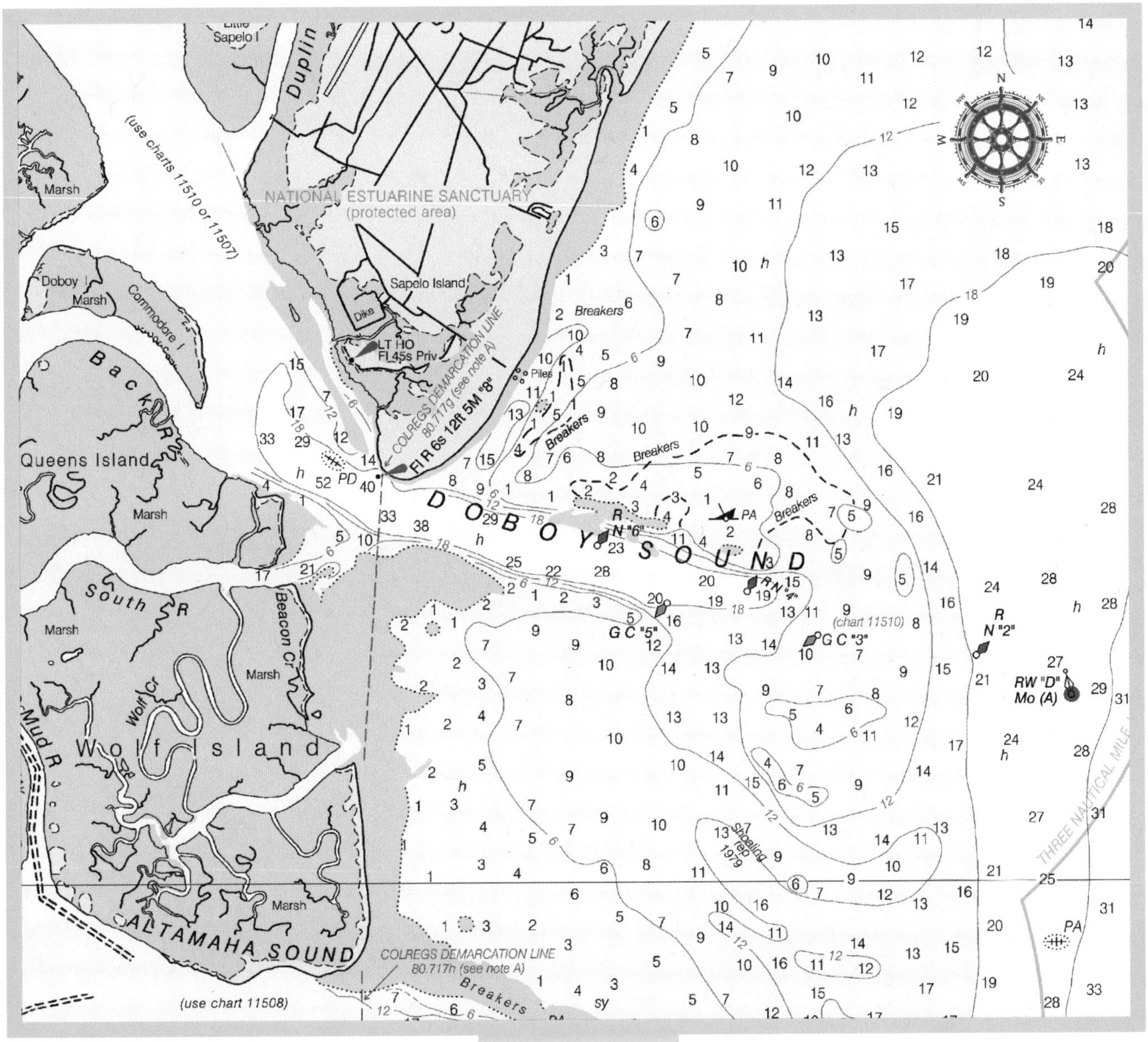

Use Chart 11509

Sea Buoy: Lighted red and white Morse (A) (RACON) whistle buoy "STS" located at N 31° 03.200'/W 81° 15.100'.

Overview: All-weather, big ship entrance to Brunswick.

Navigation: Entrance is straightforward. From the sea buoy, proceed northwesterly to quick flashing red buoy "16" on the range, then turn to port and pick up Plantation Creek Range.

Cautions & Hazards: Start from the sea buoy due to shallows that extend quite far from shore. Channel shallows very rapidly outside of the markers, and ebb current is quite strong at the mouth of the inlet. Busy entrance; keep watch for big ships transiting the inlet.

Depth: See interactive charts on Waterway Explorer at www.waterwayguide.com.

ICW Connection: ICW is immediately inside inlet at Mile 678.

Nearest Recommended Inlet: The fair weather inlet at Doboy Sound, GA, is 18 nm to the north. To the south, the big ship channel at the St. Marys Entrance is 21 nm away.

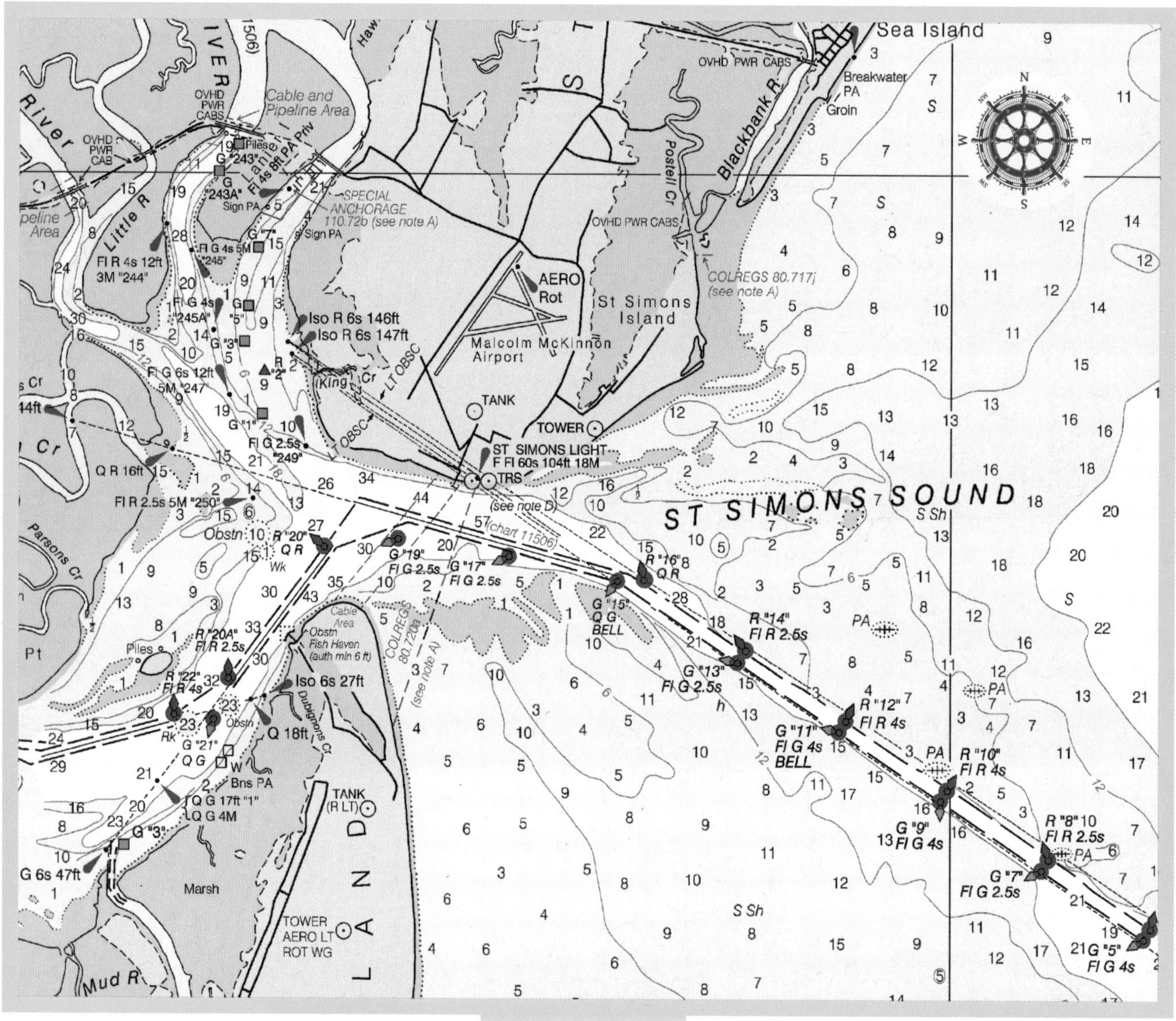

Use Chart 11502

WATERWAY GUIDE
THE CRUISING AUTHORITY
Subscription
Don't Get Left High & Dry
Safe boating and adventure on America's waterways is a click away. Subscribe to Explorer today for expert advice, navigation alerts, anchorages, fuel prices, marina listings and more all rolled up into an easy-to-use portal.
waterwayguide.com
Guide Content
Inlet - Jupiter Inlet
Jupiter Inlet
Sea Buoy: No sea buoy. Steer to waypoint N 26° 56.620'/ W 80° 03.790' (0.4 nm east of the inlet).
Overview: Fair weather inlet only. Prone to severe shoaling and cited by the USCG as "not navigable without local knowledge."
Navigation: If you must enter, proceed in a westerly direction from the waypoint to the markers on the jetties. Once inside the jetties, depths increase substantially.
Webcam: For a live view of the inlet, visit evsjupiter.com.
Cautions and hazards: Severe shoaling to both the north and south of the entrance. With any swell, mariners should divert to another inlet. The inlet is considered impassable in a northeast swell of any size.
INLETS: ST. JOHNS RIVER ENTRANCE TO ANGELFISH CREEK, FL
JUPITER INLET
Jupiter Sound
LOXAHATCHEE RIVER EXTENSION
Not a member? Join
Learn More
waterwayguide.com/learn-more

Sea Buoy: No sea buoy. Steer to a waypoint of N 30° 42.630'/W 81° 14.630' (2.5 nm seaward of the channel). Then steer to N 30° 42.690'/W 81° 21.520' to access the center of the channel at red marker "10."

Overview: Big ship and military ship inlet. Most northerly of the Florida inlets located between Cumberland Island (GA) and Fort Clinch State Park.

Navigation: Very straightforward and well marked. From red marker "10" proceed due west into Cumberland Sound.

Cautions & Hazards: Some shoal sections to the north of the channel inside the jetty. Current is very strong and dictates appropriate boat handling to compensate. Slower boats are well advised to time their passages for slack water or a favorable tide. The inlet also serves the Kings Bay Submarine Base so be on the lookout for any military craft that might be in the area. The Coast Guard has established regulated navigation areas (RNAs)

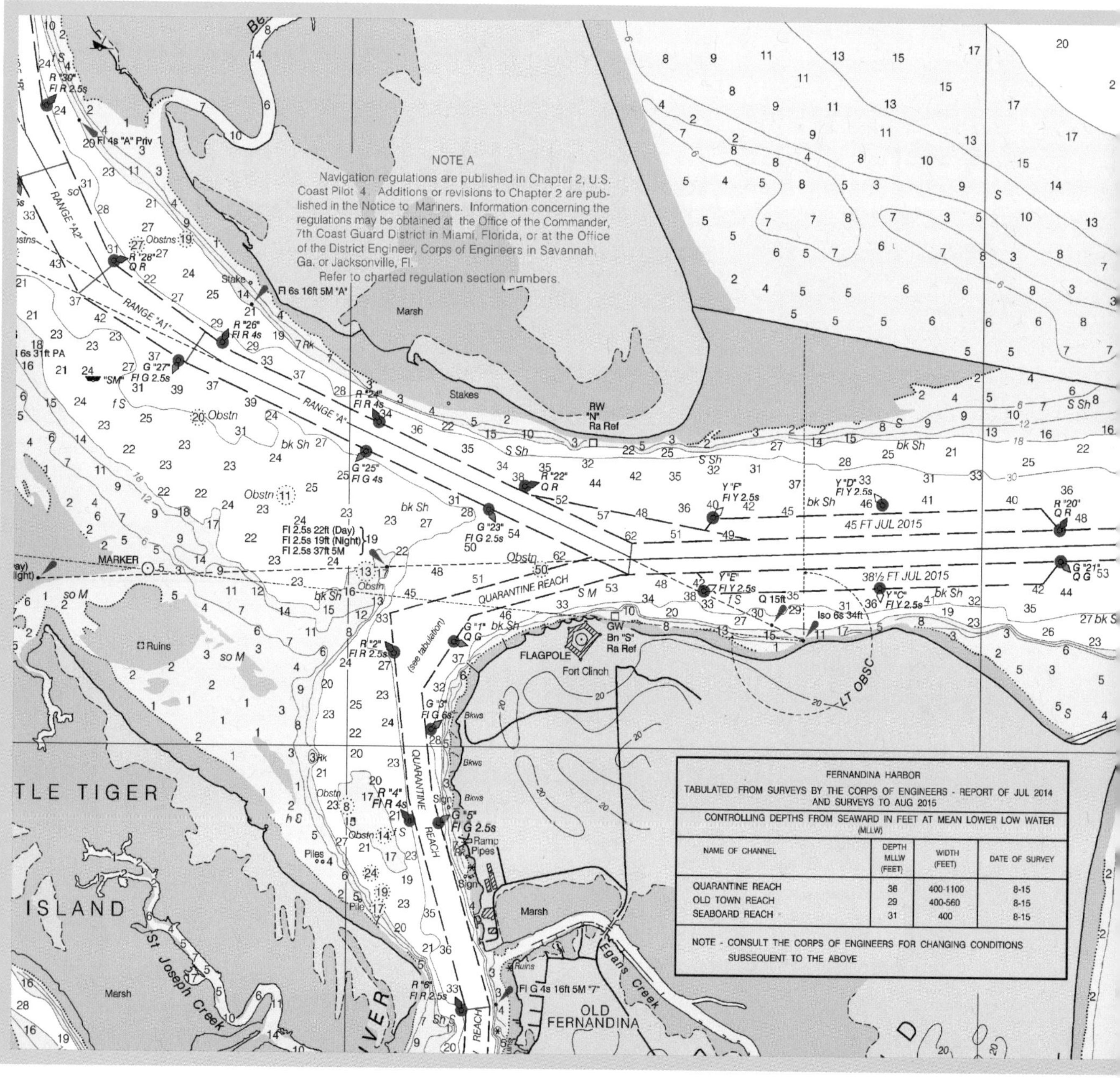

covering the St. Marys Entrance Channel, portions of the Cumberland Sound and the Atlantic Ocean that will be in effect whenever any Navy submarine (foreign or domestic) is escorted by the Coast Guard. These RNAs are necessary to help ensure the safety and security of submarines, their Coast Guard escorts and the public. No person or vessel may enter or remain within the security zone without the permission of the Coast Guard.

Depth: See interactive charts on Waterway Explorer at www.waterwayguide.com.

ICW Connection: ICW crosses the inlet at Mile 714. For either north or south, follow the banks, which remain deep outside of the channel.

Nearest Recommended Inlet: It is approximately 30 nm to the big ship inlet at the St. Marys (Cumberland Sound) Entrance.

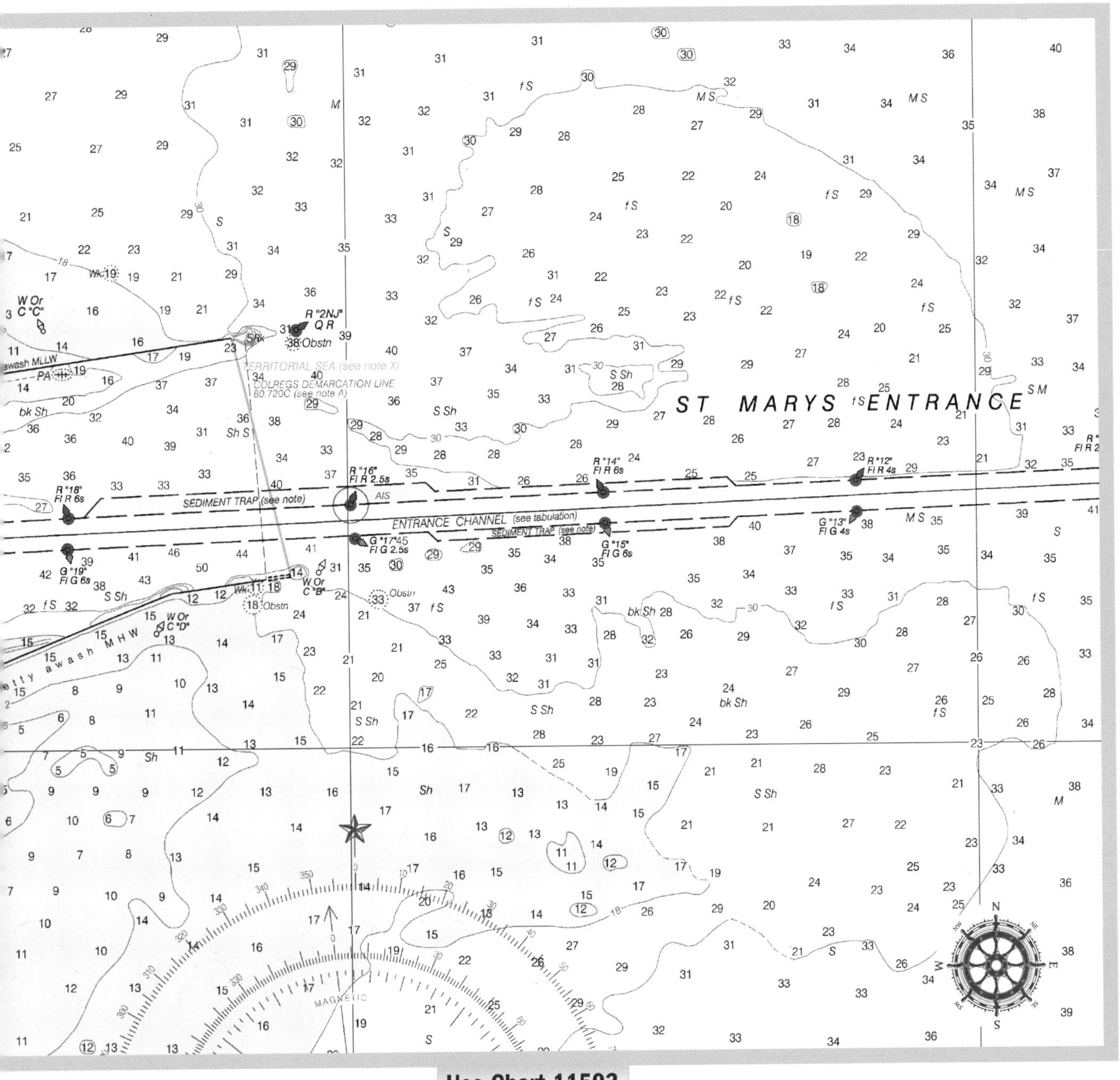

Use Chart 11503

Hampton Roads, VA to the Neuse River, NC

Chapter 1: Hampton, Norfolk & Portsmouth, VA
Chapter 2: Virginia Cut & Dismal Swamp Routes, VA/NC
Chapter 3: Side Trip: Albemarle & Roanoke Sounds, NC
Chapter 4: Albemarle Sound to the Neuse River, NC
Chapter 5: Side Trip: The Pamlico Sound & Outer Banks, NC

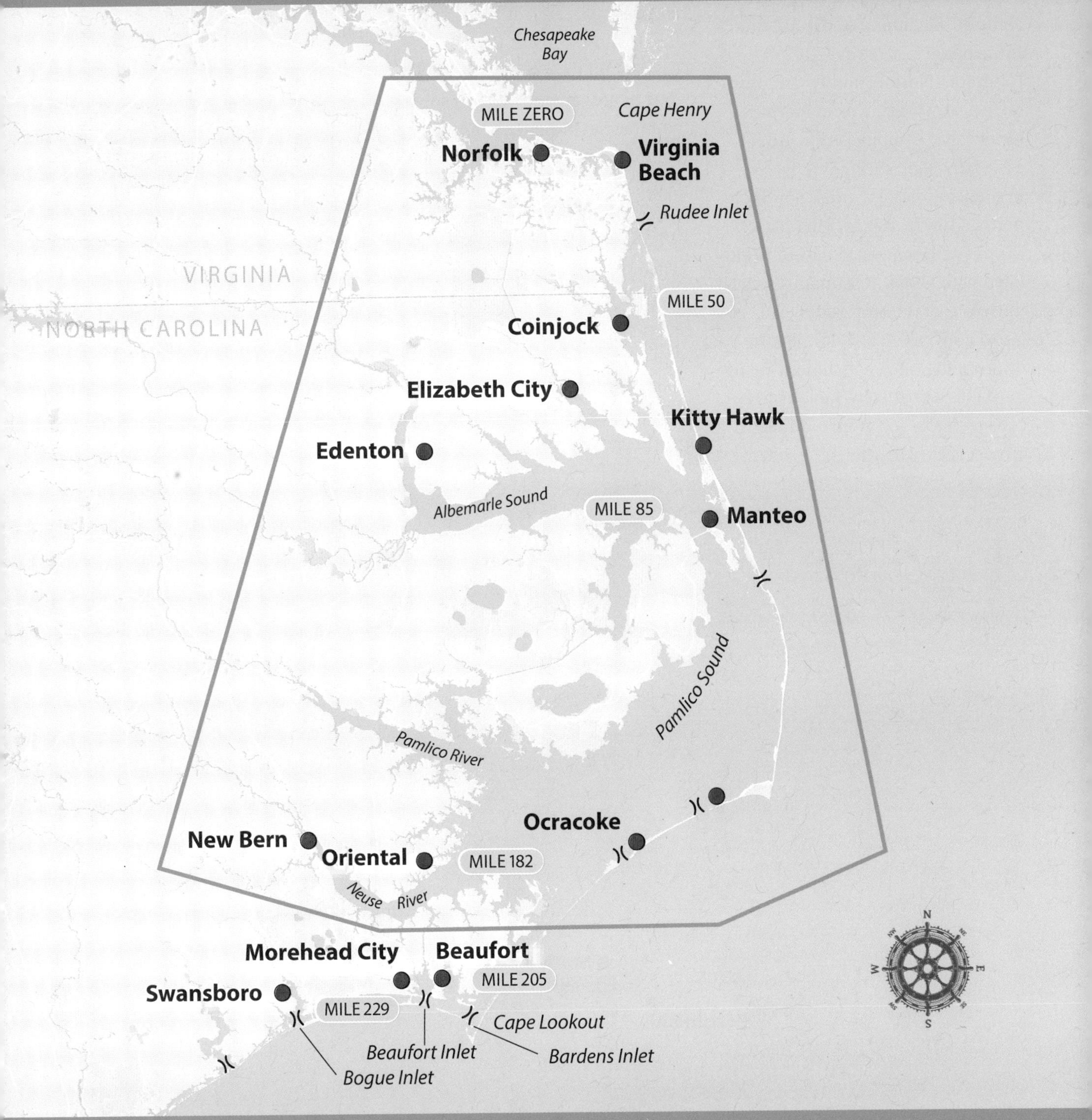

Visit Waterway Explorer at www.waterwayguide.com

ICW Mile Zero

HAMPTON ROADS

Strategically situated at Mile Zero, the "official" beginning of the Atlantic Intracoastal Waterway (AICW), Hampton, Norfolk and Portsmouth offer nearly every type of marine service and equipment and are especially good fitting-out places in preparation for a cruise south or north. They're also exciting places to visit with rejuvenated waterfronts filled with shops, restaurants, hotels, museums and historic sites. This is also a convenient area for picking up or dropping off guests and for flying in to join a boat crew. Limousine/cab service to and from Norfolk's airport is easy to arrange. If you are in Hampton or Newport News, you should also consider the Newport News/Williamsburg International Airport. It is about 25 minutes north of Hampton on I-64.

The world's merchant fleet loads and unloads cargo at the Hampton Roads and Elizabeth River piers. Colliers fill their holds with 100,000 tons of coal at a time. Even so, the commercial presence is minimal compared to the military presence. Naval Station Norfolk, the largest naval installation in the world, is homeport for the U.S. Navy's Atlantic Fleet encompassing aircraft carriers, cruisers, destroyers, frigates, support ships, nuclear submarines and admiral's barges. The Joint Expeditionary Base at Little Creek is a few miles east over land and is the world's largest amphibious base. Most of the Navy's operational aircraft are stationed at Naval Air Station Oceana in Virginia Beach. There is also a large Navy training center at Dam Neck and the Army operates Fort Story at Cape Henry. Across Hampton Roads Harbor is Langley Air Force Base. The Marines have several camps in the area. Even NATO has a headquarters in the area. All in all this area is, by far, the largest military complex in the world.

Navigating Hampton Roads

Before you can begin your journey down the AICW, you must traverse the 10-nm stretch through the Hampton Roads area. Hampton Roads Harbor begins at the line between Old Point Comfort on the north shore and Willoughby Spit to the south. Sitting on a little island in the middle of the

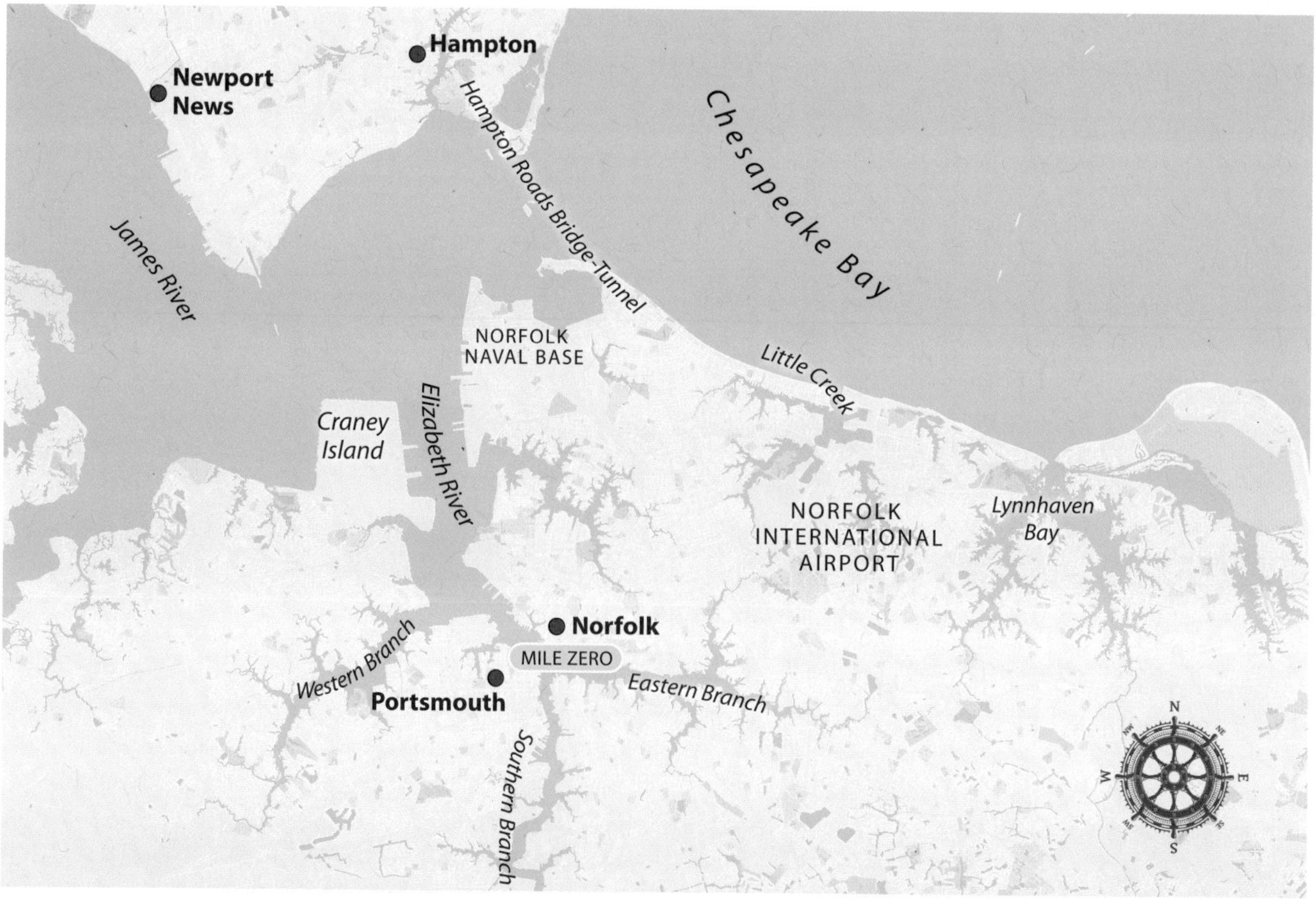

Hampton River, VA

HAMPTON AREA		Largest Vessel	VHF	Total Slips	Approach/ Dockside Depth	Floating Docks	Gas/ Diesel	Repairs/ Haulout	Min/Max Amps	Pump-Out Station
1. Bluewater Yachting Center WiFi	(757) 723-6774	200	16	200	12.0 / 12.0	F	GD	RH	30 / 100	P
2. Bluewater Yacht Yards WiFi	(757) 723-0793	80	16	200	12.0 / 8.0	F	GD	RH	30 / 100	P
3. Sunset Boating Center WiFi	(757) 722-3325	34	16	495	10.0 / 8.0	F	GD		20 / 50	P

WiFi Wireless Internet Access onSpot Dockside WiFi Facility
Visit www.waterwayguide.com for current rates, fuel prices, website addresses and other up-to-the-minute information.
(Information in the table is provided by the facilities.)

Scan here for more details:

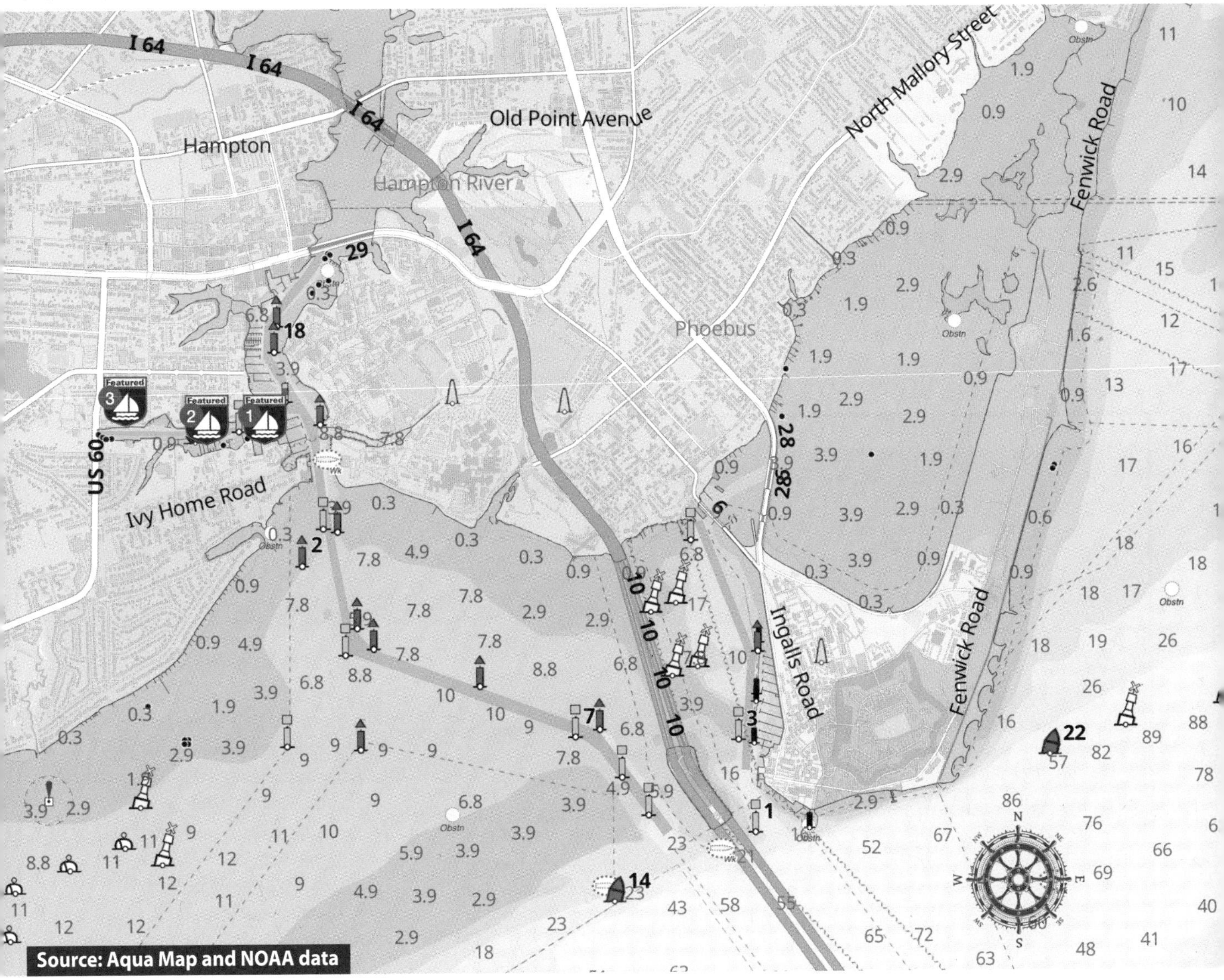

harbor's entrance is Fort Wool, which along with Fort Monroe at Hampton's Old Point Comfort, guarded the entry. Hampton Roads is the site of the famous Monitor and Merrimack naval battle of 1862, which ended in a draw between the ironclads and is one of the world's greatest natural harbors.

Mariners must find their way carefully among all the vessels and aids to navigation in this impressive nautical crossroads. Many of us cruising the waters covered by the many editions of Waterway Guide will never experience a busier harbor than Hampton Roads. It is just as busy (if not busier) than New York Harbor. Stay tuned to VHF Channel 16 and VHF Channel 13, the channel on which commercial traffic communicates. Remember that you are in deep water in this harbor and you can safely run alongside the channel (and outside it) to provide ample space between you and the many 1,000-foot container ships, submarines, aircraft carriers and commercial vessels that move through here.

NAVIGATION: Use NOAA Chart 12222. Twin 3-mile-long bridge-tunnels join the north and south sides of Hampton Roads (from Hampton to Norfolk) between Old Point Comfort and Willoughby Spit (detailed in the Chesapeake Bay edition of Waterway Guide.) Channels over the tunnels are well marked but they also serve as bottlenecks through which all boat and big ship traffic must pass. Tidal currents are usually strong here.

Proceeding south through Hampton Roads Harbor, give ships at the Norfolk Naval Station a wide berth. This area is constantly patrolled and it is advisable to favor the west side of the channel or even just outside the channel, where there is still adequate water depth. In fact, all military and commercial ships must be given a wide berth–500 yards when possible–as dictated by the Homeland Security Act.

NO WAKE ZONE

This is not a No-Wake Zone but caution should be exercised through this congested area. Before this transit, tie down as if you were going to sea. It will be choppy and confused from the many boat and ship wakes, and you will likely get rocked on your way through by an inconsiderate boater or by residual wakes that you can't avoid.

City of Hampton

At Old Point Comfort a conspicuous historical brick landmark is the former Chamberlin Hotel (now now a senior services community) marking the north side of the entrance to Hampton Roads Harbor. Fort Monroe and Hampton University are on the eastern side of Hampton Harbor. The City of Hampton, just west of Old Point Comfort, is located on both sides of the short, busy Hampton River. Founded in 1610, Hampton is the oldest English-speaking city in America and is one of Virginia's main seafood packing centers.

Hampton River, VA

HAMPTON AREA		Largest Vessel	VHF	Total Slips	Approach/ Dockside Depth	Floating Docks	Gas/ Diesel	Repairs/ Haulout	Min/Max Amps	Pump-Out Station
1. Hampton Yacht Club WiFi	(757) 722-0711	100		192	10.0 / 8.0	F		H	30 / 50	P
2. Customs House Marina WiFi	(757) 636-7772	50		60	12.0 / 11.0				30 / 50	
3. The Docks at Downtown Hampton WiFi MM 1.5	(757) 727-1276	130	16	27	12.0 / 11.0	F			30 / 100	P

WiFi Wireless Internet Access onSpot Dockside WiFi Facility
Visit www.waterwayguide.com for current rates, fuel prices, website addresses and other up-to-the-minute information.
(Information in the table is provided by the facilities.)

Scan here for more details:

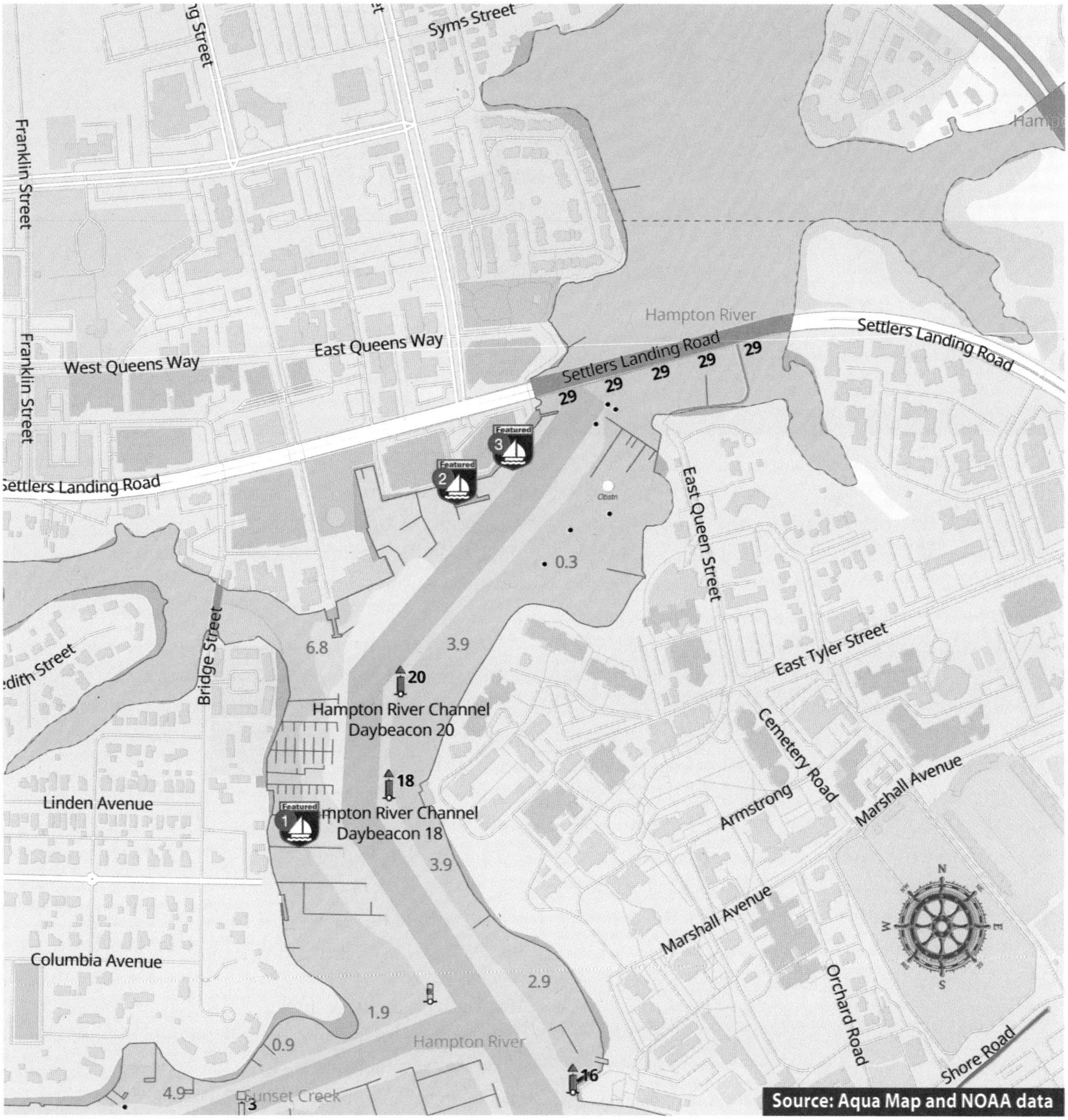

NAVIGATION: Use NOAA Chart 12222. On the north side of Hampton Roads Harbor, after you cross the twin tunnels of the **Hampton Roads Bridge-Tunnel**, pick up flashing red daybeacon "2" marking the start of the dogleg channel into the Hampton River. Take care not to cut the rip-rap too closely at the tunnel's entrance islands; some of the rocks extend out farther than expected. The channel into the Hampton River makes a turn to the south at quick flashing red light "6" and green daybeacon "7" and then to starboard at quick flashing green "11" and red daybeacon "12." Despite the curviness the channel is deep and easy to follow. (Shown as "Hampton Creek Channel" on the NOAA chart.) Both commercial and recreational boats frequently use the channel. All of the marinas are located before the 29-foot fixed vertical clearance **Settlers Landing Bridge**. The tide ranges about 2.5 feet and the current is a negligible.

See additional information about the town of Hampton in the Chesapeake Bay edition of Waterway Guide.

Dockage: The first of the facilities are on Sunset Creek, which leads off to the west from the main channel. The well-regarded Bluewater Yachting Center spans the southwest corner of the Hampton–Sunset Creek fork and features 200 floating slips for vessels up to 200 feet. They offer resort amenities, three separate high-speed fueling stations and complimentary water shuttle service to downtown. Their sister operation, Bluewater Yacht Yards, is located just beyond with world-class marine services. (Bluewater also manages the Bluewater Outer Banks Yacht Yard in Wanchese.) At the end of the navigable portion of Sunset Creek is the 6-acre Sunset Boating Center, which is a dry storage facility. They may have space for you but call ahead.

Back on the Hampton River the private Hampton Yacht Club recognizes reciprocity from other yacht clubs. Call for details. Note that the tour boat to Fort Wool uses the slip next to the Visitor's Center so don't pull in there.

The 60-slip Customs House Marina is convenient to downtown and welcomes transients. Next door is the The Docks at Downtown Hampton. Both of these offer all the usual amenities plus complimentary bicycles and pool, and spa and fitness room privileges at the Crowne Plaza Hampton Marina Hotel.

Old Point Comfort Marina, which is located at Fort Monroe, has transient slips to 50 feet available to the

Hampton Roads, VA

OLD POINT COMFORT		Largest Vessel	VHF	Total Slips	Approach/ Dockside Depth	Floating Docks	Gas/ Diesel	Repairs/ Haulout	Min/Max Amps	Pump-Out Station
1. Old Point Comfort Marina (WiFi)	(757) 788-4308	50	16	314	20.0 / 13.0	F	GD		30 / 50	P

(WiFi) Wireless Internet Access onSpot Dockside WiFi Facility
Visit www.waterwayguide.com for current rates, fuel prices, website addresses and other up-to-the-minute information.
(Information in the table is provided by the facilities.)

Scan here for more details:

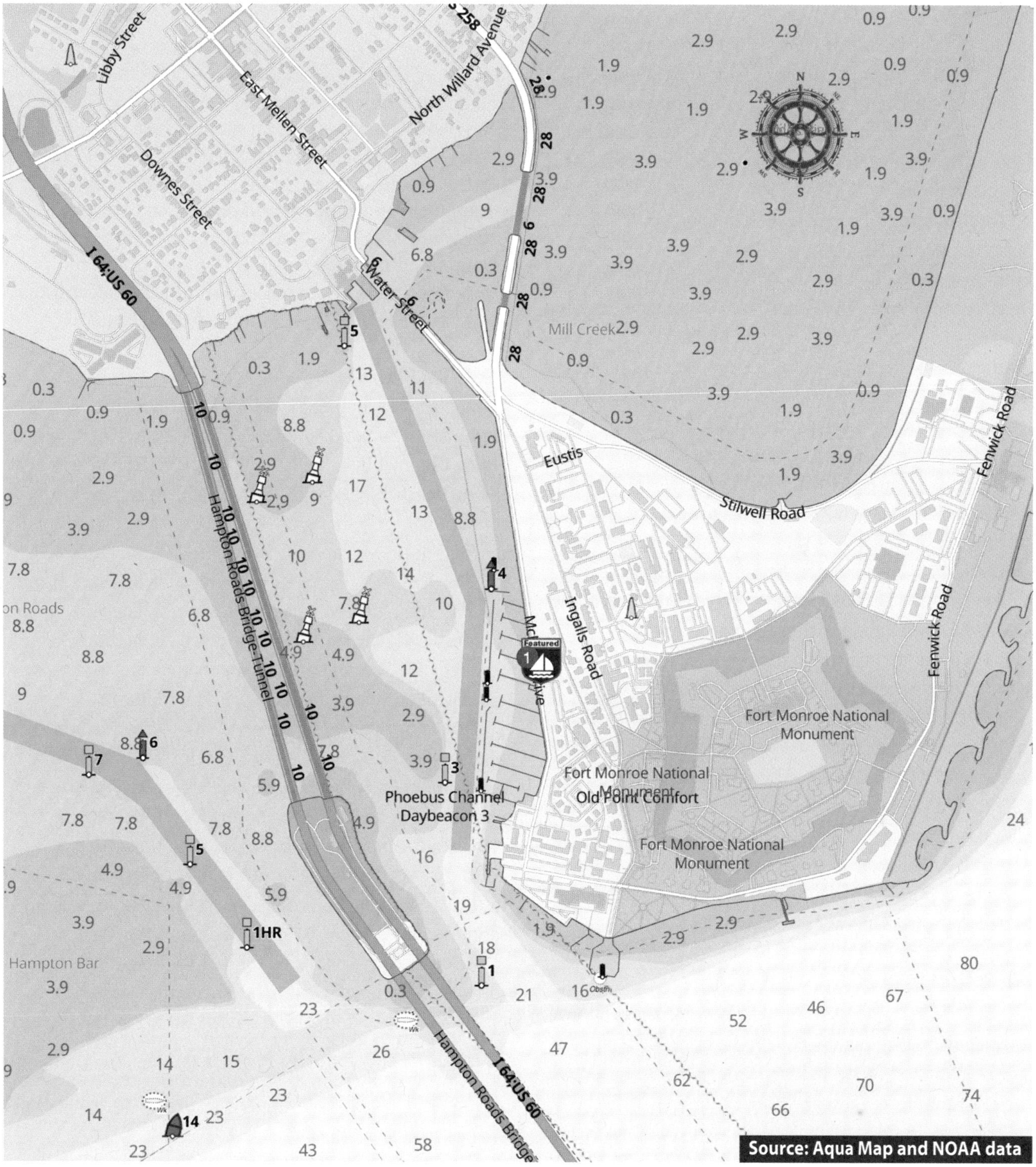

Source: Aqua Map and NOAA data

Willoughby Bay, VA

WILLOUGHBY SPIT		Largest Vessel	VHF	Total Slips	Approach/ Dockside Depth	Floating Docks	Gas/ Diesel	Repairs/ Haulout	Min/Max Amps	Pump-Out Station
1. Rebel Marina WiFi	(757) 580-6022	100	16	80	10.0 / 9.0	F			30 / 50	P
2. Willoughby Harbor Marina MM 10.7	(757) 583-4150	80	16	271	9.0 / 8.0	F			30 / 50	P

WiFi Wireless Internet Access onSpot Dockside WiFi Facility
Visit www.waterwayguide.com for current rates, fuel prices, website addresses and other up-to-the-minute information.
(Information in the table is provided by the facilities.)

Scan here for more details:

public. The fort is now a National Historic Site rather than an active base. The Officer's Club functions as the Paradise Ocean Club, offering meals and beverages to guests at the outdoor pool and a stretch of beach at daily rates or by membership (seasonal). The on-site tiki bar is especially popular.

Anchorage: There are several anchorage opportunities on the Hampton River. One is at Cedar Point just north of where Sunset Creek joins the Hampton River at Mile 196.2. The Cedar Point anchorage has good holding in 7 to 8 feet MLW in mud but is open to the northeast, south and ICW wakes. Another is opposite the downtown public docks. Boats may anchor anywhere past red daybeacon "20" on the red-marker side of the channel. Use your depth sounder to find the best spot. Do not block traffic or interfere with the private marina or with the city dock. This is not a "designated anchorage area" so be sure to use appropriate day-shape and anchor lights.

Boats that can get under the 29-foot fixed vertical clearance of the Settlers Landing Bridge at the end of the channel can find good anchorage on the Hampton River in 8 to 10 feet MLW with good holding and plenty of swing room. As always, exercise caution in shoal areas.

The City of Phoebus has a 96-foot fixed pier with a 60-foot-floating dock to encourage boaters to anchor in deeper water (Mill Creek–Old Point Comfort) and then take their dinghies to shore and visit the downtown area. Shopping, restaurants and a theater are a short walk. The well-established anchorage is open enough to have a breeze in hot weather and protected enough to cut the breeze and waves in a southwest wind.

Willoughby Bay

A less crowded and less protected layover than Hampton is available at Willoughby Bay on the opposite (south) side of Hampton Roads behind Willoughby Spit (where the Hampton Roads Bridge-Tunnel ends).

Note that helicopters from the highly active Norfolk Naval Air Station airport on the southern shore of Willoughby Bay conduct practice exercises over the water. All mariners are required to remain well clear of the helicopters, the towed devices and the area extending directly behind the aircraft for 400 yards. Do not approach or cross the area directly behind the towed device as a submerged hazard exists regardless of whether the device is in motion or stationary.

NAVIGATION: Use NOAA Chart 12222. Two marked channels take you into Willoughby Bay between Willoughby Spit and Sewells Point. The Navy-maintained South Channel by Sewells Point is in a restricted area near the carrier piers. Use the North Channel near the bridge-tunnel to enter Willoughby Bay. Be prepared for strong currents at the entrance by Fort Wool. When entering the North Channel, stay clear of green daybeacon "1" and use flashing red "2" as the entrance point. Give the green markers a wide berth, especially green daybeacons "3" through "7." Backsight the channel often as it is shallow to the east and you can easily drift out of line.

Dockage: Rebel Marina and Willoughby Harbor Marina are located on the north side of Willoughby Bay on Willoughby Spit and both have slips reserved for transients. You will need transportation for extensive provisioning or other shopping. (Rebel Marina has a courtesy car.) The biggest draw is the convenient access to the Chesapeake Bay and a spectacular 7-mile stretch of sandy beaches.

Anchorage: Anchor holding in Willoughby Bay past the marina complex (just past the entry on the north side of the bay) is good in approximately 10 feet MLW but watch for submerged, marked pilings and crab markers in the area. In addition to reported debris on the bottom, an unmarked telephone cable crosses this area. Be sure to anchor with care.

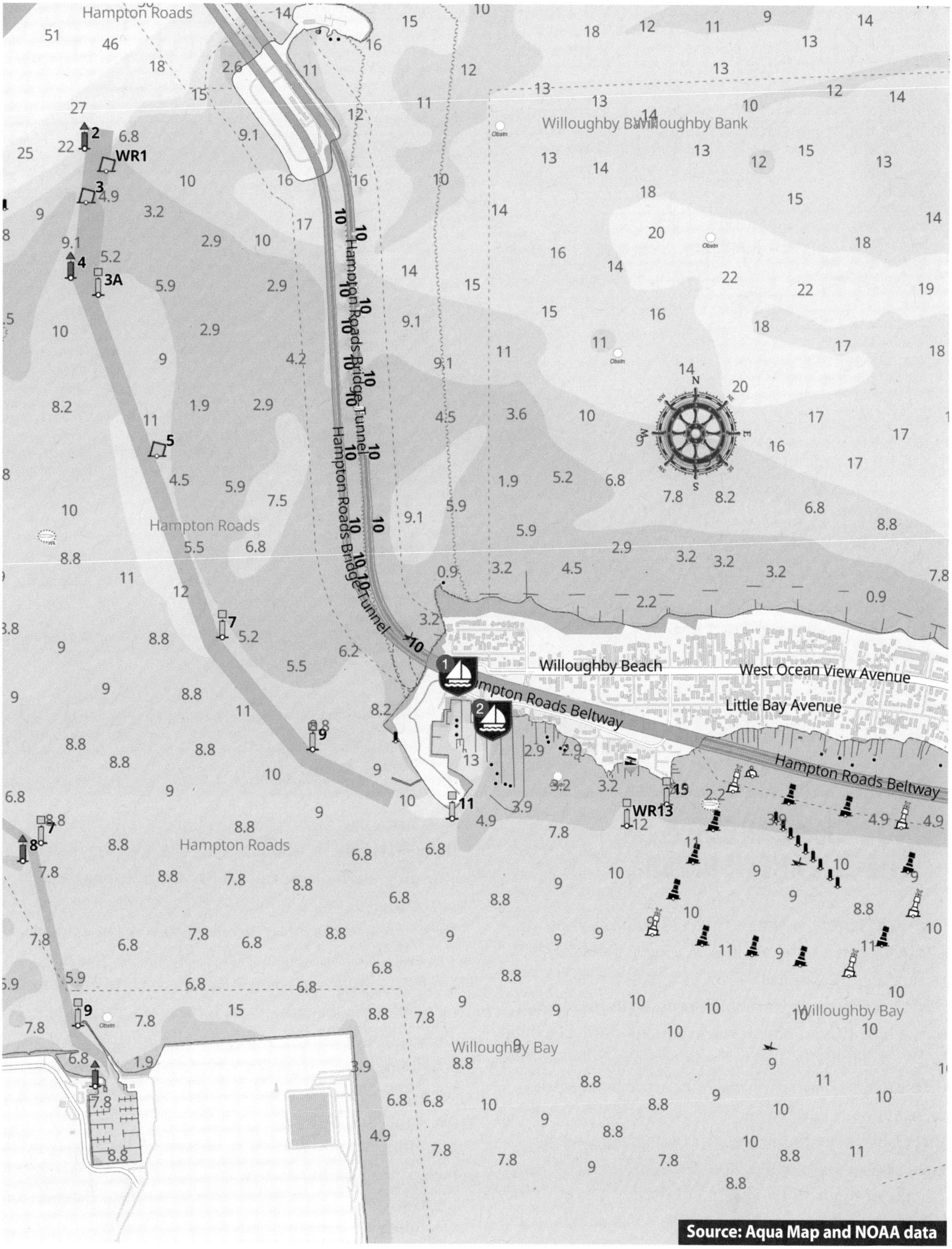

Source: Aqua Map and NOAA data

NORFOLK HARBOR & THE ELIZABETH RIVER

NAVIGATION: Use NOAA Chart 12222, 12253 or 12206. (Chart 12253 provides an inset of Norfolk Harbor and the Elizabeth River at 1:10,000 scale.) Even with all its commercial and military activity, navigating through Norfolk Harbor is relatively easy during daylight hours. If southbound from Hampton Roads, pick up the marked channel past Sewells Point at the western end of Willoughby Bay and continue on into the Elizabeth River. Southbound past Sewells Point you will see a great array of naval vessels to the east, from aircraft carriers to submarines. The harbor itself begins at Craney Island (where you should switch to NOAA Small Craft Chart 12206).

At night navigation can be a bit more difficult with all the illumination ashore making aids to navigation more difficult to detect. You will be much happier and enjoy the sights a lot more traveling in daylight. As in other large harbors it is recommended you run alongside or outside the marked channel if ship traffic is heavy. Depths alongside the channel are good. The main hazard is flotsam, which can be in the form of wooden planks or piles the size of telephone poles. If you choose to run outside the channel, use the western side until you are past the Norfolk Naval Base and port operations to the east. Patrol boats and security barriers line the Restricted Area on the eastern side of the channel (shown as a purple shaded area on your NOAA chart). From Craney Island southward remain inside the channel to avoid shallows and military or port facilities.

The Western Branch of the Elizabeth River leads off to starboard to the south of the bend in the main channel at Lamberts Point. Note the magenta restricted area on the NOAA chart east of Lovett Point on your approach to Western Branch. The 45-foot fixed vertical clearance **West Norfolk Bridge** located just west of Lovett Point makes it impossible for some sailboats to pass farther upstream. Those who can clear the fixed bridge will find depths of 15 to 20 feet all the way to the **Churchland (High Street) Bridge** with a 38-foot fixed vertical clearance.

Elizabeth River quick flashing red buoy "36" just east of Hospital Point marks Mile 0 and the beginning of the 1,243-mile-long Atlantic ICW. South of the Western Branch junction on the western side of the main Elizabeth River channel is Hospital Point, home to the nation's oldest and largest naval hospital. Beyond that are the sprawling cities of Norfolk and Portsmouth.

The current can be strong here and discourteous boaters may throw a wake that will roll you so be aware and prepared. Expect less current as you proceed from ICW Mile 0 southward. Heavy commercial traffic, bridge schedules and lock openings can also sometimes cause marked delay in arrival time so planning ahead is a good idea before proceeding southward.

Dockage: Norfolk Yacht and Country Club on the Lafayette River is private but recognizes reciprocity from some other clubs. There is a dress code for the dining areas so plan accordingly. Western Branch Diesel, Inc is conveniently located on the north side of the Western Branch of the Elizabeth River before the 45-foot fixed West Norfolk Bridge. They offer installation, service and parts for vessels of all sizes and are on site 24/7.
They also offer mobile parts and service. Virginia Boat & Yacht Service, also located on the north side of Western Branch, is a traditional working boat yard. Call ahead for slip space.

Anchorage: You can drop the hook directly across from Norfolk Yacht and Country Club and just outside the channel at red daybeacon "10" on the Lafayette River. For boats that can clear a 24-foot fixed vertical clearance **Hampton Boulevard Bridges**, additional anchorage is available farther up the river in 8 to 9 feet MLW with ample swing room and protection.

Bridges/Distances

(Approximate Statute Miles from Mile Zero, Norfolk, VA)

SM	BRIDGE NAME	CLOSED CLEARANCE	SCHEDULE
Virginia			
2.6	Belt Line Railroad Bridge	6'	UO
3.6	Norfolk & Western Railroad Bridge	10'	UO
5.8	Gilmerton Bridge	35'	OS*
5.8	Norfolk Southern #7 Railroad Bridge	7'	UO
11.3	Great Bridge Lock		
12.0	SR 168 (Battlefield Blvd.) Bridge	8'	OS*
13.9	Albemarle & Chesapeake Railroad Bridge	7'	UO
15.2	Centerville Turnpike (SR 170) Bridge	4'	SS
Albemarle-Chesapeake Canal: North Carolina			
20.2	SR 165 (North Landing)Bridge	6'	OS*
***Dismal Swamp Canal: Virginia/North Carolina**			
10.5	Deep Creek Lock		
11.1	Deep Creek Bridge (openings coordinate with lock)	4'	SS
28.0	Dismal Swamp Canal VC Foot Bridge	0'	UO
32.6	South Mills Bridge (openings coordinate with lock)	4'	SS
32.7	South Mills Lock		
47.7	Norfolk Southern Railroad Bridge	3'	UO
50.7	US 158 (Elizabeth City) Bridge	2'	OS*
North Carolina			
84.2	Alligator River (US 64) Bridge	14'	OS
125.9	Wilkerson (US 264) Bridge	64'	F
203.8	Beaufort Channel Railroad Bridge	4'	UO
240.7	Onslow Beach Swing Bridge	12'	OS*
252.3	NC 210 Hwy. Bridge	64'	F
278.1	Figure Eight Island Swing Bridge	20'	SS
283.1	SR 74 (Wrightsville Beach) Bridge	20'	SS
South Carolina			
347.3	Captain Archie Neil "Poo" McLauchlin (Little River) Swing Bridge	7'	OS
353.3	Barefoot Landing Swing Bridge	31'	OS
365.4	SCL Railroad Bridge	16'	UO
371.0	Socastee Swing Bridge	11'	OS
411.5	Estherville-Minim Canal Bridge	0'	UO
462.2	Ben Sawyer Memorial (SC 703) Bridge	31'	OS*
470.8	Wappoo Creek (SC 171) Bridge	33'	OS*
536.0	Lady's Island (Woods Memorial) Bridge	30'	OS*
579.9	Causton Bluff (Sam Varnedoe) Bridge	21'	OS*

Note: Bridges here do not include all fixed bridges (usually 65-foot vertical clearance or more).

F = Fixed

UO = Usually open

OS = Opens on signal

OS* = Opens on signal but with variations at certain times of day (e.g., during rush hour)

SS = Set schedule (e.g., on the hour and half hour, on the quarter hour, etc.)

Elizabeth River, VA

LAFAYETTE RIVER		Largest Vessel	VHF	Total Slips	Approach/ Dockside Depth	Floating Docks	Gas/ Diesel	Repairs/ Haulout	Min/Max Amps	Pump-Out Station
1. Norfolk Yacht and Country Club WiFi	(757) 423-4500			200	11.0 /	F	GD		30 / 50	P

WiFi Wireless Internet Access onSpot Dockside WiFi Facility
Visit www.waterwayguide.com for current rates, fuel prices, website addresses and other up-to-the-minute information.
(Information in the table is provided by the facilities.)

Scan here for more details:

Elizabeth River, VA

WESTERN BRANCH		Largest Vessel	VHF	Total Slips	Approach/ Dockside Depth	Floating Docks	Gas/ Diesel	Repairs/ Haulout	Min/Max Amps	Pump-Out Station
1. Western Branch Diesel, Inc	**(757) 673-7100**	**100**		**62**	**12.0 / 7.0**			**R**	**30 / 50**	
2. Virginia Boat & Yacht Service	(757) 673-7167	150		62	12.0 / 8.0			RH	30 / 50	

WiFi Wireless Internet Access onSpot Dockside WiFi Facility
Visit www.waterwayguide.com for current rates, fuel prices, website addresses and other up-to-the-minute information.
(Information in the table is provided by the facilities.)

Scan here for more details:

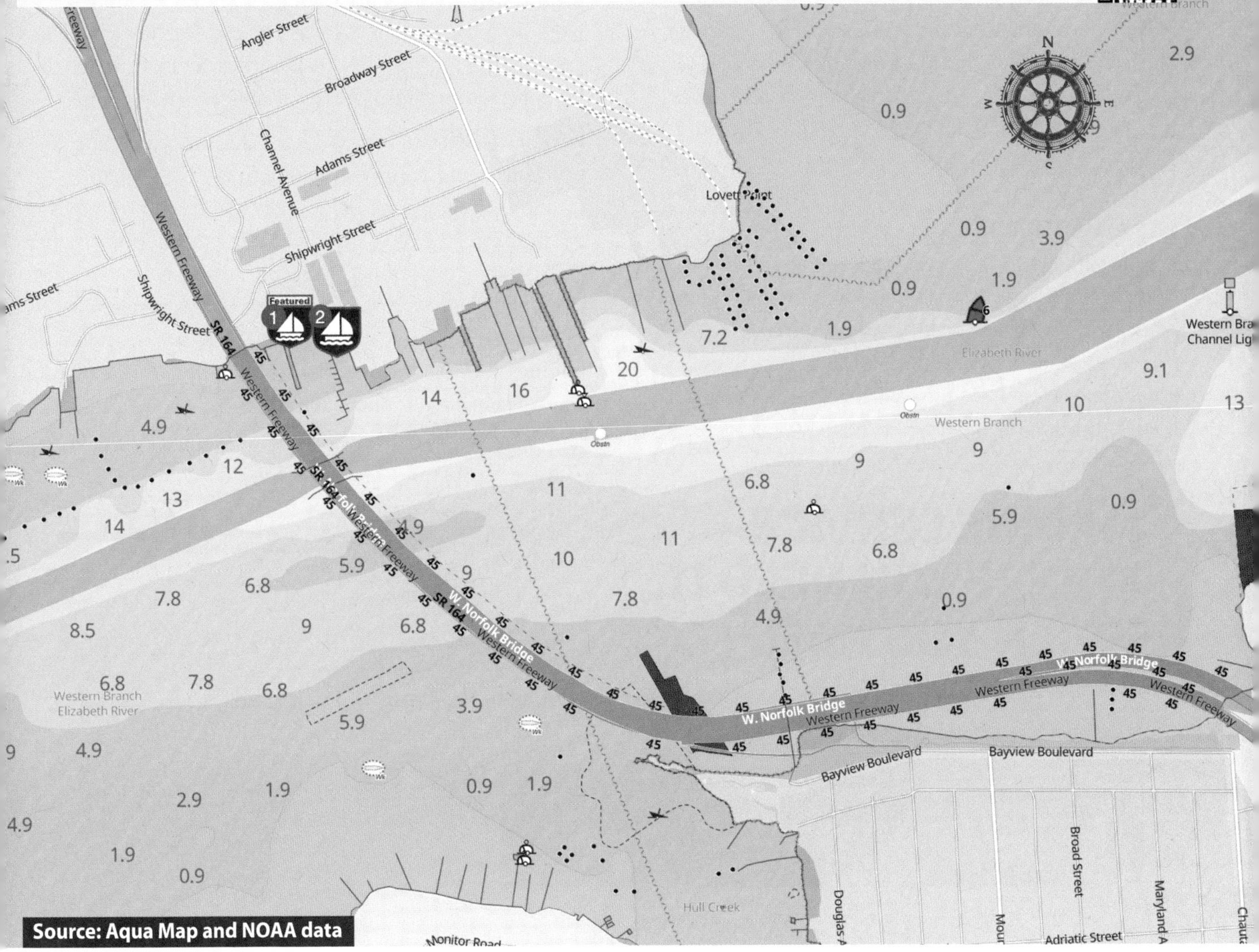

Source: Aqua Map and NOAA data

City of Norfolk

For two centuries Norfolk has been a Navy town and to this day it is flanked on north and south by ships in gray livery. Well before the U.S. Navy was established, merchant ships and sailors called Norfolk home and cargo vessels of all types with international crews still call to load, discharge and undergo repairs. With a population approaching 250,000, Norfolk is the second largest city in Virginia. (Virginia Beach is the largest with almost 450,000.) It is not surprising that Norfolk supports many of the cultural and recreational outlets associated with bigger cities. It has a symphony orchestra, several museums, professional sports teams and a downtown shopping mall full of high-end retail stores. (See "Goin' Ashore: Norfolk, VA" in this chapter for details.)

Dockage: There is a wave screen directly in front of the 50-slip Waterside Marina to provide protection for vessels moored there. Transient space is available at floating slips with access to restrooms and showers. Overnight slip holders can get transportation for provisioning arranged by the dockmaster on request. The deep-water marina can accommodate vessels to 300 feet. Waterside Marina is part of the City of Norfolk's Waterside District, which has undergone a multimillion dollar renovation. The marina is well protected and within easy walking distance of downtown venues.

There is a smaller marina facility (15 slips) for overflow close by at Nauticus, a museum and park. Call Waterside Marina for information and reservations for Nauticus Marina. You may tie up for 2 hours at no charge if you are visiting the museum. The marina can only accept vessels that do not exceed 24-foot vertical clearance due to a walking bridge that spans the opening.

City of Portsmouth

Portsmouth has long served as a key point at the beginning or end of a passage through the ICW. For many years before the city began construction on the new face it now presents to the Elizabeth River, it was a place to only to take aboard fuel and provisions before running for the less threatening open spaces of the Bay or the ICW. Today it is a destination worth exploring for its own sake. The waterfront area has been largely rebuilt and High Street is vibrant with commerce plus several museums and cultural centers. See suggestions in "Goin' Ashore: Portsmouth, VA."

America's largest warships and support vessels are often berthed in enormous floating dry docks undergoing refits directly across from Portsmouth. Shipyards and industrial piers stretch upstream as far as you can see. Towers of glass and concrete in Norfolk's business district loom above the harbor downstream. The river itself teems with traffic.

NAVIGATION: Use NOAA Chart 12206. Located directly on "Mile 0" of the ICW, Portsmouth is a convenient location to regroup for the journey south or to recoup from the rigors of "the ditch" when heading north. Pedestrian ferry service to Norfolk is available at both North Landing Dock and High Street Landing. The 150-passenger Elizabeth River Ferry drops off and picks up every 30 minutes at the Waterside District in Norfolk for $2.00 (one way). There are discounts and multi-day passes available.

Dockage: Scott Creek is home to Portsmouth Boating Center, known for its high-speed diesel pumps and reasonable fuel prices. They also offer all types of services and boat storage.

Just to the south and directly opposite Norfolk's Town Point the full-service Tidewater Yacht Marina has 100 deep-water reserved transient slips on their floating docks as well as diesel and gas fueling stations, substantial repair facilities and a well-stocked Ship Store with charts, clothing and groceries. To reach the fuel dock pass behind the breakwater from the river then turn southeast down the first fairway. The large pumps on the outermost dock are only for ferries and other large vessels. The on-site Fish & Slips Marina Raw Bar & Grille is situated above the marina store and office with a commanding view of the harbor.

Ocean Yacht Marina, a sister marina to Tidewater Yacht Marina, is 0.5 miles south with clean facilities, a professional and courteous staff and wide docks. Next door is Fairlead Structures (formerly Ocean Marine Yacht Center), a marine industrial base for both commercial and government customers. These facilities are adjacent to a large outdoor pavilion where big name entertainers regularly perform and to the Elizabeth River Ferry landing at High Street. The Olde Towne Portsmouth historic district is within walking distance.

High Street Landing in Portsmouth offer free short-term dockage for vessels 40 feet and under (36-hour limit; no more than 3 days in any 30-day period). There are no utilities. This is where the Elizabeth River Ferry drops off and picks up. Boaters should check in at the kiosk across from the High Street Landing for a list of rules and regulations. Call the Visitor Center (757-393-5111) for more information. (Note that North Street landing was under renovation in 2021 and not available for boaters.)

Anchorage: Late arrivals and those who prefer to anchor normally use the harbor's small-boat anchorage (Hospital Point) south and west of the channel at flashing red buoy "36" between the large brick naval hospital and Tidewater Yacht Marina. Anchor in 8 to 9 feet MLW in mud. Holding is only fair so don't skimp on scope. The anchorage is popular and usually holds numerous boats. The no-wake zone in the harbor keeps you relatively calm (other than occasional tug wakes or inconsiderate boaters) but strong winds in summer storms can funnel down the river.

Dinghy dockage and use of some facilities is available at the Tidewater Yacht Marina on the Portsmouth side for a fee. You can also take the dinghy to Waterside Marina on the Norfolk waterfront and make fast inside (for a small fee) if there is space.

Mile 0: Elizabeth River

For southbound boats the first 200-mile-long stretch of the AICW between Mile 0 at Norfolk and Mile 205 at Morehead City/Beaufort, NC, presents a diverse array of navigational challenges while offering equally diverse natural beauty, fascinating sights, side trips and ports of call. The route passes through a lock (or two depending on the route you choose), canals, land cuts and open-water sounds along the way. Some of the open water offers the challenges associated with long fetches, shallow depths and choppy wave action when the wind kicks up. Sailors may consider minimizing motoring time by sailing from sound to sound.

In much but not all of North Carolina (and sporadically in other ICW states) the Army Corps of Engineers has placed signs just outside the channel marking each 5-statute mile increment along the route. Note that the numbers on these signs do not necessarily correspond to the "Mile Markers" on the charts. Some are the same, some are different by a hundred yards or so and some by as much as a mile. If you are using the actual signs to determine your location in relation to a timed bridge or marina location, you may find yourself a lot closer or farther away than you thought. It is best to use the charts for this information but make sure you have the most current edition.

Reminder: All mileage on the ICW is measured in statute rather than nautical miles. (1 nm = 1.15 mile).

There are no aids to navigation in this area and none are needed as the water is deep to the shoreline. Four bridges cross this stretch: two bascule bridges, one with a 48-foot and one with a 4-foot closed vertical clearance; one fixed with a 65-foot vertical clearance; and one railroad swing bridge with a 6-foot vertical clearance. The bascule and swing bridges have restricted closures.

NAVIGATION: Use NOAA Chart 12206. Beyond Mile 0 Town Point on the Norfolk side marks the mouth of the Elizabeth River's Eastern Branch. The Eastern Branch of

GOIN' ASHORE

NORFOLK, VA

Norfolk, home of the world's largest naval base, has roots that begin at the waterfront and are entwined with it throughout history. Boaters continue to arrive daily at the waterfront, where they can tie up within walking distance of many of the City's must-see attractions. As in most larger cities, you will have no problem locating and accessing provisions and entertainment. Hampton Roads Transit connects with destinations beyond downtown and with all the cities in the Hampton Roads area via bus, light rail and ferry. Call 757-222-6100 or visit www.gohrt.com for details.

SERVICES

1. Norfolk Post Office
999 Waterside Dr. #114 (757-640-0044)

2. Solver Library
235 E. Plume St. (757-431-7491)

3. Visit NorfolK
232 E. Main St. (800-368-3097)

ATTRACTIONS

4. Armed Forces Memorial
Unique display that tells a story through examples of letters written home by servicemen and women who subsequently died in action. A good time to visit is in late afternoon, when warm light and long shadows highlight the messages, each one borne on cast bronze sheets and displayed as though strewn across the plaza at Town Point Park by the wind.

5. Chrysler Museum of Art
Esteemed museum with broad (30,000 works) collection of ancient to contemporary art including glass and sculpture at 1 Memorial Place (757-664-6200).
Also offers demos, talks, performances and classes.

6. Harbor Park Stadium
Home of the Norfolk Tides, a AAA farm team for the Baltimore Orioles known for its outstanding water views from the stands (757-622-2222).

7. MacArthur Memorial Museum
This learning center and theater celebrates the life and achievements of Gen. Douglas MacArthur and is a tribute to those who served in WWI, WWII and the Korean War. Located downtown next to the MacArthur Center mall at 198 Bank St. (757-441-2965).
Admission is free.

8. Nauticus
Maritime museum at 1 Waterside Dr. with science exhibits, an aquarium and the Wisconsin BB-64, a veteran of three wars. The Iowa Class Battleships were the largest and last battleships built before the Navy switched to aircraft carriers. Call 757-664-1000 for operating hours and information.

9. Wells Theater
Restored Beaux Arts landmark that opened in 1913 as a vaudeville theater. Home of the Virginia Stage Company (108 E. Tazewell St., 757-627-1234).

SHOPPING

10. MacArthur Center
Three stories of department stores, small shops, restaurants and a theater complex within walking distance to waterfront at 300 Monticello Ave. (757-627-6000).

11. Seldon Market
Rotating lineup of retail shops and food venues in one historical venue at 208 E. Main St. Includes 12 retail spaces, 7 pop-up booths, multiple lounges and seating areas, and a shared kitchen (757-510-2740).

MARINAS

12. Nauticus Marina
One Waterside Dr. (757-664-1000)

13. Waterside Marina
333 Waterside Dr. (757-625-3625)

the Elizabeth River curves around Norfolk's Waterside District to port, while the Southern Branch (AICW) bears to starboard around Portsmouth. Commercial traffic can be heavy in this area with tugs passing through and large commercial vessels maneuvering into and out of the docks. It is a good idea to monitor VHF Channel 13 and to call any tug or other vessel whose intentions are unclear. Sometimes listening is enough. Always yield to commercial traffic in this area.

Before reaching Town Point study your NOAA chart carefully. Many mariners mistakenly continue along the Eastern Branch thinking it is the AICW only to turn around 2 miles later when it dead ends. The AICW route follows the Southern Branch of the Elizabeth River.

Leave the large shipyard across from Portsmouth to port when heading south on the Southern Branch of the Elizabeth River. The Norfolk Naval Shipyard is farther along, also on the Portsmouth (west) side. As many signs warn, landings are not permitted. Navy and Coast Guard patrol boats guard the naval vessels docked along both sides of the river. (They don't like for you to take photos either.)

Proceeding southward you will encounter a 7-mile-long congested stretch with a 6-mph speed limit (enforced) and six bridges. Be sure to monitor VHF Channel 13, on which all commercial vessels communicate and bridge traffic is handled, as well as VHF Channel 16. Most bridges open promptly except during restricted hours. Northbound vessels leaving the lock at Great Bridge at the same time are usually required to bunch together for openings of all the bridges in this stretch, whether fast or slow, power or sail.

There are two railroad lift bridges on either side of the fixed 145-foot vertical clearance **Jordan Bridge** at Mile 2.6 and **Norfolk & Western Railroad Bridge** at Mile 3.6. Both are usually open but closures do occur. Note that a closed vertical clearance of less than 9 feet has been observed at the railroad bridge despite the published 10-foot clearance. The Belt Line Railroad Bridge is operated remotely and will be open unless a bridge is approaching.

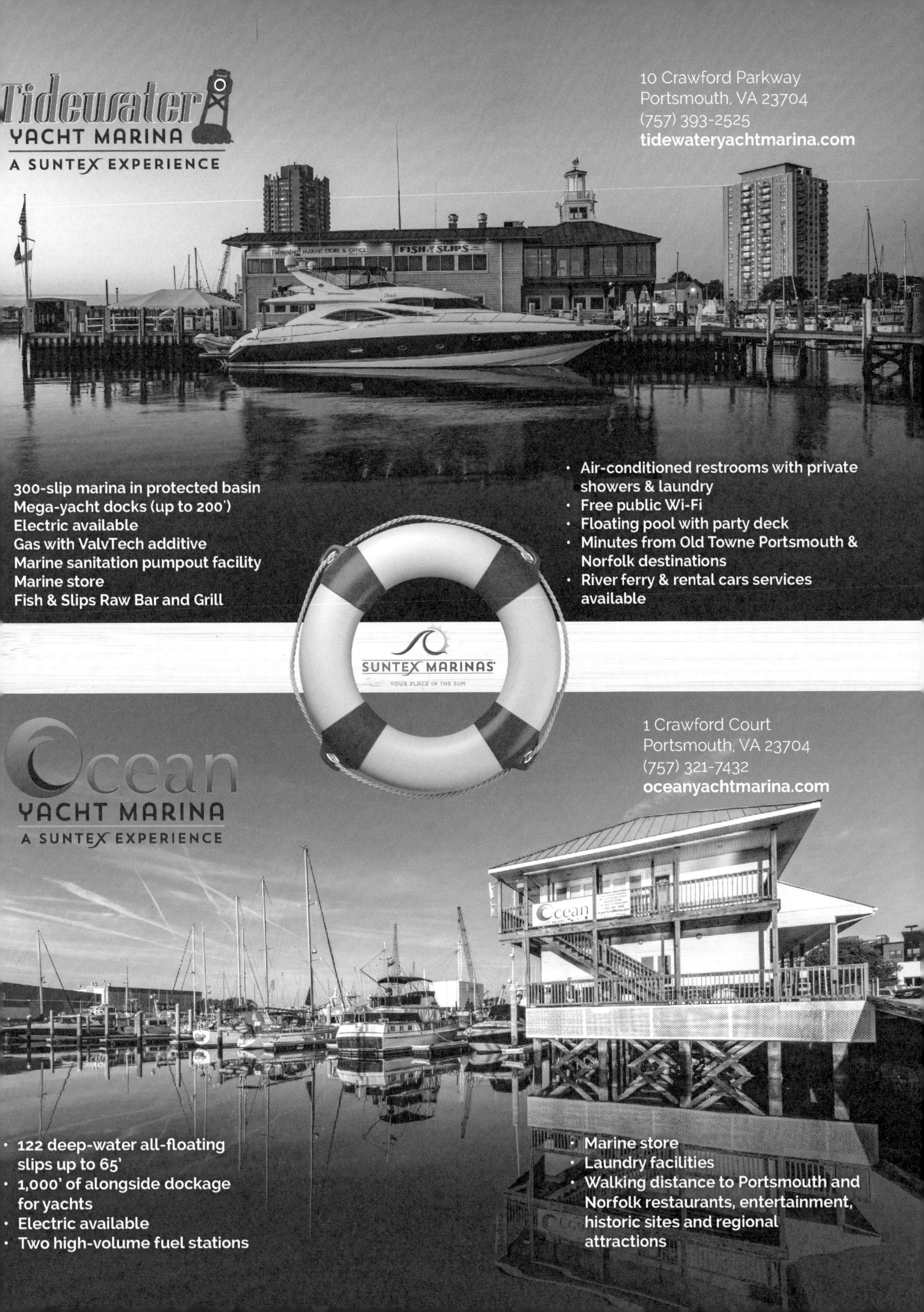

Tidewater
YACHT MARINA
A SUNTEX EXPERIENCE
10 Crawford Parkway
Portsmouth, VA 23704
(757) 393-2525
tidewateryachtmarina.com
FISH & SLIPS
300-slip marina in protected basin
Mega-yacht docks (up to 200')
Electric available
Gas with ValvTech additive
Marine sanitation pumpout facility
Marine store
Fish & Slips Raw Bar and Grill
· Air-conditioned restrooms with private showers & laundry
· Free public Wi-Fi
· Floating pool with party deck
· Minutes from Old Towne Portsmouth & Norfolk destinations
· River ferry & rental cars services available
SUNTEX MARINAS
YOUR PLACE IN THE SUN
Ocean
YACHT MARINA
A SUNTEX EXPERIENCE
1 Crawford Court
Portsmouth, VA 23704
(757) 321-7432
oceanyachtmarina.com
· 122 deep-water all-floating slips up to 65'
· 1,000' of alongside dockage for yachts
· Electric available
· Two high-volume fuel stations
· Marine store
· Laundry facilities
· Walking distance to Portsmouth and Norfolk restaurants, entertainment, historic sites and regional attractions

Elizabeth River, VA

NORFOLK		Largest Vessel	VHF	Total Slips	Approach/ Dockside Depth	Floating Docks	Gas/ Diesel	Repairs/ Haulout	Min/Max Amps	Pump-Out Station
1. Nauticus Marina	(757) 664-1000	60		15	45.0 / 20.0	F			30 / 50	P
2. Waterside Marina WiFi	(757) 625-3625	300	16	50	45.0 / 20.0	F		R	30 / 200+	P
PORTSMOUTH										
3. Portsmouth Boating Center WiFi MM 0.0	(757) 397-2092	80	16	40	8.0 / 10.0		GD	RH	30 / 50	P
4. Tidewater Yacht Marina WiFi MM 0.4	**(757) 393-2525**	**300**	**16**	**300**	**12.0 / 11.0**	**F**	**G**		**30 / 200+**	**P**

WiFi Wireless Internet Access onSpot Dockside WiFi Facility
Visit www.waterwayguide.com for current rates, fuel prices, website addresses and other up-to-the-minute information.
(Information in the table is provided by the facilities.)

Scan here for more details:

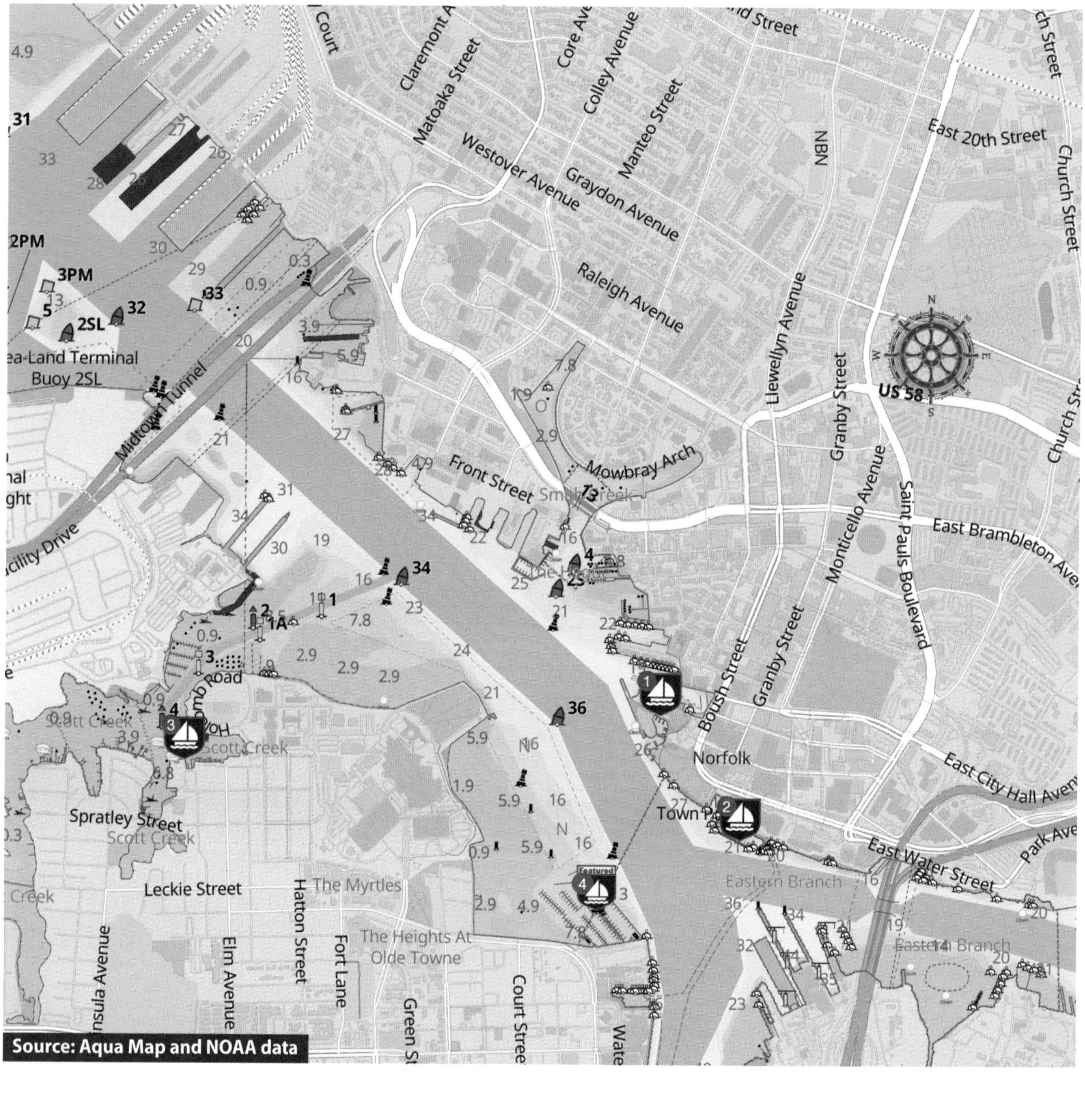

Elizabeth River, VA

PORTSMOUTH		Largest Vessel	VHF	Total Slips	Approach/ Dockside Depth	Floating Docks	Gas/ Diesel	Repairs/ Haulout	Min/Max Amps	Pump-Out Station
1. Ocean Yacht Marina WiFi **MM 1.0**	(757) 321-7432	350	16	122	45.0 / 30.0	F	GD	RH	30 / 100	P
2. Fairlead Structures (formerly Ocean Marine Yacht Center)	(757) 392-2831	235			/		GD	RH		

WiFi Wireless Internet Access **onSpot** Dockside WiFi Facility
Visit www.waterwayguide.com for current rates, fuel prices, website addresses and other up-to-the-minute information.
(Information in the table is provided by the facilities.)

Scan here for more details:

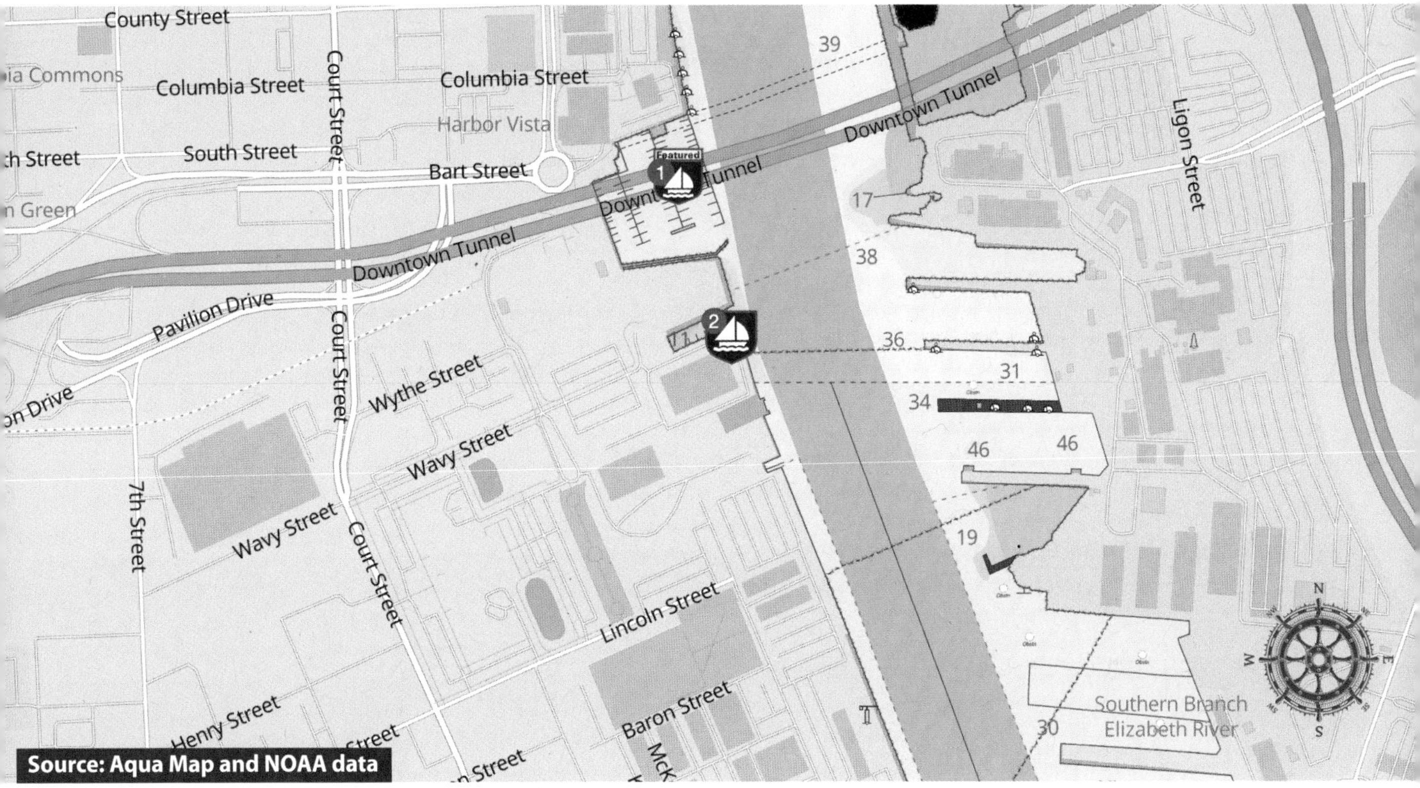

Source: Aqua Map and NOAA data

Do not mistake St. Julian Creek at Mile 4.9 for the AICW. (This is easier to do northbound than southbound when it is just north and to port of the Gilmerton Bridge.) A 45-foot-high overhead power cable also crosses this creek. Beacons warning of the power cable were placed at the mouth of St. Julian Creek after several vessels were dismasted.

The **Gilmerton Bridge** (35-foot closed vertical clearance) at Mile 5.8 opens on signal except from 6:30 a.m. to 8:30 a.m. and from 3:30 p.m. to 5:30 p.m., Monday through Friday (except federal holidays), when the bridge need not open. The adjacent **Norfolk Southern #7 Railroad Bridge** is normally open. It is important to note that the Gilmerton Bridge will not open unless the railroad bridge is open. Openings of the railroad bridge are announced on VHF Channel 13 and it is operated remotely with light, horn and audio signals when opening and closing. Be sure both bridges are open completely before you start through.

Note: Vessels traveling northbound from Great Bridge Lock will usually be required to group together for the Gilmerton Bridge opening north of the lock.

Plan departures and arrivals carefully to avoid idling in river currents for up to 3 hours while waiting for bridge openings. These bridges are situated on a bend in the river and are hard to see until you are nearly upon them. Yield to commercial traffic and listen to the radio for their intentions. If you have any questions about their movement, contact them using VHF Channel 13 and be clear and direct in your communications.

GOIN' ASHORE

PORTSMOUTH, VA

Portsmouth was founded as a town in 1752 on 65 acres of land on the shores of the Elizabeth River. The town was founded by William Crawford, a wealthy merchant and ship owner. The 65 acres were part of Colonel Crawford's extensive plantation and were constituted as a town by an enabling act of the General Assembly of Virginia. The town was named after the English naval port of the at name, and many of the streets of the new town reflected the English heritage.

SERVICES

1. Portsmouth Post Office
431 Crawford St. (757-397-5852)

2. Portsmouth Public Library
601 Court St. (757-393-8501)

3. Portsmouth Visitor Information
6 Crawford Pkwy. (757-393-5111)

ATTRACTIONS

4. Children's Museum of Virginia
Busy museum offering hands-on exhibits for kids 1-11 exploring cities, space, music, energy and the human body, plus antique trains (221 High St., 757-393-5258).

5. Elizabeth River Pedestrian Ferry
Connects the Norfolk waterfront to downtown Portsmouth across the Elizabeth River. The 150-passenger ferry leaves from 1 High St. and from 6 Crawford St. (North Landing) and runs every 30 minutes (757-222-6100).

6. Lightship Portsmouth Museum
On the waterfront at the foot of High St. (757-393-8591) is a 1915 lightship turned floating museum with displays of historic objects, uniforms, photos and models. Nearby on the waterfront is a first-order Fresnel lens.

7. Portsmouth Naval Shipyard Museum
Offers a unique perspective on U.S. history from Colonial to Civil War times and beyond. Ship models, uniforms, military artifacts and exhibits portray life from the 18th century to present day at 2 High St. (757-393-8591).

8. Railroad Museum of Virginia
Open Friday and Saturday from 10:00 a.m. to 4:00 p.m. Located at Court and Wythe Streets. Call for ticket prices (757-335-2284).

SERVICES

9. Olde Towne Drug Center Pharmacy
Household and grocery items, health and beauty aids, greeting cards and seasonal items. Free delivery on online prescription refills (600 High St., 757-393-4039).

MARINAS

10. Ocean Yacht Marina
1 Crawford Circle (757-321-7432)

11. Tidewater Yacht Marina
10 Crawford Pkwy. (757-393-2525)

Anchorage: Boats often anchor south of the Gilmerton Bridge in 9 to 13 feet MLW with good holding and protection all around. Boats often anchor here to wait out railroad bridge closures and sometimes stay all night (safely out of the waterway, of course).

NEXT STOP

You cross Mile 0 on the Atlantic ICW with little fanfare. There is no line in the water as seen on the screen during an America's Cup race, nor is there a starting horn blast. The line–were it to exist–would be located at N 36° 50.540'/W 76° 17.540' and would cross the waterway between Town Point and Tidewater Yacht Marina. From this "starting line" the ICW stretches 1,243.8 statute miles (1,080.8 nm) south to Key West, FL.

Back in the Day 1956

ICW **Mile 0-Mile 51**

At Mile 7.3, almost immediately south of the high-level **I-64 Bridge**, cruisers must choose one of two very different routes south to Albemarle Sound: the Virginia Cut route (officially the Albemarle-Chesapeake Canal) to North Landing River or the Great Dismal Swamp Canal route to Elizabeth City, NC. An Army Corps of Engineers sign, positioned on the west side of the waterway just south of the turn for Deep Creek, points the way to each route. It also states whether the canal at Dismal Swamp is open or closed and gives its controlling depth.

The Virginia Cut has deeper water and only one lock to negotiate, while the Dismal Swamp has a controlling depth of 6 feet MLW and two easy locks. During periods of low water, the Dismal Swamp Canal may be closed to navigation or have limited lock/bridge openings to protect the water levels in the Great Dismal Swamp Wildlife Refuge. It can sometimes be closed due to drought conditions or maintenance. Call the Army Corps of Engineers to confirm canal status before proceeding (757-201-7500, Option 3). The Dismal Swamp Canal Welcome Center (877-771-8333) is also a good sources of information on the status of the canal.

The Virginia Cut route winds 13 miles to the headwaters of North Landing River, on to Currituck Sound, into Coinjock Bay and then to the town of Coinjock, NC, on the North Carolina Cut. From Coinjock, the route follows the North River into Albemarle Sound. The Dismal Swamp route runs 30 miles to the headwaters of North Carolina's Pasquotank River, and then to Elizabeth City and on to the broad expanse of Albemarle Sound. The two routes rejoin near Mile 79 (after crossing Albemarle Sound) at the mouth of the Alligator River. Side trips east to the river towns of Albemarle Sound or west to the Outer Banks are covered in the "Side Trips: The Albemarle & Roanoke Sounds, NC" chapter of this guide.

ICW (VIRGINIA CUT)

Great Bridge to North Landing–ICW Mile 7 to Mile 20

Virginia Cut, the primary ICW route, is well marked and always open for navigation. The Army Corps of Engineers ICW project depth is 12 feet with a channel width of 90 feet. This route begins almost east-west and then turns north-south. The fresh-to-brackish waters have no tide but they may rise or fall with the wind. A strong northerly lowers the water and southerlies can raise it,

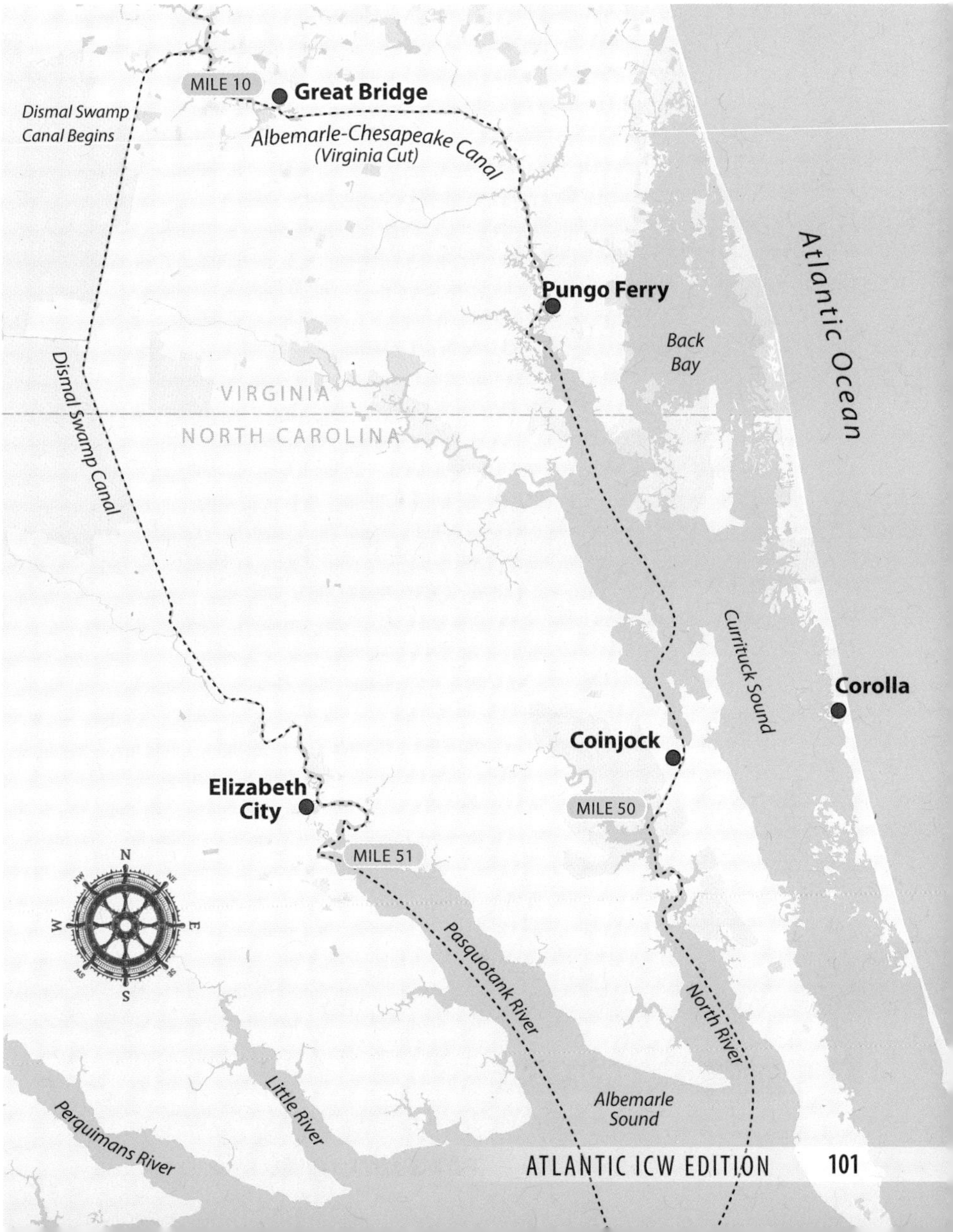

Virginia Cut, VA

GREAT BRIDGE		Largest Vessel	VHF	Total Slips	Approach/ Dockside Depth	Floating Docks	Gas/ Diesel	Repairs/ Haulout	Min/Max Amps	Pump-Out Station
1. Top Rack Marina WiFi MM 8.8	(757) 227-3041	75	16	22	20.0 / 12.0	F	GD	R	30 / 50	P

WiFi Wireless Internet Access   onSpot Dockside WiFi Facility
Visit www.waterwayguide.com for current rates, fuel prices, website addresses and other up-to-the-minute information.
(Information in the table is provided by the facilities.)

Scan here for more details:

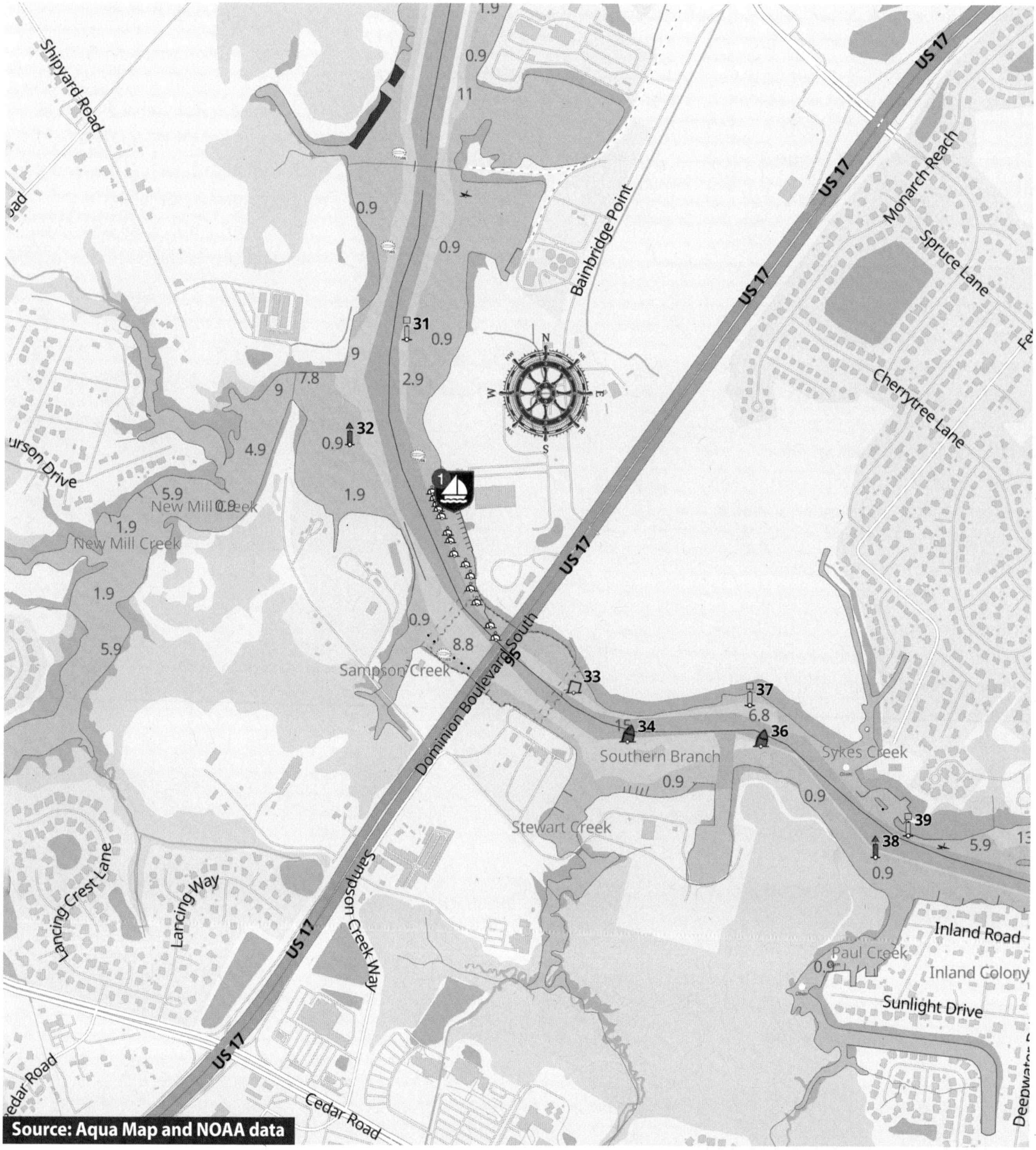

Source: Aqua Map and NOAA data

both by as much as 2 feet, so tie your lines as if you'll have that much tide. Take your time and enjoy the ride.

NAVIGATION: Use NOAA Chart 12206. The **I-64 Bridge** at Mile 7.1 has a 65-foot closed vertical clearance. An opening for taller vessels requires 24-hours advance notice. The high-rise **Veterans Bridge** at Mile 8.9 has a fixed 95-foot vertical clearance. The **Great Bridge Lock** at Mile 11.3 is the only lock on this route. The lock raises or lowers boats 2 to 3 feet with little turbulence. Delays can occur at Great Bridge Lock, especially during periods of heavy traffic. Many recreational craft lock through at once when traffic is heavy. Late arrivals should not push ahead if the line is long. The lock opens on request but coordinates with the **SR 168 (Battlefield Blvd) Bridge** just east of the lock, which opens on the hour from 6:00 a.m. to 7:00 p.m. and on request at all other times. (They respond to "Great Bridge" on the VHF.)

The Great Bridge Lock is 600 feet long, 72 feet wide and can handle tows up to 530 feet long. Since commercial traffic has first preference in locking through, it is not a good idea to push ahead of a tug, as you will probably have to wait for the vessel once you arrive. Government and commercial vessels have precedence, while fuel barges and vessels transporting hazardous materials are locked through alone. The lockmaster monitors VHF Channel 13 (757-547-3311) and can provide information on the route ahead if needed.

If the Great Bridge Lock cannot accommodate all the boats waiting and you are at the back of the line, prepare for a delay. There is room to maneuver or anchor as you wait on the west end of the lock. There is a face dock on the west side of the SR 168 (Battlefield Blvd) Bridge (on the south side of the canal) where tie-ups are allowed for up to 24 hours. This is a good spot from which to visit Great Bridge. If you are northbound and waiting at the east end of the lock and bridge, there is a face dock on the north bank that holds half a dozen boats and allows 24-hour dockage. This is the Visitor Center for the Great Bridge Battlefield and Waterways Park, which pays tribute to the Battle of Great Bridge in 1775 and includes a large stone monument (visible from the ICW) commemorating the Patriot soldiers who fought and died here. Keep the radio on VHF Channel 13 in case the lockmaster needs to contact you.

Vessels tied to the face docks on either side of the SR 168 (Battlefield Blvd) Bridge should be prepared for possible commercial traffic and a rise and fall in the water level from the displacement effect of these vessels. It is not a good idea to leave your boat unattended at these docks. There are no facilities except trash receptacles at the west docks.

Battlefield Blvd. Bridge

Virginia Cut, VA

GREAT BRIDGE		Largest Vessel	VHF	Total Slips	Approach/ Dockside Depth	Floating Docks	Gas/ Diesel	Repairs/ Haulout	Min/Max Amps	Pump-Out Station
1. Atlantic Yacht Basin, Inc. WiFi onSpot MM 12.2	(757) 482-2141	120	16	200	12.0 / 10.0		GD	RH	30 / 100	P

WiFi Wireless Internet Access onSpot Dockside WiFi Facility
Visit www.waterwayguide.com for current rates, fuel prices, website addresses and other up-to-the-minute information.
(Information in the table is provided by the facilities.)

Scan here for more details:

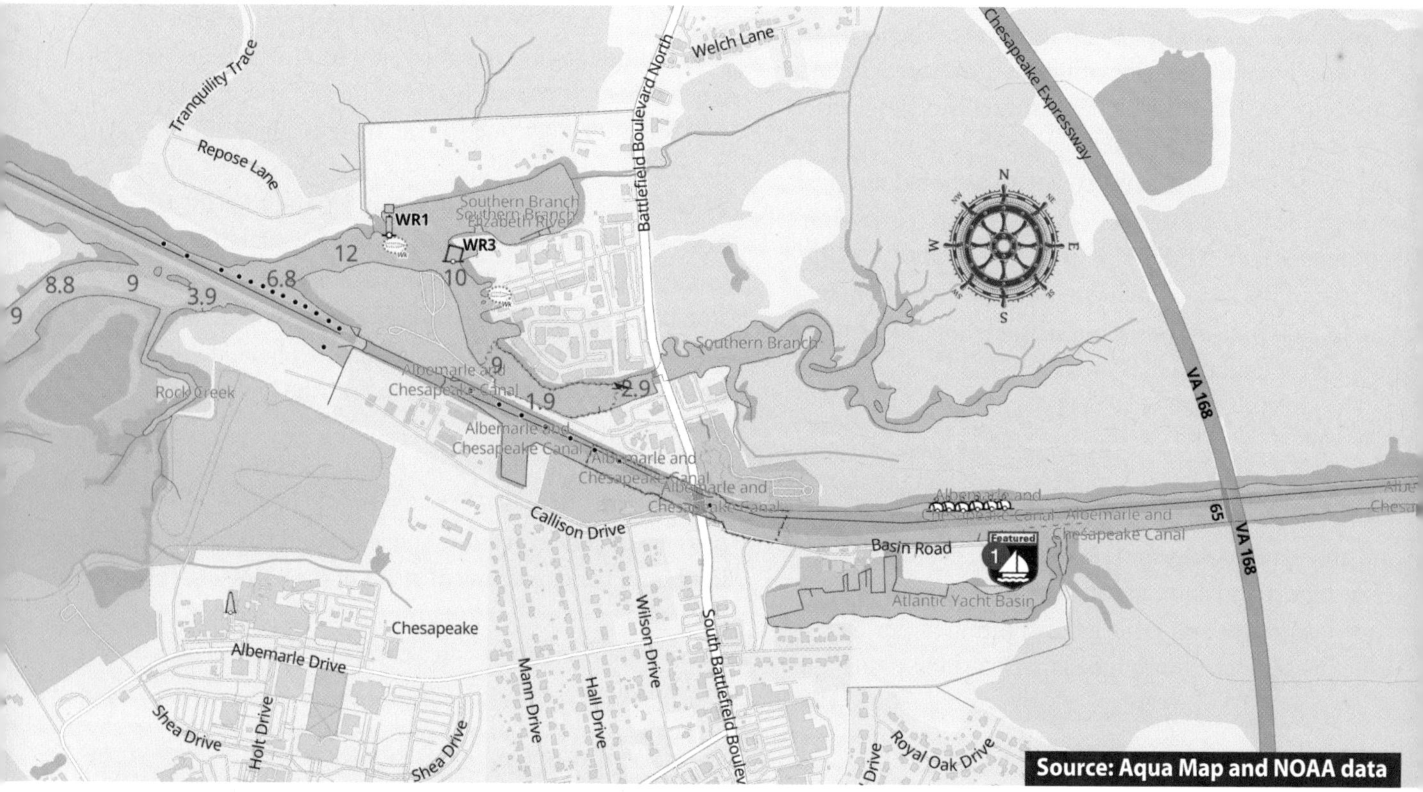

NO WAKE ZONE

A speed limit of 3 mph (actively enforced by the Virginia Marine Police) applies on the waterway until you are past the lock and bridge. It is a good idea to continue at that speed until you are well past the long face dock at the yacht basin on the south bank, east of the bridge. If you think you are about to miss the opening of the lock and bridge, do not speed. The bridgetender can delay the opening for 10 minutes if notified ahead of time on VHF Channel 13.

The remainder of the canal has no speed limit but the standard rule applies here as elsewhere: You are liable for damage caused by your wake. If yours is a big boat remember to allow for the "canal effect," a tendency of the stern to swing in toward the bank in narrow waters.

The high-rise **Chesapeake Expressway (VA 168 Bypass) Bridge** crosses the channel at Mile 13.0. The **Albemarle & Chesapeake Railroad Bridge** at Mile 13.9 is usually open unless a train is approaching. **Centerville Turnpike (SR 170) Bridge** at Mile 15.2 opens on signal from 6:30 a.m. until 8:30 a.m. and between 4:00 p.m. and 6:00 p.m., Monday through Friday (except federal holidays). From 8:30 a.m. to 4:00 p.m. the draw need only open on the hour and half-hour. The drawtender may delay the opening by up to 10 minutes to accommodate approaching vessels. Call on VHF Channel 13 to announce your intentions.

The **SR 165 (North Landing) Bridge** at Mile 20.2 has 6-foot closed vertical clearance and opens on signal except from 6:00 a.m. to 7:00 p.m., when the draw need only open on the hour and half-hour. The 5-mile distance between the Centerville Turnpike (SR 170) Bridge and SR 165 (North Landing) Bridge is slightly beyond the speed of most sailboats or slower trawlers to make neatly synchronized openings so you might as well take your time. The aging SR 165 (North Landing) Bridge has experienced numerous closures in recent years due to mechanical and electrical problems. You may want to call the bridge ahead of time at 575-482-3081 to check if it is operational.

At times of low water use caution in the areas on either side of the Centerville Turnpike (SR 170) Bridge and SR 165 (North Landing) Bridge. Stakes mark the outer limits of stumps, which go almost halfway across on the west side but not as far on the east. Occasionally stumps are unseen, unmarked and uncharted posing a constant threat to vessels.

Dockage: Top Rack Marina, north of Veterans Bridge at Mile 8.8, is a yacht brokerage offering dry storage and various marine services. The on-site Amber Lantern Restaurant offers a fine-dining experience with sunset views across the river from every seat in the house.

Atlantic Yacht Basin, Inc. is a full-service boatyard with a well-stocked marine store just east of the SR 168 (Battlefield Blvd) Bridge. This facility's long dock is along the canal (be aware of your wake in this area) and a large, protected work and storage basin is behind the wharf. If the courtesy car is not available, both local supermarkets may give you and your groceries a lift to the boatyard but check with the cashier before you start shopping. There are many restaurants within a short walk from the marina and the town of Chesapeake is very visitor friendly.

On the northwest side of the Centerville Turnpike (SR 170) Bridge at Mile 15.2 is Centerville Waterway Marina. They are a boat brokerage and service outboards.

North Landing River–ICW Mile 20 to Mile 41

About 8 miles beyond Great Bridge the heavily wooded and sparsely populated land cut leads into the headwaters of North Landing River. Recreational boat traffic increases significantly during the transient seasons in fall and spring. The cut is narrow in some areas making it almost impossible for three vessels to pass through at once. Be mindful of other vessels and not just your own schedule. Wakes are especially dangerous in narrow channels.

Virginia Cut, VA

GREAT BRIDGE		Largest Vessel	VHF	Total Slips	Approach/ Dockside Depth	Floating Docks	Gas/ Diesel	Repairs/ Haulout	Min/Max Amps	Pump-Out Station
1. Centerville Waterway Marina WiFi MM 15.2	(757) 547-4498	34	13	32	12.0 / 5.0		GD	RH	30 / 50	P

WiFi Wireless Internet Access onSpot Dockside WiFi Facility
Visit www.waterwayguide.com for current rates, fuel prices, website addresses and other up-to-the-minute information.
(Information in the table is provided by the facilities.)

Scan here for more details:

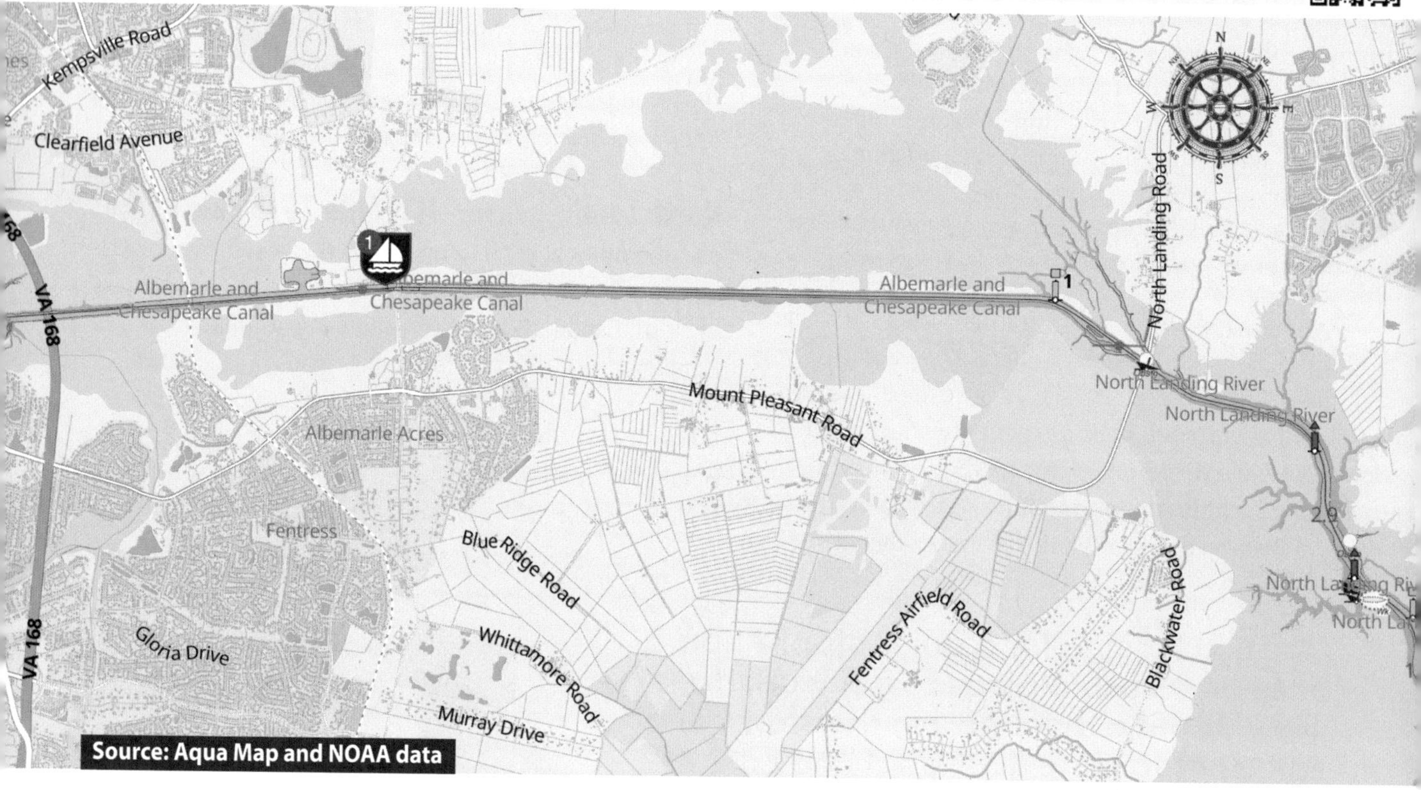

Source: Aqua Map and NOAA data

Over the years wakes have eroded the banks leaving wide shallows off the channel with stumps just below the surface. What looks like a small limb might actually be attached to a tree trunk suspended just below the surface. Give any suspect debris a wide berth. Be aware that barges and tugs use the cut and often travel at night, lighting up the area and leaving behind a rolly wake.

NAVIGATION: Use NOAA Chart 12206. The North Landing River winds leisurely southward with a dredged channel cutting through its widening waters. Watch the channel markers in the lower Virginia stretch of the river as shoals tend to encroach from the banks. The route leaves Virginia and enters North Carolina at Mile 34 between flashing green "61" and green daybeacon "63."

NO WAKE ZONE

The area on either side of the Pungo Ferry Bridge at Mile 28.3 is a posted No-Wake Zone, from the location of the now-defunct Pungo Ferry Marina immediately north of the spans through the bridge fenders to the south. Be sure to travel through this area at idle speed. Note that it is frequently patrolled by the local authorities.

Pungo Ferry (SR 726) Bridge has two tide boards on both sides of the bridge showing the charted 65-foot vertical clearance. Some sailboats, however, have reported less than 64-foot clearance here after a south wind. If in doubt contact the authorities or obtain local knowledge before proceeding. (We suggest hailing northbound vessels for tide board readings.) During the summer the beach north of the bridge is usually full of swimmers, knee-boarders and swarms of personal watercraft so proceed slowly.

Anchorage: All along North Landing River to the Pungo Ferry (SR 726) Bridge you will notice side sloughs and bypassed bends of the river, which look like secluded anchorages. Do not be tempted! All these old river loops are either silted in or may have spoil banks, submerged pilings or wrecks across them.

Boats have been observed at anchor at the Pungo Ferry oxbow on the west side of the ICW at Mile 28.5. However, it has been reported that the entrance to the anchorage has shoaled to less than 4 feet MLW. There is limited space south of the Pungo Ferry Bridge at Mile 29. Pungo Ferry Landing Park provides shore access via small floating docks and boat ramp. It is located on the east shore in the small channel across from the anchorage.

Just south of Mile 30 to starboard heading south Blackwater Creek offers a fair-weather anchorage with good holding. Enter North Landing River between that tiny marsh island and flashing red "46." A shoal of 4 to 5 feet MLW has been reported at the entrance. The charted point shown on the north side at the entrance is usually under water with just a couple of tuffs of grass showing. Favor the southern bank on entering. If you can navigate it you should find 6- to 10-foot MLW depths once inside and up the creek. Expect local outboard-powered boats rushing up and down the creek on weekends. Winds from the north quadrant can blow the water out of the creek and leave vessels firmly aground. There is little swinging room for boats longer than 35 feet.

Currituck Sound–ICW Mile 42 to Mile 49

This stretch is generally placid but Currituck Sound can develop an unpleasant chop. There is little tide but strong winds can affect water levels and create stiff currents. Government snag-boats check the cuts periodically but keep a look-out for floating debris.

NAVIGATION: Use NOAA Chart 12206. Once in Currituck Sound observe intermediate daybeacons carefully. A hedge of submerged pilings on the east side protects the narrow, dredged channel and a beam wind from the west can push you right up on them. These may be closer to the marked channel than indicated by the NOAA chart. This stretch is subject to shoaling. It is important to stay in the center of the channel and to check astern (as well as ahead) to track your progress.

The centerline channel is charted to carry 12 feet MLW. Prolonged strong northerly winds will lower the depths here by as much as 2 or 3 feet but tugs and barges drawing

Great Bridge: Locking Through

As you approach the lock, you will see either a red or a green signal light. Call the lockmaster on VHF Channel 13 to request an opening, but do not approach closer than 300 feet until the light turns green. Should your VHF call go unanswered, the horn signal for opening is two long and two short blasts. Even in cases where boats are already in line ahead of you for an opening, you should call the lockmaster and give him your boat name so that he knows how many boats are ready to lock through. If there are a lot of boats, he will direct who goes where on the lock walls.

Enter at idle speed with bow and stern lines and fenders ready to moor as directed by the lockmaster. If there are only a few boats to pass through, you will be directed to the north or (more likely) the south side of the lock. The rubber fender system on the south side of the Great Bridge Lock is excellent, which is why the lockmasters are now requesting that all recreational craft choose that side. There are cleats and bollards to loops lines around, but there are no lock attendants to help on this side. When there is an overload of recreational vessels, some will be asked to use the lock's north side. In this case, lock attendants will usually assist in getting your lines looped around the bollards.

Be aware that you will definitely need your own fenders and long dock lines when on the steel and concrete of the north side. Also, be prepared to tend your lines during the locking process, especially the stern lines as the stern may want to swing toward the center of the lock as the water level adjusts.

Note: Anyone who gets off the boat at Great Bridge Lock is required to wear a personal flotation device.

more than 9 or 10 feet regularly transit this sound with few problems.

Note that the most recent NOAA chart depicts marker "91" (Mile 40) as a daybeacon but it is actually a small can. Also in this area be alert for the ferry from Currituck, which crosses the ICW on its route to Knotts Island. The narrowest and most difficult part of this stretch is between flashing green "111" and flashing red "118." Wind-driven current will also try to push you out of the channel throughout Currituck Sound.

Shoaling to 3 feet MLW has been observed halfway into the channel at Mile 44.6 by flashing green "111." Favor the red side of the channel at the turn by red daybeacon "112."

Coinjock to Albemarle Sound–ICW Mile 49 to Mile 65

About 1 mile south of shallow Coinjock Bay the quiet hamlet of Coinjock (at Mile 50) is centered on a particularly lonely stretch of the ICW. This is a popular and welcome stop for those in need of a secure place to rest, plug in, take on reasonably priced fuel and restore basic supplies. Coinjock, named by the Indians for the berries still growing in the area, includes a hardware store, barbershop and Post Office.

NAVIGATION: Use NOAA Chart 12206. Watch for submerged logs or stumps in the channel in the stretch of Coinjock Bay between Long Point and the entrance to the North Carolina Cut, especially in the narrow cut at Long Point (near quick flashing red "116"). Vessels regularly report obstructions in the vicinity of flashing red "116" at Long Point. The boat ramp on the east side of the North Carolina Cut can be very busy on weekends. At Mile 49.9, just south of the marinas, you pass beneath the **Coinjock (US 158) Bridge**, a high-level fixed span with a 65-foot vertical clearance.

NO WAKE ZONE

Note that Coinjock is a State-posted and enforced No Wake Zone.

Check the current before tying up at the marinas in Coinjock. Although there is no tidal rise and fall here, the current is wind driven and can be strong. The wind funnels up and down the cut and the strongest current will be with northerly or southerly winds. If it is calm, consider the most recent period of strong wind in trying to determine the strength and direction of the current. If northbound check the current flow against the bridge; if southbound start checking at the first pilings you come to in the cut or at quick flashing green "123." Also don't forget to check the current before untying from one of the docks after a stay. It may be different than when you docked and can possibly cause just as much trouble when you leave as it did when you arrived.

Heavy fog can be an occasional problem in the morning, especially in the fall, although it usually burns off by 9:00 a.m. The route from Coinjock through the upper North River follows a winding but well-marked channel. Be sure to stay in the center of the narrow dredged stretch between flashing red "128" and red daybeacon "132" as it is very shallow outside the channel. Groundings occur here frequently. Heading south the river becomes wider and deeper finally reaching Camden Point and the approach to Albemarle Sound. Fish stakes extend from Buck Island southward to flashing green "155."

There are shoals encroaching the channel between green daybeacon "169" and green daybeacon "171" (Mile 65) at Camden Point on the red side of the channel. Favor the green side of the channel or just visually split green daybeacon "169" to red nun "168" for 10 feet MLW. Do not follow the chart, which depicts the channel very close to "168."

Dockage: Coinjock Marina & Restaurant has a popular restaurant on the premises and an outdoor deck where you can dine with waterfront views. The marina's wide 1,000-foot-long dock provides quiet, secure dockage with all the expected amenities including a modern bathhouse and laundry. Mechanics are on call. There is also a well-stocked convenience store. Fuel prices here are always competitive. The former Midway Marina (same owner) has some dockage with power and water and serves as overflow for Coinjock Marina & Restaurant.

Marine facilities and secure berths are scarce along this stretch of the ICW so both facilities fill up rapidly during the fall and spring transient seasons. Be prepared to be tightly packed in bow to stern and during busy times you may be

North Carolina Cut, NC

COINJOCK		Largest Vessel	VHF	Total Slips	Approach/ Dockside Depth	Floating Docks	Gas/ Diesel	Repairs/ Haulout	Min/Max Amps	Pump-Out Station
1. Midway Marina & Motel WiFi MM 49.0	(252) 453-3625	220	16	40	14.0 / 9.0		GD	R	30 / 50	P
2. Coinjock Marina & Restaurant WiFi MM 50.0	(252) 453-3271	150	16	24	12.0 / 12.0		GD	R	30 / 100	P

WiFi Wireless Internet Access onSpot Dockside WiFi Facility
Visit www.waterwayguide.com for current rates, fuel prices, website addresses and other up-to-the-minute information.
(Information in the table is provided by the facilities.)

Scan here for more details:

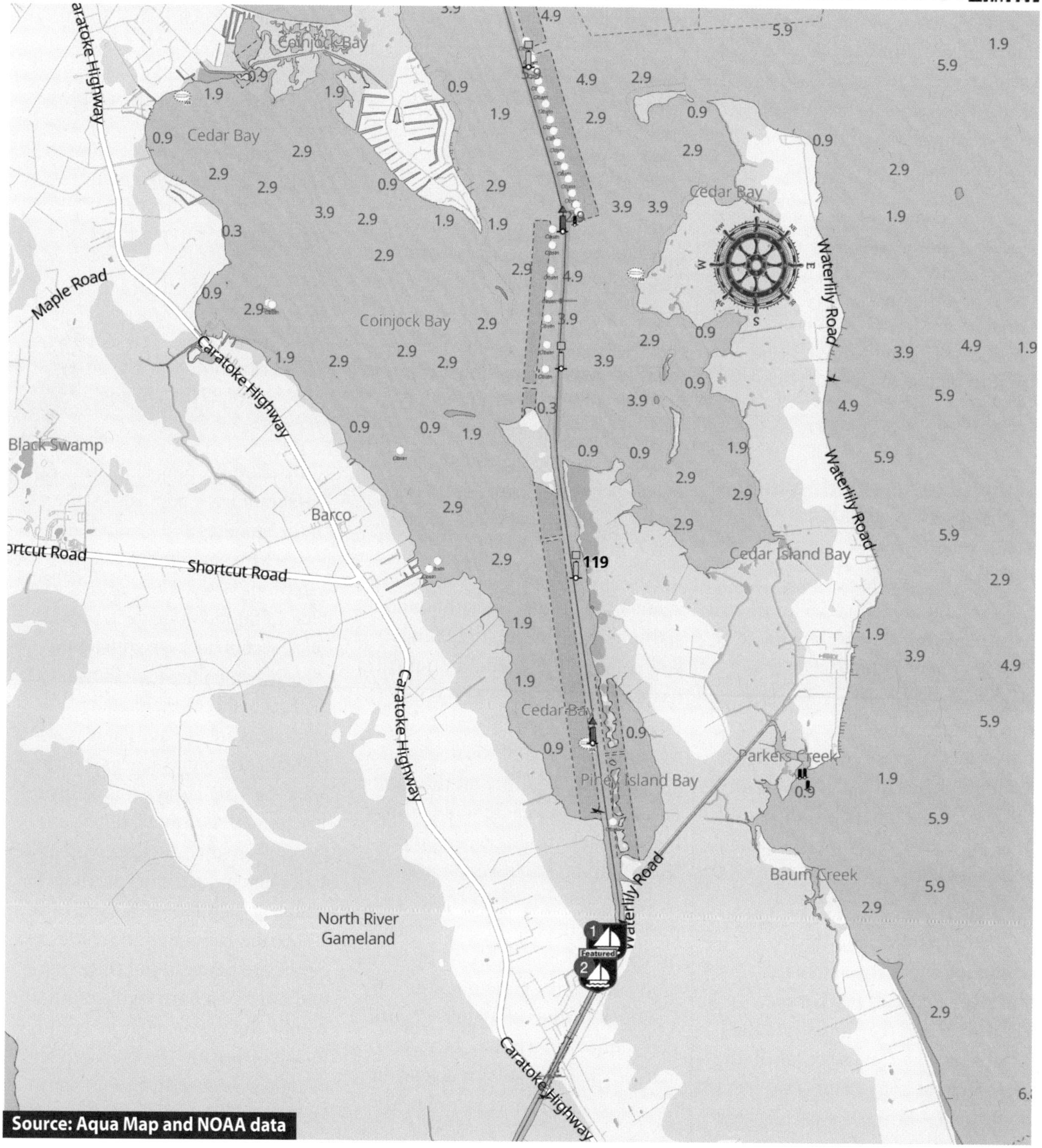

Source: Aqua Map and NOAA data

asked to let a boat tie up alongside. Making an advance call for reservations by phone or on VHF Channel 16 is advised.

Anchorage: Several North River anchorages offer good holding and reasonable protection depending on wind direction. Immediately north of Buck Island due east of quick flashing green "153" (around Mile 56.5) there is good shelter during a southerly blow with 7- to 8- foot MLW depths with good holding in mud. Boats drawing more than 5 feet should check the NOAA chart carefully to avoid shallower areas north of the anchorage area. Southeast of Buck Island there is ample anchorage room in 7- to 9-foot MLW depths with good holding in mud and good protection from the east and northeast.

Due west of quick flashing red "164" (Mile 61), Broad Creek affords excellent protection in virtually all conditions and carries 7-foot MLW depths. Once beyond the mouth of the creek boats drawing more than 5 feet should proceed slowly with an eye on the depth sounder as there have been reports of an uncharted shallow spot. In westerly winds it is possible to comfortably anchor off the mouth of Broad Creek if it is crowded or if you are too deep-drafted or large to go all the way in.

Welcome to North Carolina!

You are now in NC waters. Here you will encounter small towns, quiet anchorages and the first of the shoal spots on the ICW. The waters off Cape Hatteras are known as the "Graveyard of the Atlantic" due to the deceptively shallow water offshore here. Cape Lookout and Cape Fear to the south are delightful ports that–like the rest of the Outer Banks–are best visited from the protected inside (ICW) route with its combination of rivers, canals, bays and sounds.

Weather is a critical consideration. The best time to cruise through NC is spring and fall, and you'll have plenty of company. Hurricane season is June 1 through November 30 with a peak from early August through the end of October. Since 1851, a total of 47 hurricanes have made direct hits in the NC coast. As always, be aware of the weather around (and ahead of) you.

Important Note: It is an NC requirement that the owner or operator of a vessel that has a Marine Sanitation Device (MSD) and is in coastal waters that are either designated as a no-discharge zone or are included in a petition to the U.S. EPA to be designated as a no-discharge zone, must maintain a record of each pump-out of the MSD and the location of the pump-out facility. The no-discharge zone begins at New River Inlet and extends to the SC border. It includes the ICW and adjacent and offshore waters. See details at www.deq.nc.gov.

Great Dismal Swamp Canal, VA/NC

DISMAL SWAMP ROUTE		Largest Vessel	VHF	Total Slips	Approach/ Dockside Depth	Floating Docks	Gas/ Diesel	Repairs/ Haulout	Min/Max Amps	Pump-Out Station
1. Chesapeake Yachts Inc. MM 8.3	(757) 487-9100	200	16	10	16.0 / 8.0	F	GD	RH	30	

Wireless Internet Access onSpot Dockside WiFi Facility
Visit www.waterwayguide.com for current rates, fuel prices, website addresses and other up-to-the-minute information.
(Information in the table is provided by the facilities.)

Scan here for more details:

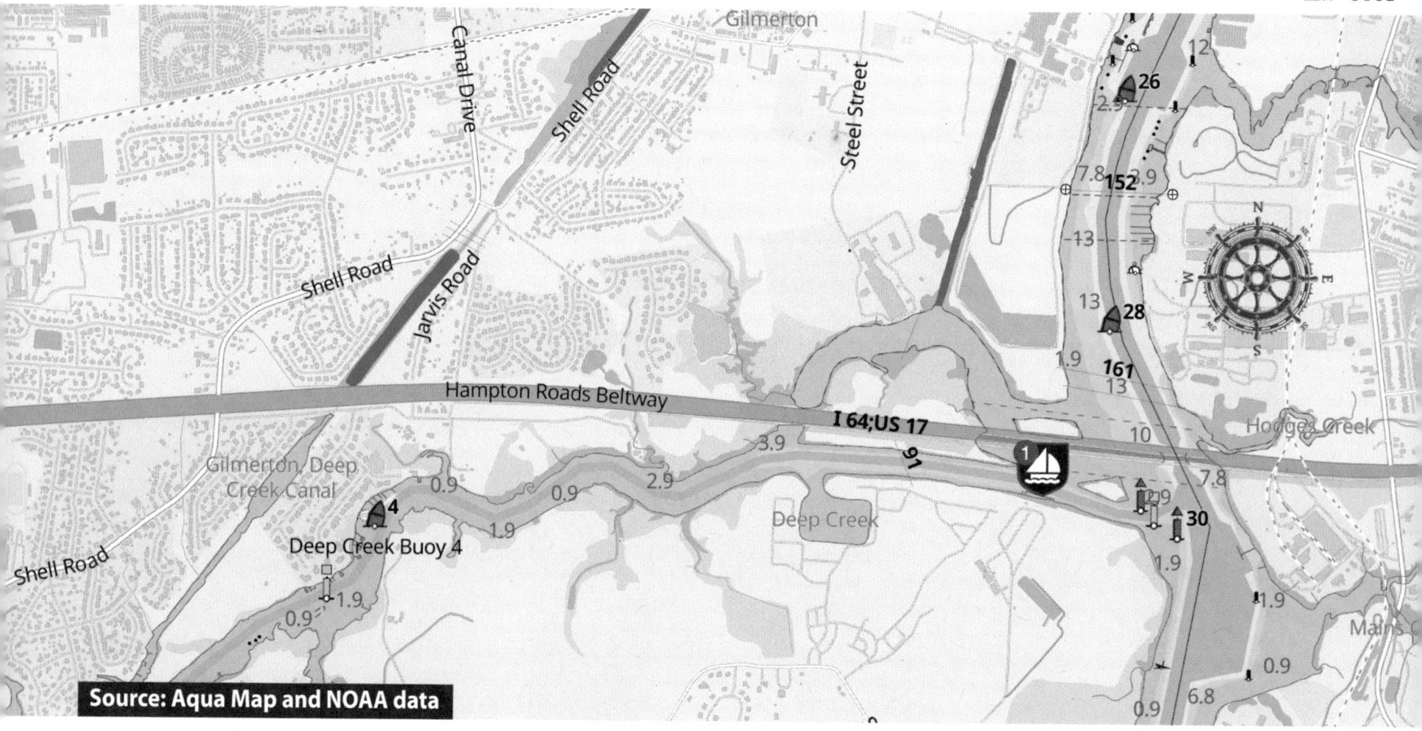

Source: Aqua Map and NOAA data

DISMAL SWAMP CANAL ROUTE

For those who choose to decide their route when already underway, the sign at ICW Mile 7.3–just past the 65-foot vertical clearance I-64 Bridge and on the west side at the entrance of the Dismal Swamp Canal–states the lock schedule, the controlling depth and whether the canal is open or closed. Information about the status of the Dismal Swamp Canal is also available from the Army Corps of Engineers at 757-201-7500 (option 3) or from the Dismal Swamp Canal Welcome Center (877-771-8333).

In 1763, George Washington first proposed draining the swamp, harvesting the timber (cypress for shipbuilding and cedar for shingles) and then farming the land. He and other prominent businessmen purchased 40,000 acres of swampland. Washington first supervised the digging for the ditch from the swamp to Lake Drummond, today known as Washington Ditch. In 1909, a lumbering company purchased the swamp and continued to harvest virgin timber until they cut the last tree down in the 1950s. In 1973, the Union Camp Company donated its swamp holding to create the Great Dismal Swamp National Wildlife Refuge.

Today, recreational boaters cruise past a number of historical sites on the Dismal Swamp Canal. The Dismal Swamp Welcome Center, Dismal Swamp State Park and Dismal Swamp Canal are all recognized with the distinction as being a designated site on the National Park Service National Underground Railroad Network to Freedom. Boats today follow the same course as James Adams' Floating Theatre, which inspired Edna Ferber to write "Showboat." It is a beautiful, unspoiled waterway and one of the prettiest on the whole ICW, while also offering the considerable benefit of being easier to transit compared to the narrow, busy, and frequently wind-driven Virginia Cut. The canal is fed primarily by freshwater drainage from Lake Drummond and its feeder system.

Great Dismal Swamp Canal, VA/NC

DISMAL SWAMP ROUTE		Largest Vessel	VHF	Total Slips	Approach/ Dockside Depth	Floating Docks	Gas/ Diesel	Repairs/ Haulout	Min/Max Amps	Pump-Out Station
1. Dismal Swamp Canal Welcome Center WiFi MM 28.0	(252) 771-8333	100			6.0 / 6.0					

WiFi Wireless Internet Access onSpot Dockside WiFi Facility
Visit www.waterwayguide.com for current rates, fuel prices, website addresses and other up-to-the-minute information.
(Information in the table is provided by the facilities.)

Scan here for more details:

NO WAKE ZONE

As a rule, skippers using this route are more interested in seeing the magnificent countryside than in making fast time. There is no speed limit here, but you are responsible for your wake. "No Wake" signs are posted in the canal proper in a stepped-up effort to reduce the problem of bank erosion. Regardless of restrictions, common sense dictates slow speed through the canal.

Great Bridge to Turner Cut

NAVIGATION: Use NOAA Chart 12206.From the sign at ICW Mile 7.3, the Dismal Swamp route heads off west of the ICW. The Deep Creek land cut leads to Deep Creek itself and the Deep Creek Lock, which introduces you to the Great Dismal Swamp Canal. The distance is approximately 51 miles from Norfolk to Elizabeth City, but the distance does not have to be covered in one day. Birds, reptiles, winged insects and bears inhabit this unique primeval forest. (Use screens and cover up before entering the canal during the summer months.)

Deep Creek Lock (Mile 10.5) raises you 8 feet in elevation, while **South Mills Lock** (at Mile 32.7) lowers you the same amount. At both locks, boats must furnish and tend their own lines. Be sure to have

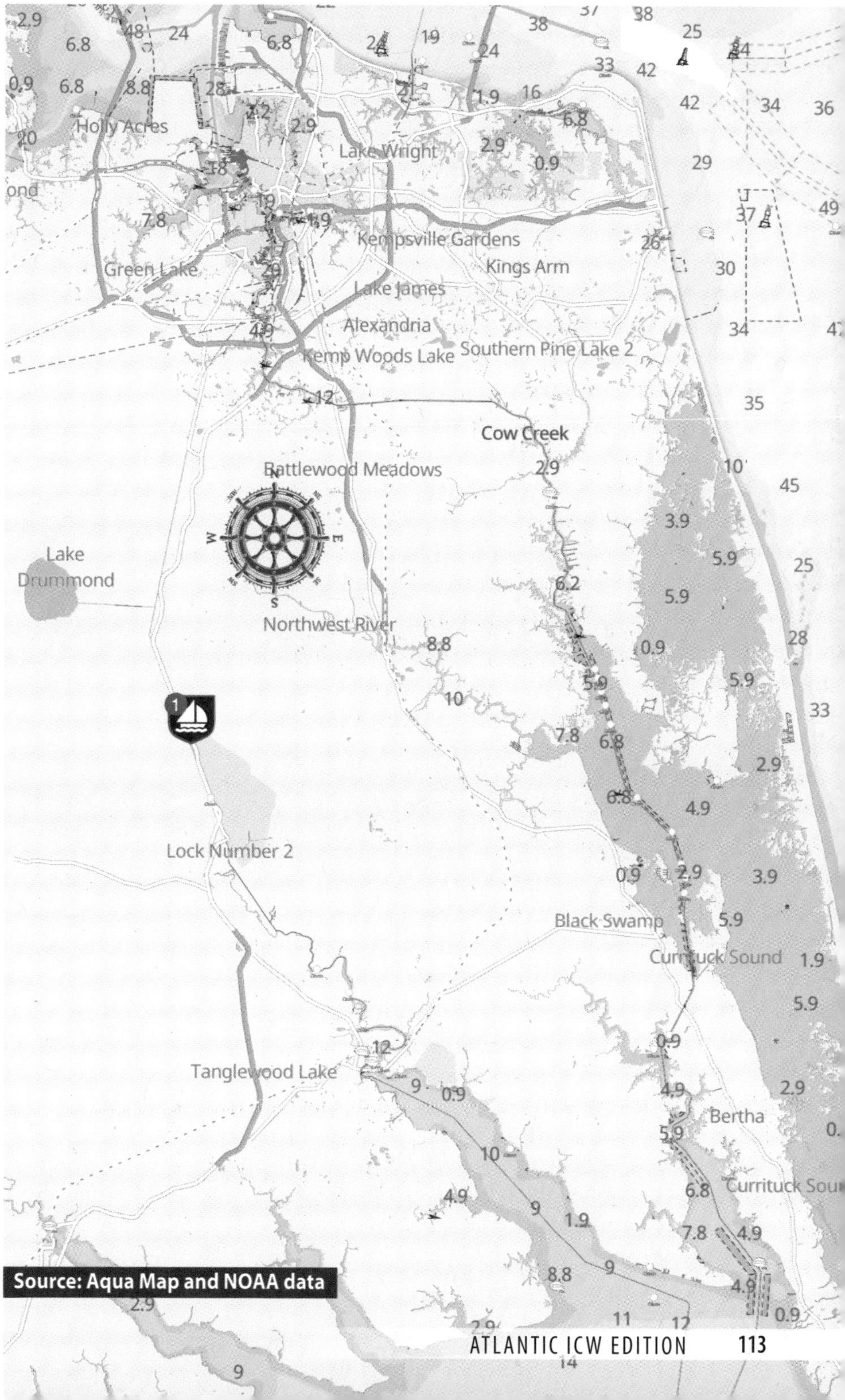

Source: Aqua Map and NOAA data

plenty of line and watch your stern, which may want to swing toward the center during the locking process. When the locks are open, the tenders will ask the draft of each vessel and warn those with drafts of more than 6 feet that they may proceed only at their own risk. Openings at **Deep Creek Bridge** at Mile 11.1 (4-foot closed vertical clearance) are coordinated with the Deep Creek Lock. Vessels are allowed to moor overnight in the canal. If you plan to stay on the bulkhead between the bridge and the lock on either side, it is courteous to notify the lockmaster on VHF Channel 13 and let him know your intentions.

The locks at Deep Creek and South Mills open four times daily (unless low water levels cause restricted openings) at 8:30 a.m., 11:00 a.m., 1:30 p.m. and 3:30 p.m. Boats entering the canal are locked first, meaning at Deep Creek Lock, southbound boats are locked first; at the South Mills Lock, northbound boats are locked first. For boats leaving the canal, the lock openings may be delayed while the entering boats are locked through. Prepare to wait before the bridge, in that case. The lockmasters do double duty as bridgetenders and open the adjacent bridges so you will have to wait for them to drive to the bridge to open it after opening the lock.

> To run the Dismal Swamp Canal in a single day, a boat traveling at 6 knots or more should enter the Deep Creel Lock at either the 8:30 a.m. or 11:00 a.m. opening. The passage to South Mills Lock is 22 miles. Once through South Mills, it is only 18 miles to Elizabeth City.

While narrow and unmarked, Deep Creek presents no unusual problems, unless there is an extremely low tide, in which case there may be a little over 5-foot depth. Travel at a reasonable speed and do not be misled by the nice-looking side waters; they are extremely shallow. Keep to the center of the main stream and give points a good berth, as shoaling is chronic. The Army Corps of Engineers has placed small pipe markers, white with a red top, along every mile of the Dismal Swamp Canal, indicating statute mileage from Norfolk. At about Mile 23, there is a sign marking the beginning of a measured nautical mile.

From Deep Creek, the Dismal Swamp Canal reaches south in two arrow-straight stretches. The feeder ditch from Lake Drummond intersects the canal toward the end of the first of these at Mile 21.5. The Dismal Swamp Canal has 6-foot depths as long as there is adequate water in Lake Drummond. This route no longer carries commercial traffic except from below South Mills (Mile 32) to Elizabeth City (Mile 50), so the stretch north of this is not as carefully maintained as it once was.

> The Army Corps of Engineers regularly cleans the ICW and clips overhanging tree limbs. Nevertheless, proceed through this area with extreme caution. Report dead heads or obstructions to lockmasters or the Visitor Center and the Corps will get out and tend to them. If you encounter a maintenance barge, you may have a wait, as there is not always ample room to pass.

We have received reports that the farmer who owns land on both sides of the canal at Mile 20.9 has permission to slide a portable steel bridge back and forth to get his livestock and farm equipment across the canal. This bridge (3 feet above the waterline) is normally only in place long enough for the farmer to accomplish his task. Be patient if the waterway is blocked when you get there. For help with this bridge call the Visitors Center (252-771-8333).

> At Mile 21.5, the Lake Drummond feeder ditch intersects the canal. If your schedule allows, you can travel the 3 miles up to Lake Drummond in a boat 16 feet or less and with a draft that is less than 3 feet. At the head of the feeder ditch, there is a free rail trolley for carrying boats less than 1,000 pounds (including dinghies) over a small peninsula into Lake Drummond.

There is a pontoon bridge south of the Visitor's Center dock at Mile 28 that allows visitors to access the Dismal Swamp State Park on the opposite side of the canal. **Dismal Swamp Canal Visitor Center Foot Bridge** is generally kept in place for pedestrians to cross and opened whenever a boat approaches. After hours, the bridge is left open for late/early boat traffic. Call 252-771-6593 or VHF Channel 13 should you need an opening. If heading south and planning to stop at the Visitor's Center dock, a courtesy call to the bridgetender will prevent an unnecessary opening.

The fixed **US 17 Highway Bridge** crosses the Dismal Swamp Canal at Mile 31.5 with 65-foot vertical clearance. South Mills Lock at Mile 32.7 opens at 8:30 a.m., 11:00 a.m., 1:30 p.m. and 3:30 p.m. and coordinates with the **South Mills Bridge** at Mile 32.6 (4-foot closed vertical clearance). An average of 2,000 recreational boats pass through the South Mills Lock annually.

Back in the Day 1960

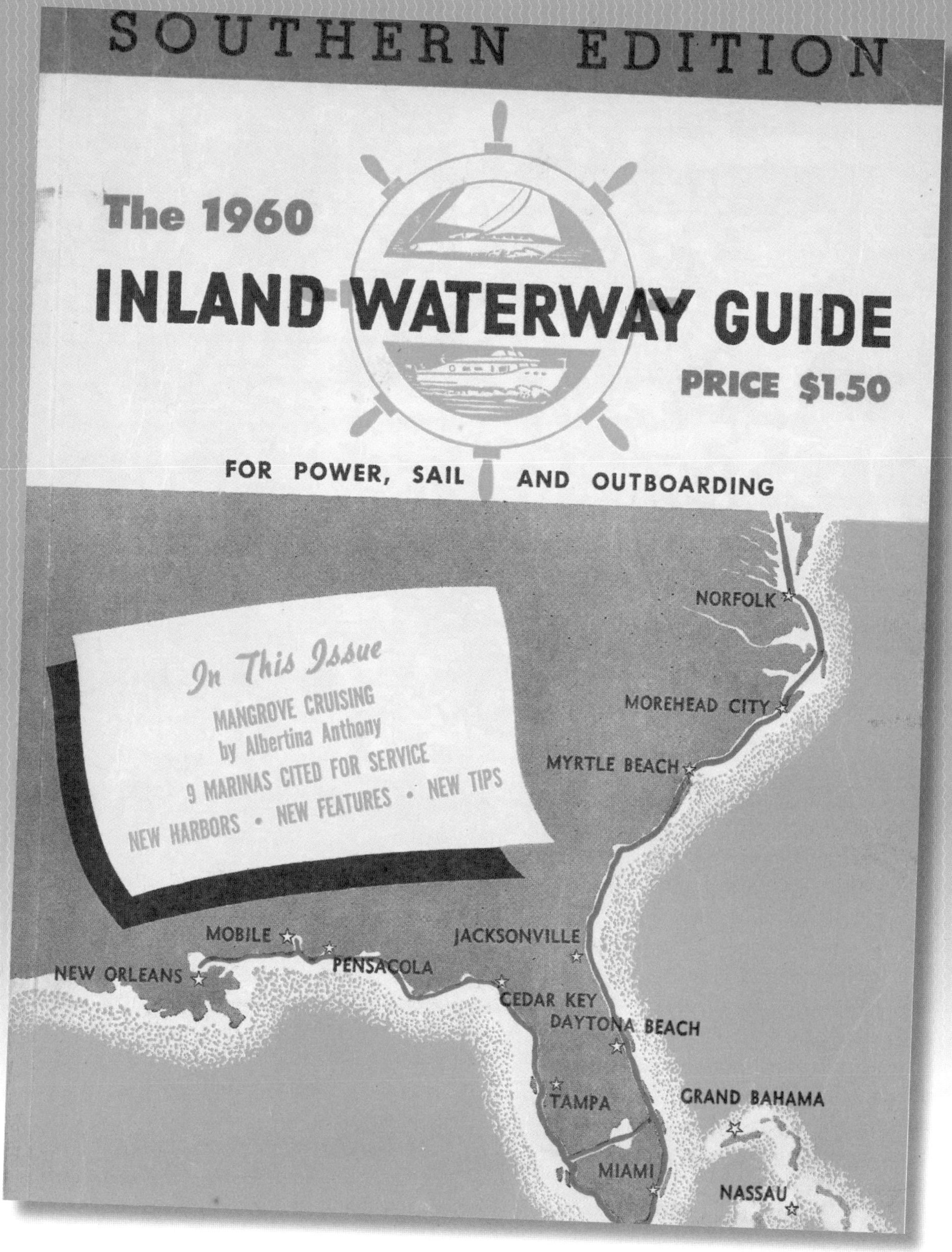

Dockage: Chesapeake Yachts Inc., located just off the main ICW channel at the northern entrance to the Dismal Swamp route at Mile 8.3, will accept transient visitors at its long floating face dock, but the facility is not set up for extensive catering to transients.

Inside the canal, on the west side in Deep Creek Lock Pond at Mile 10.7, you will find a long, wooden dock south of the locks and north of the bridge with 8-foot depths (except at the far north end). Known locally as "Elizabeth's Dock," this landing is popular with crews wanting to transit the canal the morning after a late-afternoon locking. Restaurants and shopping are nearby.

Between Miles 18 and 19, the parks department maintains Douglas Road Landing, a fixed wharf running alongside the canal for 70 feet and then another 30 feet after a jog, as a part of a hike and bike trail. There are restrooms available. At Mile 21.5, there is a small dock across from the Lake Drummond feeder ditch, which is available to cruising mariners, compliments of the Army Corps of Engineers. Rafting is permitted here. There are no recommended anchorages on this route so you may wish to take advantage of these stops.

The Dismal Swamp Canal Welcome Center (Mile 28) offers an 150-foot wharf running parallel to the canal. There are no slips but there is space for about four cruising boats to tie directly to the dock. Additional boats will raft up so be prepared to have neighbors. Power and water are not available at the dock, but clean restrooms and a water fountain are available. This is a highway rest stop as well as a State Park. The staff monitors VHF Channel 16 or can be reached by phone at 252-771-8333. You will find a friendly atmosphere here, with charcoal grills and picnic tables, bike trails with rental bikes, and a nature trail. Keep an eye out for bears, bobcats, snakes and other such "locals." If you decide to spend the night here, take time to visit the Dismal Swamp State Park Museum. It is a 3-minute walk from the dock and provides an interesting history and facts on the area (and it's air conditioned).

If you continue on through the South Mills Bridge, you may be able to find an overnight spot along the west bulkhead between the lock and the bridge, with about 6-foot MLW depths reported alongside and cleats along the middle third. There is a convenience store just west of the bridge and a family grocery store about 1 mile further west.

Turner Cut to the Pasquotank River

South Mills is the place to check your time and decide whether to lock through or to stay put for the night. It is 18 miles to Elizabeth City, and the winding, narrow, unmarked headwaters of the Pasquotank River are hazardous to run after dark. In the daytime, the tall cypress and mistletoe-festooned gum trees give the upper Pasquotank a wild and eerie splendor. Here you will see some of the most undisturbed and natural cruising grounds on the entire ICW.

NAVIGATION: Use NOAA Chart 12206. Follow the straight Turners Cut about 3 miles, where it joins the Pasquotank River. About 4 twisty miles farther the river straightens and gradually widens as markers begin to appear. Note that you are now going downstream in a river marked from seaward: Keep green to starboard (markers have yellow triangles). The first marker, green daybeacon "19," shows up suddenly around a sharp bend near Mile 41. Give all points along this route a fair berth, especially where Turner Cut enters the Pasquotank River and watch for floating debris.

> Give tows all the room you can in the narrow, straight area of Turner Cut and in the twisting upper Pasquotank River. When encountering a tow, slow down or stop, hug the bank and allow the tow as much room as possible.

> We have received a report of a 10-inch-diameter pylon embedded in the bottom north of green daybeacon "19." Approximately 1 foot of the pylon is visible above the water. Also, shoaling is a continuing problem just to the south of that, between green daybeacons "17" and "15." (Note that green daybeacon "15" is on or near shore, not at the edge of the shoal.)

Farther on at Mile 47.7, the manually operated **Norfolk Southern Railroad Swing Bridge** (3-foot closed vertical clearance) is usually left in the open position. If the bridge is closed, the drawtender will answer to horn signals. The draw is difficult to see until you are almost on top of it.

Anchorage: After transiting the canal, there are several welcome anchorage possibilities on the Pasquotank River before reaching Elizabeth City. The first, at Mile 43, is behind Goat Island at green daybeacon "13"

Pasquotank River, NC

ELIZABETH CITY AREA		Largest Vessel	VHF	Total Slips	Approach/ Dockside Depth	Floating Docks	Gas/ Diesel	Repairs/ Haulout	Min/Max Amps	Pump-Out Station
1. Lamb's Marina WiFi MM 47.2	(252) 202-4150	65	16	60	8.0 / 8.0		GD		30 / 50	

WiFi Wireless Internet Access onSpot Dockside WiFi Facility
Visit www.waterwayguide.com for current rates, fuel prices, website addresses and other up-to-the-minute information.
(Information in the table is provided by the facilities.)

Scan here for more details:

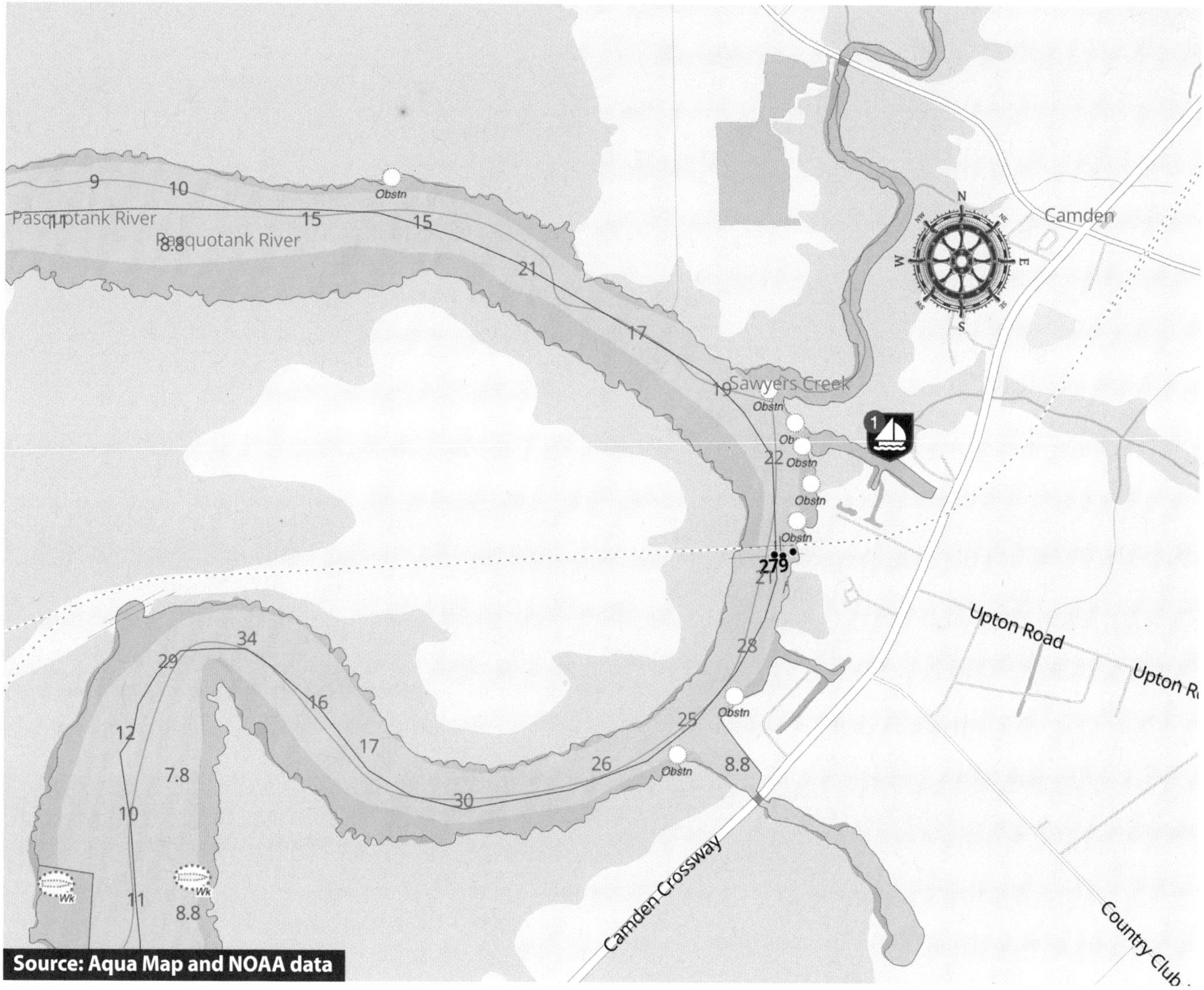

Source: Aqua Map and NOAA data

with good holding in 6- to 10-feet MLW with room for several boats. There is a small kayak dock nearby where you can land a dinghy. The second anchorage is located in the deep water of Camden Causeway Cove at Mile 48. Depths here are deeper than the 9 feet MLW shown on the NOAA charts; it is, however, open to wakes. The third is along the eastern shore near Mile 49 (Machelhe Island). This area is often used as an alternative to the Elizabeth City town docks when strong east to south winds make those docks uncomfortable.

Pasquotank River (Elizabeth City)

From the Dismal Swamp Canal Route, you emerge in Elizabeth City. Here you will find convenient dockage, friendly people and lots to see and do. See more at "Goin' Ashore: Elizabeth City, NC" in this chapter.

NAVIGATION: Use NOAA Chart 12206. Remember that you are proceeding downstream in a river marked from seaward: Keep green to starboard. (River markers have yellow triangles.) The **U.S. 158 Highway Bridge** at Mile 50.7 opens on signal, except from 7:00 a.m. to 9:00 a.m.

GOIN' ASHORE

ELIZABETH CITY, NC

Billed the "Harbor of Hospitality," Elizabeth City has long been a favorite stop for sailors going to or coming from the Chesapeake Bay area. Along the docks, you will find roses and impromptu wine parties and new friends. The harbor here beckons to sailors enjoying life in the slow lane.

SERVICES

1. East Albemarle Regional Library
100 E. Colonial Ave. (252-335-2473)

ATTRACTIONS

2. Arts of the Albemarle
Showcases fine art and traditional crafts from both regional and local artists at 516 E. Main St. (252-338-6997).

3. Moth Boat Park
Pays tribute to the Moth Boat, an 11-foot one-design sailboat designed here on the corner of Water St. and Main St. Moth Boat Regatta takes over the city's harbor in September.

4. Port Discover
Interactive science center for kids of all ages at 611 E. Main St. Call for hours and fees (252-338-6117).

5. Visitor Information/Museum of the Albemarle
Located in the Museum of the Albemarle (501 S. Water St., 252-335-1453). Over 700 artifacts, covering 400 years of local history and stories of the Native Americans, colonists, farmers and fishermen who settled in the Albemarle region (501 S. Water St., 252-335-1453).

SHOPPING

6. CVS Pharmacy
Full-service pharmacy at 101 W. Ehringhaus St. (252-338-5077).

7. Page After Page Bookstore
Great selection of North Carolina books, including nautical titles, plus art supplies, gifts, toys and stationery (111 S. Water St., 252-335-7243).

8. Todd's Pharmacy
Full-service neighborhood pharmacy at 207 S. Poindexter St. (252-335-2901).

MARINAS

9. Elizabeth City Shipyard
422 Riverside Ave. (252-335-0171)

10. Mariners Wharf
707 E. Fearing St. (252-335-5330)

Pasquotank River, NC

ELIZABETH CITY		Largest Vessel	VHF	Total Slips	Approach/ Dockside Depth	Floating Docks	Gas/ Diesel	Repairs/ Haulout	Min/Max Amps	Pump-Out Station
1. Mariners' Wharf, Elizabeth City WiFi MM 50.9	(252) 335-5330	80		14	12.0 / 15.0					
2. Elizabeth City Shipyard MM 51.2	(252) 335-0171	50		50	12.0 / 20.0			RH	30 / 50	
3. The Pelican Marina WiFi MM 51.2	(252) 335-5108	70	16	58	10.0 / 7.0				30 / 50	

WiFi Wireless Internet Access onSpot Dockside WiFi Facility
Visit www.waterwayguide.com for current rates, fuel prices, website addresses and other up-to-the-minute information.
(Information in the table is provided by the facilities.)

Scan here for more details:

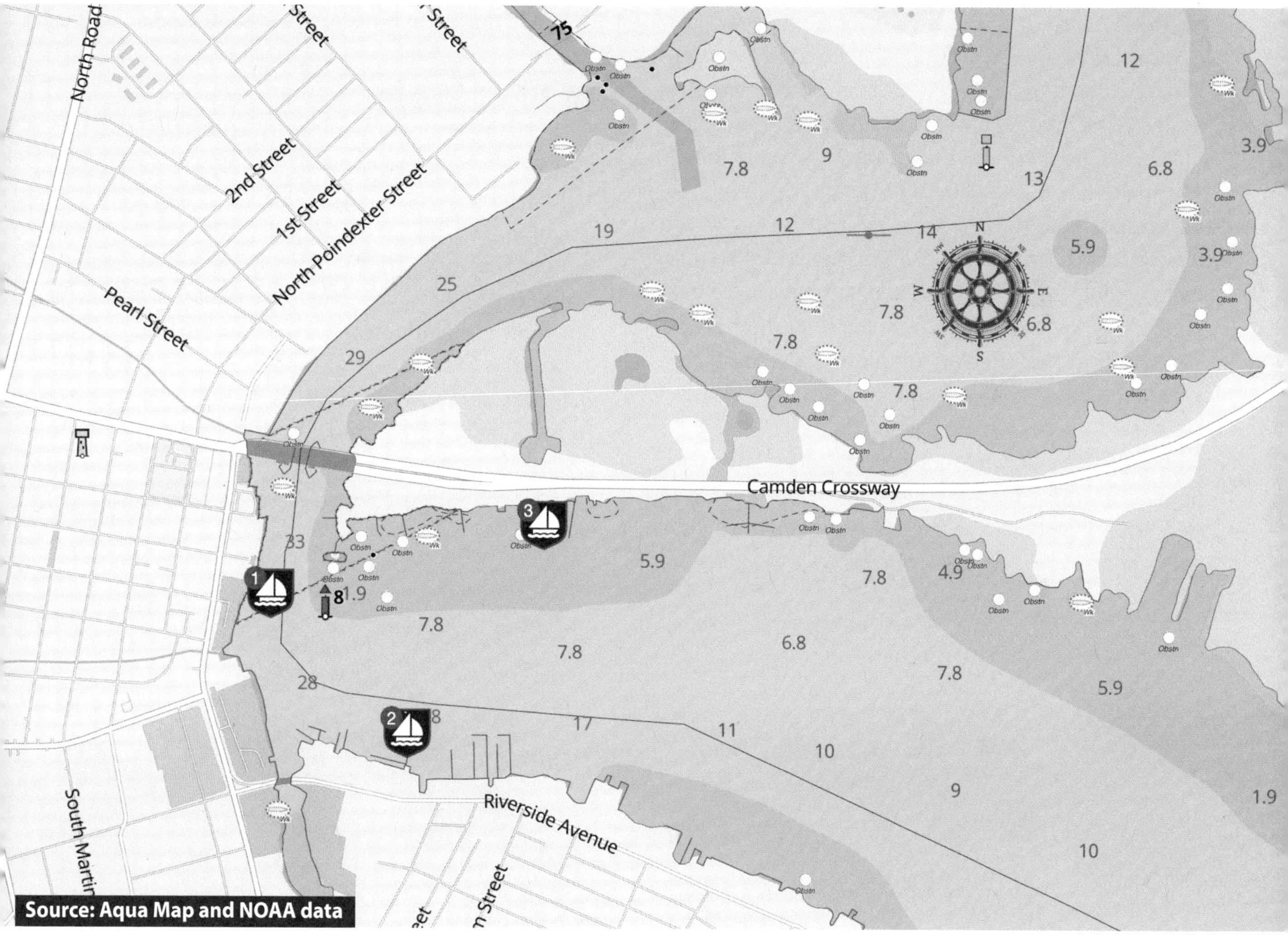

Source: Aqua Map and NOAA data

and from 4:00 p.m. to 6:00 p.m., Monday through Friday, when the draw need only open at 7:30 a.m., 8:30 a.m., 4:30 p.m., and 5:30 p.m. if vessels are waiting to pass. Call the bridgetender on VHF Channel 13 once the fast-opening bridge comes into view.

NO WAKE ZONE

The No-Wake Zone along the city is strictly enforced with a 6-mph speed limit.

Dockage: Well-protected Lambs Marina at Mile 47.2 on the Dismal Swamp Canal north of Elizabeth City has the only fuel in the area. They also have an on-site convenience store and a café. PVC pipes mark the entrance channel and fairway leading to the turning basin next to the fuel docks.

Depending on your direction, the town docks in Elizabeth City at Mile 51 mark the beginning or end of your trip through the Dismal Swamp Canal. Mariners' Wharf is right in the downtown area with 14 transient slips offered on a first-come, first-served basis. The finger piers between slips are quite short so backing in provides easier access from a boat. The outer pilings are about 35 feet from the seawall, so larger boats will need to use spring lines to stay off the wall. The slips range from 11 to 18 feet in width, and the clearance for each slip is indicated in white paint on the seawall. Strong east to south winds can cause an uncomfortable surge at the dock.

You can dispose of your trash ashore, but water or electrical hookups are not available. Comfort facilities with restrooms and hot showers are available as well as free WiFi. Bicycles are available on loan from Visit Elizabeth City, located at the nearby Museum of the Albemarle. There is a place to tie dinghies, although there are no attendants. If there are more than five boats, you may be treated to a wine and cheese party. And if you are lucky, it will be "movie night" and you can catch a classic on the huge outdoor screen from the comfort of your boat slip. Classic American films are shown on at Mariners' Wharf Tuesday evenings in June and July.

West of the city slips and along the Waterfront City Park there is a concrete/steel seawall painted with "No Dockage" signs. East of the city slips there is a short steel seawall dedicated to the U.S. armed services with the flags of every branch of service flying. Boats docking here will need sufficient fenders for the steel bulkhead. Elizabeth City Shipyard is a working boatyard. Call ahead for details.

Recently renovated The Pelican Marina is on the eastern side of the Pasquotank, south of the bridge. They have transient slips and sell some marine supplies. It is only a short walk or dinghy ride from the marina to downtown.

There is no viable anchorage here so plan to take a slip.

NEXT STOP

Depending on the route, you will find yourself approaching Albemarle Sound either from Elizabeth City or Coinjock. Once in the Sound, cruisers may choose to venture west to further explore the Albemarle Sound or east to the Outer Banks. Boaters with a schedule to keep can continue south on the ICW. Fast boats may wish to take the Croatan Sound route south and rejoin the waterway at the Neuse River. This route will save you 18 miles, but you not only have exposed waters in the Croatan Sound but also very open, exposed waters in the Pamlico Sound. Pick your weather carefully.

Elizabeth City

ICW Mile 51

THE ALBEMARLE SOUND

The Albemarle Sound runs east to west and covers 50 miles from Kitty Hawk on the Outer Banks to Edenton at the mouth of the Chowan River. An east or west wind can stir the relatively shallow waters of Albemarle Sound into a short, nasty chop, making conditions uncomfortable and sometimes dangerous. Many a prudent skipper has holed up on either side of Albemarle Sound for days waiting for the weather and seas to calm down before making the crossing. Albemarle Sound compensates by offering some picturesque and peaceful cruising waters in the tributaries along its banks. Several of these are deep and easy to enter with many good anchorages.

The Albemarle Sound is a delightful sailing and boating destination with many small towns along the numerous rivers and creeks. You can embark on a trip around the Albemarle and take advantage of special offerings from many of the marinas and municipal docks that participate in the Albemarle Loop (www.albemarleloop.com) promotional campaign.

Perquimans River (Hertford)

The Perquimans River is home to historic Hertford, NC. A port of entry as early as 1701 Hertford's records go back to a 1685 deed book. You can visit the restored Newbold-White House said to be one of North Carolina's oldest brick houses as well as other historical sites.

NAVIGATION: Use NOAA Chart 12205. Four miles to the west of green daybeacon "1L" at the mouth of Little River lies the Perquimans River and historic Hertford. Navigation is fairly straightforward up the well-marked Perquimans River. Start your approach at flashing red "2P" just south of Reed Point and then head northwest into the river, making sure to honor the markers positioned at most of the points. Eight- to 11-foot MLW depths prevail in the river proper. The **U.S. 17/NC 37 Bridge** just east of town on the Perquimans River is locally referred to as the Jim "Catfish" Hunter Bridge. If you can clear the fixed 33-foot vertical clearance bridge, there is also a swing bridge (opens on request) at the entrance to the town harbor. Call on VHF Channel 13 or 252-426-7241 from 8:00 a.m. to midnight (seasonal hours). The town manager suggests that boaters contact the town office prior to arrival at the marina at 252-426-1969.

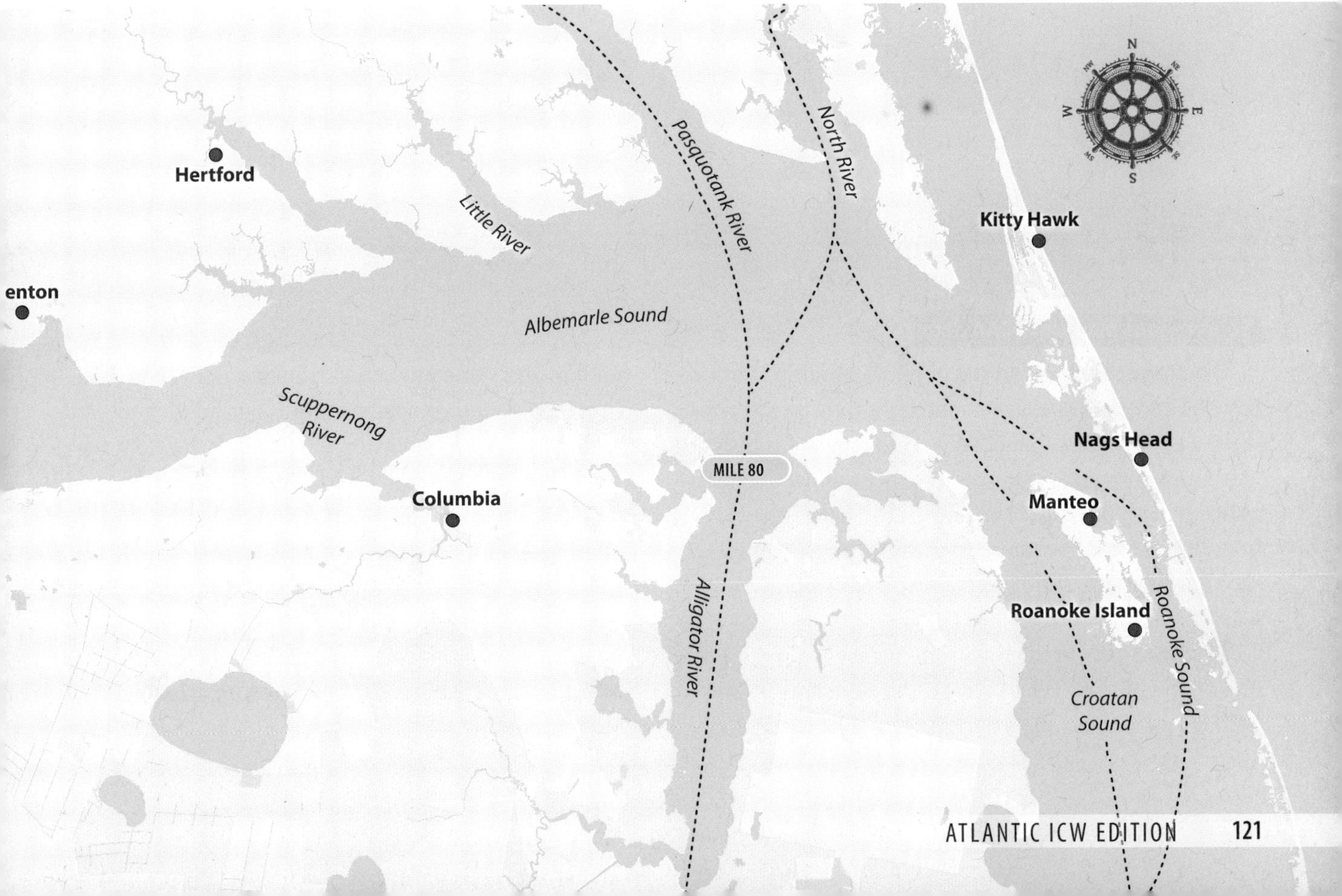

Albemarle Sound, NC

PERQUIMANS RIVER		Largest Vessel	VHF	Total Slips	Approach/ Dockside Depth	Floating Docks	Gas/ Diesel	Repairs/ Haulout	Min/Max Amps	Pump-Out Station
1. Hertford Bay Marina	(252) 426-7805			9	11.0 / 11.0				30 / 50	P

WiFi Wireless Internet Access onSpot Dockside WiFi Facility
Visit www.waterwayguide.com for current rates, fuel prices, website addresses and other up-to-the-minute information.
(Information in the table is provided by the facilities.)

Scan here for more details:

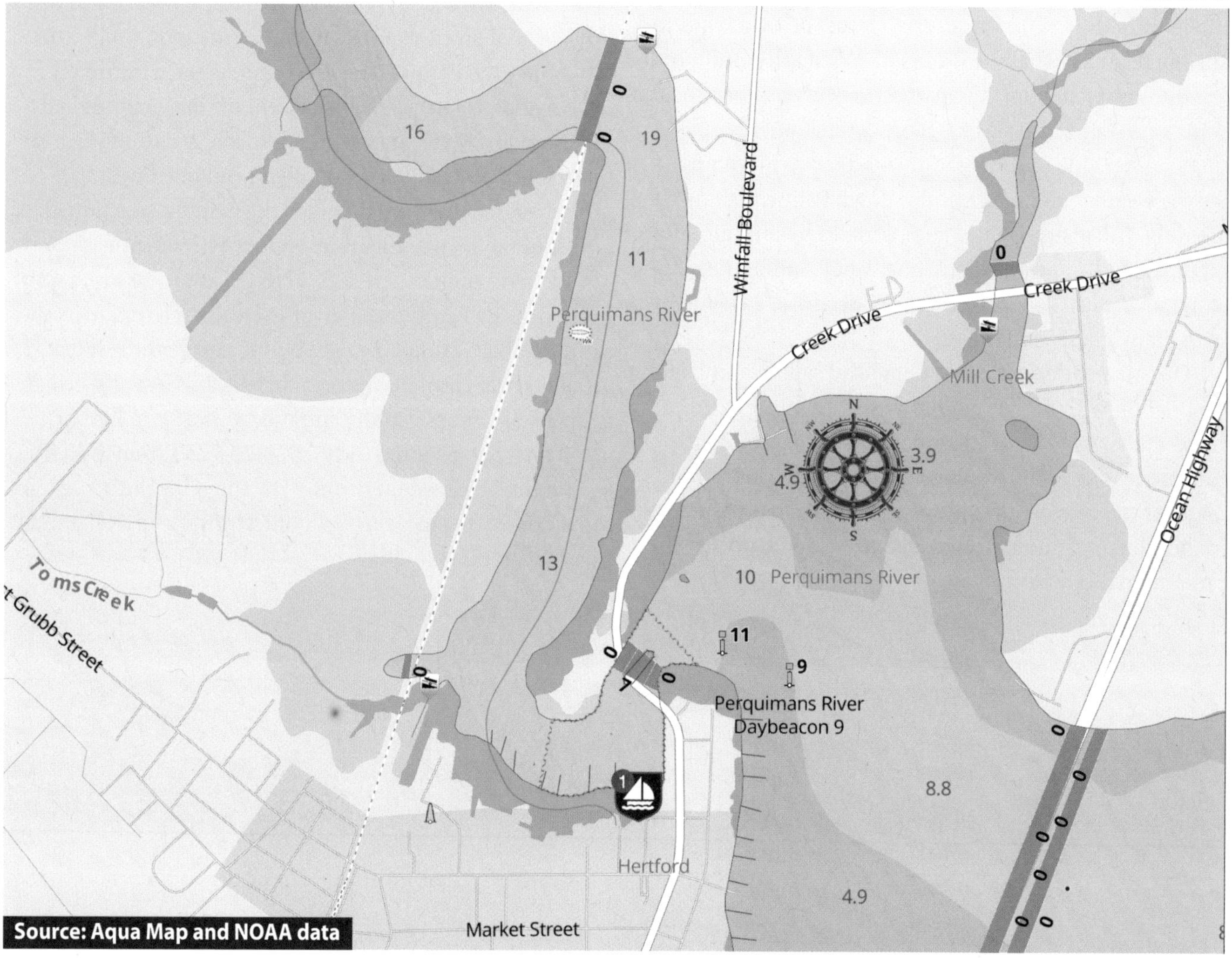

Source: Aqua Map and NOAA data

Dockage: Adjacent to the public boat ramp Hertford Bay Marina offers dockage at one of its nine fixed-pier slips, which can accommodate a wide range of transient vessels. Free electric, pump-out service and water are available with dockage. The marina is located one block from the historic downtown Hertford with restaurants, shops, a hardware store and a convenience store with groceries.

Anchorage: On the way from Elizabeth City to Little River you will pass Wharf Bay on the east shore at Mile 64. This anchorage offers 8 to 11 feet MLW with good holding and some protection from the north and east. The river's mouth is spacious, with fair holding in hard mud and makes a good stop when winds are from the east or west. Because of the long fetch anchorages could be choppy in a strong southeast wind, especially near the mouth of the river. Make sure your anchor is set well. You will be accompanied by a lot of crab pots and the friendly crabbers who stop by to check them. Depths are suitable for anchoring in the coves upriver and the scenery is lovely for those who don't mind the long trip to the upper reaches.

About 8 miles west of the Pasquotank River Entrance Light flashing green "1PR" (or 14 miles from flashing green "173" at the North River), off the north side of Albemarle Sound, you will find the entrance to Little River, which is easy to enter. The entrance is marked by green daybeacon "1L" and there is a platform to its northwest. Watch for fish net stakes. Depths in the river run 8 to 10 feet MLW but be wary of the shoals that extend from Mill and Stevenson Points at the entrance. The remainder of the river is unmarked.

The abundance of good anchorages makes Little River a natural place where groups of boaters can rendezvous. There is a good anchorage (despite a southeast exposure and a lot of crab pots) about 1 mile past Mill Point on Little River. The holding ground is good for anchoring in 7 to 9 feet MLW in Perquimans River–Halsey Bay, less than halfway between the river entrance and Hertford, and you can dinghy ashore. Here you will find 9 to 11 feet MLW with a soft mud bottom.

Yeopim River

NAVIGATION: Use NOAA Chart 12205. The Yeopim River is 6 miles west of the mouth of the Perquimans River. Enter the river from flashing green "1" and then follow the private aids northward to Albemarle Plantation. The approach to the dock is easy but pay attention to the marks. Also be aware that there are lots of crab pot buoys in the area.

Dockage: Albemarle Plantation Marina off the entrance channel to the Yeopim River offers dockage, showers and WiFi. This 166-berth marina sells competitively priced gas and diesel, and amenities include a free laundry, saltwater pool and fitness center. Clubhouse Restaurant offers fine dining and beautiful views. The more casual Dockside Café has a large deck with both screened and open areas and the menu includes wood fired pizza. The award-winning Sound Golf Links are open to visiting boaters. Call 252-426-5555 to arrange a tee time.

Albemarle Sound, NC

YEOPIM RIVER	Largest Vessel	VHF	Total Slips	Approach/ Dockside Depth	Floating Docks	Gas/ Diesel	Repairs/ Haulout	Min/Max Amps	Pump-Out Station
1. Albemarle Plantation Marina WiFi 10.0 mi. W of MM 75.0 (252) 426-4037	92	16	166	6.0/7.0		GD	R	30/50	P

WiFi Wireless Internet Access **onSpot** Dockside WiFi Facility
Visit www.waterwayguide.com for current rates, fuel prices, website addresses and other up-to-the-minute information.
(Information in the table is provided by the facilities.)

Scan here for more details:

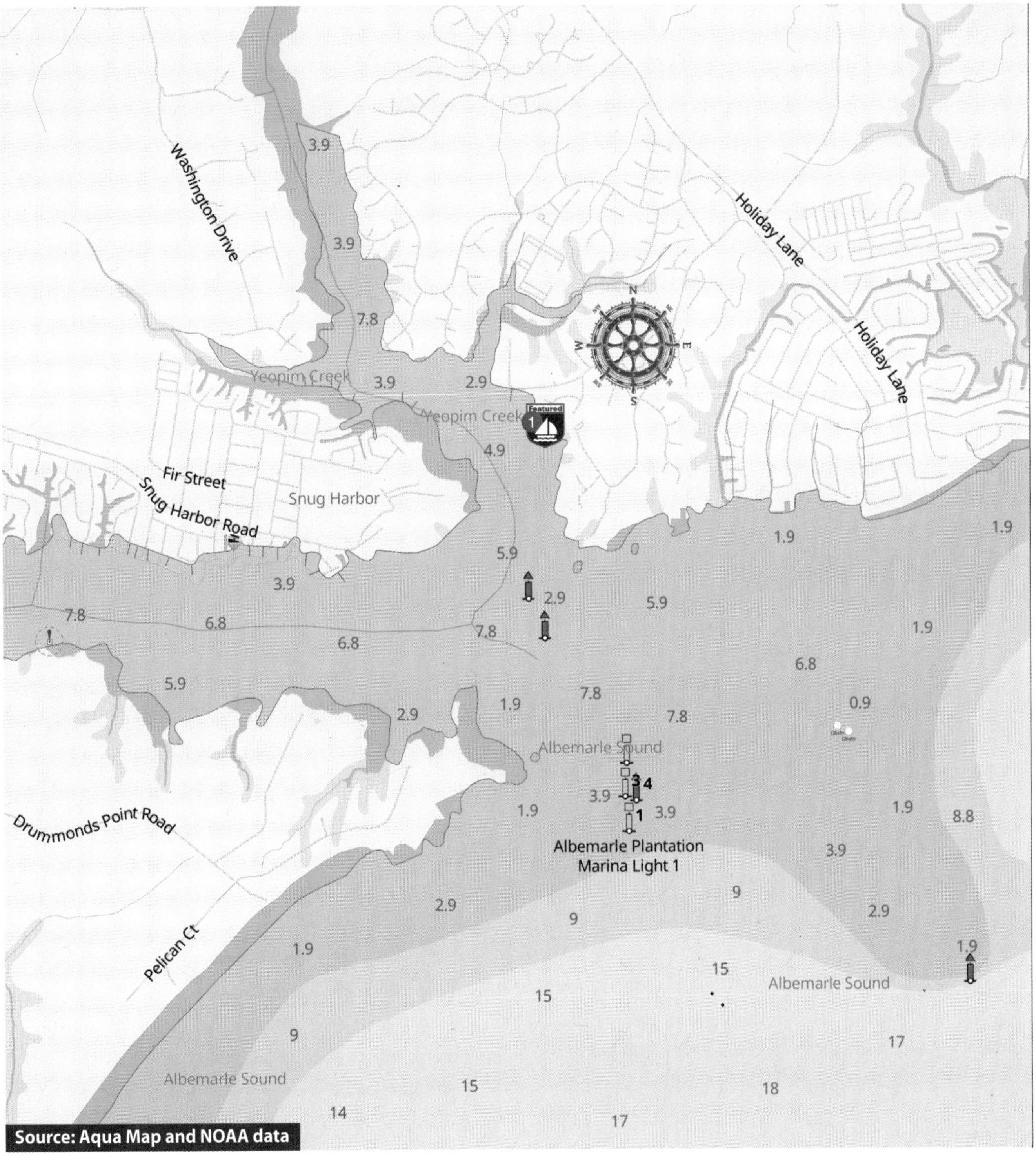

Source: Aqua Map and NOAA data

Albemarle Sound, NC

EDENTON		Largest Vessel	VHF	Total Slips	Approach/ Dockside Depth	Floating Docks	Gas/ Diesel	Repairs/ Haulout	Min/Max Amps	Pump-Out Station
1. Edenton Harbor WiFi	(252) 482-2832	130	16	9	6.0 / 6.0	F			30 / 50	
2. Edenton Marina	(252) 482-7421	85		107	6.0 / 8.0		GD		30 / 50	

WiFi Wireless Internet Access onSpot Dockside WiFi Facility
Visit www.waterwayguide.com for current rates, fuel prices, website addresses and other up-to-the-minute information.
(Information in the table is provided by the facilities.)

Scan here for more details:

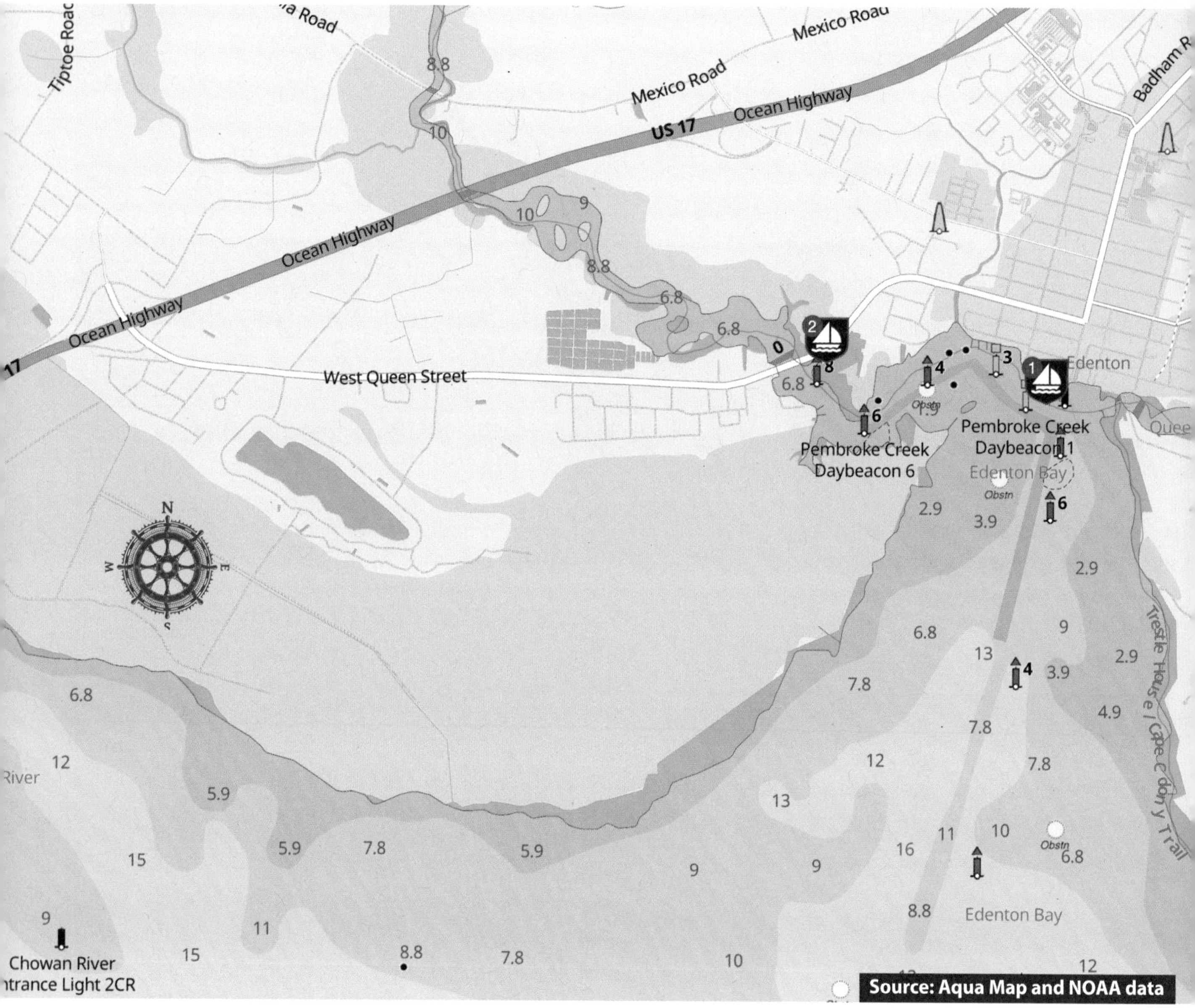

Anchorage: Yeopim River offers good anchorage in protected waters (from all directions except east). Tuck in behind Drummond Point for protection from all but east winds. Water depths are 5 to 7 feet MLW once you have cleared the well-marked entrance channel. Mind the depth sounder carefully.

Edenton & the Chowan River

Edenton is a delightful side trip from the ICW. Largely unscathed through the Revolutionary and the Civil Wars, Edenton maintains many historic colonial buildings while also being a thriving small town. The welcoming atmosphere and short entrance makes this a good

destination while exploring the western reaches of the Albemarle Sound. See more at "Goin' Ashore: Edenton, NC" in this chapter.

Three miles west of Edenton Bay the wide mouth of the Chowan River opens up with the picturesque river swinging northward for many undeveloped miles. The shores with their high wooded banks are especially scenic. These inland freshwater rivers offer many miles of delightful cruising.

NAVIGATION: Use NOAA Chart 12205. Cruising west on Albemarle Sound toward Edenton you will pass under the fixed high-rise **Albemarle Sound Bridge** (65-feet fixed vertical clearance). Overhead power lines farther upriver have a 94-foot minimum vertical clearance in the marked channel. Once you have passed the power lines, watch for flashing red "2" leading into Edenton. Reedy Point on the west side of Edenton Bay hosts submerged fish stakes as well as the taller ones seen throughout the area. The entrance is a broad funnel and the channel here is well marked with a controlling depth of 5.5 feet MLW past the turning basin.

Should you feel like exploring, the Chowan River carries 12-foot depths for 80 miles beyond the high-rise **U.S. 17 Bridge** at Emperor Landing and Edenhouse Point. It is interrupted by a 35-foot fixed vertical clearance **U.S. 13 Bridge** located 32 miles upriver at the town of Winton. Snags dictate caution, especially in the bend around Holiday Island. Beyond Winton, near the mouth of the Meherrin River, skippers need to exercise caution in the cable ferry area. Do not pass any cable ferry until it has reached the other side of the river and its cables have dropped.

There is no public dockage but there is a boardwalk that can accommodate dinghies. A short walk will bring you to the courthouse, restaurants, banks and convenience stores. The real attraction is the journey–beautiful scenery, abundant wildlife and quiet anchorages. Look for old ballast piles at creek entrances from the days that the Chowan River was a major trading link.

Dockage: The 9-slip Edenton Harbor has slips and accepts reservations. A breakwater protects the docks from the chop that can develop from a southerly breeze. Enter on the west side of the breakwater. These town docks put you in the heart of the village with restaurants and shops within easy walking distance and offers showers, pump-out service, WiFi and a courtesy car. Kayaks and canoes are available for rent at the marina office.

Dockage is also available at Edenton Marina up Pembroke Creek before the 5-foot fixed vertical clearance **W. Queen St. Bridge**. While you may see small boats anchored in or near Edenton Harbor, we cannot recommend it due to shoal water outside the channel and poor protection outside the harbor.

GOIN' ASHORE

EDENTON, NC

Sailing into Edenton Harbor is a voyage back in history. Standing on the broad-columned porch of the Penelope Barker House, you can look across Edenton Bay at a row of Revolutionary War cannons supplied by France. The Edenton Battery protects stately homes nestled among cypress trees and serves as a reminder that the town on Queen Anne's Creek began a cultural revolution that changed the future of the Colonies. From a bluff overlooking Edenton Bay and the Albemarle Sound, the open windows of shops and homes catch the full effect of the water's breeze.

SERVICES

1. **Edenton Post Office**
   100 N. Broad St. (252-482-2611)
2. **Shepard-Pruden Memorial Library**
   106 W. Water St. (252-482-4112)
3. **Vidant Family Medicine-Edenton**
   300 Court St. (252-482-2116)

ATTRACTIONS

4. Chowan County Courthouse
Oldest and most intact Colonial courthouse in the country (built in 1767) recognized as a National Historic Landmark. Host to a gala reception for President James Monroe in 1819 (101 S. Broad St., 252-368-5000).

5. Cupola House
National Historic Landmark built in 1758 for Francis Corbin, controller of customs, and restored in 1967 as a museum and formal gardens. Call for hours and fees (408 S. Broad St., 252-482-2637).

6. James Iredell House
Circa 1800 home of James Iredell, an attorney appointed (at age 39) to the first Supreme Court by President George Washington. House is two-story, "L"-shaped frame dwelling with Georgian and Federal style design elements (107 E. Church St., 252-482-2637).

7. Penelope Barker House (Welcome Center)
Home to the Edenton Historical Commission and the famous Edenton Tea Party and serves as a Welcome Center with exhibits and a gift shop (505 S. Broad St., 252-482-7800). Open daily from 10:00 a.m. to 5:00 p.m.

8. St. Paul's Episcopal Church
Built in 1736, this is the state's second oldest surviving church (101 W. Gale St., 252-482-3522). (The oldest is St. Thomas Episcopal Church in Bath.)

SHOPPING

9. Blount's Mutual Drugs
Full-service pharmacy with old-fashioned soda fountain with ice cream at 323 S. Broad St. (252-482-2127).

10. Byrum Hardware Company
Hardware store offering both the necessary (household tools) and the frivolous (gifts and decorations) at 314 S. Broad St. (252-482-2131).

11.Chowan Arts Council
Located on the waterfront at 112 W. Water St. (252-482-8005) with unique and affordable works by local and regional artists.

12. Garden of Readin'
Used book store and tea shop at 103 E. King St. (252-482-7323).

MARINAS

13. Edenton Harbor
Located at 621 W. Queen St. (252-482-7421).

Albemarle Sound, NC

ROANOKE RIVER		Largest Vessel	VHF	Total Slips	Approach/ Dockside Depth	Floating Docks	Gas/ Diesel	Repairs/ Haulout	Min/Max Amps	Pump-Out Station
1. Plymouth Landing Marina WiFi	(252) 217-2204	55	19	9	12.0 / 7.5				30 / 50	P

WiFi Wireless Internet Access onSpot Dockside WiFi Facility
Visit www.waterwayguide.com for current rates, fuel prices, website addresses and other up-to-the-minute information.
(Information in the table is provided by the facilities.)

Scan here for more details:

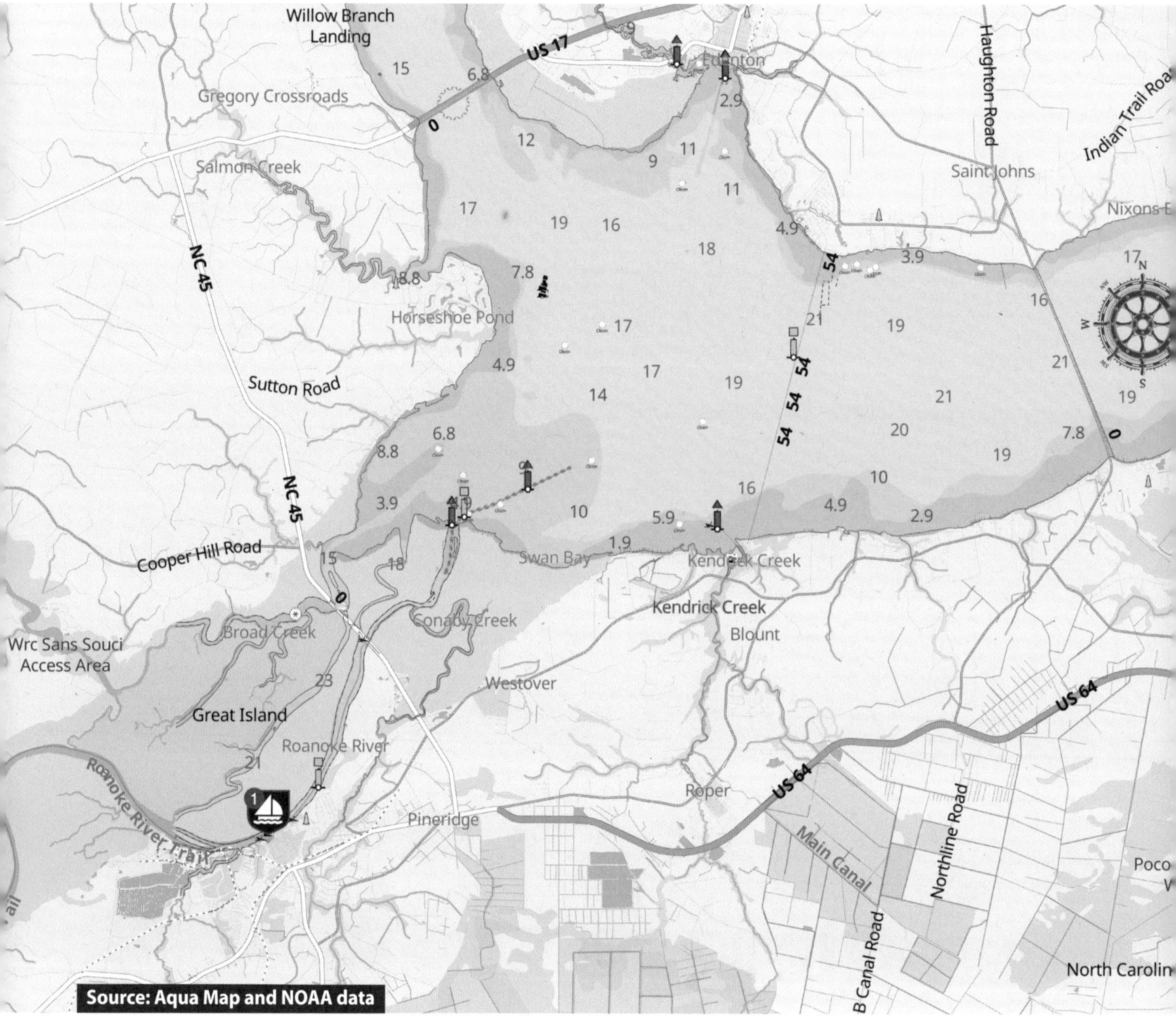

Anchorage: There is a well-protected anchorage at Rockyhock Creek with 7 to 14 feet MLW with fair holding in soft mud. It is exposed to the south. Off the north bank of the Chowan, just beyond green flashing daybeacon "13" is Bennett's Creek, which carries 11 feet at MLW and offers all-around protection.

Roanoke River (Plymouth)

Across from Edenton around Black Walnut Point, the Roanoke River leads to the southwest. The lower reaches are marked and the upper reaches are deep. There is still some commercial traffic on the river, which keeps it open. Plymouth, located 6 miles upriver, is a quaint town perfect for a diversion from the ICW or a day trip. There are restaurants within walking distance of the marina and two fine museums: Port O' Plymouth Museum (252-793-1377), which is housed in a 1923 Atlantic Coast Line train depot, and the Roanoke River Lighthouse and Maritime Museum (252-217-2204), a perfect replica of the second Roanoke River Lighthouse. Nearby the Davenport Homestead (252-797-4336) was built around 1790 and is the oldest surviving homestead open to the public in the region.

NAVIGATION: Use NOAA Chart 12205. The Roanoke River is much narrower than the Chowan River but is generally deep (about 10-foot MLW depths) and well marked. Shoaling is reported in the area of red daybeacons "8" to "12" along Rice Island. The fixed **Roanoke River Bridge** (50-foot vertical clearance) crosses the river about 2.5 miles upstream.

Dockage: Plymouth Landing Marina has floating docks with complimentary water, power and showers, while laundry and pump-out service are available for a fee. A Post Office, groceries, shopping and restaurants are nearby along Hwy. 64. Ask the dockmaster at the marina about transportation.

Anchorage: You can anchor almost anywhere along the cypress shores and marshes of Rice Island. There is a good anchorage before the Roanoke River Bridge with 10-feet MLW depths and all-around protection. On the southwest corner of the Albemarle Sound is Batchelors Bay at the confluence of the Roanoke and Cashie Rivers. This somewhat open bay has a channel with at least 7 feet MLW all the way to the 16-foot fixed vertical clearance Cashie River Bridge. The channel is narrow and there is more swing room near the mouth but less protection. You can anchor closer to the western shore in 7 to 9 feet MLW with protection from all but the northeast through east.

Scuppernong River (Columbia)

Broad, open Bull Bay forms the entrance to the scenic Scuppernong River located along the Albemarle Sound's southern shore between the Alligator River and Laurel Point. About 4 winding, well-marked miles upriver is the town of Columbia, once an important shipping point and now popular as a boating center. Sportsmen use Columbia as a year-round base to fish the waters of Albemarle Sound and the improved waterfront provides access to downtown shops and restaurants. Within a few blocks of the municipal marina there are an array of restaurant choices as well as a pharmacy, banks (with ATM), a hardware store and a Post Office.

Take the boardwalk under the highway to the large Tyrrell County Visitor Center to get situated. Just to the south is the 110,000-acre Pocosin Lakes National Wildlife Refuge and the beginning of the Scuppernong River Interpretive Boardwalk. The raised boardwalk takes you into the pristine bottomland swamp and makes a 0.75-mile loop complete with signage to explain the blackwater ecosystem.

NAVIGATION: Use NOAA Chart 12205. All sailing vessels have reached the extent of their Scuppernong excursion at the town dock due to three low bridges that cross the Scuppernong River. The first (12-foot closed vertical clearance, removable span) is immediately after the municipal Columbia Marina, while the other two are further upriver (one at Cross Landing with a 5-foot fixed vertical clearance and the other at Creswell, a removable span with an overhead cable limiting vertical clearance to 25 feet). To continue upriver past Columbia make prior arrangements for a bridge opening by calling 252-797-4468. Be aware that the projected depths upstream are just 3 feet MLW.

Dockage: The municipal Columbia Marina has transient slips available right downtown. Dockage is available for boats up to 45 feet; the pilings, however, are no more than 25 feet from the seawall. Restrooms, showers, water, shore power and pump-out service are available. Note that an uncomfortable chop can develop in a heavy northwest wind.

Albemarle Sound, NC

SCUPPERNONG RIVER		Largest Vessel	VHF	Total Slips	Approach/ Dockside Depth	Floating Docks	Gas/ Diesel	Repairs/ Haulout	Min/Max Amps	Pump-Out Station
1. Columbia Marina	(919) 495-1028	45		10	9.0 /				30 / 50	P

WiFi Wireless Internet Access onSpot Dockside WiFi Facility
Visit www.waterwayguide.com for current rates, fuel prices, website addresses and other up-to-the-minute information.
(Information in the table is provided by the facilities.)

Scan here for more details:

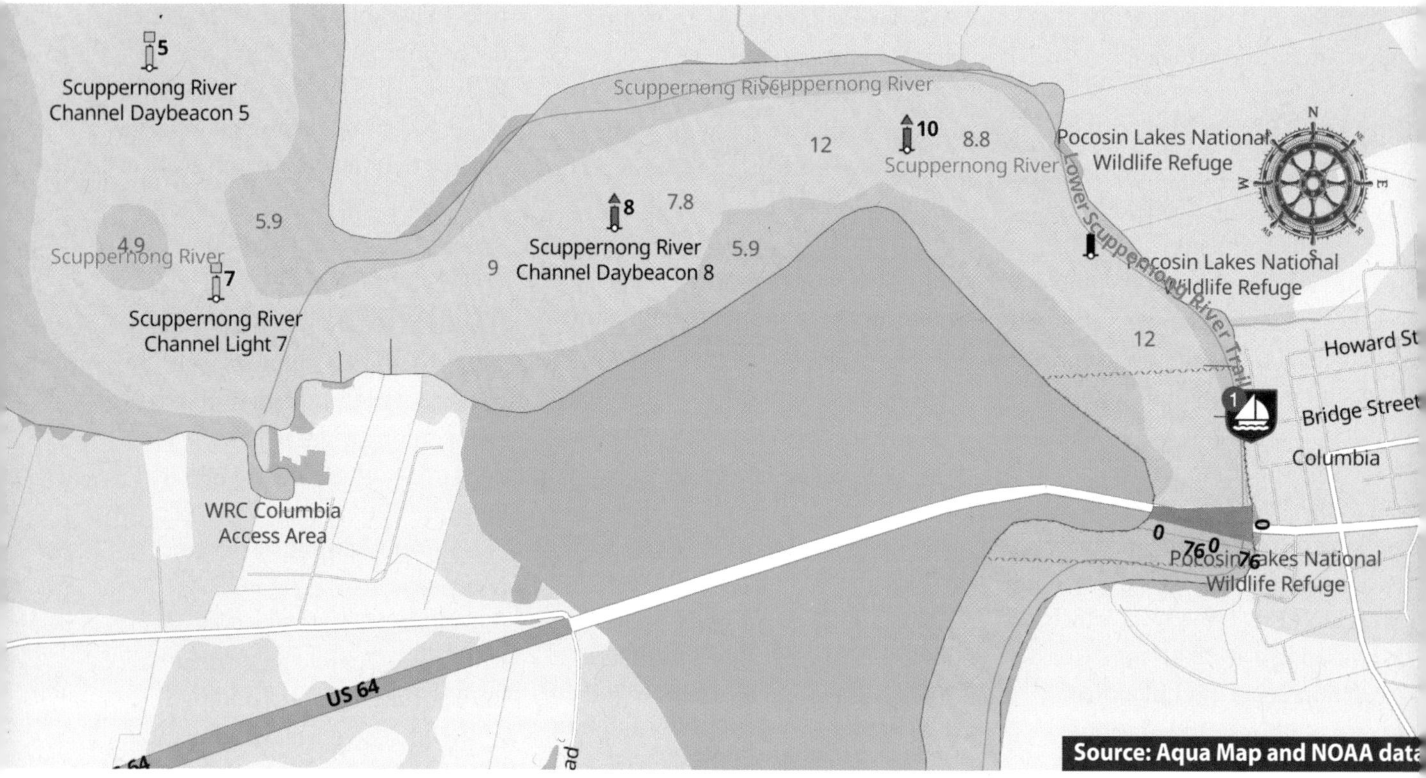

Anchorage: You will find several good anchorages in the Scuppernong River with 7 to 10 feet MLW and a mud bottom. The town of Columbia is easily accessible by dinghy. The cypress swamps of the river's upper reaches warrant exploration by dinghy or the town of Columbia's guided boat tours.

After exploring the western end of Albemarle Sound, it's decision time again. The Alligator River and the ICW proper head south and west, but the distant outline of rising dunes to the east heralds the beginning of the Outer Banks and the shorter route south.

THE ROANOKE & CROATAN SOUNDS

Roanoke Sound

Originally an instrumental route for the East Coast's first English settlers and still a popular destination for water lovers of all varieties, the Roanoke Sound separates the central Outer Banks from Roanoke Island. On the western side of the sound lies the towns of Manteo and Wanchese, which can be accessed by the Washington Baum Bridge (better known as the Manteo/Nags Head Causeway or vice versa), which stretches across the Roanoke Sound. Because Roanoke Island is bordered by two sounds–the Croatan Sound, which separates it from the mainland, and the Roanoke Sound, which separates it from the beaches–the little waterfront community is surrounded by water.

Manteo (pronounced "man-knee-oh" if you want to sound like a local) is on the northern and western sides of Shallowbag Bay off Roanoke Sound and is often overlooked by cruisers moving along the ICW but it is well worth the side trip. It is just a 5-minute taxi ride to the Outer Banks beaches and the town itself has a friendly air and much to offer. See more at "Goin' Ashore: Manteo, NC" in this chapter.

DON'T JUST CROSS THE ALBEMARLE, TAKE TIME OUT TO DISCOVER AMERICA'S BEGINNING...

Manteo Waterfront Marina

ail into the Manteo Waterfront Marina in the
storic town of Manteo on Roanoke Island
ss than one mile from Roanoke Sound.

orth and Southbound boaters will find
picturesque little village and all the
menities you would expect from a first
ass marina. Tired of driving the ICW?
ke the ALTERNATE ROUTE to the ICW and enjoy wide
pen cruising on the Albemarle and Pamlico sounds and
ve 17 miles over the traditional route between Coinjock
nd Oriental... and discover Manteo!

st off our docks is a town with shops, restaurants, inns,
ts and all the history of the first settlement in the New
orld...The Lost Colony founded in 1587!

ou'll find most everything you need within a few hundred
et of the docks, and a full shopping center with grocery,
ost office, hardware is less than 1/2 mile away.

pproach depths from Roanoke Sound are 7ft.+ except in unusual
nditions, but if you have a deep draft vessel, give us a call and we'll
e happy to help you navigate in. We can accommodate vessels up to
0 ft. and the small harbor has excellent protection from the weather.

you're not in a big rush, stick around and explore the Outer Banks
eaches, less than 5 miles away, visit the NC aquarium with the kids,
the Elizabethan Gardens and our outdoor Lost Colony play which
in its 75th year of performances! We may have lost a colony...but
ou'll find a big welcome in the town of Manteo. For more information
reservations call 252-473-3320. For reservations please go to
ockwa.com

- Transient, weekly, and monthly rates
- 30 amd 50 amp outlets at each slip
- 53 slips, accommodating boats to 140′
- A small, deep and well-protected harbor
- Modern air-conditioned showers & laundry
- WiFi and cable TV
- Adjacent to great shopping, fine dining, and elegant accommodations in Old Town Manteo

P.O. Box 246, Manteo, NC 27954-1328
252-473-3320 VHF 16 & 9
www.manteonc.gov

A Superb Marina in the Heart of Manteo
SHALLOWBAG BAY
MARINA
• Floating Slips
• Pump out
• Walk to Town
• Ship Store
• Fitness Center
• High Speed Fuel Pumps
• Short & Long-term Leases Available
• Bike Rentals
10% OFF at Stripers for boaters
The renowned Stripers Restaurant
STRIPERS
BAR AND GRILLE
(252) 305-8726
1100 b South Bay Club Drive Manteo. North Carolina 277954
Longityude: W-75 39' 54.90" / Latitud: N+35 54' 02.23" cmckenney1979@yahoo.com
Award Winning Food
Stripers Bar and Grille is an award winning service oriented 3 floor restaurant with every seat overlooking the water. The extensive food menu is enhanced by a large variety of wines, beers, cocktails and specialty drinks.
STRIPERS
BAR AND GRILLE
1100A South Bay Club Drive
Manteo, NC 27954
www.stripersbarandgrille.com

Roanoke Sound, NC

MANTEO (ROANOKE ISLAND)		Largest Vessel	VHF	Total Slips	Approach/ Dockside Depth	Floating Docks	Gas/ Diesel	Repairs/ Haulout	Min/Max Amps	Pump-Out Station
1. Manteo Waterfront Marina WiFi	(252) 473-3320	100	16	50	7.0 / 7.0				30 / 100	P
2. Marshes Light Marina WiFi	(252) 305-4737	60	16	60	10.0 / 9.0				30 / 50	P
3. Shallowbag Bay Marina WiFi	(252) 305-8726	100	16	75	7.5 / 7.0	F	GD	R	30 / 50	P

WiFi Wireless Internet Access **onSpot** Dockside WiFi Facility Scan here for more details:
Visit www.waterwayguide.com for current rates, fuel prices, website addresses and other up-to-the-minute information.
(Information in the table is provided by the facilities.)

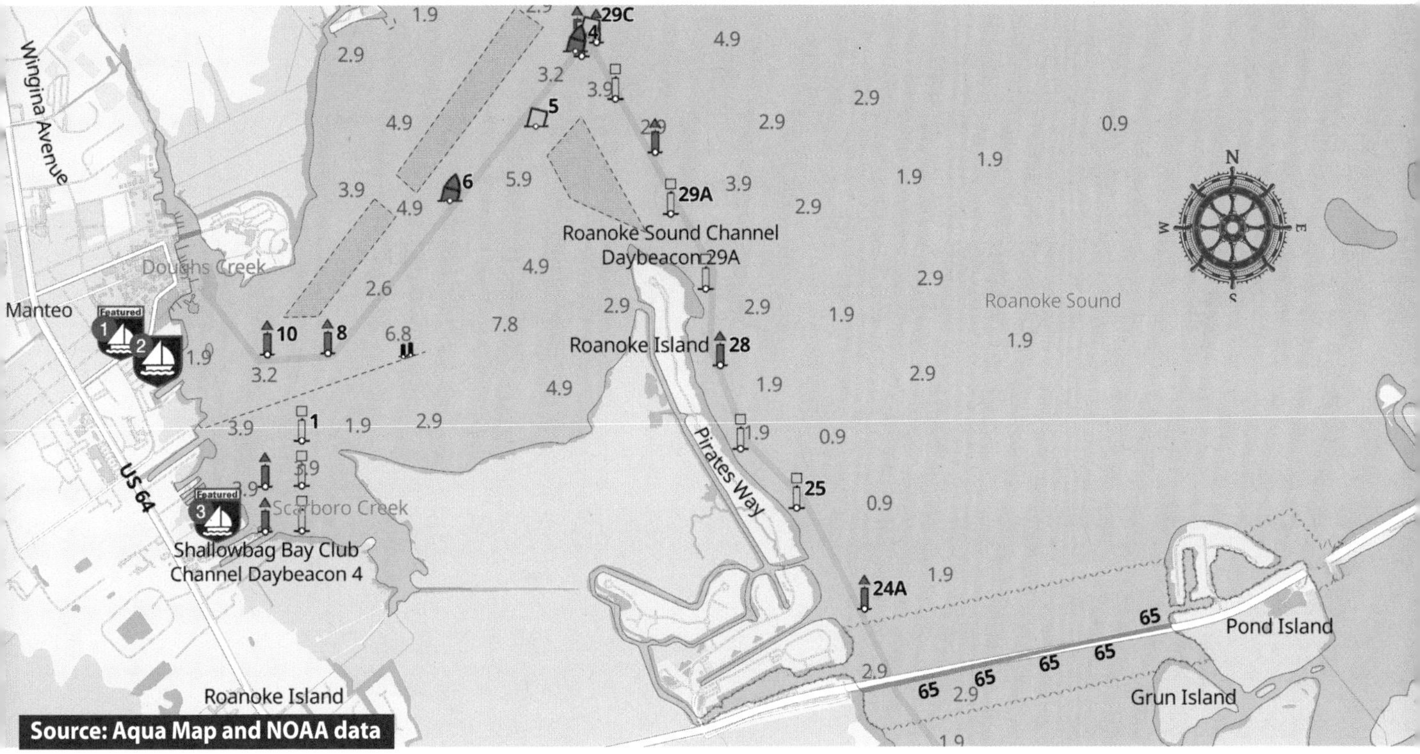

Source: Aqua Map and NOAA data

At the south end of Roanoke Island is a real commercial fishing and boat building village that is home base for several fishing companies that receive and ship the catch for the substantial oceangoing fleet that operates from here. Wanchese is the home base for the reality show "Wicked Tuna–Outer Banks" as well as several custom sportfishing boat manufacturers. You will find few amenities for recreational boaters. Silting has been an ongoing problem in the harbor so proceed cautiously.

NAVIGATION: Use NOAA Charts 12204 and 12205. From ICW Mile 70 cruise east on Albemarle Sound, setting a course to lighted "MG" at the head of Croatan and Roanoke Sounds.

Vessels that cannot clear the 44-foot fixed vertical clearance **U.S. 64 Bridge** crossing Croatan Sound can reach Manns Harbor and other Croatan Sound points via Roanoke Sound (crossed by the 64-foot vertical clearance **Washington Baum Bridge**).

To proceed to Manteo on Roanoke Sound head south from light "MG" to Croatan Sound flashing green "3CS," approximately 4 miles to the south-southeast. Continue to flashing red "42" and the well-marked Roanoke Sound channel. Proceeding southward keep the red lights and daybeacons on your port side. Use caution. It is winding and aids are not as prevalent south of Shallowbag Bay, which can be confusing, especially farther down at Oregon Inlet. South of the Manteo entrance the Roanoke Channel is crossed by

GOIN' ASHORE

MANTEO, NC

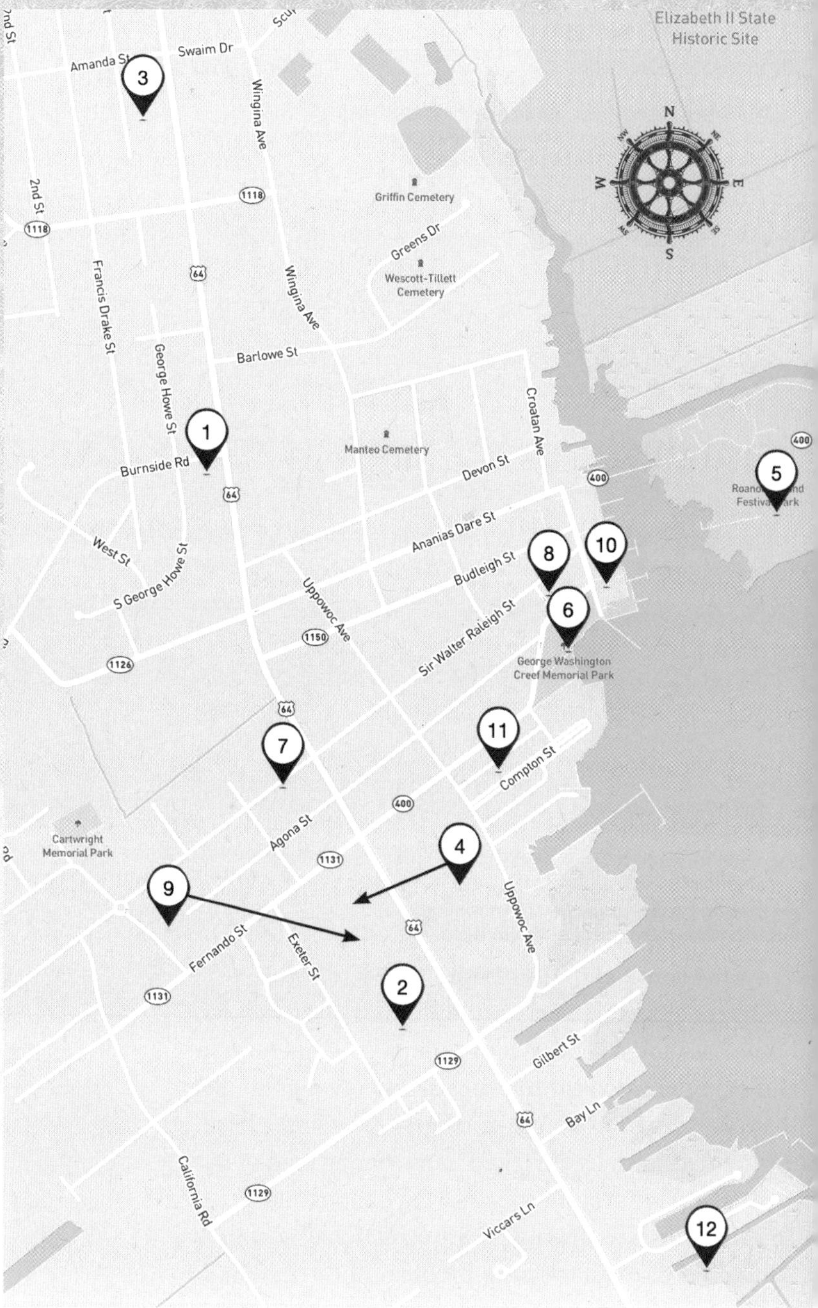

The Roanoke Marshes Lighthouse, at the entrance to Dough's Creek, is a replica of the 1877 screwpile lighthouse once found at Croatan Sound. The Manteo Weather Tower, also on the downtown waterfront, flew flags to warn locals, fishers and sailors about oncoming weather. Weather messages came in by telegraph, so Manteo's first telegraph operator, Adelphus P. Drinkwater, naturally became the first operator of the weather station and tower as well. Drinkwater took part in history when he telegraphed news to the world of the Wright Brothers' first flight. The Weather Tower is one of only five still used by NOAA to fly weather flags during the day and lights up at night.

SERVICES

1. Dare County Library
700 U.S. 64 (252-473-2372)

2. Manteo Post Office
212B U.S. Hwy. 64/264
(252-473-2534)

3. Outer Banks Family Medicine-Manteo
604 Amanda St. (252-473-3478)

4. The Wash House
Laundromat at 114 U.S. 64
(866-825-6052)

ATTRACTIONS

5. Roanoke Island Festival Park
American Indian town, settlement site and adventure museum that allows guests of all ages to experience life as an original settler in the 1500s. Costumed interpreters show how the colonists lived, worked and played. The *Elizabeth II*, a replica of a 16th-century ship, is anchored here at1 Festival Park.

6. Roanoke Island Maritime Museum
Nautical museum located on the waterfront featuring the famous shad boats built here over 100 years ago. They also have an eclectic collection of small boats including a New England Beetle Cat, a Hampton Bay One Design and a 1950s vintage outboard hydroplane. Admission is free (104 Fernando St., 252-475-1750).

SHOPPING

7. Ace Hardware
Household tools, supplies and more at 300 U.S. 64 (252-473-1444)

8. Downtown Books
Well-stocked bookstore with the goal of "putting the right book in the right hands at the right time" at 105 Sir Walter Raleigh St. (252-473-1056).

9. Piggly Wiggly
Full-service grocery chain (252-473-3727).

MARINAS

10. Manteo Waterfront Marina
207 Queen Elizabeth Ave. (252-473-3320)

11. Marshes Light Marina
301 Dartmoor Ln. (252-305-4737)

12. Shallowbag Bay Marina
1100 N. Bay Club Dr. (252-305-8726)

Roanoke Sound, NC

ROANOKE ISLAND		Largest Vessel	VHF	Total Slips	Approach/ Dockside Depth	Floating Docks	Gas/ Diesel	Repairs/ Haulout	Min/Max Amps	Pump-Out Station
1. Pirate's Cove Yacht Club & Marina WiFi	(800) 367-4728	90	78	195	10.0 / 13.0		GD	R	30 / 100	

WiFi Wireless Internet Access onSpot Dockside WiFi Facility
Visit www.waterwayguide.com for current rates, fuel prices, website addresses and other up-to-the-minute information.
(Information in the table is provided by the facilities.)

Scan here for more details:

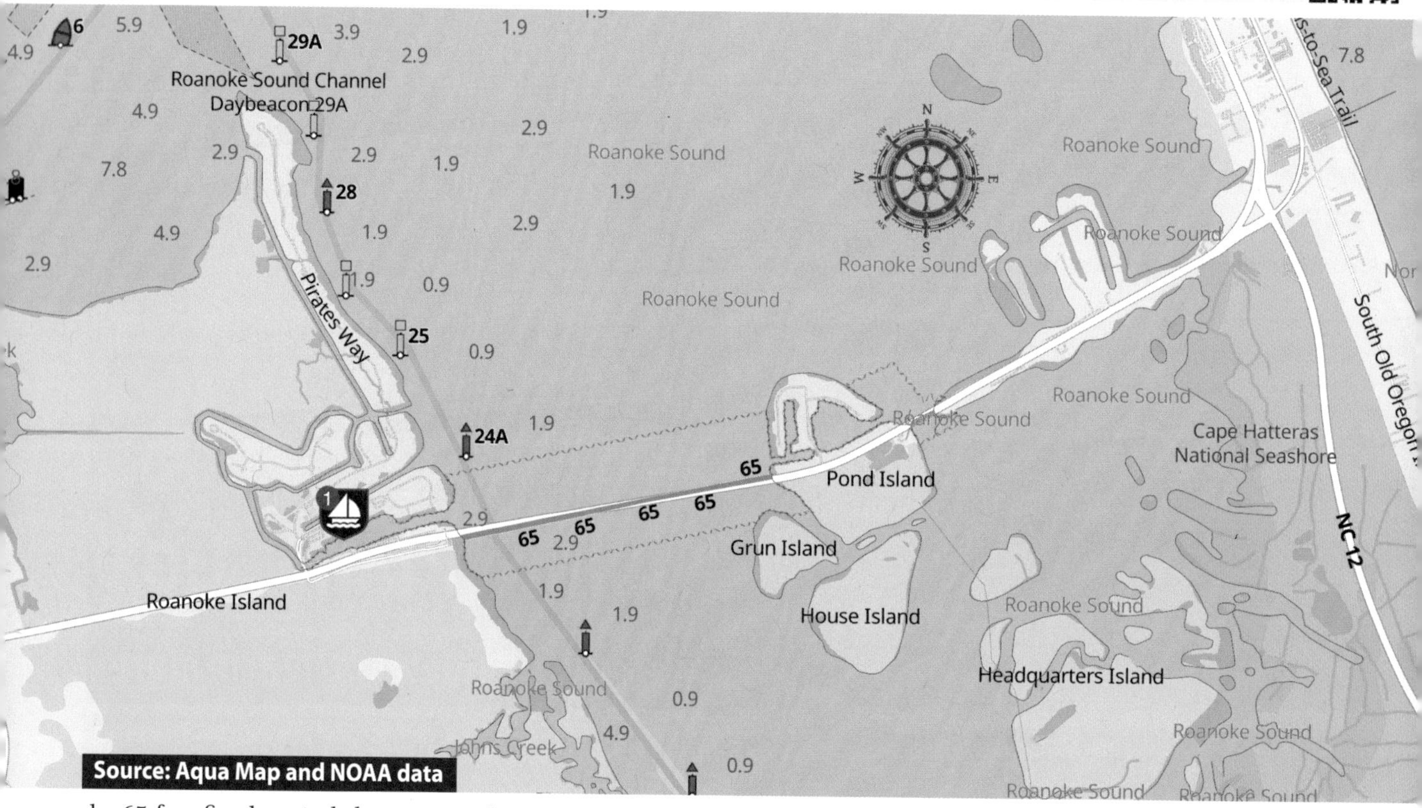

Source: Aqua Map and NOAA data

the 65-foot fixed vertical clearance Washington Baum Bridge.

Approach depths into Manteo are 7 to 12 feet MLW, despite what is noted on the latest NOAA charts. The *Elizabeth II* replica, which draws 8 feet, transits the channel frequently. Shoaling does occur at the entrance to Shallowbag Bay so slow down, mark the buoys and daybeacons carefully, and keep an eye on your depth sounder. Some chartplotters fail to show all the buoys unless zoomed in tight.

> It is helpful to know that all markers with numbers in the 20s and 30s are for the main Roanoke Bay channel, while the markers with numbers starting at "2M" belong to the Shallowbag Bay Channel.

From either direction wait to turn west to the Shallowbag Bay Channel until just north of the red "30A." Give red buoy "2M" lots of room and keep a sharp lookout for additional buoys that may have been added to mark recent shoaling. After your turn hug green daybeacons "5" and "3" for deep water. The channel broadens until red "8," where it turns west to red daybeacon "10." Most directions are figured from this last red daybeacon.

Dockage: North of red daybeacon "10" the 50-slip Manteo Waterfront Marina can accommodate vessels to 150 feet. The marina is run by the town of Manteo and has climate-controlled showers and laundry, shore power and a pump-out facility, all available for a fee payable to the dockmaster. Call on VHF Channel 16 for directions to the office, which is only manned between 10:00 a.m. and 2:00 p.m. on weekends (unless you have a reservation). Pull into a slip on the wharf ending in the brown gazebo. The marina is adjacent to many shops, inns, restaurants and the 1-mile-long town boardwalk. They can arrange repairs, haul-out, rental cars and airport shuttle service.

A set of private markers to the south lead from the red daybeacon "10" into Shallowbag Bay Marina, which accommodates vessels up to 75 feet on floating docks

Roanoke Sound, NC

WANCHESE (ROANOKE ISLAND)		Largest Vessel	VHF	Total Slips	Approach/ Dockside Depth	Floating Docks	Gas/ Diesel	Repairs/ Haulout	Min/Max Amps	Pump-Out Station
1. Bayliss Boatworks WiFi	(252) 473-9797	100	16	7	11.0 / 20.0	F	GD	RH	30 / 100	P
2. Gregory Poole Marine-Wanchese	(252) 473-1501				7.0 / 7.0			RH		
3. Outer Banks Marina	(252) 473-5344	70		45	14.0 / 14.0	F	GD	RH	30	
4. Bluewater Outer Banks Yacht Yard WiFi	**(252) 475-1420**	**90**		**6**	**14.0 / 14.0**	**F**		**RH**	**30 / 100**	

WiFi Wireless Internet Access onSpot Dockside WiFi Facility
Visit www.waterwayguide.com for current rates, fuel prices, website addresses and other up-to-the-minute information.
(Information in the table is provided by the facilities.)

Scan here for more details:

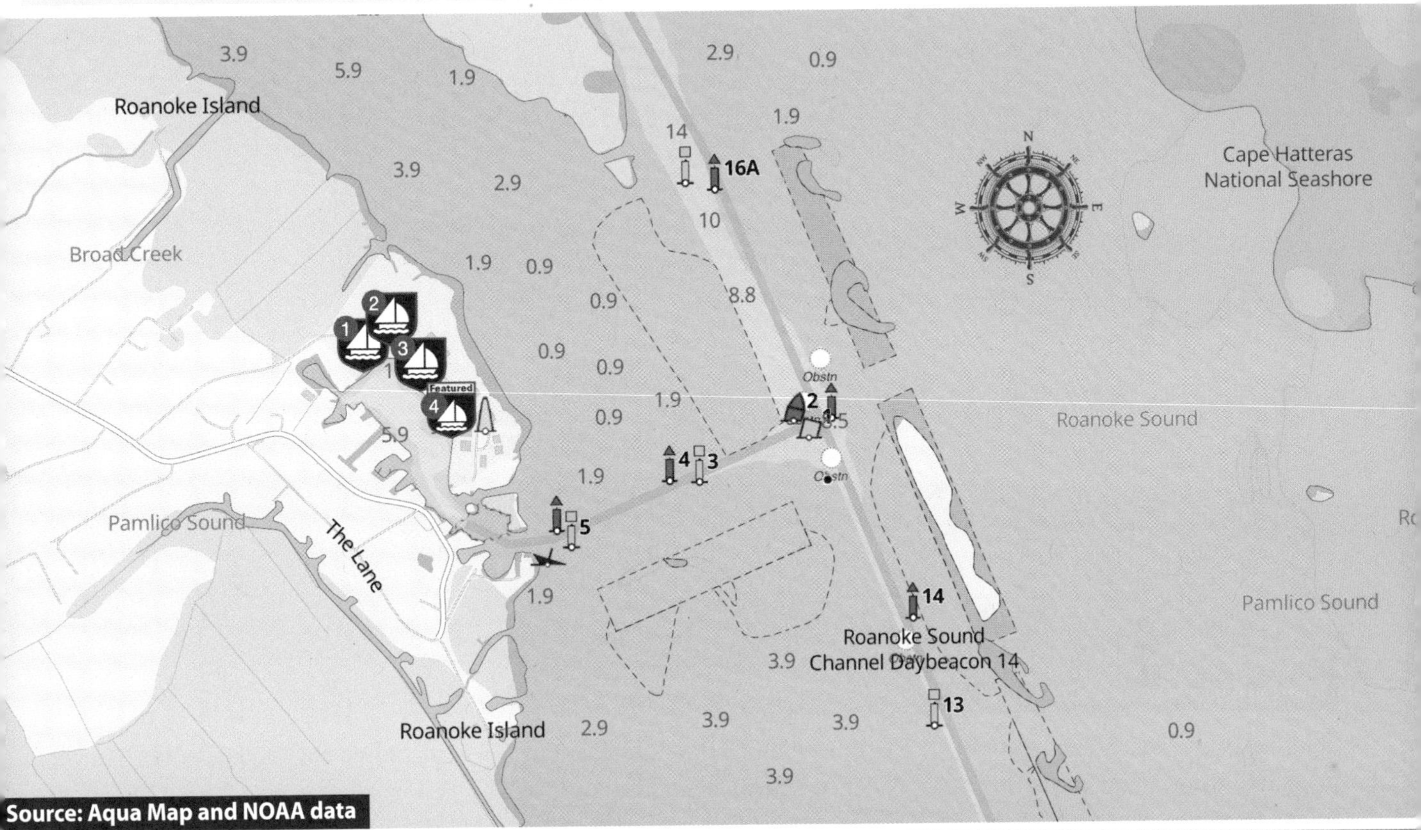

Roanoke Sound, NC

OREGON INLET		Largest Vessel	VHF	Total Slips	Approach/ Dockside Depth	Floating Docks	Gas/ Diesel	Repairs/ Haulout	Min/Max Amps	Pump-Out Station
1. Oregon Inlet Fishing Center	(252) 441-6301	65	69	55	6.0 / 6.0		GD		50	

WiFi Wireless Internet Access onSpot Dockside WiFi Facility
Visit www.waterwayguide.com for current rates, fuel prices, website addresses and other up-to-the-minute information.
(Information in the table is provided by the facilities.)

Scan here for more details:

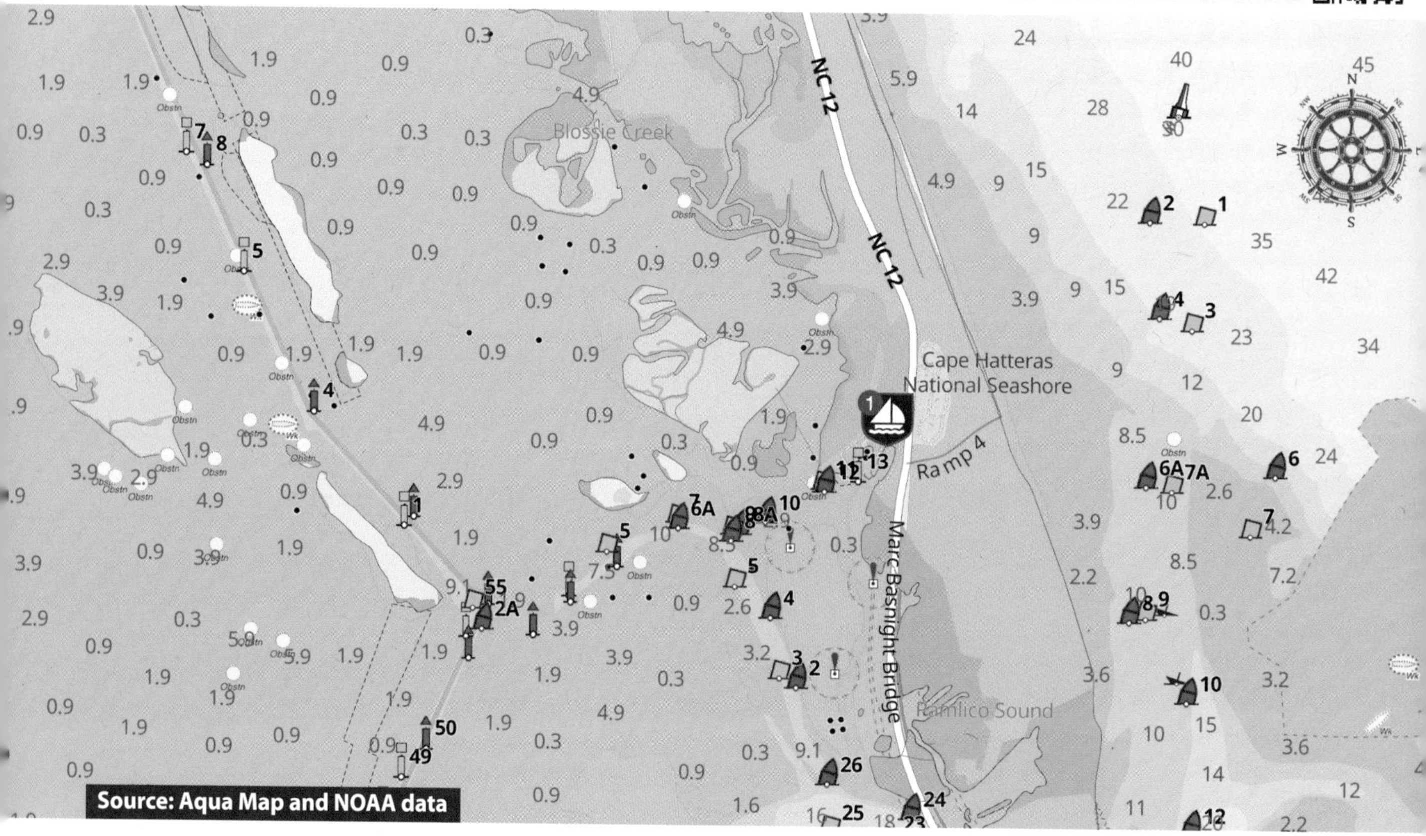

Source: Aqua Map and NOAA data

and boasts multiple fueling stations providing "in slip" fueling to most boats. They also have an on-site restaurant, pool, hot tub and laundry facilities. If you have any interest in a day of offshore fishing there are over 20 large charter boats based here that can make the run to the offshore canyons in comfort.

Marshes Light Marina is part of a waterfront community and offers some transient dockage on protected canals for (mostly power) vessels to 60 feet. Pirate's Cove Yacht Club & Marina, located just on the north side of the Washington Baum Bridge on Roanoke Island, is part of a large residential development and offers transient slips. They cater to sportfishing boats.

The town of Manteo also provides free overnight tie-up with no services on a "space available" basis with room for 3 to 4 boats on the docks between the lighthouse and the town gazebo. There is a pump-out service available and a public restroom at the nearby maritime museum.

If you need your boat fixed, Wanchese at the south end of Roanoke Island is the place. There are several yards with large travel lifts, prop shops, canvas shops, metal fabricators, and engine shops including Bayliss Boatworks, Gregory Poole Marine-Wanchese, Outer Banks Marina and Bluewater Outer Banks Yacht Yard. Bluewater's extensive facilities maintain full capabilities including engine repair, welding, machinist, metal work, wood and composite work, mechanical, electrical, electronic and complete rigging up to and including total custom construction.

Anchorage: The dockmaster for Manteo describes the anchorage area as a triangle created by three points: the red daybeacon "10" to the south, the lighthouse to the northwest and the brown gazebo to the northeast.

Anchor at Manteo in hard mud and sand in 6 to 8 feet MLW with no tide, only wind-driven changes in depth. Protection is excellent from the north and west but strong south or east winds can kick up a chop. Farther west the bottom shoals swiftly and a charted pipe restricts anchoring to the south. You can take the dinghy to the town dock for land access.

Side Trip: Oregon Inlet

NAVIGATION: Use NOAA Chart 12205. A well-defined channel with 9- to 10-foot MLW depths is used by the trawler fleet and leads south from Wanchese, 6 miles down to Oregon Inlet. It is also used by one of the East Coast's largest sportfishing fleets. Oregon Inlet is considered the most changeable of all the East Coast inlets. Be aware that aids to navigation are not charted here because they change so frequently at the Oregon Inlet intersection. This inlet regularly experiences severe shoaling and is NOT a recommended inlet. Proceed with an abundance of caution and local knowledge. Use caution transiting this area. Shoaling has been reported to 2 feet MLW in the inlet near the high-rise **Herbert C. Bonner Bridge**.

Always obtain accurate local information before attempting this inlet as it can be quite dangerous, even in calm conditions. Follow one of the local charter or fishing boats in or out of the inlet if in doubt. Do not try to run the inlet in foul weather.

Shoaling has been located in Oregon Inlet from green buoy "21A" to green buoy "25" encroaching from the south side of the channel. Water depths of 7 feet MLW have been observed. At green buoy "17" water depths of 3 feet MLW have been observed on the south side of the channel.

Dockage: Oregon Inlet Fishing Center sits north of the inlet offering fuel and transient berths and is a good resource on the Oregon Inlet channel.

Croatan Sound

Many power vessels use the Croatan Sound Route to the Pamlico Sound to circumvent the ICW and slower vessels. This open water route starts at Mile 66 after entering the Albemarle Sound from the North River and ends at Mile 169 in the Neuse River.

NAVIGATION: Use NOAA Charts 12204, 12205, 11548, 11553 and 11555. Boats that can clear the 44-foot fixed US 64 Bridge can run 4 miles down Croatan Sound (western side of Roanoke Island) from flashing green Croatan Light "3CS" to Manns Harbor (no transient facilities) on the mainland side just before the 66-foot fixed **Virginia Dare Memorial Bridge**. Check water levels carefully if your mast approaches this height. (Local knowledge says that the **U.S. 64 Bridge** actually has a vertical clearance of between 42 and 44 feet.)

After clearing both bridges in Croatan Sound heading south your next waypoint will be Roanoke Marshes flashing white 20-foot "RM." The well-marked channel carries 7- to 8-foot MLW depths. Red aids are to the west (starboard when heading south). Your subsequent waypoints from the southern end of Croatan Sound, through Pamlico Sound and ending with the Neuse River are as follows: Stumpy Point (27-foot flashing white "N"), Long Shoal (15-foot flashing red "LS2"), Bluff Shoal (40-foot isophase "BL"), Brant I Shoal (40-foot flashing white "BI") then Neuse River (24-foot flashing white "NR"). A licensed boat captain and long-time user of this route reported to us that it shaves 18 miles off the trip north or south.

Vessels that cannot clear the 44-foot fixed US 64 Bridge crossing Croatan Sound can reach Manns Harbor and other Croatan Sound points via Roanoke Sound. Old House Channel carries at least 7-foot MLW depths from Oregon Inlet west into Pamlico Sound. The channel is well marked. Carry the red lights and daybeacons on the starboard side from this point south to Pamlico Sound. The buoys change here and they can be confusing. Slow down here and sort it out before proceeding or you may find yourself aground. They can run the dredged channel east of Roanoke Island, round the island via Old House Channel in Pamlico Sound, then head north up Croatan Sound. Note that aids to navigation reverse between flashing red "4" and flashing green "OH" in Old House Channel.

NEXT STOP

Whether you choose to take the Roanoke Sound or Croatan Sound route around Roanoke Island, both converge in Pamlico Sound, leaving you poised to continue north to the Chesapeake Bay or south on the ICW.

Roanoke River Light House

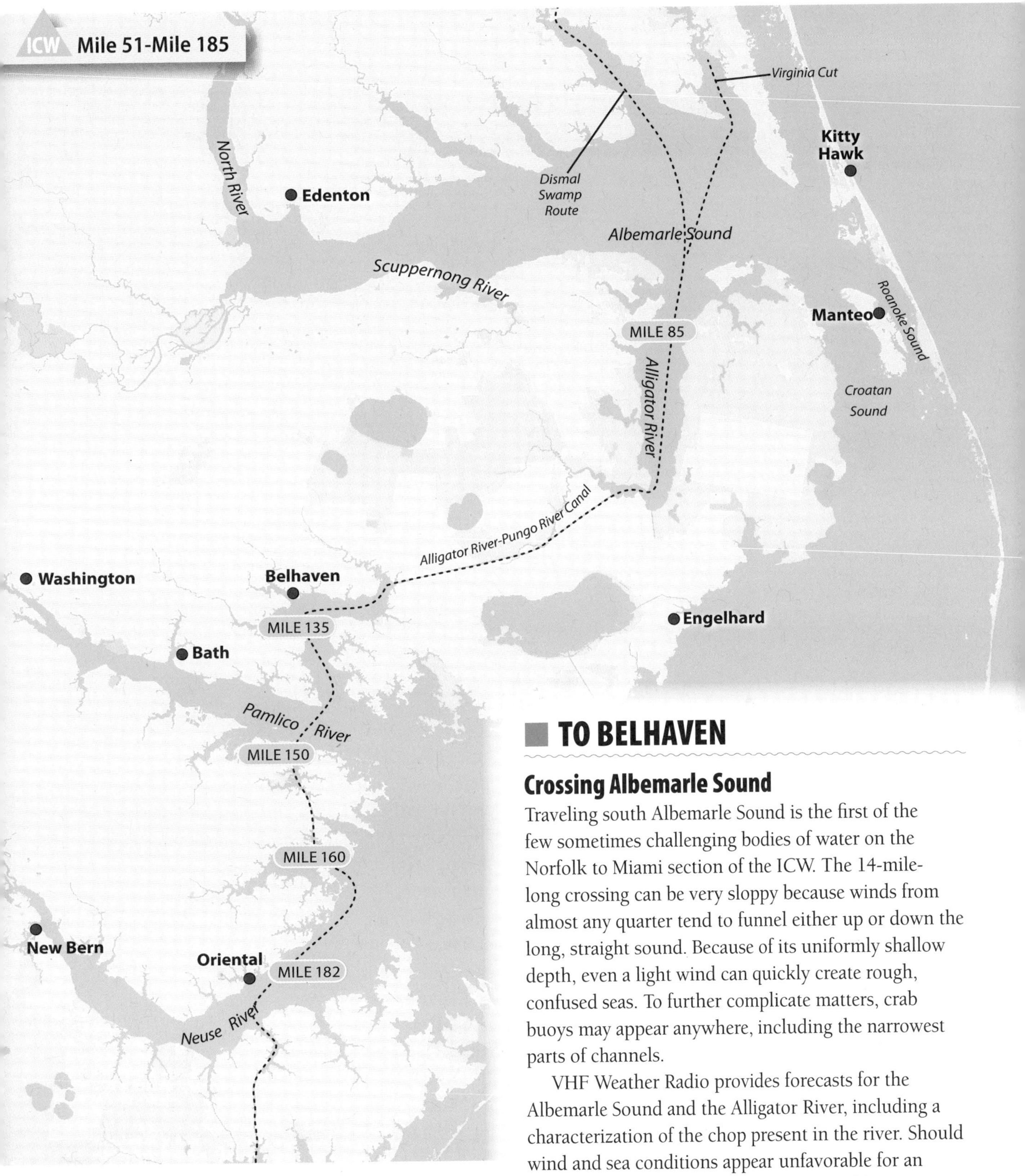

TO BELHAVEN

Crossing Albemarle Sound

Traveling south Albemarle Sound is the first of the few sometimes challenging bodies of water on the Norfolk to Miami section of the ICW. The 14-mile-long crossing can be very sloppy because winds from almost any quarter tend to funnel either up or down the long, straight sound. Because of its uniformly shallow depth, even a light wind can quickly create rough, confused seas. To further complicate matters, crab buoys may appear anywhere, including the narrowest parts of channels.

VHF Weather Radio provides forecasts for the Albemarle Sound and the Alligator River, including a characterization of the chop present in the river. Should wind and sea conditions appear unfavorable for an Albemarle crossing, prudent boaters should remain in or return to their last port, whether that be Coinjock or Elizabeth City for those coming down the ICW, or

Alligator River, NC

ALLIGATOR RIVER		Largest Vessel	VHF	Total Slips	Approach/ Dockside Depth	Floating Docks	Gas/ Diesel	Repairs/ Haulout	Min/Max Amps	Pump-Out Station
1. Alligator River Marina (WiFi) 1.5 mi. W of MM 84.0	(252) 796-0333	155	16	29	7.5 / 10.0		GD	R	30 / 100	P

(WiFi) Wireless Internet Access onSpot Dockside WiFi Facility
Visit www.waterwayguide.com for current rates, fuel prices, website addresses and other up-to-the-minute information.
(Information in the table is provided by the facilities.)

Scan here for more details:

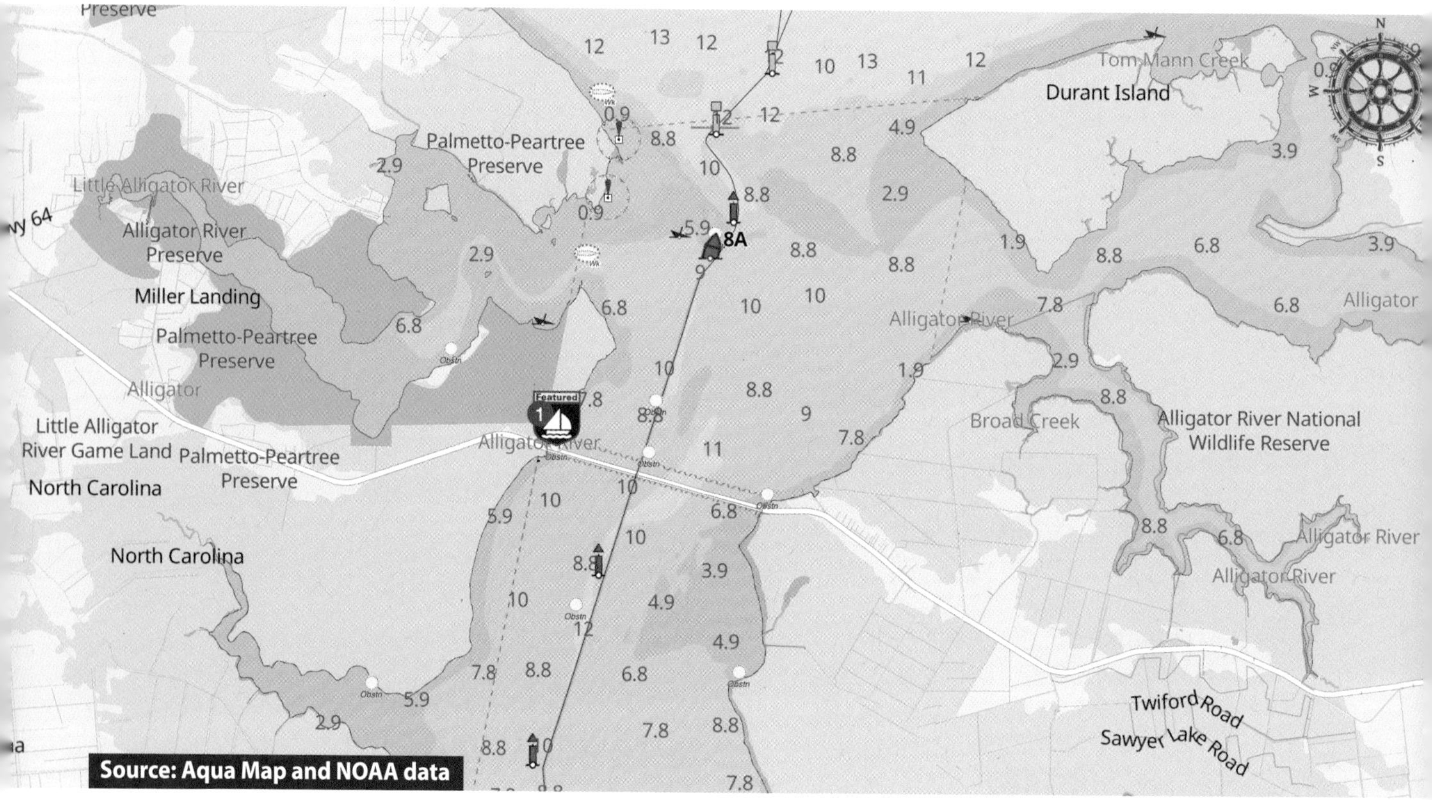

Source: Aqua Map and NOAA data

Columbia or Albemarle Plantation for those who opted to see more of Albemarle Sound.

NAVIGATION: Use NOAA Charts 12206 and 11553. Camden Point is about 19 miles from southeast Elizabeth City along the Pasquotank River. When crossing Albemarle Sound you can save a couple of miles by deserting the chart's ICW course to make for flashing green "1PR" east of Wade Point in the mouth of the Pasquotank River and then directly to flashing green "1AR" at the entrance to the Alligator River. Watch for crab pot buoys off the point.

Along the Virginia Cut route two lighted aids to navigation set the course across Albemarle Sound from the mouth of the North River: the flashing 6-second white isophase "N" to the north and flashing 4-second white "S" to the south (about 6.5 miles apart). As the course from the Dismal Swamp Canal Route from the Pasquotank River across Albemarle Sound converges with the Virginia Cut Route, the second marker, flashing 4-second white "S," will lie close to the course. It is another 3.5 miles to flashing green "1AR" at the mouth of the Alligator River.

Should you decide to cross Albemarle Sound when the wind is up, it is a good idea to call (on VHF Channel 13) the bridgetender of the Alligator River (US 64) Bridge at Mile 84.2 for a situation report. The bridge opens on signal except during unsafe conditions (in wind speeds of 34 mph or greater) when the bridgetender need not open. You should be aware of this potential obstacle before beginning your crossing. If the wind comes up en route and the bridge is closed, you have the option of ducking into Alligator River Marina just before the bridge for protection or anchoring as described in the next section. If the wind is as little as 15 mph out of a westerly direction the resulting waves can make for a very unpleasant crossing of the sound.

THE ALLIGATOR RIVER

NAVIGATION: Use NOAA Chart 11553. This heavily marked channel for the Alligator River is confusing, even to veteran ICW travelers, so be sure to slow down and take time to sort out the markers. Just before Mile 80 is the entrance marker for the Alligator River, flashing green "1AR." A wreck has been marked with a small green can buoy numbered "1A WR." Next in line to the south is quick flashing green "3," which is difficult to see approaching from either direction but is the location of the Mile Marker 80 sign.

There have been numerous groundings by vessels missing flashing green "3" and heading straight to flashing green "5." The board for flashing green "5" is visible only when approached from the correct direction.

Long Shoal Point at the mouth of the Alligator River is popular with the local hunting crowd and can be thick with duck blinds, boats and shotguns during duck season. In late fall migrating whistling swans settle onto the shallows in large flocks, a sight that is beautiful to behold. Red daybeacon "6" is just north of Long Shoal Point and quick flashing red "8" marks the shoal southeast of Long Shoal Point. Long Shoal seems to get longer with each passing year.

Flashing green "7" is just east of quick flashing red "8" and marks the eastern boundary of the ICW channel here. Make sure you honor both marks, favoring the green side. The pole from the charted former white "Danger" beacon is still on the shoal but has no boards. Favor the east side of the channel between flashing green "7" and green daybeacon "9." As you approach red buoy "8A" located between green daybeacon "9" and red daybeacon "10" stay near the red side of the channel. From here set your course for the opening span of the Alligator River (US 64) Bridge at Mile 84.2.

Always follow the markers but especially in this area as the markers are moved frequently. Up-to-date NOAA charts are a necessity for accurate navigation but are still updated less frequently than the markers are moved. Any departure from the main channel carries the risk of prop damage or worse. Do not shortcut points, do not hug the banks too closely and do approach anchorages cautiously.

The **Alligator River (US 64) Bridge** normally opens on signal but it cannot open in winds stronger than 34 knots and at the discretion of the bridgetender may remain closed in winds of lesser velocities. In either case look for a good spot to hole up in should it become necessary. Southbound boats might want to check weather conditions at the bridge and call the bridgetender on VHF Channel 13 before crossing the Albemarle. You certainly don't want to make this crossing only to find the bridge closed due to high winds. Plans are in place for a new fixed bridge to replace the swing bridge.

Drought conditions and prolonged strong winds can lower the water level throughout the Alligator River. A north or south blow can kick up 6-foot waves and make this transit very uncomfortable. While the Alligator River continues wide and deep almost to its head, snags are frequent outside the channel and boaters should follow the markers carefully. The most snags have been observed between red daybeacon "24" and green "37." An extra pair of eyes is always helpful in this area. Snags and obstructions are often partially submerged and difficult to see and you may hear other skippers reporting them to the Coast Guard on VHF Channel 16 and making Sécurité calls.

South of the Alligator River (US 64) Bridge the east bank of the river is primitive with side streams worth exploring but only by dinghy. Milltail Creek, east of the bend in the channel at quick flashing red "18" (about Mile 88), is pristine but hard to locate. Five miles upstream are the turning basin and the decaying town wharf of Buffalo City. The creek is narrow and fallen trees may lie across the creek in areas.

Dockage: At the northwestern end of the Alligator River Bridge is Alligator River Marina with a well-protected harbor and the only fuel available along the 86 miles on the Virginia Cut Route between Coinjock (Mile 50) and Belhaven (Mile 136). This friendly marina accepts transients of all sizes and offer all the usual amenities plus a convenience store and early morning breakfast and short-order favorites at the on-site restaurant. It is easily recognizable by its candy cane-striped lighthouse.

Anchorage: Little Alligator River offers limited protection on the east side of the river north of the bridge, especially in any northerly or easterly wind. There is 6 feet MLW and fair holding behind Mill Point near the mouth of the Little Alligator. It is not a spot to wait out a cold front passage nor is it a comfortable refuge if the Alligator River (US 64) Bridge cannot open because of strong winds when southbound.

If planning to stay north of the bridge for weather reasons, it is better to head further off the track to the east and anchor to the southwest side of Durant Island, the common entrance to East and South Lakes. Here you will find good shelter from northeast winds among the numerous crab pots.

Just past Briery Hall Point at the mouth of Broad Creek on South Lake offers some protection. Venture carefully into East Lake or South Lake if you draw more than 5 feet; the channel is unmarked and narrow. Although both carry 8- to 10-feet MLW depths, they shallow to 3 to 5 feet MLW just outside of the channel. Both anchorages have good holding and wind protection.

If you are northbound and there is a bridge closure, you will need to find a spot close to the southwestern end of the bridge to drop the hook and wait it out. This is not a good anchorage in a north or northeast wind so when in doubt contact the bridge. A better bet is Catfish Point at Mile 94.3, which is an excellent all-around anchorage in clay with 6- to 14-foot MLW depths.

The Alligator River in the proximity of Mile 100 is wide so choose a location that provides wind protection. In season there may be plenty of bugs and fisherman traffic early morning. It is recommended that a trip line be used when anchoring in the Alligator River due to the many snags on the bottom. Anchoring options include Newport News Point at Mile 101 with good holding in 7 to 8 feet MLW (exposed to the north) and Deep Point at Mile 102 with good holding in 7- to 8-foot MLW depths in mud (exposed to the east). When anchoring position yourself as far out of the channel as possible to stay away from maneuvering tugs and barges in this vicinity.

Tuckahoe Point (Mile 104) just before the entrance to the 20-mile-long Alligator River-Pungo River Canal offers the best all-around protection in 6- to 10-feet MLW depths. Turn to the north off the ICW between green daybeacon "49" and red daybeacon "52" and then proceed slowly to Tuckahoe Point. Do not get too close to the point; the area is foul with tree stumps. Holding, swing room and protection are good. Position yourself as far out of the channel as possible to stay away from maneuvering tugs and barges in this vicinity and show anchor lights at night.

Alligator River-Pungo River Canal–ICW Mile 105 to Mile 126

The 21-mile-long Alligator River-Pungo River Canal runs northeast to southwest. It is scenic and heavily wooded at its upper end. Do not be in a hurry or you might miss deer snacking near the shore or a black bear swimming across the channel. The occasional alligator has been spotted here as well. Farther on are areas that have burned in the past but now have their second growth. The canal is relatively narrow and boats dragging huge wakes have a tendency to damage the banks. Each year more and more trees topple into the water. Proceed slowly.

The Fairfield Canal at Mile 113.8 leads to Lake Mattamuskeet, which is part of the Mattamuskeet Wildlife

Refuge. The refuge is popular with hunters and naturalists from November through May when huge flocks of water birds gather in the lake and marshes. Arrangements to visit the refuge can be made in Belhaven.

NAVIGATION: Use NOAA Chart 11553. While enjoying the scenery and wildlife keep a lookout for stumps and snags outside of the channel. This is another area where deadheads have been spotted in the channel. Keep a watchful eye on the water when transiting this canal. It is a good idea to stick to the center of the channel and maintain a radio watch; tugs and recreational boats will frequently point out possible hazards with Sécurité calls on VHF Channel 16. Channel markers in the vicinity of the Fairfield (NC 94) Bridge at Mile 113.9 and farther west will help you maintain your mid-channel position in those areas.

The Alligator River-Pungo River Canal's controlling depth is 12 feet MLW; however, keep a close eye on the depth sounder, stick to the center of the channel and squeeze to the side carefully if you must pass another boat.

Fairfield Canal crosses the ICW just before the fixed **Fairfield (NC 94) Bridge** at Mile 113.9. The bridge has a charted 65-foot vertical clearance but we have received reports of it being closer to 64 feet. Tree stumps line both sides of the channel and there can be considerable current present here. Boats have been observed anchoring here with lines tied to shore and anchors astern. Note that this is not a recommended anchorage except in an emergency situation.

At Mile 125.9 you will pass under the high-level **Wilkerson (US 264) Bridge** (also known as the Walter B. Jones Bridge), which has 1 foot less clearance than the Army Corps of Engineers' authorized fixed vertical clearance of 65 feet at mean high water.

Sailboats with masts over 60 feet should know their exact mast height with antennas and exercise extreme caution when passing under the Wilkerson (US 264) Bridge. The slight tidal range here may or may not provide the extra clearance required for safe passage. If the tide boards are missing from this bridge, check locally for information.

Pungo River (Belhaven)–ICW Mile 126 to Mile 145

Belhaven (which translates as "beautiful harbor") is a popular rest stop for ICW travelers. The town sits among old forests and wide creeks, good anchorages and dark water. It offers the charm of an historic small town life with pastoral views and many opportunities to observe wildlife. Drop anchor or tie up at the town dock or one of the marinas and take a short walk into town where you will find shops, restaurants and the museum. You will pass beautiful Victorian homes along Belhaven's tree-lined streets, many with their windows open to catch the river breeze. Read more at "Goin' Ashore: Belhaven, NC" in this chapter.

NAVIGATION: Use NOAA Charts 11553 and 11554. Flashing green "59AR" east of the Wilkerson (US 264) Bridge is the last ICW marker before the Pungo River marking system takes over. Green daybeacon "27PR" is the first Pungo River marker with red daybeacon "28" just to its south. The river is easy to follow, although floating logs and submerged obstacles require caution. During periods of extreme low water the tips of several submerged pilings are sometimes visible along the channel between the Wilkerson Bridge and flashing green "23" on the north edge of the channel.

Heading southwest on the Pungo River stay in the channel and give flashing green "21" a wide berth to avoid the chronic shoaling extending from the western bank. The channel is well marked up to Belhaven's entrance channel, which is reached by heading northwest from flashing red "10" in the Pungo River.

> Note that flashing red "10" has a 4 second light, not "QR" as shown on the charts.

The approach to the full-service marinas and boatyards of Belhaven is easy and well marked. On approach to Pantego Creek reduce your speed and wake just beyond green daybeacon "3" and red daybeacon "4." The channel carries 9-foot MLW depths along the centerline. At Belhaven the Pungo River makes a 90-degree turn to the south for the 10-mile run to the Pamlico River.

> Heading south into the Pungo River the buoys suddenly reverse with green aids to starboard but still with the familiar ICW yellow triangles and squares marking the boards to signify they are ICW markers. This is because you are going downstream here on the Pungo River, which is marked from seaward.

Pungo River, NC

BELHAVEN AREA		Largest Vessel	VHF	Total Slips	Approach/ Dockside Depth	Floating Docks	Gas/ Diesel	Repairs/ Haulout	Min/Max Amps	Pump-Out Station
1. Dowry Creek Marina WiFi MM 132.0	(252) 943-2728	200	16	73	9.0 / 9.0		GD	R	20 / 200+	P

WiFi Wireless Internet Access onSpot Dockside WiFi Facility
Visit www.waterwayguide.com for current rates, fuel prices, website addresses and other up-to-the-minute information.
(Information in the table is provided by the facilities.)

Scan here for more details:

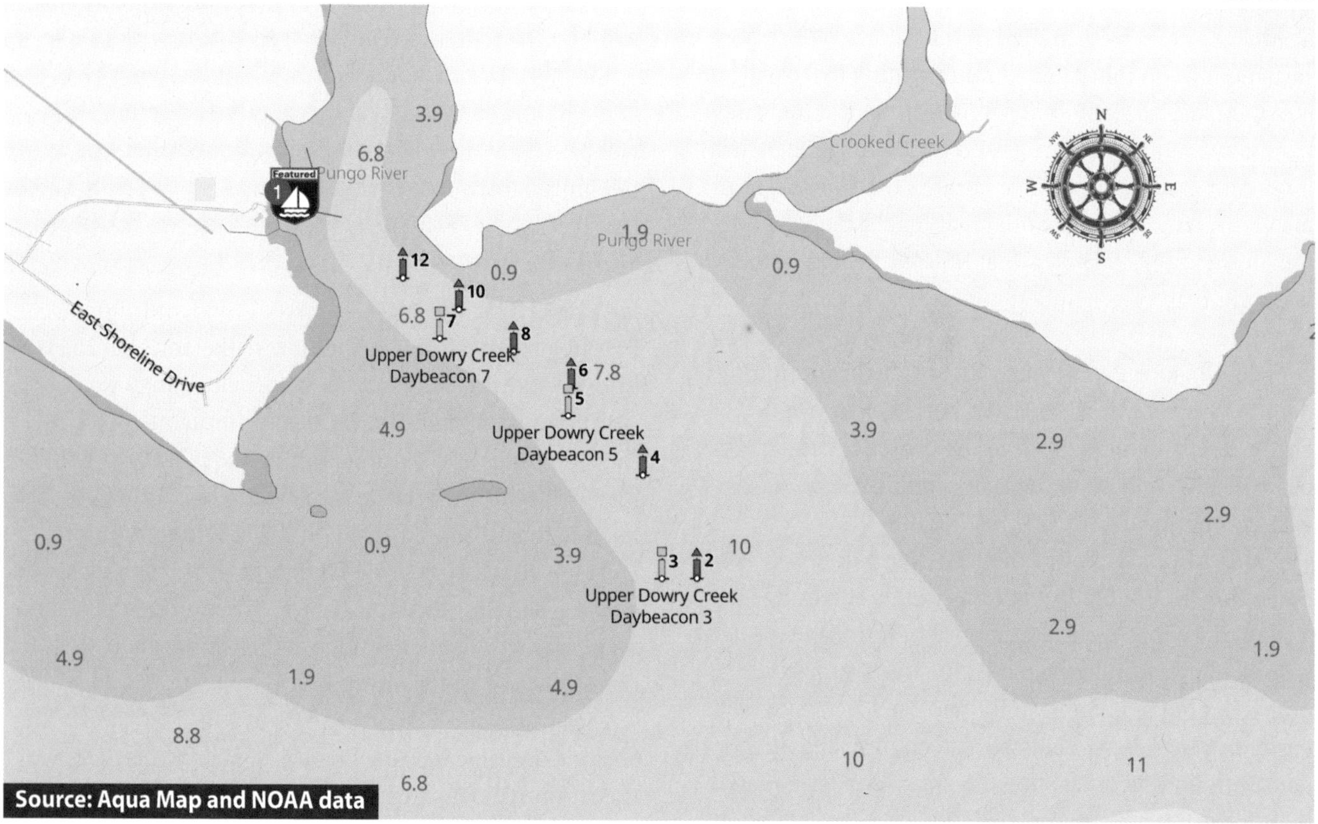

Source: Aqua Map and NOAA data

Dockage: After exiting the Alligator River-Pungo River Canal the well-regarded Dowry Creek Marina is just north of the channel at green daybeacon "15" (Mile 131.6). The marked entrance channel has a minimum depth of 8 feet MLW. Experienced deckhands will help you dock. The marina offers transient slips with amenities such as WiFi, a laundry, a swimming pool, tennis courts and a courtesy car. Major upgrades to the docks and power were completed in 2019.

Just north on Pantego Creek is River Forest Boatyard/ Shipyard, a full-service shipyard specializing in prop and shaft repair, hull painting, electrical repairs and all types of marine overhauls. They have a full-time mechanic and diver, plus a 40-ton lift. DIY boaters are welcome. Rental cars are available and they have complimentary golf carts for getting around town. Nearby TJ's Marina & Boatyard offers repairs and may have space for you.

Immediately inside the charted Belhaven storm barrier to the right (via a marked channel) is River Forest Manor and Marina. The renovated manor and detached bungalows can accommodate those looking for a land vacation or a location for meeting friends and family. The marina has transient slips with water and power, plus complimentary laundry, a tennis court and electric golf carts.

Belhaven Marina is to the north with slips and offers some repairs. They are known for their clean heads and showers with soap and towels. They also offer a free laundry. Immediately to the north are the Belhaven Town Docks At Wynne's Gut with power (30 amp) and water. A nice boater lounge, restrooms and showers are only available when the Chamber of Commerce is open (closed Saturday, Sunday and Monday). Payment for the town docks can be made by calling the dockmaster at Belhaven

35°31.98'N 076°32.16'W

Dowry Creek Marina

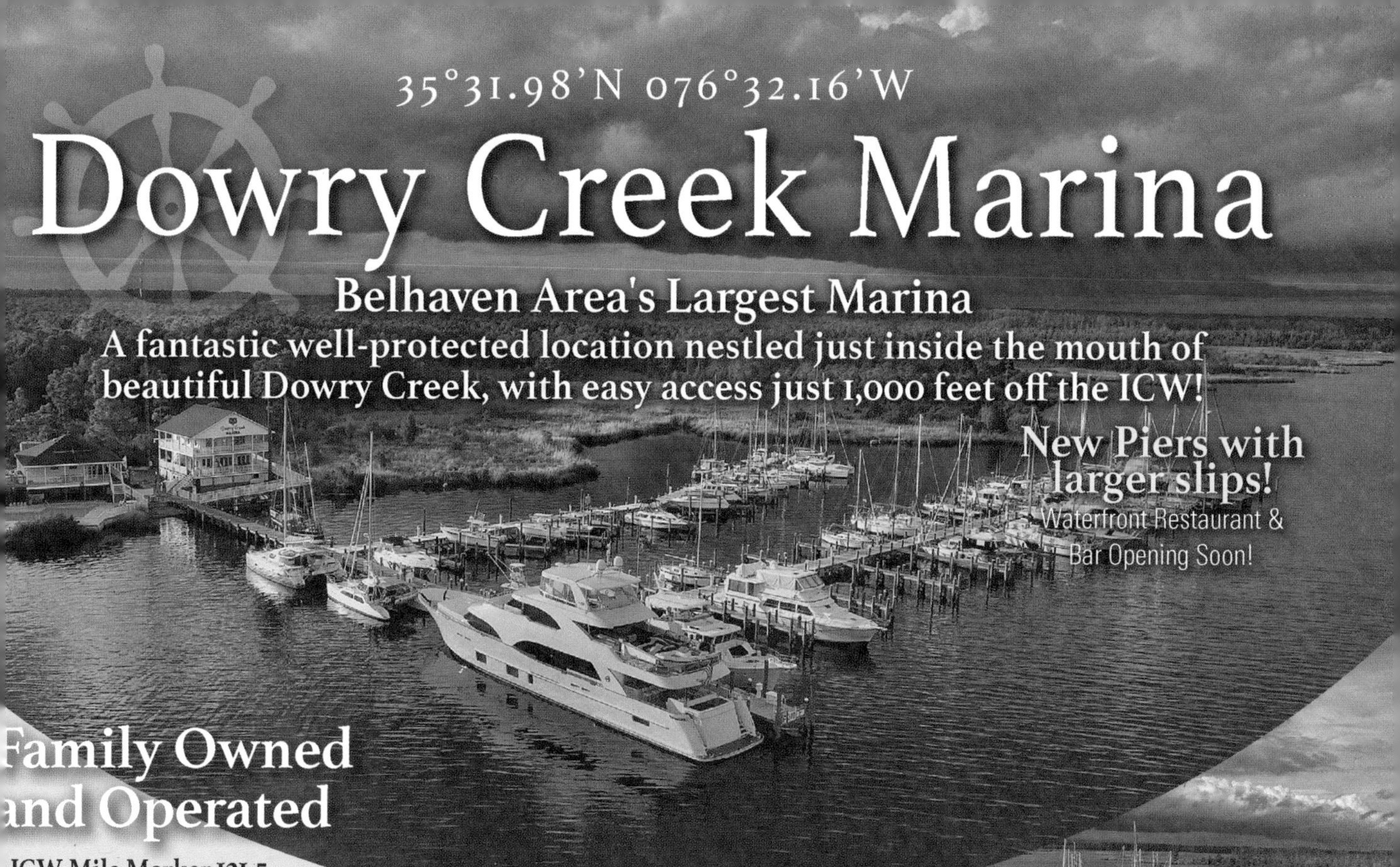

Belhaven Area's Largest Marina

A fantastic well-protected location nestled just inside the mouth of beautiful Dowry Creek, with easy access just 1,000 feet off the ICW!

New Piers with larger slips!

Waterfront Restaurant & Bar Opening Soon!

Family Owned and Operated

- ICW Mile Marker 131.5 Three miles north of Belhaven
- Bear 350° at Pungo River G "15" to proceed through our well-marked and lighted 9' deep channel
- Last stop heading north entering - and first stop heading south - exiting the 22-mile Alligator River Canal
- Gas & High Speed Diesel - great pricing & volume discounts - fuel dock holds boats up to 125 ft with 8 ft draft - late night fueling available w/advance notice
- Large clean air-conditioned showers and bathrooms
- Free Laundry and WiFi throughout
- Expanded & well-stocked ship store - food, snacks, drinks, beer, wine, ice, and LP Tank Refill Station open 7 days a week
- Loaner Cars & Complimentary Local Shuttle available; longer-distance rides available for a fee

Open Dawn to Dusk

Available 24/7 for late arrivals with dock staff to assist

Special Rates for Weekly, Monthly & Annual Slip Rentals

Heated saltwater swimming pool available free for boater use!

DOWRY CREEK MARINA

110 Spinnaker Run Road, Belhaven, NC 27810

Your Hosts

Steve, Connie, Teresa, Nicole & Zac Zeltner

E-mail: DowryCreek@gmail.com

www.dowrycreekmarina.com • 252-943-2728

Pungo River, NC

BELHAVEN		Largest Vessel	VHF	Total Slips	Approach/ Dockside Depth	Floating Docks	Gas/ Diesel	Repairs/ Haulout	Min/Max Amps	Pump-Out Station
1. TJ's Marina & Boatyard WiFi	(252) 943-3333			40	6.5 / 6.5			RH	30 / 50	P
2. River Forest Boatyard/Shipyard WiFi 1.6 mi. W of MM 136.0	(252) 943-2151	65	16		8.0 / 8.0			RH	15 / 50	P
3. River Forest Manor and Marina WiFi MM 136.0	**(252) 943-0030**	**140**	**16**	**31**	**9.0 / 9.0**		**GD**	**R**	**30 / 100**	**P**
4. Belhaven Marina WiFi 0.25 mi. W of MM 136.0	(252) 944-0066	150	16	23	9.0 / 9.0		GD	R	30 / 50	
5. Belhaven Town Docks At Wynne's Gut WiFi MM 136.0	(252) 944-0066		16	5	7.0 / 6.0				30	P
6. Belhaven Cooperage Town Docks MM 135.5	(252) 944-0066	50		8	7.0 / 6.0					

WiFi Wireless Internet Access **onSpot** Dockside WiFi Facility
Visit www.waterwayguide.com for current rates, fuel prices, website addresses and other up-to-the-minute information.
(Information in the table is provided by the facilities.)

Scan here for more details:

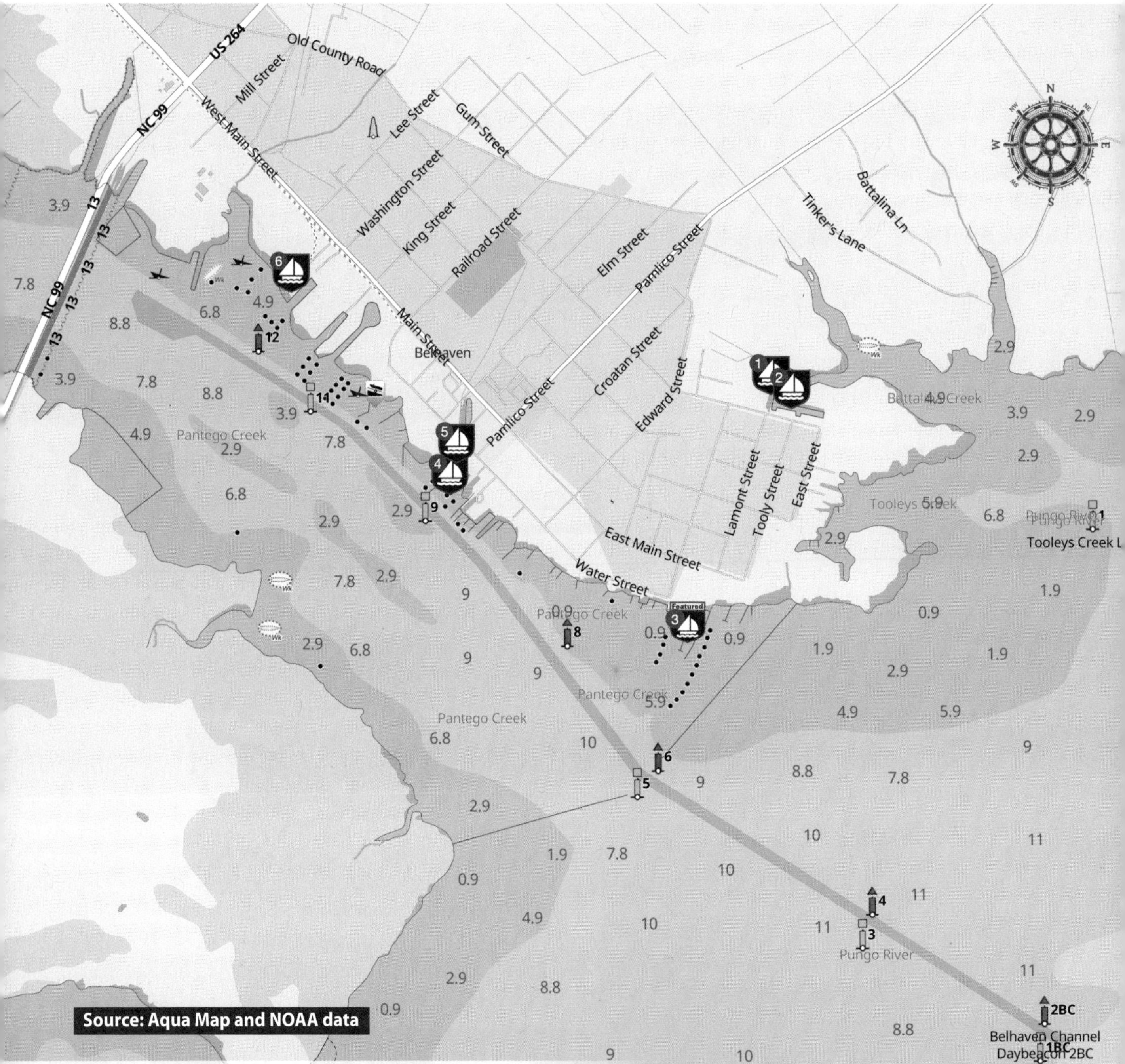

Pungo River, NC

PUNGO CREEK		Largest Vessel	VHF	Total Slips	Approach/ Dockside Depth	Floating Docks	Gas/ Diesel	Repairs/ Haulout	Min/Max Amps	Pump-Out Station
1. Pungo Creek Marina WiFi MM 135.0	(252) 964-3777	110	16	48	10.0 / 10.0		GD		30 / 50	

WiFi Wireless Internet Access onSpot Dockside WiFi Facility
Visit www.waterwayguide.com for current rates, fuel prices, website addresses and other up-to-the-minute information.
(Information in the table is provided by the facilities.)

Scan here for more details:

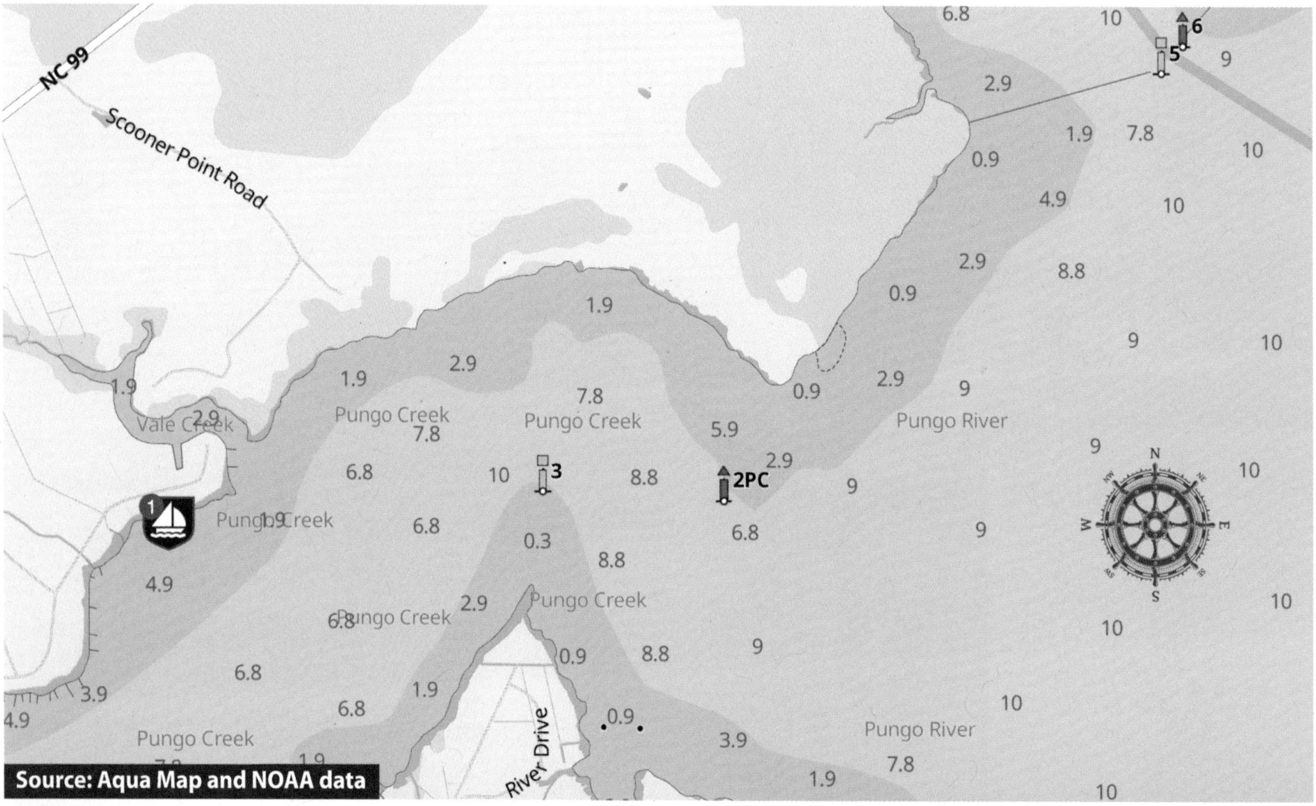

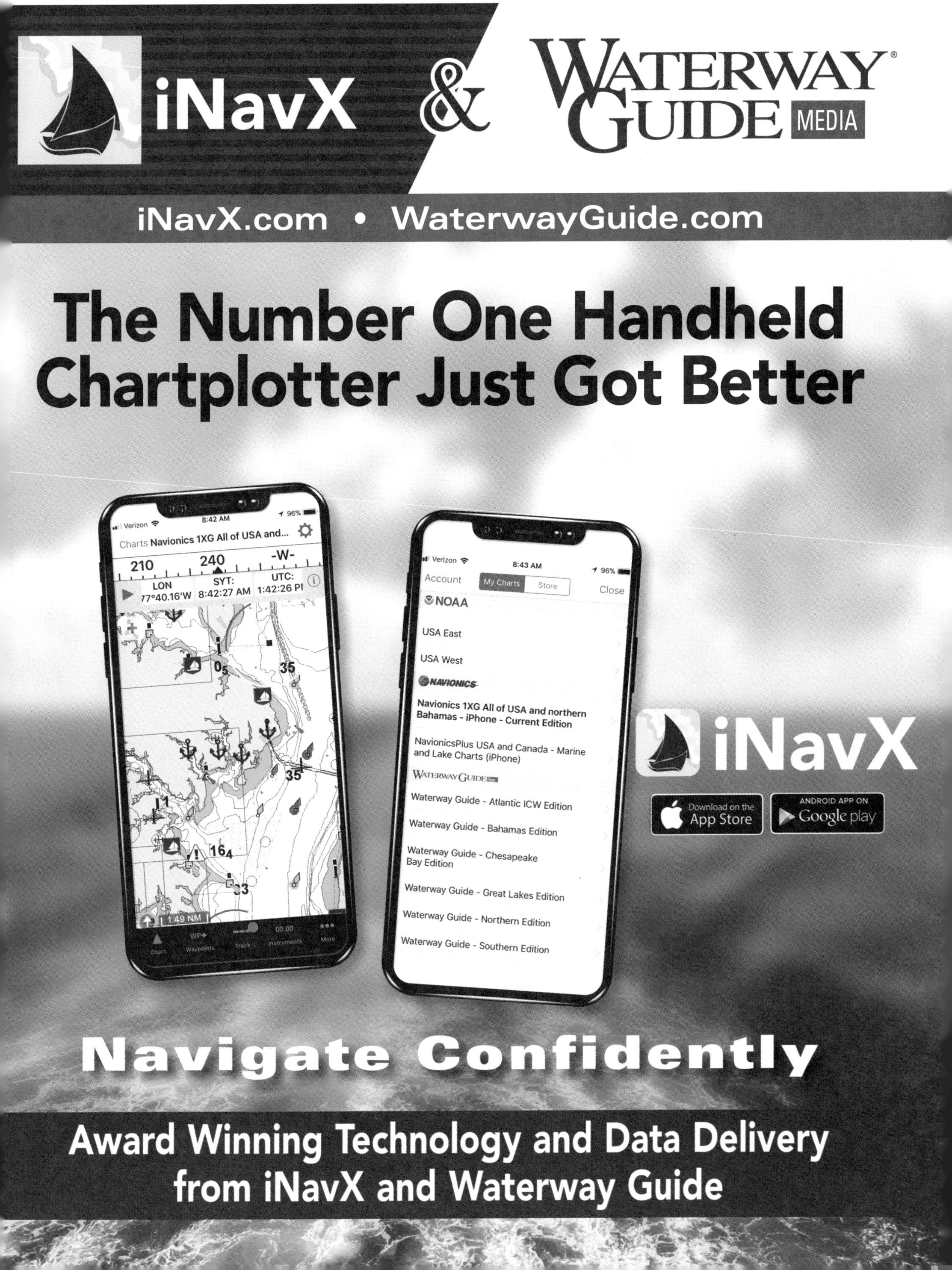
iNavX
&
WATERWAY GUIDE MEDIA
iNavX.com • WaterwayGuide.com
The Number One Handheld Chartplotter Just Got Better
Charts Navionics 1XG All of USA and...
NOAA
USA East
USA West
NAVIONICS
Navionics 1XG All of USA and northern Bahamas - iPhone - Current Edition
NavionicsPlus USA and Canada - Marine and Lake Charts (iPhone)
Waterway Guide - Atlantic ICW Edition
Waterway Guide - Bahamas Edition
Waterway Guide - Chesapeake Bay Edition
Waterway Guide - Great Lakes Edition
Waterway Guide - Northern Edition
Waterway Guide - Southern Edition
iNavX
Download on the App Store
ANDROID APP ON Google play
Navigate Confidently
Award Winning Technology and Data Delivery from iNavX and Waterway Guide

GOIN' ASHORE

BELHAVEN, NC

When Daniel Latham built a hunting and fishing camp in 1868 on what is now the River Forest Manor, Jack's Neck was little more than a small settlement inhabited by a few farmers and fishermen. In time, the town changed its name to Belhaven and with the addition of a rail spur from the Norfolk and Southern Railroad, and the port's location near the Pamlico Sound, the town became a vital transportation artery for the distribution of goods throughout eastern North Carolina. Today, the town's businesses mainly serve the surrounding farming communities, the local residents and tourists. Many of the grand homes built in the late 1800s and early 1900s remain standing today, the largest of which is River Forest Manor (circa 1904), which was recently renovated.

SERVICES

1. Belhaven Chamber of Commerce
293 E. Water St., Ste. 202
(252-943-3770)

2. Belhaven Post Office
614 W. Old Country Rd.
(252-943-2364)

3. Belhaven Public Library
333 E. Main St. (252-943-2993)

4. Vidant Multispecialty Clinic–Belhaven
598 W. Old County Rd.
(252-943-0600)

ATTRACTIONS

5. Belhaven Mainstreet Landing
Free Blue Grass, Country, Gospel and Rock & Roll jams every Tuesday (6:30 to 8:30 p.m.). Bring an instrument or just come and enjoy the music. Traveling musicians welcome (226 Main St., 252-945-7028).

6. Riddick & Windley Hardware
Old-fashioned hardware store carrying just about everything, including great wine selection, ice and a nice selection of stainless fasteners for marine use (235 Pamlico St., 252-943-2205).

SHOPPING

7. Sarah's of Belhaven
Large selection of hand-painted gifts and collectibles, most with nautical theme at 265 Main St. (828-708-0600).

MARINAS

8. Belhaven Marina
332 E. Water St. (252-944-0066)

9. Belhaven Town Docks at Wynne's Gut
268 E. Water St. (252-944-0066)

10. River Forest Boatyard/Shipyard
843 E. Pantego St. (252-945-5579)

11. River Forest Manor and Marina
738 E. Main St. (252-943-0320)

Belhaven, NC: Birthplace of the ICW

Poised on the estuary of the Pamlico Sound up the Pungo River at the mouth of Pantego Creek, Belhaven is a delightful destination for day boaters and cruisers who will find small town hospitality and history throughout the treelined streets and waterfront marinas.

In September 1928, the Alligator River–Pungo River Canal was completed and opened. This was the last remaining link to complete the 1,090-mile Atlantic Intracoastal Waterway from Norfolk to Miami. 20,000 people descended on the tiny town of Belhaven for the dedication ceremonies. The Navy sent two seaplanes, the Coast Guard dispatched several cutters and the Army hovered a blimp to join officials from Washington, DC, who were present for the festivities. On the 75th anniversary of the canal's completion in 2013, Belhaven was designated "The Birthplace of the ICW" by the Atlantic Intracoastal Waterway Association. The town celebrates this distinction and the waterway's completion with an annual ICW Celebration that includes a chowder tasting, street festival, flotilla with antique boats and traditional Blessing of the Boats ceremony.

Belhaven's restaurants and businesses have garnered great reviews from cruisers and visitors who appreciate the ambience and character of the small North Carolina town. A landmark that has stood for over a century is the River Forest Manor & Marina. Commissioned in 1899 by John Aaron Wilkinson, president of the J.L. Roper Lumber Company and vice president of Norfolk and Southern Railroad, the River Forest Manor & Marina has undergone extensive restoration to showcase its original beauty and splendor.

Once a must-visit destination for celebrities, politicos and wealthy stakeholders including American actor and dancer James Cagney, businessman Harvey Firestone and British model Twiggy, the River Forest Manor & Marina fell into disrepair and closed in 2011. It was purchased in 2014 by a group of visionary Belhaven residents and investors intent on transforming the property back to a grand mansion for entertaining, hosting lavish parties and welcoming visitors from all over the world.

Consider a visit to Belhaven, whether by boat or by land. The beautiful harbor town, local marinas and River Forest Manor & Marina are off the beaten path but well worth exploring.

Marina (252-944-0066). He will come to you or you can go to him. There is a maximum 72-hour stay.

Also owned by the town is Belhaven Cooperage Town Docks, just past red daybeacon "12" on Pantego Creek. The fixed docks (no water or electrical service) are available on a first-come, first-served basis with a maximum stay of 72 hours.

Pungo Creek Marina to the south at Mile 135 offers transient slips. This quiet marina also offers canoes for rent, great fishing, picnic tables and a BBQ. Steer between red daybeacon "2PC" and flashing green "3" and then run southwest of Windmill Point. Crab pot buoys are scattered throughout the creek; work your way in carefully.

Anchorage: When the wind is up the best protection in the area can be found in the headwaters of the Pungo River, just north of the lower end of the Alligator River-Pungo River Canal in 7 to 10 feet MLW among crab pots. Anchor north of flashing green "23" (Mile 127.3). Minding the depth sounder you can pick your way for some distance into the river. The bottom is uneven, soft and given to hump-like shoals even in what is ostensibly the center channel. It may be difficult at first to get the anchor to set but it will usually dig in tightly by backing down. This anchorage gets high marks for its protection and there is a sandy beach for shore access for the dog. This is a large anchorage area with space for many boats so spread out upriver if the first cove is crowded.

Scranton Creek on the south side of the Pungo River at Mile 129.5 has good holding in mud in 8 to 10 feet MLW. It is exposed to the west. Local knowledge advises that you stay in the middle of the creek due to sunken pilings beneath the surface along both sides.

Satterthwaite Point at Mile 130 has good holding. The views are nice and you are unlikely to ever have anyone anchor on top of you. Northbound and westbound tugs can be disconcerting until you adjust to them bearing down on you before making the turn in the ICW. Wakes are not an issue as they dissipate before reaching anchored boats.

Another anchorage is available across the river in the center of Upper Dowry Creek (Mile 131.6), north of Dowry Creek Marina. The creek carries 5- to 6-foot MLW depths for about a 0.25 mile north of the mouth. Secure holding in clay and a short fetch make this

location a favorite retreat for local skippers when even the most severe storms approach. You can arrange for facilities use with Dowry Creek Marina for a modest daily fee. Several smaller side creeks along the Pungo River have adequate depths for anchoring shallow-drafted boats.

Once inside the storm barrier at Belhaven you can anchor northwest of the channel in Pantego Creek in 7- to 9-foot MLW depths with fair holding. This is a popular spot despite considerable wave action when the wind picks up, as it often does in the afternoon. This is not a good anchorage in wind from any southerly quadrant. Care should be taken to avoid a shoal in front of the (closed) hospital.

To access the dinghy landing follow Wynn's Gut past Belhaven Town Docks At Wynne's Gut and under the Water Street Bridge (7-foot fixed vertical clearance, depending on tide). The Belhaven Mainstreet Landing is to starboard with 130 feet of dockage suited for dinghies or small powerboats visiting downtown sites.

Pungo Creek (behind Windmill Point) and Jordan Creek have anchoring potential. Jordan Creek is 5 miles south of Pungo Creek and to the south and east of the flashing red "4" at Mile 140. The entrance is marked but has a bar and should not be attempted without local knowledge if you draw more than 5 feet. (You will see large sailboats inside.) Favor the green side of the channel. Jordan Creek offers protection from all but strong easterly winds. Good holding can be found in main bowl or to north at the fork.

SIDE RIVER: PAMLICO RIVER

Sixty-five miles (via the ICW) south of Albemarle Sound lays the northwestern prong of Pamlico Sound, which reaches up to meet the Pamlico River. The Pamlico River is wide and easily navigable to Washington, NC, where the Pamlico River becomes the Tar River. This wide, beautiful river is lined with wooded banks and one industrial site–a phosphate mine on the south side of the river a little more than 10 miles from the ICW.

NAVIGATION: Use NOAA Charts 11553 and 11554. If you are southbound, the entrance to the Pamlico River from the ICW is around the junction flashing red (2+1) "PR" (Mile 146) marking the shoal off Wades Point at the mouth of the Pungo River. Do not attempt to cut inside the marker unless you are very familiar with the area. Take care not to hit the unmarked, unlighted Mile 145 marker on the east side of the Pungo River prior to Wades Point.

The Pamlico River ferry runs year-round between Aurora and Bayview. Keep your eyes open and stay out of its way.

South Creek

South Creek lies just west of the small charted Indian Island on the south shore of the Pamlico River. Deep and well marked all the way to the town of Aurora, this is an excellent creek for exploration or anchorage, but be aware that there are no facilities for transient boaters. Dinghies can tie to the former town docks, which are now leased by North Carolina Fish and Wildlife.

Downtown Aurora is about three blocks from the waterfront. The Aurora Fossil Museum (400 Main St., 252-322-4238) located near the head of South Creek off the Pamlico River is well worth a visit. It houses a collection of shark teeth, whalebones and other fossils. Visitors can sift through fossil bed soil (compliments of the nearby phosphate mine) and find their own souvenir shark teeth, free of charge.

NAVIGATION: Use NOAA Chart 11554. When approaching Aurora the channel narrows and depths shoal to 5 to 7 feet MLW. Follow the daybeacons carefully and save any shallow-water exploration for your dinghy.

Anchorage: South Creek offers numerous anchorage possibilities off of the well-marked channel but has no protection from the east or west. Nearby Bond Creek to the south (at the town of South Creek) has good holding in soft mud with 7 to 9 feet MLW.

Bath Creek

The waterfront at the little historic town of Bath on the north shore of the Pamlico River is well worth a visit, especially if you are a history buff. Founded in 1696 and established in 1705 it is listed as the oldest town in North Carolina. Bath's most notorious citizen was Edward Teach, also known as Blackbeard (the pirate). Standing in front of the historic Bonner House and looking south across the bay it is easy to see why Blackbeard selected Bath and Plum Point as his base of operation:

Pamlico River, NC

BATH CREEK		Largest Vessel	VHF	Total Slips	Approach/ Dockside Depth	Floating Docks	Gas/ Diesel	Repairs/ Haulout	Min/Max Amps	Pump-Out Station
1. Bath Harbor Marina (WiFi)	(252) 923-5711	60	16	43	6.0 / 8.0				30 / 50	

(WiFi) Wireless Internet Access (onSpot) Dockside WiFi Facility
Visit www.waterwayguide.com for current rates, fuel prices, website addresses and other up-to-the-minute information.
(Information in the table is provided by the facilities.)

Scan here for more details:

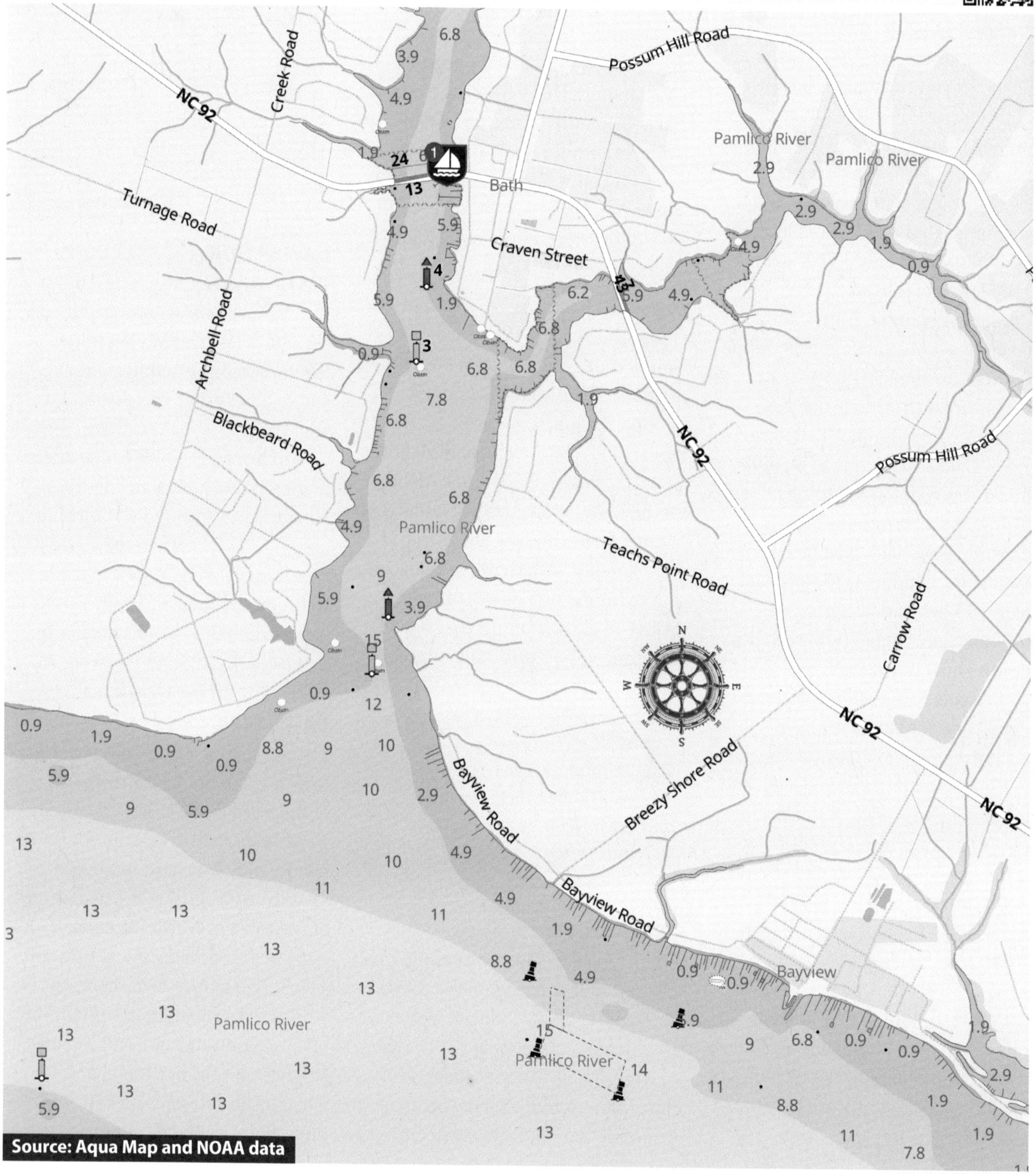

Source: Aqua Map and NOAA data

Pamlico River

privacy. That much has not changed. You can find information about Blackbeard and Bath at the Historic Bath Visitor Center (252-923-3971) between Main St. and Harding St. just one block from the water.

NAVIGATION: Use NOAA Chart 11554. You can set a northerly course into Bath Creek beyond the ferry crossing and 3 miles northwest of flashing red "4" off Gum Point. Avoid the fish stakes at the entrance and be wary of any possible submerged pilings after clearing flashing green "1" at the entrance. The harbor is easy to enter if you mind the NOAA chart and watch out for the crab pots around flashing green "1" and red daybeacon "2" (Plum and Archbell Points).

Dockage: Pass green daybeacon "3" and flashing red "4" to reach dockage at Bath Harbor Marina just to the south of the **NC 92 (Bath Creek) Bridge** (13-foot fixed vertical clearance) and have at least 6-foot MLW approach depths. (Bridge clearance has been observed to be closer to 14.5 feet.)

To starboard just before the bridge Bath Harbor Marina has slips for vessels to 60 feet and hotel rooms to rent. There are no utilities at the state dock but dockage is complimentary for 72 hours. You will need to fill out a free permit application at the Historic Bath Visitor Center.

Anchorage: Back Creek (to starboard off Bath Creek) provides a protected anchorage with good holding and depths of 6 to 7 feet MLW up to the fixed **NC 92 (Back Creek) Bridge** (7-foot vertical clearance). Ice cream, cold beer and a casual grill (burgers, hot dogs, shrimp burger) are at Quarterdeck Marina by the bridge. Gas is also available for shallow-draft boats.

You can drop the hook inside Archbell and Plum Pt. on the east and west sides of the creek at the mouth. Expect 4- to 6-foot MLW depths and pull in far enough to be out of the way of any passing traffic.

Pamlico River, NC

BROAD CREEK		Largest Vessel	VHF	Total Slips	Approach/ Dockside Depth	Floating Docks	Gas/ Diesel	Repairs/ Haulout	Min/Max Amps	Pump-Out Station
1. Broad Creek Marina	(252) 946-4924	38		100	4.0 / 4.0				30	P
2. McCotters Marina & Boatyard WiFi **20.7 mi. W of MM 146.0**	**(252) 975-2174**	**65**	**16**	**180**	**6.0 / 6.0**			**RH**	**30 / 50**	**P**
3. Washington Yacht & Country Club WiFi	(252) 402-5153	55		177	6.0 / 6.0		GD		30 / 50	P

WiFi Wireless Internet Access onSpot Dockside WiFi Facility
Visit www.waterwayguide.com for current rates, fuel prices, website addresses and other up-to-the-minute information.
(Information in the table is provided by the facilities.)

Scan here for more details:

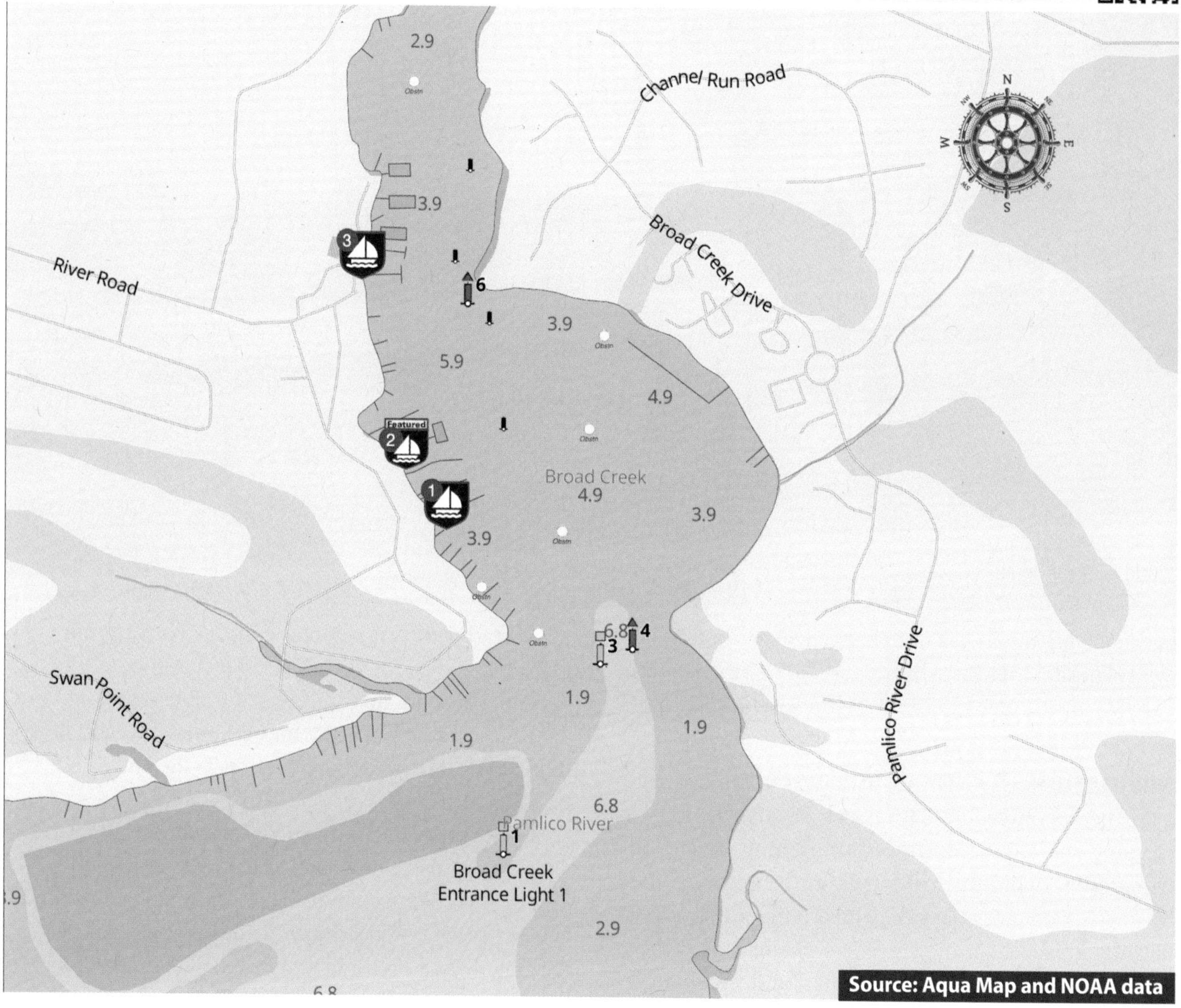

Broad Creek

Broad Creek is 7 miles to the west of Bath. Several hundred sail and powerboats make Broad Creek their home port and it is the main boating center for Washington located 7 miles farther to the north-northwest.

NAVIGATION: Use NOAA Chart 11554. Broad Creek's entrance is well marked and easy to negotiate from the east. Steer in a northwesterly direction from flashing green "7" (in the main Pamlico River channel off Maules Point) until flashing green "1" is visible north of the main channel and then follow the channel to green daybeacon "3" and flashing red "4." Note the spoil areas south of the entrance. If coming from the west steer east past the red daybeacon "8" before turning north then turn northwest once on a line between flashing green "7" in the main channel and flashing green "1" in the Broad Creek channel. There is no room for anchoring here.

Dockage: To starboard you will see the Pamlico Plantation private docks (no transient dockage). To port are Broad Creek Marina and McCotters Marina & Boatyard. Broad Creek Marina is a small-boat marina with 4-foot approach and dockside depths that can accommodate boats to 38 feet.

Locally-owned and operated McCotters Marina & Boatyard has haul-out facilities and can handle repairs and upgrades, storage and boat sales. Their canvas department can fabricate custom dodgers, biminis, enclosures, awnings and sail covers, plus restore upholstery and cushions. They may have a transient slip for you; call ahead.

Washington Yacht & Country Club is beyond red daybeacon "6." (Give the marker good clearance.) The over 50-year-old club offers transient dockage and amenities to members of reciprocating clubs. The club features a championship 18-hole golf course, fine dining and tennis courts.

Washington

This small community of just under 10,000 residents has a maritime culture all its own with dozens of colorful crab statues lining the downtown streets, hundreds of boats–both big and small–lining the waterfront and miles of open Tar and Pamlico River views extending in virtually every direction. Here you will find a sprawling waterfront with stores, businesses and the historic haunts of pirates. Read more about Washington at "Goin' Ashore: Washington, NC" in this chapter.

NAVIGATION: Use NOAA Chart 11554. The NOAA chart shows plenty of water in the Pamlico River even outside the channel until flashing red "14." From here markers "16," "17," "18" and "19" lead to the

Pamlico River, NC

CHOCOWINITY BAY		Largest Vessel	VHF	Total Slips	Approach/ Dockside Depth	Floating Docks	Gas/ Diesel	Repairs/ Haulout	Min/Max Amps	Pump-Out Station
1. Cypress Landing Marina-PRIVATE (WiFi)	(252) 975-3955	42	16	222	7.0 / 6.0	F			30 / 50	P
WASHINGTON										
2. Moss Landing Marina (WiFi)	(252) 623-1314	60	16	52	10.0 / 15.0	F			30 / 50	P
3. Washington Waterfront Docks (WiFi)	(252) 940-1231	80	16	36	14.0 / 18.0				30 / 50	P

(WiFi) Wireless Internet Access onSpot Dockside WiFi Facility
Visit www.waterwayguide.com for current rates, fuel prices, website addresses and other up-to-the-minute information.
(Information in the table is provided by the facilities.)

Scan here for more details:

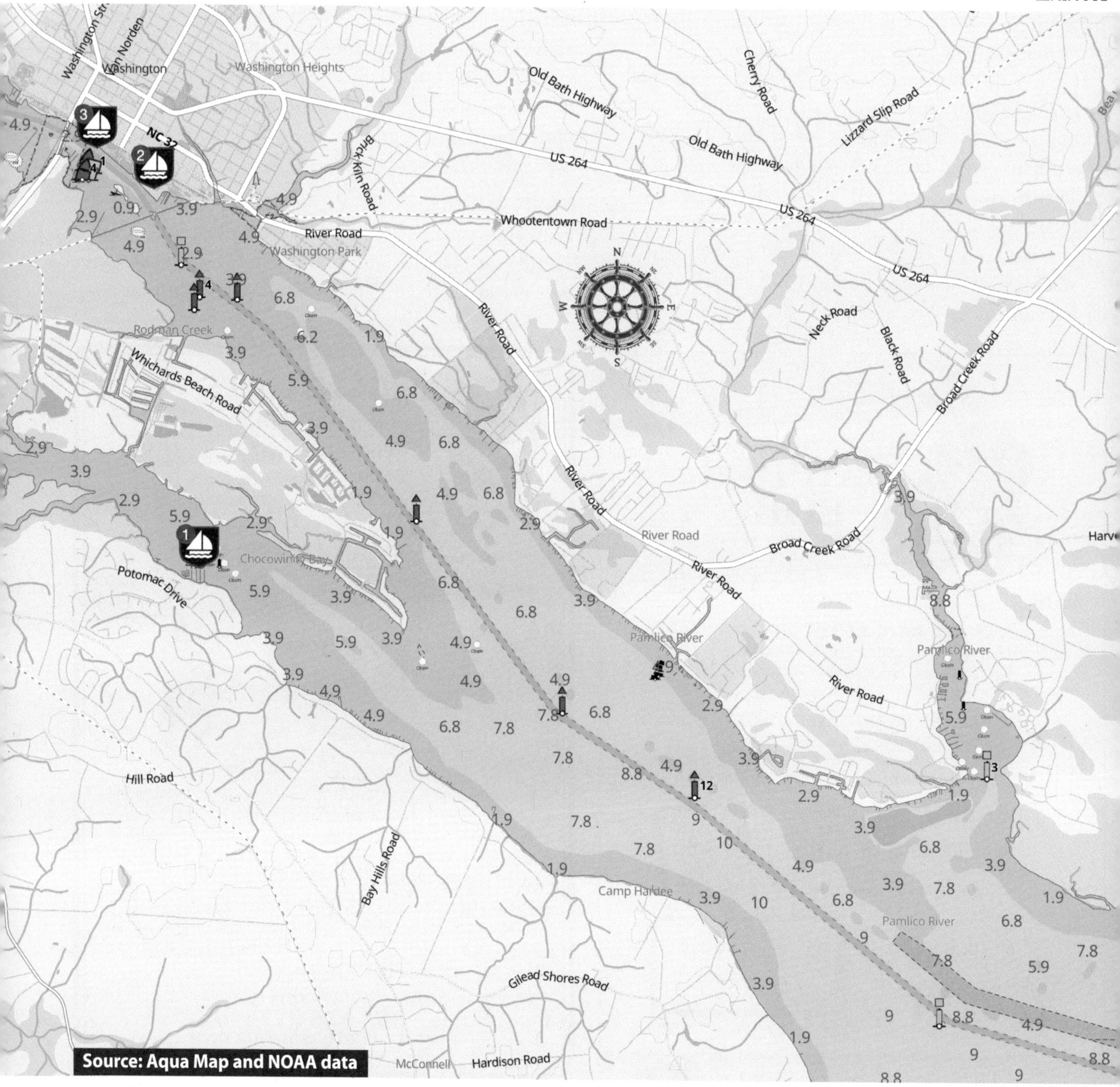

Source: Aqua Map and NOAA data

Norfolk Southern Railroad Bridge. The bridge has 7-foot closed vertical clearance and is usually open; however, it may be closed between 7:30 a.m. and 10:30 a.m. on weekdays and Saturday. Past the Norfolk Southern Railroad Bridge is the Washington riverfront located to starboard before the **U.S. 17 Business Bridge** (6-foot closed vertical clearance), which will open with 24-hour notice. US 17 Business Bridge marks the confluence of the Pamlico River and the Tar River and the river actually changes names at this point. When approaching the town keep Castle Island to port and stay within the 9-foot MLW channel.

Dockage: Moss Landing Marina is part of an upscale condo complex. They offer deeded slips in a gated facility but may be able to accommodate you; call ahead. Transient slips with electricity, water and WiFi are available at Washington Waterfront Docks. Reservations are accepted. The lighthouse building has climate-controlled heads and showers and a laundry (fee charged). Short-term docking also is available for $10.00 for up to six hours. Free dockage may be available for up to 48 hours along bulkheads on the east end of the waterfront. Water and electricity are not available. A fee is charged for stays longer than 48 hours. Cypress Landing Marina to the south at Chocowinity Bay is private.

Anchorage: Boats anchor off the waterfront bulkheads in Washington when slips are full but there is no protection here; it is completely open to wind and wakes. Be sure to stay out of the channel. A floating dinghy dock is located at the west end of the waterfront near the lighthouse building. Boats anchored in the harbor may use the dinghy dock and the heads and showers once registered with the Washington Waterfront Docks attendant.

Blackbeard the Pirate

You will find many references to Edward Teach (also known as Blackbeard) in this guide. The Pamlico Sound and River were his home waters and the scene of much of his pirating on his flagship, the *Queen Anne's Revenge*.

Supposedly born in Bristol, England, Teach had friends in high places, was quite the lady's man (with as many as seven wives) and had great successes as a pirate. He became a renowned pirate, known for his thick black beard and fearsome appearance; it was reported that he tied lit fuses under his hat and into his beard to frighten his enemies.

Blackbeard's pirate forces terrorized the Caribbean and the southern coast of North America and were notorious for their cruelty. Sometime in June 1718, Blackbeard and at least 20 members of his crew passed through Ocracoke Inlet, NC, entered Pamlico Sound and headed for the town of Bath on the Pamlico River. There he met with Governor Charles Eden who agreed to pardon Blackbeard on behalf of England in exchange for a share of his sizable booty and a promise that he would stop pirating.

When Teach began pirating again, Governor Alexander Spotswood of Virginia dispatched a British naval force under Lieutenant Robert Maynard to North Carolina to deal with Blackbeard. On November 22, Blackbeard's forces were defeated, and he was killed in a bloody battle of Ocracoke Island. Rumor has it that his treasure is buried at Springers Point on Ocracoke. This is now a National Park Service Preserve, so you need not bring your metal detector or shovel.

GOIN' ASHORE

WASHINGTON, NC

First called Forks of the Tar, the city name was changed in 1776 in honor of Gen. George Washington. Because it was America's first city to be named for Gen. Washington, it is sometimes referred to as "The Original Washington" or "Little Washington" to avoid confusion. The entire waterfront of Washington is listed in the National Register of Historic Places.

SERVICES

1. **Brown Library**
   122 Van Norden St. (252-946-4300)
2. **Washington-Beaufort Chamber of Commerce**
   102 W. Stewart Pkwy. (252-946-9168)
3. **Washington Post Office**
   222 W. 2nd St. (252-946-0128)

ATTRACTIONS

4. **North Carolina Estuarium**
   Aquarium with unique exhibits about the Pamlico-Tar River System featuring over 200 exhibits, living aquariums and a gift shop (223 E. Water St., 252-948-0000). Special programs throughout the year. River tours of the estuary (seasonal) require reservations.
5. **Washington Waterfront Underground Railroad Museum**
   Explores slavery, the function of the underground railroad in the local area and escapes to freedom from the Washington waterfront and overland routes. Part of National Park Service Underground Railroad-Network To Freedom. Located on the corner of Gladden St. and W. Main St. (252-833-0995).

SHOPPING

6. Nauti Life
Offers home and boat decor plus clothing and accessories (112 W. Main St., 252-940-1986).

7. River Walk Gallery
Gallery with a variety of fine art and high quality craft from local artists including jewelry, ceramics, metal work, paintings and fabric arts. Also hosts classes and events at 139 E. Main St. (252-974-0400).

8. Washington Wine and Gourmet
This is a provisioning possibility with wine, craft beer, gourmet food, cheese and vinegars and olive oil at 220 W. Main St. (252-974-2870).

9. West Marine
Chain store specializing in boating accessories and parts at 330 Bridge St. (252-975-6688).

MARINAS

10. Moss Landing Marina
227 E. Water St. (252-944-3045)

11. Washington Waterfront Docks
301 W. Stewart Pkwy. (252-940-1231)

TO THE NEUSE RIVER

Pamlico River Crossing–ICW Mile 145 to Mile 165

The ICW follows the broad lower reach of the Pungo River to the junction of the Pamlico River. (Markers are still reversed, green to starboard going south; continue running the yellow squares and triangles.) The markers in the lower Pungo River are spaced far apart and sometimes difficult to locate but the river is wide and adequately deep.

NAVIGATION: Use NOAA Charts 11553, 11554 and 11548. The Pamlico River crossing is straight and is usually an easy run; however, conflicting currents meet at the junction of the Pungo and Pamlico Rivers. When easterly or westerly winds are strong and gusty the crossing of the Pamlico River can be rough and wet. Confused seas are common, especially within a mile or so of Wades Point flashing red "PR," which is located around Mile 145.7. Watch for flashing red (2+1) 18-foot light with red over green triangular boards on three sides (all marked "PR") on a multi-pile structure. It can be difficult to locate, especially if northbound from Goose Creek.

After crossing the Pamlico River to Goose Creek, aids to navigation return to the ICW configuration of red-to-starboard running south. This is especially important when entering Goose Creek, where red daybeacon "4" marks the southeastern edge of a 3-foot MLW shoal and submerged piles. There is also shoaling between green daybeacons "5" and "7" so be sure to stay in the middle of the channel.

At Mile 157.2 the area surrounding the **Hobucken (NC 33/304) Bridge** and the Coast Guard Station is a No-Wake Zone. The bridge is concrete and the underside arches slightly towards the center. There are no bridge boards. The bridge is charted at 65-foot fixed vertical clearance but is closer to 64 feet at mean high water. There can be a considerable wind-driven current here.

At about Mile 159 the land cut (canal) ends at Gale Creek, an arm of the Bay River. Use caution in transiting Gale Creek, which is naturally winding though the channel is charted as arrow-straight.

Neuse River, NC

HOBUCKEN		Largest Vessel	VHF	Total Slips	Approach/ Dockside Depth	Floating Docks	Gas/ Diesel	Repairs/ Haulout	Min/Max Amps	Pump-Out Station
1. R. E. Mayo Seafood Marine Supply 157.3	(252) 745-5331	90	16		12.0 / 6.0		GD		30	

WiFi Wireless Internet Access onSpot Dockside WiFi Facility
Visit www.waterwayguide.com for current rates, fuel prices, website addresses and other up-to-the-minute information.
(Information in the table is provided by the facilities.)

Scan here for more details:

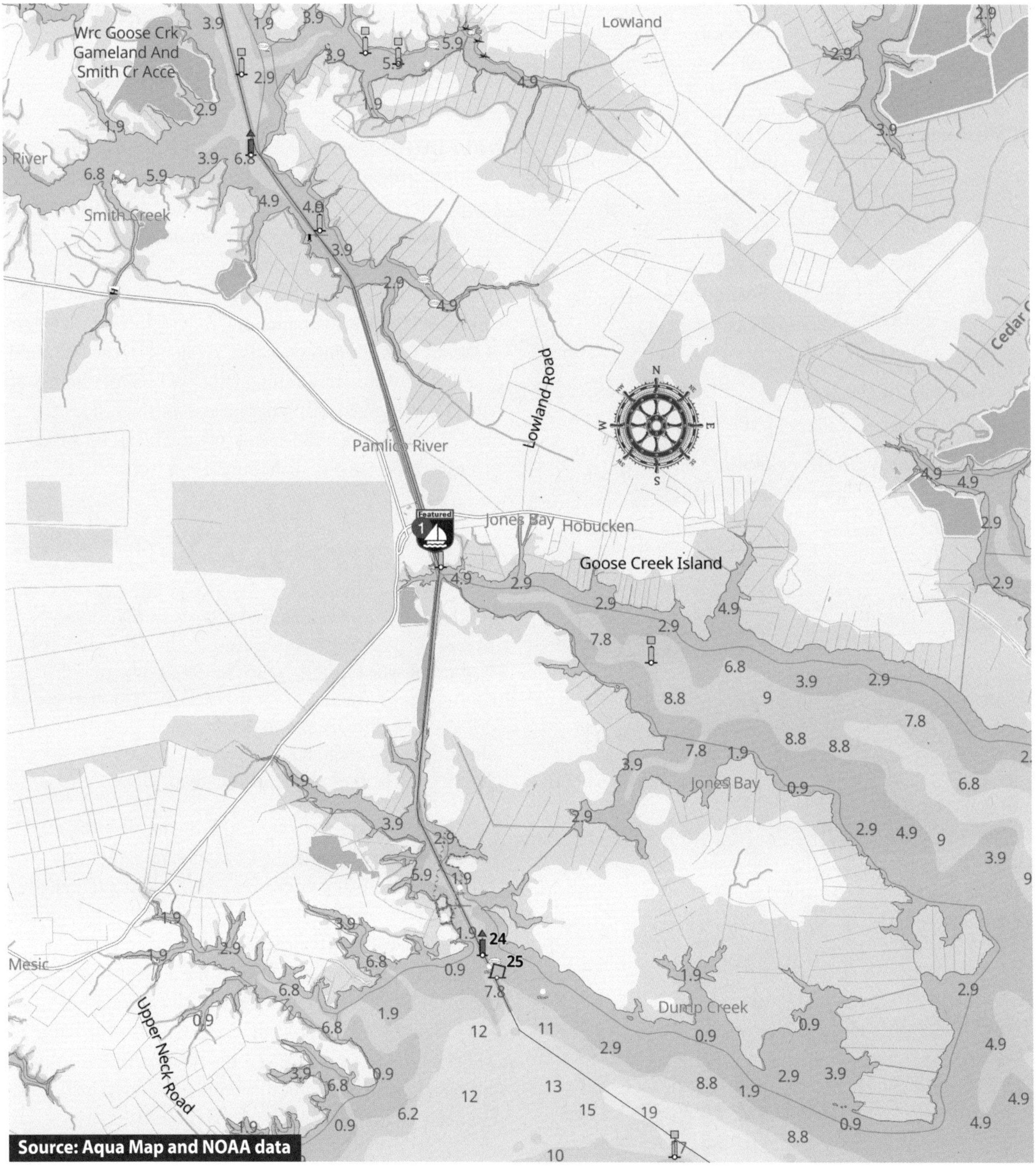

Source: Aqua Map and NOAA data

Neuse River, NC

BAYBORO		Largest Vessel	VHF	Total Slips	Approach/ Dockside Depth	Floating Docks	Gas/ Diesel	Repairs/ Haulout	Min/Max Amps	Pump-Out Station
1. Hurricane Boatyard WiFi	(252) 745-3369	60		17	8.0 / 6.5	F		RH	30	P

WiFi Wireless Internet Access onSpot Dockside WiFi Facility
Visit www.waterwayguide.com for current rates, fuel prices, website addresses and other up-to-the-minute information.
(Information in the table is provided by the facilities.)

Scan here for more details:

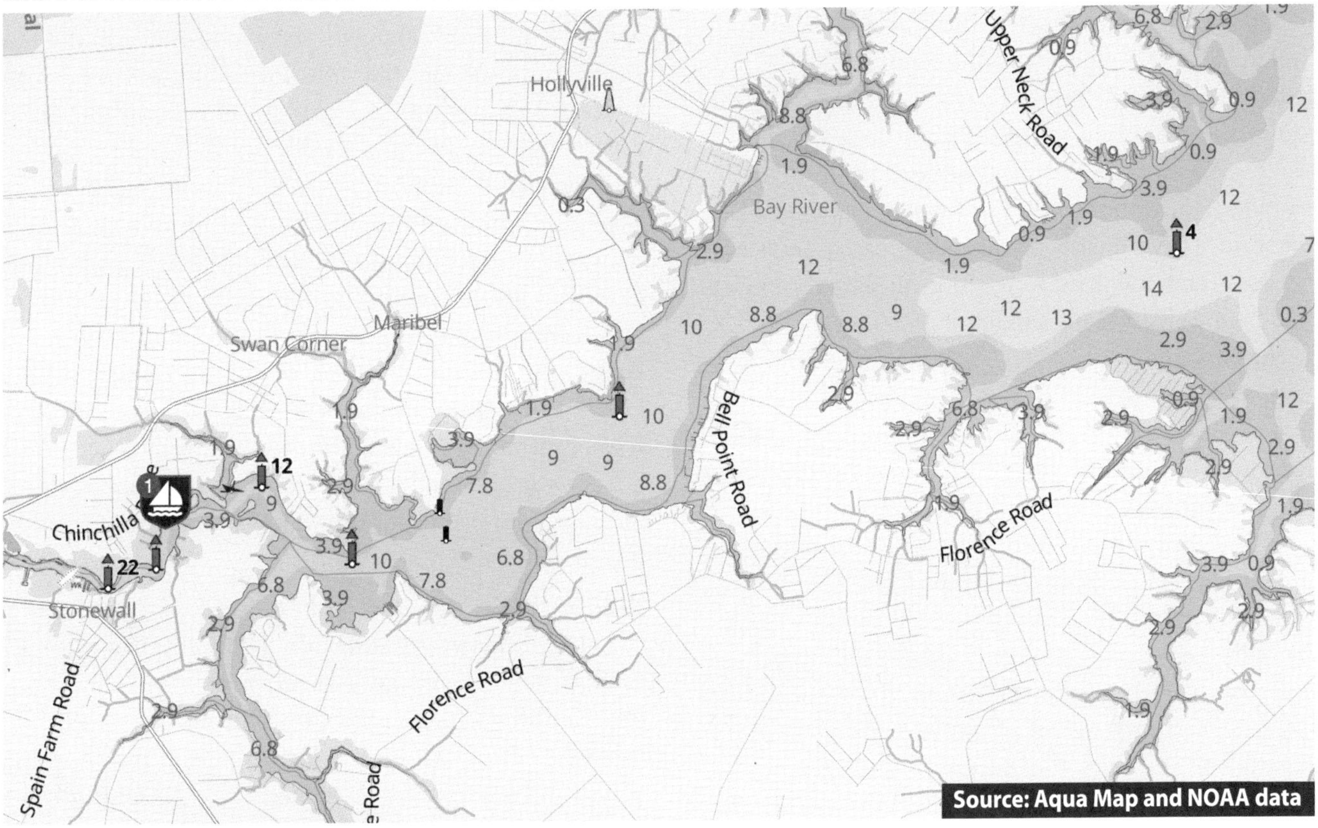

Shoaling is encroaching on the channel on the red (west) side of the channel between flashing red "22" and green daybeacon "23" at Hobucken. Boats have reported grounding hard here. It is also a good idea to keep clear of Gale Creek Point, which is continually building out and encroaching on the channel. Depths outside the markers are a scant 0.5 foot MLW in places.

Be on the lookout for crab pot floats that may be present in the channel between green "25" and green "27" at the end of the cut before Bay River. From Gale Creek the ICW cuts 5 miles down Bay River to Maw Point and Maw Point Shoal (near Mile 165), which continues to build out into the Neuse River. The Hobucken Coast Guard station can give you information on conditions around Maw Point (252-745-3131). When strong winds blow down the Bay River wave action can be almost as bad as on the much larger Neuse River.

Southeast along the Bay River, Pine Tree Point is marked by flashing green "3" to starboard (Mile 162.2) and then by flashing green "1," which marks the shoaling off Deep Point. Do not pass too close to flashing green "1" as shoaling has been reported to extend slightly into the channel from the marker. Like the Pungo River the marking system for the Bay River is numbered from seaward (i.e., the colors of the markers are reversed with green on starboard going south until the Neuse River Junction).

Maw Point and the Neuse River are often easier to run in the morning just after dawn when surface winds may be lighter so anchoring in Bay River the night before is a good idea. Adequate depths run well upriver to the quaint and quiet towns of Vandemere ("village by the sea") and Bayboro. To reach Bayboro proceed past Vandemere continuing to follow the markers carefully, especially green daybeacon "11" and red daybeacon "12." Do not mistake red daybeacon "14" for red daybeacon "12" or you will find yourself in 4-foot MLW depths along the southwest shore.

Dockage: The commercial facilities at R. E. Mayo Seafood Marine Supply are on the south side of the Hobucken (NC 33/304) Bridge (Mile 157.2). Dockage is available at this is a working shrimp dock and they will pack fresh and fresh frozen seafood in any quantity you like. Hurricane Boatyard in Bayboro has a great DIY boatyard. They can also provide full or partial service if needed. Transients have access to clean showers and a small but well-stocked chandlery.

Anchorage: You can anchor along Gale Creek (approximately Mile 159) west of flashing red "22" in 4- to 6-foot MLW depths. An underwater electric cable runs from the mainland to the Jones Island Club, a private lodge on the island shore just east of green daybeacon "23." A sign in the bay warns "Danger High Voltage" so do not anchor here. When leaving Gale Creek do not mistake the Bay River markers that lead west to Vandemere for those leading southeast to the Neuse River. Another convenient nearby anchorage is in the Bay River at Bear Creek (Mile 160.8) in 7 to 10 feet MLW with a mud bottom and exposure from the east to the south.

There is a good anchorage to the south in Bonner Bay. To reach Bonner Bay, exit the ICW at quick flashing green "27" (Mile 161) and head southwest. Feel your way in via the unmarked channel with the depth sounder and go up Long Creek (the left fork) to anchor in 9 to 11 feet MLW with good holding in mud. It is a beautiful secluded anchorage with no structures in sight but it can be buggy in the summer months.

Although there are no amenities, you can anchor off Vandemere village dock on Bay River with exposure from the southeast to the southwest. Stay clear of the channel because shrimp boats use it. Steer toward the village docks from flashing green "5" and drop the anchor in 9 to 10 feet MLW. An east to southeast wind can create rough conditions. Show an anchor light at night and always ask permission to tie up the dinghy if you go ashore.

Neuse River to Oriental–ICW Mile 162 to Mile 182

The Neuse is a large river that is open to the Pamlico Sound and can get rough. Check the weather and proceed with respect. First-timers should run compass courses and use radar or GPS whenever possible. A southwest wind can make the 18-mile run to Oriental at Mile 182 a very wet ride. A fall northwester, however, will leave the river calm with the wind coming from the shore. At those times the wide, lovely Neuse River can be a pleasant change from the narrow land cuts of the ICW, especially for sailors who want to shake out the sails.

Oriental has become widely known as the "Sailing Capital of North Carolina" and locals claim sailboats outnumber people three to one, although boating facilities in the area also attract visiting power boaters. The sheltered creeks provide immediate access to the country's second largest estuary and sailing, cruising and gunkholing areas. Local marinas welcome transients and offer supply and repair capabilities to handle virtually any requirement. This is a popular place and space is limited so reservations are recommended. Plan your trip with "Goin' Ashore: Oriental, NC" in this chapter.

NAVIGATION: Use NOAA Chart 11548. Maw Point Shoal introduces you to the Neuse River. Follow the magenta line carefully as you make the 90-degree turn around the Neuse River Junction Light, a 15-foot flashing red light (6-sec intervals). Use special caution here. The three red flashing lights (uncharted) in the prohibited area of Rattan Bay can be confused with the entrance light. More importantly there are 30 miles of open water between Maw Point and the Outer Banks. Winds out of the east make it rough and if you are not careful, you could be set onto the shoal.

If on station, flashing green "1" (off Deep Point) and flashing red "2" (off Maw Point Shoal) make a shortcut inside the Neuse River junction light but do not use it if brisk winds make Maw Point Shoal a lee shore. Even though depths are at least 8 feet along this shortcut route, crab traps are scattered throughout the area and require attention. From Bay River flashing green "1" off Deep Point run a course that will put you at least 0.25 mile off flashing red "2" and then head for flashing red "4" off the tip of the shoal extending from Piney Point (at Mile 172.3) on a south-southwesterly course.

If heading west to the Neuse River from Pamlico Sound through the Brant Island Slue, be aware that shoaling to 3 feet MLW has been reported in the area off the southeast

tip of the charted shoal across from daybeacon "1." Also there has been ongoing discussion about extending the existing Marine Corps bombing range to include Brant Island Shoals. This would effectively prevent all vessels from crossing Brant Island Shoal through the Brant Island Slough, forcing them to go all the way around the end of Brant Island Shoal.

Northbound boats will appreciate the anchorages in Broad Creek (ICW Mile 173) off the Neuse River's western shore. This is also home to the amenity-rich Grace Harbor at River Dunes, a destination in itself. The white danger marker "BW" guides skippers bound for Broad Creek around the extending shoal south of Piney Point. Shoals at Piney Point and Gum Thicket Shoal continually build out. The danger beacon marks the tip of the shoal between flashing red "4" and the warning daybeacon platform. Do not mistake the more slightly dilapidated white warning daybeacon for flashing red "4" off Piney Point. Depths inshore of the platform are less than 2 feet MLW in spots. All markers off Piney Point should be left well to the north.

Boats bound for Broad Creek should exit the ICW halfway between red daybeacon "4" and red "6" on the Neuse River and follow the markers into Broad Creek. Give green daybeacon "3" a wide berth. Be on the lookout as there may be numerous crab pot floats in the creek.

Marine facilities at Oriental begin at Mile 181 where a marked entrance leads to Whittaker Creek. There are more markers here than shown on the NOAA chart and they make it easy to stay on the range (not charted), which can be picked up on entry. Be sure to give flashing green "5" a wide berth before turning left into the facility-lined creek. Depths of 8 feet MLW are reported for the channel; nevertheless, southwesterly winds can lower this depth, and some shoaling persists in the area around and south of flashing green "5." Boats coming from the north can head straight for the 15-foot-high flashing red "6" and join the channel there. It is best to call ahead to the marina of your choice to check for current depths and steering directions at time of entry. Mind the crab traps and do not be surprised to see them in mid-channel. Oriental has no tide to contend with, only the wind-driven ups and downs of eastern and western storms.

Just to the southwest of the entrance to Whittaker Creek on the Neuse River a well-marked

GOIN' ASHORE

ORIENTAL, NC

Life moves slowly in this welcoming village. Boats and bikes rest against dock pilings and porch railings. Talking and walking may not be considered official recreational activities in most towns, but in Oriental, they fit with the feel of a quaint waterfront town where biking, sailing, kayaking, fishing, and boating are popular pastimes. Long known as the "Sailing Capital of North Carolina," Oriental is blessed with wide waters, steady winds and easy access to dozen of creeks and estuaries.

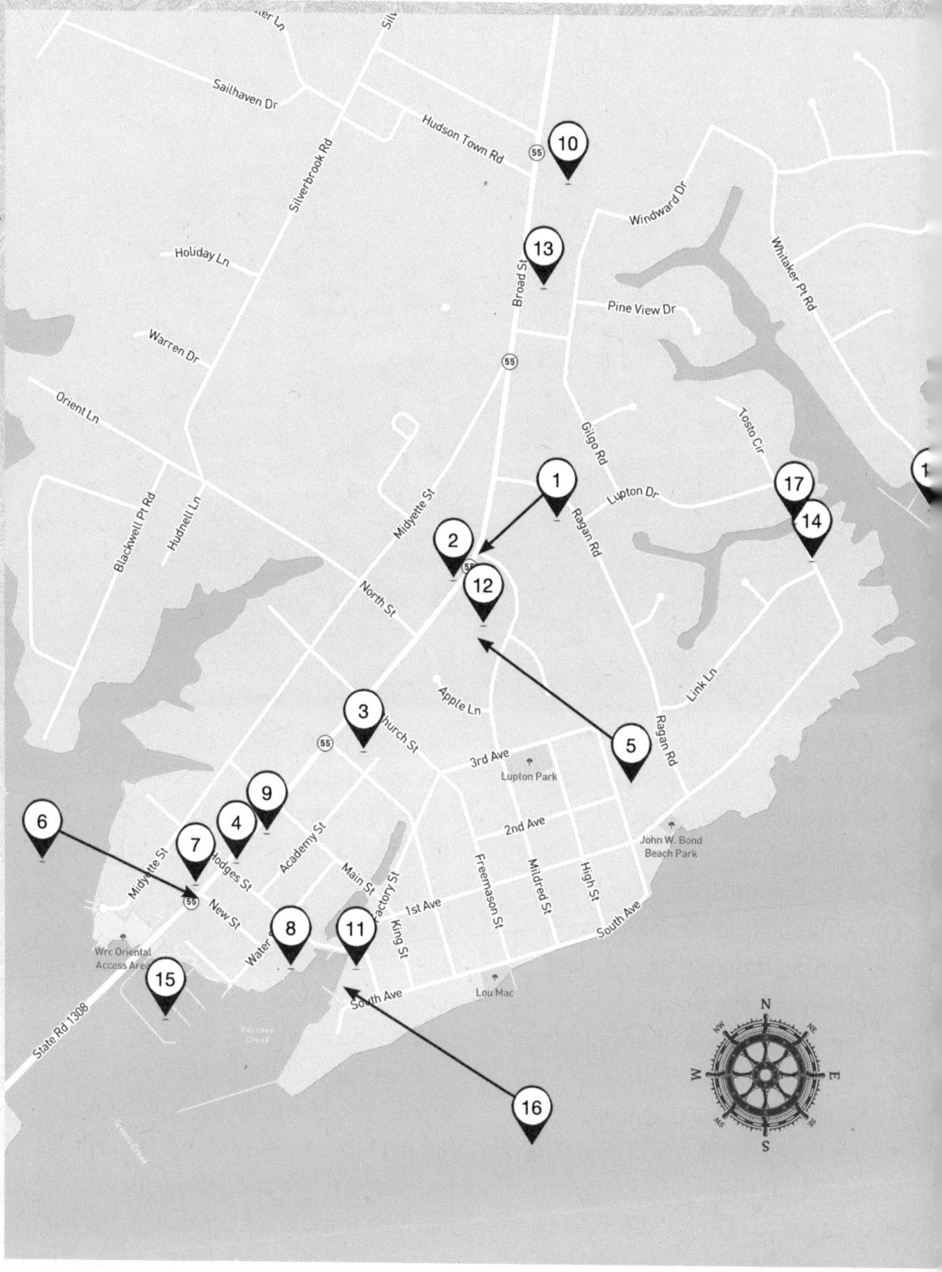

SERVICES

1. **CCHC Oriental Medical Center**
   901 Broad St. (252-249-2888)
2. **Oriental Post Office**
   809 Broad St. (252-249-0454)
3. **Oriental Town Hall**
   507 Church St. (252-249-0555)
4. **Oriental Village Veterinary Hospital**
   407 Broad St. (252-249-2149)

ATTRACTIONS

5. **Oriental's History Museum**
   Displays model skiffs, oyster scoops, the bronze porthole from its namesake, *S.S. Oriental*, a Wurlitzer juke box and much more documenting Oriental's history at 802 Broad St. (252-249-3340). Pick up a Historic Walking Tour brochure and follow the route past over 70 historical buildings and sites.

SHOPPING

6. **Down East Canvas & Gallery**
   Located at the foot of the bridge, this is a combination canvas shop and art gallery (301 Broad St., 252-249-1004). Open Tuesday through Saturday (year-round).
7. **Hodges Street Sail Repair**
   Sail repair, cleaning and canvas work close to Town Dock (603 Hodges St., 252-249-0739).

8. Inland Waterway Provision Company
Marine supplies, including some that can be ordered in advance, as well as local meats, eggs, dairy and produce and beer and wine. They also offer a Cruisers Corner, where visitors can chill out or warm up with free WiFi and a swap bookcase (305 Hodges St., 252-249-1797).

9. Nautical Wheelers
Cruiser favorite with locations in Oriental and New Bern offering nautical gift items, clothing, shoes and jewelry. They also sell wine and frequently host wine tastings on the porch at 411 Broad St. (252-249-0359).

10. Piggly Wiggly
Grocery store at 1400 Broad St. (252-249-3100) that provides a convenient "Piglet" shuttle for pick-ups and drop-offs.

11. The Village Gallery
Features works in oil, pastels, acrylic, photography, jewelry, watercolor, pottery, glass and more, which you can buy directly from the juried artists (300 Hodges St., 252-249-0300).

12. Village Hardware & Marine Supply
Hardware, marine supplies, home provisions and great customer service (804 Broad St., 252-249-1211).

13. West Marine
Boating parts and accessories, apparel and fishing supplies (1104 Broad St., 252-249-3200).

MARINAS

14. Deaton Yacht Service
1306 Neuse Dr. (252-249-1180)

15. Oriental Harbor Marina
518 S. Water St. (252-671-9692)

16. Oriental Marina & Inn
103 Wall St. (252-249-1818)

17. Sailcraft Marina
1400 Tosto Circle (252-249-1754)

18. Whittaker Creek Yacht Harbor
415 Whittaker Point Rd. (252-670-3759)

Neuse River, NC

BROAD CREEK		Largest Vessel	VHF	Total Slips	Approach/ Dockside Depth	Floating Docks	Gas/ Diesel	Repairs/ Haulout	Min/Max Amps	Pump-Out Station
1. Grace Harbor at River Dunes WiFi onSpot MM 173.0	(252) 249-4908	125	16	400	7.0 / 9.0	F	GD		30 / 200+	P
2. Ensign Harbor Marina	(252) 249-0823	40			/ 5.5					

WiFi Wireless Internet Access onSpot Dockside WiFi Facility
Visit www.waterwayguide.com for current rates, fuel prices, website addresses and other up-to-the-minute information.
(Information in the table is provided by the facilities.)

Scan here for more details:

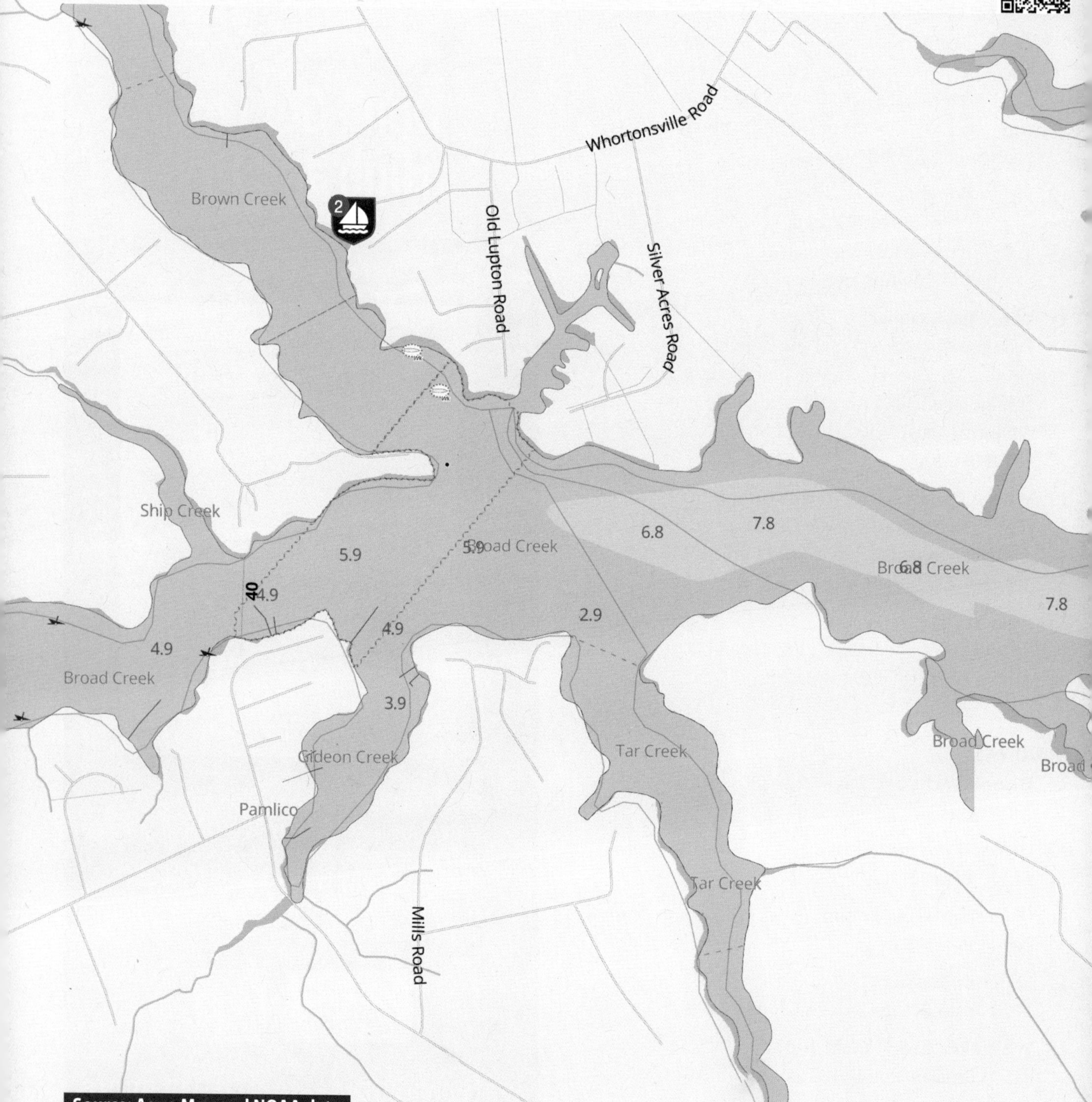

Source: Aqua Map and NOAA data

Silverwood Road
Green Creek
1.9
Pittman Creek
Pittman Creek
4.9 Neuse River
Paradise Shores Road
3.9
6.8
2.9
4.9
2.9
2.9
Neuse River
2.9
3.9
2.9
6.8
0.9
0.9
6.8
3
8.8
Broad Creek
5.9
6.8
Broad Creek
2A
1.9
2.9
5.9
6.8
1
Broad Creek Light 1
8.8
9
Neuse River Kayak Trail
4
7.8
1.9
3.9
0.9
Neuse River Kayak Trail
8.8
0.9
Ballast Point
Kayak Trail
Neuse River
7.8
Neuse River
Broad Creek
11
Broad Creek
0.9
10
6.8
11

Neuse River, NC

WHITTAKER CREEK		Largest Vessel	VHF	Total Slips	Approach/ Dockside Depth	Floating Docks	Gas/ Diesel	Repairs/ Haulout	Min/Max Amps	Pump-Out Station
1. Whittaker Pointe Marina WiFi MM 181.0	(252) 249-1750	100	16	53	8.0 / 9.0				30 / 50	
2. Whittaker Creek Yacht Harbor WiFi 1.7 mi. NW of MM 181.0	(252) 670-3759	140	16	140	7.0 / 8.0			R	30 / 50	

WiFi Wireless Internet Access   onSpot Dockside WiFi Facility
Visit www.waterwayguide.com for current rates, fuel prices, website addresses and other up-to-the-minute information.
(Information in the table is provided by the facilities.)

Scan here for more details:

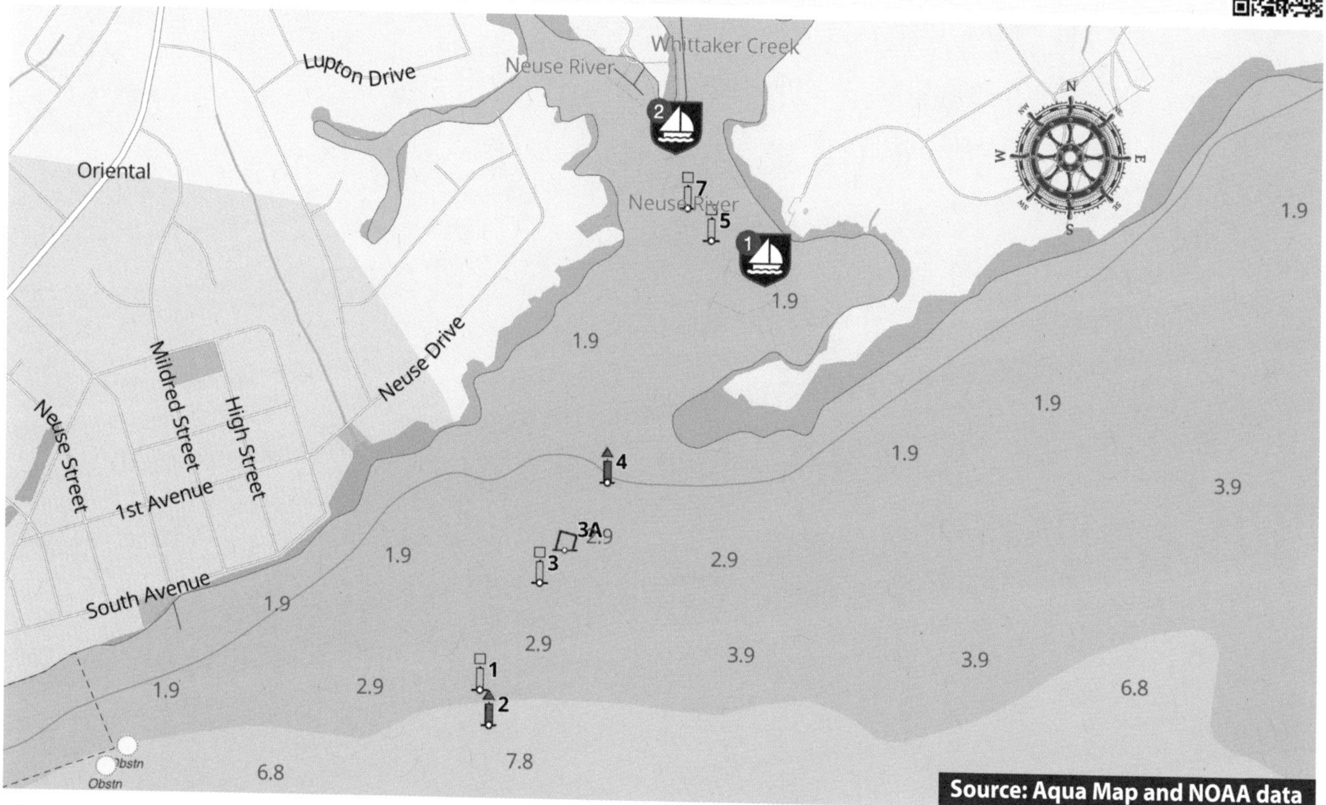

Source: Aqua Map and NOAA data

channel carrying 8.5 feet MLW leads to the basin confluence of Smith Creek and Greens Creek immediately beyond the fixed **Oriental Road (NC 1308) Bridge** spanning the junction.

Oriental Road (NC 1308) Bridge is not on the ICW and only has a vertical clearance of 45 feet. Do not attempt to navigate up Greens Creek to the anchorage or marina if your vessel's air draft exceeds 40 feet. Also, note that charted depths in these creeks can be misleading. Wind and weather can raise (as well as lower) the water level appreciably in this area. If winds have been out of the west or southwest for any length of time, a drop in water levels of as much as 3 feet is possible. Sound your way in.

Dockage: Grace Harbor at River Dunes is reached by heading northwest from the ICW halfway between flashing reds "4" and "6" and then following the marked channel into Broad Creek. Give the markers at least 50 yards as you pass. The marina is on the port side of the creek at red daybeacon "4." Entry is through a private, well-maintained and marked, bulkheaded channel with charted 8-foot MLW depths. Unless you have the latest updates on your electronic charts you will not see the channel marked so follow the private markers. The floating docks at Grace Harbor at River Dunes have full-length finger piers and 8 feet MLW. They offer resort-type amenities including croquet on the green, tennis and billiards. A courtesy car is available for the 10-mile trip into Oriental and its many services and amenities. Ensign Harbor Marina to the north on Brown Creek can accommodate vessels to 40 feet.

Neuse River, NC

WHITTAKER CREEK		Largest Vessel	VHF	Total Slips	Approach/ Dockside Depth	Floating Docks	Gas/ Diesel	Repairs/ Haulout	Min/Max Amps	Pump-Out Station
1. Sailcraft Marina WiFi	(252) 249-1754	50		39	7.0 / 6.0			R	30 / 50	
2. Sailcraft Service WiFi MM 181.0	(252) 249-0522	65	16	12	8.0 / 7.0			RH	30 / 50	
3. Zimmerman Marine - Oriental WiFi MM 181.0	(252) 249-1180	65	16	29	7.0 / 7.0			RH	30 / 50	P

WiFi Wireless Internet Access onSpot Dockside WiFi Facility
Visit www.waterwayguide.com for current rates, fuel prices, website addresses and other up-to-the-minute information.
(Information in the table is provided by the facilities.)

Scan here for more details:

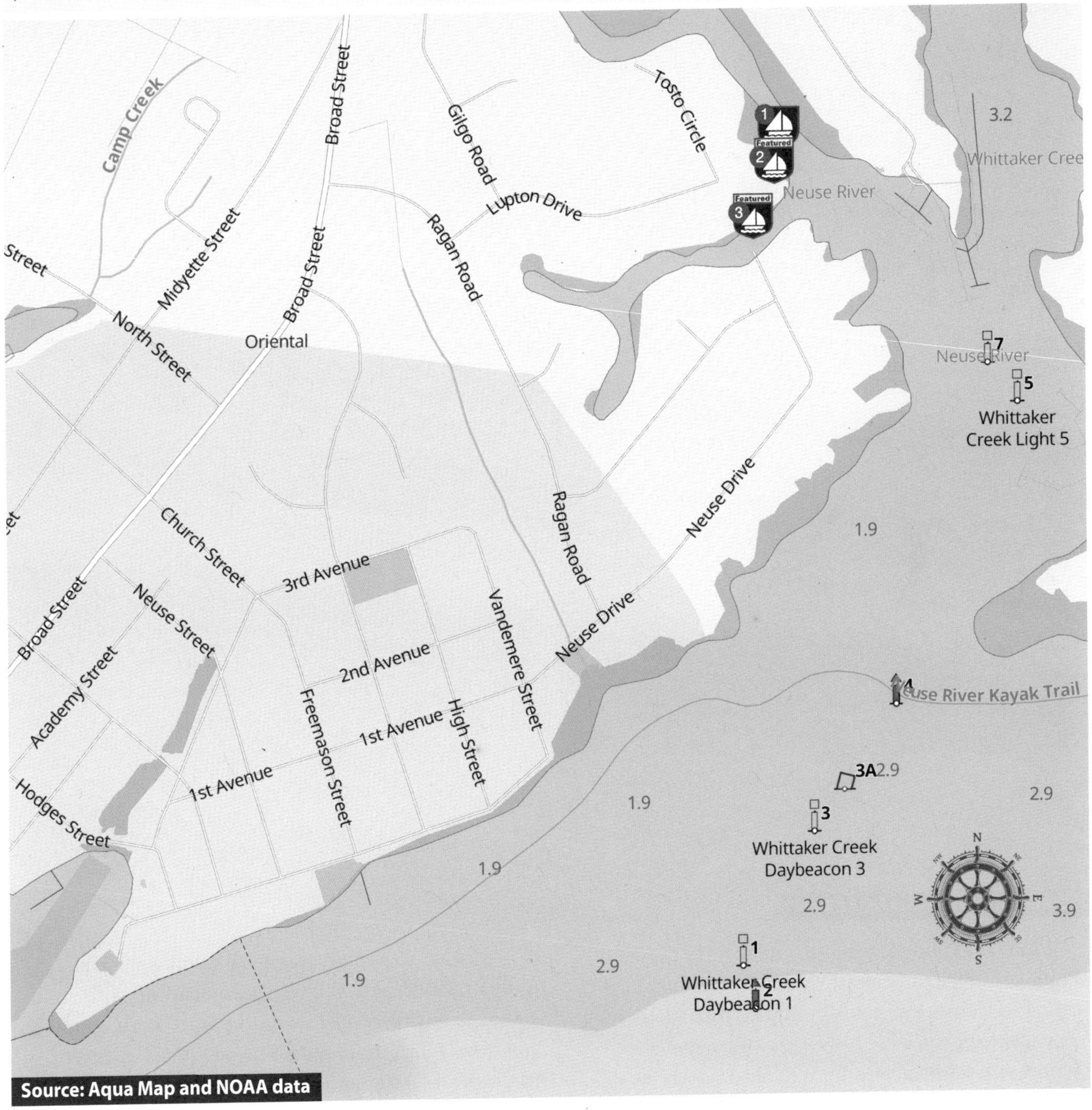

Source: Aqua Map and NOAA data

Neuse River, NC

ORIENTAL		Largest Vessel	VHF	Total Slips	Approach/ Dockside Depth	Floating Docks	Gas/ Diesel	Repairs/ Haulout	Min/Max Amps	Pump-Out Station
1. Oriental Marina & Inn (WiFi) **1.9 mi. NW of MM 181.5**	**(252) 249-1818**	**100**	**16**	**27**	**8.0 / 6.5**		**GD**		**30 / 50**	
2. Oriental Harbor Marina (WiFi) MM 182.0	(252) 249-0777	100	16	110	8.0 / 6.0				30 / 50	P
SMITH CREEK										
3. Blackwell Point Marina (WiFi) MM 182.0	(252) 725-7865	50	16	10	6.0 / 6.0	F			20	

(WiFi) Wireless Internet Access **onSpot** Dockside WiFi Facility
Visit www.waterwayguide.com for current rates, fuel prices, website addresses and other up-to-the-minute information.
(Information in the table is provided by the facilities.)

Scan here for more details:

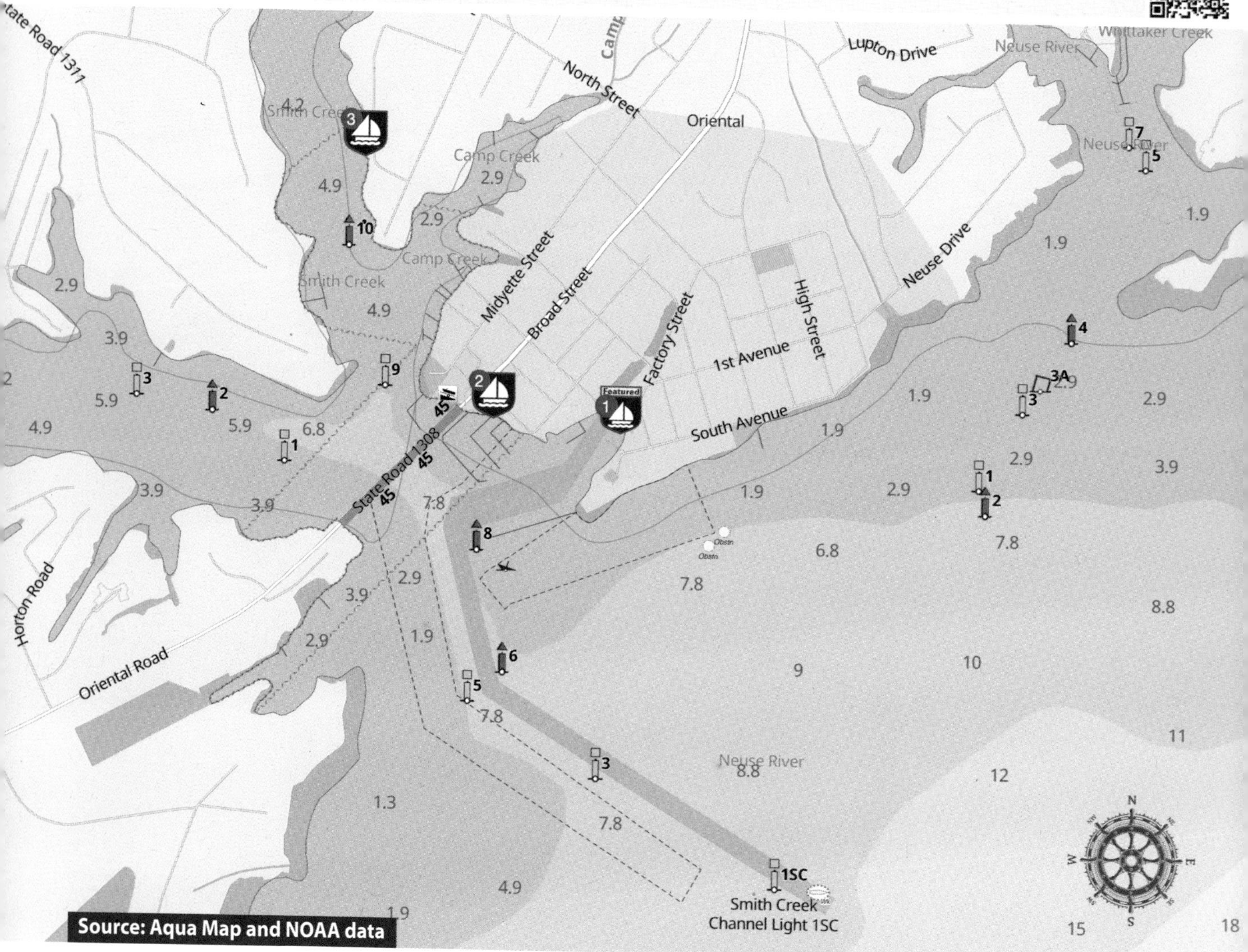

Whittaker Pointe Marina is located at the mouth of Whittaker Creek on the east side of the entrance. The marina welcomes transients in a quiet, park-like setting. They will loan you a courtesy van to provision after helping you settle in. Nearby Whittaker Creek Yacht Harbor is immediately visible just inside the point. The 140-slip marina reserves 10 transient slips.

Upstream to port on an arm of Whittaker Creek, Sailcraft Service is a well-respected boatyard with complete repair services including woodwork, welding and metal fabrication, plumbing and HVAC, painting, mechanical service and cleaning and detailing. DIY boaters are welcome. Sailcraft Marina is nearby with 39 slips. They welcome transients. Call ahead.

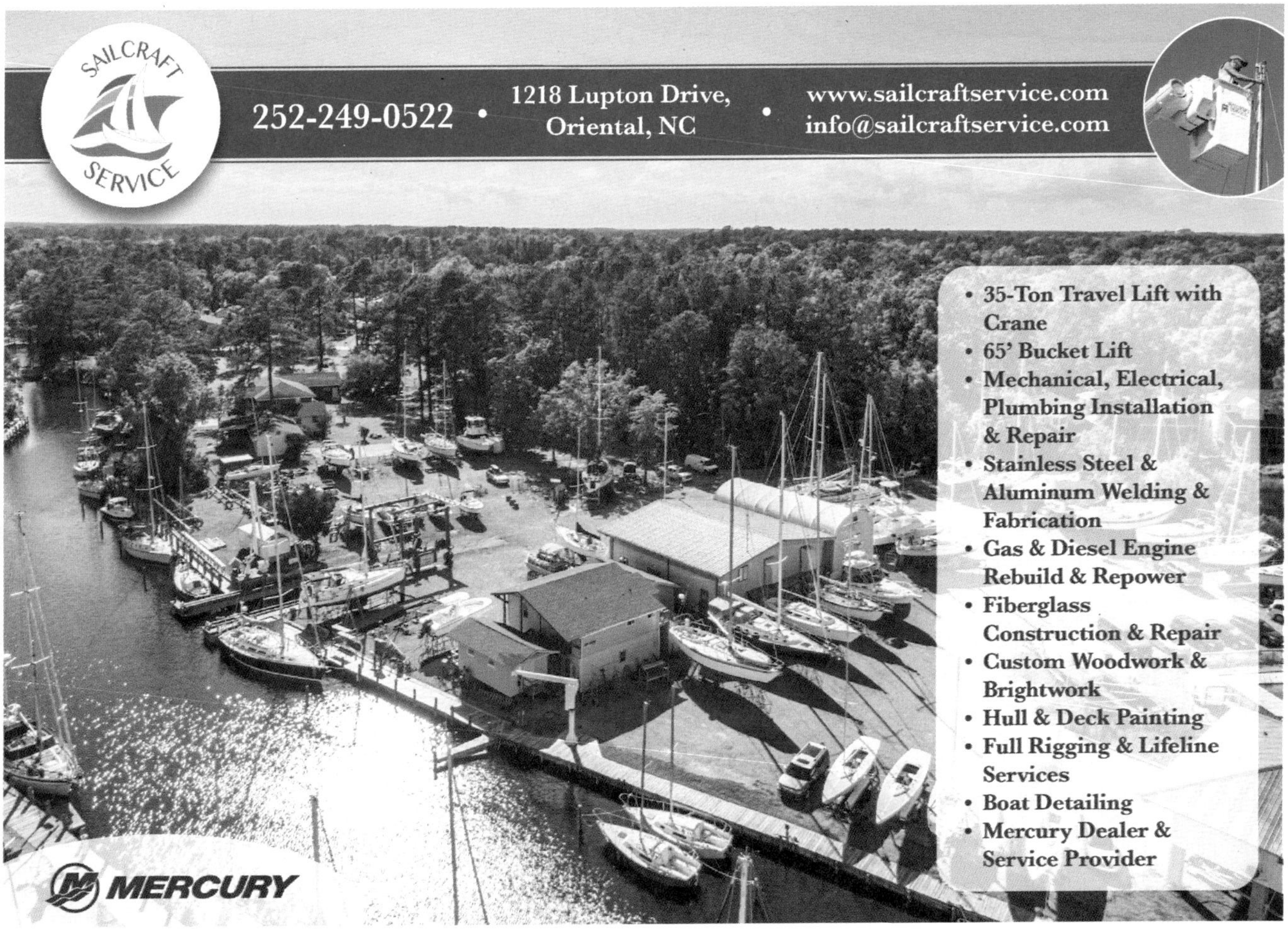
SAILCRAFT SERVICE
252-249-0522
1218 Lupton Drive,
Oriental, NC
www.sailcraftservice.com
info@sailcraftservice.com
• 35-Ton Travel Lift with Crane
• 65' Bucket Lift
• Mechanical, Electrical, Plumbing Installation & Repair
• Stainless Steel & Aluminum Welding & Fabrication
• Gas & Diesel Engine Rebuild & Repower
• Fiberglass Construction & Repair
• Custom Woodwork & Brightwork
• Hull & Deck Painting
• Full Rigging & Lifeline Services
• Boat Detailing
• Mercury Dealer & Service Provider
MERCURY

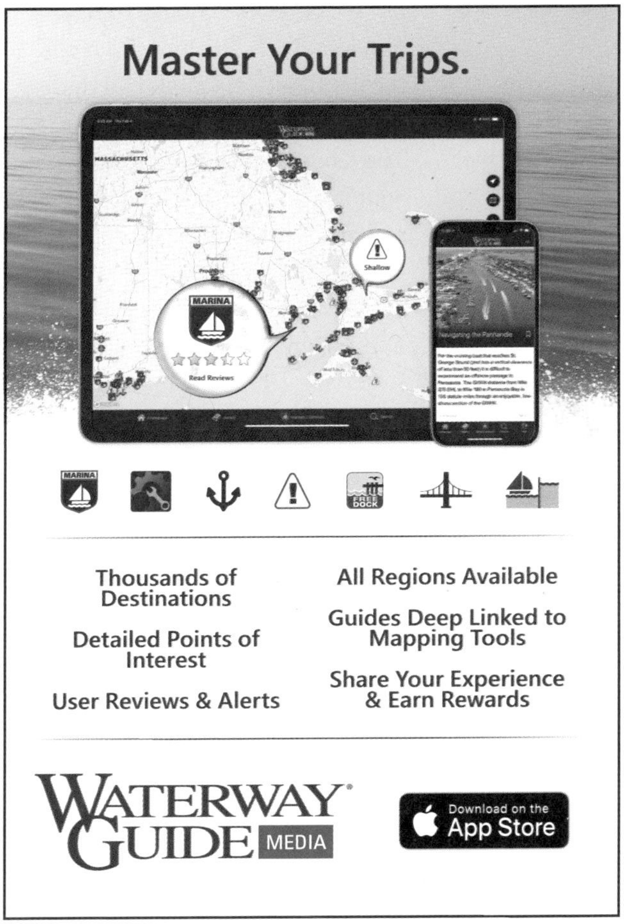
Master Your Trips.
Shallow
MARINA
Read Reviews
Thousands of Destinations
Detailed Points of Interest
User Reviews & Alerts
All Regions Available
Guides Deep Linked to Mapping Tools
Share Your Experience & Earn Rewards
WATERWAY GUIDE MEDIA
Download on the App Store

Inland Waterway Provision Company
• Marine Supplies
• Fishing Gear
• Safety Gear
• Inflatable Boats
• Kayak Rentals
• Gifts
• Fresh Local Produce & Meats, Beer & Wine
Oriental, NC • 252-249-1797
iwpc@dockline.net
InlandWaterwayProvisionCompany.com

Oriental MARINA & INN
HODGES STREET ON THE WATER, ORIENTAL
Your Best Stopover
Oriental Marina & Inn
Oriental, North Carolina
All Suite Inn
• Nightly Rates
• 1, 2, 3 Bedroom & ADA
• Kitchenettes
• All Waterfront Balconies
Transient Boat Slips
• Per Foot Charge
• Up to 105' X 25'
• Water, Power
• Wireless Internet
• Flotillas Welcome • Fuel Dock • Pool • Laundry • Showers
• Tiki Bar • Toucan Grill and Fresh Bar • ALL ABC PERMITS
• We now have additional slips • 440' Face Dock — Vessels to 150'
252-249-1818 • MM 182 ICW VHF 16 • www.orientalmarina.com

Zimmerman Marine-Oriental (formerly Deaton Yacht Service Inc.) is a full-capacity boatyard located across the canal. They have on-site mechanics and 24-hour towing service, plus they allow DIY. (Zimmerman's has six other yards in Holden Beach, NC; Southport, NC; Deltaville, VA; Mobjack Bay, VA; Herrington Harbour, MD; and Charleston, SC.)

Oriental's harbor (known locally as Raccoon Creek) lies immediately to starboard after passing flashing red "8" at the end of the rock jetty south of Whittaker Point. This harbor is tight with the distance between the north and south shores being not much more than a generous fairway. Note that the breakwater here only minimally protects the harbor from a bouncy and uncomfortable chop when the winds blow over 10 knots across the 5-mile fetch of the Neuse River. Oriental Marina & Inn manages the the 110-slip Oriental Harbor Marina. They offer boat repair and cleaning and can accommodate vessels to 100 feet. The face docks are immediately adjacent to the channel under the bridge going upriver, which gets considerable traffic, especially on weekends. Unfortunately this is NOT in a "No Wake" area resulting in bumpy conditions on the face dock.

To reach the amenity-rich Oriental Marina & Inn follow the dredged channel past the Oriental Yacht Club to the north, which is usually packed with boats (but no transient slips) and proceed straight ahead to the marina. This is actually a complex of facilities consisting of docks, an inn and lounge, a swimming pool with a tiki bar and the on-site Toucan Grill & Fresh Bar (252-249-2204), famous for fresh seafood meals (open for lunch and dinner).

There are two town docks in Oriental Harbor on either side of Oriental Marina & Inn. Oriental Town Dock #1 has approximately 80 feet of dockage and is complimentary for up to 48 hours and has a 7-day maximum stay. There is no shore power or water but there are clean restrooms next to the dock and you may pay for use of the showers at Oriental Marina & Inn. Directly at the end of the harbor channel is a second public pier (Oriental Town Dock #2) with room for just a few boats and a free pump-out station. This is directly across the street from The Bean, a popular coffee shop and gathering place (252-249-4918).

Blackwell Point Marina may be an option for those who can fit under the fixed 45-foot vertical clearance Oriental Road (NC 1308) Bridge to access Smith Creek. This is very well protected. Call ahead for slip availability.

Anchorage: If the free town docks are full you can anchor in soft mud with 5- to 8-foot MLW depths in the Oriental anchorage. This is exposed to the south. Several boats are usually at anchor but there is generally room for more as long as you are careful to stay out of the resident shrimp boat's channel. Holding is poor without good scope. Check with other anchored boats to be sure you don't anchor within their swing circle. The long seawall for Oriental Harbor Marina is reserved for transient moorage so leave space for boats coming and going from the seawall while also staying outside the route under the bridge.

Anchorage is possible in Smith Creek and Greens Creek if you can travel beyond the 45-foot vertical clearance of the fixed Oriental Road (NC 1308) Bridge and handle controlling depths of 4.5 to 5 feet MLW. The length of the creek is open to southerly winds. Should you choose to explore these or other side creeks be aware that depths may be less than charted due to shoaling. Proceed slowly and sound your way in.

Side Trip: Upriver to New Bern

The Neuse River provides a delightful side trip for anyone with the time and inclination. The southwestern prong of Pamlico Sound leads up the Neuse River to New Bern where the Trent River comes in. A trip up river can be a great time or a real challenge, depending on wind direction. The wind's direction and strength (not the moon) cause the tide fluctuations in the upper Neuse River. No tables or regular schedules can be established but water depths change by a foot or two in each direction. Overall the depth is adequate for all drafts but pay attention to your charts. The Cherry Point Marine Corps Air Station occupies the Hancock Creek and Slocum Creek areas on the south side of the river.

New Bern is 21 miles from flashing green "1AC," which is near ICW Mile 185 at the mouth of Adams Creek. The town offers visitors hospitality and Southern charm with the best of modern conveniences. New Bern's greatest assets are its natural resources: abundant water, steady winds and a vibrant waterfront. This is a river town not a coastal city. In New Bern you will find park benches and city sidewalks, restaurants and brick storefronts adorned with polished brass. This is the home of Pepsi-Cola and best-

Neuse River, NC

MINNESOTT BEACH		Largest Vessel	VHF	Total Slips	Approach/ Dockside Depth	Floating Docks	Gas/ Diesel	Repairs/ Haulout	Min/Max Amps	Pump-Out Station
1. Wayfarers Cove Marina & Boatyard WiFi MM 185.0	(252) 249-0200	55		150	6.5 / 7.0			RH	30 / 50	P

WiFi Wireless Internet Access onSpot Dockside WiFi Facility
Visit www.waterwayguide.com for current rates, fuel prices, website addresses and other up-to-the-minute information.
(Information in the table is provided by the facilities.)

Scan here for more details:

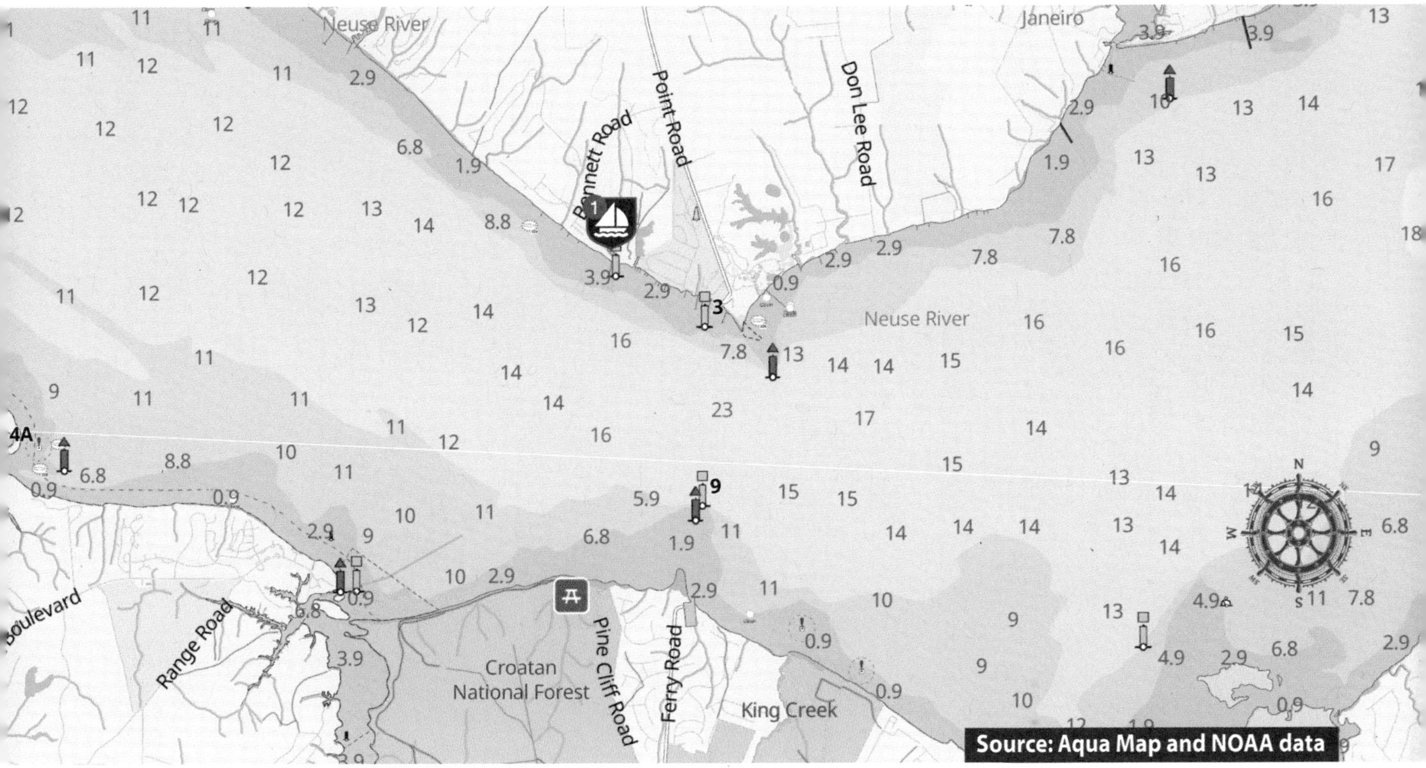

Source: Aqua Map and NOAA data

selling author Nicholas Sparks. It is the state's first capital and the final port of call for those seeking small-town living without the big-box feel. See more at "Goin' Ashore: New Bern, NC" in this chapter.

NAVIGATION: Use NOAA Chart 11552. The channel up the Neuse River to New Bern is well marked and easy to navigate. The lighted clock tower on City Hall is an excellent landmark. The 65-foot fixed vertical clearance **U.S. 17/NC 55 Bridge** (also known as the Neuse River Bridge) to the south of New Bern is visible for about 10 miles. Be aware that strong northeasterly winds can raise the water level resulting in reduced bridge clearance.

Alfred Cunningham (U.S. 70) Bridge at Mile 0 in the Trent River has 14-foot closed vertical clearance and opens on the hour and half hour, Monday through Friday, from 6:00 a.m. to 10:00 p.m., except from 7:30 a.m. to 8:30 a.m. and from 4:00 p.m. to 6:00 p.m., when the draw need not open. It will open on signal at all other times.

The Norfolk & Southern Railroad Bridge (5-foot closed vertical clearance) also crosses the Trent River. This bridge is usually open except for during the infrequent train crossings. Two thousand feet upstream are the twin fixed **US 17/U.S. 70 Hwy. Bridges** (45-foot vertical clearances). Note that winds may affect water levels and there may be less than the charted 45-foot clearances.

Dockage: About 7 miles up the Neuse River from Oriental at Minnesott Beach is Wayfarers Cove Marina & Boatyard, offering a well-protected alternative to a stopover in Oriental. They can accommodate vessels to 50 feet and offer repairs (plus DIY). Call ahead for slip availability. Across the river, 6 miles southwest of Mile 185, Matthews Point Marina at Mitchell Creek is part of a campground and RV park and has six reserved transient slips.

Neuse River, NC

MITCHELL CREEK		Largest Vessel	VHF	Total Slips	Approach/ Dockside Depth	Floating Docks	Gas/ Diesel	Repairs/ Haulout	Min/Max Amps	Pump-Out Station
1. Matthews Point Marina (WiFi) 6.0 mi. SW of MM 185.0	(252) 444-1805	46	16	110	6.5 / 6.5		GD	R	30 / 50	P

(WiFi) Wireless Internet Access onSpot Dockside WiFi Facility
Visit www.waterwayguide.com for current rates, fuel prices, website addresses and other up-to-the-minute information.
(Information in the table is provided by the facilities.)

Scan here for more details:

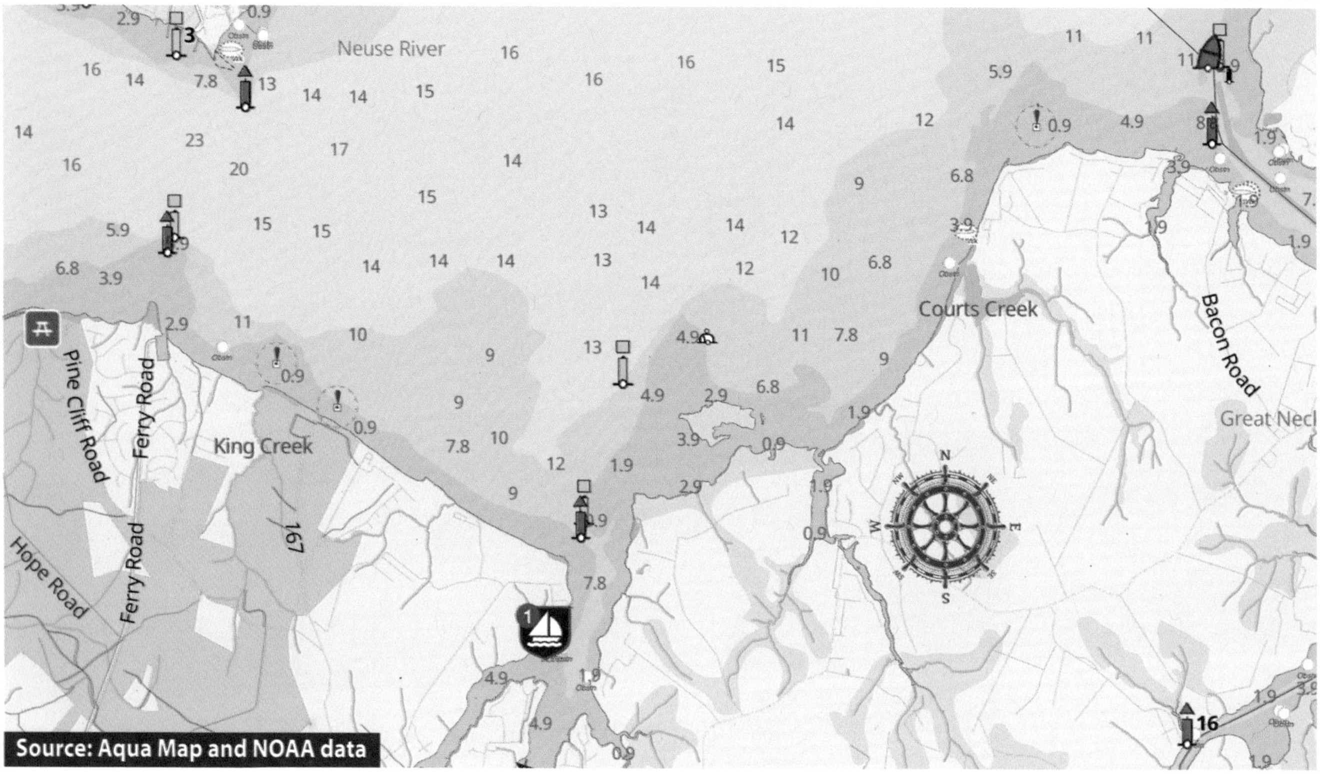

Neuse River, NC

NORTHWEST CREEK		Largest Vessel	VHF	Total Slips	Approach/ Dockside Depth	Floating Docks	Gas/ Diesel	Repairs/ Haulout	Min/Max Amps	Pump-Out Station
1. Northwest Creek Marina WiFi MM 185.0	(252) 638-4133	60	16	274	8.0 / 12.0		GD		30 / 50	P

WiFi Wireless Internet Access onSpot Dockside WiFi Facility
Visit www.waterwayguide.com for current rates, fuel prices, website addresses and other up-to-the-minute information.
(Information in the table is provided by the facilities.)

Scan here for more details:

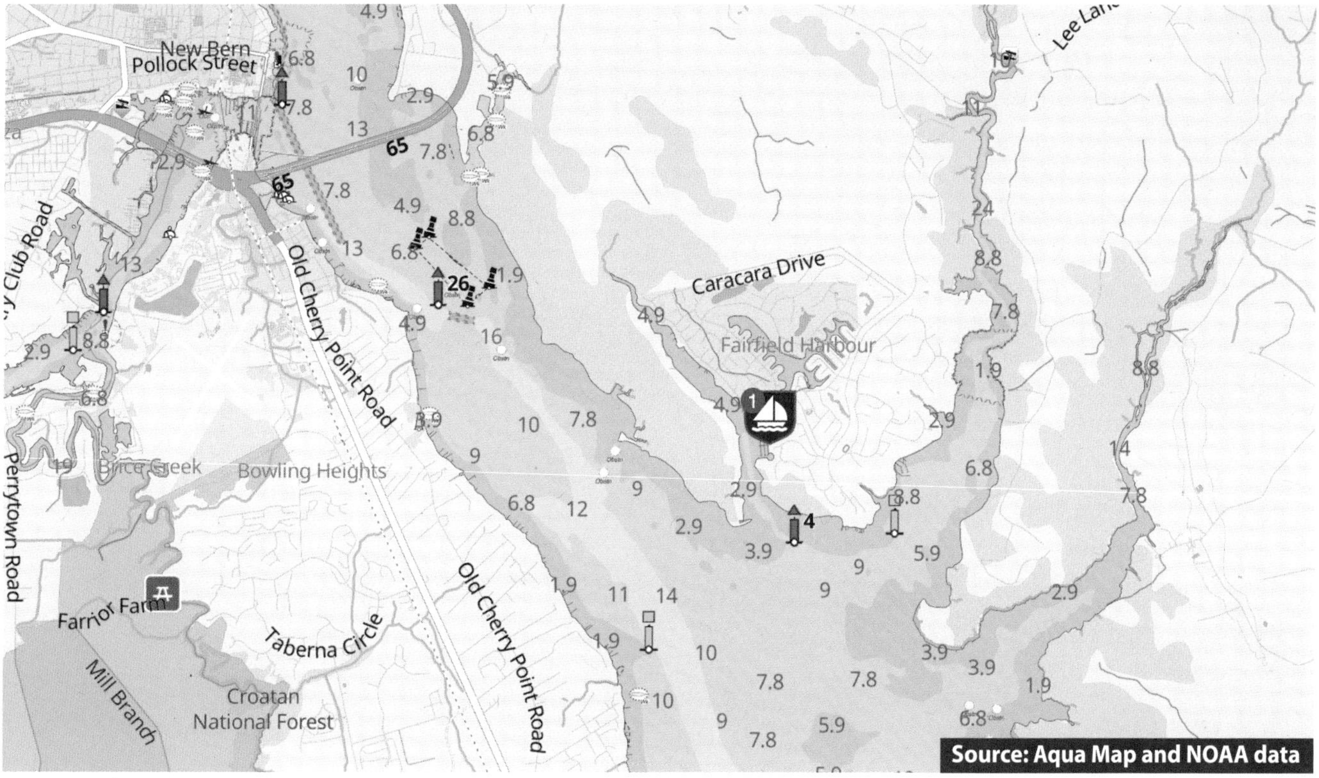

Source: Aqua Map and NOAA data

GOIN' ASHORE

NEW BERN, NC

From the downtown marinas you can walk and explore all of the historic downtown of New Bern. New Bern is a town of firsts. It was North Carolina's first capital, and the home of the state's first printing press, as well as its first publicly chartered school, its first motion picture theater, and was also the first town to hang electric Christmas lights above city streets. Be aware that New Bern residents are quick to point out that Caleb Bradham's soda pop (Pepsi-Cola) has a better kick than the "other" brand.

SERVICES

1. **Craven-Pamlico-Carteret Library**
   400 Johnson St. (252-638-7800)
2. **New Bern-Craven County Convention & Visitors Bureau**
   203 S. Front St. (252-637-9400)
3. **New Bern Post Office**
   233 Middle St. #101 (252-638-6921)

ATTRACTIONS

4. **Birthplace of Pepsi Cola**
   New Bern residents are quick to point out that Caleb Bradham's soda pop (Pepsi-Cola), first developed here in 1898, has a better kick than the "other" brand. Stop in the Pepsi Store at 256 Middle St. (252-636-5898) for a free sample and judge for yourself!
5. **Craven Arts Council & Gallery Bank of the Arts**
   Features monthly exhibits of painting, sculpture, photography and pottery (317 Middle St., 252-638-2577).
6. **New Bern Firemen's Museum**
   You will find early steam pumpers, a brass sliding pole and an extensive collection of early fire-fighting equipment (408 Hancock St., 252-636-4087).
7. **Tryon Palace Historic Site and Gardens**
   The 13-acre estate includes the palace (a mansion), the George W. Dixon House, the John Wright Stanly House, stables, a series of landscaped gardens and the Academy Museum. Demonstrations of the period include cooking, blacksmithing and weaving. Originally built between 1767 and 1770, Tryon Palace was the first permanent capitol of the Colony of North Carolina and a home for the Royal Governor and his family. Adjacent to Tryon Palace is the North Carolina History Center, a large and impressive museum with many interactive exhibits. One price gets you into the museum (a must-see) and the Tryon Palace (610 Pollock St., 252-639-3500).

SHOPPING

8. **Galley Stores and Marina**
   Gourmet provisioning establishment on the waterfront with provisions for the boat and a wide selection of wine, beer and gifts (300 E. Front St., 252-633-4648).

9. Mitchell Hardware
Authentic turn-of-the-century hardware store with a little bit of everything, including books and gifts (215 Craven St., 252-638-4261).

10. Nautical Wheelers
Nautical home decor and gift items, clothing, shoes and jewelry plus specialty wines at 202A Craven St. (252-514-2553) with a second location in Oriental.

11. The Boathouse
Carries a selection of nautical books and gifts (220 Middle St., 252-633-5501).

MARINAS

12. Galley Stores Marina
300 E. Front St. (252-633-4648)

13. New Bern Grand Marina Yacht Club
101 Craven St. (252-638-0318)

Neuse River, NC

DUCK CREEK		Largest Vessel	VHF	Total Slips	Approach/ Dockside Depth	Floating Docks	Gas/ Diesel	Repairs/ Haulout	Min/Max Amps	Pump-Out Station
1. Duck Creek Marina & Boatyard	(252) 638-1702	45		60	7.0 / 6.0			H	30	

WiFi Wireless Internet Access onSpot Dockside WiFi Facility

Visit www.waterwayguide.com for current rates, fuel prices, website addresses and other up-to-the-minute information.

(Information in the table is provided by the facilities.)

Scan here for more details:

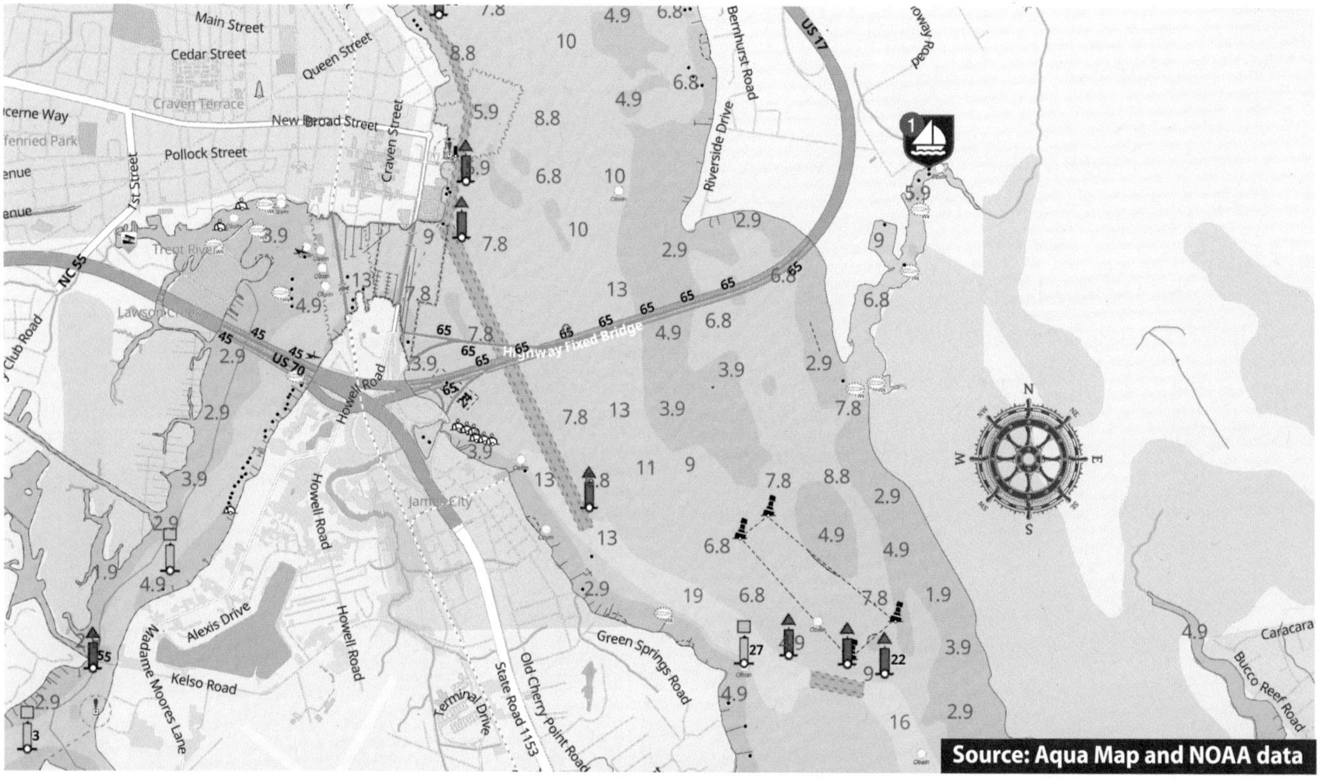

Neuse River, NC

BRIDGETON		Largest Vessel	VHF	Total Slips	Approach/ Dockside Depth	Floating Docks	Gas/ Diesel	Repairs/ Haulout	Min/Max Amps	Pump-Out Station
1. Bridgeton Harbor Marina WiFi	(252) 349-1194	150		135	7.0 / 10.0	F		RH	30 / 50	P

WiFi Wireless Internet Access onSpot Dockside WiFi Facility
Visit www.waterwayguide.com for current rates, fuel prices, website addresses and other up-to-the-minute information.
(Information in the table is provided by the facilities.)

Scan here for more details:

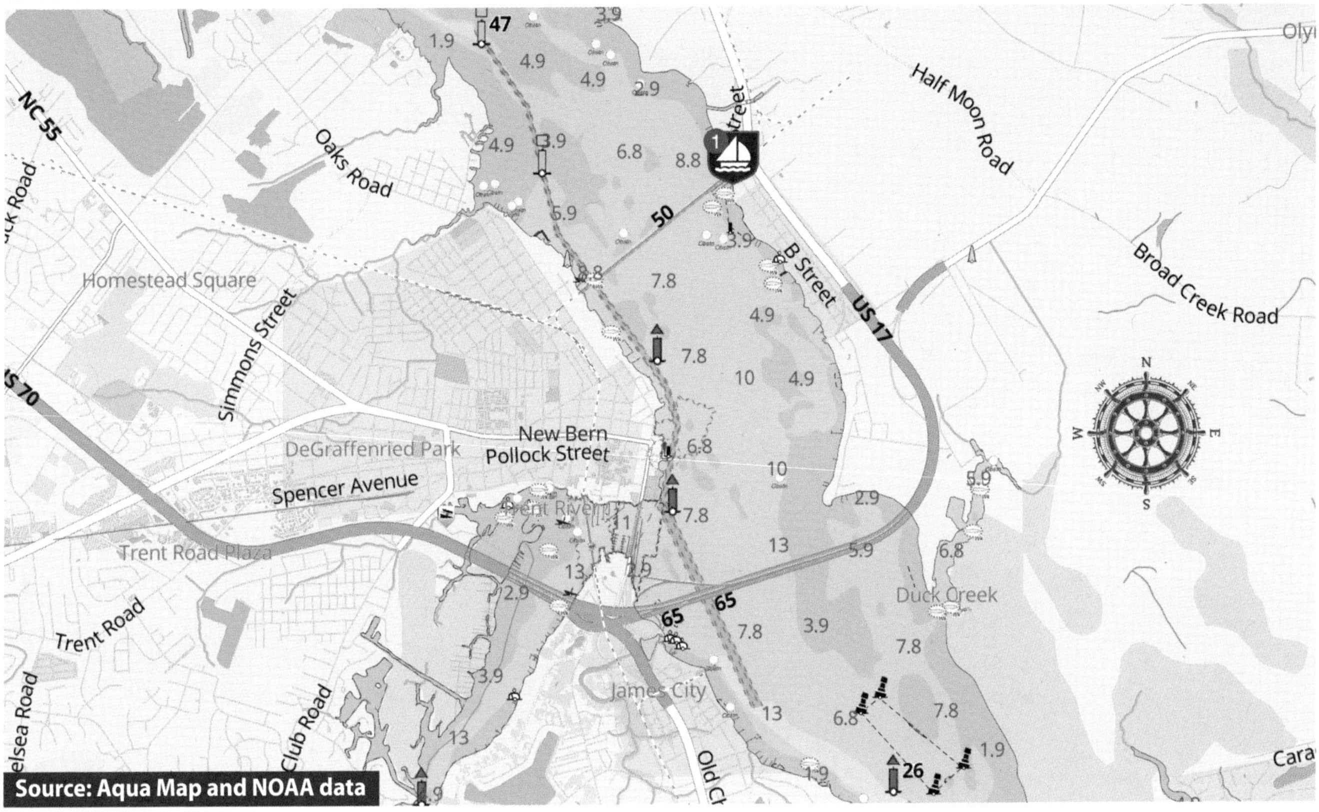

Source: Aqua Map and NOAA data

Closer to New Bern (4 miles southeast) is the well-protected Northwest Creek Marina. The marina has 274 slips and can accommodate yachts up to 60 feet with the usual amenities. Beyond the marina is Fairfield Harbour, a private community on a deepwater canal. Farther up the Neuse River but before the fixed 65-foot vertical clearance US 17/NC 55 Bridge is Duck Creek Marina & Boatyard. They are a well-regarded repair yard but only maintain two transient slips. Call ahead.

Across the Neuse River from New Bern and before the **Neuse River Railroad Bridge** (usually open) is Bridgeton Harbor Marina with slips on floating docks for vessels to 150 feet. They are a bit off the beaten path but have all the usual amenities in a quiet and secure residential neighborhood.

Galley Stores Marina is located directly on the channel on the Neuse River, north of the Trent and Neuse River intersection. This facility offers full-service transient dockage and has an on-site gourmet store featuring wine, beers and specialty items including daily "gourmet to go" meals.

Marine facilities on the Trent River are convenient to all the amenities of New Bern. New Bern Grand Marina Yacht Club has a 1,000-foot face dock with 12-foot MLW depths inside a protected breakwater. The marina is located in front of the waterfront DoubleTree Hotel by Hilton and all the hotel amenities are available to marina guests including the fitness center and pool. This is a convenient location for crew changes or for accommodating visiting family and friends. They also offer free day dockage to visit historic New Bern.

Between the Alfred Cunningham (US 70) Bridge and the The Norfolk & Southern Railroad Bridge on the south side of the Trent River is BridgePointe Hotel and

Neuse River, NC

NEW BERN		Largest Vessel	VHF	Total Slips	Approach/ Dockside Depth	Floating Docks	Gas/ Diesel	Repairs/ Haulout	Min/Max Amps	Pump-Out Station
1. Galley Stores Marina WiFi MM 185.0	(252) 633-4648	100	16	25	/	F	GD		30 / 50	P
2. New Bern Grand Marina Yacht Club WiFi	**(252) 638-0318**	**200**	**16**	**223**	**12.0 / 12.0**	**F**			**30 / 100**	**P**

WiFi Wireless Internet Access onSpot Dockside WiFi Facility
Visit www.waterwayguide.com for current rates, fuel prices, website addresses and other up-to-the-minute information.
(Information in the table is provided by the facilities.)

Scan here for more details:

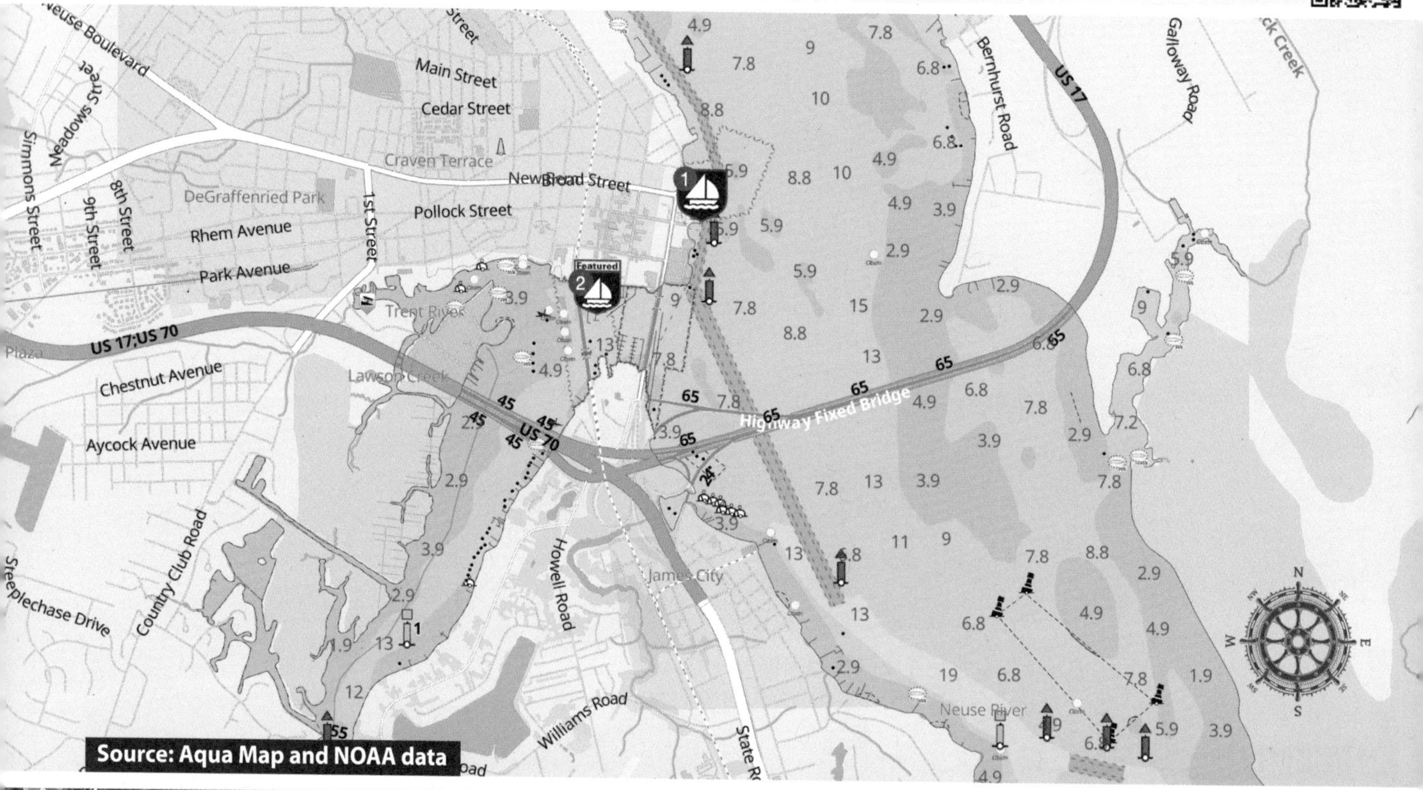

Source: Aqua Map and NOAA data

"Bern" is the old Germanic word for bear, which is the symbol of New Bern. Founded by Swiss and German settlers in the 1700s, New Bern is home to over 50 bear statues dressed in every imaginable costume. They are colorful, entertaining, and photogenic.

Marina with 125 slips on floating docks with a wave attenuator. The marina facilities and docks were closed for renovations at press time in 2021. Call ahead for current operating status.

While there is a no wake zone here locals appear to ignore it and law enforcement seems to be nonexistent. On weekends you will rock and roll due to wakes. It's easy to stay off the boat should the wakes kick up. Extensive shopping, restaurant and bars and an excellent market are nearby. Across Front Street from Union Point is a convention center, which hosts the Visitor Center.

Anchorage: There are places all along the Neuse River to tuck in and several good creeks on both side. Sound your way in and anchor according to wind direction.

NEXT STOP

Back on the ICW, we follow Adams Creek to the historic seaport of Beaufort and then on to Morehead City, where you could spend weeks exploring or just relaxing on the beautiful beaches of the "Crystal Coast." But first, we take a side trip to explore the expansive waters of the Pamlico Sound and Outer (and Lower) Banks of North Carolina.

ICW Mile 146

PAMLICO SOUND

Pamlico Sound, the second largest ICW estuary after the Chesapeake Bay, is 65 miles south of Albemarle Sound (via the ICW) and deserves the same amount of respect. The afternoon sea breeze, combined with prevailing southwesterlies, can often produce winds in excess of 20 knots and a short, steep chop that can fairly be called "vicious."

In November migratory waterfowl transiting the Atlantic Flyway visit the refuge area halfway between Englehard and Swan Quarter (also written as Swanquarter at times including on NOAA charts). Swan Quarter is the seat of Hyde County and the trading center for this area. It is also an embarkation point for ferries crossing Pamlico Sound to Ocracoke Island.

NAVIGATION: Use NOAA Chart 11555. If you are southbound, the entrance to the Pamlico River from the ICW is around the junction flashing red (2+1) "PR" (Mile 146) marking the shoal off Wades Point at the mouth of the Pungo River. Do not attempt to cut inside the marker unless you are very familiar with the area. Take care not to hit the unmarked, unlighted Mile 145 marker on the east side of the Pungo River prior to Wades Point.

Pamlico Sound markers are generally 5 to 15 miles apart so we strongly recommend that you run compass courses or GPS routes between them. Currents, often set up by the wind, can cause you to drift 10 to 15 degrees off course. Where these currents begin and end is impossible to predict but they are indeed there so check your position continually. Pamlico Sound, like any large sound, is a good area in which to use the GPS. An alternative route to the ICW via the Croatan and Roanoke Sounds is covered in "Side Trip: The Albemarle & Roanoke Sounds, NC."

Dockage: On the western shore of Pamlico Sound (north of the intersection with Pamlico River) is the well-marked Far Creek leading to Big Trout Marina. A small "southern comfort food" café is on site with pork chops, butter beans, mac and cheese...you get the idea (lunch only. The marina reports 5-foot MLW dockside depths and

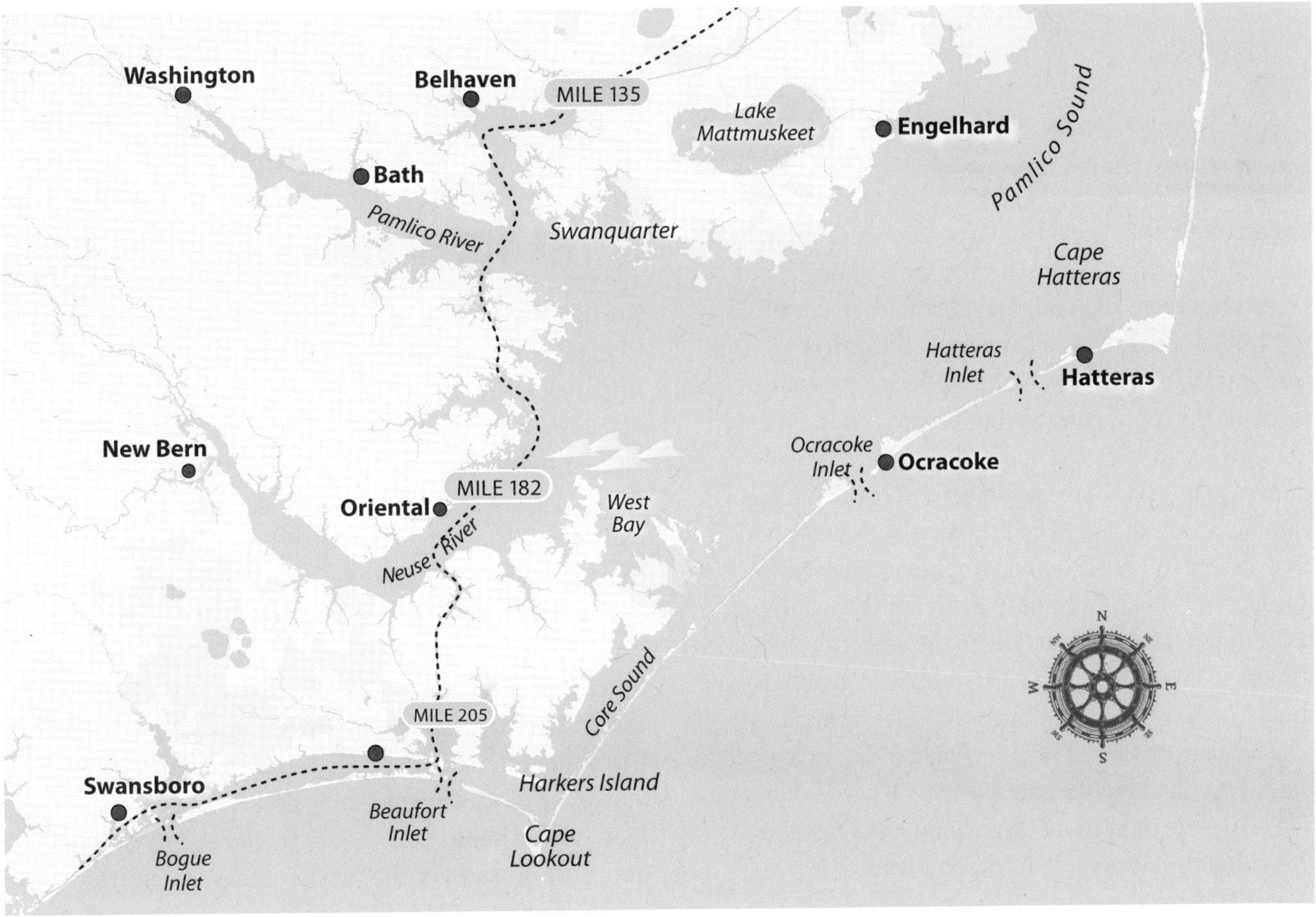

Pamlico Sound, NC

FAR CREEK		Largest Vessel	VHF	Total Slips	Approach/ Dockside Depth	Floating Docks	Gas/ Diesel	Repairs/ Haulout	Min/Max Amps	Pump-Out Station
1. Big Trout Marina	(252) 925-6651	60	18	25	6.0 / 5.0				30	

WiFi Wireless Internet Access onSpot Dockside WiFi Facility
Visit www.waterwayguide.com for current rates, fuel prices, website addresses and other up-to-the-minute information.
(Information in the table is provided by the facilities.)

Scan here for more details:

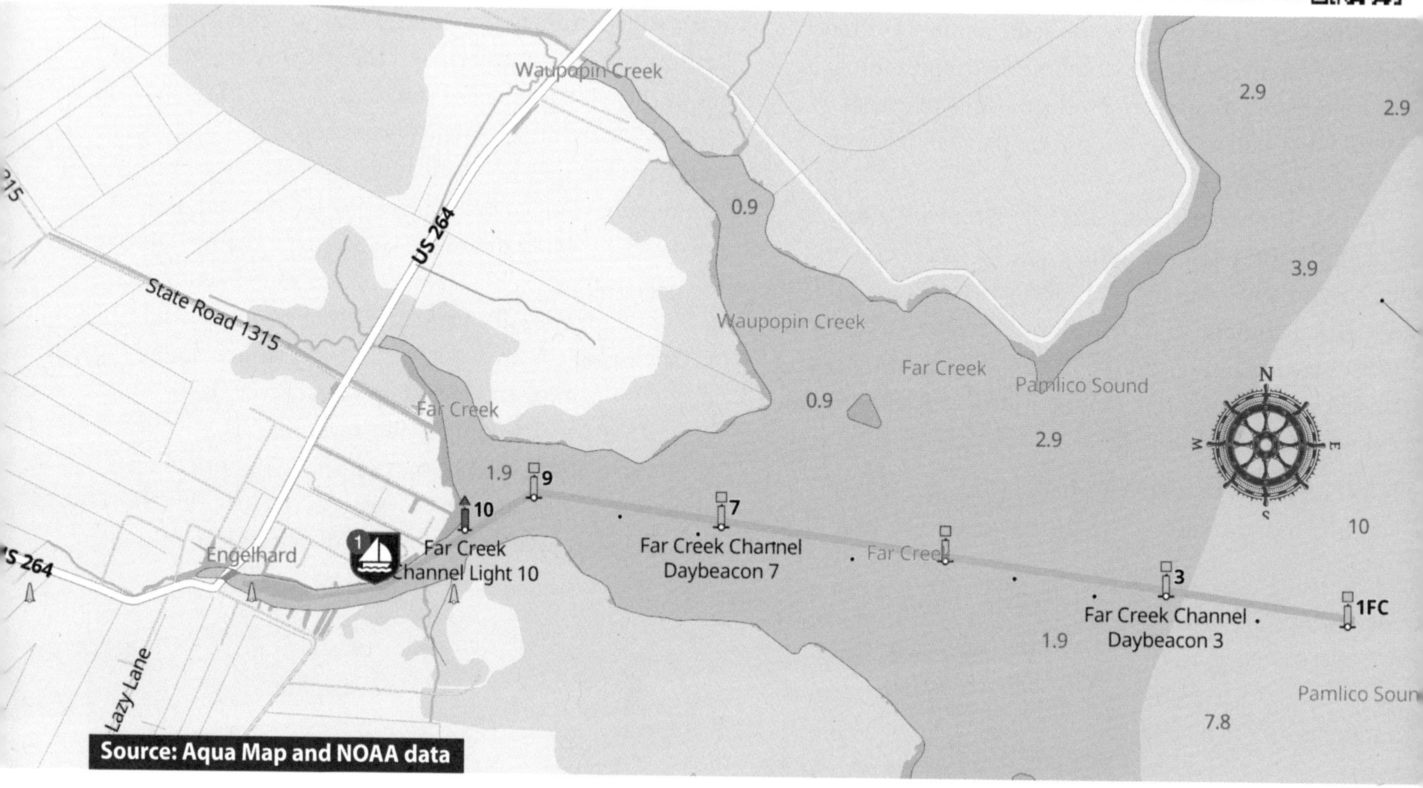

Source: Aqua Map and NOAA data

can accommodate boats to 60 feet. Groceries, a hardware store and a hotel are nearby in the town of Englehard.

Anchorage: The Long Shoal River to the north of Big Trout Marina offers anchorage in 6 to 8 feet MLW in hard mud with a bit of wave break due to the encroaching shoals at the south entrance but no protection from the north.

Wysocking Bay to the south beyond Far Creek has a hard mud bottom and marshy borders with protection from chop except from the south to southeast. From July to April this harbor is likely to be busy with commercial fishing boats. Juniper Bay, the next bay to the west, can be followed upriver to good protection and 6-foot MLW depths in soft mud. This location can be buggy on still summer nights.

The many bays west of Swan Quarter Bay look good on the NOAA chart but they are low marsh, have soft bottoms and offer little protection. Large commercial trawlers use this entrance so be especially diligent here.

THE OUTER BANKS

North Carolina's Outer Banks, a long strip of barrier islands, are unlike any other islands along the Mid-Atlantic coast. Vulnerable to wind and wave, they extend in a crescent from the Virginia state line bending farther and farther out to sea until Cape Hatteras and then abruptly sweep back west, leaving an exposed and dangerous cape. They finally meet with the mainland at Cape Lookout near Morehead City and Beaufort.

The Outer Banks enclose Currituck, Albemarle, Roanoke, Croatan, Pamlico and Core Sounds (in that order). As an alternative to the better-protected ICW route that cuts across Albemarle and Pamlico Sounds, this route offers higher speeds, more opportunity to sail and some of the most pristine and wild scenery on the East Coast should you choose to go ashore. Currituck and Core Sounds, at the two extremes, are narrow, shoal and suitable only for small or shoal-draft craft with local knowledge.

The northern end of the Outer Banks has been a popular summer resort for generations with many cottages, condominiums and commercial services. Below Nags Head the Cape Hatteras National Seashore stretches the length of the barrier islands to meet Cape Lookout National Seashore at Core Sound beyond Ocracoke. The wild beaches, dunes, marshes and woodlands are preserved as National Seashores and are interrupted in only a few places by villages and private property holdings. The Outer Banks are truly one of our nation's natural treasures and well worth your time to explore and enjoy.

The best way to see the Outer Banks is from the inside (not from the Atlantic) and the best time is summer when the sounds are relatively placid. The waters in the sound is often shoal and channels near inlets shift rapidly. Although channels are marked, they may not be entirely reliable after a storm. Off-channel waters are sprinkled with crab floats and fishnet stakes, which warrant a wide berth.

For those who would like to avoid the wide-open waters of Pamlico Sound but also wish to see more of North Carolina's treasures, the Pamlico and Neuse Rivers both offer excellent waters, anchorages and historic towns for exploration. These waterways are described in "Albemarle Sound to the Neuse River, NC."

Hatteras Island

Hatteras Island is the longest of the barrier islands, stretching from Oregon Inlet south and around the elbow of Cape Hatteras to Hatteras Inlet. Occupied since the 1700s by European settlers the community has always lived off the sea. In 1846 a hurricane opened Hatteras Inlet to the ocean and the community began to thrive. Damage from various storms has at times separated Hatteras Village from the remainder of Hatteras Island.

While there is still a commercial fishing industry here, charter sport fishing is the lifeblood of the community. It is a short run from the island out to the deep waters of the Gulf Stream where the marlin, swordfish and sailfish wait to be caught.

Start your visit at the north end of town in the old Weather Station, which has been restored and now serves as the Hatteras Visitor Center. This was an active weather

Graveyard of the Atlantic

The treacherous waters off the NC Outer Banks have earned the nickname "Graveyard of the Atlantic" due to the over 600 shipwrecks scattered across the ocean floor here. So many shipwrecks occurred that the government eventually required that lifesaving stations be built every 7 miles along the coast of the Outer Banks. These stations and their personnel would later become the U.S. Coast Guard.

From the Outer Banks north to the southern entrance of Chesapeake Bay off the Virginia coastline, two forces collide to create stormy, dangerous seas on a regular basis. One of those forces is the Labrador Current, which is an arctic stream of icy water that originates off the coast of Greenland. The other is the Gulf Stream, which contains warm waters from the Caribbean. When these two forces collide, rough seas and dense fog are usually the result.

In addition to severe weather, these areas have strong currents that can cause sandbars to shift, making it hard to navigate. It is believed that Blackbeard the Pirate used these factors to his advantage to keep from being captured. There is no doubt that this section of the Atlantic Ocean is extremely dangerous.

The first recorded shipwreck in the area occurred in 1526 at the mouth of the Cape Fear River. Explorers were attracted to the area because it was wild and new. It quickly became known as a dangerous spot for mariners, though, as ships began to encounter the deadly conditions often present in the area. Legend has it that the wild Spanish mustangs of the Outer Banks got there by swimming ashore from sinking colonial ships.

The Graveyard of the Atlantic Museum, located in Hatteras Village at 59200 Museum Dr. (252-986-0726), focuses on the history of this area and features many artifacts recovered from area shipwrecks. Blackbeard's ship, Queen Anne's Revenge, was discovered here in 1996. Parts of the ship are on display at the North Carolina Maritime Museum in Beaufort, NC.

Pamlico Sound, NC

HATTERAS ISLAND		Largest Vessel	VHF	Total Slips	Approach/ Dockside Depth	Floating Docks	Gas/ Diesel	Repairs/ Haulout	Min/Max Amps	Pump-Out Station
1. Hatteras Boatyard	(252) 995-4331	55	7	9	6.0 / 6.0			RH	30	

Wireless Internet Access onSpot Dockside WiFi Facility
Visit www.waterwayguide.com for current rates, fuel prices, website addresses and other up-to-the-minute information.
(Information in the table is provided by the facilities.)

Scan here for more details:

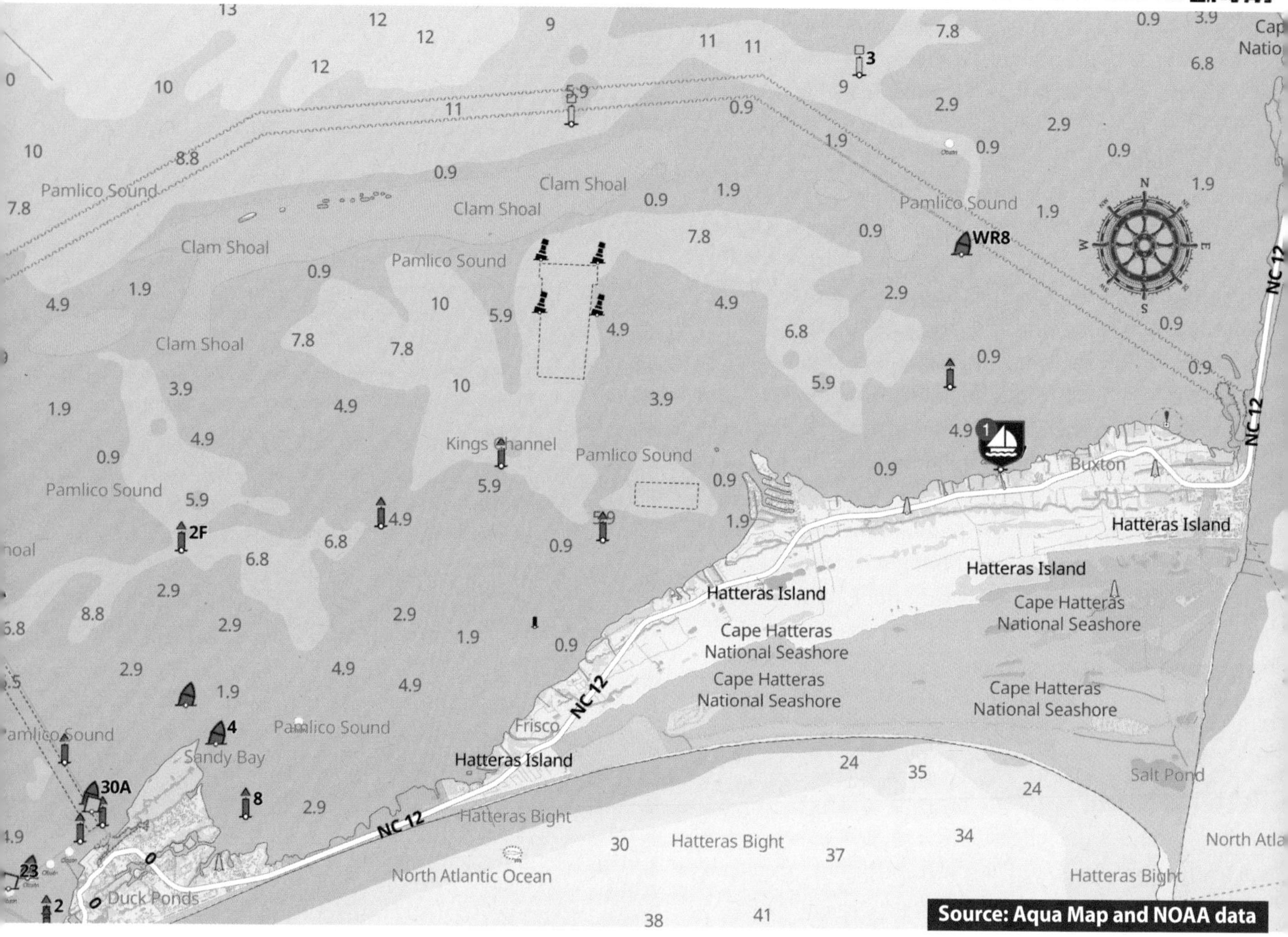

station from 1901 until 1946 and issued the first hurricane warnings ever in the U.S. Its radio operator happened to pick up the SOS from the Titanic the night she sank. A guided tour of Hatteras Village includes 20 historic sites and markers.

Since the 1500s more than 600 ships have wrecked along the treacherous coastline surrounding Cape Hatteras. The Graveyard of the Atlantic Museum at Hatteras Village features displays on shipwrecks and North Carolina's maritime history. Do not fail to visit the circa 1870 Cape Hatteras Lighthouse (10 miles from Hatteras Village). To protect it from beach erosion, it was moved 2,900 feet inland in 1999. (It is the largest structure of its kind ever moved.) The view from its top toward famous Diamond Shoals is an unforgettable sight. It is 268 steps to the top but definitely worth the effort. Climbing hours are 9:00 a.m. to 4:30 p.m. daily. Tickets (available on site for a fee) are required.

NAVIGATION: Use NOAA Chart 11555. The Pamlico Sound side of the island is shoal for a considerable distance out from the shore. Approach Hatteras Village from Pamlico Sound (flashing red "42 RC") via long, well-marked Rollinson Channel. The channel was last charted

Pamlico Sound, NC

HATTERAS BASIN		Largest Vessel	VHF	Total Slips	Approach/ Dockside Depth	Floating Docks	Gas/ Diesel	Repairs/ Haulout	Min/Max Amps	Pump-Out Station
1. Oden's Dock	(252) 986-2555	75	1	25	6.0 / 10.0		GD		30 / 50	
2. Village Marina Hatteras WiFi	(252) 986-2522	70	1	23	7.0 / 6.0		G		30 / 100	
3. Hatteras Harbor Marina WiFi	(800) 676-4939	60	1	44	7.0 / 6.0		D		30 / 100	

WiFi Wireless Internet Access onSpot Dockside WiFi Facility
Visit www.waterwayguide.com for current rates, fuel prices, website addresses and other up-to-the-minute information.
(Information in the table is provided by the facilities.)

Scan here for more details:

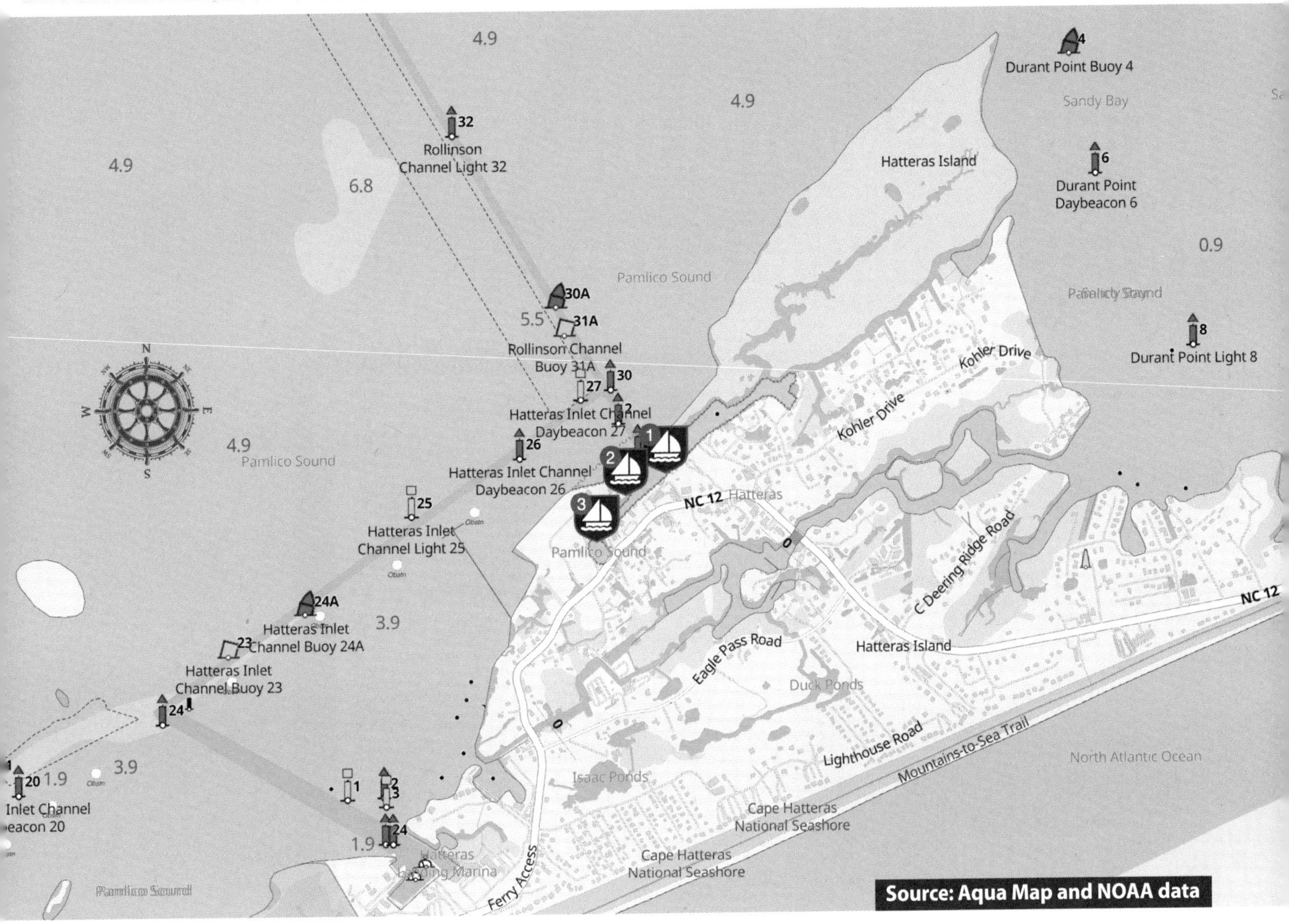

at 4 feet MLW in a May 2015 survey but slightly deeper mid-channel depths have been recently observed. Leave red markers to port.

The Pamlico Sound is big, open water and can get rough. If you are going to venture to the Outer Banks and visit Hatteras and Ocracoke, check your weather window carefully. This is one of those places you can get stuck for many days if bad weather blows in. (There are much worse places to get stuck in our opinion.) Be sure to call ahead and check the status of transient dockage before making your way to Hatteras Village.

Storms have eroded about 1 mile off the point of Hatteras Island, widening the inlet. The Coast Guard has temporarily discontinued numerous navigation aids in the vicinity of Hatteras Inlet due to shoaling. The current navigational aids in this section of the waterway do not accurately mark navigable water due to limited channel depth and reduced channel width. This inlet is frequently dredged; however, seas push sand into the shorter channel faster than dredges can clear it. We do not advise attempting Hatteras Inlet

Pamlico Sound, NC

HATTERAS ISLAND SOUTH		Largest Vessel	VHF	Total Slips	Approach/ Dockside Depth	Floating Docks	Gas/ Diesel	Repairs/ Haulout	Min/Max Amps	Pump-Out Station
1. Teach's Lair Marina Inc. WiFi	(252) 986-2460	70		85	6.0 / 6.0		GD		30 / 50	
2. Hatteras Landing Marina WiFi	(252) 986-2077	90		37	9.0 / 9.0		GD		30 / 50	P

WiFi Wireless Internet Access onSpot Dockside WiFi Facility
Visit www.waterwayguide.com for current rates, fuel prices, website addresses and other up-to-the-minute information.
(Information in the table is provided by the facilities.)

Scan here for more details:

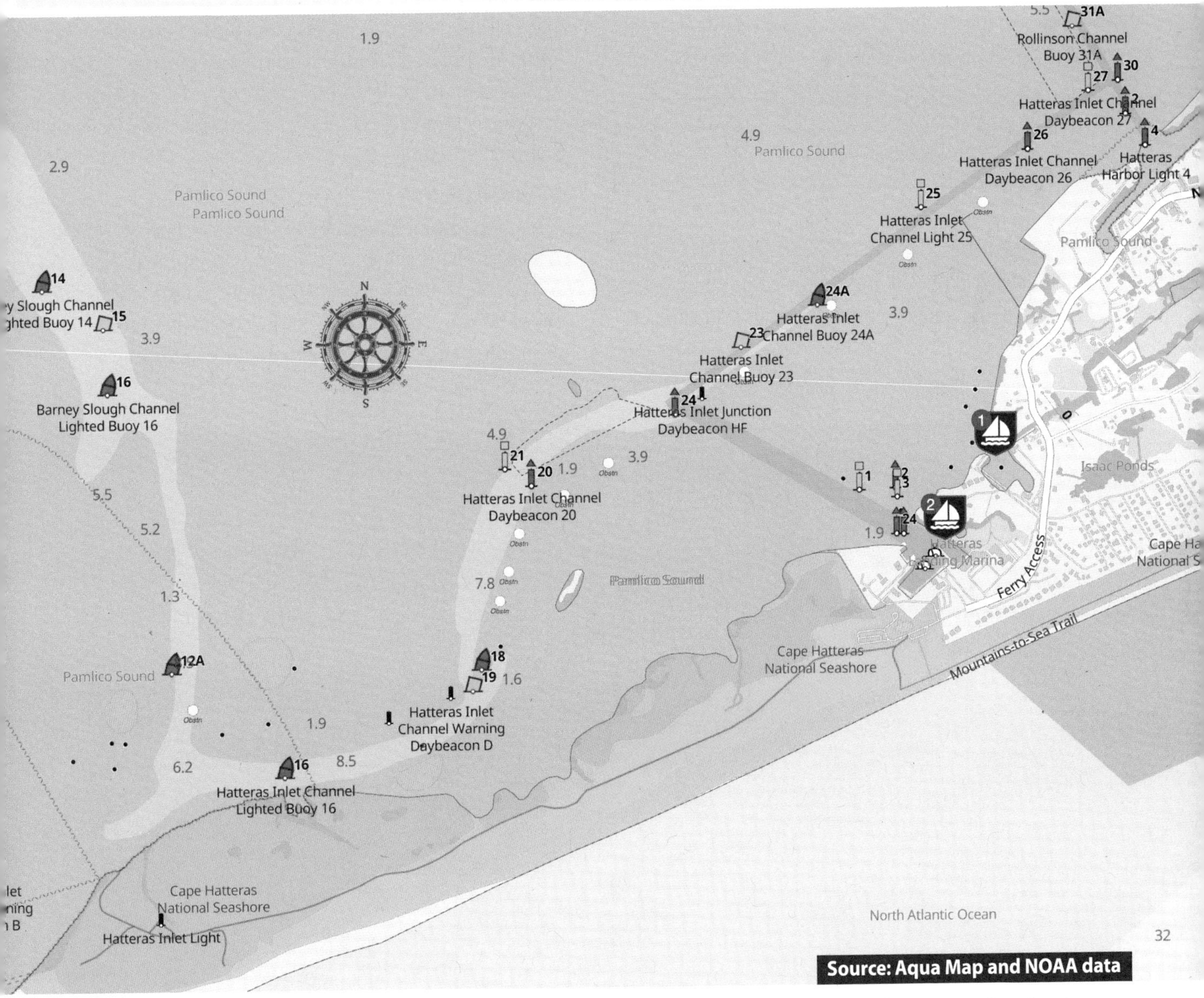

without local knowledge, as the twisting channel shifts regularly and may shoal to 4-foot MLW depths or less.

Dockage: Hatteras Boatyard offers slips and professional boatyard services and a comfortable and casual place for DIY boat owners. Hatteras Basin to the south is breakwater protected and the facilities here cater to serious sportfishermen and accept transient boaters. Hatteras Marlin Club is a private social club but they report that they have transient slips. Call ahead. The 25-slip Oden's Dock has amenities like water and electric hookups, access to showers and quick access to Breakwater Restaurant (252-986-2733) as well as many other Hatteras Village businesses. Village Marina Hatteras has 23 slips available and can accommodate boats up to 70 feet. They also offer dry storage. Hatteras

Harbor Marina is a well-protected, full-service marina with a 20 boat charter fleet as well as deep-water transient slips to accommodate boats up to 60 feet.

In a separate basin to the south Teach's Lair Marina Inc. has transient slips and is the base of several fishing charters. It is managed by the same folks who run Hatteras Landing Marina in the next basin to the south, which is surrounded by a community of fine stores and eateries and extensive boardwalks to the ocean and sound. The marina is well appointed with 9-foot MLW depths in the basin.

Keep an eye out for the car ferries that run in and out of this basin from 5:00 a.m. until midnight. The schedule changes seasonally. See details at NC Dept. of Transportation (www.ncdot.gov/divisions/ferry).

Ocracoke Island

Ocracoke Island is the last link in the Cape Hatteras National Seashore and is about as close as you can get to out-island cruising in North Carolina. The anchorage is well protected, bordered by beautiful beaches with a marine forest and an ancient lighthouse. Read more at "Goin' Ashore: Ocracoke Island, NC" in this chapter.

Although motels, cottages, shops and restaurants cater to a large number of tourists, most of the island's longtime residents strive to preserve the small-town atmosphere and staunchly defend its merits. The road wasn't paved until 1957 when regular ferry service began. Geography is also a contributing factor. Ocracoke has a road but no bridge so access is by boat or aircraft only. Motorists must take a ferry from Swan Quarter, Cedar Island or Hatteras Island. A car ferry and a passenger-only ferry runs between Hatteras and Ocracoke Islands with a seasonal schedule.

NAVIGATION: Use NOAA Chart 11555. Big Foot Slough Channel, routinely used by the large car ferries coming from the mainland, carries minimum depths of 10 feet MLW. It is the obvious choice for deep-draft vessels and those lacking current local knowledge. The channel shoals constantly and portions are frequently dredged.

Pamlico Sound, NC

OCRACOKE		Largest Vessel	VHF	Total Slips	Approach/ Dockside Depth	Floating Docks	Gas/ Diesel	Repairs/ Haulout	Min/Max Amps	Pump-Out Station
1. Ocracoke National Park Service Docks	(252) 475-8316	60		15	7.0 / 7.0				30 / 50	
2. Anchorage Inn & Marina WiFi	(252) 928-6661	100	16	35	10.0 / 9.0		GD		30 / 50	
3. Down Creek Marina	(901) 491-0111			1	12.0 / 8.0				30 / 50	

WiFi Wireless Internet Access onSpot Dockside WiFi Facility
Visit www.waterwayguide.com for current rates, fuel prices, website addresses and other up-to-the-minute information.
(Information in the table is provided by the facilities.)

Scan here for more details:

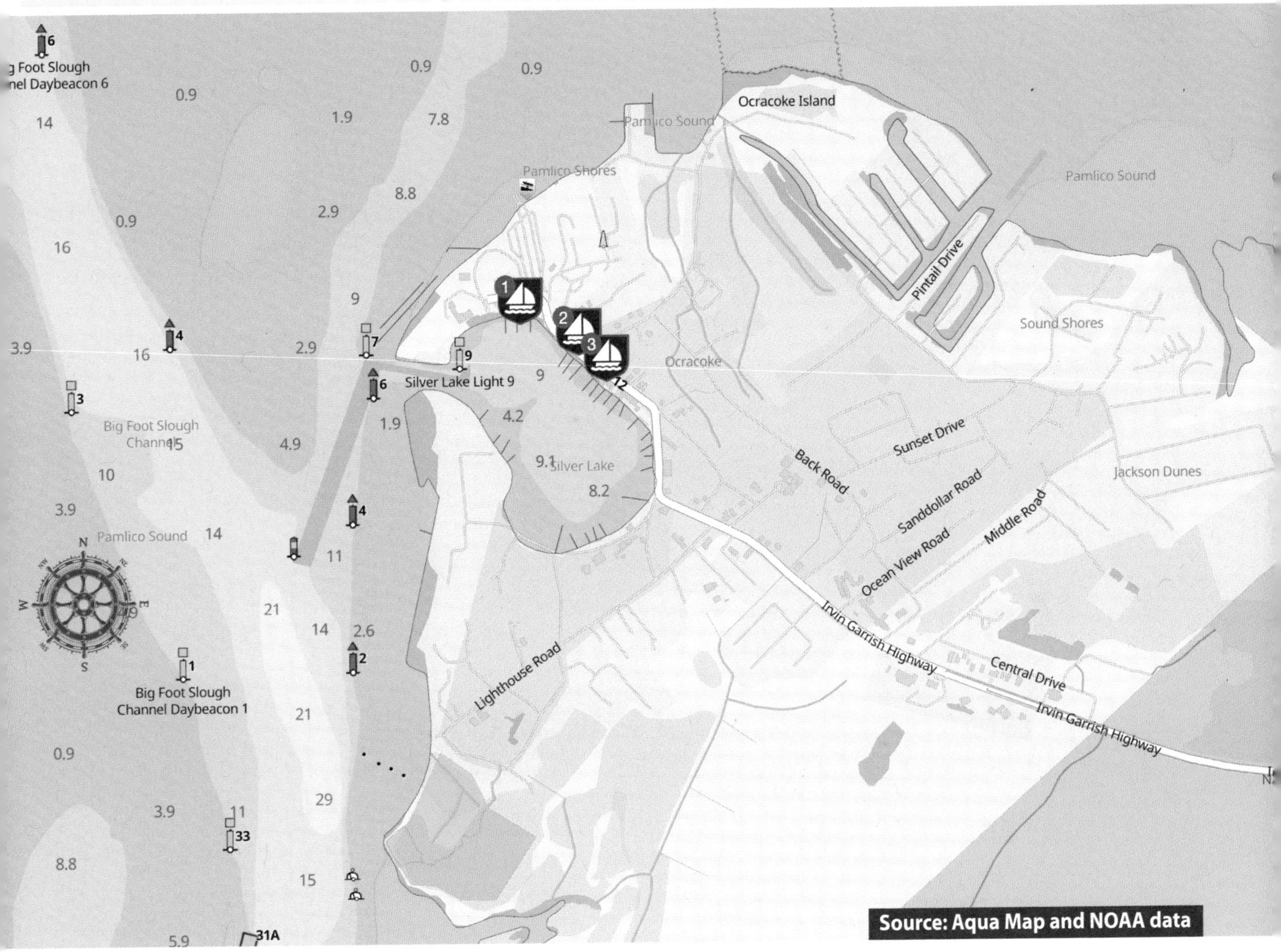

Source: Aqua Map and NOAA data

Be careful not to confuse the Nine Foot Shoal Channel markings for the Big Foot Slough Channel. The most confusing spot is where the Big Foot 6-second flashing red "8" marking the channel into Ocracoke appears close by the Nine Foot 2.5-second flashing red "4." Heading toward the "4" may put you hard aground. Binoculars will be handy for checking the number to ensure you don't head toward the wrong red.

Shoaling has been reported between red daybeacon "10" and green buoy "11." Temporary buoys mark where shoals encroach on the channel so keep a lookout for red nuns and green cans with a letter suffix (although those are sometimes missing or off station). Two steel pipes protruding far above the water near flashing green "13" at the channel entrance will be visible from the sound well before the channel becomes evident. These pipes are part of a sunken dredge boat that appears (both on the

GOIN' ASHORE

OCRACOKE ISLAND, NC

Exuding a Cape Cod ambiance, Ocracoke Island is peppered with pirate legends and a rich nautical heritage. You will hear Ocracokers speaking with an old English "brogue," a unique dialect passed down from the early settlers of the Outer Banks. (Remember that to the locals, you are the one speaking with an accent!) In 2019, a passenger-only ferry began round-trip service between Hatteras and Ocracoke Islands. The schedule changes seasonally. A one-way trip takes about 70 minutes. View a schedule at www.ferry.ncdot.gov.

SERVICES

1. Ocracoke Library
225 Back Rd. (252-928-4436)

2. Ocracoke Island Visitor Center
38 Irvin Garrish Hwy. (252-475-9701)

3. Ocracoke Post Office
1122 Irvin Garrish Hwy. (252-928-4771)

ATTRACTIONS

4. British Cemetery
Four British sailors who perished in the sinking of the HMS Bedfordshire are buried here. Tradition dictated that they be buried on British soil, so the small graveyard was leased to Great Britain in perpetuity. It is cared for by the U.S. Coast Guard (234 British Cemetery Rd., 252-473-2111).

5. Ocracoke Lighthouse
Lighthouse overlooking Silver Lake and the Pamlico Sound. The first light station was built on the island in 1803, but 20 years later was destroyed by lightning and replaced with the current lighthouse (360 Lighthouse Rd., 252-473-2111).

6. Ocracoke Preservation Society Museum
Museum at 49 Water Plant Rd. (on National Park Service property) displaying photographs, artifacts and exhibits pertaining to island life and culture (252-928-7375). A small gift shop exhibits works from local artists. Upstairs is a small research library.

SHOPPING

7. Books To Be Read
Housed in 1898 cottage with selection of books, handcrafted items and unique gifts (34 School Rd., 252-928-3936).

8. Ocracoke True Value
Household tools, supplies and more at 950 Irvin Garrish Hwy. (252-928-4911).

9. Zillie's Island Pantry
Bar and retail shop with large selection of global wines, craft beers, gourmet snacks, cheeses and gift items (538 Back Rd., 252-928-9036). Features wine and beer tastings and a relaxed deck.

MARINAS

10. Anchorage Inn & Marina
205 Irvin Garrish Hwy. (888-295-1128)

11. Down Creek Marina
260 Irvin Garrish Hwy. (901-491-0111)

12. Ocracoke National Park Service Docks
Hwy. 12 (252-928-5111)

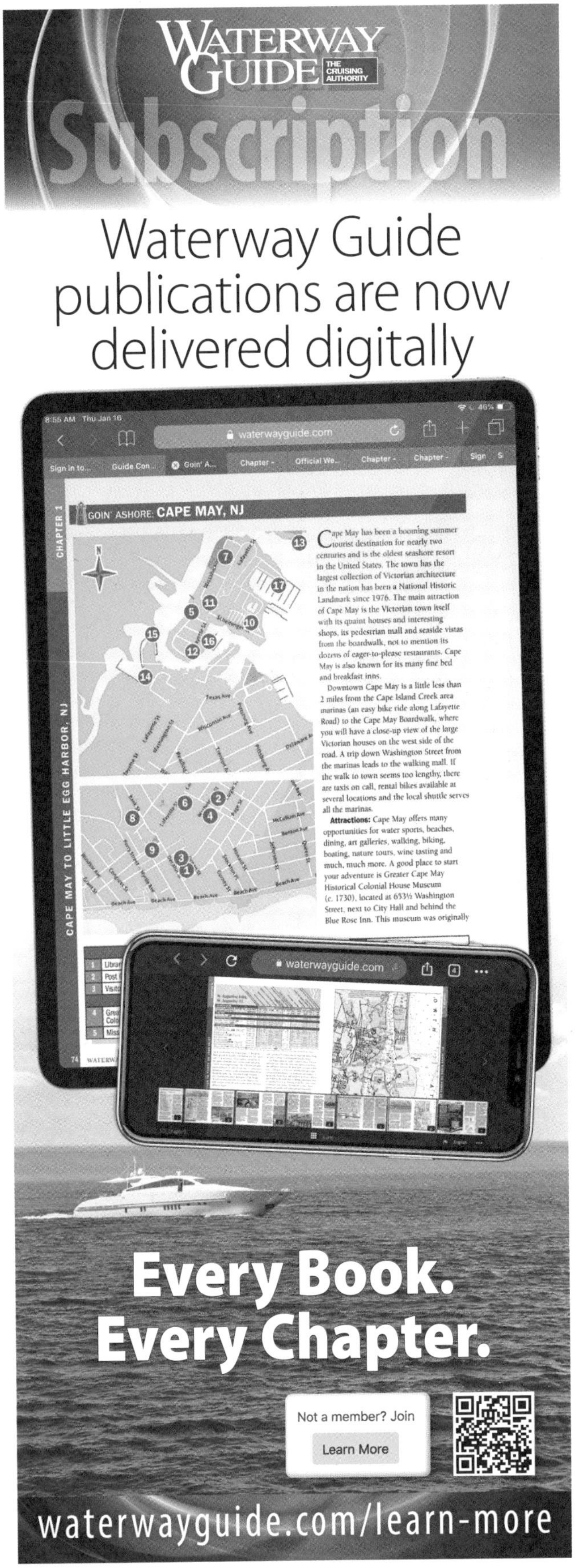

Back Sound

HARKERS ISLAND		Largest Vessel	VHF	Total Slips	Approach/ Dockside Depth	Floating Docks	Gas/ Diesel	Repairs/ Haulout	Min/Max Amps	Pump-Out Station
1. Harkers Island Fishing Center Motel & Marina WiFi	(252) 728-3907	48	69	70	4.0 / 6.0		GD	RH		

WiFi Wireless Internet Access onSpot Dockside WiFi Facility
Visit www.waterwayguide.com for current rates, fuel prices, website addresses and other up-to-the-minute information.
(Information in the table is provided by the facilities.)

Scan here for more details:

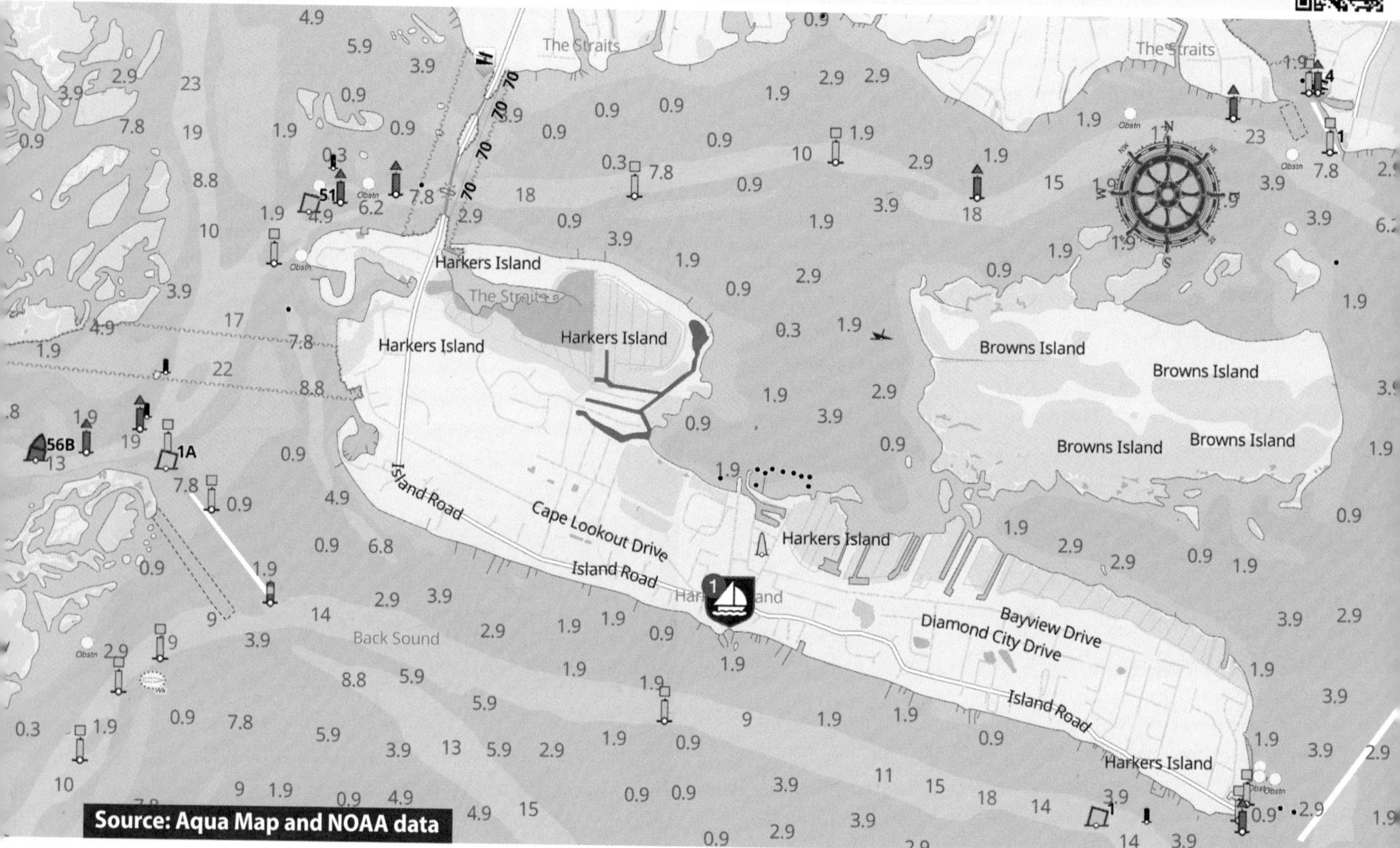

Source: Aqua Map and NOAA data

NOAA chart and on first sighting) to be a partial obstruction. In fact the wreck is located off to the east side of the channel. There is also a charted 6-foot MLW spot in that vicinity as shown on NOAA Chart 11550 (by flashing red "NB").

Dangers are not restricted to shoaling. Dredges work just outside the temporary buoys and ferry traffic is a regular and serious hazard. If possible, time your trip to enter the channel after any exiting ferry traffic or to follow incoming ferries.

Ocracoke's harbor, known as Silver Lake (or Cockle Creek by locals), is entered using a secondary channel that heads north from a junction marker. The marker has a 6-second flashing red light and a red-over-green "SL" board. Once south of the junction marker head north along the entrance channel, which is well marked and straightforward, keeping reds on the starboard side. Stay in the middle of the channel but watch for ferries. Prop thrust from the ferries can cause a considerable current inside Silver Lake.

Ocracoke Inlet can be an alternative to the long diversion to Beaufort when heading north or south around Cape Hatteras, but this is not an inlet to be attempted under anything but the most benign conditions and only with local knowledge. Although protected from the north, shoaling is constant and breakers on both sides are evident in nearly all conditions. Check with Coast Guard Sector North Carolina via VHF Channel 16 for current conditions before using the inlet at or near low tide.

Dockage: The Ocracoke National Park Service Docks are located near the Park Service offices on the port side of the Silver Lake entrance between two ferry docks. Rates are reasonable with discounts for senior citizens possessing a Park Service

"Golden Age Passport." Enter these transient docks between two clusters of huge pilings and tie up alongside sturdy piers faced with large, widely spaced bollards. (These were originally built for PT boats during World War II.) In the summer the maximum allowable stay here is two weeks. There is room for about a dozen transients on a first-come, first-served basis. Expect some surge here as the ferry enters and departs.

The 35-slip Anchorage Inn & Marina has space for transients with a swimming pool and bike rentals. This can be a busy place during in-season weekends; it is best to call ahead for reservations. Nearby Down Creek Marina is home to Denison Yachting but has some transient space. Call ahead. Note that there is a no laundry service on the island.

Anchorage: Silver Lake is a perfectly protected harbor with anchoring depths of 7 to 13 feet MLW, except in the shallow cove to the southwest. Holding is good but watch for a weedy bottom, which can give a false sense of security. There are also reports of debris on the bottom. Make certain you set your anchor well. There is ample room for those who want to drop a hook, even on summer weekends. Be sure to anchor away from the ferry channel and dock.

There are two dinghy docks–the National Park Service dock and a community dock. These provides easy access to groceries, restaurants and shops. Many restaurants and coffee shops offer outdoor seating and are pet friendly. Note that many of the restaurants and stores are closed between November and March.

Harkers Island & the Lower Banks

When locals talk about the Harkers Island area they usually include the adjacent mainland villages fronted by The Straits, which separates the island from the mainland. This marshy region is known as "Down East" and has a total of only 3.8-square miles.

The Harkers Island Visitor Center at the east end of the island also serves as home to the National Park Administrative Offices and Headquarters (252-728-2250). They have an interactive map of the Cape Lookout National Seashore Park, exhibits and seasonal programs.

NAVIGATION: Use NOAA Chart 11545. To the south 27-mile-long Core Sound runs behind the narrow ocean barrier of Core Banks. Once part of the ICW route, it was abandoned when the land cuts that link the present ICW were dredged. Cruising boats now usually bypass the sound due to the very shallow water: 3.5-foot draft is the limiting factor when transiting Core Sound. Drum Inlet is closed to navigation.

The channels in Core Sound call for local knowledge and there are only a few wide-spaced markers. Shallow-draft boats less than 25 feet long can reasonably consider cruising here. Shoaling to 3 feet MLW has been reported across the channel between Core Sound flashing red "5" and red daybeacon "5A."

Harkers Island Bridge with a 14-foot closed vertical clearance crosses The Straits. (Opens on signal.) An offshoot channel before the bridge, which is marked and has 6-foot MLW depths, leads to Marshallberg after flashing green "42A" (a private aid). This is strictly small-boat territory; otherwise, rent a car in Morehead City and take the "long way around" to visit this area.

Dockage: Harkers Island Fishing Center Motel & Marina may have a slip for vessels to 48 feet. This is accessed from the south side of the island via a channel with 3- to 4-foot MLW depths. Seek local knowledge and plan to enter with a rising tide if needed.

Lookout Bight

One of the most beautiful anchorages of the Carolinas, Lookout Bight offers a secure place to set the hook in all but the most inclement weather within the protective arm and elbow of the cape. Miles of unspoiled, dune-backed beaches of the Cape Lookout National Seashore provide the perfect setting to search for shells of the giant whelk or watch the antics of laughing gulls, a variety of terns, willets, dunlins, cavorting oystercatchers and the inimitable working patterns flown by resident black skimmers. Look for the wild horses on nearby Shackleford Banks, where they have roamed since the 1500s when a failed colony released the horses. They have fended for themselves and prospered ever since. Cape Lookout Lighthouse has been a landmark for the coast since 1812.

While arriving in Cape Lookout Bight on your own vessel is the better way to see the bight, you can also go by passenger ferry from Beaufort or Harkers Island. The Island Express Ferry runs daily (year round). The schedule is seasonal.

NAVIGATION: Use NOAA Chart 11545. Cape Lookout is best accessed from the ocean from Beaufort Inlet, although it can be accessed in a shoal-draft vessel via Back Sound, which leads between Shackleford Banks (part of Rachel Carson Reserve) and Middle Marsh. This is strictly small-boat territory.

Barden Inlet has shoaled to an average channel depth of less than 3 feet MLW. Under the current condition of the inlet, the aids to navigation can no longer be configured to safely mark a passable channel and the aids to navigation have been discontinued. Two Danger Shoal Buoys are at each end of the removed section. Mariners are advised to use extreme caution while navigating this area.

At the eastern end of Cape Lookout a dredged channel leads to Lookout Bight and Cape Lookout. Coming from the ocean, the entrance buoy to the Bight (flashing red "4") is located 6.2 miles from flashing red "6" on an east-southeasterly course coming from Beaufort Inlet. Beaufort Inlet is discussed in more detail in Chapter 6, "Beaufort to Southport, NC."

Anchorage: During summer months most skippers anchor just east of Power Squadron Spit at Lookout Bight, taking advantage of prevailing southwesterly breezes with a short fetch. Holding is excellent in thick mud at depths ranging from 8 to 26 feet MLW. Anchor for up to 14 days within the boundaries of Cape Lookout National Seashore. For a grand view, climb to the top of the Cape Lookout Lighthouse (open through late September).

The distinctive black-and-white diamond pattern on the Cape Lookout Lighthouse helps you locate your position. Black diamonds indicate you are north or south of the light, while white diamonds indicate you are east or west.

NEXT STOP

The next section gets you back on your way south on the ICW bound for Morehead City and beyond to Charleston, SC. This succession of dredged channels and shallow sounds doesn't allow for much sailing but the scenery makes up for it. You will begin to feel the pull of the tides, which become progressively greater as you head towards Georgia, where they peak at an impressive 9 feet.

Beaufort, NC to Isle of Palms, SC

Chapter 6: Beaufort to Southport, NC

Chapter 7: Lockwoods Folly, NC to McClellanville, SC

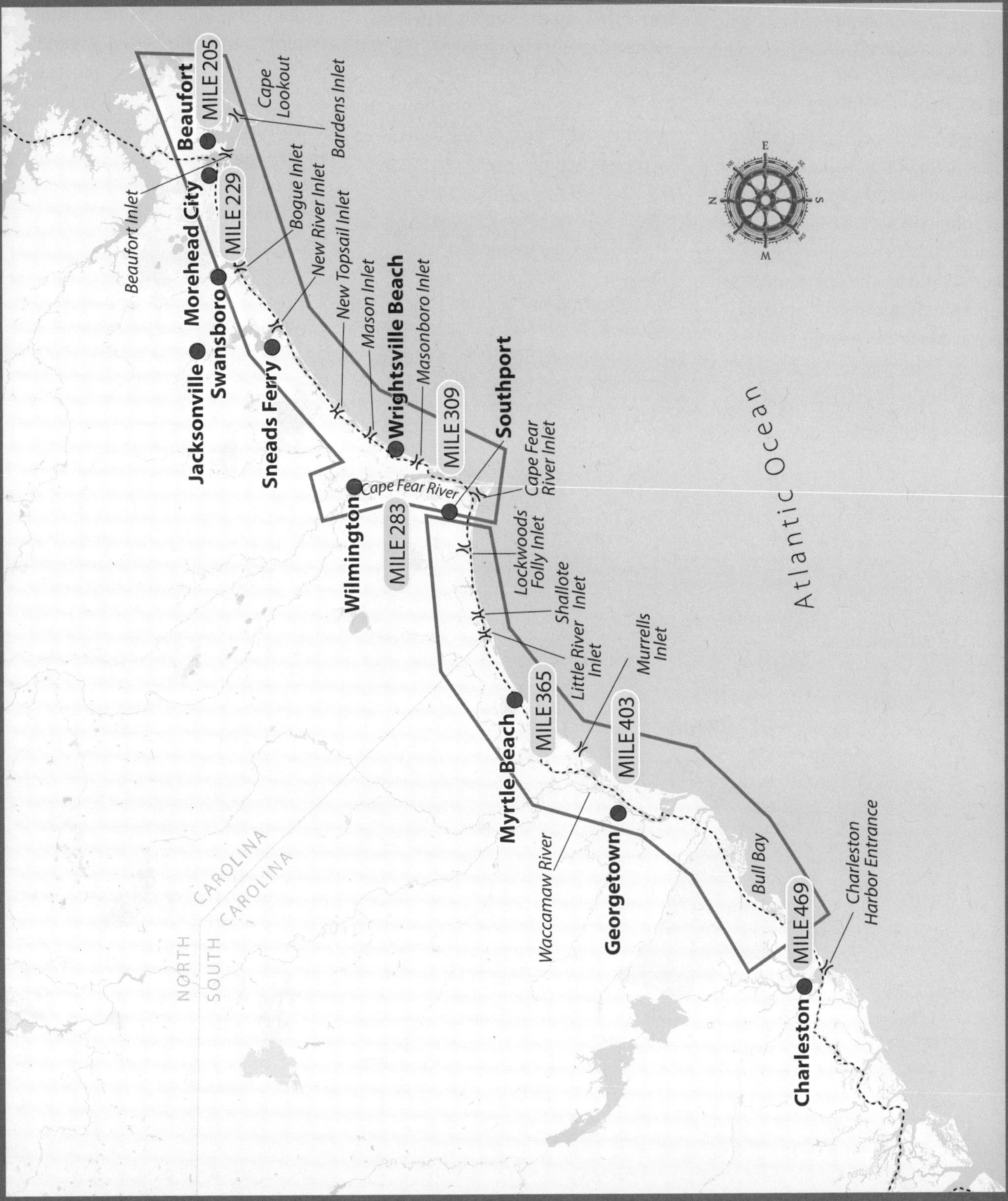

Visit Waterway Explorer at www.waterwayguide.com

TO BEAUFORT & MOREHEAD CITY

Roughly 265 miles along the ICW from Bogue Sound in North Carolina to Charleston, SC, this passage will slowly reveal different kinds of waterways and scenery. The wide, deep waters of the North Carolina sounds are behind you and the route now follows a succession of dredged channels through small sounds, shallow sloughs and salt marshes, all connected by a series of land cuts. Halfway along the passage North Carolina gives way to South Carolina and you begin to enter the aptly named "Lowcountry."

Cruising Conditions

This section of the ICW has more than its fair share of bridges, particularly in the stretch between Swansboro and Georgetown (SC). Seventeen of these are fixed high-level bridges. Some bridges open only once an hour and your trip may be delayed by their schedules.

Boats with masts taller than 65 feet must run outside from Beaufort Inlet, NC, to Georgetown or Charleston, SC, both of which have safe big-ship entrances.

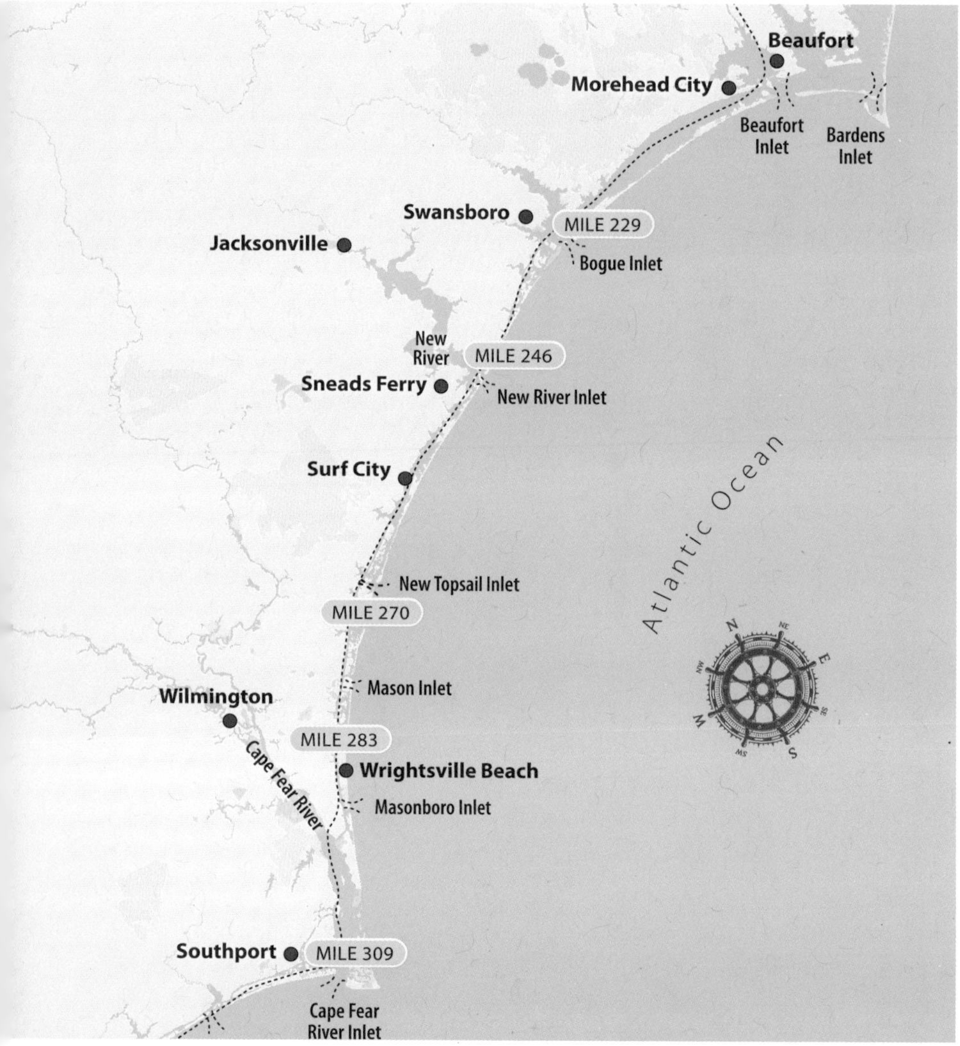

Shoaling continues to be an issue in some sections of this stretch of the ICW. While we cover these areas in detail in this section, certain areas require your utmost attention and are noted in the guide by "navigation alerts." Several of the problem areas were dredged in the 2017 and again in 2019 including the channel near Browns Inlet, Mason Inlet, Carolina Beach Inlet, Lockwoods Folly Inlet and Shallotte Inlet. When shoaling becomes a problem the Army Corps of Engineers does its best to survey these areas and frequently gives specific GPS waypoints that you can use to avoid the shoals. Be aware that conditions may change between the survey date and the time you pass through.

While the mile marker figures do not change, aids to navigation are frequently relocated and additional aids added to reflect the current deep part of navigable channels especially near inlets. If a marker or two on your chart appears to be on the wrong side of the magenta line, don't be alarmed. In most cases the marker has been moved as conditions have changed and is in the correct position on the chart. It is our recommendation that you always follow the markers and not the magenta line unless you have extremely reliable local information. Also check the *Local Notice to Mariners* (www.navcen.uscg.gov) for possible changes in the markers.

Bridge Openings

ICW bridges will not delay openings if boats are already waiting so you must know your speed and calculate your transit carefully; slow boats may not be able to synchronize their passages with the openings. Bridges in VA and NC respond on VHF Channel 13, while SC and GA bridgetenders monitor VHF Channel 09. It is a good idea to monitor both.

Tidal Currents

Keeping an eye on tidal currents is important in this area. Beginning at Morehead City you suddenly encounter tide and tidal current conditions quite different from those on the run down from Norfolk. The 3-foot tidal fluctuation becomes progressively greater and peaks at 9 feet in Georgia. It is important to have accurate tide and current information available when traveling this portion of the ICW.

NOAA offers tidal information online at www.tidesonline.nos.noaa.gov.

Tidal currents grow stronger as you head south and are strongest around inlets, bridges and converging waterways, which have a side-sweeping effect. Try to visualize beforehand which way the current might push (or pull) your boat and consider how an ebb or flood tide might affect the situation. Learn to check your course astern from the relative position of the markers and steer to compensate. Places where the side-setting effect of the current can be serious are detailed in the text.

When approaching a bridge with the current have your boat under control and do not move in too close while waiting for the bridge to open. There is no regulation on these waters as to which boat has the right-of-way passing through bridges, but it is generally accepted that a boat going against the current should yield to one going with the current. It is foolish and dangerous to contest the channel with another boat under any circumstance.

Be careful to follow the marked channel, particularly on a falling tide as going aground then can be serious. Your boat might wind up high and dry, allowing for the possibility of a swamping when the tide begins to rise.

Adams Creek to Beaufort, NC–ICW Mile 185 to Mile 200

Beaufort and its sister city, Morehead City, are two of the most popular stopovers between Norfolk and Florida. Beaufort is well known as a transient stop with numerous marinas and service facilities that can handle the needs of cruisers, both power and sail. Morehead City is a renowned commercial and sportfishing center with a large fishing charter fleet year-round. Note that tides and currents now begin to be a major consideration as you proceed south on the ICW in close proximity to the coast.

NAVIGATION: Use NOAA Chart 11541. The ICW route leaves the Neuse River at Mile 185 and enters Adams Creek. Do not be tempted to cut inside Garbacon Shoal flashing green "7" in the Neuse River (Mile 180.6) when approaching Adams Creek. The fishermen's markers off Winthrop Point indicate nets just below the surface. Follow the magenta line on the NOAA chart around flashing green "1AC" (Mile 183.8), which marks the entry to Adams Creek, and make a dogleg approach. You will then be on a range for 1.5 miles.

The aids to navigation along Core and Adams Creeks are located 30 to 35 feet outside the channel limits. Although the chart shows 8-foot MLW depths in Adams Creek opposite marker "9," cutting this corner puts you in 6-foot MLW depths. In general the marks are widely spaced here. Flashing red "8A" helps with this. Where you have a green on one side and a red a long way farther along, go almost to the green before changing course for the red. Unlike the common practice of marking the inside edges of turns and shoals, the channel markers are usually set on the outside edge. This makes it tempting to cut the corners but it is safer to follow the legs to their full natural extensions before making your turns.

Flashing red "18" at Mile 191.3 is the last marker before the canal, which is unmarked but holds good 12-foot MLW depths. Keep to the center of the channel except when passing other boats or being passed. This area was last dredged in 2019.

Adams Creek is connected to Core Creek at Mile 195.8 via the Adams Creek Canal, a 5-mile-long land cut that ends at the headwaters of Core Creek below the **Core Creek (NC 101) Bridge**. Adams Creek Canal is mostly undeveloped. Keep an eye out for deer, eagles and other wildlife along the way. Adams and Core Creeks as well as the canal may have floating debris so keep a close eye on the course ahead.

There is a huge residential development on the Adams Creek Canal north of the Core Creek Bridge with numerous docks extending toward the ICW channel. Tidal currents from the Beaufort Inlet begin to appear in the vicinity of the bridge. Currents are particularly strong around the bridge, at Bock Marine just below the bridge

Adams Creek, NC

ADAMS CREEK CANAL		Largest Vessel	VHF	Total Slips	Approach/ Dockside Depth	Floating Docks	Gas/ Diesel	Repairs/ Haulout	Min/Max Amps	Pump-Out Station
1. Sea Gate Marina WiFi MM 193.3	(252) 728-4126	60	16	70	6.0 / 6.0		GD		30 / 50	P
2. Bock Marine WiFi MM 196.0	(252) 728-6855	75	16	7	8.0 / 8.0			RH	15 / 50	

WiFi Wireless Internet Access onSpot Dockside WiFi Facility
Visit www.waterwayguide.com for current rates, fuel prices, website addresses and other up-to-the-minute information.
(Information in the table is provided by the facilities.)

Scan here for more details:

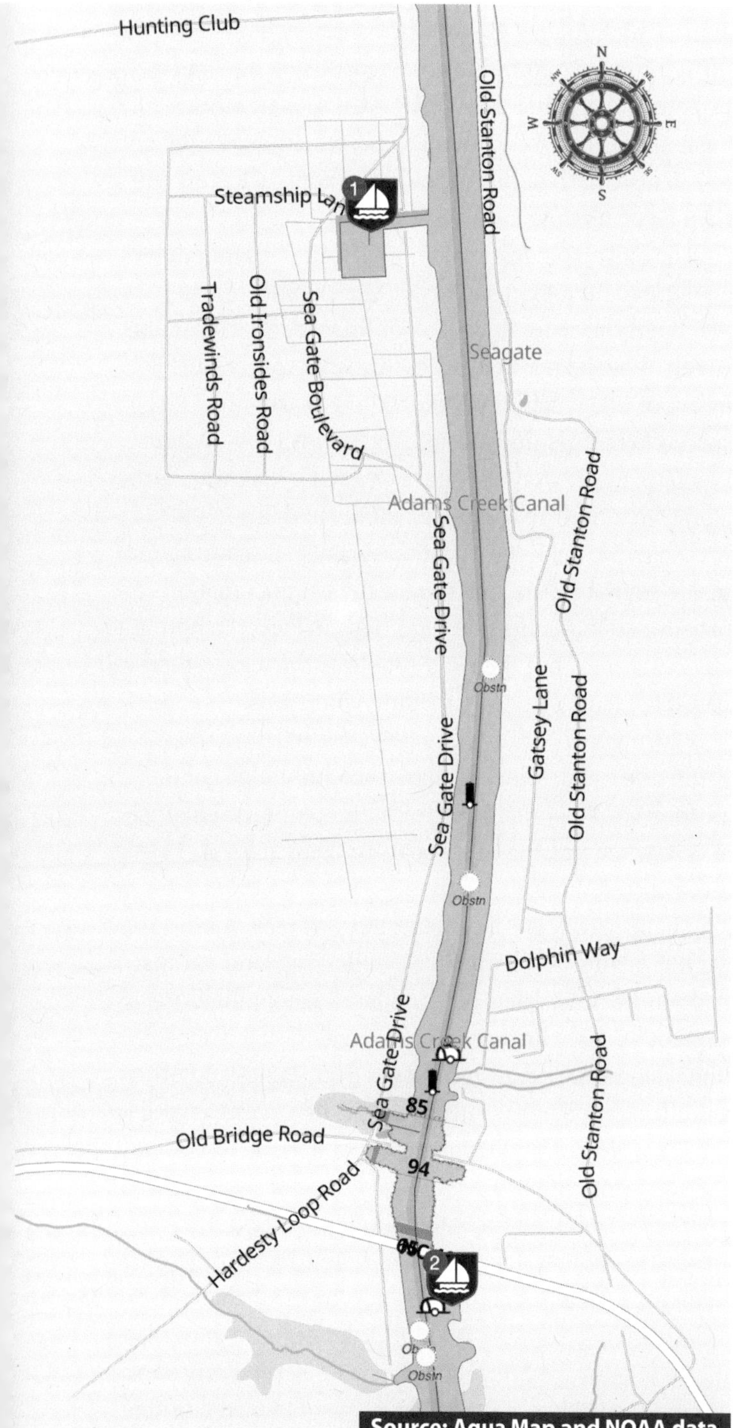

Source: Aqua Map and NOAA data

and at the outside docking area at Jarrett Bay Boatworks. Strong wind-driven currents can be felt as well in the Adams Creek Canal and into lower Adams Creek in certain conditions. From the Core Creek (NC 101) Bridge to the Morehead City/Beaufort area at Mile 205, ebb current provides strong assistance to southbound craft.

At Mile 199.3 the ICW route turns to the southeast after flashing red "24." From there follow the Newport River as it makes several dogleg turns. At Mile 200.7 you can continue on the ICW to Morehead City or to take a side trip to Beaufort, using the channel to port and keeping red daymarker "2" to starboard.

The split between the ICW and the channel to Beaufort causes much confusion. On the ICW heading south pass red daybeacon "28" and red daybeacon "30" (shown on the NOAA chart as a red nun) to starboard then pass flashing green (2+1) junction marker "RS" to port and red nun buoy "30A" starboard. Also note that "30A" has been relocated. If your chart does not show it across from the junction buoy, then your chart is out of date.

There may be additional uncharted buoys between flashing green "29" and green daybeacon "31." To further complicate matters shoaling to 5 feet MLW has been observed in this area. Mariners are advised to use extreme caution while navigating this area.

Dockage: At Mile 193.3 Sea Gate Marina is located on the west side of the Adams Creek Canal with slips. The marina is part of a neighborhood association. Just beyond the Core Creek (NC 101) Bridge (Mile 195.8), the family-run Bock Marine has repair and service capabilities and welcomes DIY boaters. The tidal flow can make docking demanding but you will find plenty of helping hands.

Jarrett Bay Boatworks, a Down East Carolina custom builder and full-service boatyard, operates a large facility in the Jarrett Bay Marine Industrial Park at Mile 198 on

Adams Creek, NC

JARRETT BAY MARINE INDUSTRIAL PARK		Largest Vessel	VHF	Total Slips	Approach/ Dockside Depth	Floating Docks	Gas/ Diesel	Repairs/ Haulout	Min/Max Amps	Pump-Out Station
1. Jarrett Bay Boatworks WiFi MM 198.0	(252) 728-7100	125	16	15	12.0 / 9.0	F	GD	RH	15 / 100	P
2. Western Branch Diesel-Beaufort MM 198.0	(252) 504-2185				/			R		
3. Bluewater Yacht Sales-Beaufort	(252) 728-2645			8	/			RH		
4. Gregory Poole Marine Power MM 198.0	(252) 504-2640	350	16		/			R	30	
5. Banks Boatworks WiFi MM 198.0	(252) 728-7358	150			12.0 / 9.0			RH	30 / 100	P
6. Beaufort Inlet Boatyard WiFi MM 198.5	(252) 728-2541	100	16	4	7.0 / 5.0	F		RH	15 / 50	

WiFi Wireless Internet Access **onSpot** Dockside WiFi Facility
Visit www.waterwayguide.com for current rates, fuel prices, website addresses and other up-to-the-minute information.
(Information in the table is provided by the facilities.)

Scan here for more details:

Core Creek. With a 175-acre yard, a 200-ton lift and a 12-foot-deep basin, the service department at Jarrett Bay Boatworks can handle virtually any project on vessels up to 130 feet in length or a draft of up to 10 feet. Transient dockage is available for vessels up to 125 feet including nine 22-foot-wide slips fronting the ICW. A well-stocked Ship Store is on site.

Adjacent to Jarrett Bay is Western Branch Diesel-Beaufort, one of the largest power dealers on the East Coast. They have a fully stocked parts department and respond to after-hour emergencies. In the same marine industrial park are Gregory Poole Marine Power (offering engine repair) and Bluewater Yacht Sales-Beaufort (boat brokerage).

Banks Boatworks lovingly restore classic powerboats from the 1920s through the 1960s. Beaufort Inlet Boatyard is also in the Jarrett Bay Marine Industrial Park with repairs and may have space for you. Call ahead.

Anchorage: Just beyond the straight stretch of the first range in Adams Creek and behind quick flashing green "9" is the mouth of Cedar Creek (Mile 187.6), a good anchorage for vessels with drafts of 6 feet or less with more room than you might think from the chart. The secret is to go farther in where you get good protection from a south wind. Anchor towards the south shore and east of the 5-foot line as shown on the charts. There is about 7 feet MLW as you snug up behind the point of land to protect you from a south wind. There is a strip of sand on the south shore for pet relief. Be sure to pick up when done. Shrimp boats leave this harbor at all hours (day and night) in season. Many years ago a sailboat sunk in this anchorage. The wreck of a sailboat is approximately 150 to 200 yards to the east-northeast of flashing green "9A"and is marked by white PVC poles.

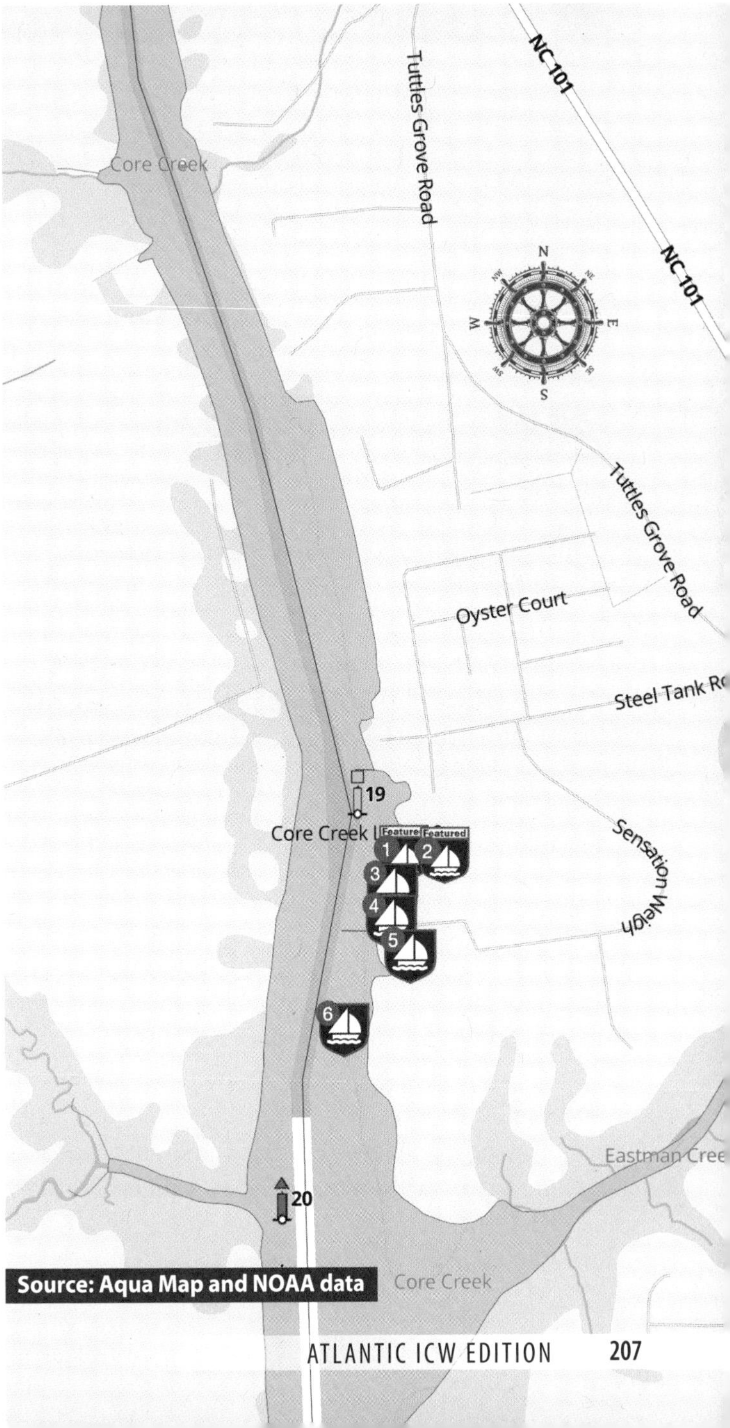

Source: Aqua Map and NOAA data

Although the chart shows only 5 feet MLW, 6-foot MLW depths or better are available in the much more protected Jonaquin Creek farther back to port off Cedar Creek. It provides all-around protection with excellent holding. Back Creek (Mile 189)–1.5 miles south of Cedar Creek–can provide excellent protection from southwest and northeast winds and wakes from the ICW for boats drawing 4.5 feet or less. There are no other protected anchorages until you reach Beaufort and Morehead City.

Beaufort, NC

Founded in 1709 the charming city of Beaufort, NC (pronounced "BO-fort" not "BEW-fort" as in the SC town) preserves traces of its nautical history as a backdrop to a thriving modern boating center. Beaufort is home to yachts of all descriptions year-round, either moored out or tied up along the town side of the waterfront channel. During the fall passage-making sailboats dominate the scene with preparations for ocean voyages from this major jumping-off point for trips to the Caribbean.

Long hailed as the "Gateway to the Caribbean," Beaufort is often cooled by a brisk sea breeze. Then in the fall, as the western edge of the Gulf Stream veers to within 40 miles of the inlet, fresh northwest winds carry eager sailors into the Atlantic. It is a four-day sail to the Bahamas and one day more to Bermuda. This close proximity to the Atlantic trade routes was not lost on the early settlers and to this day Beaufort is still receiving cargo and sailors from afar. It is a great walking town with eclectic shops, good restaurants and a waterfront full commercial fishing vessels, shrimpboats, kayaks and paddleboards as well as pleasure boats of all sizes. Read more at "Goin' Ashore: Beaufort, NC" in this chapter.

The North Carolina Maritime Museum Conservation Lab, located northwest of the marina repair yard on Russell Slough Channel (referred to locally as the Gallants Channel) is a receiving and conservation area for the artifacts brought up from the nearby wreck of Blackbeard's Queen Anne's Revenge. It is not open to the public although there are occasional guided tours of the

GOIN' ASHORE

BEAUFORT, NC

In Beaufort, the town is the culture and its seascape the canvas. A flourishing arts community of painters, photographers, sculptors and writers reside here, as evidenced by the numerous galleries, all within walking distance of the docks. To see the town from a different point of view, the popular Beaufort Ghost Walk covers approximately nine blocks and lasts around one hour. You will be entertained by pirate guides, who will regale you with an enjoyable assortment of chilling stories about ghost ships and haunted houses. Tours start at 108 Middle Ln. (252-772-9925).

SERVICES

1. **Austin Veterinary Animal Hospital**
   1550 Lennoxville Rd. (252-838-9028)

2. **Seaside Family Practice**
   407 Live Oak #1 (252-728-2328)

ATTRACTIONS

3. **Beaufort Historic Site**
   The 1713 Beaufort Towne is depicted in a 12-block area in the National Register of Historic Places that includes the Carteret County Courthouse (the oldest wood-framed courthouse in North Carolina); the Old Jail with 28-inch-thick walls and legends of active ghosts; and the Apothecary & Doctors Office, housing a unique collection of medicinal and pharmaceutical artifacts. The Welcome Center and gift shop are located at 130 Turner St. (252-728-5225).

4. **North Carolina Maritime Museum**
   Features an active boatbuilding program and environmental education programs (315 Front St., 252-504-7740). The Maritime store carries nautical and coastal books, gifts, prints and souvenirs. The Annex facility on Gallants Channel (next to Town Creek Marina) features an exhibit on North Carolina shipwrecks. Photographs and artifacts include from the wreck of Queen Anne's Revenge, Blackbeard's flagship.

5. Old Burying Ground

Beneath the shade of live oak trees at 400 Ann St. (252-728-5225), the weathered tombstones chronicle the heritage of Beaufort and the surrounding coast. Listed on the National Register of Historic Places, the cemetery was deeded to the town in 1731 by Nathaniel Taylor. Union soldiers, Confederate soldiers, freed African-Americans and slaves all rest together here.

SHOPPING

6. Barbour's Marine Supply

Chandlery and machine shop catering to commercial and sport fishermen, boat yards and DIY individuals at 410 Hedrick St. (252-728-2136). Celebrated 100 years of service in 2019.

7. Coastal Community Market

Health-food store carrying organic fruits and veggies, grass-fed beef, pasture raised chicken and pork, and local eggs as well as organic coffees and teas. Located just few blocks from the waterfront at 606 Broad St. (272-728-2844).

8. Scuttlebutt Nautical Books

A legendary fixture on the Beaufort waterfront since 1993 at 433 Front St. (252-728-7765) specializing in "nautical books and bounty" such as charts, guidebooks and nautical gifts and gear. They ship, offer gift certificates and accommodate special orders.

9. The General Store

Just what the name implies: Enjoy ice cream, fudge (32 flavors) and other treats while you shop for Guy Harvey, Simply Southern and Columbia Sportswear, as well as toys and souvenirs. They also have a coin-operated laundry (515 Front St., 252-728-7707).

MARINA

10. Beaufort Dock Marina

500 Front St. (252-728-2503)

Beaufort, NC

TOWN CREEK AREA		Largest Vessel	VHF	Total Slips	Approach/ Dockside Depth	Floating Docks	Gas/ Diesel	Repairs/ Haulout	Min/Max Amps	Pump-Out Station
1. Gallants Channel	(252) 728-2762	100		20	12.0 / 12.0	F			30 / 50	
2. Town Creek Marina WiFi 1.3 mi. S of MM 202.0	(252) 728-6111	180	16	71	10.0 / 10.0	F	GD	RH	30 / 100	P
3. Beaufort Yacht Basin WiFi	(252) 504-3625	100	16	74	7.0 / 5.5	F			30 / 50	P
4. Homer Smith Docks and Marina WiFi onSpot	(252) 728-2944	150	16	95	10.0 / 8.0	F	GD		30 / 100	P
5. Beaufort Inn WiFi 1.7 mi. E of MM 202.3	(252) 728-2600	45		12	12.0 / 5.0				30	
TAYLOR CREEK										
6. Beaufort Docks Marina WiFi MM 202.0	(252) 728-2503	250	16	98	16.0 / 16.0	F	GD	R	30 / 100	P

WiFi Wireless Internet Access onSpot Dockside WiFi Facility
Visit www.waterwayguide.com for current rates, fuel prices, website addresses and other up-to-the-minute information.
(Information in the table is provided by the facilities.)

Scan here for more details:

Town Creek Marina
Russell Slough
ICW
Beaufort Docks Marina
Town Creek
Bulkhead Channel
Beaufort

65'
92'
65'
82'
142'
95'
112'

Beaufort, NC

TAYLOR CREEK		Largest Vessel	VHF	Total Slips	Approach/ Dockside Depth	Floating Docks	Gas/ Diesel	Repairs/ Haulout	Min/Max Amps	Pump-Out Station
1. Loggerhead Marina - Boathouse Marina WiFi MM 202.0	(252) 838-1524	100	16	30	15.0 / 12.0	F	GD	RH	30 / 200+	P

WiFi Wireless Internet Access onSpot Dockside WiFi Facility
Visit www.waterwayguide.com for current rates, fuel prices, website addresses and other up-to-the-minute information.
(Information in the table is provided by the facilities.)

Scan here for more details:

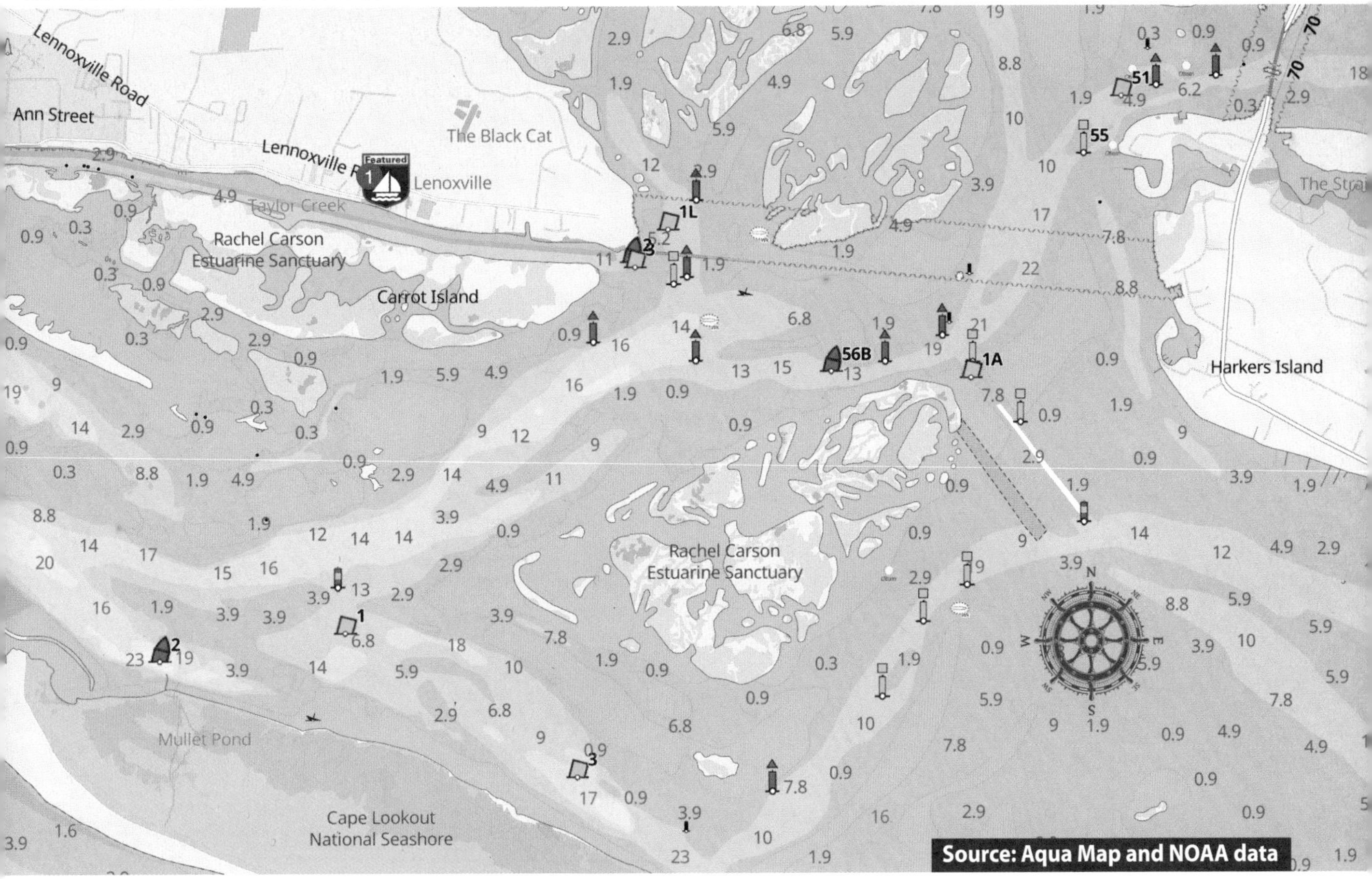

Beaufort, NC

RADIO ISLAND		Largest Vessel	VHF	Total Slips	Approach/ Dockside Depth	Floating Docks	Gas/ Diesel	Repairs/ Haulout	Min/Max Amps	Pump-Out Station
1. Radio Island Marina MM 203.9	(252) 726-3773	35		8	5.0 / 4.0	F	G	RH	30	

WiFi Wireless Internet Access onSpot Dockside WiFi Facility
Visit www.waterwayguide.com for current rates, fuel prices, website addresses and other up-to-the-minute information.
(Information in the table is provided by the facilities.)

Scan here for more details:

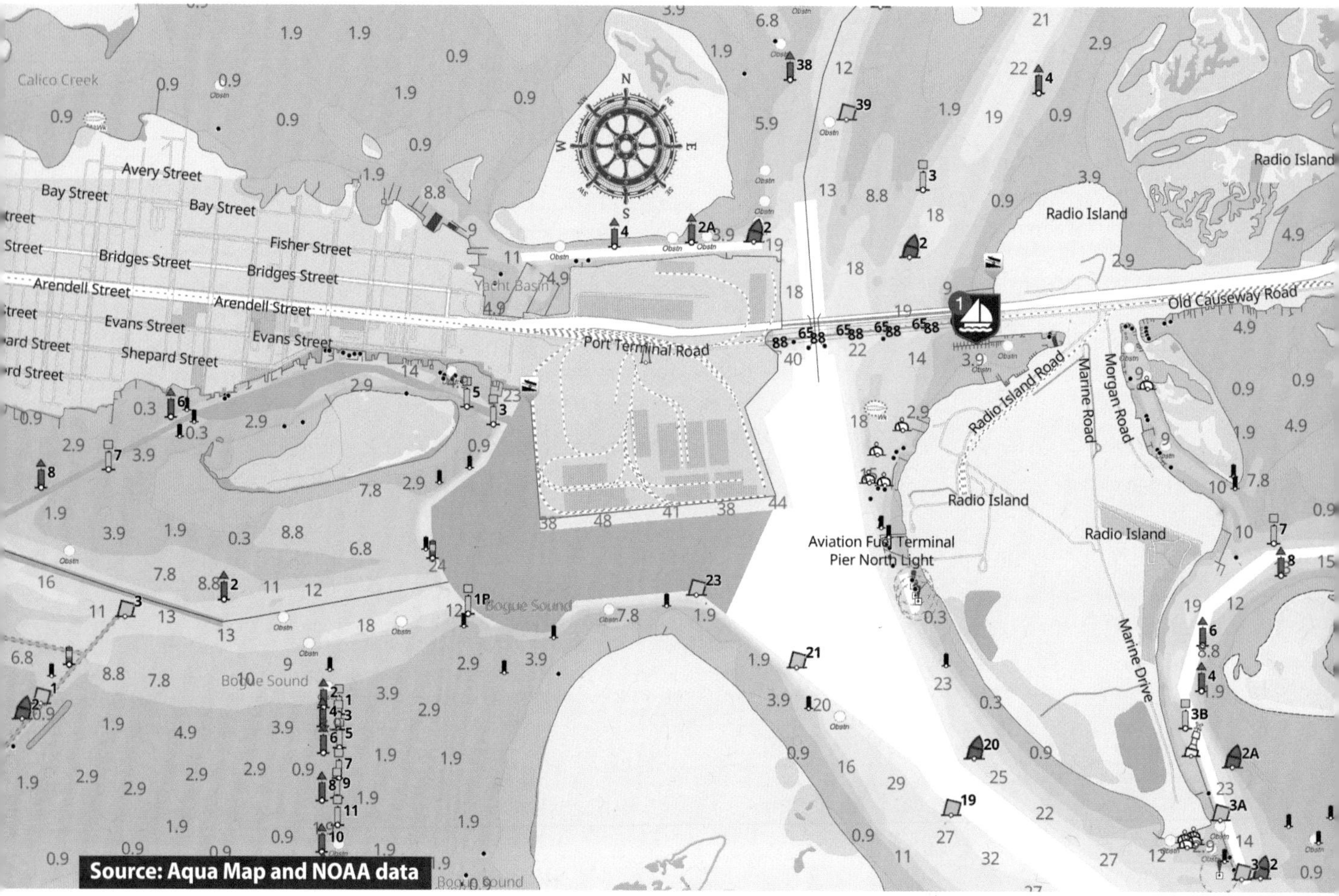

premises. This facility has a new bulkhead on the creek and there has been considerable expansion ashore.

NAVIGATION: Use NOAA Chart 11545. Southbound vessels heading for Town Creek should depart the ICW by passing daybeacon "28," red daybeacon "30" (shown on the latest NOAA chart as a nun buoy), flashing green (2+1) junction marker "RS" and red daybeacon "2" to starboard (Mile 200.8) then follow the Russell Slough Channel east of the ICW and west of Russell Creek.

Favor the green side of the channel at red daybeacon "4" and after making the turn to starboard at flashing green "5" plot a course to green daybeacon "7." Red nun buoy "6A" beyond red daybeacon "6" assists you in reaching green daybeacon "7." Where "8" used to be there is now a lighted junction marker, flashing "RG" with red at the top and green at the bottom of its board. Once past green daybeacon "7" turn immediately to port toward red daybeacon "10" and continue southeast on Gallants Channel to quick flashing red "12" to Town Creek.

Southbound vessels on the ICW headed to Taylor Creek can bear south and follow the Russell Slough Channel markers to the Beaufort waterfront. (Note that Russell Slough Channel is known locally as "Gallants Channel" where it passes Gallants Point and leads towards the bridge.) The new 65-foot fixed vertical clearance **U.S. 70 Bridge** (also known as Gallant Channel Bridge) replaced the old bridge to the south, which has been removed. Note that the overhead power lines remain in place. They are charted with an 87-foot vertical clearance but have been observed to be closer to 85 feet.

Note that the western end of Taylor Creek has shoaling when approaching from the north. Contact the dockmaster for local knowledge.

If northbound on the ICW and bound for Beaufort, turn southeast from the turning basin into the Morehead City Channel. Heading toward the inlet round the southern tip of Radio Island and pick up quick flashing red buoy "2," the entrance marker to Beaufort. (This is the same approach if traveling north from Beaufort Inlet.)

Remember that the numerous range markers for the entrance from the Beaufort Inlet are different from the red or green ICW lateral system or the lateral markers for the inlet. Some boats have mistaken these range markers (especially at night) for other navigation aids in this area, realizing the error only once they have run aground.

Dockage: There are several great marinas in the Town Creek area. Gallants Channel is an annex of the North Carolina Maritime Museum (www.ncmaritimemuseumbeaufort.com). Although it is a bit removed from the facilities of Beaufort (1 mile from the waterfront), it does have attractive transient pricing. It offers floating docks with water and power but no heads, showers or other facilities.

The full-service Town Creek Marina is located on Town Creek Basin at Mile 202, where you can find transient dockage or take on gas or diesel in-slip or at their fuel docks. This is a major repair facility with state-of-the-art floating docks and premiere amenities. The popular City Kitchen restaurant is above the marina office and is a great spot for catching the sunset. The marina provides a courtesy car for trips to provision or the Beaufort waterfront.

Beaufort Yacht Basin may have space for you on their floating docks. They cater to sportfishers, powerboats and sailboats in an attractive and comfortable environment. Homer Smith Docks and Marina is nearby with some transient space and even though it is a working dock, they have many attractive cruiser amenities. Beaufort Inn on the south side of the Gallants Channel Bridge has 6 reserved transient slips (with 5-foot MLW dockside depths).

The largest and most convenient marina to town is Beaufort Docks Marina, where the marina slips along Front St. are adjacent to the sights, sounds and activities of downtown Beaufort and convenient to all the waterfront attractions, businesses and services. Beaufort Docks Marina has 98 slips with floating piers maintained solely for transients. There are 25 restaurants and ample shopping within a short walk and the marina offers free WiFi and an adjacent laundry. The marina has diesel fuel available in-slip and multiple courtesy cars for trips around town.

Loggerhead–Boathouse Marina at Front Street Village bills itself as "part boat storage facility, part yacht club." They offer a variety of amenities and have a complete Ship Store. The on-site 34° North Restaurant (252-838-7250) is open to the public and offers a weekend brunch menu on Saturday and Sunday (reservations recommended). There is also a boutique hotel on site. Trolley service into Beaufort is available.

Anchorage: Boats sometimes anchor to the northwest of Town Creek Marina in 6 to 12 feet MLW. Anchorage space is minimal, however, due to the remains of sunken boats in the anchorage and a few private moorings. The holding is poor and the anchorage is exposed to the northwest. Anchoring space here is further limited by the docks and shoreside activities at the North Carolina Maritime Museum. You can, however, land your dinghy on the small sandy beach to the southwest. The anchorage in Taylor Creek is very limited; you may not be able to find space to drop the hook. Keep this in mind as you plan ahead.

The swift tidal current and the close quarters dictate that you use caution when anchoring. Anchor only on the southern side of the channel and consider using a Bahamian moor. Be mindful of the precipitous shoaling along the southern side of the anchorage. Large excursion vessels use the channel at all hours to get to their docks upstream and the Coast Guard frowns on anchored boats that encroach upon the channel.

The town dock across the street from the Post Office has a convenient floating dinghy dock; look for the gazebo at the shore end. The bathhouse at the western end of the Beaufort Docks Marina is available for a modest charge. There is a second dinghy dock two blocks away at the foot of Orange Street.

Beaufort Inlet

Beaufort Inlet is a big ship inlet that is wide, deep and very well marked. From the Beaufort Inlet area you can take the dinghy and do some real exploring. The long dinghy trip east through Taylor Creek out into Back Sound past Harkers Island and down to Cape Lookout provides a glimpse of North Carolina that transients do not often witness. This trip is for anyone with a large, sturdy, fast and reliable dinghy or shoal-draft cruiser and time on their schedule to play. On the return trip, follow Shackleford Banks on the inside from Middle Marsh to the inlet. There is some beautiful, clear water with many deserted sandy islands, quaint shoreline and plentiful wildlife including birds, fish and turtles. Be sure to leave time to explore Cape Lookout.

NAVIGATION: Use NOAA Chart 11541. To reach the Beaufort Inlet from Taylor Creek head west out of the creek following the marked channel that swings to port past Radio Island and then joins the Morehead City and inlet channels. The inlet channel leads south past Shackleford Banks then south-southwest out to sea. Lights on the Shackleford Range markers at night are bright green and skippers should identify them when making a night entry through the inlet. The range markers are much brighter than channel markers and have different characteristics. An offshore jaunt to the south from Beaufort Inlet to Masonboro Inlet at Wrightsville Beach is approximately 73 miles, while the inside route is about 70 miles.

Dockage: Radio Island Marina is mainly a yacht brokerage that may be able to accommodate you in a pinch.

Morehead City

Like its sister city, Beaufort, Morehead City is a strategic spot on the southeast coast and it has become a favorite for offshore skippers heading north to avoid the rigors of Cape Hatteras and with ICW boaters heading south and looking forward to some free travel along the open Atlantic. Thus a large marine community serving both commercial and recreational boats flourishes here. All repairs–from electronics and propellers to diesel engines–are available at Morehead City and the waterfront is packed with restaurants to feed the crew. See more at "Goin' Ashore: Morehead City, NC" in this chapter.

NAVIGATION: Use NOAA Charts 11545 and 11541. Southbound vessels heading for Morehead City on the ICW pass daybeacon "28," red daybeacon "30," flashing green (2+1) junction marker "RS" and continuing on the well-marked Newport River channel. (Note that the

Morehead City, NC

MOREHEAD CITY		Largest Vessel	VHF	Total Slips	Approach/ Dockside Depth	Floating Docks	Gas/ Diesel	Repairs/ Haulout	Min/Max Amps	Pump-Out Station
1. Morehead City Yacht Basin WiFi **0.7 mi. W of MM 203.5**	**(252) 726-6862**	**200**	**16**	**88**	**12.0 / 8.0**	**F**	**GD**		**30 / 100**	**P**
2. Portside Marina WiFi MM 205.0	(252) 726-7678	150	16	25	35.0 / 10.0	F	GD	RH	30 / 100	P
3. Dockside Yacht Club-PRIVATE WiFi MM 203.9	(252) 247-4890	80	16	75	14.0 / 14.0	F			30 / 50	P
4. Sanitary Fish Market & Restaurant MM 204.9	(252) 247-3111	55		15	12.0 / 12.0					
5. Morehead Gulf Docks 0.7 mi. W of MM 204.9	**(252) 726-5461**	**130**	**16**	**9**	**14.0 / 14.0**	**F**	**GD**		**30 / 50**	
6. Morehead City Transient Docks WiFi	(252) 725-5025	50	16	10	8.0 / 8.0	F			20 / 50	
7. Russell Yachts 0.7 mi. N of MM 205.0	(252) 240-2826	100		5	12.0 / 12.0			RH	30	

WiFi Wireless Internet Access **onSpot** Dockside WiFi Facility
Visit www.waterwayguide.com for current rates, fuel prices, website addresses and other up-to-the-minute information.
(Information in the table is provided by the facilities.)

Scan here for more details:

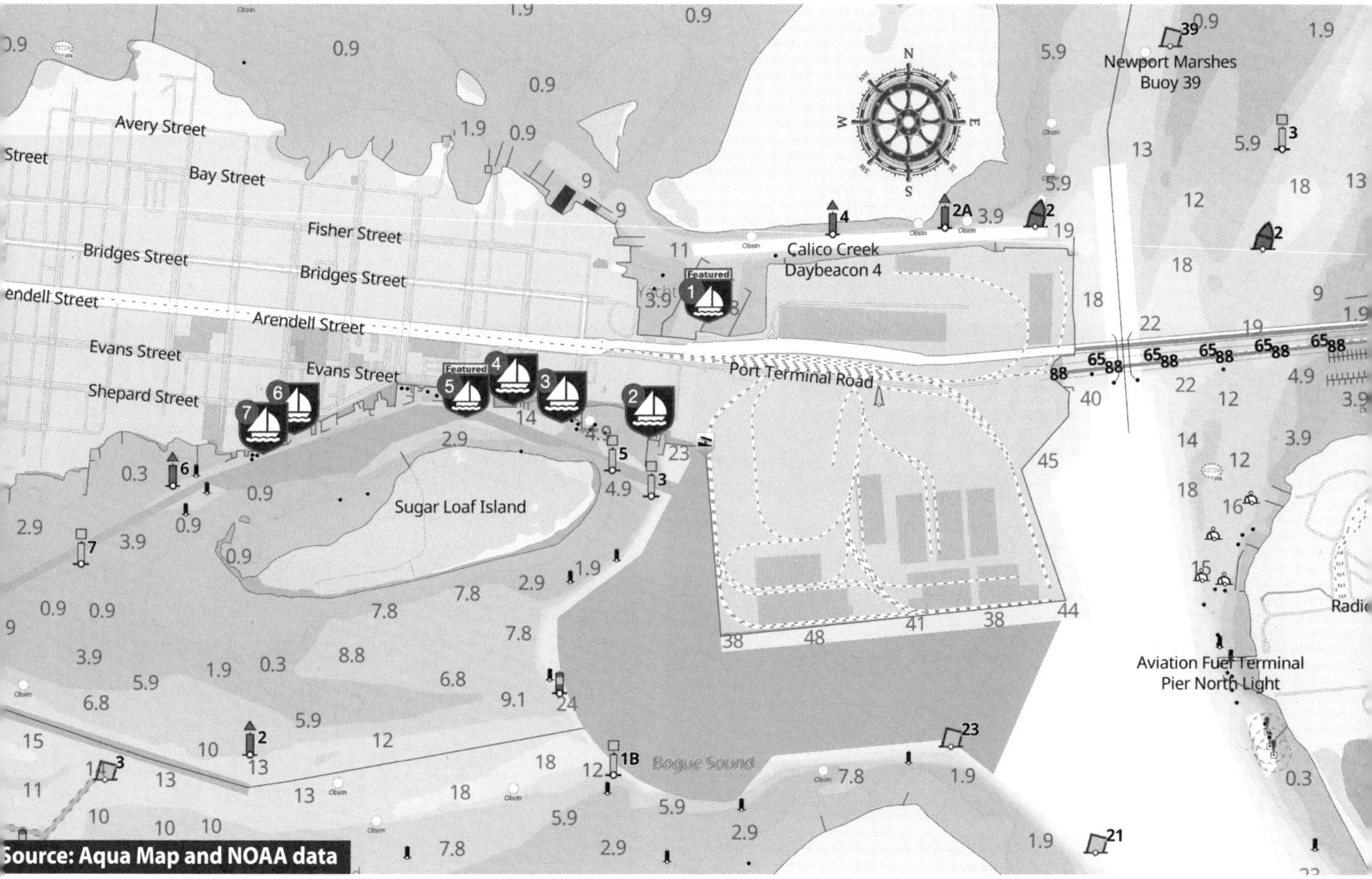

Source: Aqua Map and NOAA data

NOAA chart mistakenly shows daybeacon "30" as a red nun.) The ICW channel that leads down the Newport River to the bridges at Mile 203.8 is holding its depths (12 feet MLW) but has a very strong crosscurrent (1 to 2 knots). The shoal to the west is bare at low tide (rather than 2 feet MLW as indicated on the NOAA chart) so be sure to stay in the channel. There may be additional uncharted buoys in this area.

Proceed under the **Beaufort Channel (U.S. 70) Bridge** (65-foot fixed vertical clearance) and adjacent **Beaufort Channel Railroad Bridge** (4-foot closed vertical clearance, usually open) between Beaufort and Morehead City (Mile 203.8). The horizontal opening at the Beaufort Channel (US 70) Bridge is very narrow with strong current and is made more difficult by the narrow opening of the railroad bridge on the other side. This is a "one boat at a time" passage.

As a peninsula Morehead City has two waterfronts. Morehead City Yacht Basin is the only facility for recreational vessels on the back (north) side of the Morehead City waterfront. From the north leave the ICW about 0.25 mile north of the Beaufort Channel (US 70) Bridge and adjacent Beaufort Channel Railroad Bridge at Mile 203.8, turning west into Calico Creek at red nun "2," the next red marker south of the flashing red "38." Do not confuse this buoy with the red nun buoy on Chimney Island Channel farther north and east of the bridges. Leave red markers to starboard on the way in.

The Morehead City waterfront proper (on the south side of the peninsula) is approached from the ICW by taking a sharp turn to the west around the Port Terminal Turning Basin (at Mile 204.2) before reaching the junction light "MC" at Mile 205 (where the marker numbers start over). Stay well off the bulkhead and be alert for ship and tug traffic around the terminal.

NO WAKE ZONE

Local authorities and the Coast Guard enforce a No-Wake Zone here 24 hours a day.

The channel between Sugar Loaf Island and Morehead City carries at least 7 feet MLW to the west end where it shallows dramatically. A channel is shown on some charts leading back to the ICW to the west but depths reach as low as 5 feet MLW in spots. At low tide or in a deep-draft vessel, returning to the ICW via the channel east of Sugar Loaf Island is the safer, if slower, option.

High-speed reversing tidal currents rip through this area. Ebb tide begins at the Beaufort Channel Bridge and the adjacent railroad bridge (Mile 203.8) 11 minutes after the times given for Charleston Harbor. If you leave Morehead City southbound at low water slack, you can carry the flood tide south to around Mile 220. This is especially advantageous for smaller and slower boats.

Dockage: The "back way" into Morehead City's north side (above the Beaufort Channel (US 70) Bridge) has a well-marked canal, Calico Creek, which holds 9.5-foot MLW depths and leads directly to the well-protected Morehead City Yacht Basin. The facility has been around since 1947 and has played host to Ernest Hemingway, along with legions of other renowned sportsmen, and is the original home of the Big Rock Blue Marlin Tournament. Transient dockage on well-maintained floating docks and in-slip fueling is available. Amenities include an on-site laundry facility, clean restrooms and spacious showers plus a comfortable lounge/office area overlooking the harbor.

Proceeding under the Beaufort Channel (US 70) Bridge and then entering Morehead City's waterfront from the Turning Basin, you will encounter a large number of establishments including marinas, commercial docks and seafood restaurants. The uninhabited Sugar Loaf Island and marshland to port strike a natural counterpoint. Keep in mind the high-speed reversing tidal currents that rip through this area. All of these facilities can pose a docking challenge when the tidal current is running at 3 to 4 knots. Check with the dockmaster before you approach.

Traveling west from the Turning Basin (on the south side) the full-service Portside Marina is the first facility to starboard behind a protective breakwater. They have deep-water slips and dockage for vessels up to 125 feet. Dockside Yacht Club in the next basin is private. Sanitary Fish Market & Restaurant, a large retail seafood market and popular restaurant, offers face-dock moorage (without service or dockside amenities). Do take the time to stop and eat here; the portions are huge and the food (mostly seafood) is fresh. They are most well-known for their hush puppies.

Morehead Gulf Docks are in the heart of Morehead City and can accommodate vessels to 130 feet on their face dock with 13-foot MLW dockside depths. They have a well-stocked chandlery, where in addition to tackle and clothing, they also sell coffee, ice cream, snacks and some groceries. Transients are welcome.

Morehead City Transient Docks are to the west. The municipal dock are managed by Morehead City Parks and Recreation Department. They have 10 slips for vessels to 50 feet with 8- to 10-foot MLW dockside depths. Complimentary dockage is available for up to 4 hours. (No free overnight dockage.) Russell Yachts is nearby with a few transient slips. Call ahead.

Anchorage: Swing room is limited but anchoring is possible in the lee of Sugarloaf Island with good holding in 7 to 8 feet MLW (despite the 3.5 feet MLW designated on the NOAA chart). Several vessels appear to be permanently anchored fore-and-aft, decreasing the amount of space available and requiring some careful consideration of placement in order to remain distant from the non-swinging boats.

TO NEW TOPSAIL INLET

Cruising Conditions–Bogue Sound

Below Morehead City the ICW follows Bogue Sound almost 25 miles to Swansboro (Mile 229), the port for Bogue Inlet. The ICW channel to Swansboro is marked with daybeacons and lights; green and red are staggered with few exceptions.

The Bogue Sound route is by no means monotonous. Covered with tall pines and windswept oaks, the high mainland side is dotted with beautiful homes, many with private docks along the sound. Dolphins often frequent the sound's lower portion and goats sometimes appear on the spoil islands. You can also expect to see people digging for clams (although clamming is banned in some places so check before you join them). Opposite the

GOIN' ASHORE

MOREHEAD CITY, NC

Morehead City was originally called Shepherd's Point and marked the confluence of Newport River, Bogue Sound and Beaufort Inlet. Governor John Motley Morehead envisioned a great commercial hub, so he designed a town built around city blocks with a system of alleys between each block in the form of an "H." In this way, all houses and businesses could be serviced from the alleys. Each block contained 16 lots, and much of that "Philadelphia plan" remains today.

SERVICES

1. **Carteret County Chamber of Commerce**
   801 Arendell St. #1 (252-726-6350)

2. **Webb Memorial Library and Civic Center**
   812 Evans St. (252-726-3012)

ATTRACTIONS

3. **History Museum of Carteret County**
   Houses a collection of local artifacts and an excellent research library with over 10,000 books and publications at 1008 Arendell St. (252-247-7533). The museum store offers books on a wide variety of subjects and unique gifts for children and adults.

4. **Olympus Dive Center**
   For an up close look at history, try deep sea diving. Depending on conditions, you may be able to dive on an 18th-century schooner, cargo ship, British fishing trawler, World War I gunboat or German submarine. The dive shop is located at 713 Shepard St. (252-726-9432).

SHOPPING

5. **Almost Southern Marine**
   Specializing in marine hardware and other boating/trailer needs at 410-C Arendell St. (252-622-4074).

6. **Carteret County Curb Market**
   On the corner of 13th and Evans Streets is the oldest continuously operating curb market in North Carolina. Stalls open each Saturday through Labor Day at 7:30 a.m. Come and pick from fresh vegetables, local seafood, cut flowers and baked goods.

7. **Dee Gee's Gifts & Books**
   A great selection of nautical books, fiction, non-fiction and works by local authors at 508 Evans St. (252-726-3314).

MARINAS

8. Dockside Yacht Club
301 Arendell St. (252-247-4890)

9. Morehead City Transient Docks
807 Shepard St. (252-725-5025)

10. Morehead City Yacht Basin
208 Arendell St. (252-726-6862)

11. Morehead Gulf Docks
611 Evans St. (252-726-5461)

12. Portside Marina
209 Arendell St. (252-726-7678)

13. Russell Yachts
903 Sheppard St. (252-240-2826)

14. Sanitary Fish Market and Restaurant
501 Evans St. (252-247-3111)

Morehead City Moorings

Bogue Sound, NC

PELETIER CREEK		Largest Vessel	VHF	Total Slips	Approach/ Dockside Depth	Floating Docks	Gas/ Diesel	Repairs/ Haulout	Min/Max Amps	Pump-Out Station
1. 70 West Marina MM 209.2	(252) 726-5171	55	16	70	5.0 / 5.0		GD	RH	30 / 50	
2. The Harbor Master Inc. MM 209.2	(252) 726-2541	50	16	30	8.0 / 5.0	F		RH	30	
3. Taylor Boat Works MM 209.2	(252) 726-6374	55		8	4.6 / 6.0			RH	30 / 50	
4. Coral Bay Marina MM 209.2	(252) 247-4231	45		18	5.0 / 5.0	F	G	R	30	

WiFi Wireless Internet Access onSpot Dockside WiFi Facility
Visit www.waterwayguide.com for current rates, fuel prices, website addresses and other up-to-the-minute information.
(Information in the table is provided by the facilities.)

Scan here for more details:

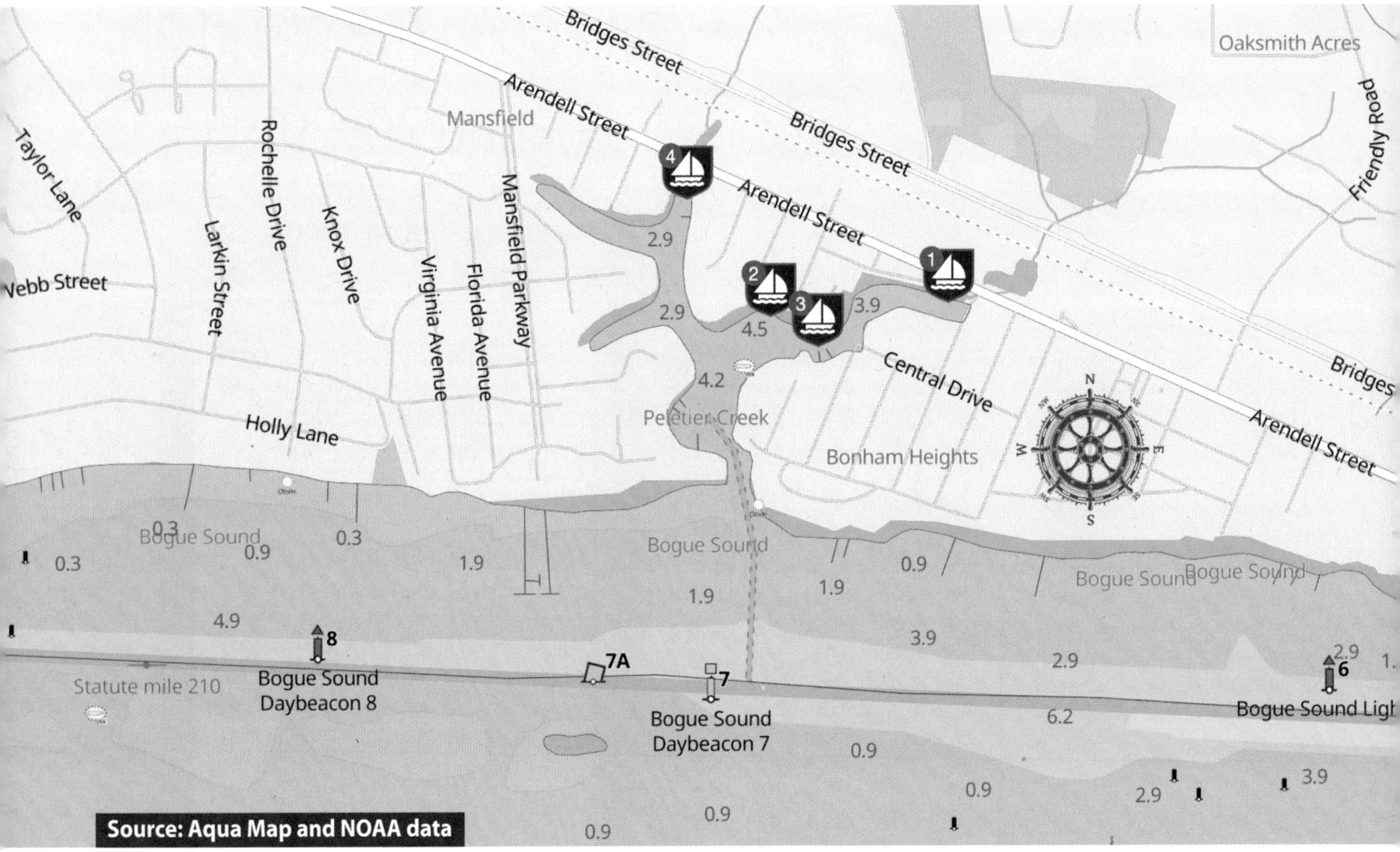

Source: Aqua Map and NOAA data

mainland Bogue Banks stands in stark contrast. From the ICW this long barrier island no longer appears as a dense growth of scrub pine and myrtle. More and more, however, vacation homes, condominiums and resorts are covering the sand dunes.

Farther down Bogue Sound waters alongside the channel turn shoal with the bottom just inches below the surface. Commercial watermen sometimes wade rather than work from their boats and often the workboats are deliberately grounded on tiny islets.

If your vessel draws 4 feet or more and you want to continue southbound down the ICW from Morehead, go back east around Sugar Loaf Island to the Morehead City Harbor's entrance then follow the buoys carefully to rejoin the ICW channel. The western exit of the Morehead basin, which is adequately marked, has been sounded at depths from 12 to 4.5 feet MLW in different portions of the channel and carries a raging current.

Currents and tides are something to contend with here. Be aware of tides and the timing of their occurrences; you can use them to your advantage with proper planning. However, where there are ocean inlets the currents will change at and between each one. Fast boats will see many floods and ebbs on any given day. Slower boats may be able to use a flood to find the turnaround point then take the ebb to the next inlet.

Bogue Sound, NC

SPOONER CREEK		Largest Vessel	VHF	Total Slips	Approach/ Dockside Depth	Floating Docks	Gas/ Diesel	Repairs/ Haulout	Min/Max Amps	Pump-Out Station
1. Spooners Creek Marina-PRIVATE (WiFi) MM 210.0	(252) 726-2060	100		85	6.0 / 8.0	F	GD		30 / 50	P

(WiFi) Wireless Internet Access **onSpot** Dockside WiFi Facility
Visit www.waterwayguide.com for current rates, fuel prices, website addresses and other up-to-the-minute information.
(Information in the table is provided by the facilities.)

Scan here for more details:

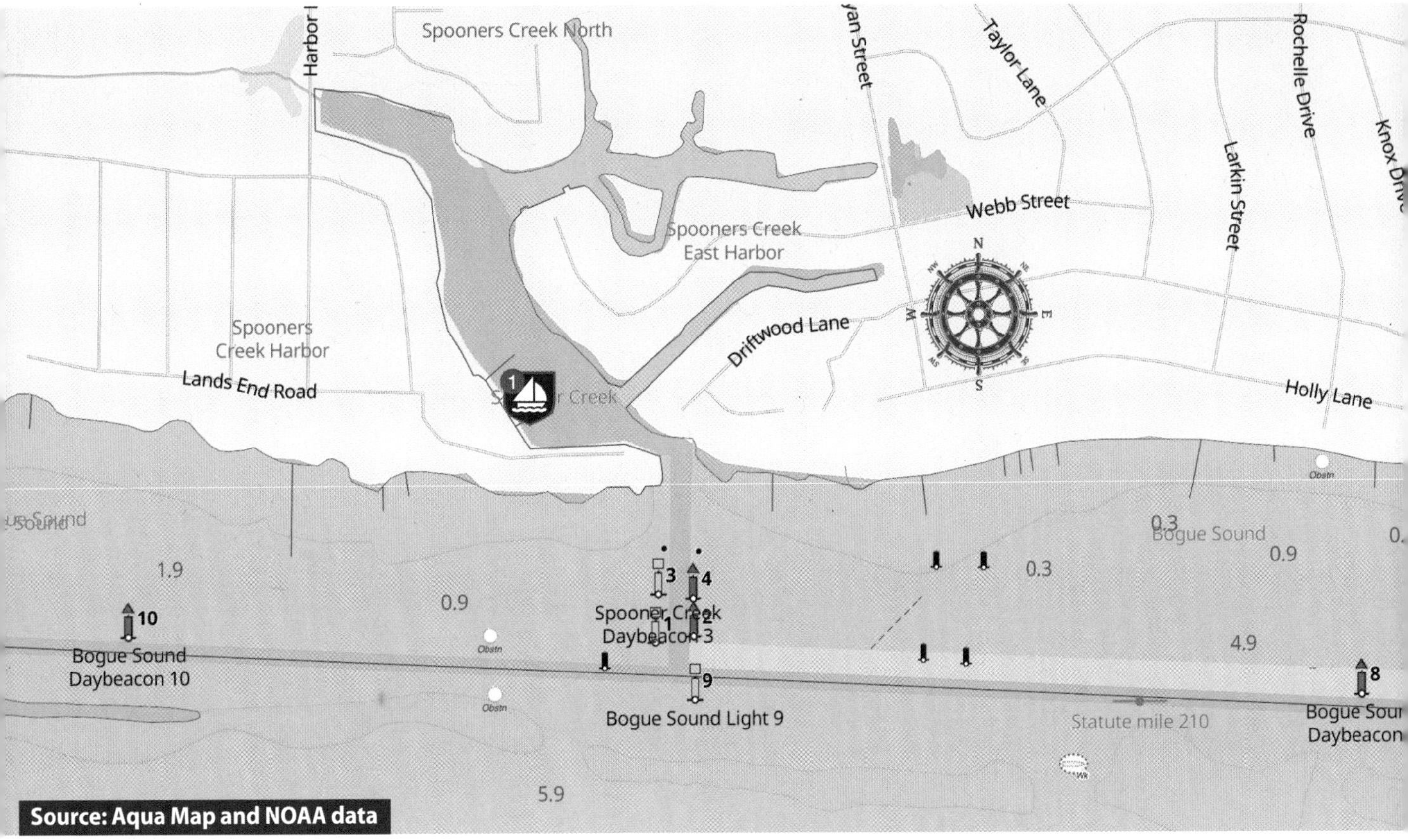

Source: Aqua Map and NOAA data

The channel through Bogue Sound is narrow so it is a good idea to set your depth sounder alarm at 8 feet. If it sounds and the depth continues to decrease, slow down. This method helps you stay in the channel and spot shoal areas. With its sometimes scattered shoaling and shallow water outside the channel, Bogue Sound is a good place to use this technique.

The aids to navigation in Bogue Sound on to New River and then to the Cape Fear River are located 30 to 35 feet outside the channel limits. This is yet another good reason never to cut marks too closely. Many areas between Morehead City and Swansboro are subject to shoaling, despite frequent dredging. Encroaching shoals are frequently marked with temporary floating aids to navigation until dredging can correct problems. If you see a stationary beacon and a temporary floating marker of the same identification (sometimes the temporary marker will be designated with an "A" or a "B"), honor the temporary marker. Additionally, if the original marker was lighted, it will be extinguished and the light on the temporary marker should be honored. Of course, it is always advised to travel in the safety of daylight whenever possible and use the most recent (print-on-demand) NOAA charts.

Another hazard of Bogue Sound is that a strong wind on your beam can set you on the often-hard edge of the dredged channel. Watch behind you and be sure to steer toward the windward side of the channel so if you go aground the wind will help push you off. Keep current with the *Local Notice to Mariners* (www.navcen.uscg.gov) regarding shoaling in this stretch.

Swansboro Area, NC

SWANSBORO AREA		Largest Vessel	VHF	Total Slips	Approach/ Dockside Depth	Floating Docks	Gas/ Diesel	Repairs/ Haulout	Min/Max Amps	Pump-Out Station
1. Dudley's Marina (WiFi) MM 228.7	(252) 393-2204	75	16	26	6.0 / 4.0		GD	RH	30 / 50	

(WiFi) Wireless Internet Access onSpot Dockside WiFi Facility
Visit www.waterwayguide.com for current rates, fuel prices, website addresses and other up-to-the-minute information.
(Information in the table is provided by the facilities.)

Scan here for more details:

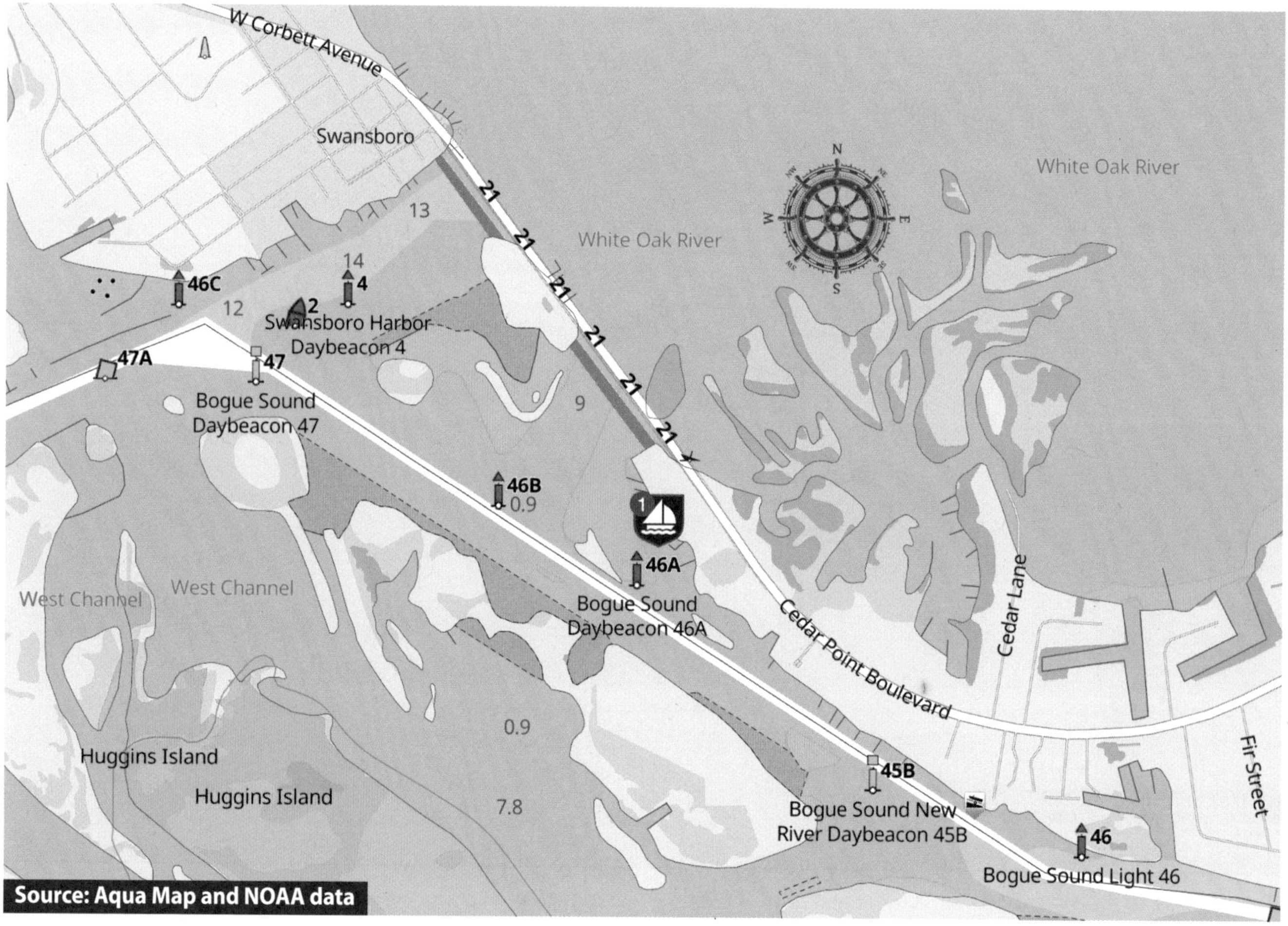

Source: Aqua Map and NOAA data

Bogue Sound to Swansboro–ICW Mile 206 to Mile 228

NAVIGATION: Use NOAA Charts 11541 and 11534. At Mile 206 the markers to the side channels in Atlantic Beach become very confusing. Be sure to sort them out before proceeding along the ICW or up one of the side channels. To reach the westernmost of Morehead City's services from Bogue Banks follow the marked ICW channel through the **Atlantic Beach Bridge** at Mile 206.7 (65-foot fixed vertical clearance). (Note that the tide boards and cruisers consistently report 2 to 3 feet less than the charted 65-foot fixed vertical clearance at this bridge.)

Do not mistake the "Resume Speed" sign just before (east of) the bridge for green daybeacon "3A." The sign is in shallow water and boats have gone aground here by making that mistake. You may see small powerboats taking this marked side channel through Money Bay (south of ICW green daybeacon "3") but it carries just 1.5-foot MLW depths. This is strictly small-boat territory.

Peletier Creek at Mile 209 is a couple of miles west of Morehead City and considered part of the city. The Peletier Creek marinas and anchorage are popular with locals and transients who can handle the 3-foot MLW

Swansboro Area, NC

SWANSBORO		Largest Vessel	VHF	Total Slips	Approach/ Dockside Depth	Floating Docks	Gas/ Diesel	Repairs/ Haulout	Min/Max Amps	Pump-Out Station
1. Church St. Town Dock (WiFi) MM 229.0	(910) 326-2600	100		10	8.0 / 8.0	F			30 / 100	P
2. Casper's Marina (WiFi) MM 229.3	(910) 326-4462	180	16	20	16.0 / 14.0		GD		30 / 50	

(WiFi) Wireless Internet Access onSpot Dockside WiFi Facility
Visit www.waterwayguide.com for current rates, fuel prices, website addresses and other up-to-the-minute information.
(Information in the table is provided by the facilities.)

Scan here for more details:

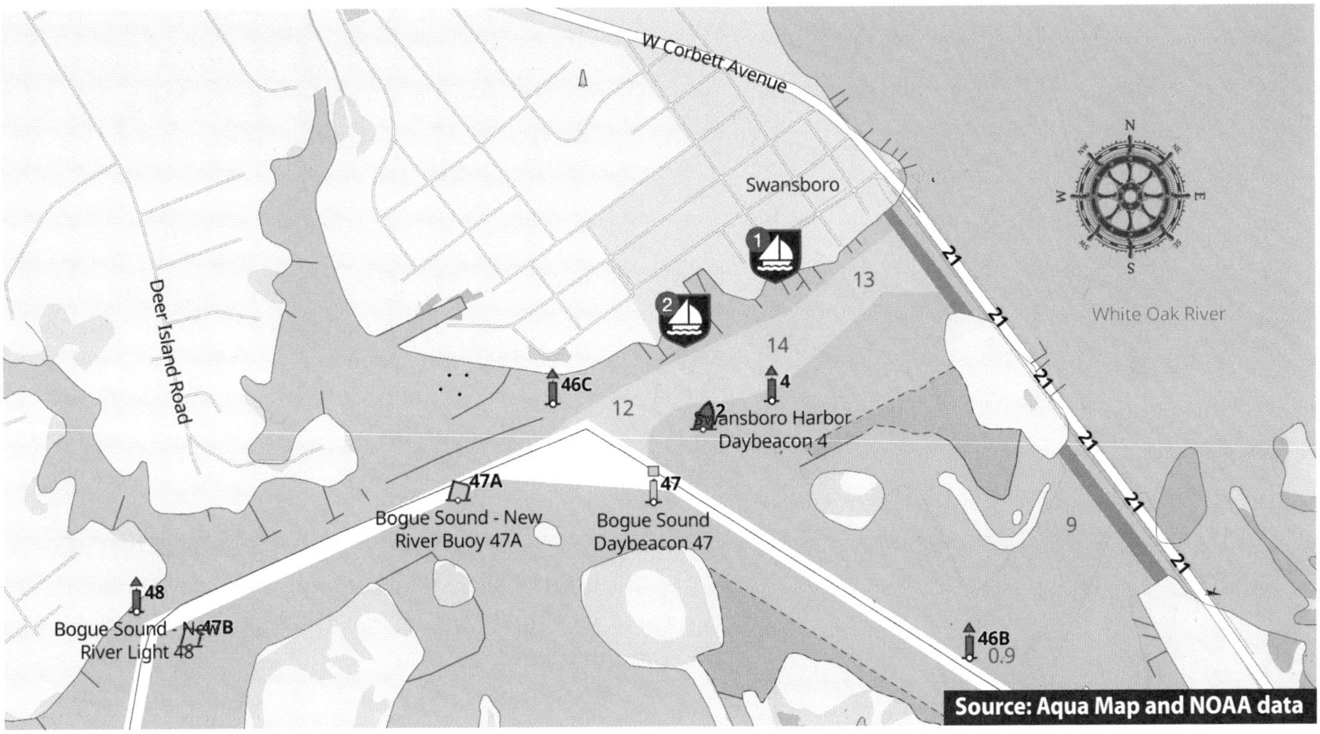

approach depths. Once inside the depths increase some, making the creek accessible to deeper boats that can time their arrival and departure for higher tides. Leave the ICW just east of green daybeacon "7."

One mile west of Peletier Creek on the ICW nice homes and docks surround the large basin at Spooner Creek (or "Spooners Creek" as it is referred to by locals). A marked entrance channel off the ICW at flashing green "9" leads to the marked entrance channel, which is reported to be 7 feet MLW but is prone to shoaling. Watch for crosscurrents when entering channel. High tide is approximately 2.5 hours later here than at Beaufort.

Despite recent dredging, there are several areas of caution along the ICW in this area.

- **Mile 209:** Dredging spoils are washing into the channel from the green side all along this stretch of the ICW from green daybeacon "7" at Peletier Creek to green daybeacon "15." Shoaling to 6.5 feet MLW has been observed.
- **Mile 210.5:** Dredging has been completed to 8 feet MLW by Spooner Creek but this is a difficult passage with winds of 15 knots or greater as there is wave action coming between the two islands to the south to push you off track, not to mention oncoming boats in the narrow passage.
- **Mile 224.4:** Going south from red daybeacon "40" stay centered until halfway to red nun "40A" then watch your depth and feel your way between two shoals for 8.1 feet MLW.

Currents in Bogue Sound occasionally run swiftly at velocities up to 1 to 2 knots. Slow boats leaving Morehead City during the last part of the flood tide usually catch

New River, NC

SWAN POINT		Largest Vessel	VHF	Total Slips	Approach/ Dockside Depth	Floating Docks	Gas/ Diesel	Repairs/ Haulout	Min/Max Amps	Pump-Out Station
1. Swan Point Marina WiFi MM 247.0	(910) 327-1081	100	16	40	8.0 / 5.0			RH	30 / 50	
2. New River Marina MM 247.0	(910) 327-2106	90	16	13	6.0 / 9.0		GD	R		

WiFi Wireless Internet Access onSpot Dockside WiFi Facility
Visit www.waterwayguide.com for current rates, fuel prices, website addresses and other up-to-the-minute information.
(Information in the table is provided by the facilities.)

Scan here for more details:

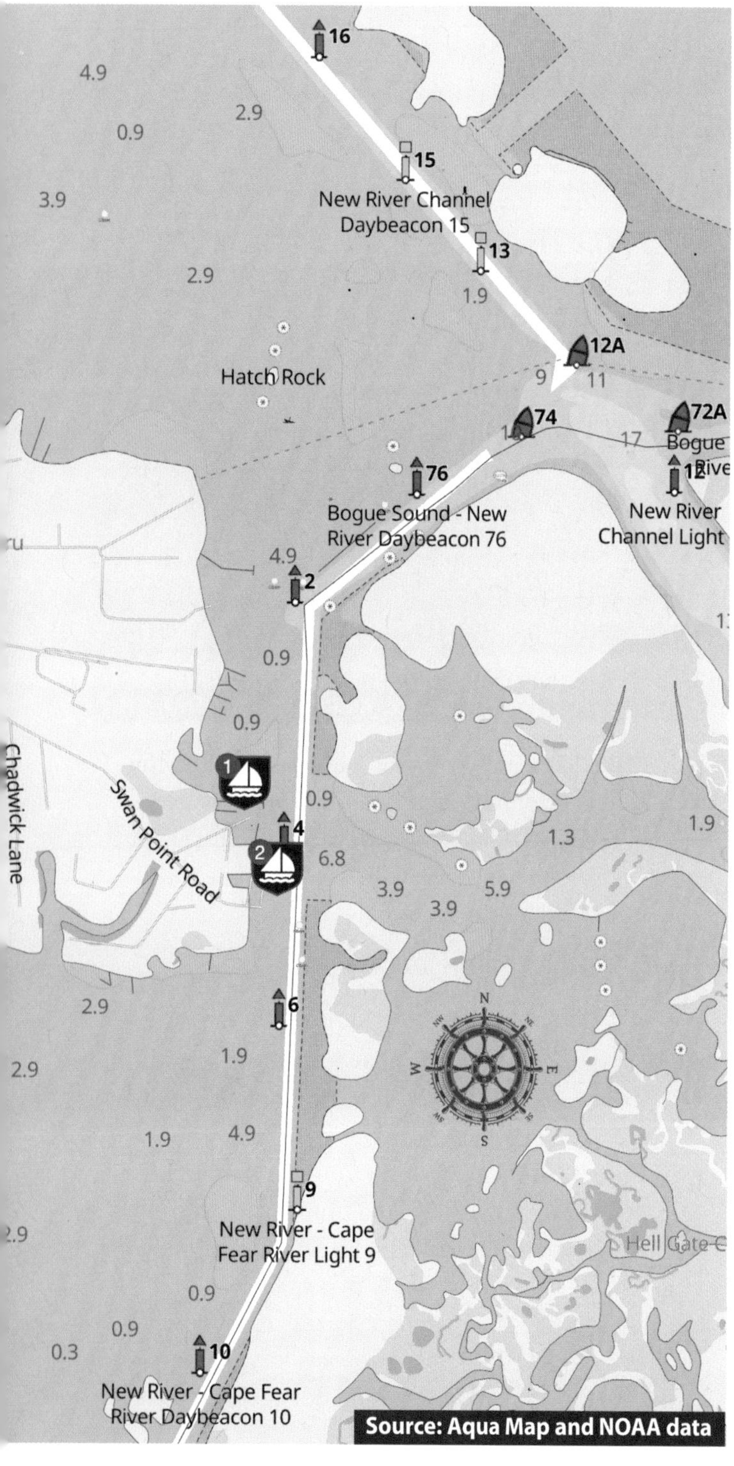

the first of the ebb tide at about Mile 220. Then a fair tide carries to the point where Bogue Inlet meets at Swansboro a few miles below the **B. Cameron Langston Bridge** (65-foot fixed vertical clearance), which is known locally as either the Cedar Point or the Emerald Isle Bridge. From here to Mile 290 current reversals at the various inlets work to cancel each other out.

Favor the mainland side when crossing Bogue Inlet, since the area is subject to shifting bars and shoaling. This inlet is subject to severe shoaling (as low as 4 feet MLW) and should not be attempted by cruising boats without local knowledge.

Dockage: Peletier Creek has several boatyards but not many transient slips. Services and repairs are available at Taylor Boat Works and The Harbor Master Inc. West Marina specializes in dry storage. Coral Bay Marina is a yacht brokerage. Spooners Creek Marina to the south is private.

Anchorage: It is possible to drop the hook in 4 to 8 feet MLW depths (once past the 3-foot MLW entrance) in Peletier Creek. Boats sometimes anchor in the middle of the widest part of Spooner Creek but the area offers poor holding in soft mud. Go past the condominium development and anchor in the basin. You will see a boat ramp and small floating dock. These are private and should not be used to go ashore. Numerous private docks on Spooner Creek reduce anchorage space.

Swansboro–ICW Mile 228

Popular with inland anglers Swansboro also has a sizable charter fishing fleet of considerable commercial importance because of its inlet. Swansboro is a friendly little town with a few good dining spots, convenient provisioning and numerous small antiques shops all making it increasingly popular as a tourist destination. Read more at "Goin' Ashore: Swansboro, NC" in this chapter.

NAVIGATION: Use NOAA Chart 11541.

NO WAKE ZONE

Local boaters traditionally considered the area from red daybeacon "44" to flashing red "48" (Mile 227 to Mile 229) a No-Wake Zone; however, the signs have been removed and there are no speed/wake restrictions. There are two marinas in the area, however, and (as always) you should control your wake.

In approaching Swansboro be wary of crosscurrents and their side-setting effect, particularly on the ebb. Here and at other places like it the flow out of the river accelerates the current. Stay to mid-channel favoring the mainland side between green can "45A" and red daybeacon "46B" and keep an eye on the depth sounder. This area is regularly dredged but is a persistent shoaling problem.

Directly off the ICW at the mouth of the White Oak River is Swansboro. The ICW turns abruptly west and the turn is marked on its outside corner by flashing red "46C." If bypassing Swansboro while heading south pass green daybeacon "47" and continue toward flashing red "46C" until green can buoys "47A" and "47B" are lined up then turn west.

The entrance to the secondary channel to Swansboro is marked by red nun buoy "2," which should be left to starboard on entry. Do not miss the nun buoy and head straight for red daybeacon "4." Although clearly charted these marks seem to confuse newcomers. An immediate grounding awaits those who attempt to go between these markers.

Dockage: Approaching Swansboro, cruising boaters can tie up comfortably or have most hull and engine repairs handled at Dudley's Marina, which has a large-boat marine railway at Mile 228.7. They offer dockside fueling, a well-stocked bait and tackle store and a courtesy car. They are family-owned and -operated and have been in business since 1938. (You can't miss the large facility with their name on the front.) Call ahead for exact depths and directions.

Church St. Town Dock is run off-site by Swansboro Parks & Recreation and one of their 10 slips can be reserved online. There is a maximum 5-night stay. The docks host eco-tours and cruises in season. Dockage is available at the 20-slip Casper's Marina, located adjacent to Swansboro's Historic District. A short-term tie-up for breakfast or lunch is available for a small fee.

Anchorage: There is a tight anchorage if needed between Casper's Marina and the NC 24 Bridge (fixed vertical clearance 12 feet) at Swansboro. Holding is fair and the current is swift. We recommend backing down hard on your anchor so you don't end up dragging into the bridge. It may be difficult to get the anchor initially set. Exposure from the northeast and southwest may make for a bumpy stay and wakes can be common. There is a free dinghy dock at the end of Main Street.

Swansboro to New River Inlet–ICW Mile 229 to Mile 246

NAVIGATION: Use NOAA Chart 11541. Departing from Swansboro the ICW zigzags its way southwest with two noteworthy bends–one at quick flashing red "48" and another at flashing green "49" at Mile 230. Neither marker is on the exact edge of the turn so exercise care not to cut or overshoot the channel.

Around Mile 232 a narrow marked channel leads southeast to Hammocks Beach State Park at Bear Island. Watch for shoaling on the northwest side of flashing green "55" off Sanders Creek at Mile 231. There is less than 7 feet MLW. Note that the chronic shoaling at Browns Inlet (Mile 238.2) has been alleviated due to dredging in 2019 and the markers have been moved to mark the newly dredged channel.

From Mile 235 to the New River at Mile 246 the ICW cuts through the U.S. Marine Corps' Camp Lejeune military reservation where signs along the way prohibit landing. Camp Lejeune extends about 18 miles upstream on the New River, almost to Jacksonville.

The ICW through Camp Lejeune is occasionally closed for artillery, small-weapons firing and beach-landing exercises. The affected area is from just south of red daybeacon "58" (Mile 235.2) to Mile 240 north of the Onslow Beach Swing Bridge. Prominent lighted signs stand at both ends of the range area. All navigable waters between the south bank of Bear Creek and the north bank of Browns Inlet are strictly off-limits due to highly sensitive unexploded ordnance in the area. Boaters may proceed through the inlet (without stopping) during periods of non-military use.

GOIN' ASHORE

SWANSBORO, NC

Located along the shoreline where the White Oak River joins the ICW, this "Friendly City by the Sea" is a quaint waterfront community with a rich, maritime history dating back to the 1700s. Recent years have also brought tourism to this quaint town but its maritime history and quiet waterfront remain the same. While there is a relaxed pace to this small, seaside town, finding something fun to do in the warm coastal sun is as easy to do as finding the perfect seafood dinner with a view.

SERVICES

1. **Mandala Yoga Center**
   In addition to yoga and spa services, the center offers kayak and standup paddleboard (SUP) rentals and guided tours. And, of course, they offer SUP Yoga (preregistration required) at 208 W. Main St. (910-325-3600).

2. **Med First Primary & Urgent Care**
   718 W. Corbett Ave. (910-326-5588)

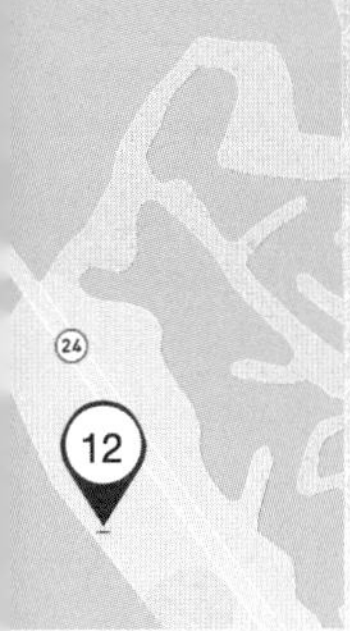

3. Swansboro Animal Hospital
130 Phillips Loop Rd. (910-325-8227)

4. Swansboro Post Office
664 W. Corbett Ave. (910-326-5959)

ATTRACTIONS

5. Bicentennial Park
The best way to see Swansboro's historic downtown, the Croatan National Forest, Hammocks Beach State Park and other historic landmarks is to bike along the 25-mile Bicentennial Bicycle Trail. It starts at the harborside Bicentennial Park. While there, check out the statue of Capt. Otway Burns, an American privateer during the War of 1812 and later an NC State Senator born in Swansboro.

SHOPPING

6. Bake Bottle & Brew
Sells wine, beer, coffee and sweets at 147 N. Front St. (910-325-7550).

7. Piggly Wiggly
Grocery chain at 715 W. Corbett Ave. (910-326-8500).

8. Walgreens
Drugstore chain with health and beauty aids, prescriptions and mini-mart basics at 702 W. Corbett Ave. (910-325-0038).

9. Western Auto
Auto parts store with hand tools, batteries and lubricants at 636 W. Corbett Ave. (910-326-5565).

MARINAS

10. Casper's Marina
301 S. Water St. (910-326-4462)

11. Church St. Town Dock
137 Front St. (910-326-2600)

12. Dudley's Marina
106 Cedar Point Blvd. (252-393-2204)

Topsail Island Area, NC

TOPSAIL ISLAND	Largest Vessel	VHF	Total Slips	Approach/ Dockside Depth	Floating Docks	Gas/ Diesel	Repairs/ Haulout	Min/Max Amps	Pump-Out Station
1. Topsail Island Marina MM 261.0	60		15	10.0 / 8.0	F	GD			

WiFi Wireless Internet Access onSpot Dockside WiFi Facility
Visit www.waterwayguide.com for current rates, fuel prices, website addresses and other up-to-the-minute information.
(Information in the table is provided by the facilities.)

Scan here for more details:

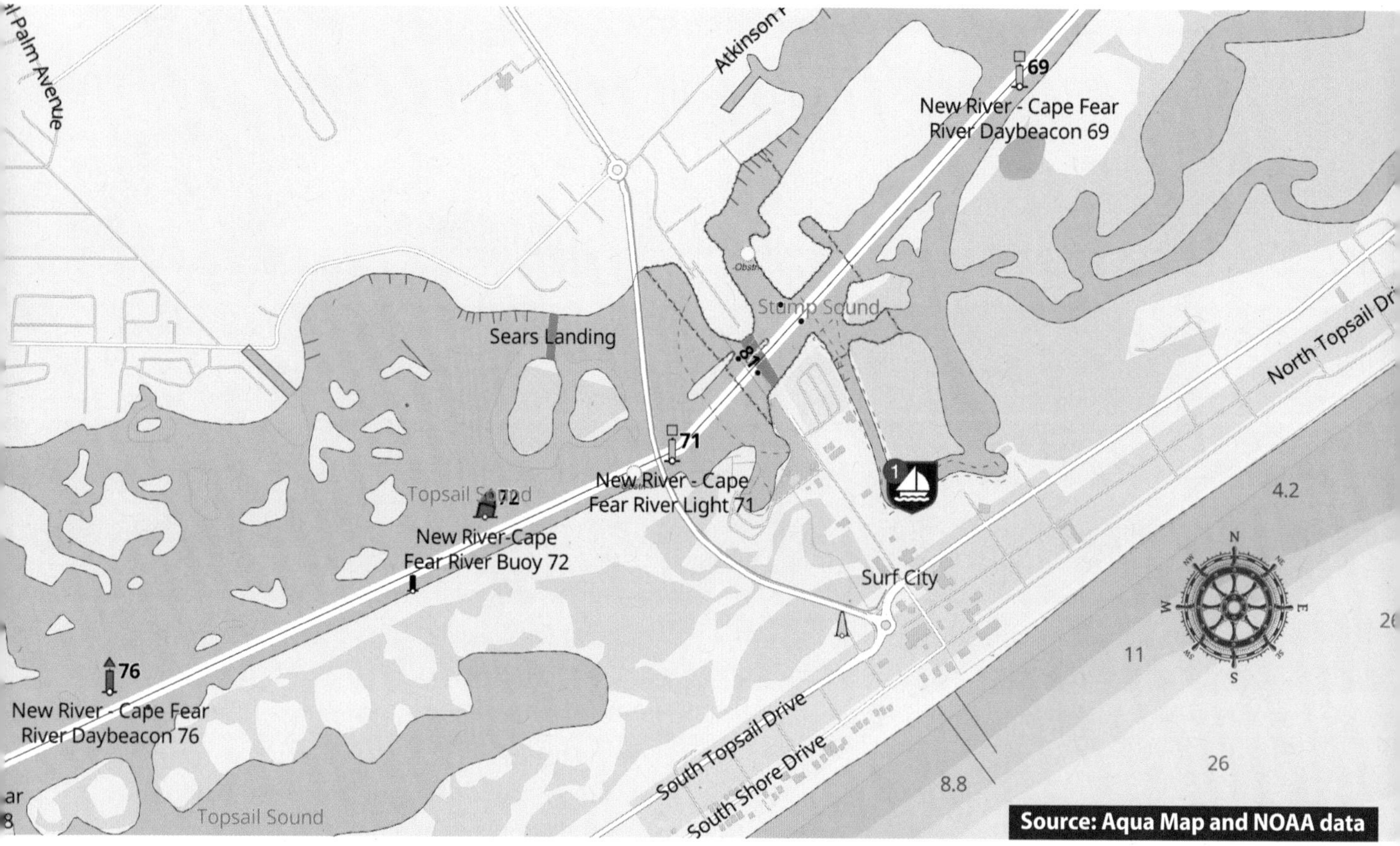

At the southern end of the Camp Lejeune range at Mile 240.7 is the **Onslow Beach Swing Bridge** (12-foot closed vertical clearance), which is owned and operated by the Marine Corps. The bridge opens on signal except between 7:00 a.m. to 7:00 p.m. when it need only open on the hour and half-hour. The drawtender will only open for vessels actually at the bridge at the appointed times and only if you contact them on VHF Channel 13 to request an opening. This bridge is very slow to open (openings usually take about 8 to 10 minutes). Use the northwest side, which swings away from boats heading south. Note that sails must be furled during a bridge opening.

Even though you have passed the danger area when through the bridge there can be heavy military activity along the sides of the ICW to the south, where the Marines practice amphibious landings.

Watch for shallow water near the edge of the channel in the long straight stretch below the Onslow Beach Swing Bridge. Shoaling has been observed by green daybeacon "65A" and the marker should be passed by 50 to 60 feet. Take great care through this area as the shoaling has been rapid and is continuing.

Anchorage: About 2 miles north of the three-way junction where the ICW, New River and New River Inlet channel meet a large dredged basin in Mile Hammock Bay (Mile 244.5) offers a very good and popular anchorage. The entrance channel has adequate depths for deep-draft vessels to enter the channel (10 to 12 feet MLW) and to anchor inside. Do not go too far east of the eastern wharf where depths are only 1 or 2 feet MLW. Except

Topsail Island Area, NC

HAMPSTEAD		Largest Vessel	VHF	Total Slips	Approach/ Dockside Depth	Floating Docks	Gas/ Diesel	Repairs/ Haulout	Min/Max Amps	Pump-Out Station
1. Anchors Away Boatyard MM 264.0	(910) 270-4741	70		2	6.5 / 6.5			RH	15 / 50	
2. Harbour Village Marina Inc. WiFi MM 267.0	(910) 270-4017	100	16	192	8.0 / 7.0	F	GD		30 / 50	P

WiFi Wireless Internet Access onSpot Dockside WiFi Facility
Visit www.waterwayguide.com for current rates, fuel prices, website addresses and other up-to-the-minute information.
(Information in the table is provided by the facilities.)

Scan here for more details:

for a few soft spots holding is very good in the area. Stay clear of the docks; an Army Corps of Engineers dredge often ties there.

> This is Marine Corps property and civilians are prohibited from going ashore. Frequent military activity and exercises in this basin can sometimes be interesting to observe. Note that a helicopter, Osprey aircraft or inflatable full of well-armed marines may buzz you.

New River Inlet to New Topsail Inlet–ICW Mile 246 to Mile 270

In this stretch to Topsail Beach and beyond a wide expanse of channel and slough-threaded marsh separates the ICW from barrier beaches. Most of these small waterways dead-end inside the barrier beach dunes. (Watch for side-setting currents and shoaling where these meet the ICW.) Others provide access to small inlets and some are even deep enough for anchoring if you feel adventurous.

A Coast Guard patrol boat may check on you if you anchor near the channel. The bottom is very sandy here and currents can run swiftly. Because of increased hurricane activity over the past decade, last year's good anchorage may be too shallow this year or a formerly shoaled entrance channel may have been scoured deep. The ICW channel tends to shoal near small inlets. Deep-draft boats should proceed cautiously in such areas.

The countryside begins to change in this section. Inlets appear with more frequency and the high wooded shores gradually become lined with year-round houses and vacation cottages. Because this is popular fishing and boating territory, most homes have their own boats at docks snuggled up side creeks or in dredged private channels. Some of these small communities have landings but they are not set up to handle transients.

NAVIGATION: Use NOAA Charts 11541 and 11542. At the junction of the New River Inlet and the ICW at Mile 246 be prepared for strong side currents and favor the ocean side. Be aware of changing depths in the area. Take time beforehand to sort out markers as the upriver channel buoys can be confusing. Note that red buoys are used to mark inshore shoals at the junction of the ICW and inlet channels. These are moved as required to show deep water limits.

At this point New River, with a well-marked channel, heads off sharply to starboard. Shoaling has been reported to a depth of 2 feet MLW in the channel. The Coast Guard moves temporary markers to show best water but has discontinued some of the permanent ones. We do not recommend use of this inlet by cruising vessels.

> To avoid shoaling at Mile 244 favor green can "71" while staying 150 to 200 feet off the southern shore (but no more). Next pass red nun "72A" to starboard and aim for red nun "74," passing it to starboard by 100 feet. Then return to the center of the channel.

It is possible to journey up the New River to the Marine Corps training base, Camp Lejeune, and on to the City of Jacksonville. Some areas of the New River above its intersection with the ICW are shoal. Seek local knowledge before heading up this river. Below New River, the ICW doglegs and the marina facilities at Mile 247 become visible. Just north of red daybeacon "4" you will find a mix of local recreational boats, small-scale commercial fishermen and cruisers.

The route from Swan Point runs southwest along a mostly straight dredged path for about 10 miles to the **NC 210 Highway Bridge** (64-foot fixed vertical clearance) at Mile 252.3. The fixed 65-foot **Surf City (NC 50) Bridge** at Mile 260.7 was completed in 2019 and replaces the Surf City Swing Bridge. All the remains of the old bridge have been removed and the area has been dredged.

At junction flashing green "BC" at about Mile 263.5 a marked channel makes off to the southeast and meanders along the backside of the barrier island, past Topsail Beach to New Topsail Inlet. Used extensively by locals this scenic side trip is suitable only for shallow-draft boats (despite depths shown on the NOAA chart).

New Topsail Inlet is primarily used by local fishermen. The Coast Guard has reported significant shoaling throughout the inlet. Several aids to navigation have been discontinued and any remaining are unreliable. Mariners should use extreme caution while navigating this area.

Dockage: South on the ICW at Swan Point you may find transient dockage at Swan Point Marina or New River Marina. There is a small store with a few staples and fishing tackle at Swan Point Marina, which has 4-foot MLW dockside depths. Immediately south of red daybeacon "4," the fuel dock at New River Marina faces the ICW and has just two reserved transient slips. Deep-draft vessels should call ahead for docking information. There may be space for larger vessels when the fuel pumps have closed for the evening. They also offer some repairs.

Nearby Topsail Island Marina at Mile 261 before the Surf City (NC50) Bridge offers all fuels but no transient slips. Anchors Away Boatyard at Mile 264 is a DIY and full-service boat yard that also offers boat storage. Their certified specialists are knowledgeable and professional.

A channel at Mile 267 on the mainland side leads into the well-maintained Harbour Village Marina, which is private but will rent a slip to you if one is available. You must call ahead (at least one day in advance). They will provide a drone video of the approach and marina, written directions for tie up and a picture of the marina layout.

Anchorage: On the way south you will pass several loading basins used by pulpwood barges many of which are abandoned and shoaled so we do not recommend anchoring there. For a proper anchorage leave flashing green "BC" to starboard to head for the anchorage off Sloop Point. Follow the channel markers favoring the red (east) side of the channel around the curve and anchor in sand between red daybeacon "14" and green daybeacon "15" in 6 feet MLW. At the foot of Humphrey Ave. is a small public beach. You can land a dinghy and walk across the peninsula to the ocean beach.

TO SNOWS CUT

New Topsail Inlet to Masonboro Inlet–ICW Mile 270 to Mile 288

Wrightsville Beach is a burgeoning water-oriented community and for the ICW traveler it is well worth a visit. The ICW itself is only part of what Wrightsville Beach has to offer. See details at "Goin' Ashore: Wrightsville Beach, NC" in this chapter. Motts Channel has more marinas, while Banks Channel offers secure, if busy, anchorages as well as a public (during daylight only) group of floating docks.

NAVIGATION: Use NOAA Chart 11541. Continuing from New Topsail Inlet at Mile 270 to Wrightsville Beach at Mile 283 the ICW channel is straight, well marked and easy to run.

When approaching green "105" at Mile 274.4 from either the north or south favor the red side to avoid the developing shoal on the green side of the channel.

Figure Eight Island Swing Bridge at Mile 278 (20-foot closed vertical clearance) opens on the hour and the half-hour, 24 hours a day. The bridge will not open when the sustained wind is stronger than 30 miles per hour and can remain closed at the discretion of the bridgetender in bad weather.

In the 5 miles between the **SR 74 Bridge** (also known as Wrightsville Beach Bridge) at Mile 283 and the Figure Eight Island Swing Bridge, the route is straightforward, although aids to navigation are fewer and farther apart. When the marshes flood at high tide it is hard to make out the channel. At such times monitor your chart plotter closely and run compass courses between marks.

Going through Middle Sound after mid-afternoon watch for commercial mullet fishermen with their nets stretched across the channel. (It is hard to identify even on the most up-to-date NOAA charts but extends from around Mile 278 to Mile 283.) Ordinarily fishermen tend to the nets and promptly lower them so that approaching boats can pass over them. To be on the safe side boaters should travel at a reasonable speed and allow ample time for the nets to reach the bottom. The Coast Guard at Wrightsville Beach has stated that the nets are to be at least 6 feet below the surface and always tended.

Mason Inlet at Mile 280.2 was dredged in the spring of 2019 but it has already shoaled. Favor the red side of the channel for 6.8 MLW. It is mostly used by local fisherman as it is prone to shoaling.

At Mile 283.1, SR 74 Bridge has a charted 20-foot closed vertical clearance but it has been observed to be closer to 14 feet MLW. The bridge opens on signal, except between 7:00 a.m. and 7:00 p.m. when it need only open on the hour. (This does not hold true if there is a race or other special event so call ahead at 910-256-2886.)

The current picks up as you approach the SR 74 Bridge and then reverses just north of the bridge making it difficult for slower vessels to correctly time arrivals at the bridge. Sailboats and slower trawlers have a difficult time making the 5 miles between this and the Figure Eight Island Swing Bridge to the south. Currents are particularly strong directly at the bridge and at the marinas adjacent

Wrightsville Beach, NC

WRIGHTSVILLE AREA		Largest Vessel	VHF	Total Slips	Approach/ Dockside Depth	Floating Docks	Gas/ Diesel	Repairs/ Haulout	Min/Max Amps	Pump-Out Station
1. Wrightsville Beach Marina WiFi MM 283.3	(910) 256-6666	200	16	100	15.0 / 15.0	F	GD		30 / 100	P
2. Bridge Tender Marina WiFi MM 283.3	(910) 256-6550	200	16	65	18.0 / 18.0	F	GD		30 / 100	P
3. MarineMax Wrightsville Beach MM 284.0	(910) 256-8100	100	16		/	F		RH		
4. Atlantic Marine MM 284.0	(910) 256-9911	26	16		8.0 / 5.0	F	G	RH	30	
5. Seapath Yacht Club & Transient Dock WiFi MM 284.0	(910) 256-3747	150	16	190	8.0 / 10.0	F	GD		30 / 50	P

WiFi Wireless Internet Access onSpot Dockside WiFi Facility
Visit www.waterwayguide.com for current rates, fuel prices, website addresses and other up-to-the-minute information.
(Information in the table is provided by the facilities.)

Scan here for more details:

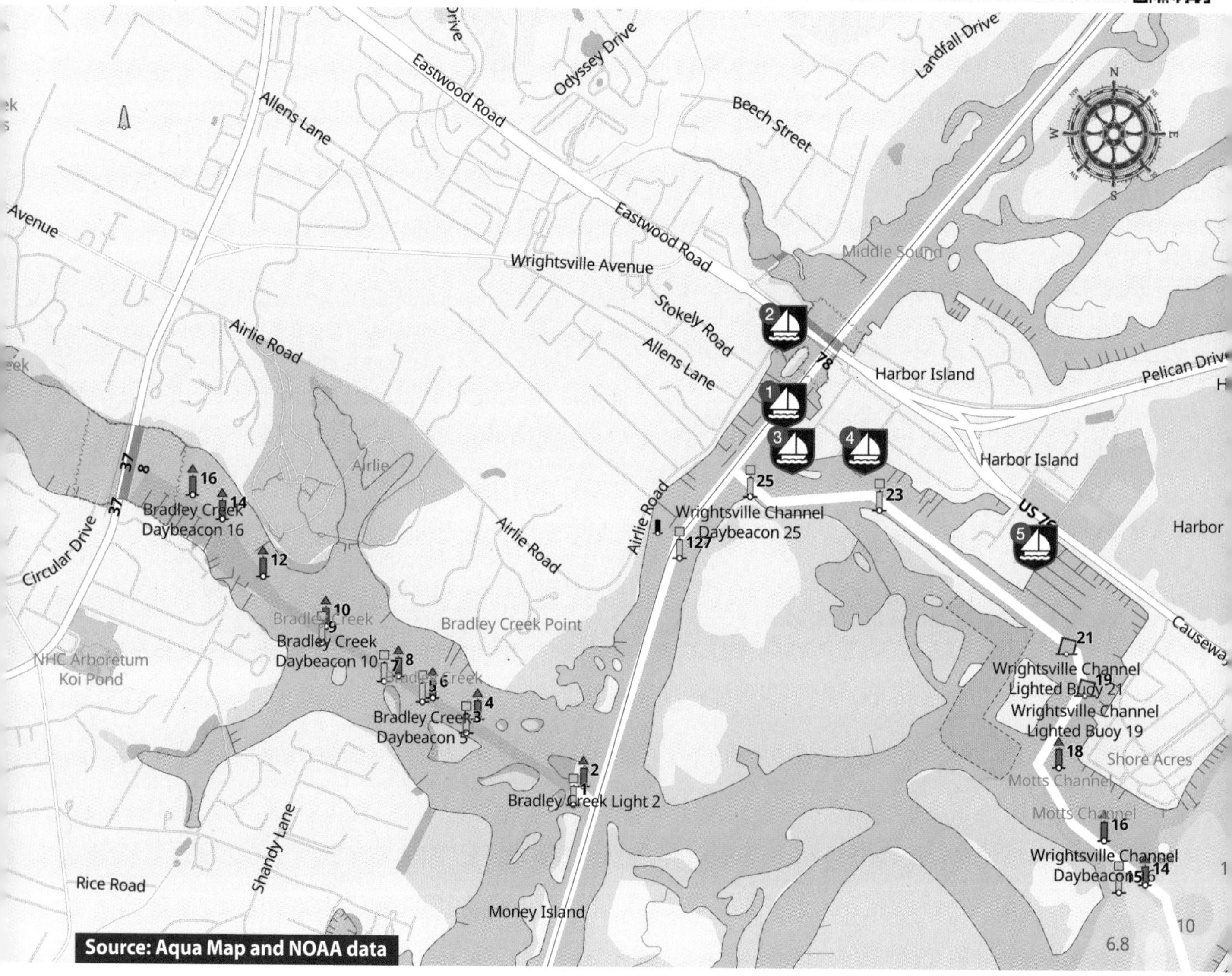

to the ICW below the bridge. Exercise care in holding for this bridge on either side.

You may receive instructions to bunch with other boats during the unrestricted hours. Traffic from a busy launching ramp just north of the SR 74 Bridge adds to the congestion. Boats waiting on the south side of the bridge will also see congestion from marina traffic and Motts Channel.

There are several areas of concern on the ICW south of Masonboro Inlet. See detailed tracks at Waterway Explorer (www.waterwayguide.com).

- **Mile 285–**Shoaling to 7.6 feet MLW has been observed 300 feet north of green can "129" in the middle of the channel. You can avoid the developing shoal by favoring the red side if you need the depth at low tide.
- **Mile 287.5–**There is shoaling to 5.0 feet MLW in the middle of the channel 500 feet north of green daybeacon "135." Move over to the red side of the channel for 9.7 feet MLW.
- **Mile 288.4–**Favor the red side of the channel 500 feet north of flashing green "137" to avoid shoaling to 5.1 feet MLW on the green side.

Motts Channel is south of the SR 74 Bridge at Mile 284 and runs east from the ICW at green daybeacon "25" (not an ICW number) to Banks Channel, which extends southwest to Masonboro Inlet. Note that when you use these channels you are off the ICW and away from its marking system. Refer to the NOAA chart for buoy information before leaving the ICW. The area is wide with good water depths.

Masonboro Inlet, NC, is the first major inlet south of Beaufort and is popular with sportfishermen. It is an uncomplicated entrance protected by jetties on both sides and has good depths within. Depths are maintained at 12 feet in the 400-foot-wide channel running midway between the jetties. The uncharted buoys in Masonboro Inlet are frequently relocated. Once inside, if you are heading to Wrightsville Beach, bear to starboard at green and red daybeacon "WC" into Banks channel and then turn to port at Motts Channel bit farther up. If Masonboro is your destination, continue straight ahead.

Deep-draft boats can enter the Banks Channel anchorage area via Masonboro Inlet to Shinn Creek (10- to 15-foot MLW depths) at Mile 285.1. The Coast Guard maintains dockage on Banks Channel just north of Masonboro Inlet and responds quickly to emergency calls. The channel from the inlet to Shinn Creek is marked and readily passable. On summer weekends, however, this area resembles Fort Lauderdale and is packed with boats of all types.

Note that when you use these channels, you are off the ICW and away from its marking system. Refer to the NOAA chart for buoy information before leaving the ICW. The area is wide with good water depths.

When turning off the ICW into Shinn Creek, watch for current set, and treat ICW green can "129" (Mile 285.1) as a green marker for the ICW as well as for Shinn Creek, which is marked with red on the right coming from the sea. Cut halfway between green can "129" and the sandy north shore of Shinn Creek for 8 feet MLW. Check the most recent Army Corps of Engineers survey for Shinn Creek Crossing.

Just south of Mile 285 on the ICW strong crosscurrents can make it difficult to maintain a mid-channel course. Favor the ocean side of the main channel on the flood tide and the mainland side on the ebb. Tidal range is from 3 to 4 feet.

Dockage: Several marinas are right on the ICW after the SR 74 Bridge and navigation is straightforward. Just south of the bridge on the mainland side Bridge Tender Marina has a 350-foot floating dock making overnight dockage convenient and easily accessible. They also have a state-of-the-art fuel pumping. The venerable Bridge Tender Restaurant offers fine dining. Reservations are recommended (910-256-4519).

Across the waterway is the full-service Wrightsville Beach Marina on Harbor Island. Be sure to follow marina docking instructions here regarding the current. There are always plenty of hands to help as you approach. The Bluewater Waterfront Grill (910-256-8500) is adjacent to the marina and several others are within one block.

MarineMax Wrightsville Beach and Atlantic Marine are on the turn into Motts Channel. Both are primarily yacht brokerages that offer some repairs. Call ahead for slip availability. The well-maintained Seapath Yacht Club & Transient Dock is located farther east on the northern side of the channel. They welcome transients and offer full amenities.

GOIN' ASHORE

WRIGHTSVILLE BEACH, NC

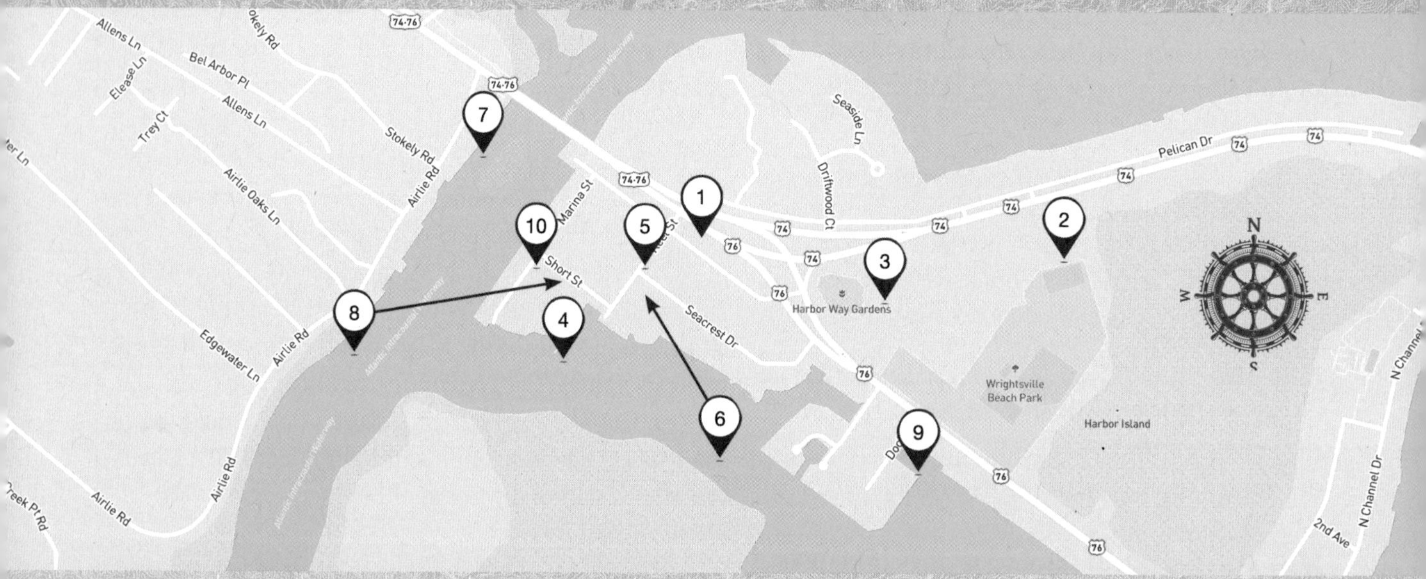

For cruisers, Wilmington (west side of the ICW) and Wrightsville Beach (east side of the ICW) offer a convenient stopover for replenishing, dining or sightseeing. Marinas line both sides of the ICW beginning immediately south of the Wrightsville Beach Bascule Bridge and just off the ICW on Motts Channel, but a word of caution: This is a popular stopover so make a reservation in advance.

SERVICES

1. **Wrightsville Beach Post Office**
   206 Causeway Dr. (910-256-0159)

ATTRACTIONS

2. **Wrightsville Beach Museum of History**
   Located in the 1909 Myers Cottage at 303 W. Salisbury St. (910-256-2569) the museum preserves and shares the history of Wrightsville Beach. Exhibits include a shell collection, maps from the 1920s and a scale model of Wrightsville Beach circa 1910 with a running trolley car.

SHOPPING

3. **Farmers Market**
   Held from May 15 to October 30 from 8:00 a.m. to 1:00 p.m. on Mondays with fresh, locally grown produce at the Wrightsville Beach Municipal Complex (910-256-7925).
4. **Motts Channel Seafood**
   This wholesaler will be happy to put together a seafood sampler of fresh shrimp, fish steaks and scallops. You are likely to find locally grown produce out front to accompany your meal (120 Short St., 910-256-3474).
5. **Redix**
   A good bet for basic fishing supplies, beachware and beverages at 120 Causeway Dr. (910-256-2201). They also carry over-the-counter medicines. There are numerous other surf and beachwear shops along the beach road.

MARINAS

6. **Atlantic Marine**
   101 Keel St. (910-256-9911)
7. **Bridge Tender Marina**
   1418 Airlie Rd. (910-256-6550)
8. **MarineMax Wrightsville Beach**
   130 Short St. (910-256-8100)
9. **Seapath Yacht Club & Transient Dock**
   330 Causeway Dr. (910-256-3747)
10. **Wrightsville Beach Marina**
    6 Marina St. (910-256-6666)

Snows Cut Area, NC

MASONBORO		Largest Vessel	VHF	Total Slips	Approach/ Dockside Depth	Floating Docks	Gas/ Diesel	Repairs/ Haulout	Min/Max Amps	Pump-Out Station
1. Masonboro Yacht Club and Marina WiFi MM 288.2	(910) 791-1893	60	16	103	7.0 / 7.0	F		H	30 / 50	

WiFi Wireless Internet Access onSpot Dockside WiFi Facility
Visit www.waterwayguide.com for current rates, fuel prices, website addresses and other up-to-the-minute information.
(Information in the table is provided by the facilities.)

Scan here for more details:

Anchorage: A favorite (but busy) anchorage is in the bight just southwest of the Motts Channel junction with Banks Channel (south flashing red "15") inside the protective arm of Wrightsville Beach. There are 12- to 15-foot MLW depths with a fine sand ("mucky") bottom, which will require you to back down hard on your anchor for a good set. This is exposed to wakes and wind from the southwest. Expect lots of traffic even at night so leave the lights on–both anchor and navigational, if possible.

An equally good anchorage lies northeast of Motts Channel and south of **Causeway Drive Bridge** (8-foot fixed vertical clearance) between Harbor Island and Wrightsville Beach. This anchorage has a varied type of bottom in 10-foot MLW depths. The shallower parts have a very hard bottom with poor holding, while the deeper areas have a softer bottom and usually will hold with some extra work in backing down.

In both anchorages boats will swing, sometimes rather wildly, with the current rather than the wind unless the wind is quite strong. Those dropping the hook here should plan accordingly. Expect lots of boat traffic. You can dinghy to the municipal docks located just south of the Causeway Drive Bridge on the beach side. There is a grocery store and other amenities nearby.

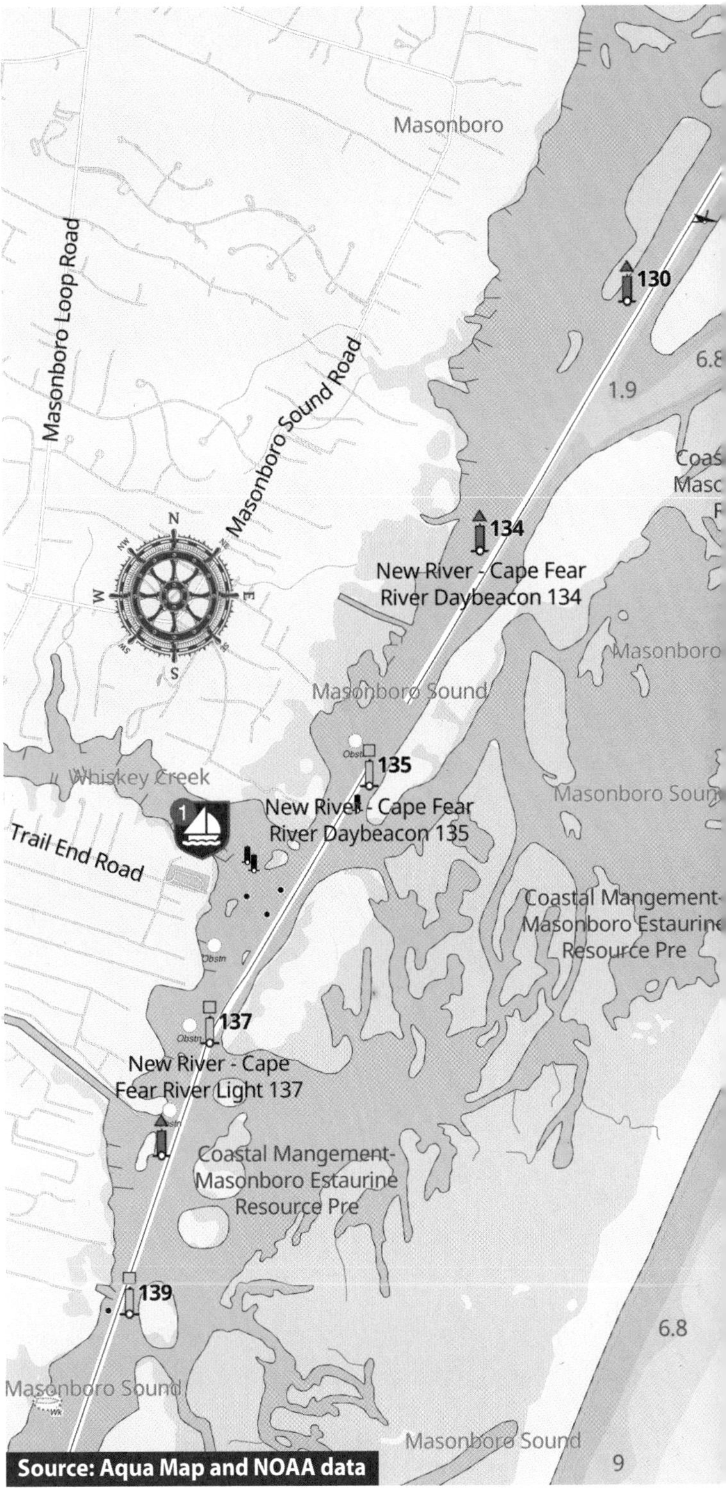

Source: Aqua Map and NOAA data

Masonboro Inlet to Snows Cut– ICW Mile 288 to Mile 298

Below Wrightsville Beach the route follows a dredged channel through a succession of marshy sloughs for about 12 miles to Snows Cut (Mile 295), the connecting link with the Cape Fear River. Continuing straight in Myrtle Grove Sound at Mile 295 will take you to Carolina Beach. This is one of the state's busiest (and oldest) summer resorts but its grocery stores and restaurants stay open off-season as well.

NAVIGATION: Use NOAA Charts 11541 and 11534. Through Masonboro Sound and Myrtle Grove Sound

Snows Cut Area, NC

CAROLINA BEACH AREA		Largest Vessel	VHF	Total Slips	Approach/ Dockside Depth	Floating Docks	Gas/ Diesel	Repairs/ Haulout	Min/Max Amps	Pump-Out Station
1. Carolina Beach Yacht Club & Marina WiFi MM 295.0	(910) 458-5053	100	16	69	6.0 / 6.0	F	GD		30 / 50	P

WiFi Wireless Internet Access onSpot Dockside WiFi Facility
Visit www.waterwayguide.com for current rates, fuel prices, website addresses and other up-to-the-minute information.
(Information in the table is provided by the facilities.)

Scan here for more details:

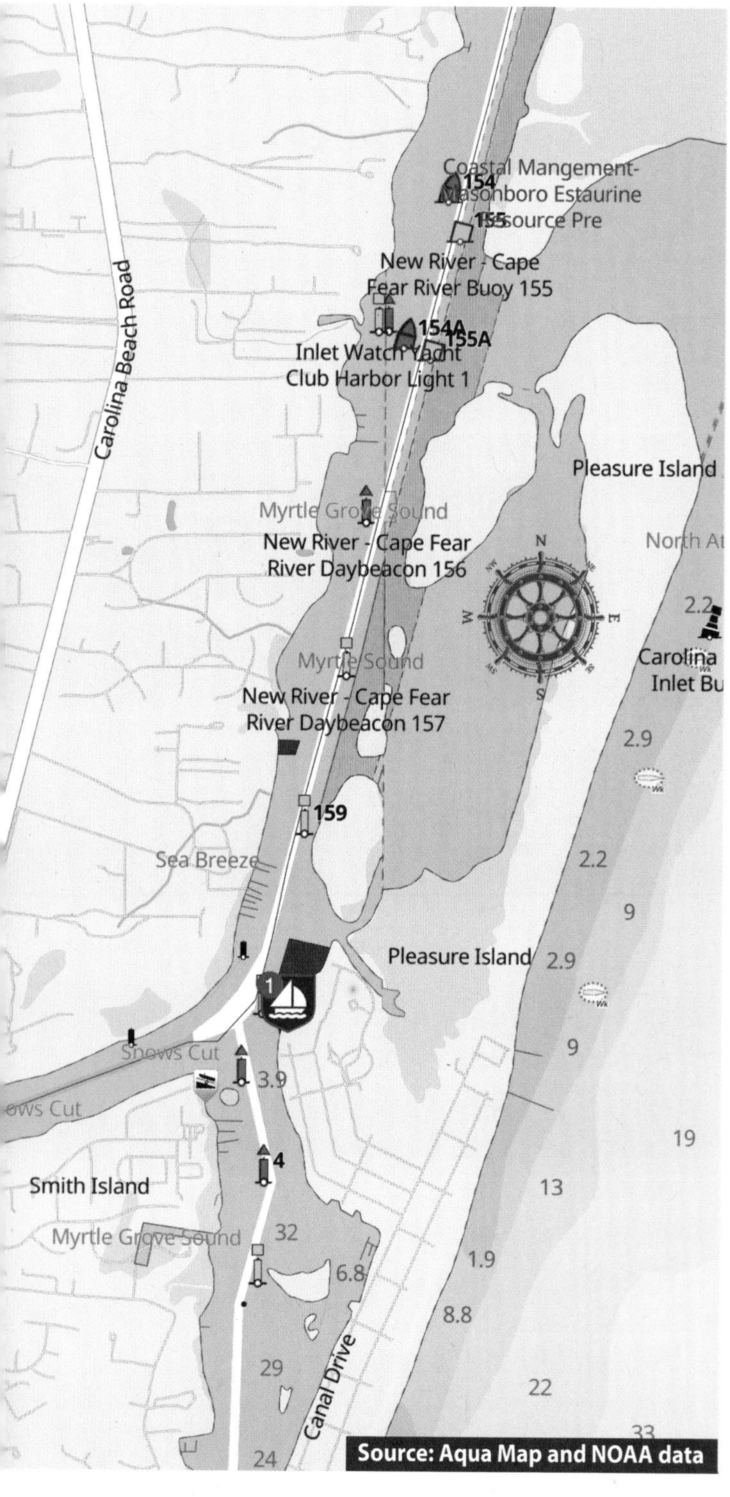

Source: Aqua Map and NOAA data

the route runs straight and narrow. Despite dredging in 2019, shoaling frequently occurs here especially at the many junctions where side creeks cross the ICW and temporary buoys are placed to mark the shallow areas. Caution and local knowledge are advised.

Carolina Beach Inlet (Mile 293.5) is closed due to shoaling to 2 feet MLW. The Coast Guard has pulled all the navigational aids until further notice. This is a local knowledge, small-boat inlet in the best of conditions and should be avoided until the buoys are reset after dredging (date undetermined). Mariners should use extreme caution while navigating this area.

At Mile 295 immediately before the ICW turns to enter Snows Cut a deep, well-marked channel leads to Carolina Beach and the marinas.

> Shoaling has been observed between red daybeacons "172 and "174." The Coast Guard has placed moveable red markers to mark shoaling and a sand bar (visible at low tide). Shoaling has also been observed by flashing red "168." Depths as low as 3 feet MLW encroach from the northern edge of the channel extending into the channel. Exercise caution.

Favor the green side of the channel between red daybeacon "162" and green "161A." Then favor the red side of the channel when passing "161A" (keeping well off the marker) and favor the green side when passing red "162A" (again, passing well off the marker). The route follows a zigzag course at the southern exit and the current can run 2 to 3 knots so exercise caution.

The high-rise Snow's Cut (US 421) Bridge (65-foot vertical clearance) and the overhead power cables (68-foot vertical clearance) just west of the bridge at Mile 295.7 should provide enough room for most. Exercise care here, however, as the current runs strong at the bridge and eddies can make boat handling difficult. On top of that, be prepared for a lot of local boat traffic.

Snows Cut Area, NC

CAROLINA BEACH AREA		Largest Vessel	VHF	Total Slips	Approach/ Dockside Depth	Floating Docks	Gas/ Diesel	Repairs/ Haulout	Min/Max Amps	Pump-Out Station
1. Carolina Beach NC Mooring Field	(910) 386-1492	55			30.0 / 14.0	F				P
2. Mona Black Marina WiFi MM 295.0	(910) 232-0211	60		24	20.0 / 20.0	F			30 / 50	P
3. Carolina Beach Boatyard & Marina WiFi	(910) 707-1007	60	16		20.0 / 10.0	F		RH	30 / 50	
4. Federal Point Yacht Club Marina WiFi	(910) 458-4201	90		110	15.0 / 25.0	F			30 / 50	P

WiFi Wireless Internet Access onSpot Dockside WiFi Facility
Visit www.waterwayguide.com for current rates, fuel prices, website addresses and other up-to-the-minute information.
(Information in the table is provided by the facilities.)

Scan here for more details:

Stay in the channel as parts of this area tend to shoal.

There is frequent dredging in this area so expect to see tugs towing long runs of dredging pipe. These can be as long as 0.25 mile and can completely block Snows Cut to navigation. Listen to "Sécurité" broadcasts from tows before entering Snows Cut.

Dockage/Moorings: Five miles south of Wrightsville Beach at Whiskey Creek (Mile 288.2), the Masonboro Yacht Club and Marina is visible to starboard. The marina has floating docks with transient dockage. Its two-story clubhouse has a fantastic view, along with showers and laundry facilities. This is home to an exceptional community of active sailors and recreational boaters.

At the north entrance to Snows Cut (Mile 295) you will find Carolina Beach Yacht Club & Marina to port with transient and long-term slips. Be aware that the fuel and transient dock is just off the ICW beyond flashing green "161" and should be passed without a wake. Although this is a 2-mile dinghy ride from the "business end" of Carolina Beach, there are good bus service connections into Wilmington (6 miles away).

More marine services and facilities are available on the channel south of the north entrance to Snows Cut including the popular Carolina Beach Mooring Field. The 10 moorings are located beyond green daybeacon "5" and the small grassy island beyond and can accommodate boats between 26 and 55 feet. There is a beach across the street with public restrooms and outside showers. A dinghy dock is located to the south of the mooring field (near mooring number 1). Moorings are available on a first-come, first-served basis. Pick up a mooring then call 910-667-0004.

The 24-slip Mona Black Marina to the south has some reserved transient space but is mostly a liveaboard facility. Carolina Beach Boatyard & Marina is a working boatyard offering all types of repairs. Call

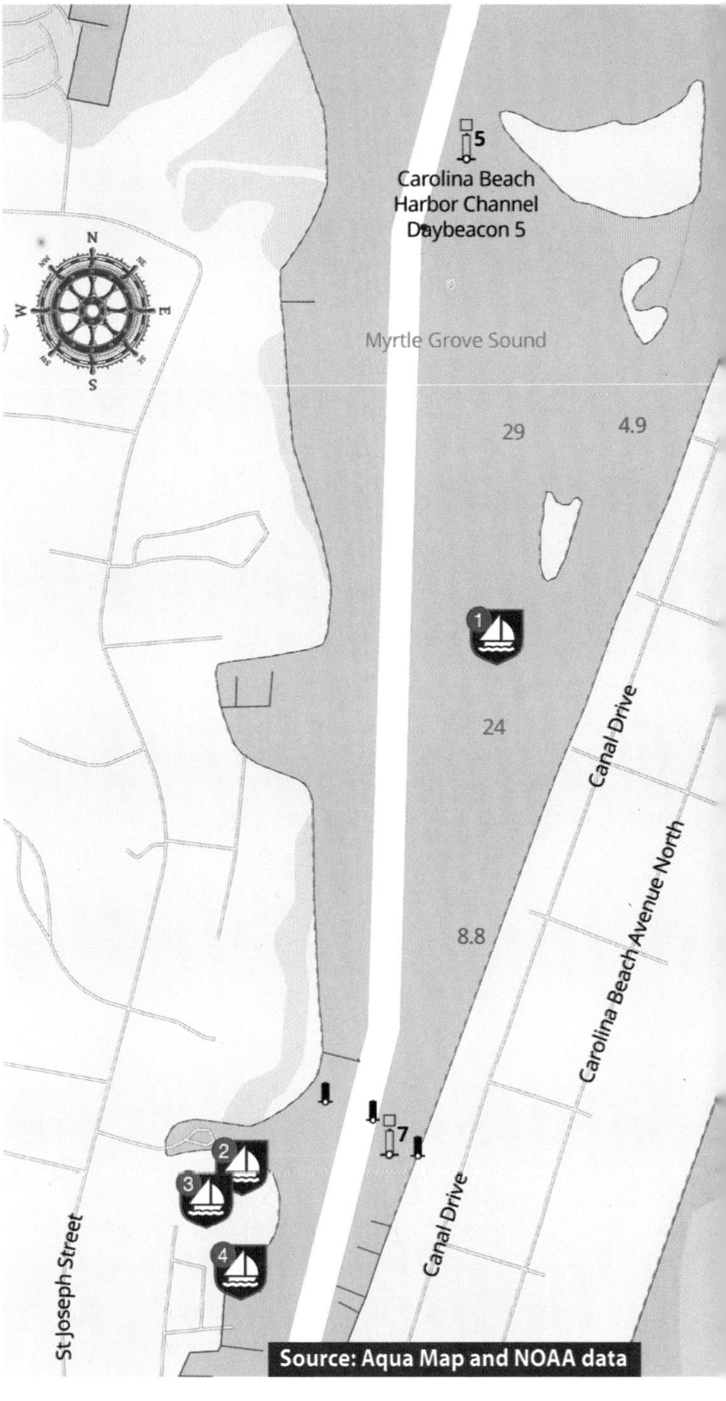

Snows Cut Area, NC

CAROLINA BEACH AREA		Largest Vessel	VHF	Total Slips	Approach/ Dockside Depth	Floating Docks	Gas/ Diesel	Repairs/ Haulout	Min/Max Amps	Pump-Out Station
1. Carolina Beach Municipal Marina	(910) 386-1492	25		7	/	F				P

Wireless Internet Access onSpot Dockside WiFi Facility
Visit www.waterwayguide.com for current rates, fuel prices, website addresses and other up-to-the-minute information.
(Information in the table is provided by the facilities.)
Scan here for more details:

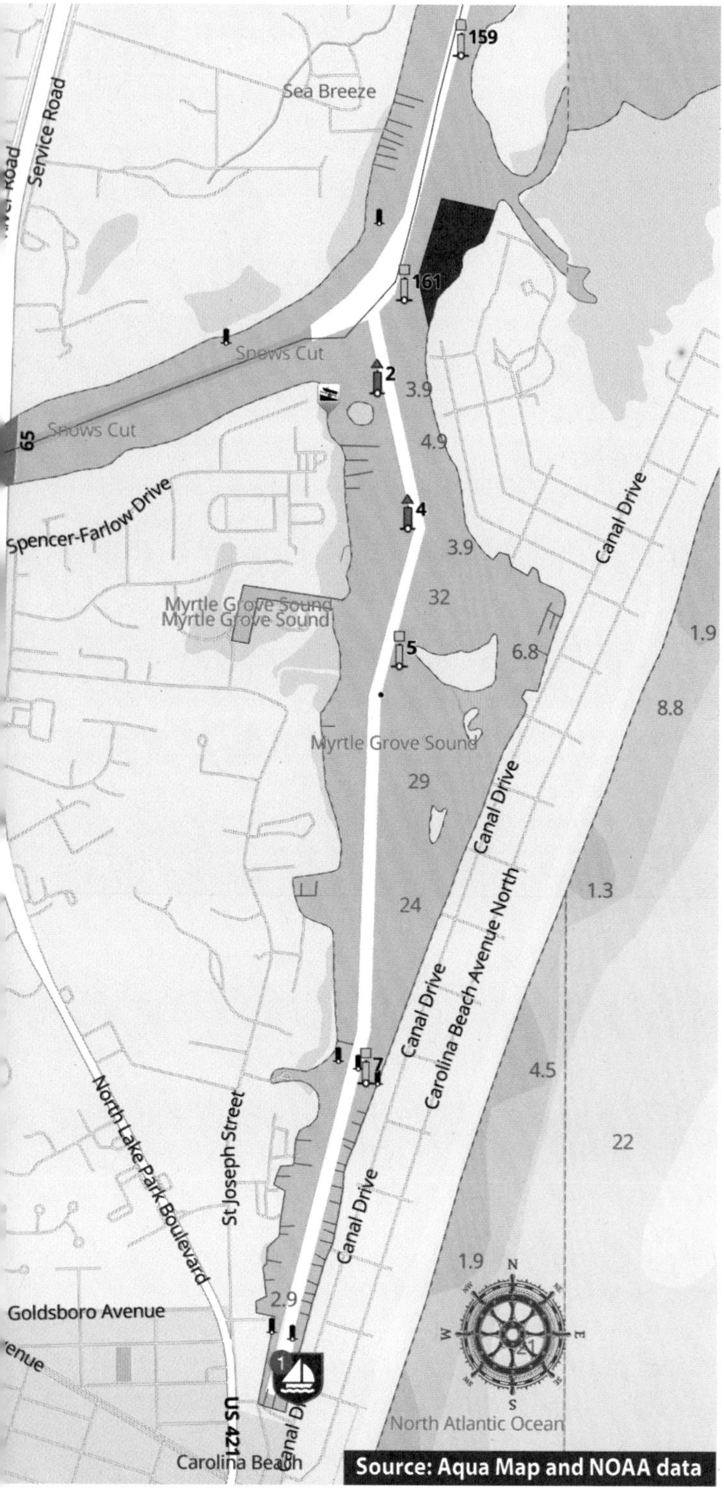

Source: Aqua Map and NOAA data

ahead. The well-appointed Federal Point Yacht Club Marina is walking distance to restaurants and shopping and has bikes on site for rental. At the south end of the channel Carolina Beach Municipal Marina has a 3-hour docking limit.

The marina at Carolina Beach State Park is in a basin at the southeast end of Snows Cut with a secluded camping area and miles of hiking trails. Fishing and camping supplies are available at the marina store along with restroom and laundry facilities. The largest boat accommodated is 48 feet.

Anchorage: The entire bight at Carolina Beach (south of Snows Cut and behind the beach) has more than adequate water off the marked channel except where specifically noted on the NOAA chart. Be aware of sharp shoaling and submerged pilings in the harbor near red daybeacon "4." North of green daybeacon "5" and the grassy island it marks, a deep, 30-foot hole provided long-scope anchorage for boats with plenty of rode.

South of green daybeacon "5" and north of the large moorage area sign, there is room for several boats in 14 feet MLW. Boat traffic, particularly on summer weekends, is intense. Holding is fair here but be prepared for an eddy effect under certain wind and tide conditions. From here it is easy to get an early morning start through Snows Cut and down the Cape Fear River.

Side Trip: Wilmington, Cape Fear River

While you could use a rental car to drive from Wrightsville Beach to Wilmington, the 15-nm trip upriver on the deep, well-marked shipping channel provides an easy passage with interesting features. Renting a car from Wrightsville Beach might still be your best bet if you want to see the surrounding area. For a small taste of what is there see "Goin' Ashore: Wilmington, NC" in this chapter.

NAVIGATION: Use NOAA Chart 11537. Do not be tempted by the channel shown on the NOAA chart that runs northwest from Snows Cut (just after red nun "162A") and joins the shipping channel farther north.

Snows Cut Area, NC

CAROLINA BEACH AREA		Largest Vessel	VHF	Total Slips	Approach/ Dockside Depth	Floating Docks	Gas/ Diesel	Repairs/ Haulout	Min/Max Amps	Pump-Out Station
1. Carolina Beach State Park MM 297.1	(910) 458-7770	48	16	54	5.0 / 4.0	F	GD		30 / 50	

WiFi Wireless Internet Access onSpot Dockside WiFi Facility
Visit www.waterwayguide.com for current rates, fuel prices, website addresses and other up-to-the-minute information.
(Information in the table is provided by the facilities.)

Scan here for more details:

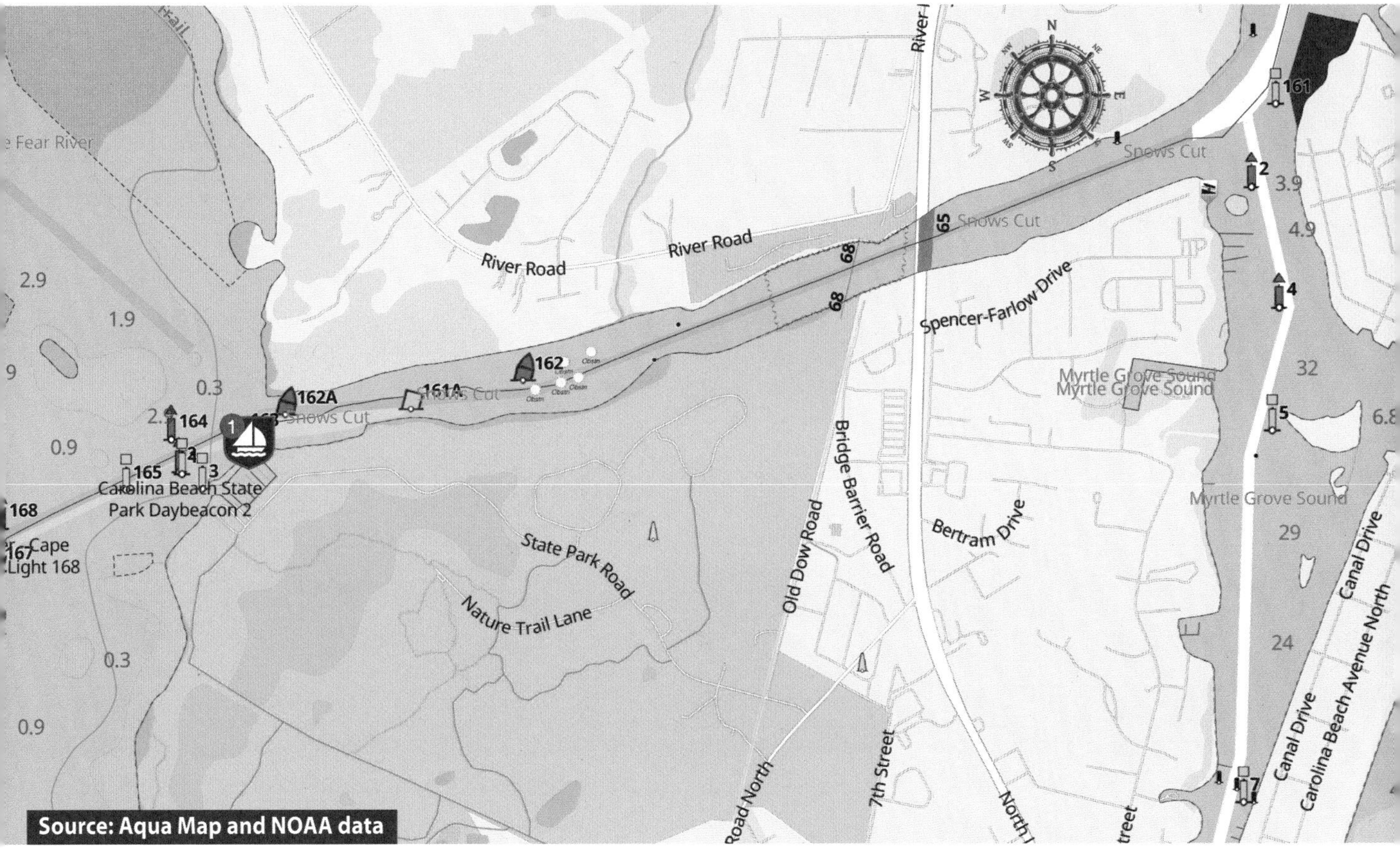

Source: Aqua Map and NOAA data

Local commercial fisherman and towing companies indicate this has silted in to less than 2 feet MLW.

From Snows Cut set a course southwest to join the main Cape Fear River shipping channel at green daybeacon "33" then turn north toward Wilmington. The main shipping channel is wide and well marked with several charted ranges. Note, however, that numerous ranges have been changed recently and may not correspond with those on your NOAA chart.

Note that the buoys are reversed from the normal ICW system when you reach the Cape Fear River at Mile 299. From here, look for yellow squares and triangles. Keep the yellow triangles on your starboard side (even if the aid is painted green) and leave the yellow squares to port when traveling south.

The easiest way to make this upriver run is to go with the flood tide but be prepared for a rough chop if the wind is against the current. Conditions will improve in the upper reaches where the river narrows but currents will be strong during the ebb tide.

Cape Fear Memorial Bridge crosses the river south of the marinas. It has 65-foot closed vertical clearance and opens on signal (except during special events) for large ships. The bridgetender monitors VHF Channel 18. To the north is **Isabelle Holmes Bridge** with 40-foot closed vertical clearance. The draw opens on signal, except from 6:00 a.m. to 6:00 p.m., when the draw only opens at 10:00 a.m. and 2:00 p.m. for waiting vessels.

Dockage: Upriver at flashing green buoy "59" (approximately 7 nm north of ICW Mile 297) a well-marked channel leads off to starboard to Wilmington Marine Center (Marina & Service). Even with a tidal

GOIN' ASHORE

WILMINGTON, NC

The heart of downtown Wilmington is its riverfront. Once a bustling wharf of warehouses, boatsheds, docks and stables, today, a cluster of shops and restaurants span several city blocks along the Cape Fear River. The 1-mile-long Riverwalk follows the borders of the Cape Fear River and provides beautiful views framed with antebellum homes wrapped in picket fences, jasmine and magnolias. The wooden walkway passes shops and restaurants as well as a number of landmarks, including the *USS North Carolina Battleship* and the Cape Fear Memorial Bridge.

SERVICES

1. **Downtown Medical Center**
   1615 Doctor's Circle (910-762-5588)

2. **New Hanover County Public Library**
   201 Chestnut St. (910-798-6300)

3. **Wilmington and Beaches Convention and Visitors Bureau**
   505 Nutt St., Unit A (910-341-4030)

4. **Wilmington Post Office**
   152 N. Front St. (910-313-3293)

ATTRACTIONS

5. **Battleship North Carolina**
   The *USS North Carolina* is one of Wilmington's best-known attractions. Visitors can tour the main deck, interior rooms and 16-inch gun turrets. There is a Roll of Honor in the wardroom listing the names of North Carolinians who died in the line of duty during World War II. The site also features a gift shop, visitor's center and picnic area at 1 Battleship Rd. (910-399-9100).

6. Bellamy Mansion Museum
This home is a great example of antebellum architecture at 503 Market St. (910-251-3700). After the fall of Fort Fisher in 1865, Federal troops used the home as their headquarters. Inside, you will find historical exhibits, arts and exhibitions. Carriage and walking tours begin out front.

7. Burgwin-Wright House
This historic home (circa 1770) is distinguished by wrap-around, two-story porches and Colonial-style tiered gardens. The massive ballast-stone foundation at 224 Market St. is the remains of an abandoned town jail (910-762-0570).

8. Cape Fear Museum of History and Science
With an original opening date of March 1898, in one room of the Wilmington Light Infantry building, this is the oldest history museum in North Carolina (814 Market St.). Inside there is a 20-foot-tall Giant Ground Sloth skeleton, a miniature recreation of the second battle of Fort Fisher and a room dedicated to native son and basketball great Michael Jordan (910-798-4370).

SHOPPING

9. Old Wilmington City Market
Established in 1880, this collection of eclectic and unique merchandise is offered by local artists, vendors and specialty shops (120 Front St., 910-399-3674).

10. The Cotton Exchange
At the turn of the century, cotton was still king and one of the largest and busiest cotton export companies in the world was located at 321 N. Front St. Today, eight restored buildings, connected by brick walkways and open-air courtyards, house 30 unique specialty shops and restaurants, each a charming reflection of the style and feel of Wilmington's 19th-century working port days (910-343-9896).

MARINAS

11. Port City Marina
10 Harnett St. (910-251-6151)

12. Wilmington City Docks
302 Willard St. (910-520-6875)

Cape Fear River, NC

WILMINGTON AREA		Largest Vessel	VHF	Total Slips	Approach/ Dockside Depth	Floating Docks	Gas/ Diesel	Repairs/ Haulout	Min/Max Amps	Pump-Out Station
1. Wilmington Marine Center WiFi 7.0 mi. N of MM 297.0	(910) 395-5055	120	16	106	5.5 / 5.0	F	GD	RH	30 / 50	P

WiFi Wireless Internet Access onSpot Dockside WiFi Facility
Visit www.waterwayguide.com for current rates, fuel prices, website addresses and other up-to-the-minute information.
(Information in the table is provided by the facilities.)

Scan here for more details:

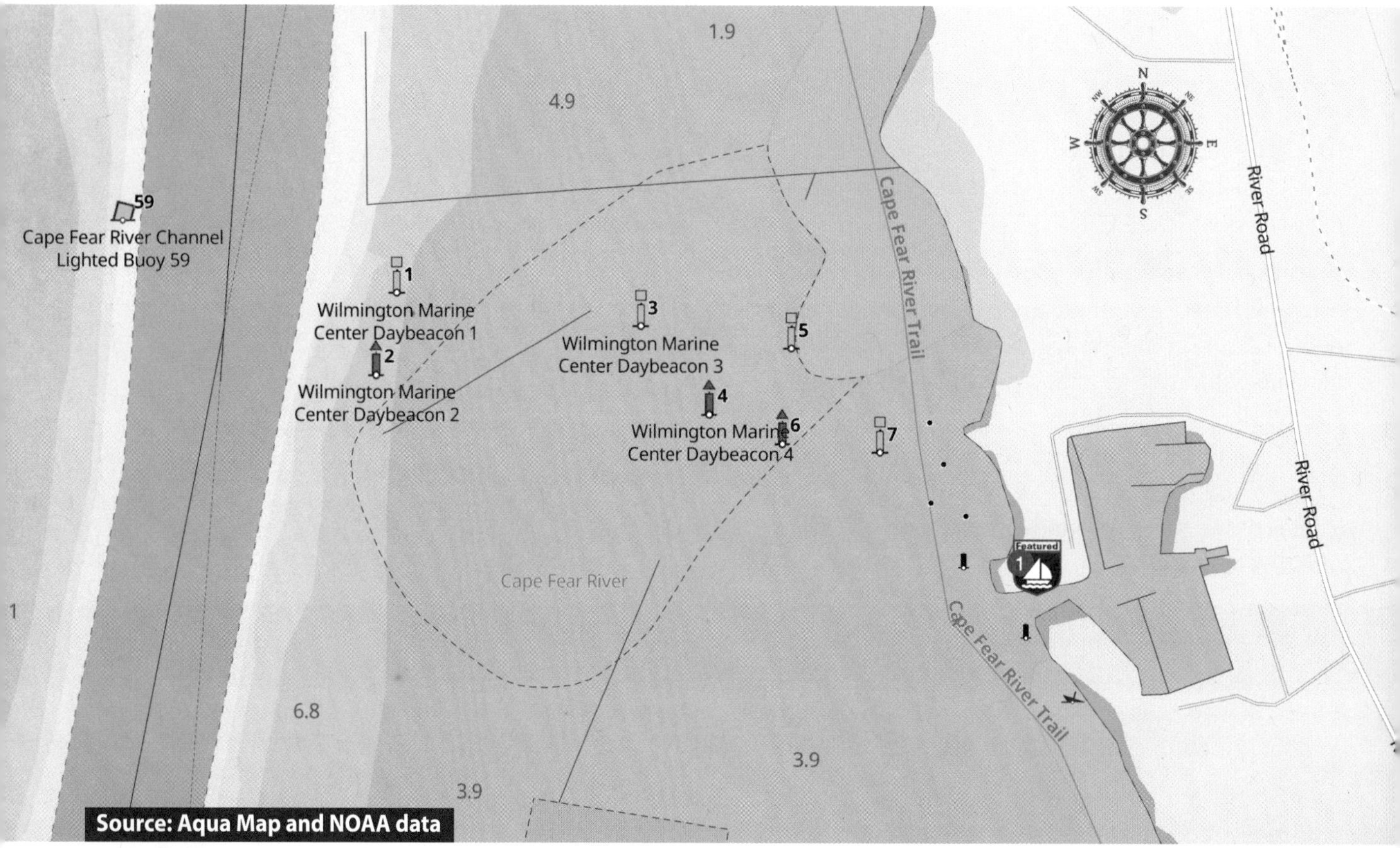

Source: Aqua Map and NOAA data

Cape Fear Memorial Bridge

Cape Fear River, NC

WILMINGTON		Largest Vessel	VHF	Total Slips	Approach/ Dockside Depth	Floating Docks	Gas/ Diesel	Repairs/ Haulout	Min/Max Amps	Pump-Out Station
1. Wilmington City Docks (WiFi) 13.6 mi. N of MM 297.0	(910) 520-6875	100	16	30	38.0 / 16.0	F			30 / 50	P
2. Port City Marina (WiFi)	(910) 251-6151	250	16	86	25.0 / 6.5	F	GD		30 / 200+	P
3. Sawmill Point Marina (WiFi) 14.0 mi. N of MM 297.0	(910) 772-9277	50		50	40.0 / 20.0	F			30 / 50	
4. Cape Fear Marina (WiFi) 14.4 mi. N of MM 297.0	(910) 772-9277	175	16	75	40.0 / 20.0	F			30 / 100	P
5. Off The Hook Yacht Services (WiFi) 14.4 mi. N of MM 297.0	(910) 772-9277	175	16	75	40.0 / 18.0	F		RH	30 / 100	P

(WiFi) Wireless Internet Access onSpot Dockside WiFi Facility
Visit www.waterwayguide.com for current rates, fuel prices, website addresses and other up-to-the-minute information.
(Information in the table is provided by the facilities.)
Scan here for more details:

range of about 4 feet, deep-draft vessels find good water depths. The facility can also accommodate multihulls. This marina has full transient facilities, floating docks and pump-out service. Yard capabilities include bottom painting, electrical, plumbing, fiberglass repair and complete yacht painting services. They are also a certified Mercury Outboard sales and service dealer.

The convenient and affordable Wilmington City Docks are located north of the Cape Fear Memorial Bridge, just across from flashing green "63" with transient dockage, public restrooms and a nearby laundry. The docks are located downtown in the center of the Historic District with museums, shops, restaurants and nightlife all within walking distance. Port City Marina to the north can accommodate boats up to 250 feet with a 10-foot dockside depth on concrete floating slips. They call themselves "the marina in the middle of it all."

Sawmill Point Marina has floating docks for vessels to 50 feet with water and power at each slip and offers direct access from the Wilmington Riverwalk.

A short distance upriver beyond the Isabelle Holmes Bridge (40-foot closed vertical clearance) you can find transient slips on floating docks at Cape Fear Marina. They offer a fully equipped dock house with shower and laundry facilities. The facility is located in a rural area that is restricted to residential and recreational use (no charter fishing boats, tour boats or scuba dive boats). Off The Hook Yacht Services is a yacht brokerage.

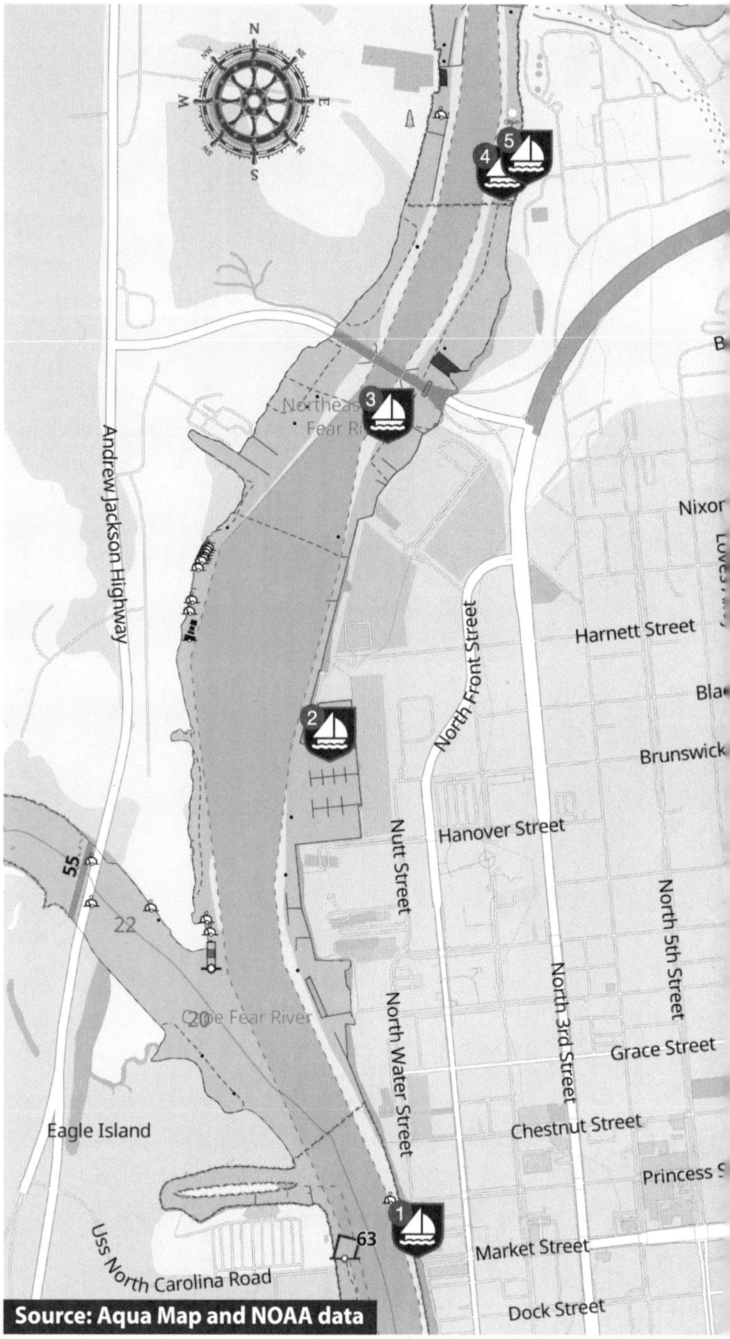

Source: Aqua Map and NOAA data

Bald Head Island, NC

BALD HEAD ISLAND		Largest Vessel	VHF	Total Slips	Approach/ Dockside Depth	Floating Docks	Gas/ Diesel	Repairs/ Haulout	Min/Max Amps	Pump-Out Station
1. Bald Head Island Marina WiFi 2.8 mi. S of MM 309.0	(910) 457-7380	115	16	175	8.0 / 7.0	F	GD		30 / 100	P

WiFi Wireless Internet Access onSpot Dockside WiFi Facility
Visit www.waterwayguide.com for current rates, fuel prices, website addresses and other up-to-the-minute information.
(Information in the table is provided by the facilities.)

Scan here for more details:

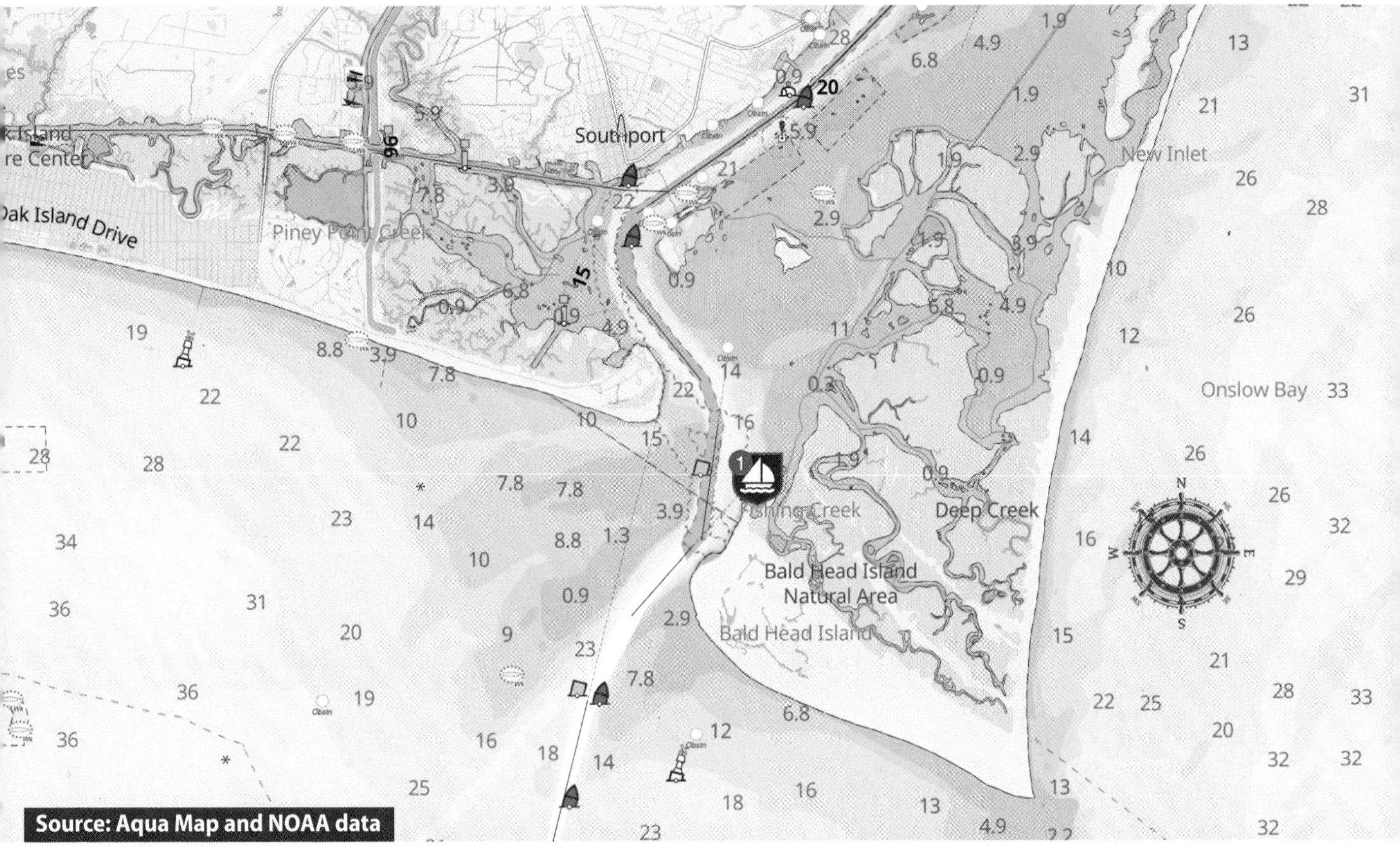

Source: Aqua Map and NOAA data

Southport Area, NC

DEEP POINT		Largest Vessel	VHF	Total Slips	Approach/ Dockside Depth	Floating Docks	Gas/ Diesel	Repairs/ Haulout	Min/Max Amps	Pump-Out Station
1. Deep Point Marina (WiFi) MM 307.0	(910) 269-2380	100	16	82	6.0 / 6.0	F	GD		30 / 100	P

(WiFi) Wireless Internet Access onSpot Dockside WiFi Facility
Visit www.waterwayguide.com for current rates, fuel prices, website addresses and other up-to-the-minute information.
(Information in the table is provided by the facilities.)

Scan here for more details:

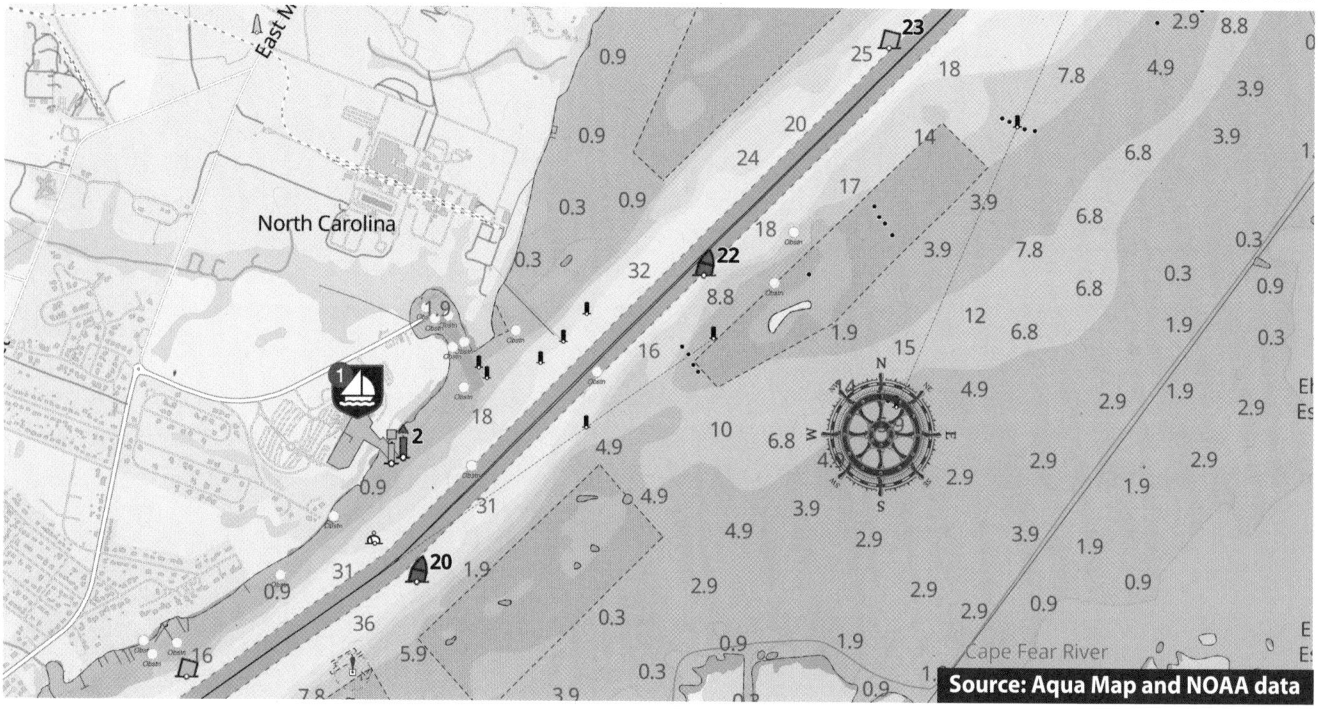

Source: Aqua Map and NOAA data

TO SOUTHPORT

Snows Cut to Southport–ICW Mile 298 to Mile 309

Back on the ICW the route to Southport leads through Snows Cut and down the Cape Fear River. A good procedure along this 12-mile downstream run to Southport is to run compass courses for each leg to assist in identifying the navigational aids that mark the course. The color of the marks changes from side to side and also the numbering changes as you continue down the Cape Fear River. Studying your charts before departure is, as always, a very wise decision.

NAVIGATION: Use NOAA Chart 11534. South of Snows Cut additional buoys have been added in the Cape Fear River, increasing the ease of maintaining a visual ICW channel course from the helm. The numerous ranges used by the large ships in the Cape Fear River have been changed recently and may not correspond with those on your NOAA chart.

Remember that the buoys are reversed from the normal ICW system when you reach the Cape Fear River at Mile 299. From here look for yellow squares and triangles. Keep the yellow triangles on your starboard side (even if the aid is painted green) and leave the yellow squares to port when traveling south.

Between Mile 299 and 302 on the west side of the Cape Fear River you will pass the Army's Military Ocean Terminal at Sunny Point with its three large piers. This is a restricted area protected by a security barrier marked by mooring dolphins connected to each other with cables with three openings for ships to pass. Each dolphin pile shows a white light and white and orange sign worded "Danger Restricted Area." This is the largest ammunitions port in the U.S. and is patrolled by smaller vessels. Steer clear of this area.

Also of note in navigating the Cape Fear River is the Fishers Island Ferry, which makes regular runs across the river between Federal Point (Mile 303.5) and the

Southport Area, NC

SOUTHPORT		Largest Vessel	VHF	Total Slips	Approach/ Dockside Depth	Floating Docks	Gas/ Diesel	Repairs/ Haulout	Min/Max Amps	Pump-Out Station
1. Southport Marina WiFi MM 309.3	(910) 457-9900	200	16	200	8.0 / 8.0	F	GD			P
2. Zimmerman Marine - Southport Yard WiFi	(910) 477-9044				8.0 / 6.0	F	G	RH	30 / 100	P
3. Indigo Plantation & Marina WiFi MM 310.0	(910) 269-2380	80	16	65	10.0 / 8.0	F			30 / 50	P

WiFi Wireless Internet Access onSpot Dockside WiFi Facility
Visit www.waterwayguide.com for current rates, fuel prices, website addresses and other up-to-the-minute information.
(Information in the table is provided by the facilities.)

Scan here for more details:

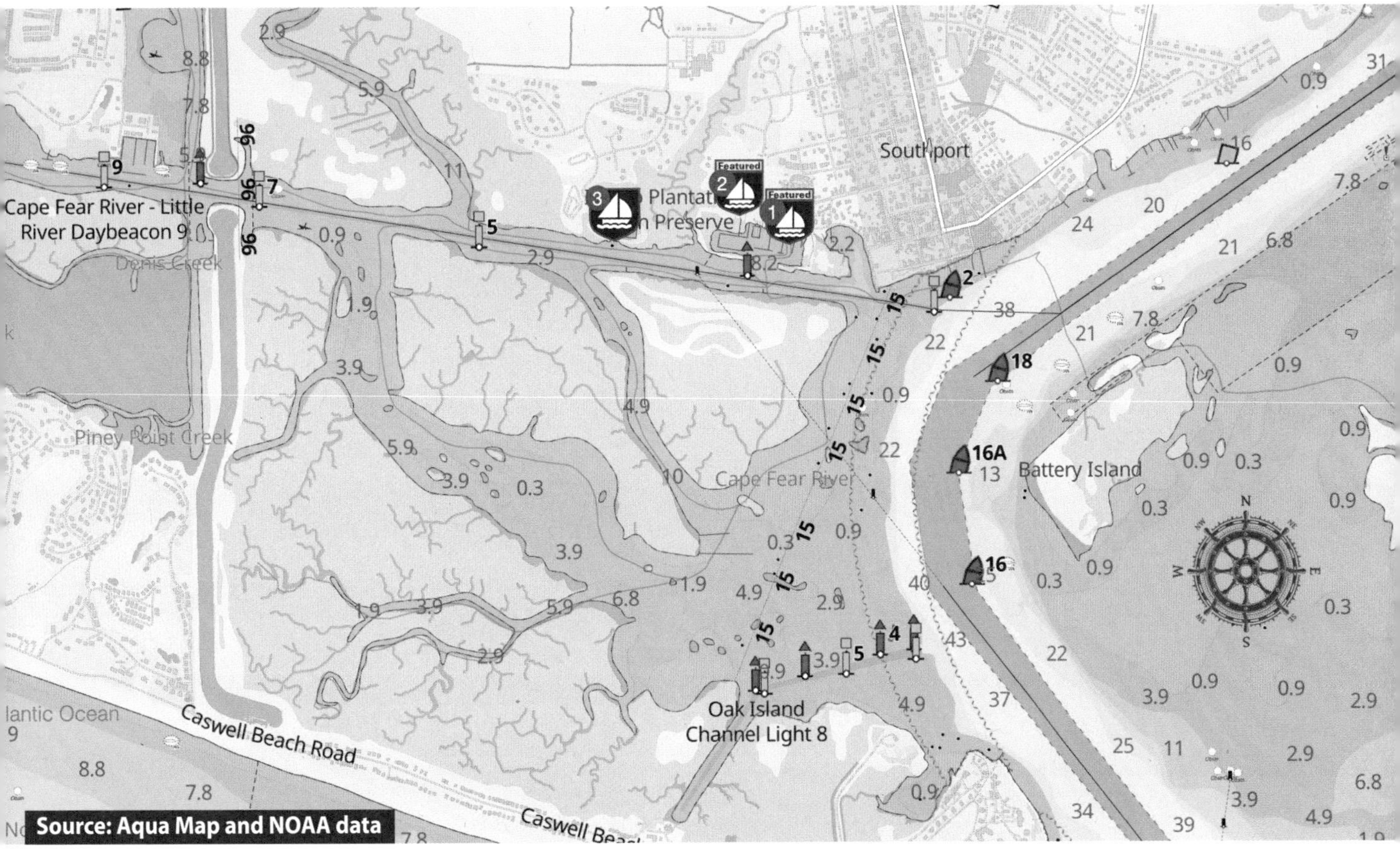

Source: Aqua Map and NOAA data

Ferry Terminal just north of Price Creek (Mile 306.5). You may also encounter large ships going to and from the port of Wilmington.

Southport is another spot where you can't go wrong if you arrive at or before low-water slack, going either north or south. Currents can run in excess of 2 knots during flood tide. Low-water slack before flood tides occurs in the river off Southport 1 hour and 16 minutes after the time listed in the tide tables for Charleston Harbor. If you ride the maximum ebb down the Cape Fear River, you will be facing into a wicked current as you turn into the ICW at Southport. If you have a favorable current in Snows Cut, it will be against you in the Cape Fear River. When the tide and wind are opposing batten down for a wet, uncomfortable ride to Southport.

Side Trip: Cape Fear River Entrance

The Cape Fear River Entrance is the first port south of Morehead City suitable for all sizes of oceangoing vessels via a major deepwater channel. This is a well-marked big ship channel that is protected from the north and an easy entrance day or night. This is one of several good inlets for snowbirds heading south should conditions deteriorate.

NAVIGATION: Use NOAA Chart 11534. If you wish to exit the ICW and continue outside on the outside, bear south at flashing red "18" between Southport and Bear Island and follow the well-marked channel for the Cape Fear River Entrance. For those headed north it is wise to stay on the ICW to avoid a significant detour around Frying Pan Shoals, which extend 30 nm out

into the Atlantic. Because of Jay Bird Shoals, buoys on Cape Fear's main shipping channel should be observed and the Western Bar Channel should be avoided. Many charts still show the old entrance channel to the west of the new channel that replaced it. Follow the markers.

The current is very strong; time your entrance to take advantage of the tides. Northbound in slower boats would be well-advised to check the tides before attempting the Cape Fear Rivers strong currents. This is a busy inlet so keep a constant watch posted for big ships.

Side Trip: Bald Head Island

Bald Head Island on the northeastern shore at the mouth of the Cape Fear River offers a destination marina and shore development well worth the 2-mile diversion off the ICW. Its remoteness (accessible only by water), 14 miles of wide, unspoiled beaches and magnificent dunes, alongside meandering creeks through diverse forests and waving marsh grass makes this natural barrier island stand out. If a walk on a pristine, deserted beach is your thing, then Bald Head is your place. Except for a few service vehicles, there are no cars on the island so transportation is by foot, bicycle and electric cart. You can rent bikes and carts on the island to reach shopping, restaurants and the beaches. All Bald Head beaches are public with access via paths from the road. You will pass several trail heads along the way marking trails that wind through the forest and marsh.

While you are exploring be sure to stop by Old Baldy, the original Cape Fear Lighthouse and the Keeper's House and one of the oldest standing lighthouses (built in 1817). You can climb the 108 steps and the ladder to the lantern room for a wonderful view of the entire area.

NAVIGATION: Use NOAA Chart 11534. Bald Head Island is easily reached either from the ICW, which turns to the west at Southport or from the ocean. It is an excellent jumping-off or landing point to or from a voyage south. Bald Head Island's deep-dredged and well-marked channel lies southeast of flashing green "13A" on the Smith Island

GOIN' ASHORE

SOUTHPORT, NC

Southport was originally named Smithville after Benjamin Smith who served under Gen. George Washington in the Revolutionary War. The first Spanish explorers arrived in 1521 and settled up the Cape Fear River in what became known as Brunswick Town. In the early 1700 Southport was a harbor for pirates, including Stede Bonnet, the "Gentleman Pirate," who was a frequent visitor. What began as a small fishing and military town has blossomed into a community for retirees and commuters working in Wilmington.

SERVICES

1. **Dosher Memorial Hospital**
   924 N. Howe St. (910-457-3800)
2. **Fort Johnston-Southport Museum & Visitor's Center**
   203 E. Bay St. (910-457-7927)
3. **Margaret and James Harper, Jr. Library**
   109 W. Moore St. (910-457-6237)
4. **Southport Post Office**
   206 E. Nash St. (910-457-4633)

ATTRACTIONS

5. Keziah Memorial Park
Lovely place for a walk and home to an ancient gnarled oak has been estimated to be more than 800 years old. Native Americans may have bent the young tree to mark the trail to their fishing grounds. The tree took root a second time, thus developing the unusual formation; you can't miss it (113 W. Moore St.).

6. North Carolina Maritime Museum
Dedicated to the history of the Lower Cape Fear Region and containing a detailed and fascinating collection that covers shipwrecks, piracy, the Civil War, commercial fishing, hurricanes and a number of other natural and manmade events that have left a permanent mark on the North Carolina coast (204 E. Moore St. 910-457-0003).

7. Old Brunswick County Jail Museum
Restored two-story brick jailhouse (circa 1904) featuring quarters with period artifacts at 318 E. Nash St. (910-457-7927).

8. Old Smithville Burying Ground
History buffs will want to visit this 1792 cemetary founded before the town at 401 E. Moore St. Managed by the Southport Historical Society (910-457-7927).

SHOPPING

9. Duck Duck Goose
Carries unique, gifts for home and garden made in southeastern NC. Painted glassware, custom birdhouses, local books and soaps and lotions are among the offerings at 106 E. Moore St. (910-454-0643).

10. NAPA Auto Parts of Southport Auto & Marine
Parts, tools and accessories (including some boating supplies) available at 721 N. Howe St. (910-457-5022).

11. Ocean Outfitters
Sportswear, footwear, beach chairs and sunglasses are among the offerings at 121 E. Moore St. (910-457-0433).

MARINAS

12. Southport Marina
606 W. West St. (910-457-9900)

13. Zimmerman Marine
606 W. West St. (910-477-9044)

Southport, NC

Southport Area, NC

OAK ISLAND		Largest Vessel	VHF	Total Slips	Approach/ Dockside Depth	Floating Docks	Gas/ Diesel	Repairs/ Haulout	Min/Max Amps	Pump-Out Station
1. Safe Harbor South Harbour Village WiFi MM 311.4	(910) 454-7486	200	16	153	15.0 / 12.0	F	GD	R	30 / 100	
2. American Fish Shop & American Marine Construction MM 312.0	(910) 457-5488				/			RH		

WiFi Wireless Internet Access onSpot Dockside WiFi Facility
Visit www.waterwayguide.com for current rates, fuel prices, website addresses and other up-to-the-minute information.
(Information in the table is provided by the facilities.)

Scan here for more details:

Source: Aqua Map and NOAA data

SAFE HARBOR SOUTH HARBOUR VILLAGE AWAITS
Two Waterside Restaurants
Bathhouses, Showers & Laundry
Courtesy Bikes
Complimentary Parking
Dog Park
Home Port Events
Scan with your mobile camera
or visit SHMARINAS.COM
SAFE HARBOR
– SOUTH HARBOUR VILLAGE –
4909 Fish Factory Road
Southport, NC 28461
910.454.7486

WATERWAY GUIDE THE CRUISING AUTHORITY
Subscription
Don't Get Left High & Dry
Safe boating and adventure on America's waterways is a click away. Subscribe to Explorer today for expert advice, navigation alerts, anchorages, fuel prices, marina listings and more all rolled up into an easy-to-use portal.
Not a member? Join
Learn More
waterwayguide.com
Jupiter Inlet
INLETS: ST. JOHNS RIVER ENTRANCE TO ANGELFISH CREEK, FL
JUPITER INLET
Jupiter Sound
LOXAHATCHEE RIVER EXTENSION
waterwayguide.com/learn-more

Southport Area, NC

OAK ISLAND		Largest Vessel	VHF	Total Slips	Approach/ Dockside Depth	Floating Docks	Gas/ Diesel	Repairs/ Haulout	Min/Max Amps	Pump-Out Station
1. St. James Marina WiFi onSpot MM 315.0	(910) 253-0463	120	16	155	7.0 / 7.0	F	GD	RH	30 / 50	P

WiFi Wireless Internet Access onSpot Dockside WiFi Facility
Visit www.waterwayguide.com for current rates, fuel prices, website addresses and other up-to-the-minute information.
(Information in the table is provided by the facilities.)

Scan here for more details:

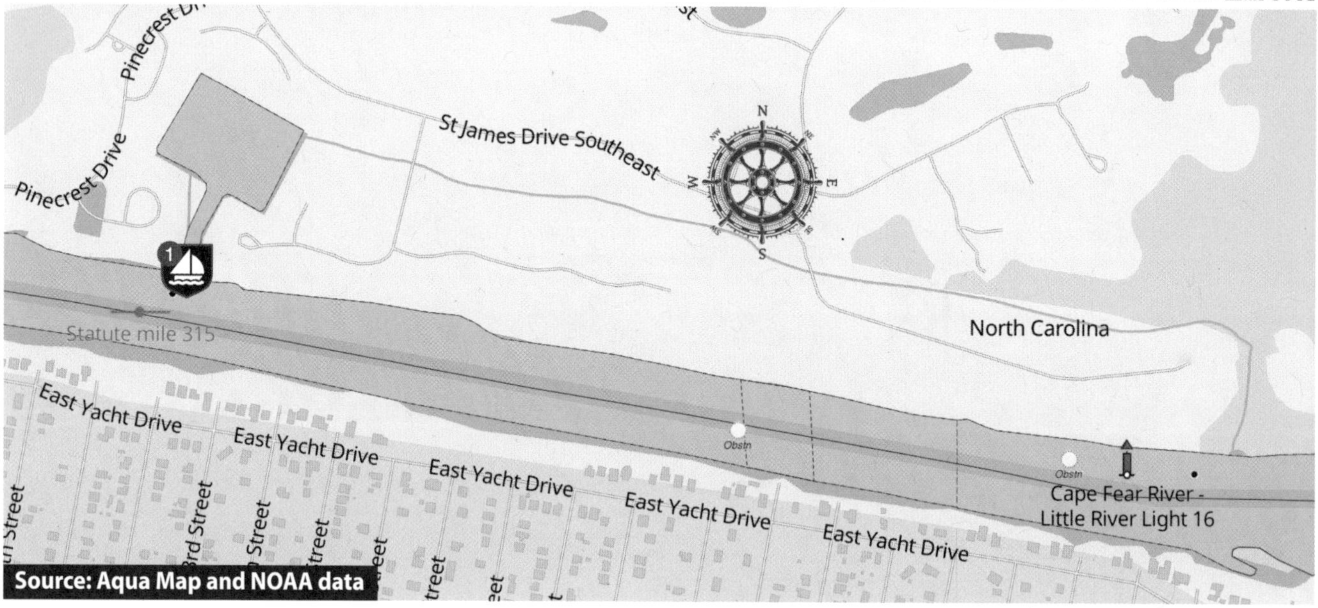

Range of the Cape Fear River (east of Jay Bird Shoals). The ebb and flood currents range from 2 to 3 knots and run perpendicular to the island's entrance channel. The entrance channel is narrow and care must be exercised to maintain control of your vessel in the current. Do not try to enter if another boat is exiting the channel fairway.

Dockage: Bald Head Island Marina is located in a 10-acre protected harbor with neatly lined floating docks and surrounded by an adorable village. Along with dockside conveniences such as showers, laundry facilities, some groceries, boating supplies and casual dining, Bald Head Island Marina guests may purchase temporary memberships at the Bald Head Island Club for superb golf, tennis, pool and croquet facilities and elegant dining, and at the private Shoals Club for fine and casual dining, swimming in the crystal clear salt water pool and direct beach access with chairs and umbrellas provided. The marina can accommodate vessels to 115 feet and 8-foot drafts. Call ahead for availability, docking instructions and assistance (monitoring VHF Channel 16). There is no room for anchoring in the enclosed basin.

Southport & Oak Island–ICW Mile 309 to Mile 311

About 2 miles north of the Cape Fear River Inlet (to the Atlantic) the ICW leaves the river, takes a hard turn to the west, enters a dredged land cut and arrives in the peaceful little village of Southport. Southport's numerous restaurants and much of its business district are within easy walking distance of the waterfront. The downtown combines all the charm of a laid-back coastal village with historic southern architecture and style. (See "Goin' Ashore: Southport, NC" in this chapter for details.

A "drive on" (car) ferry terminal is 2 miles north of Southport and runs to the tip of Fort Fisher at the mouth of the Cape Fear River. The enjoyable 45-minute one-way trip is filled with unique, beautiful views and is a bargain at $5 per carload.

From Oak Island through Long Beach you will pass through several small towns and a series of beach developments. You will likely encounter numerous small fishing boats testing the waters for red fish and flounder. These are also some of the most beautiful sections of the ICW.

Oak Island Lighthouse offers sweeping views over Caswell Beach and Bald Head Island. Tours to the second level (12 steps up to a solid concrete floor) are offered during the summer months on Wednesdays and Saturdays. Reservations are not required but if you wish to take a tour to the top (up 131 steps to an outside balcony) we recommend making a reservation (and well in advance). All tours are free.

NAVIGATION: Use NOAA Chart 11534. Shoaling has been observed along Southport's waterfront and the nameless island just southwest of the village so stay in the channel. When entering the ICW channel from the Cape Fear River, there is no shortcut. The two rectangular condo buildings on the point at Southport make a prominent landmark.

Oak Island (NC 133) Bridge (65-foot fixed vertical clearance) at Mile 311.8 is the first bridge encountered after Snows Cut. There is another high-level bridge–**Middleton Street Bridge** with 67-foot fixed vertical clearance–between Oak Island and the mainland at Mile 316.8 (at Swains Cut).

From Mile 310 to Mile 396 below Myrtle Beach, the National Ocean Service (NOS) tables do not provide information on currents. In general the flood runs south in this area but expect current reversals as you pass inlets.

Dockage: At Mile 307 the modern Deep Point Marina offers comfortable dockage along with easy ocean, ICW and river access. They sell all fuels and have clean showers, a pool (seasonal) and laundry facilities in an impressive Harbor Master facility, which also houses an on-site store that sells snacks and ice. The marina is adjacent to the Bald Head Island Mainland Ferry Terminal.

A short distance into the southbound ICW land cut a channel opens to the right at flashing red marker "2A" into Southport Marina, one of the largest and most amenity-laden marinas in North Carolina. The full-service marina has over 200 in-water protected slips with deep water access, a well-appointed Ship Store and a fuel dock. They also have a 220 unit dry-storage facility. Note that Southport Marina was heavily damaged during Hurricane Isaias in summer 2020 but rebuilding plans were in place within a few weeks. Overnight dockage was not allowed as of summer 2021 but the dinghy dock was available. Call ahead.

Zimmerman Marine–Southport Yard is located at Southport Marina and offers full boat repair services from rigging to mechanical and electrical and including carpentry and fiberglass. (They have six other yards in Oriental, NC; Holden Beach, NC; Deltaville, VA; Mobjack Bay, VA; Herrington Harbour, MD; and Charleston, SC.) A public boardwalk surrounds the marina along the bulkhead as part of Southport's Riverwalk. It is a five-minute walk into downtown.

The floating docks at the entrance to the basin are private and associated with the condos on the point. Dockage is sometimes available at a few of the private slips in the town basin. (Check the posted signs.) Past these docks and in front of Provision Company there are four slips for dining patrons. If you eat there you can stay overnight at the dock. There is no water or power and it may be noisy when the restaurant is full. Nearby Fishy Fishy (910-457-1881) may also have dockage for diners.

Indigo Plantation & Marina has limited transient space immediately south on the ICW. This is home to the Indigo Plantation Yacht Club. The road to town from here is not direct, making a taxi ride necessary for shopping or dining out.

At Mile 311 (daybeacon green "9"), Safe Harbor South Harbour Village offers a spacious 500-foot facing dock parallel to the ICW that can accommodate boats up to 200 feet. They offer all fuels, pump-out stations, ice and oil on the face dock. The on-site Rusty Hooks Dockside Grill has great food (try the signature fish tacos), a bar and live music, while Joseph's Italian Bistro offers fine dining with European decor. Safe Harbor South Harbour Village is known for being cruiser- and pet-friendly. Reservations are recommended.

American Fish Shop & American Marine Construction occupies the docks on the west side of the ICW north of the Oak Island (NC 133) Bridge (65-foot vertical clearance) at Mile 311.8. This is a full-service boat yard with competitive pricing.

St. James Marina at Mile 315 is another full-service marina with everything you need right on site. They have 50 reserved transient slips for vessels to 120 feet and a dry storage facility. They also sell all fuels. This is part of a large residential development and includes three golf courses, a small general store, a gift shop and an on-site restaurant.

Anchorage: The Southport Basin at the beginning of the land cut is shallow (3- to 7-foot MLW depths) with poor holding and is open to the south and ICW wakes. The entrance to Dutchman Creek at Mile 310.2 has shoaled, as has the anchorage on the west side of Pipeline Canal (north of red "8" at Mile 311). In short, this is a good area to plan on taking a slip.

NEXT STOP

Looking ahead, boaters will find some true "ditch" cruising, punctuated by side-setting inlets. When you reach Myrtle Beach at Mile 346, you may want to spend a few days enjoying the many amenities and public beaches. Then it's on to the beautiful Waccamaw River as you move toward Charleston and the Lowcountry.

ICW Mile 321-Mile 456

TO MYRTLE BEACH, SC

NO WAKE ZONE

No Wake Zones, Idle Speed Zones and various Speed Limit restrictions are in effect throughout the waterways included in this chapter. Exercise diligence in knowing the regulations by observing signs and other markers. Enforcement is always present. As always, be courteous to other vessels.

Approaching Lockwoods Folly Inlet, the shoreline shifts to low marshland extending back to scrub trees. Along the banks at Holden Beach just below the inlet an increasing number of houses have appeared on the ocean side of the ICW. This section carries heavy commercial and recreational boat traffic, particularly on weekends, and there are long stretches of No-Wake Zones.

If you make the passage in late June when North Carolina rivers are open for fishing, you will find a lot of boat traffic. Boats vary from outboard-powered skiffs and center consoles with families aboard to miniature shrimp boats. Although the traffic is chaotic and some skippers are uncooperative, one reward is that a fresh shrimp or fish meal is readily available at almost any tie-up.

ICW Bridges will not delay openings if boats are already waiting, so you must know your speed and calculate your transit carefully; slow boats may not be able to synchronize their passages with the openings.

Lockwoods Folly Inlet Area–ICW Mile 321 to Mile 325

NAVIGATION: Use NOAA Chart 11534. Just past Mile 321 the ICW crosses the junction of Lockwoods Folly Inlet and Lockwoods Folly River. The proximity of the ICW to the ocean in this area makes conditions extremely changeable at both Lockwoods Folly Inlet crossing and Shallotte Inlet crossing a few miles farther south. Strong

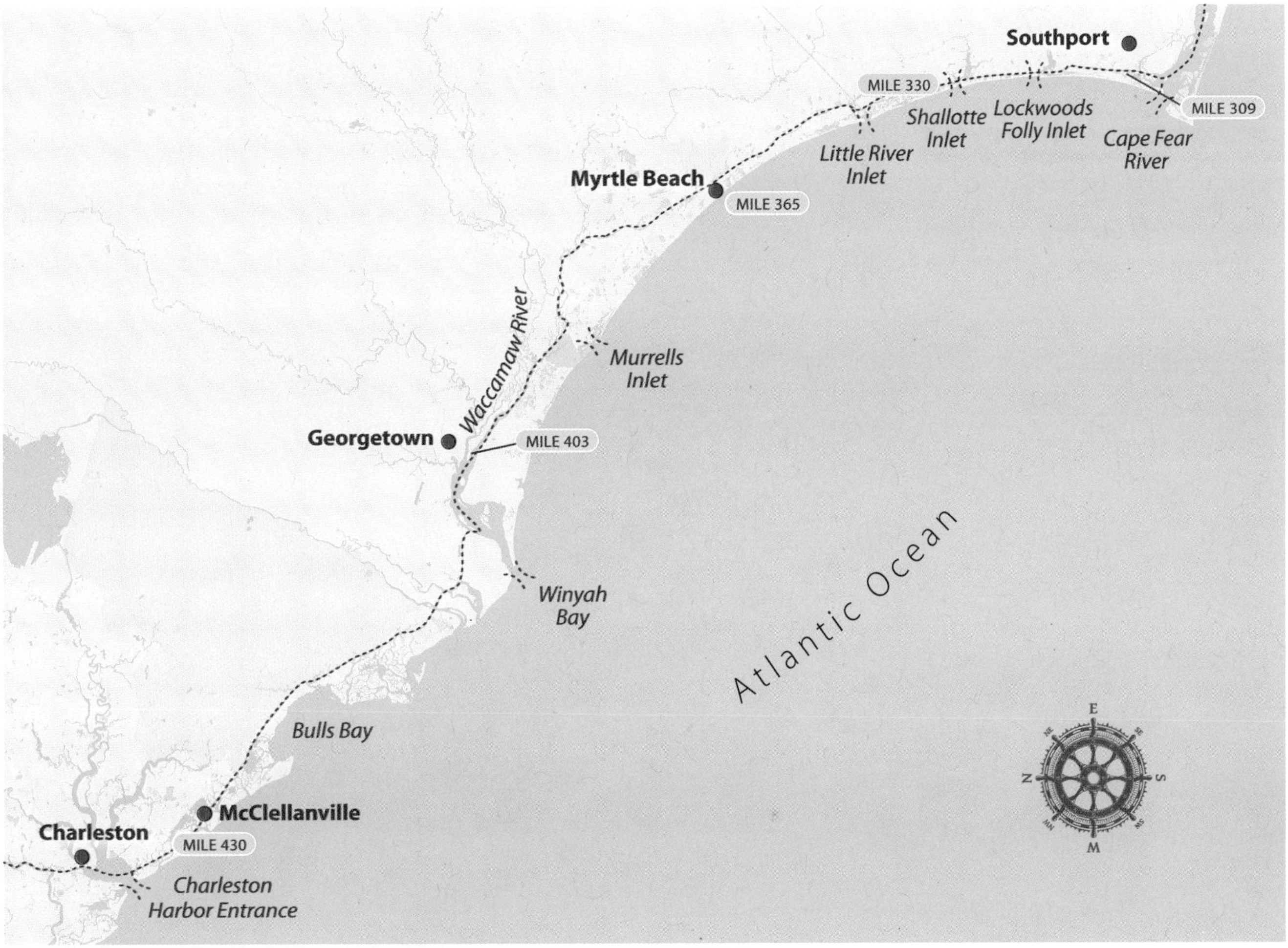

Lockwoods Folly Inlet, NC

HOLDEN BEACH		Largest Vessel	VHF	Total Slips	Approach/ Dockside Depth	Floating Docks	Gas/ Diesel	Repairs/ Haulout	Min/Max Amps	Pump-Out Station
1. Zimmerman Marine - Holden Beach MM 322.5	(910) 842-5488	72		8	/			RH	30 / 50	
2. Holden Beach Marina MM 324.0	(910) 842-5447	50	16	15	6.0 / 6.0	F	GD	R	30 / 50	
3. Holden Beach Transient Dock (WiFi) MM 324.0	(910) 842-6488			3	/	F			20 / 50	P

(WiFi) Wireless Internet Access onSpot Dockside WiFi Facility
Visit www.waterwayguide.com for current rates, fuel prices, website addresses and other up-to-the-minute information.
(Information in the table is provided by the facilities.)

Scan here for more details:

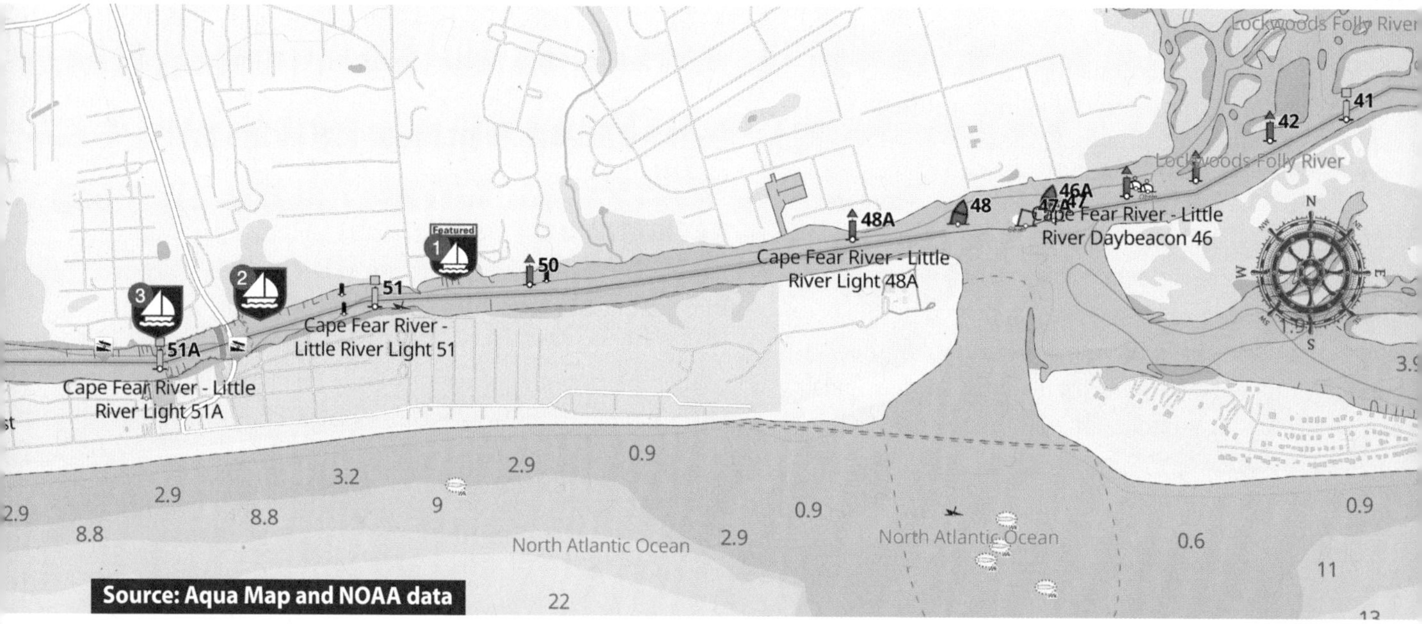

Source: Aqua Map and NOAA data

ebb and flow currents alone continually move the sand, while storms off the ocean can reshape the bottom in hours. Be aware of crosscurrents and adjust your heading as required.

The channel past Lockwoods Folly Inlet usually has extra floating markers (which can be readily moved) that are not shown on the NOAA chart, plus other charted markers may be missing. As always, honor the marks. Look for the ICW yellow triangles and squares so you do not confuse the inlet markers with those for the ICW.

At Mile 323.6 you will pass under the **Holden Beach (NC 130) Bridge** (65-foot fixed vertical clearance). This area has more boating traffic each year, especially during spring and summer. This is not a good place to anchor. Plan to take a slip.

Dockage: Zimmerman Marine–Holden Beach offers full boat repair services from rigging to mechanical and electrical and including carpentry and fiberglass. (Zimmerman's has six other yards in Oriental, NC; Southport, NC; Deltaville, VA; Mobjack Bay, VA; Herrington Harbour, MD; and Charleston, SC.)

Holden Beach Marina just above Mile 323 is primarily a dry-stack marina but they do reserve a few of their 15 slips for transients. You can walk to a grocery store and several restaurants. The nearby Provision Company (910-842-7205) has good seafood, a casual atmosphere, dockage and live music on weekends. The municipal Holden Beach Transient Dock is at Mile 324 with just three slips (72 hour limit). Call ahead.

Shallotte Inlet to Little River Inlet–ICW Mile 325 to Mile 341

At both Holden Beach and Ocean Isle Beach, long colonies of oceanfront houses (many on stilts) are on Florida-style dredged canals from the ICW to the ocean. Houses on the mainland side are more substantial, spaced farther apart and appear among the trees facing toward the ocean beach. You need to stay in the middle of the channel in this area due to rapid shoaling outside the channel.

The name Shallotte was derived from the original settlement name Charlotte, and is pronounced "sha-LOTE" (with a long "o" sound).

Welcome to South Carolina!

The canals and dredged cuts of NC give way to the wide river mouths, large sounds and coastal inlets of SC. The natural waterways are deep to the banks of low, marshy grasslands that are backed by hummocks of trees, including stately moss-covered oaks. At low tide, the vast salt marshes will teem with bird life.

Beyond Charleston, there is a noticeable increase in tidal currents and heights. The tidal range runs about 8 feet and depths can change quickly. Shoaling is an issue in some areas, and strong tidal currents throughout the region can change depths overnight. This section of the ICW also has many bridges, including many fixed high-level (65-foot vertical clearance) bridges. All SC bridges monitor VHF Channel 09. Be aware of the South Carolina Department of Transportation (SC DOT) Hurricane Evacuation Rule (posted on most opening bridges): Draw and swing bridges will not open when wind reaches a sustained 25 knots or if mandatory evacuation is ordered. During periods of strong winds, these bridges may be closed. (Swing bridges are especially vulnerable to damage from high winds.) Boats with taller masts must run outside from Beaufort, NC, to Georgetown or Charleston, SC, both of which are safe, big ship inlets. Be sure to refer to the Waterway Explorer at www.waterwayguide.com for navigational alerts, tidal information and bridge restrictions and schedules.

Little River, SC

SEASIDE		Largest Vessel	VHF	Total Slips	Approach/ Dockside Depth	Floating Docks	Gas/ Diesel	Repairs/ Haulout	Min/Max Amps	Pump-Out Station
1. Ocean Isle Marina & Yacht Club WiFi MM 335.5	(910) 579-6440	75	16	28	12.0 / 6.0	F	GD	RH	30 / 100	P

WiFi Wireless Internet Access **onSpot** Dockside WiFi Facility
Visit www.waterwayguide.com for current rates, fuel prices, website addresses and other up-to-the-minute information.
(Information in the table is provided by the facilities.)

Scan here for more details:

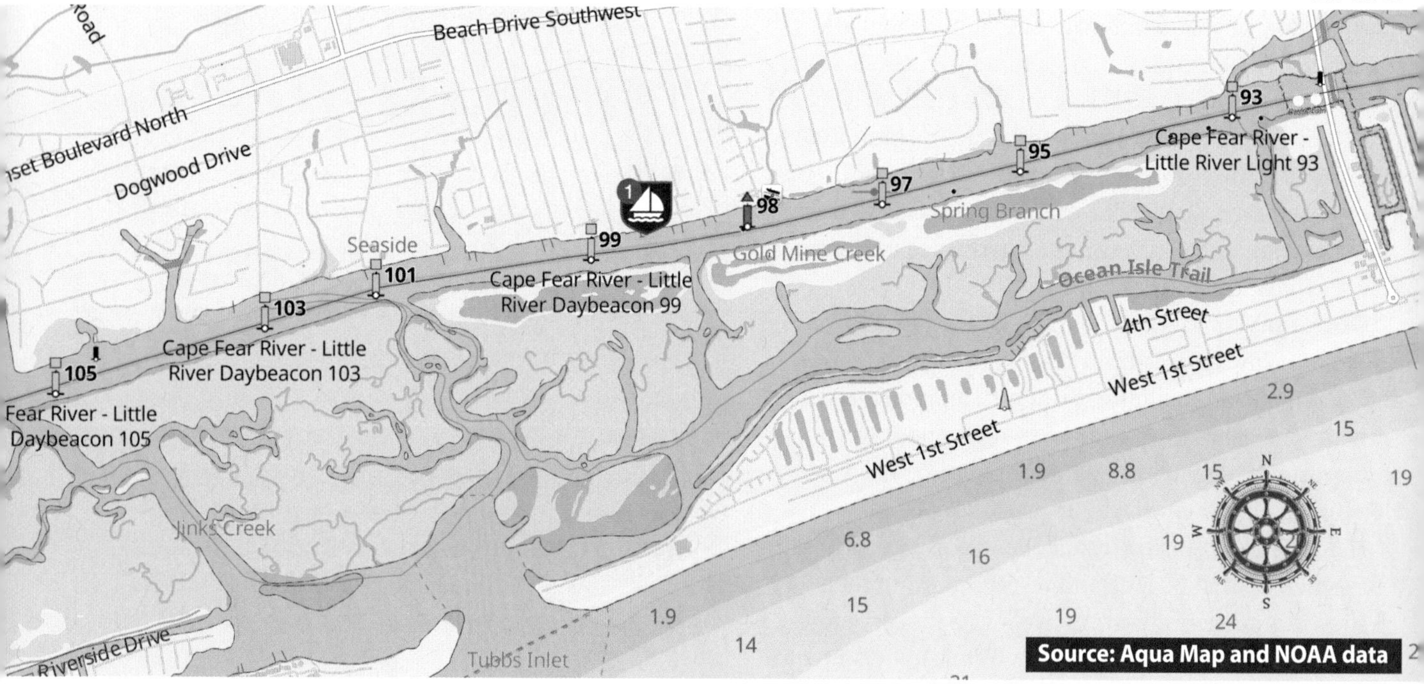

NAVIGATION: Use NOAA Chart 11534. The Shallotte River makes off northward at Mile 329.6 and carries 3- to 5-foot MLW depths to the rural town of Shallotte, NC. Call Coastal Machine and Welding on VHF Channel 16 for advice if you are considering venturing up the Shallotte River, which has a spring tidal range of 6 feet.

On the ICW at Shallotte Inlet, boaters can expect a sudden lateral push from the current coming through the inlet during a rising tide. You will experience a "pull" toward the ocean during an ebb tide. This pushing and pulling is more likely to put you aground than any shoaling along the ICW channel.

> Keep in mind that one storm can completely change the inlet. Because of this, the Coast Guard is likely to move green can "81" to mark the movement of the shoal.

Shallotte Inlet has been dredged. Stay in the middle of the channel and do not hug any buoys. Despite the recent dredging we do not advise use of Shallotte Inlet, even with local knowledge. This inlet is used primarily by local small fishing boats.

The next 8 miles are straightforward. Ocean Isle (NC 904) Bridge at Mile 333.7 is a fixed 65-foot span. Between the Mannon C. Gore (Sunset Beach) Bridge at Mile 337.9 and the Little River intersection with the ICW at Mile 343, stay in mid-channel to avoid the frequent shoals, which often crop up where various creeks cross to the ocean. Flashing green daybeacons "117" and "119" are out of the water about 20 feet up on the bank at very low tide so give both a wide berth.

Dockage: Ocean Isle Marina & Yacht Club is located at Mile 335.5 in Seaside. This facility mostly caters to sportfishing boats and offers repairs, storage, rentals and fishing charters. There are no viable anchorage areas along this stretch.

Little River Inlet to Pine Island Cut–ICW Mile 341 to Mile 349

Just inside the South Carolina State Line the ICW crosses Little River, which offers relatively easy and well-marked access to the ocean through the well-maintained channel between jetties. Little River Inlet, SC, is deep, wide and busy with a steady flow of tourist and fishing boats.

The village of Little River is a good stopping point for boats coming from the north or south. About a one-day run from Wrightsville Beach to the north and just before the long stretch of the ICW behind Myrtle Beach, it is the northern gateway to popular vacation resorts, which line the ocean beach for more than 20 miles as you head south. The mild climate has attracted permanent residents as well as vacationers. It also attracts anglers who come to patronize its charter fishing boats as well as golfers, who come to take on the 100-plus golf courses. This area is very busy with small boats, especially on weekends and holidays.

NAVIGATION: Use NOAA Chart 11534. Little River Inlet, SC, has jetties and is relatively stable. This inlet is used regularly by casino boats and head boats docked at Little River (SC). Casino boats are not required to have

Captain Archie "Poo" McLauchlin (Little River) Swing Bridge

Little River, SC

COQUINA HARBOR		Largest Vessel	VHF	Total Slips	Approach/ Dockside Depth	Floating Docks	Gas/ Diesel	Repairs/ Haulout	Min/Max Amps	Pump-Out Station
1. Cricket Cove Marina WiFi MM 345.0	(843) 249-7169	50	16	73	10.0 / 7.0	F	GD		30 / 100	P
2. Coquina Yacht Club WiFi MM 346.0	(843) 249-9333	102	16	87	8.0 / 8.0	F			30 / 50	P
3. Myrtle Beach Yacht Club WiFi MM 346.0	**(843) 249-5376**	**75**	**16**	**153**	**8.0 / 10.0**	**F**	**GD**		**30 / 100**	**P**
4. Lightkeepers Marina WiFi onSpot MM 346.0	(843) 249-8660	80	16	125	6.0 / 6.0	F			30 / 50	P

WiFi Wireless Internet Access onSpot Dockside WiFi Facility
Visit www.waterwayguide.com for current rates, fuel prices, website addresses and other up-to-the-minute information.
(Information in the table is provided by the facilities.)

Scan here for more details:

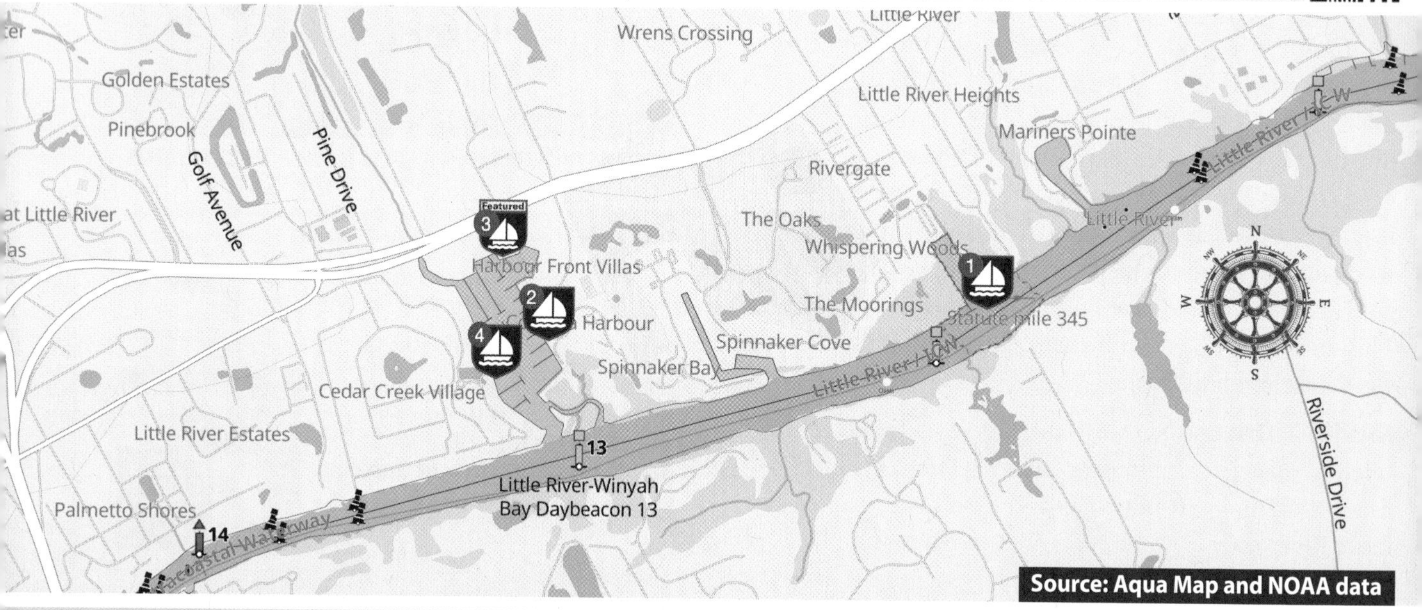

North Myrtle Beach Area, SC

NORTH MYRTLE BEACH		Largest Vessel	VHF	Total Slips	Approach/ Dockside Depth	Floating Docks	Gas/ Diesel	Repairs/ Haulout	Min/Max Amps	Pump-Out Station
1. Grande Harbour Marina MM 346.0	(843) 427-7934	48	16		13.0 / 8.5	F	G	RH		
2. Cherry Grove Marina (formerly Anchor Marina) MM 347.0	(843) 427-7008	48	16	100	7.0 / 6.0	F		RH	30 / 50	
3. Harbourgate Resort & Marina WiFi MM 347.7	(843) 249-8888	150	16	100	8.0 / 6.0	F	GD	R	30 / 50	P

WiFi Wireless Internet Access onSpot Dockside WiFi Facility
Visit www.waterwayguide.com for current rates, fuel prices, website addresses and other up-to-the-minute information.
(Information in the table is provided by the facilities.)

Scan here for more details:

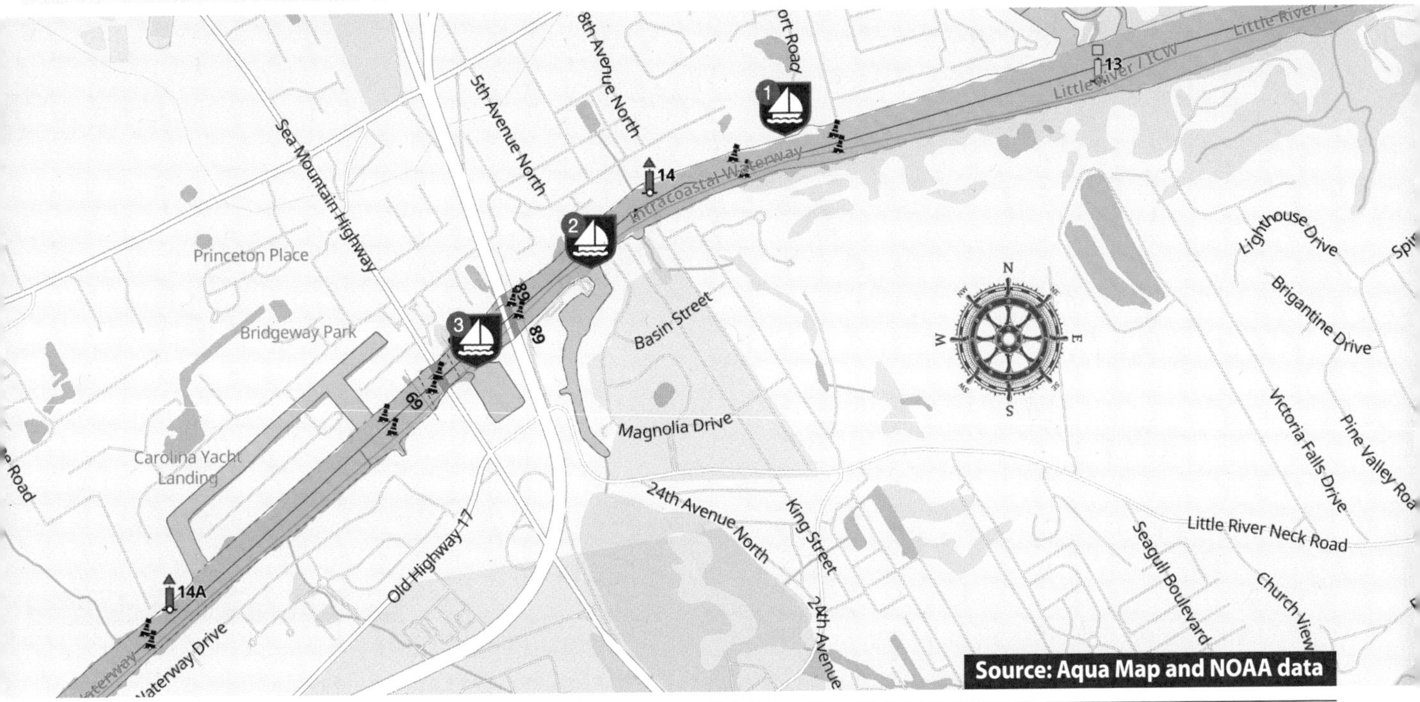

AIS transponders and many do not. There is a 5-foot shoal just off the east jetty that is awash at low tide. Note that the aids to navigation are frequently moved here to mark shifting shoals. Seek local knowledge before traversing the inlet.

About 1 mile above the junction of the ICW and the channel from the Little River Inlet, the route crosses the border from North Carolina into South Carolina (Mile 340.9). You can assume that you are in South Carolina when you make the turn below flashing red daybeacon "116."

Nixon Crossroads has two bridges: **Nixon Crossroads Bridge** at Mile 347.2 (fixed vertical clearance 65 feet) and the **Captain Archie Neil "Poo" McLauchlin (Little River) Swing Bridge** at Mile 347.3 with a closed vertical clearance of 7 feet. (The Little River Swing Bridge was renamed in 2018 after a lifelong resident.) The bridge opens on request. The Captain Poo Swing Bridge is old and frequently in need of repair.

> The Nixon Crossroads Bridge and the Captain Archie Neil "Poo" McLauchlin (Little River) Swing Bridge denote the dividing line between fresh and saltwater. Southwest of the bridges where the water becomes fresh you need a freshwater fishing license to do any angling.

> Keep an eye out for a "Danger Submerged Rock" sign just northeast of the The Nixon Crossroads Bridge, about one-third of the way out into the channel from the east (or ocean) side. Be careful of shoals along both sides of the waterway and submerged obstructions (likely pilings) on the ocean side for the 0.25 mile below the Captain Archie Neil "Poo" McLauchlin (Little River) Swing Bridge.

Dockage: Cricket Cove Marina at Mile 345 has one of the largest indoor dry storage facilities in the Myrtle Beach area. The popular Snooky's (843-249-5252) is on site.

North Myrtle Beach, SC

NORTH MYRTLE BEACH		Largest Vessel	VHF	Total Slips	Approach/ Dockside Depth	Floating Docks	Gas/ Diesel	Repairs/ Haulout	Min/Max Amps	Pump-Out Station
1. North Myrtle Beach RV Resort and Marina WiFi	(843) 390-4386	35	9	36	8.0 / 5.0	F	GD	H	30 / 50	P

WiFi Wireless Internet Access onSpot Dockside WiFi Facility
Visit www.waterwayguide.com for current rates, fuel prices, website addresses and other up-to-the-minute information.
(Information in the table is provided by the facilities.)

Scan here for more details:

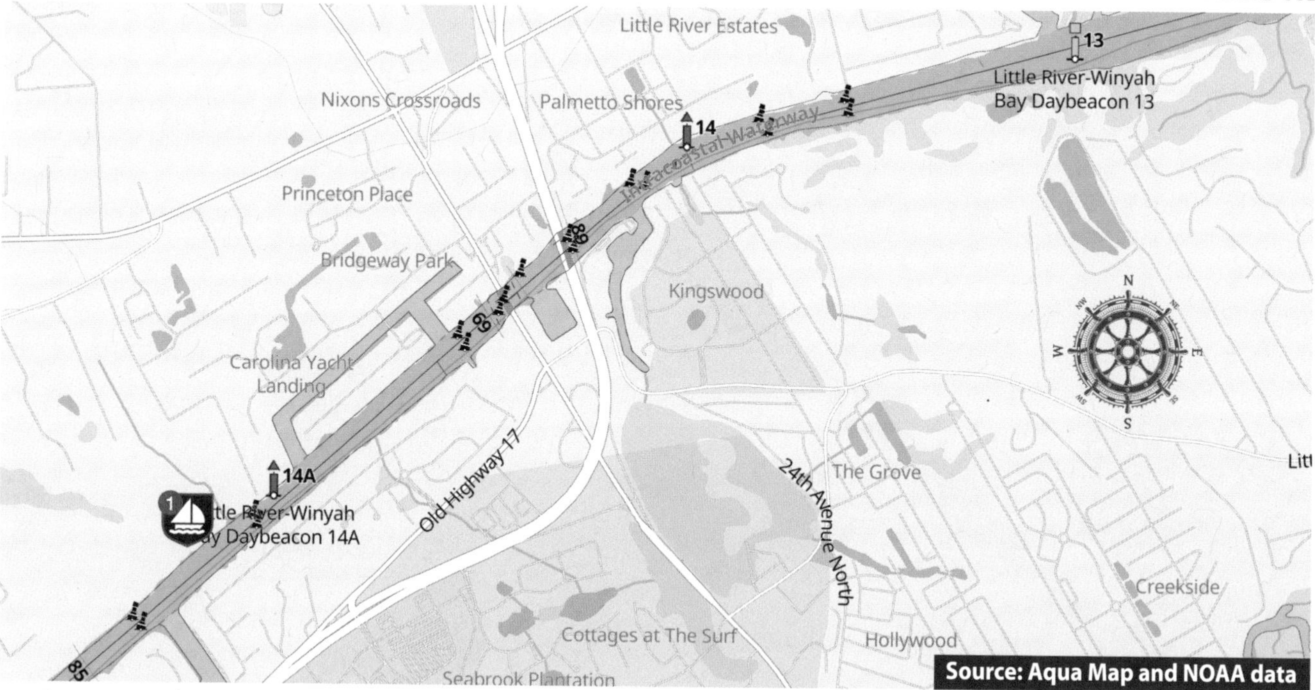

Coquina Harbor, a large deepwater basin on the west side of the ICW at Mile 346 (green daybeacon "13") is home to three marinas serving transients: Coquina Yacht Club, Myrtle Beach Yacht Club and Lightkeepers Marina. Southbound boaters need to go slightly south of this entrance and come back to the north and enter at an angle. Do not try to cut the corner on this well-marked channel; it is shallow outside the entrance markers. Deep-draft vessels should call ahead for entrance information. A black and white lighthouse replica marks the harbor entrance. The entire harbor is surrounded by a 3-mile boardwalk.

Transients to 46 feet are welcome at the well-regarded Myrtle Beach Yacht Club at Coquina Harbor. They have all the usual amenities plus a large pool, laundry room and a restaurant (the Officers Club), which you can visit as a guest of the marina manager. Coquina Yacht Club and Lightkeepers Marina also have ample reserved transient space but it's a good idea to call ahead. By the way, don't be

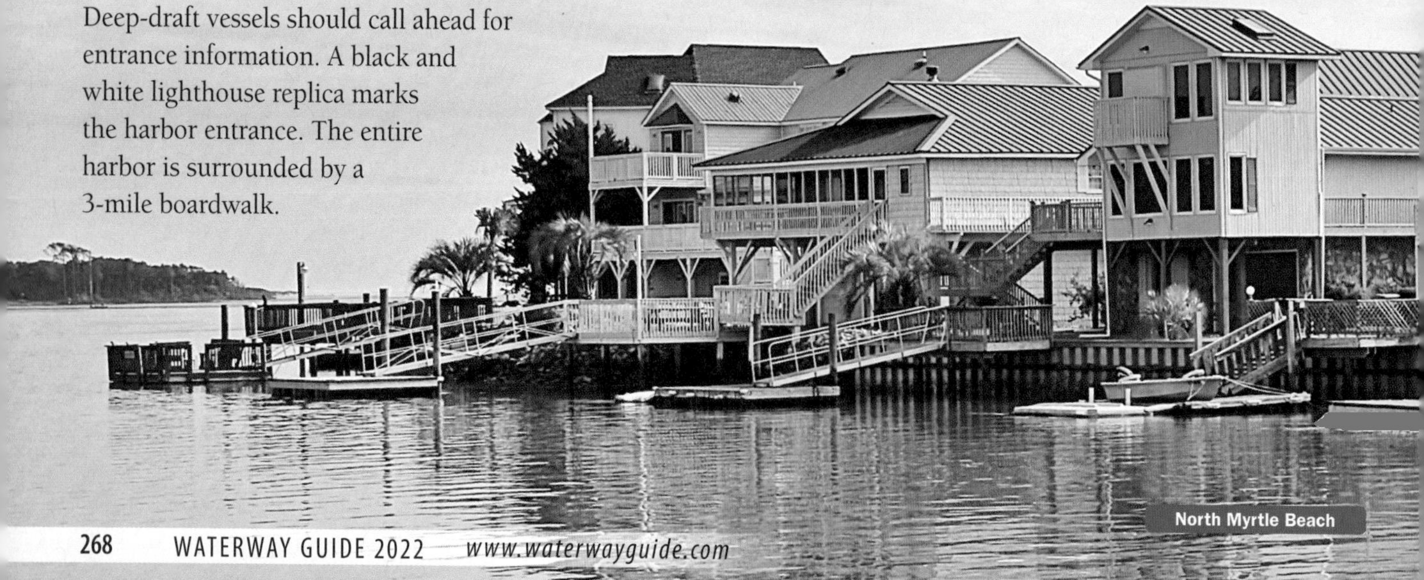
North Myrtle Beach

Myrtle Beach Area, SC

BAREFOOT LANDING		Largest Vessel	VHF	Total Slips	Approach/ Dockside Depth	Floating Docks	Gas/ Diesel	Repairs/ Haulout	Min/Max Amps	Pump-Out Station
1. Barefoot Marina WiFi MM 354.0	(843) 390-2011	150	16	142	8.0 / 12.0	F	GD		30 / 50	P

WiFi Wireless Internet Access onSpot Dockside WiFi Facility
Visit www.waterwayguide.com for current rates, fuel prices, website addresses and other up-to-the-minute information.
(Information in the table is provided by the facilities.)

Scan here for more details:

surprised if someone on a floating tiki bar motors over to offer you a drink after you dock!

Grand Harbor Marina at Mile 346 offers boat storage (to 32 feet) and services but no transient slips. Cherry Grove Marina (formerly Anchor Marina) is located just before the Nixon Crossroads Bridge (Mile 347.2) on the south side of the ICW with complete repair capabilities but only a few transient slips. Harbourgate Resort & Marina directly on the ICW at Mile 347.7 (between the bridges) is part of a condominium complex. They welcome transients on their floating docks. A large shopping plaza with groceries and a West Marine is within walking distance.

Just south of the two bridges is North Myrtle Beach RV Resort and Marina with covered dry storage to 48 feet and 38 wet slips that can accommodate boats to 35 feet with resort amenities.

Anchorage: You can anchor in Calabash Creek on the mainland side of the junction between the ICW and Little River Inlet at Mile 342. At extreme low tides the entrance bar carries around 5 feet. You will be subject to wakes from the ICW if you anchor toward the mouth of the creek. This is a pleasant spot otherwise with a golf course on the wooded northern shore.

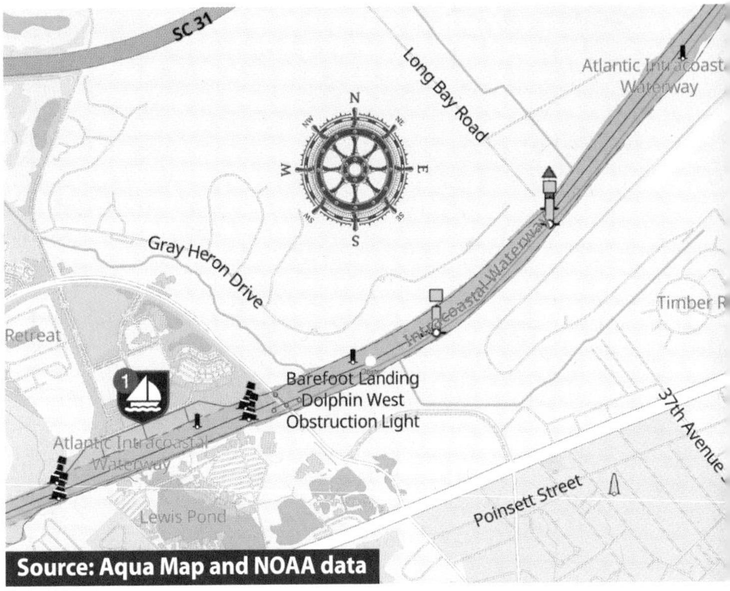

Source: Aqua Map and NOAA data

Give Calabash Creek red daybeacon "2A" (not the ICW red daybeacon "2," which features the distinctive ICW yellow triangle) a wide berth to avoid the shoal at the entrance. Then turn toward the row of charted dolphins and drop the hook near the north side of the center of the river. There is increasing shoaling on the opposite

Myrtle Beach Area, SC

GRANDE DUNES		Largest Vessel	VHF	Total Slips	Approach/ Dockside Depth	Floating Docks	Gas/ Diesel	Repairs/ Haulout	Min/Max Amps	Pump-Out Station
1. Marina at Grande Dunes WiFi MM 357.0	(843) 315-7777	120	16	126	12.0 / 8.0	F	GD		30 / 100	P

WiFi Wireless Internet Access onSpot Dockside WiFi Facility
Visit www.waterwayguide.com for current rates, fuel prices, website addresses and other up-to-the-minute information.
(Information in the table is provided by the facilities.)

Scan here for more details:

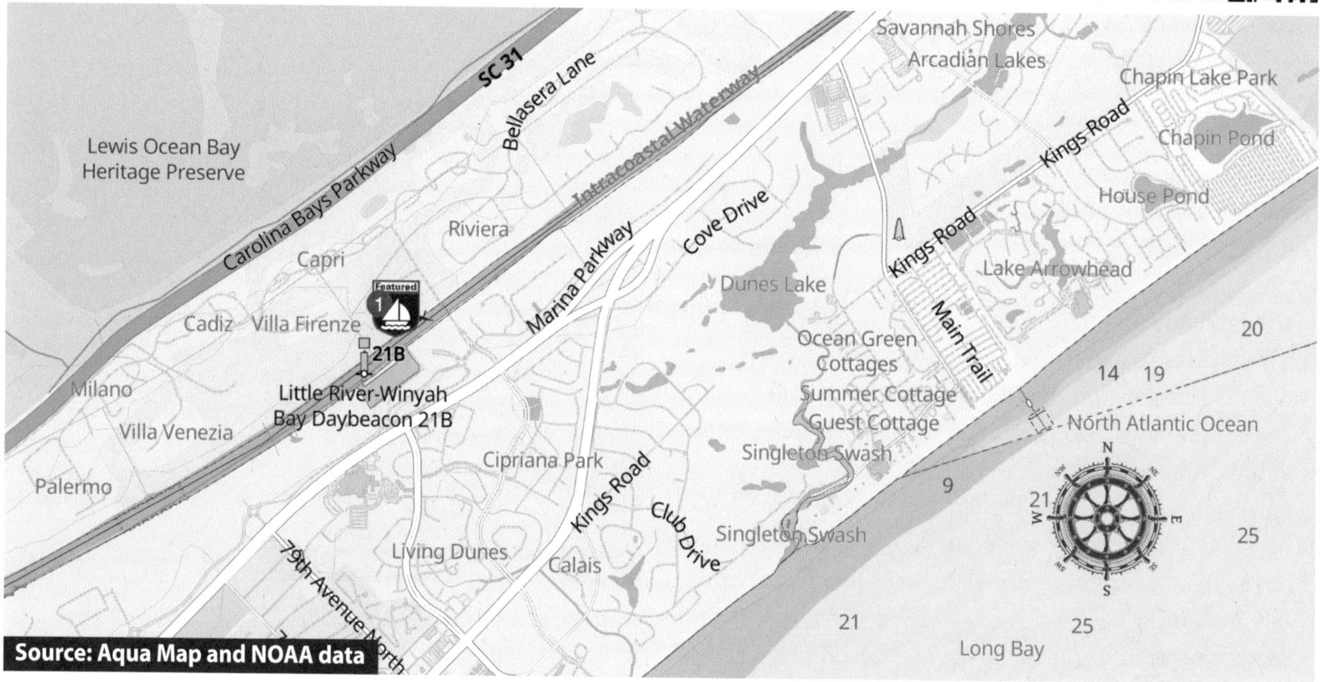

shore just upstream of the dolphins. Do not anchor near the creek entrance as other vessels may arrive after you. Use two anchors in bad weather or if the anchorage is too crowded for normal swinging room. As always, show an anchor light. Shrimp boats and sightseeing vessels, whose wakes may disturb you, use the channel at night.

Pine Island Cut to Myrtle Beach–ICW Mile 349 to Mile 354

Below Little River the ICW route enters a 26-mile-long high-banked land cut known as Pine Island Cut. For some unexplained reason, its name is not on the NOAA chart, labeled only as "Intracoastal Waterway."

NAVIGATION: Use NOAA Chart 11534. There is a tall white sign ("Danger Rocks") that marks the start and the ending of this stretch of the waterway. New development and clearing along this once-heavily wooded area give the illusion that the channel is wider than it really is. Be extremely careful to remain in the center of the channel.

The stretch between ICW Mile 349 to around Mile 352 is known as the "Rock Pile" due to the rock ledges along both sides of the channel. A number of charted daybeacons mark the most worrisome of the rock ledges, many of which are visible only at low tide. Not all of them are marked so keep a sharp watch.

Check on VHF Channels 13 or 16 for any tug or barge traffic passing through the area. Stay in the center of the channel and follow the markers. It is wise to make a "Sécurité" call on VHF Channels 13 or 16. Keep to mid-channel and watch for shoaling at bends and places where drainage ditches enter the waterway. When passing or being passed by another boat, do not crowd too close to the edge of the channel. Keep an eye out for flotsam and snags. Numerous trees have toppled into the cut. There is heavy development along much of this stretch. **Robert Edge Parkway Bridge** (also known as North Myrtle Beach Connector Bridge) with 65-foot fixed vertical clearance crosses the ICW at Mile 349.1.

Myrtle Beach Area–ICW Mile 354 to Mile 374

Barefoot Landing at Mile 354 (North Myrtle Beach) is a large complex featuring two theaters, plus over a dozen restaurants and 100 plus specialty shops. This open air "mall" has ponds, bridges, turtles, alligators and birds in addition to shopping and dining.

There has been almost continuous new shoreside development between Barefoot Landing at Mile 354 and about Mile 362 on both sides of the ICW. Golf is very popular here with over 100 courses in the greater Myrtle Beach area. Single-family homes, docks and huge condominium developments surrounding golf courses line much of the ICW. Supermarkets, marine supplies and restaurants are within walking distance of most marinas and are too numerous to list here, which is why there is no Goin' Ashore for Myrtle Beach. They do a better job than we can at Visit Myrtle Beach (www.visitmyrtlebeach.com).

NAVIGATION: Use NOAA Chart 11534. The **Barefoot Landing Swing Bridge** (31-foot closed vertical clearance) crosses at Mile 353.3. The bridgetender at the swing bridge monitors VHF Channel 09, and the bridge opens on signal. Two dolphins are on the edges of the channel on the east side of the bridge between the bridge and the docks.

Just beyond Barefoot Landing you will pass under the **Conway Bypass (SC 22) Bridges** (65-foot fixed vertical clearance) at Mile 355.5. Shoaling has been observed near the drainage ditches between this bridge and the bridges at Mile 365.4. At Mile 356 cables for an overhead gondola giving access to a now defunct golf course across the ICW may look too low for comfort but the clearance is at least 67 feet as clearly charted.

At Mile 357.5 is **Grande Dunes Bridge** (65-foot fixed vertical clearance) spanning both sides of the ICW. Be careful not to confuse the small floating markers at the two entrances to the Marina at Grande Dunes just south of the bridge with ICW markers. Should you need it, Grand Strand Medical Center (843-692-1000) is located adjacent to the Grand Dunes development.

Another fixed 65-foot high-rise bridge, **Grissom Parkway Bridge**, is at Mile 360.5. At Mile 361.5 favor the

Myrtle Beach Area, SC

MYRTLE BEACH		Largest Vessel	VHF	Total Slips	Approach/ Dockside Depth	Floating Docks	Gas/ Diesel	Repairs/ Haulout	Min/Max Amps	Pump-Out Station
1. Hague Marina WiFi MM 368.2	(843) 293-2141	100	16	20	6.0 / 6.0			RH	30 / 50	

WiFi Wireless Internet Access onSpot Dockside WiFi Facility
Visit www.waterwayguide.com for current rates, fuel prices, website addresses and other up-to-the-minute information.
(Information in the table is provided by the facilities.)

Scan here for more details:

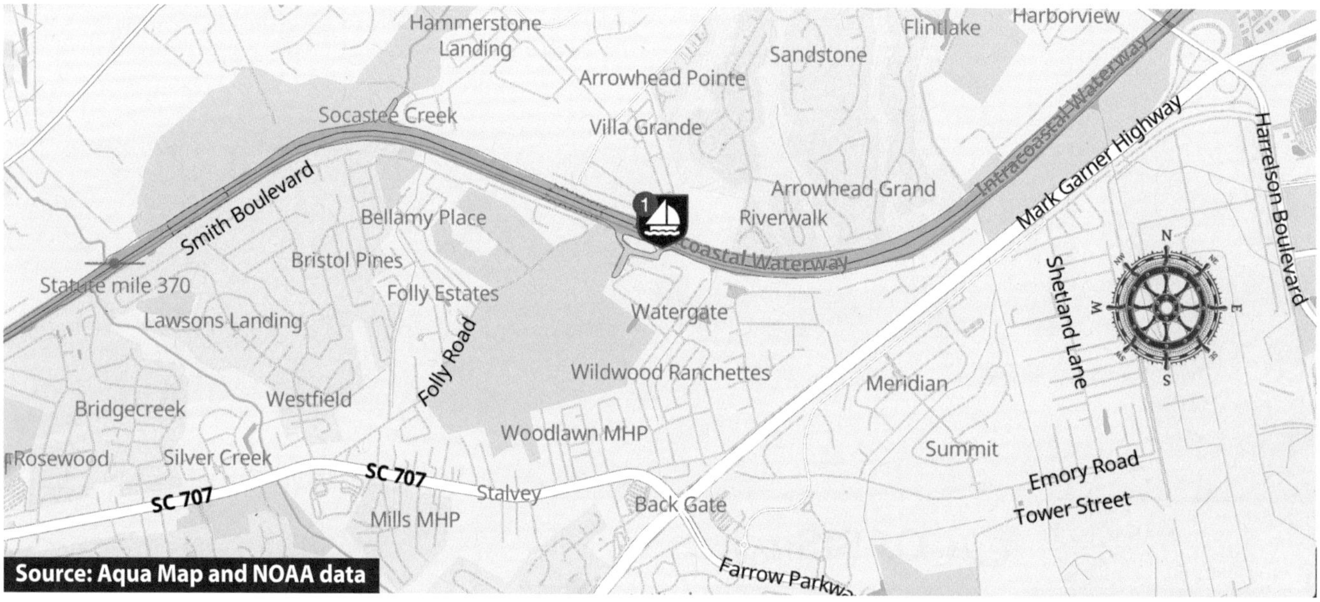

Source: Aqua Map and NOAA data

green side and pass the docks by 30 feet for 7 feet MLW. At Mile 362.5 between green daybeacons "23" and "25" there is a very conspicuous shoal at another drainage ditch on the north side of the ICW. Additional markers are near Mile 363 to mark shoaling.

The fixed 65-foot **U.S. 501 Bridge** crosses the ICW at Mile 365.4 along with a **SCL Railroad Bridge** (16-foot vertical clearance), which remains open. ICW veterans and commercial skippers refer to these two bridges as the "Combination Bridges."

At Mile 366 numerous cypress stumps and a lone tree encroach into the north side of the ICW from the extensive stone riprap meant to prevent soil erosion around one of the many condominium developments along this stretch. The 65-foot **Fantasy Harbor Bridge** at Mile 366.4 is the connector to access the defunct Freestyle Music Park.

At Mile 369 there is shoaling to 4 feet MLW on the red side of the channel by the creek. Just stay in the middle of the channel for 11.5 feet MLW.

Socastee Swing Bridge (which opens on request) at Mile 371.0 has an official closed vertical clearance of 11 feet, although its tide board shows less. It opens on request. Use the southeast draw. The Socastee (pronounced "sock-a-stee") Swing Bridge is old and frequently in need of repair. Call the drawtender on VHF Channel 09 or by phone (843-302-8640) for up-to-date status. **Socastee (SC 544) Highway Bridge** at Mile 371.3 frequently has less than the charted 65 feet of clearance due to high rainfall during storms, especially after a hurricane. A graph that shows bridge clearance versus water gauge height can be found online at Socastee Water Gauge Height (www.waterdata.usgs.gov). Sailboats with tall masts should check conditions carefully here.

The new (in 2019) **Carolina Bays Parkway (SC-31) Bridge** crosses the ICW at Mile 372.3 with 65-foot closed vertical clearance.

Dockage: Free daytime dockage is available at The Dock at Barefoot Landing. This is a great place to stop for lunch or shopping but absolutely no overnight docking is allowed. There is some current, and you will be docking with the current on the beam.

Barefoot Marina is across the ICW from the shopping area. Access to a huge pool, private showers and well-

Myrtle Beach Area, SC

MYRTLE BEACH		Largest Vessel	VHF	Total Slips	Approach/ Dockside Depth	Floating Docks	Gas/ Diesel	Repairs/ Haulout	Min/Max Amps	Pump-Out Station
1. Osprey Marina (WiFi) MM 373.0	(843) 215-5353	300	16	119	10.0 / 9.0	F	GD	H	30 / 50	P

(WiFi) Wireless Internet Access **onSpot** Dockside WiFi Facility
Visit www.waterwayguide.com for current rates, fuel prices, website addresses and other up-to-the-minute information.
(Information in the table is provided by the facilities.)

Scan here for more details:

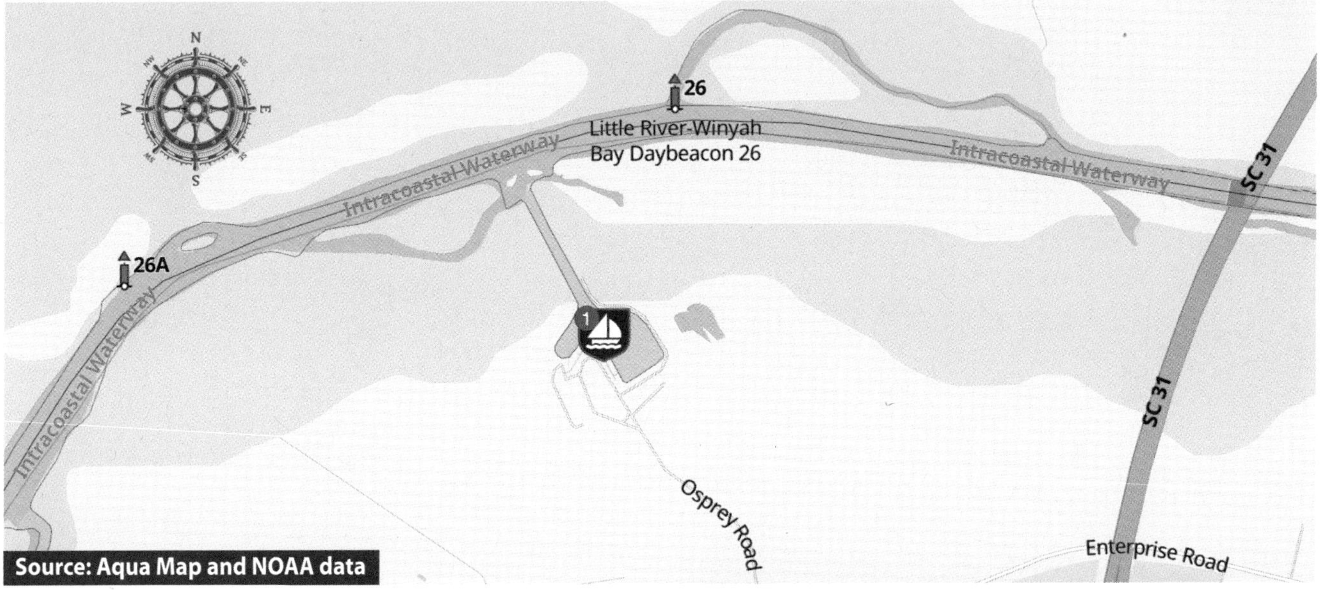

Source: Aqua Map and NOAA data

priced laundry are among the perks here. The marina provides free transportation (by golf cart) to Barefoot Landing (1 mile walk across bridge) or you can dinghy across the river and tie up for even easier access.

Marina at Grande Dunes at Mile 357 offers a protected harbor for vessels up to 120 feet. The marina is also the trailhead for scenic walkways along the ICW. Several dining options are within walking distance as is a grocery store and other shopping.

At around Mile 368 a No-Wake Zone protects the two entrances to Hague Marina in a protected basin off the ICW. This is a well-kept boat yard that can locate hard-to-find parts and has a skillful service staff. They keep a few reserved transient slips.

The family-oriented Osprey Marina, located at red daybeacon "26" (Mile 373), has floating transient slips, pump-out service and a dockmaster's building with showers, laundry and a well-stocked Ship Store. The entrance to the protected basin is well marked and has 10-foot MLW depths. This marina is an ICW favorite with consistently low fuel prices.

Once in a slip here, expect a welcome from dozens of turtles looking for a handout. This may be your first experience with "southern" turtles and yes, they do know how to beg. If you don't happen to have turtle food aboard, they are glad to accept hush puppies, crackers, pet food or anything else you throw their way.

Anchorage: The upper Waccamaw River is laden with great anchorages. This is one of the most rewarding areas to anchor south of the Chesapeake Bay, but bass-boat fishermen may sometimes come full-bore around the bends, so bear that in mind when picking your spot. Always use your anchor light. Also be aware the bugs can be troublesome in this area of the river. Screens are a must all the time.

TO MCCLELLANVILLE, SC

When you talk to cruisers about their favorite rivers there seem to be several that are always mentioned for their beauty: the Hudson, Tennessee, St. Johns and Waccamaw seem to be on everyone's list. The Waccamaw River, which starts at Mile 374, is deep to its wooded banks and is easily the most scenic part of the ICW. Moss-draped

Waccamaw River, SC

BUCKSPORT		Largest Vessel	VHF	Total Slips	Approach/ Dockside Depth	Floating Docks	Gas/ Diesel	Repairs/ Haulout	Min/Max Amps	Pump-Out Station
1. Bucksport Plantation Marina & RV Resort WiFi MM 36	(843) 397-5556	200	16	50	20.0 / 8.0	F	GD		30 / 50	P

WiFi Wireless Internet Access onSpot Dockside WiFi Facility
Visit www.waterwayguide.com for current rates, fuel prices, website addresses and other up-to-the-minute information.
(Information in the table is provided by the facilities.)

Scan here for more details:

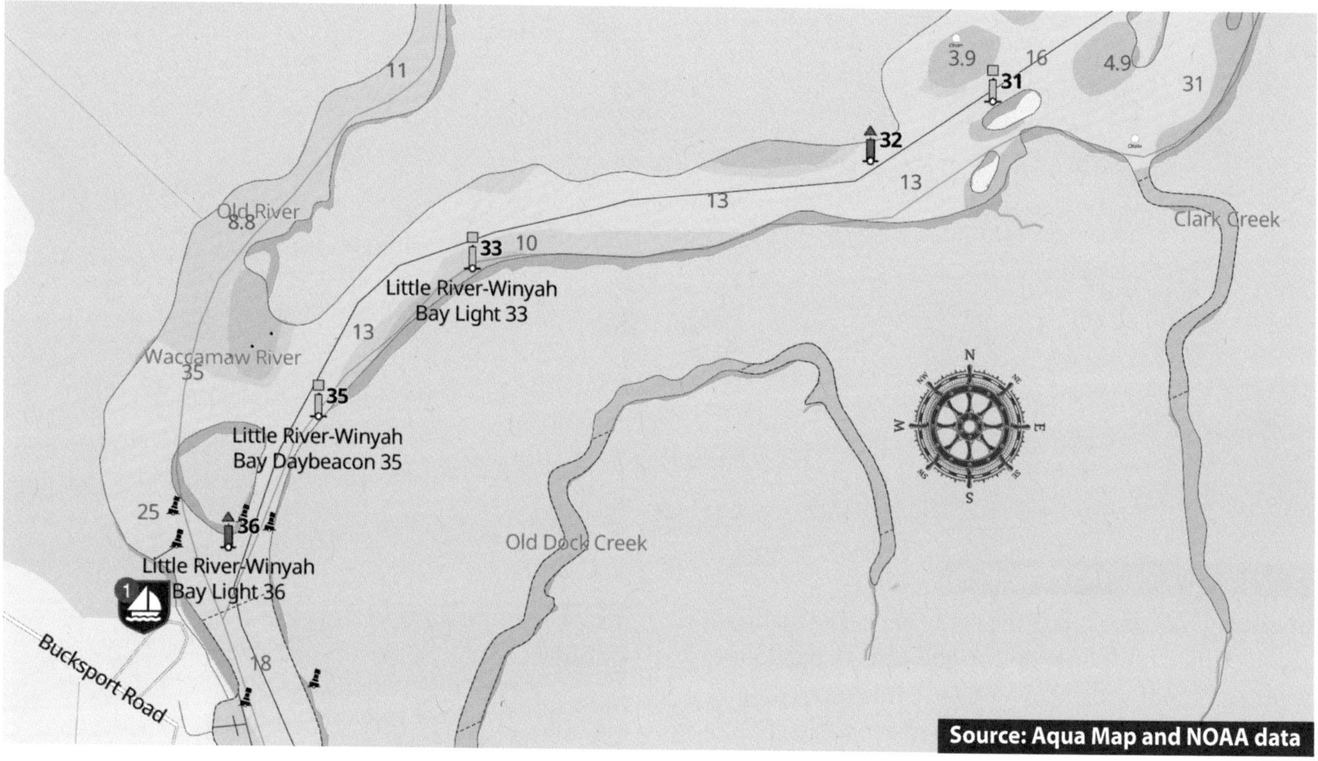

Source: Aqua Map and NOAA data

cypresses line its side streams and turtles sometimes sun themselves along the shore. Wildflowers of all descriptions grow in cypress stumps and the water looks like tea. Your boat's bow will get a brown mustache but that is easy to remove with lemon juice or a commercial cleaner. Ospreys abound and there are some eagles. Peaceful anchorages are plentiful.

Side Trip: Upriver to Conway–ICW Mile 375

Conway is a beautiful and interesting side trip 15 miles north of the ICW. The upper Waccamaw River, while not completely charted, is well marked. Stay to the outside of the bends and be prepared to face a speeding bass boat or two as you round the curves. Set your depth sounder alarm and hold down your speed. The **U.S. 501 Bypass Bridge** south of Conway has a 65-foot fixed vertical clearance. The bridge to the north (**Main St. Bridge**) has no clearance gauge but charts show a charted 35 feet of vertical clearance. You'll find some eclectic shops and good cafés in this quaint southern town.

NAVIGATION: Use NOAA Chart 11534. At Enterprise Landing (Mile 375) the ICW enters the upriver waters of Waccamaw River. Note that at Mile 375.2 charted green daybeacon "1" appears on the red-marker side of the channel. Its location can be confusing until you realize that it is not an ICW marker but actually the first in a series of aids that mark the upper Waccamaw River leading off to the north and to Conway. Although the ICW route continues downriver on the Waccamaw, the upriver 15-mile-long stretch to Conway carries 4.5-foot MLW depths. This section of the Waccamaw is highly trafficked by local boats. Tugs with tows frequently announce their presence in the narrow and winding upper Waccamaw River with a "Sécurité" call on VHF Channel 16 or occasionally on VHF Channel 13.

Waccamaw River, SC

WACHESAW LANDING		Largest Vessel	VHF	Total Slips	Approach/ Dockside Depth	Floating Docks	Gas/ Diesel	Repairs/ Haulout	Min/Max Amps	Pump-Out Station
1. Wacca Wache Marina WiFi MM 383.0	(843) 651-2994	150	16	100	25.0 / 8.0	F	GD	H	30 / 100	P

WiFi Wireless Internet Access **onSpot** Dockside WiFi Facility
Visit www.waterwayguide.com for current rates, fuel prices, website addresses and other up-to-the-minute information.
(Information in the table is provided by the facilities.)

Scan here for more details:

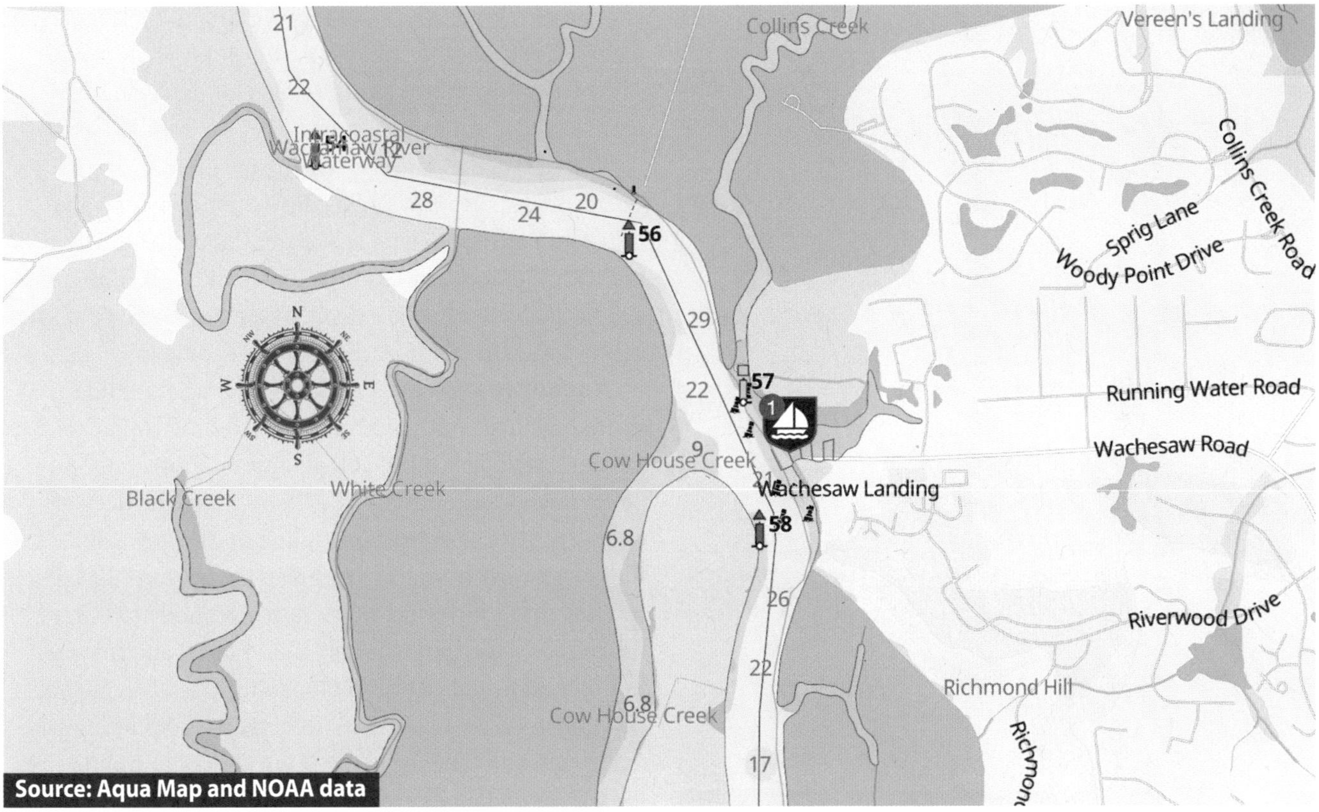

Source: Aqua Map and NOAA data

Watch for flotsam along the entire length of the Waccamaw River. It can vary from harmless bundles of reeds to a whole tree or a water-soaked log (or deadhead) with only the top exposed.

Dockage: Conway has a city marina that mostly caters to local boats, usually in the 30-feet-or-less category. Call 843-248-1713 for details.

Anchorage: At Conway you can anchor upriver between the high-level US 501 Bypass Bridge and the Main St. Bridge (35-foot fixed vertical clearance) in 5 to 6 feet MLW with good holding in mud. Make sure you stay out of the channel. From here you can dinghy to shore and the town of Conway.

Bucksport to Pawleys Island–ICW Mile 375 to Mile 388

Enterprise Landing at Mile 375 was once the departure point for huge shipments of yellow pine and cypress. This was the domain of Capt. Henry Buck, who brought over 100 shipwrights from Bucksport, ME, to Bucksport, SC, where they built the 210-foot sailing ship *Henrietta*, which carried cargo worldwide for over 30 years. Bucksport lies on a sharp bend where the Waccamaw River begins to widen, making navigation easier.

NAVIGATION: Use NOAA Chart 11534. There is a large, busy public boat ramp on the southeast side of the ICW at Enterprise Landing north of green daybeacon "27A" (around Mile 375) so watch for small-boat traffic. There is also a series of private docks here extending toward the ICW channel. Slower boats will carry a fair current all the way to Georgetown (Mile 403) when leaving Enterprise

Waccamaw River, SC

PAWLEYS ISLAND		Largest Vessel	VHF	Total Slips	Approach/ Dockside Depth	Floating Docks	Gas/ Diesel	Repairs/ Haulout	Min/Max Amps	Pump-Out Station
1. Safe Harbor Reserve Harbor WiFi MM 388.2	(843) 235-8262	60	16	50	6.0/6.0	F	GD	H	30/50	P

WiFi Wireless Internet Access onSpot Dockside WiFi Facility
Visit www.waterwayguide.com for current rates, fuel prices, website addresses and other up-to-the-minute information.
(Information in the table is provided by the facilities.)

Scan here for more details:

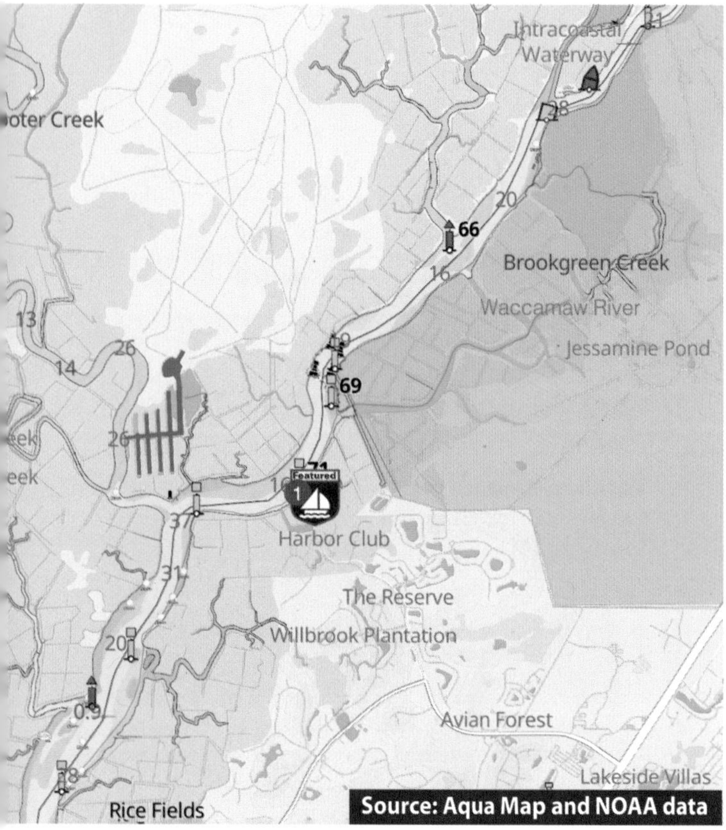

Source: Aqua Map and NOAA data

Landing about 1.5 hours after high tide.

South of Mile 385 the Waccamaw River becomes wider and straighter, making navigation easier but it is important for slow boats to note that tidal currents here can have an impressive effect on your progress. Coming north during a wet spring, boats should respect the ebb tide, which is accelerated by spring rain runoff. Conversely, there may be no advantage on flood tide when offset by this runoff.

It is interesting to note that the address at Wachesa Landing is actually Murrells Inlet, SC, although the inlet is several miles away and not connected by water to the ICW. The village of Murrells Inlet is a popular fishing resort with many seafood restaurants and good shopping opportunities.

Dockage: Bucksport Plantation Marina & RV Resort, located on the west side at the bend in the river at Mile 377, is easy to access and typically has good prices on gas and diesel. The on-site restaurant (Captain Buck's) is open daily with an outdoor tiki bar and live music (seasonal). The marina also offers kayak rentals for exploring the more shallow waters in the area.

Wacca Wache Marina at Wachesaw Landing, 6 miles below Bucksport, provides a convenient fuel dock and transient berthing. There is a current to contend with so it is worth it to look north of the fuel dock to see if there is a spot available on the face dock. The marina also boat sales and rentals and is home to a tour boat company

Anchorage: There is a good anchorage in mud at the oxbow just south of Enterprise Landing (Mile 374.8) with at least 6 feet MLW and all-around protection. A better anchorage option is at Mile 375.5 in the deeper oxbow north of Enterprise Landing on the north side of the river across from flashing green daybeacon "29." The holding is fair in 13 feet MLW near the southern part of the oxbow. This spot will hold 3 or 4 boats and may be full on a weekend. We recommend the use of an anchor trip line in case you snare a submerged stump or log and make sure your anchor is set. It is a short run up the river to the county launching ramp where you can dinghy your pet ashore.

One of the prettiest, most secluded anchorages anywhere is at Prince Creek east of the ICW across from flashing red "44" at Mile 380.4. The north and south entrances both have approximately 15-foot MLW depths but neither end offers protection from ICW wash. The lower end is wide enough to warrant only one anchor but you may need two at the upper end or narrower parts. If you give the points of Prince Creek a wide berth, you can run the length of Longwood Island and rejoin the ICW south of Mulberry Landing at flashing green "53" (at Mile 381.7).

Just south of the northern entrance to Prince Creek (Mile 381.2), you may turn west off the ICW at flashing red "48" marking the entrance to Bull Creek. Give this marker a very wide berth. This has better holding and more swing room than other anchorages on the

Waccamaw River, SC

PAWLEYS ISLAND		Largest Vessel	VHF	Total Slips	Approach/ Dockside Depth	Floating Docks	Gas/ Diesel	Repairs/ Haulout	Min/Max Amps	Pump-Out Station
1. Heritage Plantation Marina WiFi MM 394.0	(843) 237-3650	200	16	40	30.0 / 30.0	F			15 / 50	P

WiFi Wireless Internet Access onSpot Dockside WiFi Facility
Visit www.waterwayguide.com for current rates, fuel prices, website addresses and other up-to-the-minute information.
(Information in the table is provided by the facilities.)

Scan here for more details:

Waccamaw River. Anchor in at least 15 feet MLW with a mud bottom. Go up past the first bend to avoid the wake of ICW traffic and anchor where depths suit. Hunters frequent this area in season so prepare to awaken early to the sound of shooting in season.

A secluded anchorage is available at Mile 383.5 in Cow House Creek. This is somewhat exposed to the north and south but has excellent holding (7 to 12 feet MLW) and is very scenic. It is a great spot to watch the alligators and other wildlife, which is why we don't recommend swimming here!

Pawleys Island to Georgetown–ICW Mile 388 to Mile 403

Pawleys Island at Mile 388 on the ICW is known for its beaches, sand dunes and hammocks. The original Pawleys Island Hammocks (www.pawleysislandhammocks.com) has been in the business of producing rope hammocks since 1889 and that's still their mainstay along with fabric hammocks and hammock-inspired swings. At the opposite end of this stretch is Butler Island (near Mile 396), a scenic natural area.

NAVIGATION: Use NOAA Chart 11534. There are no special alerts along this route, other than two long private community docks that extend into the channel in the Butler Island area where the river narrows and the ICW channel turns around the east side of the island. The ends of both docks are marked with flashing white lights.

Dockage: At flashing green daybeacon "71" (Mile 388) is the entrance to Safe Harbor Reserve Harbor, which is part of an upscale development near Pawleys Island. The location gives you access to the beach, river and pool as well as resort-style amenities for vessels to 60 feet. Heritage Plantation Marina to the south at Mile 394 is directly on the ICW at Pawleys Island. This

Georgetown Area, SC

GEORGETOWN HARBOR		Largest Vessel	VHF	Total Slips	Approach/ Dockside Depth	Floating Docks	Gas/ Diesel	Repairs/ Haulout	Min/Max Amps	Pump-Out Station
1. Georgetown Landing Marina WiFi MM 402.0	(843) 546-1776	200	16	171	19.0 / 17.0	F	GD		30 / 100	
2. Hazzard Marine WiFi onSpot 0.9 mi. N of MM 403.0	(843) 527-3625	200	16	37	10.0 / 9.0	F	GD	RH	30 / 50	P
3. Georgetown Dry Stack Marina WiFi 1.0 mi. N of MM 403.0	(843) 546-1700	80	16	20	10.0 / 9.0	F	GD		30 / 50	
4. Harborwalk Marina WiFi onSpot 1.1 mi. N of MM 403.0	(843) 546-4250	200	16	50	12.0 / 10.0	F	GD		30 / 100	P

WiFi Wireless Internet Access onSpot Dockside WiFi Facility
Visit www.waterwayguide.com for current rates, fuel prices, website addresses and other up-to-the-minute information.
(Information in the table is provided by the facilities.)

Scan here for more details:

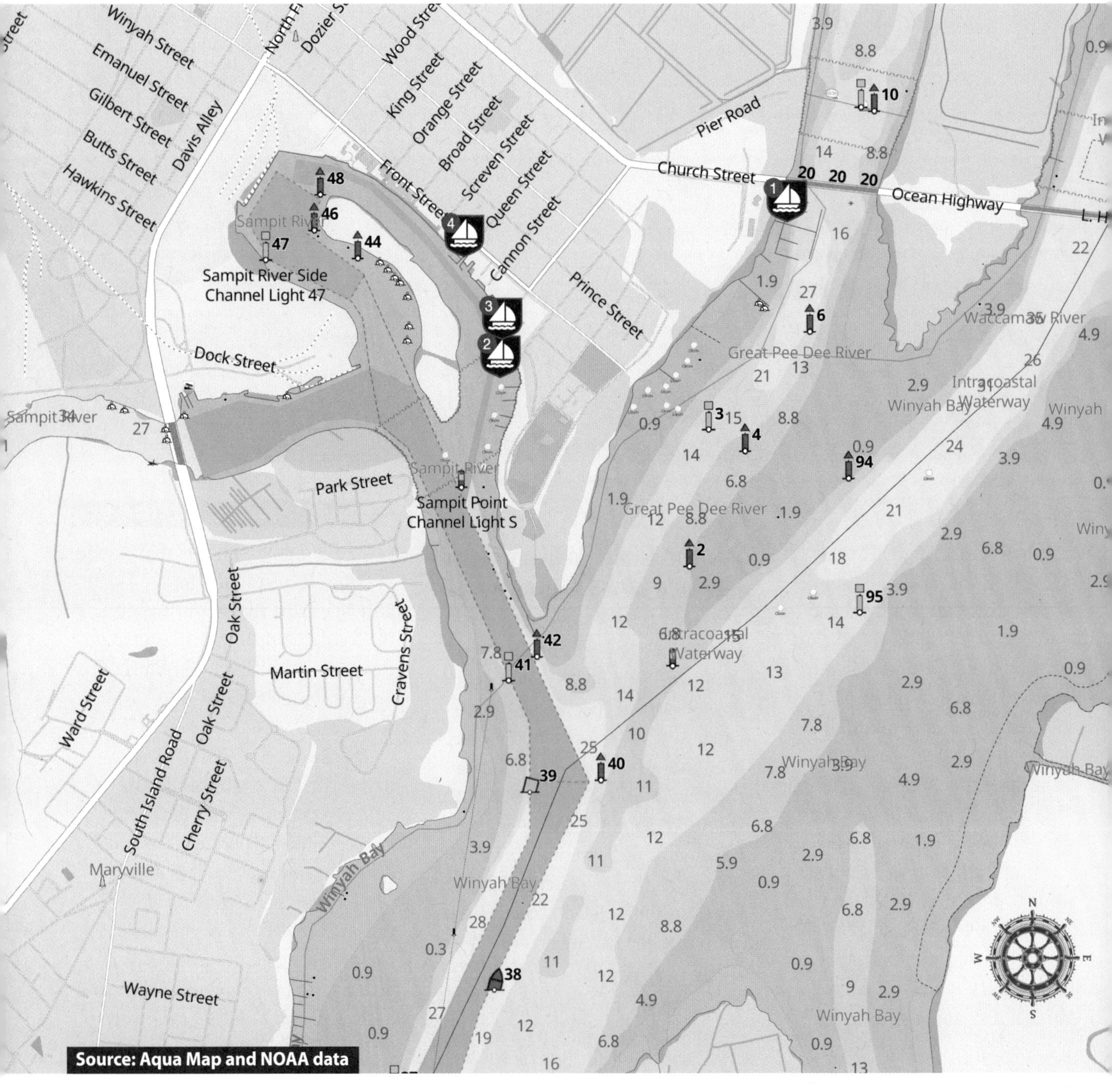

friendly marina is also part of an upscale gated community. They may have space for you but call ahead.

Anchorage: A good spot to drop the hook is at Mile 389 in Lower Thorofare, which carries 14-foot MLW depths. Turn up Thoroughfare Creek at flashing green daybeacon "73" and anchor in 10 to 13 feet MLW with a sandy bottom. Be aware that Thoroughfare Creek is heavily used by locals on the weekends and it may not be the same tranquil spot it is during the week.

Schooner Creek at Mile 393.1 has depths of at least 8 feet MLW with protection in all directions. Enter in mid-channel proceeding up to where the creek widens slightly just before the sharp bend to starboard.

At Mile 395 you can anchor in at least 9 feet MLW in Jerico Creek with good holding in mud. (The creek has 8-foot charted MLW depths at the entrance but deepens as you proceed.) Turn into Jericho Creek at Mile 394.9 before flashing green daybeacon "83."

Good protection from northwest winds can be found at Butler Island. Pass green can "1" to port and then proceed into the unnamed cove between Contentment Island and Butler Island. There is good holding in 15- to 30-feet MLW depths but use an anchor trip-line near the island. If you anchor on the channel side north of Butler Island, you will be jostled by wakes from fast-moving boats.

On the north end of Butler Island there is an underwater high voltage cable crossing. It is indicated on the chart as a cable area and there are signs ashore but they are difficult to read. Avoid this area when choosing your anchorage.

Georgetown Harbor–ICW Mile 403

The stretch of the Waccamaw River that includes Georgetown has become increasingly popular. There has been a proliferation of tour boats of many types–even amphibious craft–along the river and around the inlet at Winyah Bay. There are island tours, plantation tours and wilderness tours. Even vessels that create minimum wake should give these tour boats a slow pass. Read more at "Goin' Ashore: Georgetown, SC" in this chapter.

NAVIGATION: Use NOAA Chart 11534.The high-level **Ocean Highway (US 17) Bridge** (65-foot fixed vertical clearance) at Mile 402.1 is a short distance above Georgetown on the Waccamaw River. After passing under the bridge take the time to sort out the markers leading to the Georgetown Harbor entrance channel. Four bodies of water converge below the big shoal extending south from Waccamaw Point: Waccamaw River, Winyah Bay, Great Pee Dee River and Georgetown's Sampit River. The buoys can be confusing. Near the junction of the four bodies of water is flashing red daybeacon "W." Read your chart carefully and do not cut behind this daybeacon, which sits in 5 feet MLW. Leave it to starboard.

The channel into Georgetown Harbor is wide and deep with at least 9-foot MLW depths. Once off the ICW and heading toward the harbor the channel for yachts and small commercial craft bears off to starboard just before flashing red "S." The Sampit River turns abruptly to port and Factory Basin is straight ahead. If your intention is to visit Georgetown take the channel to starboard. Exercise some care and do not cut too close to the starboard shore, which is infested with broken and submerged pilings. Once abeam of the first docking area, the harbor is relatively clear of obstacles.

The upper reaches of the small but attractive Sampit River are readily open to exploration. Beyond the twin-span high-level Rosen (US Hwy. 17) Bridge, the river is unmarked and uncharted.

The Great Pee Dee River channel is marked with red and green daybeacons leading upriver toward Georgetown Landing Marina, which is just before the Ocean Highway (US 17) Bridge (West) with 20-foot fixed vertical clearance at Mile 402. The Coast Guard station at Georgetown is next to the marina.

Dockage: The 171-slip Georgetown Landing Marina on the Great Pee Dee River is a good option when the Georgetown Harbor is full. Note that it is somewhat exposed, which can make the long face dock uncomfortable in a south wind. If the fully-stocked marine store doesn't already have what you need, they can help you arrange transportation to the many local supermarkets, hardware and general stores for provisioning.

Hazzard Marine in Georgetown Harbor is the only repair and refit facility between the Myrtle Beach area, 40 miles to the north, and Charleston, 65 miles to the south. The marina can accommodate vessels to 200 feet. Georgetown Dry Stack Marina next door accepts transients if space is available.

The well-regarded Harborwalk Marina is directly adjacent to Georgetown's business district. Floating docks with shore power and WiFi are available as well as

GOIN' ASHORE

GEORGETOWN, SC

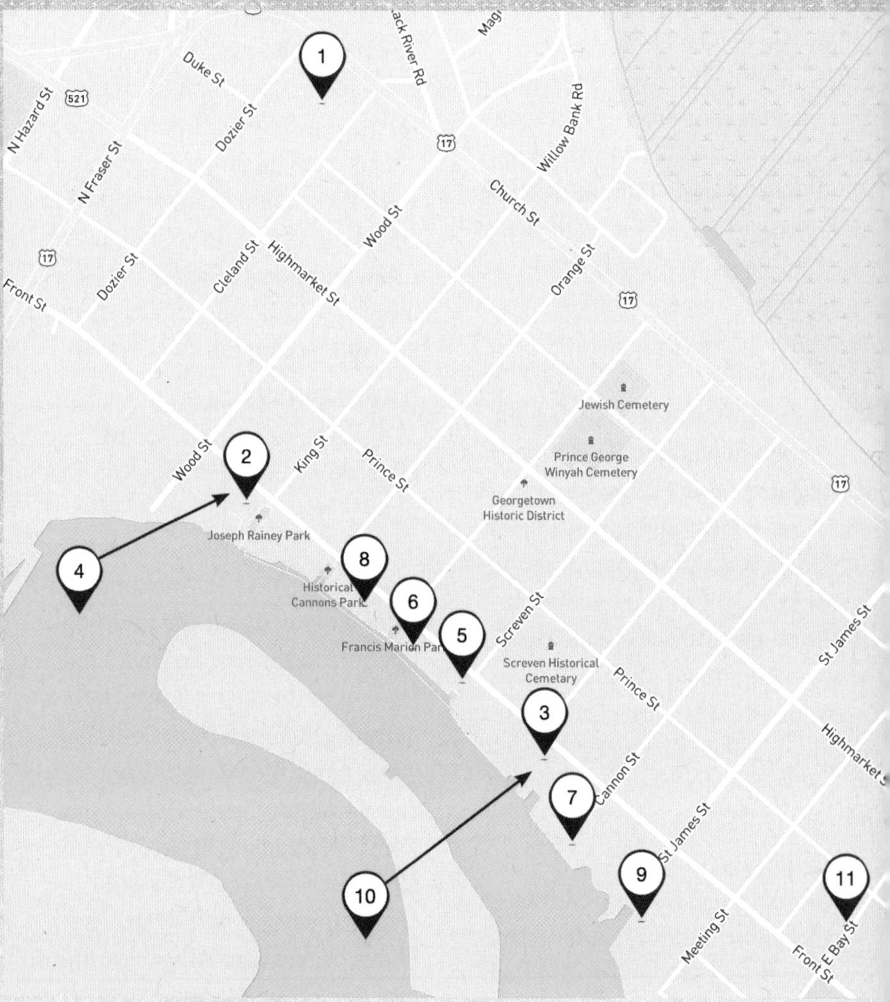

Georgetown's entire downtown is a National Historic District, where visitors can stroll along the live oakshaded streets and adjacent neighborhoods, admiring the city homes of former plantation owners. There are 63 downtown homes on the National Historic Register. The town and its residents welcome transients with a wealth of services, including good restaurants and interesting shopping. The third weekend in October is a great time to be in Georgetown for the Georgetown Wooden Boat Show, hosted by the Georgetown Harbor Historical Association. Proceeds go toward adding exhibits to the maritime museum.

SERVICES

1. **Georgetown County Library**
   405 Cleland St. (843-545-3300)
2. **Harborwalk Veterinary Hospital**
   1001 Front St. (843-546-3355)

ATTRACTIONS

3. **Georgetown Chamber of Commerce**
   Located at 531 Front St. (843-546-8436). A Trolley Tour leaves from 814 Front St. to tour the revitalized downtown. The narrator provides a good story of the town's history. The marinas can supply the packets of information when you register for dockage.
4. **Kaminski House Museum**
   A visit to the Kaminski House Museum at 1003 Front St. should be part of your itinerary. Built in 1769 by a local merchant, it is now used as a teaching tool for the area's history. Admission by tour only. Museum shop on site. Call for hours and fees (843-546-7706).
5. **Rice Museum**
   Another must-stop is the Rice Museum (originally the Old Market built in 1842) at 633 Front St., which includes a 45-minute guided tour about the local rice culture, featuring the 1842 Clock Tower and the Kaminski Hardware Building. The third floor of the Rice Museum houses the skeleton of America's oldest known vessel, Brown's Ferry, an 18th-century all-purpose freighter. The whole history of this area is linked to rice, and there is no better and more enjoyable way to find out all about that than to tour the Rice Museum. Call for hours or to book a tour at 843-546-7423.

6. South Carolina Maritime Museum

This small museum at 729 Front St. features photographs, documents, artifacts and interactive exhibits related to South Carolina's maritime history. Exhibits include the prized Fresnel lens of the old North Island lighthouse, a photographic representation of the chronology of the Port of Georgetown and a model of the Henrietta, the largest wooden ship ever built in South Carolina. The ship was 201 feet long and the top of her mainmast was 147 feet above the deck. Free admission. Call for hours at 843-520-0111.

SHOPPING

7. Independent Seafood Market

Georgetown has its own shrimp dock and fishing fleet and that freshly caught seafood is available at 1 Cannon St. (843-546-6642).

8. Waterfront Books

This full-service bookstore at 815 Front St. has an eclectic mixture of new and used books, cards, gifts, magazines, newspapers and art by local artists. While they specialize in used books, they can special order any titles and will gladly ship to any location (843-546-2665).

MARINAS

9. Georgetown Dry Stack Marina

18 St. James St. (843-546-1700)

10. Harborwalk Marina

525 Front St. (843-546-4250)

11. Hazzard Marine

200 Meeting St. (843-527-3625)

Winyah Bay, SC

GEORGETOWN AREA		Largest Vessel	VHF	Total Slips	Approach/ Dockside Depth	Floating Docks	Gas/ Diesel	Repairs/ Haulout	Min/Max Amps	Pump-Out Station
1. Belle Isle Yacht Club & Marina WiFi MM 405.9	(843) 546-1423	55	16	80	5.0 / 7.0	F	GD		30 / 50	P

WiFi Wireless Internet Access onSpot Dockside WiFi Facility
Visit www.waterwayguide.com for current rates, fuel prices, website addresses and other up-to-the-minute information.
(Information in the table is provided by the facilities.)

Scan here for more details:

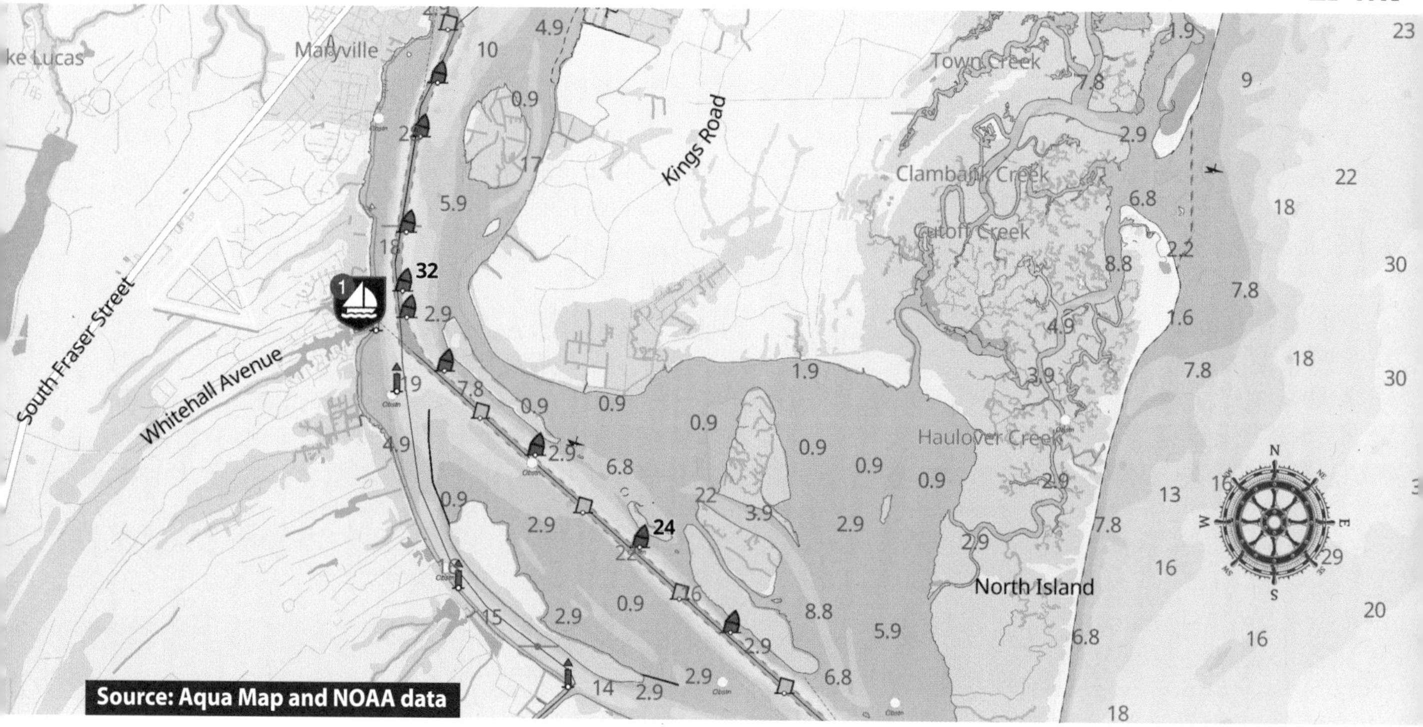

climate-controlled private restrooms/showers and laundry facilities. They can accommodate vessels up to 200 feet. The marina is just a short walk from restaurants, museums and shopping. The knowledgeable and helpful staff can help you decide what to explore.

Anchorage: There are several local boats anchored at Georgetown but there is still room for transients to anchor. The bottom is deep mud in this location; however, if you set your anchor well in 10 feet MLW, it can be delightful. Shore access is easy thanks to the two public docks along the Harborwalk. The docks will accommodate anything from a dinghy to a 60-footer but both have signs indicating daytime use only, which is strictly enforced. One is at the south end of the walk behind the clock tower at Lafayette Park and the other is in the middle of the walk at Francis Marion Park (next to the South Carolina Maritime Museum). Either can be reached from the more northern anchorage as well.

Over the years, the "main channel" to the abandoned steel mill has shoaled to less than 2 feet MLW. If inbound for the Steelmill Channel anchorage nearest the mill, the safest approach is to take the channel through town. Keep the bifurcated "S" light to port and keep close to the docks.

Winyah Bay–ICW Mile 403 to Mile 410

NAVIGATION: Use NOAA Chart 11534. For boats making the ocean run along the coast, Winyah Bay is the first shipping inlet south of the Cape Fear River and Southport, NC.

If you bypass Georgetown to go down Winyah Bay, note that the aids to navigation at the junction of Georgetown's harbor channel and the ICW are colored and numbered as from seaward. Three miles below Georgetown at Mile 406 the ICW route leaves the Winyah Bay ship channel, bears off to the south and continues down the well-marked Western Channel to just past Mile 410. The ICW marking system resumes at the Western Channel.

It pays to watch the tide here and enter or leave with the current. Low-powered boats headed north should leave Georgetown 1 hour after slack tide before flood tide at Charleston to carry a fair current up the Waccamaw River. The Western Channel to the inlet, although unmarked beyond the ICW turn into the Estherville-Minim Creek Canal, is true to its charted depths.

If Winyah Bay Entrance is your goal, follow the main shipping channel beginning at Frazier Point. If you should end up in the wrong channel, note the shoal between the two channels and be cautious. There are swift currents and whirlpools on the ebb tide. The tremendous volume of water that passes through the jetties at this entrance should not be underestimated. Use caution, especially on the ebb tide with opposing winds. To make matters worse much of the south jetty is visible only at low water. Use extreme caution.

Dockage: The marked entry channel to Belle Isle Yacht Club & Marina is just to the west of the ICW at Mile 406. Amenities include two swimming pools, two tennis courts and a private oceanfront clubhouse at Pawleys Island (20 minutes away). Also on site is an activity building spanning a mid-18th century rice irrigation canal.

Anchorage: Currents in the Western Channel are strong–up to 3 knots on the ebb. Don't be tempted to anchor here. You can drop the hook behind the unnamed marshy island at the north end of the Estherville-Minim Canal in 10 feet MLW with good holding. There is a strong current but if you drag it would be in the current direction, not toward the shore. Expect traffic in the morning in season.

Estherville-Minim Canal to McClellanville Area–ICW Mile 410 to Mile 439

This area was one of the primary territories of Francis Marion (a.k.a. "The Swamp Fox") during the American Revolution. He earned a reputation for harassing the British troops and then disappearing into the swamp. Several attempts by the British to capture him failed.

If time permits, do visit the small community of McClellanville. There is a museum by the fire tower, a few shops and some restaurants. The town also boasts some amazing live oak trees draped with Spanish moss. Near the marina is the Deerhead live oak (www.treessc.org/deerhead-oak), which is over 150 feet tall and 36 feet in circumference and estimated to be over 1,000 years old.

NAVIGATION: Use NOAA Charts 11534 and 11518. The ICW makes a sharp departure southward from the Western Channel at flashing red daybeacon "2" into the Estherville-Minim Creek Canal. The creek was dredged in 2020 but still requires careful navigation.

Despite recent dredging (late 2020), shoaling has been observed at the entrance to the Estherville-Minim Creek Canal. Split flashing red "2" and the shore for 17-foot MLW depths. Stay centered in the channel when entering the canal.

At Mile 411.5 **Estherville-Minim Canal Bridge** is open to vessel traffic except when a vehicle needs to cross (infrequent). Watch for flashing yellow lights on sign. In the open position the floating bridge rests against the east bank of the river. Continuing south on the ICW the channel turns to starboard just past Mile 415 and immediately crosses Minim Creek where it enters a long cut with shoal edges.

Be careful of strong currents at Mile 420 when crossing the Santee River. It shallows to 8.2 feet MLW. Favor the green side of the channel and take care not to be swept into the shoal area at the southern end.

Shrimp boats have been observed using a surprisingly well-marked channel across from Jeremy Creek to access Five Fathom Creek (Mile 430). If you want to explore the Cape Romain area, it is an easy run to the ocean on this route.

The ICW at McClellanville was dredged to 12 MLW from flashing green "35" to flashing green "43" but has shoaled in some spots to 4.2 MLW. Do not hug the markers; pass them at least 50 feet off. Note: Be sure to load the latest Bob423 Southport to Savannah Long Track at Waterway Explorer (www.waterwayguide.com).

Be careful to stay in the middle of the channel as it shallows rapidly along the edges. In general stay 50 feet off all marks, go slow and test the depths side to side. The bottom is soft mud. With a strong east wind, the water can be a foot higher and with a west wind, a foot lower. A deviation of 30 feet can result in a change in depth of up to 2 feet.

McClellanville, SC

MCCLELLANVILLE		Largest Vessel	VHF	Total Slips	Approach/ Dockside Depth	Floating Docks	Gas/ Diesel	Repairs/ Haulout	Min/Max Amps	Pump-Out Station
1. Leland Oil Company WiFi 0.5 mi. N of MM 430.0	(843) 887-3641	75	16	8	10.0 / 6.0	F	GD		30 / 50	

WiFi Wireless Internet Access onSpot Dockside WiFi Facility
Visit www.waterwayguide.com for current rates, fuel prices, website addresses and other up-to-the-minute information.
(Information in the table is provided by the facilities.)

Scan here for more details:

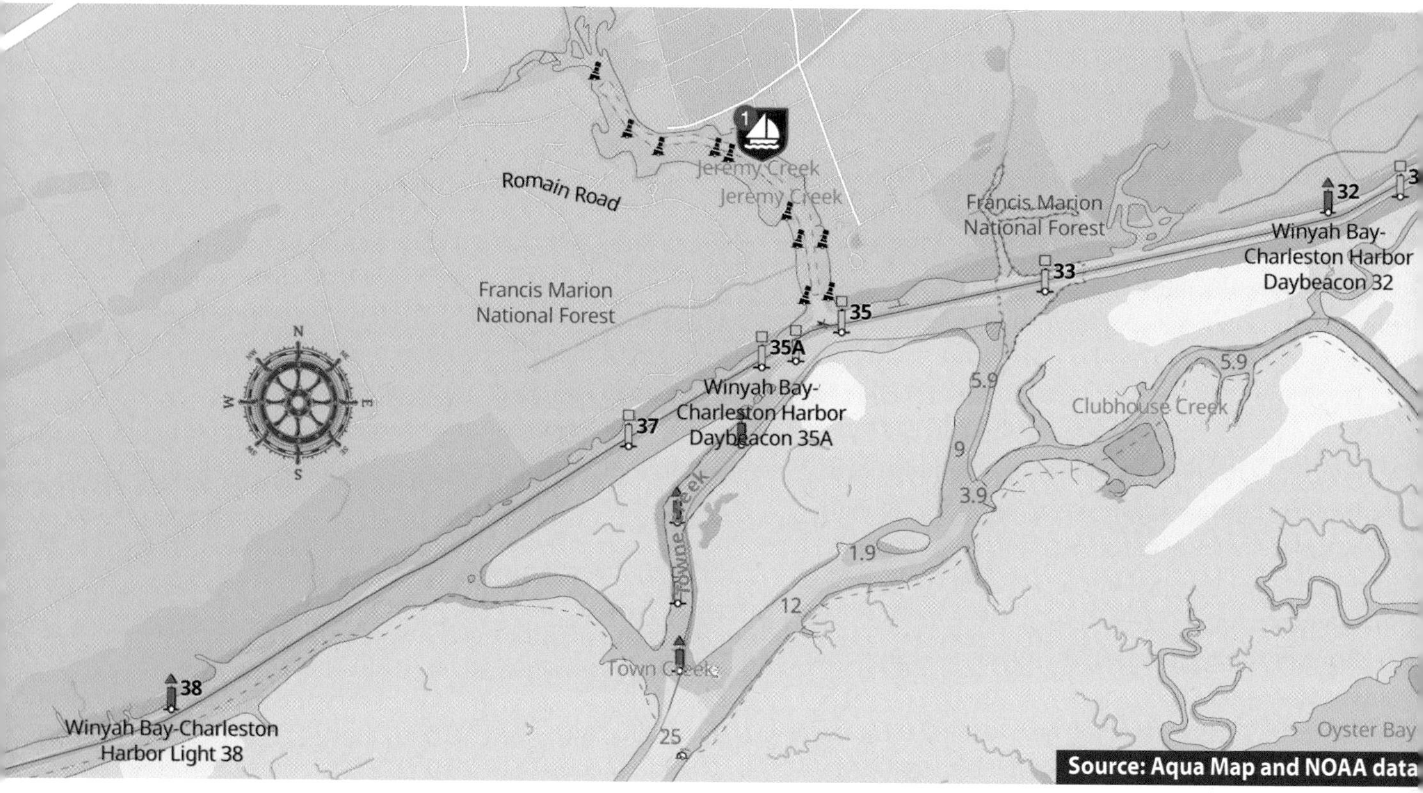

Source: Aqua Map and NOAA data

From Mile 436 the ICW follows another land cut (Mathews Cut) for about 10 miles. On the mainland side Francis Marion National Forest Recreation Area offers picnic areas, campsites and a boat ramp but no facilities for transient boaters. The ICW channel between Mile 437 and Mile 456 is among the straightest stretches along the entire ICW. Be sure to mind the markers. At Mile 444 watch your wake and exercise caution when passing Andersonville.

Shoal water has been observed by green daybeacon "47" (stay off by 200 feet) and flashing red "48" (stay off by 120 feet)at Mile 435.7 so stay in the middle of the channel.

Dockage: Jeremy Creek leading to McClellanville has been dredged to 10 feet MLW. Leland Oil Company in McClellanville provides dockage. They only have 8 slips so most boats emulate the shrimpers by rafting up, particularly during the annual shrimp festival each spring.

Anchorage: Although it has a good deal of tidal current, Minim Creek is the best anchorage for many miles to come. Either side of the creek has good holding but the west side just below Mile 415 offers excellent protection with 8- to 20-foot MLW depths and all-around protection. You will have to dodge the crab pots and bugs will come visit at dusk but your reward will be a beautiful sunset and sunrise. The east side of Minim Creek has 8- to 11-foot MLW depths with excellent holding in mud and protection from all but north and southeast.

The anchorage on the west side of the South Santee River at Mile 420.1 (behind Brown Island) has 10- to 12-foot MLW depths, a sand and mud bottom and excellent holding. Crab pots usually line both sides of the river. Several channels lead off the ICW just past Mile 425 but don't be tempted; depths are suspect for anchoring.

There are many uncharted side creeks but these are of questionable depths for the tidal range. Five Fathom Creek near McClellanville is pristine. Leave the ICW at green daybeacon "25" and proceed south about 0.50 mile on Town Creek. When you get to Five Fathom Creek turn to port (north) and go up Five Fathom a hundred yards or more to anchor in 15 feet MLW. This gets you out of the main channel and is a wonderful anchorage. (Do have your bug screens ready.) Like all creeks in this area, this creek is deep with strong currents. Be prepared for a rather eerie experience as the shrimpers come and go; you can only see the marsh grass and not the creeks they are in so they appear to be moving through the grass.

Proceeding 2 miles south on Five Fathom Creek will afford another anchorage spot at its intersection with Bull River. Depths vary so sound your way in. There are many "lost" crab pots and lines on the bottom in Five Fathom Creek. Use an anchor retrieving line and have a wire cutter ready as some lines are steel.

You can anchor east of the ICW at Mile 435.6 in Awendaw Creek opposite flashing red daybeacon "48." Go around the bend heading east and anchor in the 12-foot MLW spot shown on the NOAA chart. The bottom is sand and the anchorage is protected from waves but not wind. There is space for several boats. Your boat position will reverse in a good current. There is shore access for pets at an oyster pile at the eastern end of the anchorage at any time other than high tide.

At Mile 439 there is good holding in sand in Graham Creek with protection from waves and slightly higher elevation on the west-southwest bank for reasonable wind protection. Approach the creek near red daybeacon "64" and proceed south down Graham Creek. Anchor midstream in 10-foot MLW depths or better up to the bend.

NEXT STOP

Charleston is another 35 miles south along a straight dredged cut with marshes to the east. Watch for persistent shoaling, especially where natural creeks cross the ICW. Plan to stop and enjoy this historic and beautiful city with its burgeoning yachting facilities.

Photo courtesy of Sail Folly

Charleston, SC to St. Marys, GA

Chapter 8: Charleston Area

Chapter 9: Stono River to Ossabaw Sound, GA

Chapter 10: St. Catherines Sound to St. Marys, GA

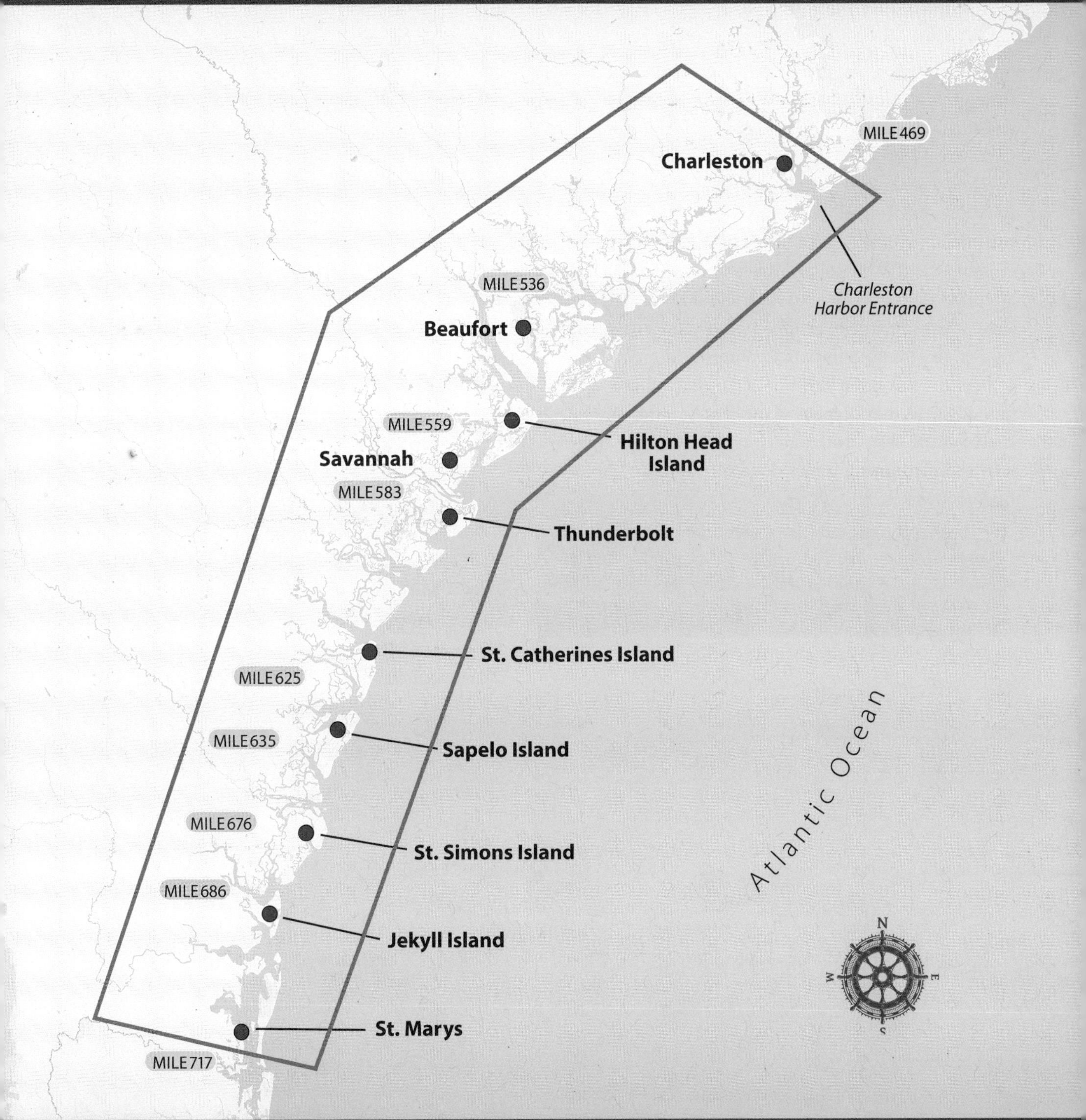

Visit Waterway Explorer at www.waterwayguide.com

ICW Mile 456-Mile 475

ISLE OF PALMS TO CHARLESTON

The ICW north of Charleston offers wide scenic marsh views to the east and alternating marsh and forest on the west. Here the dredged ICW channel cuts through low marshy islets, across several small rivers and finally through a long land cut before reaching Charleston Harbor.

Numerous marsh streams and small rivers cross the ICW channel from all directions in this area. All of these can affect the tidal current flow and the side currents crossing the ICW channel. Slow boats need to pay more attention than fast ones but both should be aware that shoal areas can and do creep out near these crossings. The charted depths are somewhat optimistic along this stretch so be more precise in keeping to the channel at low tide. Our advice is that keeping in the center of the channel is always the best. If the water gets too "skinny," then start slightly moving from side to side in an attempt to find good water.

From Mile 415 to about Mile 450 the National Ocean Service does not provide tidal current information. Generally the flood tidal current runs north. From Mile 450 to Mile 460 the current reversals cancel each other out.

This is not a No-Wake Zone but caution should be exercised through this congested area. Before this transit, tie down as if you were going to sea. It will be choppy and confused from the many boat and ship wakes, and you will likely get rocked on your way through by an inconsiderate boater or by residual wakes that you can't avoid.

To Isle of Palms–ICW Mile 439 to Mile 469

At Mile 456.7 you pass through a land cut between Isle of Palms on the ocean side and Goat Island on the mainland side. The two islands are quite different. The Isle of Palms is well developed with golf courses, resort hotels and restaurants, while Goat Island was formerly inhabited by only a few hearty souls who commuted to their jobs by boat. Now, although the island remains relatively isolated, more and more weekend getaway cottages have appeared on Goat Island.

NAVIGATION: Use NOAA Charts 11521, 11523 and 11523.

- **Mile 441–**There is a stretch of shallow water down to 6.9 feet MLW from red daybeacon "64" to flashing green "65" in Graham Creek. Be careful to stay in the middle of the channel, it shallows rapidly along the edges.
- **Mile 448–**Shoaling to 5 feet MLW has been observed in the middle of the channel at flashing red "86." You can avoid the shoal area by going outside the channel on the green side for 7.8 MLW.

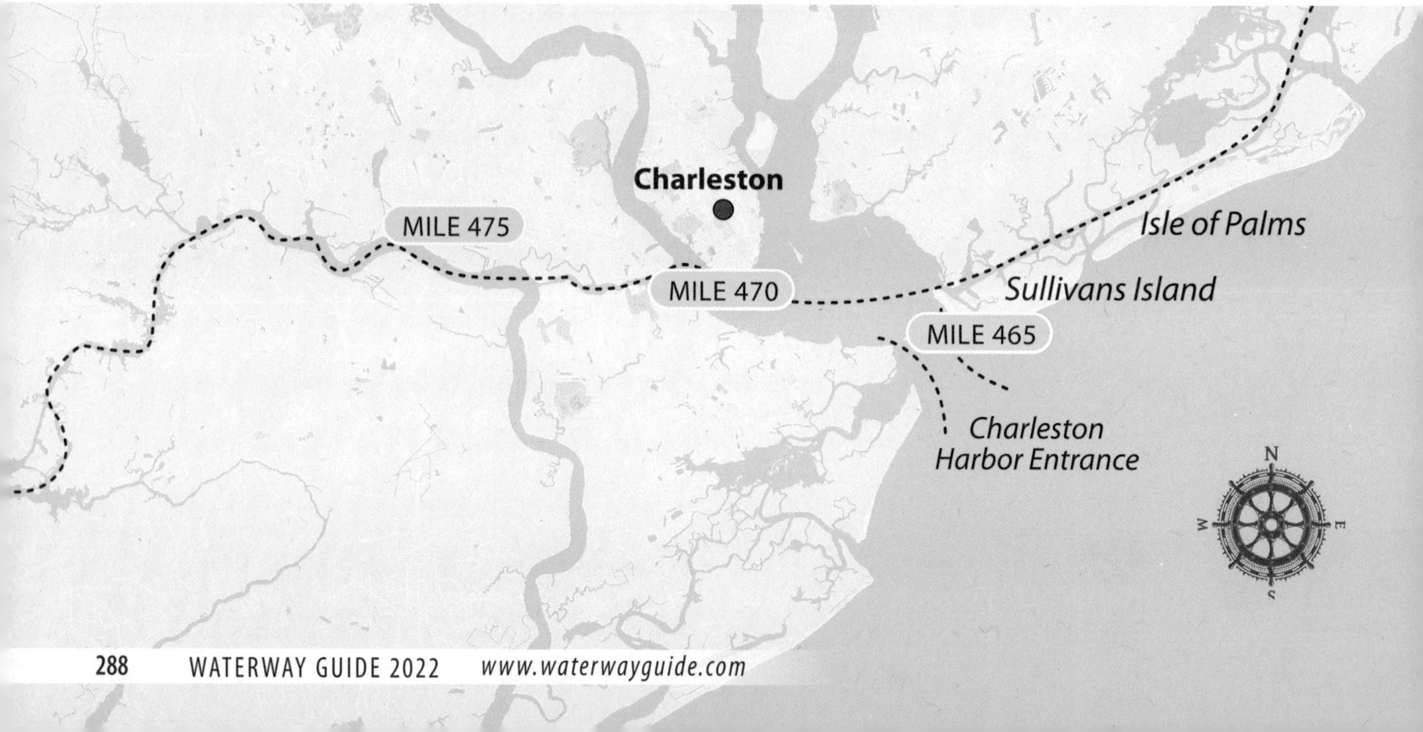

- **Mile 449–**Favor the red side of the channel and stay off flashing green "89" by 150 feet. There is shoaling to 5 feet MLW along the green edge of the channel through here.
- **Mile 452–**Shoaling has been reported between green daybeacon "97" and flashing green "99" on green side of channel. Favor the red side and proceed slowly.

At Mile 458.9, **Isle of Palms Connector Bridge** (65-foot fixed vertical clearance) crosses over the ICW to the Isle of Palms community. Based on stains on the tide boards there may only be 63 to 64 feet of clearance at high tide. **Ben Sawyer Memorial (SC 703) Bridge** (31-foot vertical clearance) at Mile 462.2 opens on signal, except from 7:00 a.m. to 9:00 a.m. and 4:00 p.m. to 6:00 p.m. year-round Monday through Friday (except federal holidays) when the draw need not open. The bridge need only open on the hour from 9:00 a.m. to 7:00 p.m. on weekends and holidays. Use the western span.

Isle of Palms was dredged to 12 MLW in 2019; however, there are some undredged (7-foot MLW) spots between the Isle of Palms Connector Bridge and the Ben Sawyer Memorial (SC 703) Bridge.

Dockage: At Mile 456 near flashing red “116” is the municipal Isle of Palms Marina with transient slips on floating docks and an easy to access fuel dock. The on-site Morgan Creek Grill offers spectacular views and sunsets, as well as two creative kitchens and menus, giving you the choice of a fine dining experience or a casual open experience that even your dog will love. There are few provisions or amenities on the island but the well-stocked Marina Market has everything you might need. This is a pleasant stop close to but out of the hustle and bustle of Charleston.

Just through the Ben Sawyer Memorial (SC 703) Bridge (31-foot vertical clearance) (Mile 462.5) on the mainland side is Toler's Cove Marina. This is part of a private condominium development but transients are welcome if space is available. It is best to call ahead on VHF Channel 16 for slip availability.

Anchorage: You will find several lovely spots to drop the hook along

Charleston Area, SC

ISLE OF PALMS		Largest Vessel	VHF	Total Slips	Approach/ Dockside Depth	Floating Docks	Gas/ Diesel	Repairs/ Haulout	Min/Max Amps	Pump-Out Station
1. Isle of Palms Marina WiFi MM 456.5	(843) 886-0209	220	16	55	12.0 / 12.0	F	GD		30 / 50	P

WiFi Wireless Internet Access onSpot Dockside WiFi Facility
Visit www.waterwayguide.com for current rates, fuel prices, website addresses and other up-to-the-minute information.
(Information in the table is provided by the facilities.)

Scan here for more details:

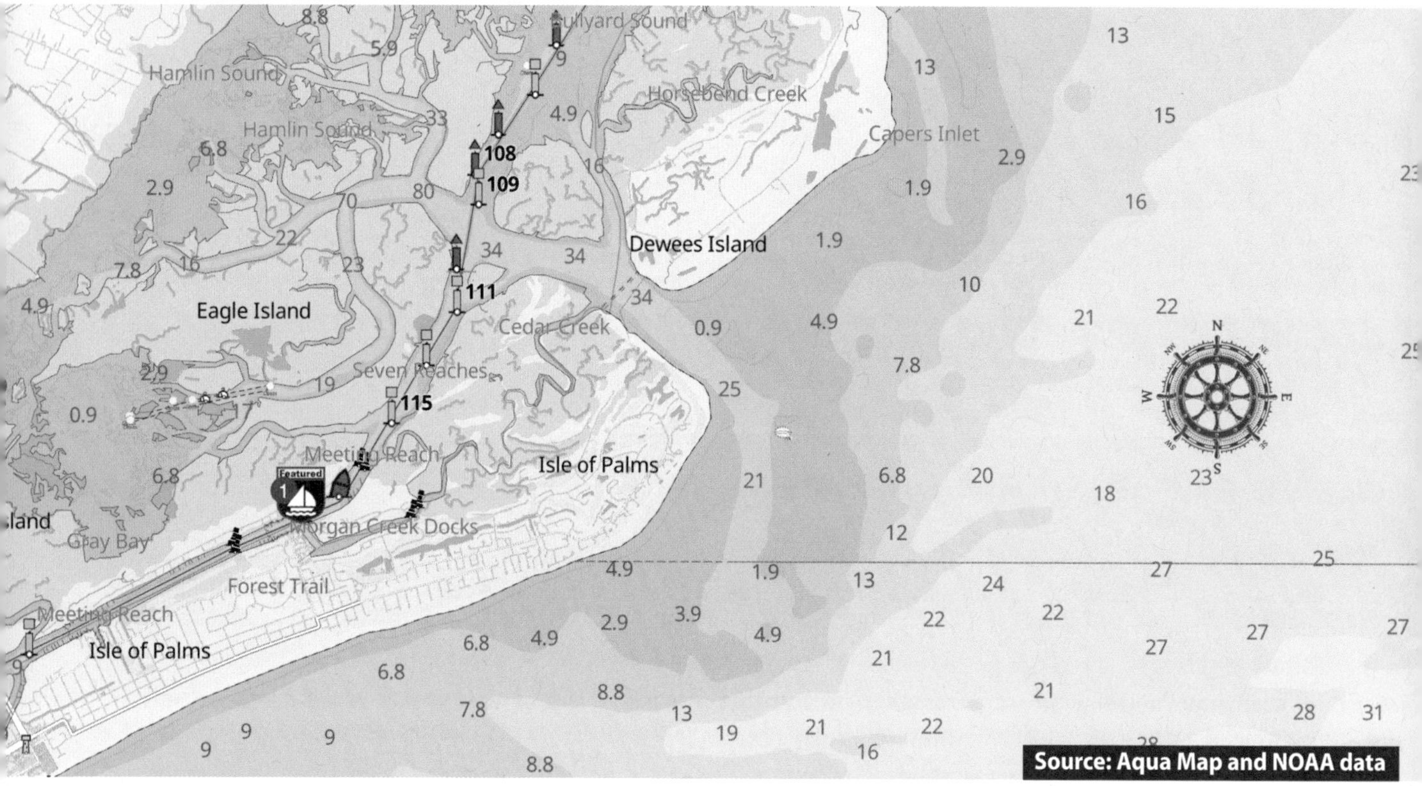

the way to Isle of Palms. Price Creek at Mile 448 is a local favorite for weekend and holiday outings. Feel your way in near flashing red daybeacon "86" below the islet blocking the entrance (submerged at high tide) then proceed a short distance to a suitable spot in 15- to 20-foot MLW depths with a sandy bottom. Proceeding seaward, this winding creek widens into Price Inlet.

Because of its proximity to Capers Island Heritage Preserve, Whiteside Creek at Mile 451.1 is a favorite overnight anchorage for skippers who are ready for an ocean swim or a hike along the beach. Whiteside Creek can get extremely congested during the spring and fall. It is too deep for anchoring at the bend and shoals unpredictably upriver of the bend. Depths are generally shallower before the bend than shown on the NOAA chart. Take the dinghy to the park dock at the western tip of Capers Island. A trail from the dock leads to an ocean beach after passing an impounded lake, which is home to numerous alligators. (No swimming!)

Dewees Creek (Mile 455) is wide and deep but the current flows swiftly and a commuter boat from the mainland serves the island residents. Bear these things in mind when dropping the hook. On the opposite side of the ICW at Mile 455 is an anchorage behind Big Hill Marsh with deep (12 to 17 feet) water and protection from wind and wakes from all but the east. To reach the anchorage, you must navigate around the east side of Big Hill Marsh by turning to port at green daybeacon "109" and following the deep-water channel around.

Dewees Island is privately owned so cruising boaters should not venture above the high-water line while walking on the beach. If you take the unnamed branch to the north 0.25 mile in and go around the bend to the west, you'll find a nice anchoring spot in 20 to 30 feet MLW with good holding in mud in Unnamed Creek. Or you can proceed up Dewees Creek to Hamlin Sound to Eagle Island and anchor in 15 to 25 feet MLW with a mud bottom.

At Mile 456, north of Isle of Palms Marina, Seven Reaches Creek offers 7-foot MLW depths with good holding in mud. To the south Hamlin Creek at Mile 458 offers a protected anchorage off the south side of the ICW near green daybeacon "117." Anchor before the 28-foot fixed vertical clearance Isle of Palms Connector Bridge in 7 to 10 feet MLW with good holding in sand. It is exposed to the northeast.

Inlet Creek at Mile 461 is a regular stop for cruisers heading north or south. It offers fair holding in at least 11 feet MLW and is exposed to the south. This is the last good anchorage before the large and busy Charleston Harbor, which you will want to enter in daylight if possible.

Side Trip: Mount Pleasant

The original village of Mount Pleasant is a picture-perfect community of tree-lined streets with large, handsome and lovingly maintained homes. This is home of the Patriots Point Links (843-881-0042), well known for its spectacular views of the city, Fort Sumter and ships arriving from all over the world. South along the ICW just before Charleston Harbor a well-marked channel arcs northward inside Crab Bank, leading to Mount Pleasant and Shem Creek. Depths in the Mount Pleasant Channel are at least 8 feet MLW. The closest facilities are Charleston Harbor Resort & Marina and Zimmerman Marine–Charleston at Patriots Point (described in the next section).

Charleston Area, SC

SULLIVANS ISLAND		Largest Vessel	VHF	Total Slips	Approach/ Dockside Depth	Floating Docks	Gas/ Diesel	Repairs/ Haulout	Min/Max Amps	Pump-Out Station
1. Toler's Cove Marina WiFi MM 462.3	(843) 881-0325	110	16	140	8.0 / 8.0	F	GD		30 / 50	

WiFi Wireless Internet Access onSpot Dockside WiFi Facility
Visit www.waterwayguide.com for current rates, fuel prices, website addresses and other up-to-the-minute information.
(Information in the table is provided by the facilities.)

Scan here for more details:

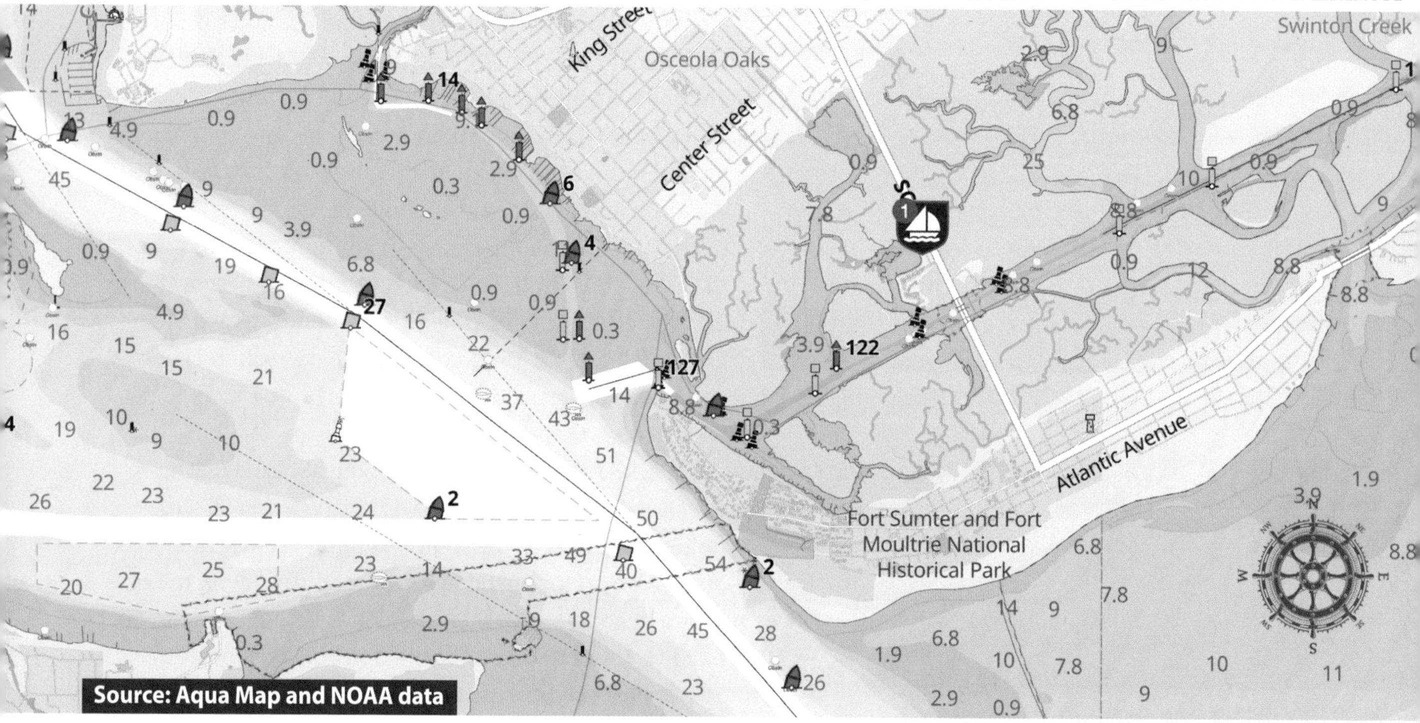

Charleston Harbor Entrance

On April 12, 1861, Capt. Abner Doubleday fired the first Union shot of the Civil War defending Fort Sumter in Charleston Harbor. The fort fell to the Confederates 34 hours later and remained in their hands for the duration of the war. The Union placed it under siege for over 550 days and conducted 5 major bombardments, which effectively flattened the fort, but they never retook it.

It is difficult to enter the Charleston Harbor Entrance from the ocean and not take note of Fort Sumter on the northeastern tip of James Island. Private boats should not attempt to tie up at the fort. According to the National Park Service, all ladders, cleats and lines are for the use of ferries and tour boats. You can either beach or anchor your boat on the western side of the fort.

Once in the harbor you can follow the well-marked channel to reach the facilities on the Cooper River at Patriots Point or Town Creek as well as those on the Ashley River. Be alert for commercial traffic when crossing the harbor and give these big vessels plenty of room.

NAVIGATION: Use NOAA Chart 11525. This is a heavily used ship channel and there is a great deal of commercial traffic here day and night. Smaller vessels are advised to stay to the edge of the channel until reaching the inlet jetties. When entering Charleston Harbor from the ICW–anytime after low-water slack tide to about 2 hours before high-water slack for Charleston Harbor–the current will give slower boats a healthy boost up to the marinas on the Ashley River. When leaving Charleston to head north, slow boats should leave a couple of hours before low-water slack tide for an easier run.

The sea buoy for Charleston Harbor Entrance is 10 nm farther out than necessary for recreational craft. A waypoint at N 32° 42.860'/W 79° 47.550' between green buoy "15" and red buoy "16" saves considerable time, although southbound vessels need to be aware of the shoaling to the north and guide their course appropriately, coming in on a southwesterly heading.

Follow the markers in and if continuing south on the ICW bear to the west on the South Channel Range. Those northbound or heading for the Cooper River continue using the Mount Pleasant Range and follow it out of the channel, watching for flashing green "1" about 0.25 mile to the east marking the entrance to the northbound ICW. During daylight the entrance markers and the forest of harbor buoys leading to Charleston Harbor are easy to sort out. If yours is a first-time passage, however, it is best to run rough compass courses without shortcutting any of the buoys.

Starting at flashing red daybeacon "130" set a course for flashing yellow buoy "L" (Mile 465) to the South

Charleston, SC

PATRIOTS POINT		Largest Vessel	VHF	Total Slips	Approach/ Dockside Depth	Floating Docks	Gas/ Diesel	Repairs/ Haulout	Min/Max Amps	Pump-Out Station
1. Charleston Harbor Resort & Marina WiFi onSpot	(843) 284-7062	200	16	459	12.0 / 12.0	F	GD		30 / 100	P
2. Zimmerman Marine - Charleston	(843) 849-2458				/			R		
COOPER RIVER										
3. Charleston Maritime Center 0.5 mi N of MM 467.0	(843) 853-3625	180	16	30	30.0 / 20.0	F	GD		30 / 50	P

WiFi Wireless Internet Access onSpot Dockside WiFi Facility
Visit www.waterwayguide.com for current rates, fuel prices, website addresses and other up-to-the-minute information.
(Information in the table is provided by the facilities.)

Scan here for more details:

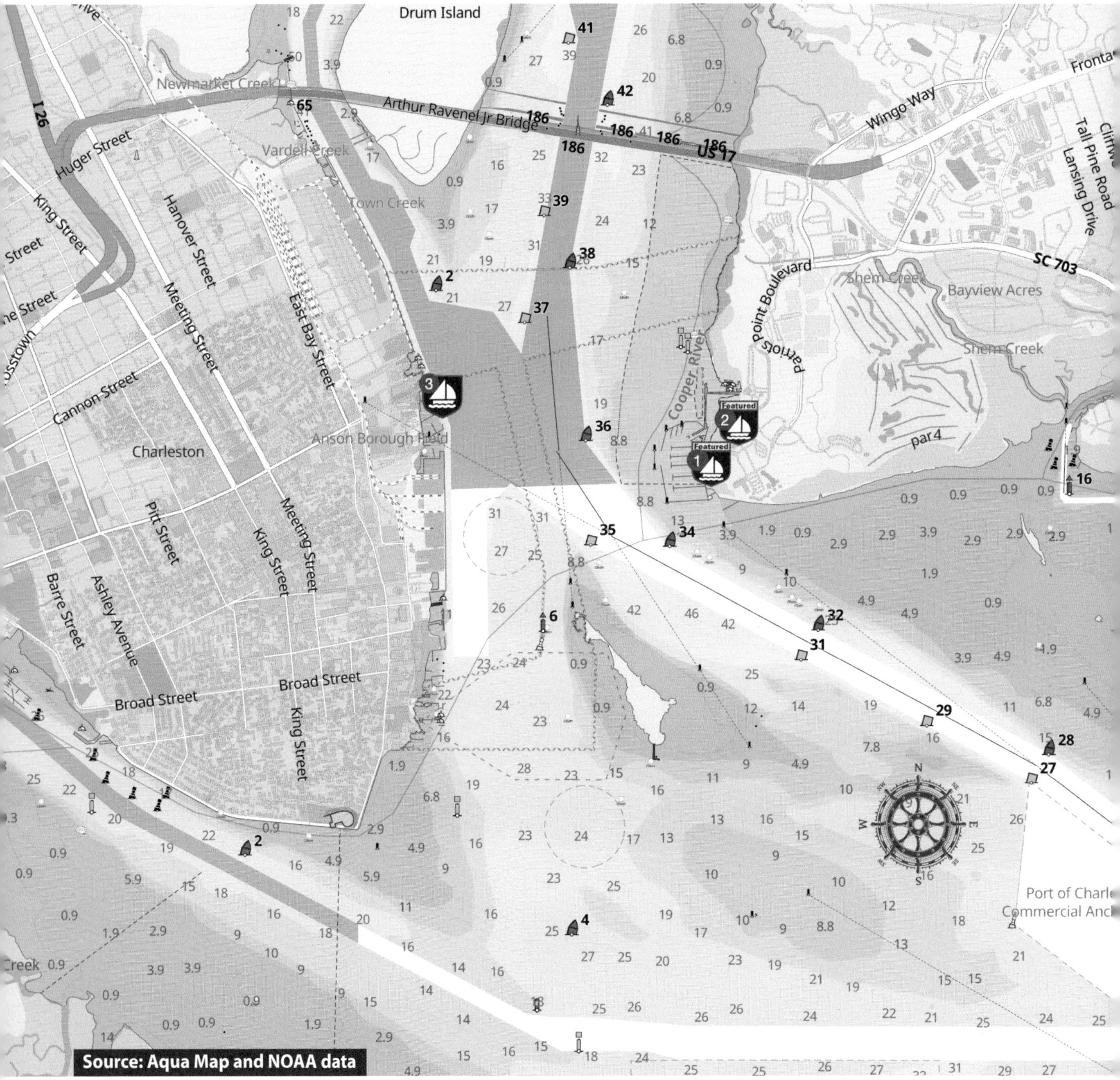

Source: Aqua Map and NOAA data

CHARLESTON HARBOR
RESORT & MARINA

CHARLESTON'S ONLY RESORT STYLE MARINA

Three Phase 480v Power • On Spot Wifi
High Speed Fueling • Full Service Marina
24-hr Gym • Top Rated Spa
Complimentary Shuttle to Downtown Charleston

Mount Pleasant • South Carolina • 29464
843.284.7062 • Marina@CharlestonHarborResort.com
www.CharlestonHarborMarina.com

Charleston, SC

COOPER RIVER		Largest Vessel	VHF	Total Slips	Approach/ Dockside Depth	Floating Docks	Gas/ Diesel	Repairs/ Haulout	Min/Max Amps	Pump-Out Station
1. Cooper River Marina WiFi	(843) 406-6966	150	16	200	45.0 / 25.0	F			30 / 100	P
2. Cooper River Boatyard	(843) 554-7775	90	16		48.0 / 10.0	F	D	RH	30 / 50	

WiFi Wireless Internet Access onSpot Dockside WiFi Facility
Visit www.waterwayguide.com for current rates, fuel prices, website addresses and other up-to-the-minute information.
(Information in the table is provided by the facilities.)
Scan here for more details:

Charleston, SC

WANDO RIVER		Largest Vessel	VHF	Total Slips	Approach/ Dockside Depth	Floating Docks	Gas/ Diesel	Repairs/ Haulout	Min/Max Amps	Pump-Out Station
1. Safe Harbor City Boatyard (WiFi)	(843) 884-3000	125	16		15.0 / 10.0	F		RH	30 / 50	

(WiFi) Wireless Internet Access (onSpot) Dockside WiFi Facility
Visit www.waterwayguide.com for current rates, fuel prices, website addresses and other up-to-the-minute information.
(Information in the table is provided by the facilities.)

Scan here for more details:

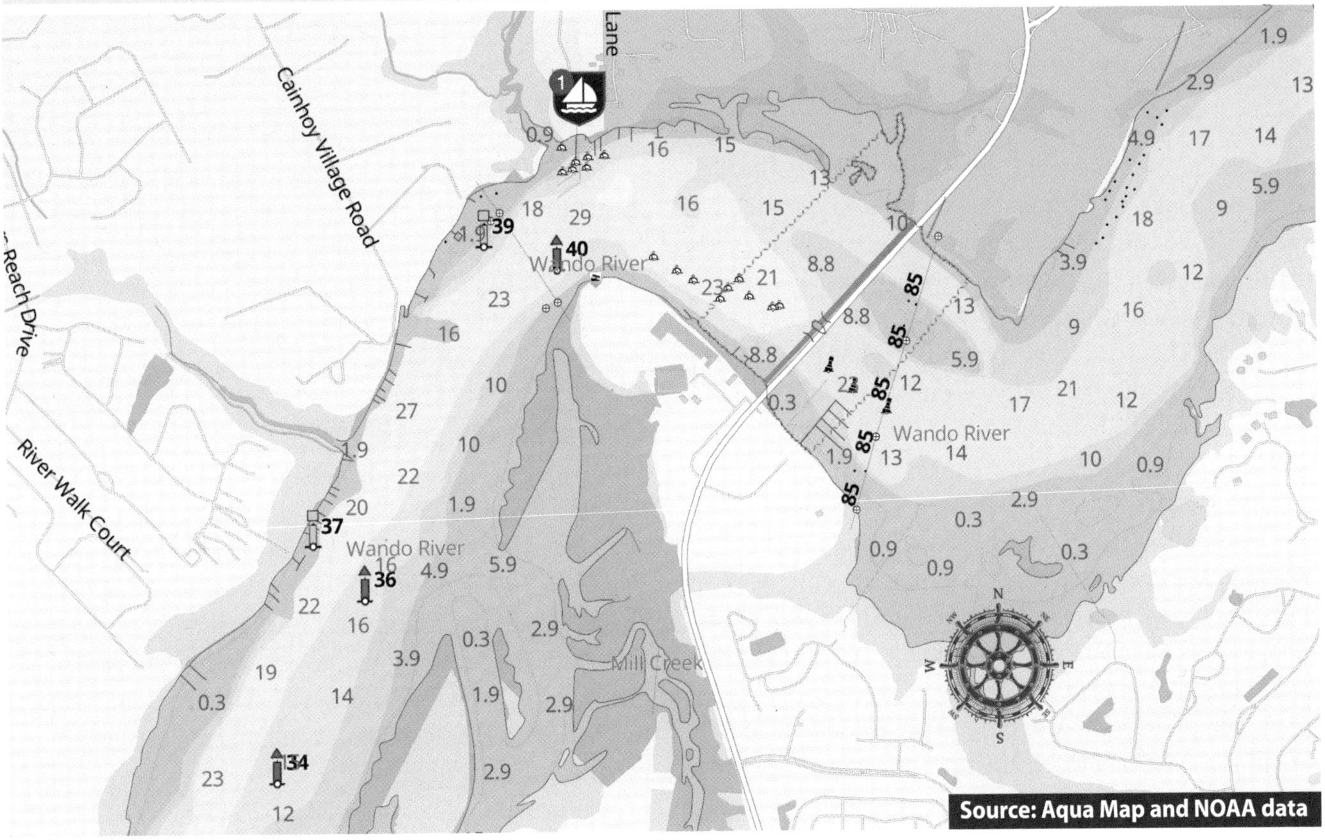

Channel Range. There is plenty of water depth in the area, which is frequently dredged. Follow your chart's ICW magenta line to the Ashley River and allow for the stiff current (about 3 knots at flood). If the current is flowing contrary to a wind of any strength, prepare yourself for a rough crossing.

If Charleston Harbor is busy (which it normally is), you may want to leave the ICW and take a shortcut by skirting the southern edge of the charted Middle Ground to pick up the ICW again at flashing red buoy "BP" south of Potts Shoal using flashing yellow buoy "L" as a mid-way point.

Charleston (Cooper River)

On the east side of Charleston's peninsula the Cooper River enters from the north to meet the harbor at Shutes Folly Island, where historic Castle Pinckney stands. On the east side of the Cooper River at Hog Island is Patriots Point, where the aircraft carrier *USS Yorktown*, the submarine *USS Clamagore* and the destroyer *USS Laffey DD-736* are permanently berthed and open for tours. See "Goin' Ashore: Charleston, SC" in this chapter for more information.

NAVIGATION: Use NOAA Chart 11524. Above Drum Island the Wando River feeds into the Cooper from the northeast. **Arthur Ravenel Jr. Bridge** over the Cooper River at Drum Island has a vertical clearance of 186 feet, and where the same highway crosses Town Creek on the west side of Drum Island the vertical bridge clearance is 65 feet.

Dockage: Charleston Harbor Resort & Marina at Patriots Point is a destination in itself but it is also a convenient place to dock for easy access to the adjoining Patriots Point Naval & Maritime Museum. Turn in at

Charleston, SC

ASHLEY RIVER		Largest Vessel	VHF	Total Slips	Approach/ Dockside Depth	Floating Docks	Gas/ Diesel	Repairs/ Haulout	Min/Max Amps	Pump-Out Station
1. Safe Harbor Charleston City WiFi **MM 469.5**	**(843) 723-5098**	**300**	**16**	**415**	**20.0 / 25.0**	**F**	**D**		**30 / 200+**	**P**
2. Charleston Yacht Club - PRIVATE MM 469.5	(843) 722-4968				/ 8.0	F				
3. Ripley Light Yacht Club WiFi MM 469.0	(843) 766-0908	100		83	5.0 / 6.0	F			30 / 100	P
4. The Harborage at Ashley Marina WiFi onSpot MM 469.5	(843) 722-1996	120	16	230	15.0 / 22.0	F	GD		30 / 100	P
5. Safe Harbor Bristol	(843) 723-6600	70	16	145	15.0 / 22.0	F			30 / 50	P

WiFi Wireless Internet Access **onSpot** Dockside WiFi Facility
Visit www.waterwayguide.com for current rates, fuel prices, website addresses and other up-to-the-minute information.
(Information in the table is provided by the facilities.)

Scan here for more details:

quick flashing red buoy "34" for the a slip on the floating docks or to take on gas and diesel at the 24-hour fuel dock near the entrance. Amenities include a water taxi to Charleston and a free shuttle to a well-stocked gourmet grocery store nearby in Mount Pleasant. The on-site restaurant, The Charleston Harbor Fish House (843-284-7070), has a rooftop bar with a great view. This marina hosts the famous Charleston Race Week sailing regatta, which draws hundreds of boats.

Zimmerman Marine–Charleston is located here offering full boat repair services from rigging to mechanical and electrical and including carpentry and fiberglass. (They have six other yards in Deltaville, VA; Mobjack Bay, VA; Herrington Harbour, MD; Oriental, NC; Southport, NC; and Holden Beach, NC.)

On the western shore of the Cooper River south of Drum Island is the municipal Charleston Maritime Center with some transient dockage adjacent to Liberty Square. The current at this marina can be challenging but it is convenient to most of the sightseeing attractions. A free trolley that serves the downtown area stops in front of the South Carolina Aquarium, which is next to the marina. Charleston is a working commercial harbor and you can expect some surge from the passing ships when docked at the Maritime Center.

Farther north at the entrance to Shipyard Creek is Cooper River Marina with 200 slips (35 reserved for transients) on floating docks. They can accommodate vessels to 42 feet (long term) or 150 feet (transients) and have a well-stocked store, climate-controlled showers and laundry facilities and pump-out service. This is a county-owned and -operated facility. North of Drum Island on the west side of Clouter Creek Reach is Cooper River Boatyard, which offers an array of boat repair and maintenance services.

The well-protected Safe Harbor City Boatyard is located about 20 miles up the Wando River from Drum Island. The full-service boatyard offers complete yacht repair and service. While this facility may be a bit off the beaten path, they offer mobile service at any Charleston area marina even emergency after-hours service.

Charleston (Ashley River)

The Ashley River forms the west fork of the two rivers that flow along the peninsula of downtown Charleston. Note that the ICW leaves the Ashley River and enters Wappoo Creek across from and just past the Coast Guard Station in Charleston. The shoreline along the city side of the Ashley River, marked by the row of colonial mansions, is known as The Battery. The name dates back to Charleston's earliest days when gun emplacements protected the city here.

On the west side of the Ashley River above the **James Island Expressway Bridge** (56-foot vertical clearance) and the **U.S. 17 (Ashley River) Bridges** (18- and 14-foot closed vertical clearances, respectively) is Charles Towne Landing at Old Town Creek. This is the site of the first permanent English settlement in South Carolina. This historic site recreates the colonists' daily lives and includes a full-scale replica of the trading vessel Adventure and is worth a visit if you are spending a few days in Charleston.

Additionally several beautiful plantation homes and gardens–including Middleton Place, Drayton Hall, Magnolia Plantation and Gardens and the Audubon Swamp Gardens–are upriver on the Ashley. Both Charles Towne Landing and the plantations are best visited by car. The historic downtown lends itself to the horse-drawn carriage tours but many of the areas attractions are outlying and will require transportation.

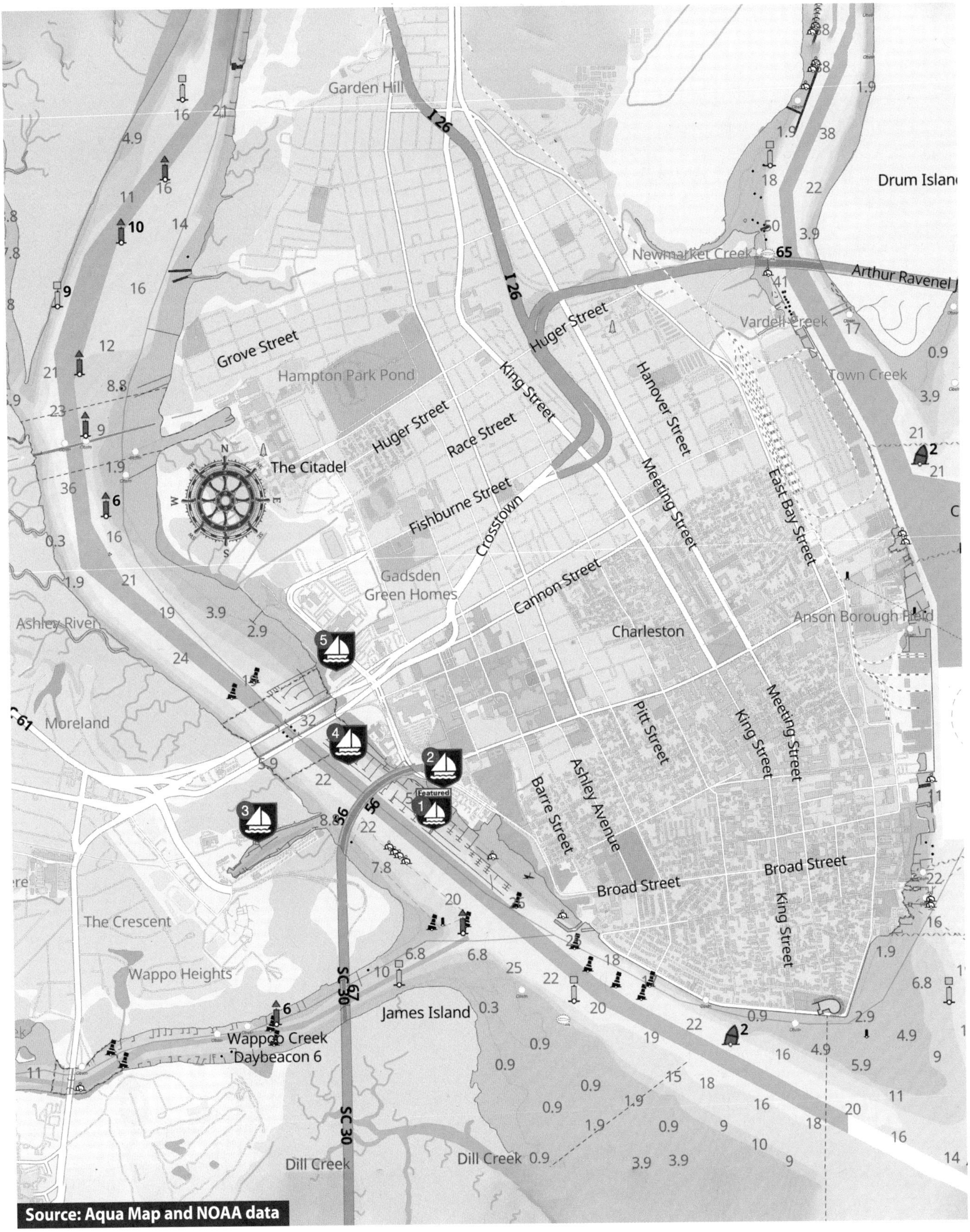

Source: Aqua Map and NOAA data

NAVIGATION: Use NOAA Charts 11524. When heading into the Ashley River from the Charleston Harbor Inlet there are two clearly charted ranges–the South Channel and the Ashley River Approach–to assist you. This area is frequently dredged. Note that the current can be extremely swift, from 1 to 2 knots, with tides ranging 4 to 6 feet in this area. Check the currents and winds carefully before entering any of the marinas and call for assistance if needed. Space during the traveling seasons can be at a premium, so reservations are highly recommended.

The marinas are located south of the James Island Expressway Bridge (56-foot vertical clearance) on the Ashley River. If you wish to cruise past the marinas and cannot clear the twin US 17 (Ashley River) Bridges with their respective 18- and 14-foot controlling vertical clearances, you will need to call ahead to request the bridges openings. The bridges open on signal daily, except from 4:00 p.m. to 9:00 a.m., when the draws will only open if at least 12-hour notice is given. The bridges are 0.10 of a mile apart. Beyond the turning basin the Ashley River's minimal depths prohibit all but small shallow-draft boats from proceeding. The Coast Guard base is to starboard about 1 mile up the river beyond The Battery.

Strings of crab pots have been observed near the breakwater by the Coast Guard Station on both sides of the channel. They are barely visible, green on top and black on their side at or just below the water. The "tell-tale" wake they leave in strong currents will reveal their location.

Dockage: A convenient walkway under the James Island Expressway Bridge connects Safe Harbor Charleston City, Charleston Yacht Club (private) and The Harborage at Ashley Marina.

Safe Harbor Charleston City at Mile 469.5 welcomes transients of all sizes. They offer 3,000 feet of floating docks with high-speed diesel fueling stations, deep-draft slips with no height limitations and an impressive floating bathhouse with laundry. The Mega Dock (the main floating dock of the marina) is almost 0.25 mile long and, as the name suggests, you can expect to find megayachts tied there. Safe Harbor Charleston City also has a full-service convenience store, an internet café and a marina courtesy van that makes hourly trips to the downtown area and daily trips to West Marine. The marina is also home to the popular

Charleston, SC

NORTH CHARLESTON		Largest Vessel	VHF	Total Slips	Approach/ Dockside Depth	Floating Docks	Gas/ Diesel	Repairs/ Haulout	Min/Max Amps	Pump-Out Station
1. Dolphin Cove Marina WiFi	(843) 744-2562	60	16	85	35.0 / 8.0	F	G	RH	30	P
2. Loggerhead Marina - RiversEdge Marina WiFi	(843) 554-8901	45	16	60	5.0 / 5.0	F	G	H	30 / 50	P

WiFi Wireless Internet Access onSpot Dockside WiFi Facility
Visit www.waterwayguide.com for current rates, fuel prices, website addresses and other up-to-the-minute information.
(Information in the table is provided by the facilities.)

Scan here for more details:

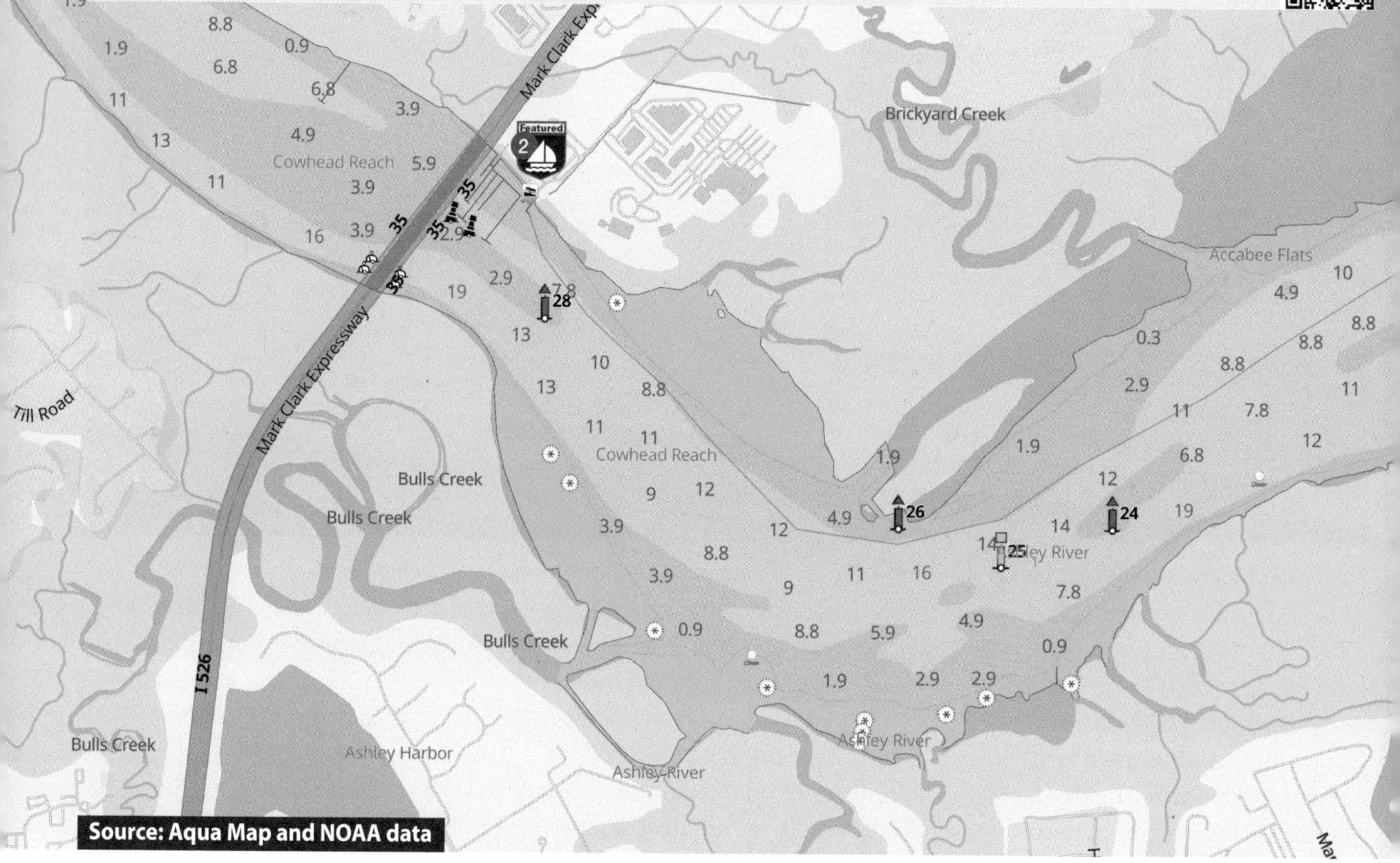

Source: Aqua Map and NOAA data

Variety Store Restaurant (843-723-6325). Charleston Yacht Club is private and does not accommodate transients but members of reciprocal clubs are welcome in their clubhouse.

The full-service The Harborage at Ashley Marina is north of the 56-foot fixed vertical clearance James Island Expressway Bridge and is capable of accommodating vessels up to 150 feet. The marina has high-speed fuel pumps, WiFi, pump-out service and a laundry as well as a courtesy shuttle to take transients to and from many of downtown Charleston's most popular attractions. There are plenty of restaurants within walking distance and groceries within 2 miles. The marina is adjacent to two hotels, making it a great location for hosting visitors or crew changes. Across the Ashley River (on the west side) is the 83-slip Ripley Light Yacht Club, which caters to sportfishing vessels. They report 5-foot MLW approach depths; call ahead for transient space.

Safe Harbor Bristol is located past the Ashley River Bridges and adjacent to the Citadel. It was designed and engineered for easy docking with 128 wet slips for boats less than 70 feet (14-foot maximum vessel height/air draft) and 63 drive-on docks for boats from 12 to 20 feet. They have a mobile pump-out station, cable and water at every slip and welcome transients.

Farther north on the Ashley River across from Duck Island is Dolphin Cove Marina, which offers some boat repairs and may have transient space (to 65 feet). This

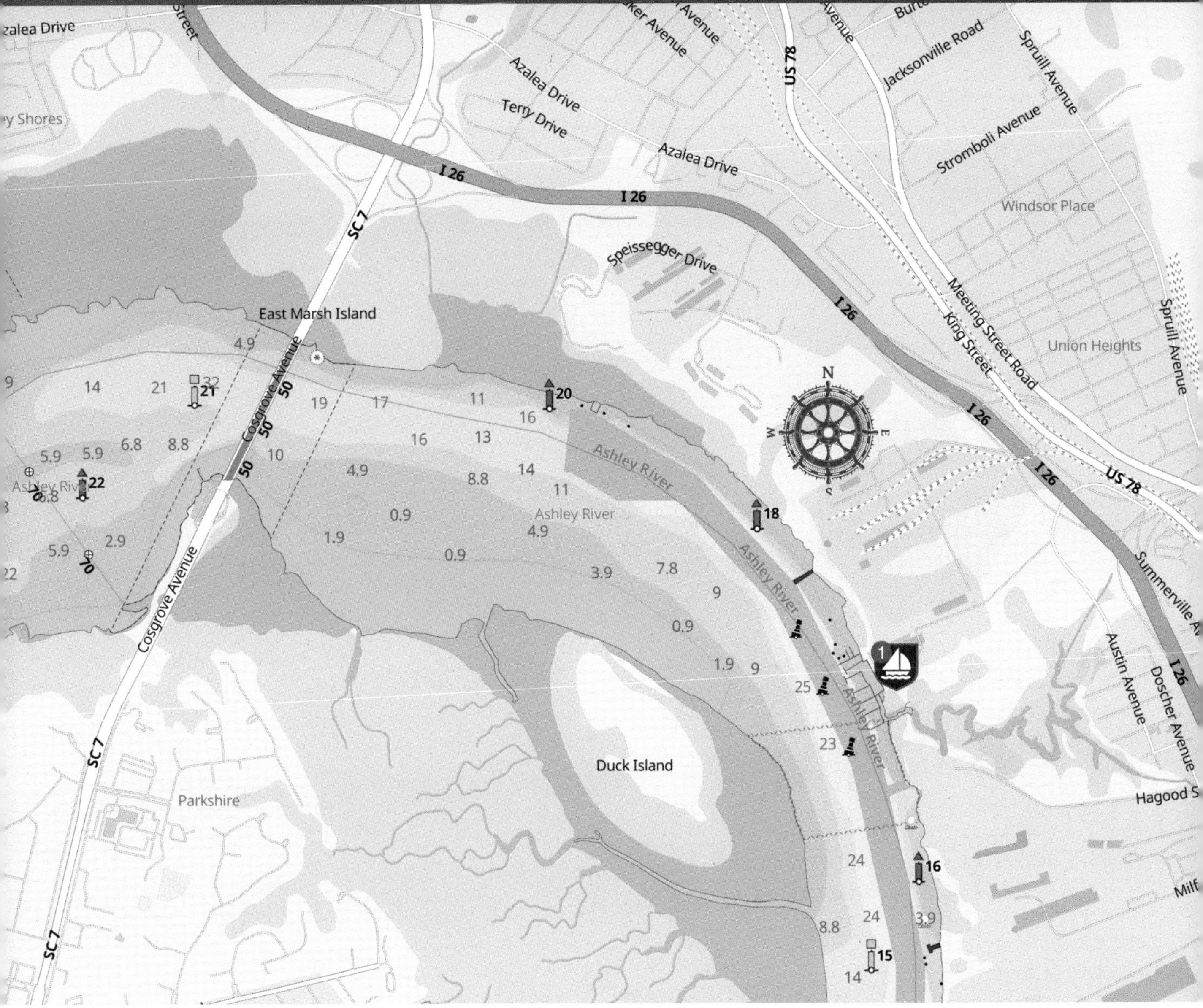

marina primarily caters to liveaboards and is one of the most economical in the area (but with less amenities). They also have a fully enclosed drystack.

A little farther north on the Ashley River, past the **SC 7 (Cosgrove Avenue) Bridge** (with a fixed vertical clearance of 50 feet) and before the **General William C. Westmoreland (I-526) Bridge** (with a fixed vertical clearance of 35 feet), you will find Loggerhead Marina–RiversEdge Marina. They offer indoor and outdoor dry storage for boats up to 36 feet and wet slips for boats up to 40 feet.

Anchorage: Boats swing differently in the current here so pay careful attention to how the boats around you are swinging (some on a single anchor, some on two; some on rode, some on chain) when you set the hook.

There are three popular anchorages directly on the Ashley River. There is a large designated anchorage on NOAA Chart 11524 across from Safe Harbor Charleston City (near the Wappo Creek entrance). It has good holding in mud (12 to 20 feet MLW) and is exposed to the northwest and southeast. You should also be aware that there are a lot of snags on the bottom.

Another anchorage is in the small area adjacent to the Coast Guard Station and before Safe Harbor Charleston City in 10 feet MLW with a mud bottom. It is exposed to the northwest through the southeast. There are a handful of long-term-anchored boats here taking up most of the useful space. Watch for crab pots.

Just north of the channel entrance to Ripley Light Yacht Club between the high rise and the bascule bridges

GOIN' ASHORE

CHARLESTON, SC

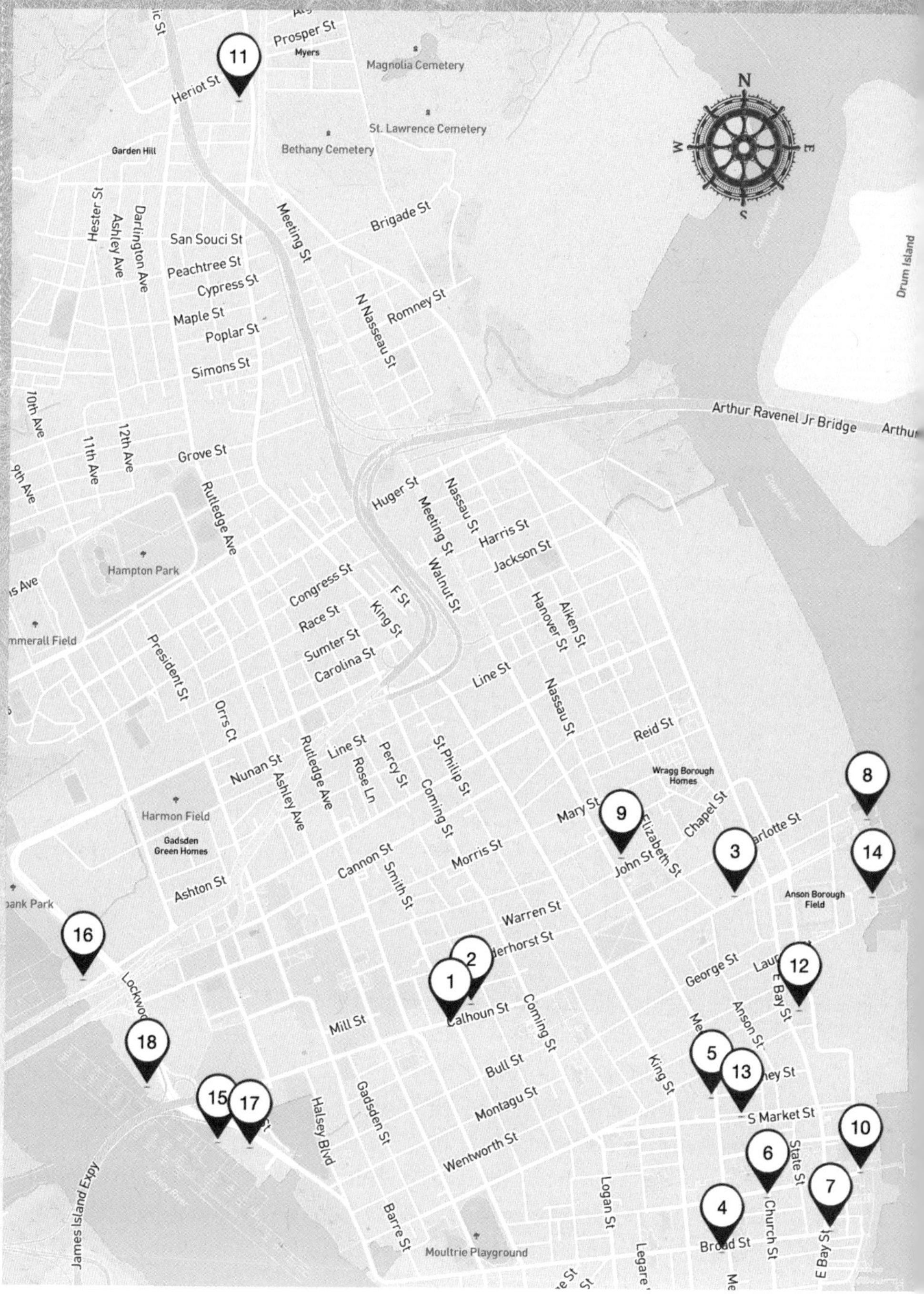

Charleston is a favorite destination for cruisers, offering superb protection in bad weather, and with its numerous marinas and boatyards, an excellent stopover point to attend to you and your boat's needs. Charleston's "Museum Mile" boasts six museums, five nationally historic homes, four scenic parks, numerous historic churches, the Old Market and City Hall. Frequent tours by the Historic Charleston Foundation and the Preservation Society offer a peek inside the old homes and their glorious gardens. Do take one of the ghost tours if you have time. Even if it does not make your hair stand on end, you will have a new insight into the city's past. (Example: The cobblestone streets in the historic district were built from the rocks used as ship's ballast.)

SERVICES

1. **Access Urgent**
   233 Calhoun St.
   (843-853-8870)
2. **All Creatures Veterinary Clinic**
   224 Calhoun St.
   (843-579-0030)
3. **Charleston County Public Library**
   68 Calhoun St.
   (843-805-6930)
4. **Charleston Post Office**
   83 Broad St. (843-727-1129)
5. **Charleston Visitor Information**
   211 Meeting St.
   (843-573-4849)

ATTRACTIONS

6. **Dock Street Theater**
   This is a "must see" if only to see its stunning interior. Reopened in 1937, the theater is the first building in the U.S. designed specifically for theatrical performances (135 Church St., 843-577-7183).

7. **Old Exchange Building**
Costumed docents lead tours daily every half hour between 9:30 a.m. and 5:00 p.m. of this historic building that once housed a Revolutionary prison, known as the Provost Dungeon (122 E. Bay St., 843-727-2165).

8. **South Carolina Aquarium**
Liberty Square houses the aquarium where residents include an American alligator, playful river otters, bright green moray eels and horseshoe crabs. There are numerous exhibits (of both aquatic and wildlife), a 6,000-gallon stingray tank and the two-story, 385,000-gallon Great Ocean tank, which houses a 220-pound loggerhead sea turtle and several tiger sharks. The best times to visit are weekdays before 11:00 a.m. or after 2:00 p.m. Call ahead for admission fees (843-577-3474).

9. **The Charleston Museum**
"America's first museum," founded in 1773 by the Charleston Library Society, has changing exhibits and artifacts about South Carolina and also Confederate history. Located at 360 Meeting St. Call for hours and ticket prices (843-722-2996).

10. **Waterfront Park**
The famous Pineapple fountain is located at this eight-acre park that runs one-half mile alongside the Cooper River at Vedue Range. Snag a swing on the pavilion-covered pier to bide your time or finish your gelato from just across the street (Belgian Gelato at 8 Venue Range, 843-743-5043).

SHOPPING

11. **East Bay True Value Hardware**
Full-service hardware store for parts and tools (18 Society St., 843-577-9196).

12. **Harris Teeter**
Full-service grocery store with deli and bakery items (290 E. Bay St., 843-722-6821). This location also boasts an on-site wine bar and a Starbucks.

13. **Historic Charleston City Market**
The four-block city market at 188 Market St. is over 200 years old and was actually a market for food items, not slaves, as commonly thought. (The Slave Market is a few blocks away.) This may now be the best spot to see the sweet grass basket weavers at work. There are many and the variety of their work is impressive. Open daily at 9:30 a.m.

MARINAS

14. **Charleston Maritime Center**
10 Wharfside St. (842-853-3625)

15. **Charleston Yacht Club**
17 Lockwood Dr. (843-722-4968)

16. **Safe Harbor Bristol**
145 Lockwood Dr. (843-723-6600)

17. **Safe Harbor Charleston City**
17 Lockwood Dr. (843-723-5098)

18. **The Harborage at Ashley Marina**
33 Lockwood Dr. (843-722-1996)

Charleston

is an anchorage with 12 to 25 feet MLW with good holding in mud. Note that it is exposed to the northwest and southeast, is also home to a lot of local boats and is usually congested.

Anchored vessels may dock a dinghy at Safe Harbor Charleston City for a fee, at the nearby boat ramp or possibly at the private Charleston Yacht Club. With the strong current, do factor the current into your trip ashore.

> Charleston Waterkeeper offers a mobile pump-out service in the lower Charleston Harbor. They will come to your slip or location at anchorage and pump out your holding tank for free. Pump-out service is performed once per week on weekends. All requests for pump-out service must be received by 5:00 p.m. on Friday. Boat owners do not need to be present. Call 843-608-9287 to schedule.

WAPPOO CREEK & STONO RIVER

Wappoo Creek–ICW Mile 469 to Mile 475

From Mile 472 at Elliott Cut to Mile 535 at Beaufort, SC, the South Carolina Lowcountry scenery is lush and beautiful with water birds and marsh grass creating picture-postcard sights everywhere you look. Beaufort is a beautiful stopping place and the next community of any size past Charleston.

NAVIGATION: Use NOAA Charts 11518. Continuing down the ICW on the Ashley River opposite the Safe Harbor Charleston City you enter Wappoo Creek, which then leads into narrow Elliott Cut. Immediately inside Wappoo Creek's northern entrance at Mile 469.9 is **James Island Expressway Bridge** (official fixed vertical clearance of 67 feet but there are no tide boards), followed by the **Wappoo Creek (SC171) Bridge** (33-foot closed vertical clearance) at Mile 470.8. The draw here will open on signal except from 6:00 a.m. to 9:29 a.m. and 3:31 p.m. to 7:00 p.m., Monday through Friday (except federal holidays), when the draw need not open. Between 9:30 a.m. and 3:30 p.m., Monday through Friday (except federal holidays), the draw need only open on the hour or the half-hour. A boat ramp is on the north side of the Wappoo Creek (SC171) Bridge.

NO WAKE ZONE

This entire section through Elliott Cut is a patrolled No-Wake Zone. Almost every pier has a sign saying, "Slow, you are responsible for your wake." Go as slowly as you can, even though it may be difficult when the strong current is dead against you.

Ebb tide begins at the Wappoo Creek entrance 45 minutes before it begins at Charleston Harbor. You must be able to maintain steerage when the current is with you. For slower southbound boats the best time to leave Charleston for Beaufort is toward the end of a flood tide. Moreover, a passage through Elliott Cut's narrow channel against a 2- to 4-knot current can guarantee an all-too-memorable experience. Slower auxiliary-powered craft may prefer to wait until the current moderates.

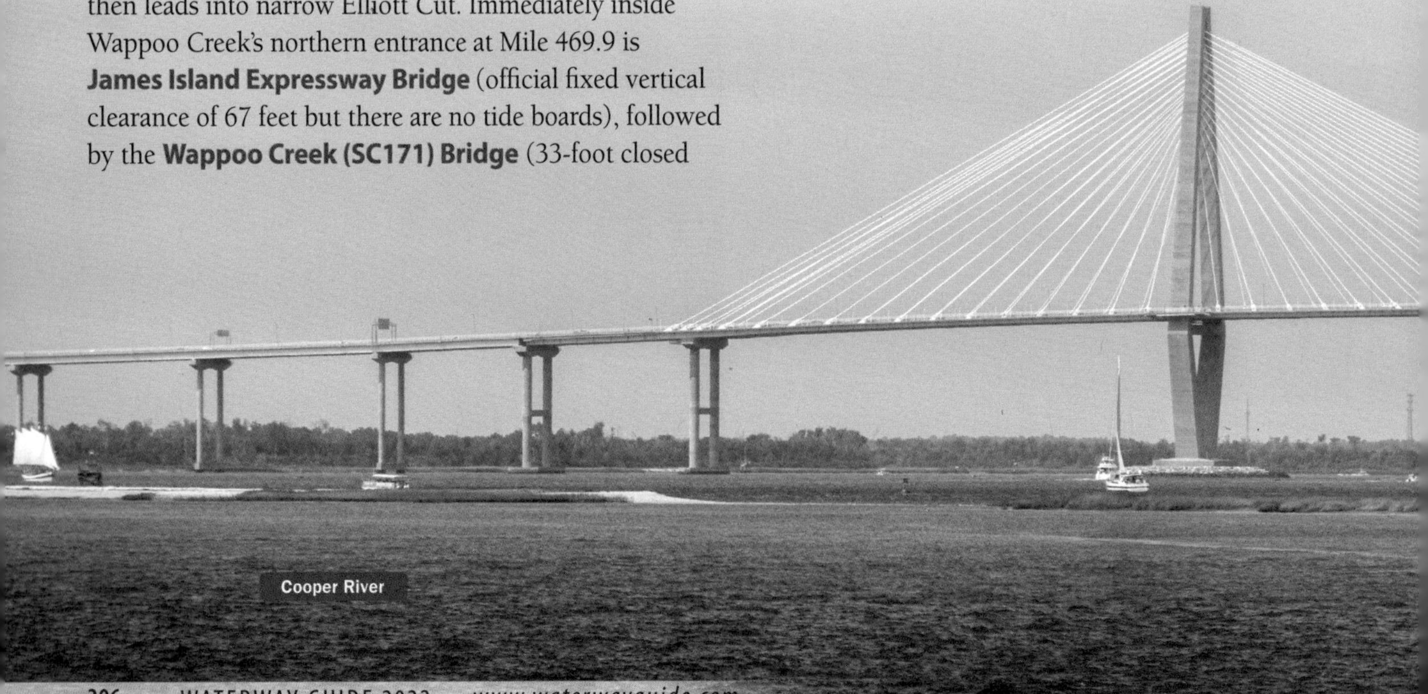

Cooper River

Anchorage: The most protected overnight anchorage in the Charleston area at Mile 471 is just beyond the Wappoo Creek (SC171) Bridge (33-foot closed vertical clearance, restricted schedule) in 11 to 15 feet MLW behind the unnamed small island. This anchorage is very narrow and not very large (with space for only a few small to mid-size cruising boats) and subject to strong current. It is a long dinghy ride to downtown but it is a quiet, secluded spot for those who get there early. It is in a residential area with private docks on the south side.

Stono River–ICW Mile 472 to Mile 484

From Elliott Cut, which leads from Charleston, SC, south to the Stono River, the ICW route continues along the Stono River for about 12 miles to the Beaufort, SC, area.

NAVIGATION: Use NOAA Chart 11518. From Elliott Cut the ICW enters the Stono River just beyond Mile 472. Shoaling has been reported at the confluence of Elliott Cut and the Stono River near red daybeacon "18." The ICW channel up the Stono River begins with green daybeacon "19A." Make sure you are using the most up-to-date charts.

Downstream on the Stono River leads to the Folly and Kiawah Rivers, frequented by local recreational boaters. Folly and Kiawah Islands are home to several ocean resorts with beaches, shopping, restaurants and several golf courses.

A short distance beyond the **John F. Limehouse Highway Bridge** at Mile 479.3 (65-foot fixed vertical clearance), the Stono River narrows and the ICW channel follows a winding path past Johns Island. When heading north through the starboard side of the channel at the Limehouse Bridge be aware of small-boat traffic coming from the busy boat ramp north of the bridge.

Just beyond Mile 480 red daybeacon "40" marks a shoal off the creek to the north. This marker appears to be in the wrong place but it is not. Give it space as a shoal extends slightly farther into the channel from the creek. The current usually reverses at this point.

Dockage: A short side trip south from Elliott Cut down the Stono River brings you to St. Johns Yacht Harbor. They offer "yacht club amenities in a family-friendly environment." The facility sells non-ethanol gas and diesel and has laundry facilities, a ship and sundries store, free in-slip pump-out services and a saltwater pool. They also offer a courtesy car. This is just before the 65-foot fixed vertical clearance **Paul J. Gelegotis (Stono) Bridge**.

Stono River Area, SC

STONO RIVER		Largest Vessel	VHF	Total Slips	Approach/ Dockside Depth	Floating Docks	Gas/ Diesel	Repairs/ Haulout	Min/Max Amps	Pump-Out Station
1. St. Johns Yacht Harbor WiFi 1.0 mi. S of MM 472.5	(843) 557-1027	120	16	224	25.0 / 8.0	F	GD		30 / 50	P

WiFi Wireless Internet Access onSpot Dockside WiFi Facility
Visit www.waterwayguide.com for current rates, fuel prices, website addresses and other up-to-the-minute information.
(Information in the table is provided by the facilities.)

Scan here for more details:

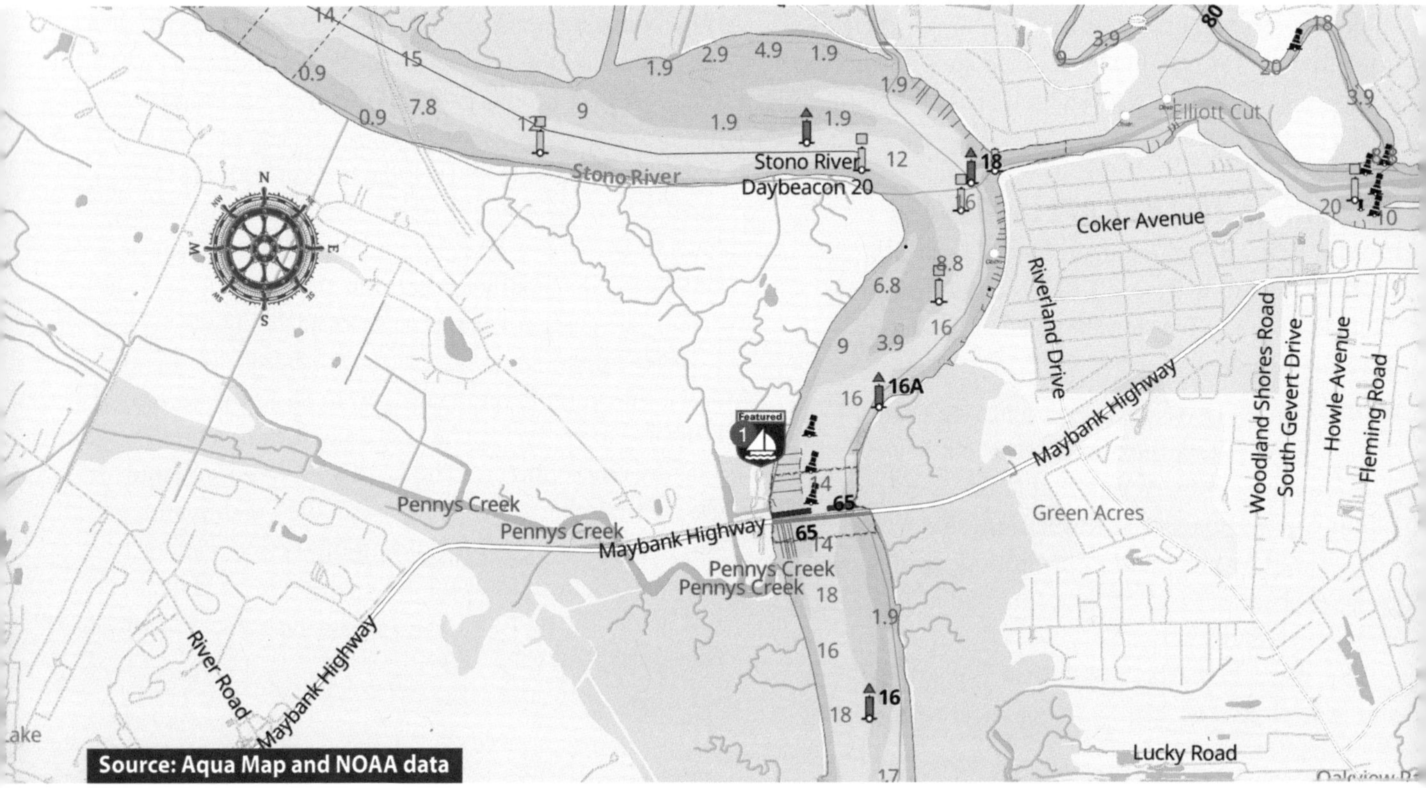

Paul J. Gelegotis (Stono) Bridge

St. Johns
Yacht Harbor

Stono River Area, SC

STONO RIVER		Largest Vessel	VHF	Total Slips	Approach/ Dockside Depth	Floating Docks	Gas/ Diesel	Repairs/ Haulout	Min/Max Amps	Pump-Out Station
1. Ross Marine MM 476.0	(843) 559-0379	150	16	40	12.0 / 12.0	F	D	RH	30 / 50	

WiFi Wireless Internet Access onSpot Dockside WiFi Facility
Visit www.waterwayguide.com for current rates, fuel prices, website addresses and other up-to-the-minute information.
(Information in the table is provided by the facilities.)

Scan here for more details:

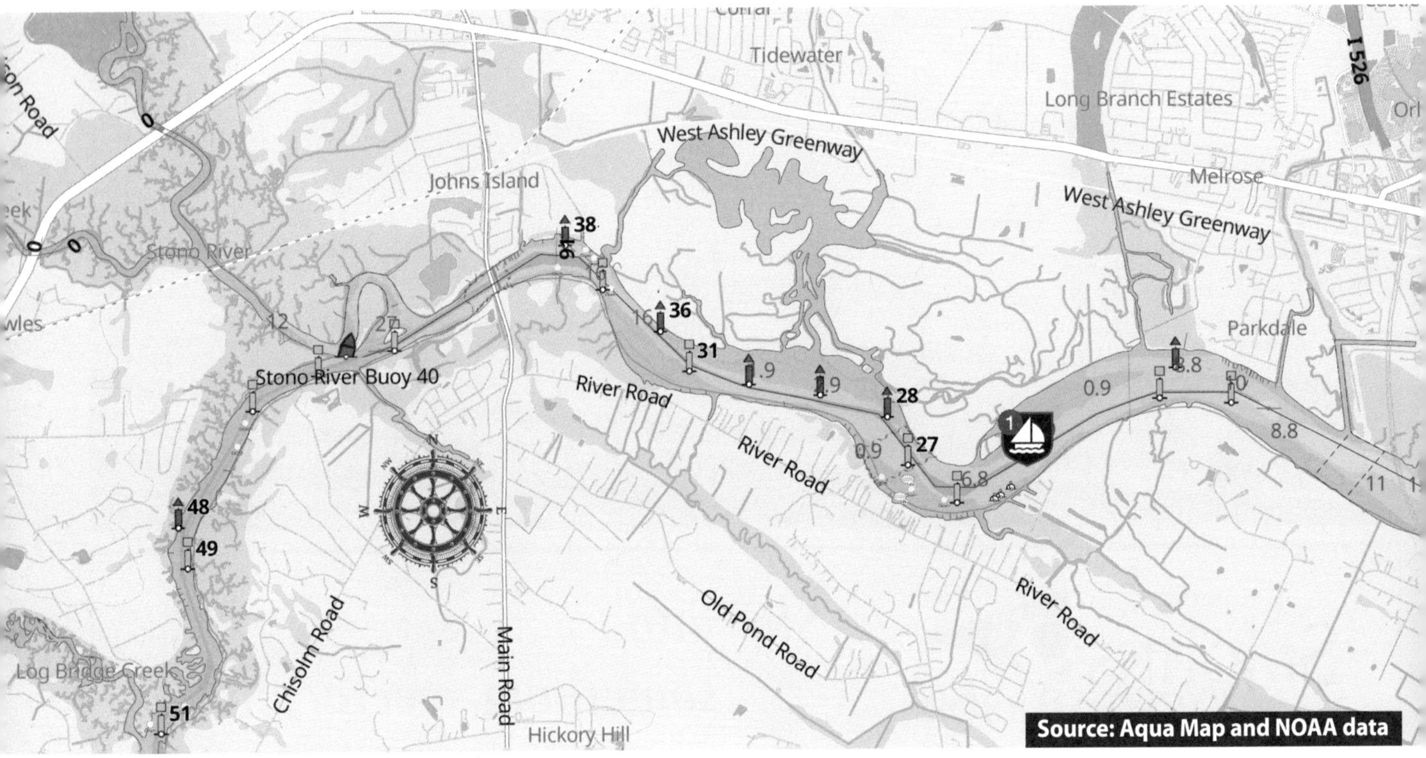

Continuing about 3 miles along the ICW near flashing green daybeacon "25" to port (Mile 476) is Ross Marine. This full-service yacht repair yard is equipped to handle major repairs on any size boat with a crane and a lift.

Anchorage: The best anchorage in this area is across the Stono from red daybeacon "16A" (at Mile 472.6 behind Buzzards Roost Point) in the 10-foot MLW charted area near St. Johns Yacht Harbor. There can be considerable current in the river; however, there is excellent holding here in clay.

Anchorage is also available up the Stono River at Mile 475.5 (before Ross Marine) with 8-foot MLW depths with good holding in mud but with minimum wake and wind protection. At Mile 479.8 at Johns Island there is another somewhat protected spot on the north shore for more shoal-draft vessels with 4 to 6 feet MLW.

NEXT STOP

Ahead on your southbound journey down the ICW lies the lush and lovely Lowcountry. The following chapters offer trips off the ICW via the North Edisto River or South Edisto River to Seabrook and Edisto Islands, respectively. Different in character and amenities, each has something to offer. Back on the ICW, Beaufort and Hilton Head, SC, await your arrival.

ICW Mile 456-Mile 475

TO BEAUFORT, SC

This stretch of lush and lovely South Carolina marsh is teeming with wildlife. The delicate colors of the grasses and the unique scents wafting off the marsh make cruising through these parts a unique experience. You are now in open country.

Wadmalaw to Dawho River–ICW Mile 484 to Mile 497

NAVIGATION: Use NOAA Chart 11518. The ICW leaves the Stono River at Mile 485 and enters a short land cut leading to the headwaters of the Wadmalaw River. The tides meet at Church Flats at Mile 485 (so named for the practice of going to church on the flood tide and coming home on the ebb.) Near red daybeacon "78A" there are (charted) submerged rocks on both sides of the channel.

Several aids to navigation mark the shoals on the Wadmalaw River between flashing red daybeacon "82" and green daybeacon "101." Run the long stretch between red daybeacon "92" and flashing red daybeacon "94" on a compass course and swing wide to the outside on curves. If transiting at mid to high tide, check your position with respect to the current along the way to avoid the mud flats to the north and in deep water. Swing wide toward flashing red daybeacon "94" and avoid the shortcut to green daybeacon "95." Red daybeacons "98" and "100" indicate a shoal area that is visible at low tide but can be difficult to spot at high tide. These two markers need to be given a wide berth.

Anchorage: There is another at Mile 487 at New Cut Landing, which is especially popular during the spring and fall. The holding here is good in about 15 feet MLW and the anchorage is fairly well protected. To reach this anchorage turn off the ICW at green "77" and proceed east into Church Creek for less than 0.50 mile, taking care to stay an equal distance from the shores. Low tide will reveal the hidden oyster beds on the north side and shallow mud flats on the south side. However, dropping anchor in the middle of the creek will give you plenty of swing room and depth to handle the tide change. This anchorage offers a lovely panoramic view of the sunset and sunrise.

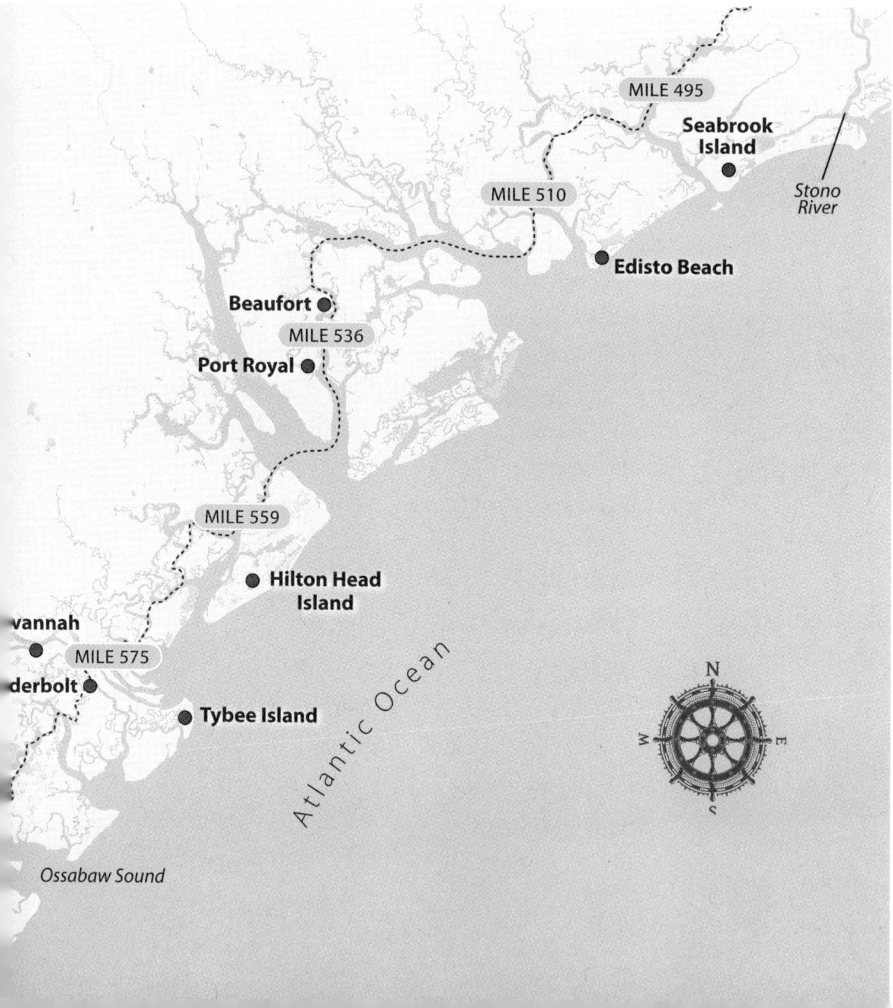

Side Trip: North Edisto River Inlet

NAVIGATION: Use NOAA Chart 11522. About 6 miles south of the ICW on the North Edisto River you can head up swift-running Bohicket Creek to the village of Rockville and Seabrook Island, both popular weekend destinations with Charleston-based boaters. A side trip with access to the ocean can be made by continuing down the North Edisto River, which is well charted and easy to run, except for shoaling along both riverbanks. North Edisto River Inlet is a straight shot with a charted shoal section (5 foot MLW) near flashing red "6."

Up-to-date tide information is available online from NOAA (www.tidesandcurrents.noaa.gov).

Edisto River, SC

BOHICKET CREEK		Largest Vessel	VHF	Total Slips	Approach/ Dockside Depth	Floating Docks	Gas/ Diesel	Repairs/ Haulout	Min/Max Amps	Pump-Out Station
1. Bohicket Marina & Market WiFi 7.2 mi S of MM 497.0	(843) 768-1280	150	16	200	14.0 / 14.0	F	GD		30 / 100	P

WiFi Wireless Internet Access onSpot Dockside WiFi Facility
Visit www.waterwayguide.com for current rates, fuel prices, website addresses and other up-to-the-minute information.
(Information in the table is provided by the facilities.)

Scan here for more details:

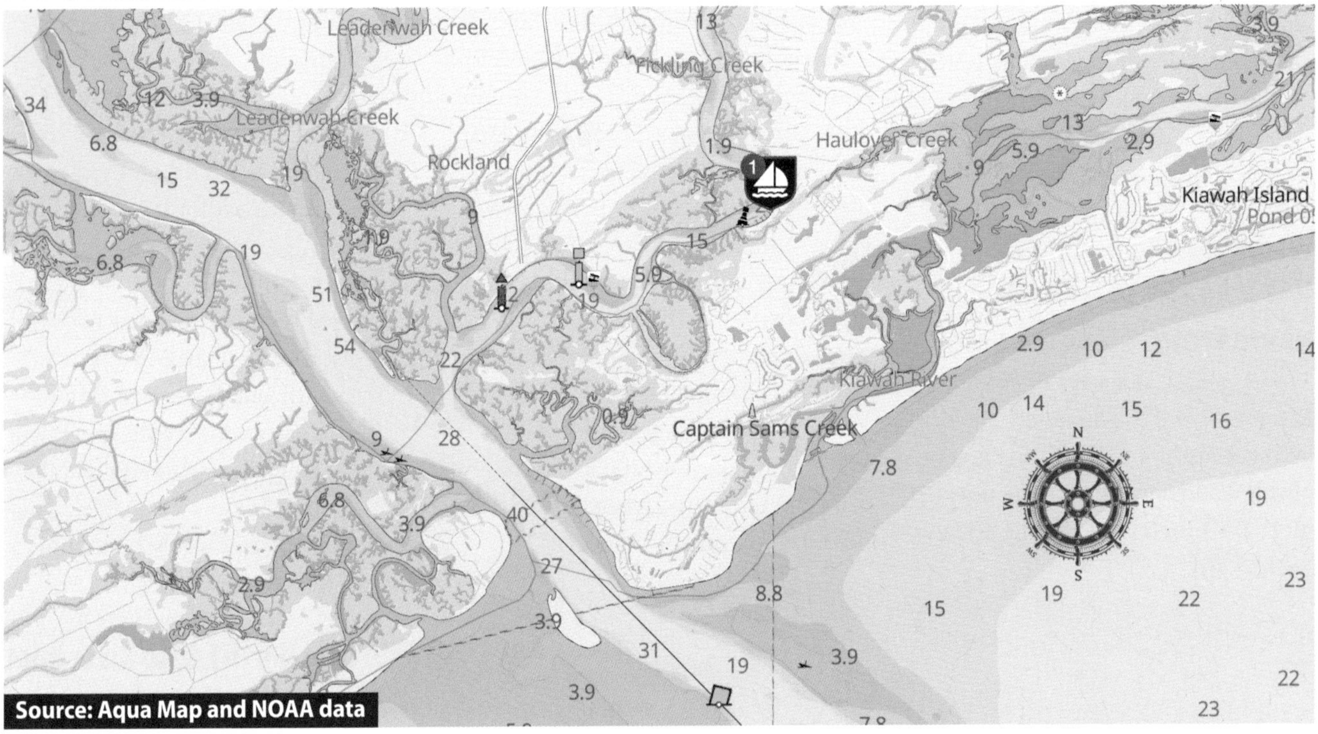

Source: Aqua Map and NOAA data

Dockage: Bohicket Marina & Market lies just north of the village of Rockville on Bohicket Creek off the North Edisto River. Maximum ebb and flood currents call for both advance planning and dockside help to assure a smooth docking and departure. The marina has dockage to 50 feet. Shopping and restaurants are available at the on-site Market. Adams Creek, located off the north side near the mouth of Bohicket Creek, is the home of Marine Propulsion Inc., which offers yacht repairs and marine supplies but no transient dockage.

Anchorage: At Mile 495 leave the ICW and turn to starboard to enter Toogoodoo Creek. Use great caution when entering Toogoodoo Creek as there are large areas of mud banks on both sides at its entrance. You will find good holding in 10- to 15-foot MLW depths in packed mud. You will also be subjected to some wakes from passing fisherman but that settles down in the early evening.

If you continue on the ICW for another 0.50 mile, you will find Tom Point Creek with 8 to 20 feet MLW and good holding. Note that there is an uncharted shoal on the outside bend with less than 3 feet MLW. Stay in the center of the channel.

Steamboat Creek, to the south on the west side of the North Edisto River, has an excellent anchorage in 17-plus feet MLW with a clay bottom but you might encounter some snags on the bottom. There is limited protection from the wind until you are well into the creek. There is also a boat ramp in this creek that has a small dock where you can land dinghies to exercise your pets.

Dawho River to South Edisto River– ICW Mile 497 to Mile 504

NAVIGATION: Use NOAA Chart 11521. The ICW briefly follows the North Edisto River where it intersects the Wadmalaw River at flashing red "108." Stay in the center of the river, slightly favoring the southern bank. Note that green daybeacon "109" is not shown on some charts. Enter the ICW channel at the Dawho River at flashing

Edisto River, SC

ADAMS CREEK		Largest Vessel	VHF	Total Slips	Approach/ Dockside Depth	Floating Docks	Gas/ Diesel	Repairs/ Haulout	Min/Max Amps	Pump-Out Station
1. Marine Propulsion Inc. WiFi MM 495.0	(843) 559-1025	100	16	17	8.0 / 16.0	F		RH	30 / 50	

WiFi Wireless Internet Access onSpot Dockside WiFi Facility
Visit www.waterwayguide.com for current rates, fuel prices, website addresses and other up-to-the-minute information.
(Information in the table is provided by the facilities.)

Scan here for more details:

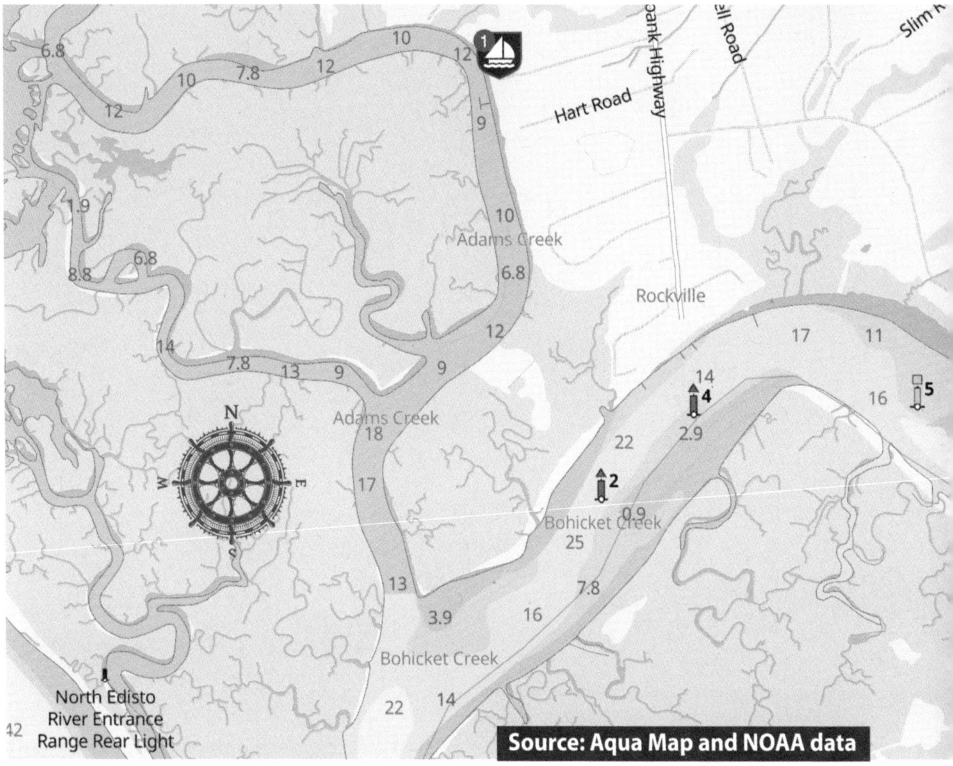

Source: Aqua Map and NOAA data

red buoy "110" at White Point (Mile 496.7). (Green "109" is not shown on some charts.) Remember that at low tide floating aids in areas of extreme tidal range will pull in the direction of the current, away from their anchored position.

There are two routes through Dawho River. The northern route is the officially designated ICW channel route. It is at least 150 feet wide and carries 9.9 feet MLW. A southern route carries 9.3 feet MLW but is only 90 feet wide. The recommended route is the northern route since it is straight and at least twice as wide as the southern route. Also, the southern route has many turns that are not marked with buoys, which makes it difficult to follow with current and wind. If you stray outside the narrow (90-foot wide) channel, you can expect to see 3 feet MLW immediately.

The ICW enters a land cut at Mile 501.3 just before the **McKinley Washington Jr. (SR 174) Bridge** with a published fixed vertical clearance of 65 feet but closer to 63- to 64-foot according to the tide boards. A portion of the old swing bridge is used as a fishing pier.

South of the McKinley Washington Jr. (SR 174) Bridge there is shoaling to 5 feet MLW on the red side. Favor the green side of the channel for 9 feet MLW.

Beyond the bridge the ICW passes through narrow North Creek and Watts Cut before emptying into the broad and swiftly flowing South Edisto River.

Watts Cut was dredged in 2019 but has already started to shoal to 6.2 feet MLW. The best track does not follow the visual center of the channel but moves from side to side for the deepest water. See details at Waterway Explorer (www.waterwayguide.com). Proceed with care.

Anchorage: At Mile 501 you will notice a pair of sloughs coming into the Dawho River from the north. These little slivers of water actually connect behind marshland to form an oxbow. Do not be tempted to try to anchor in either slough as shoals become bare at low tide.

Just south of the McKinley Washington Jr. (SR 174) Bridge, it is possible to anchor in the approach to Fishing Creek. Be aware that the charted depth at its entrance is 4 feet MLW and that there are charted submerged piles outside the ICW channel here. If you decide to enter Fishing Creek, favor the red daybeacon "132" side when entering. You will find at least 9-foot MLW depths inside and good holding, despite some current. There is

Edisto River, SC

EDISTO ISLAND		Largest Vessel	VHF	Total Slips	Approach/ Dockside Depth	Floating Docks	Gas/ Diesel	Repairs/ Haulout	Min/Max Amps	Pump-Out Station
1. The Marina at Edisto Beach WiFi 4.5 mi. S of MM 511.0	(843) 631-5055	55	16	72	17.0 / 12.0	F	GD		30 / 50	

WiFi Wireless Internet Access **onSpot** Dockside WiFi Facility
Visit www.waterwayguide.com for current rates, fuel prices, website addresses and other up-to-the-minute information.
(Information in the table is provided by the facilities.)

Scan here for more details:

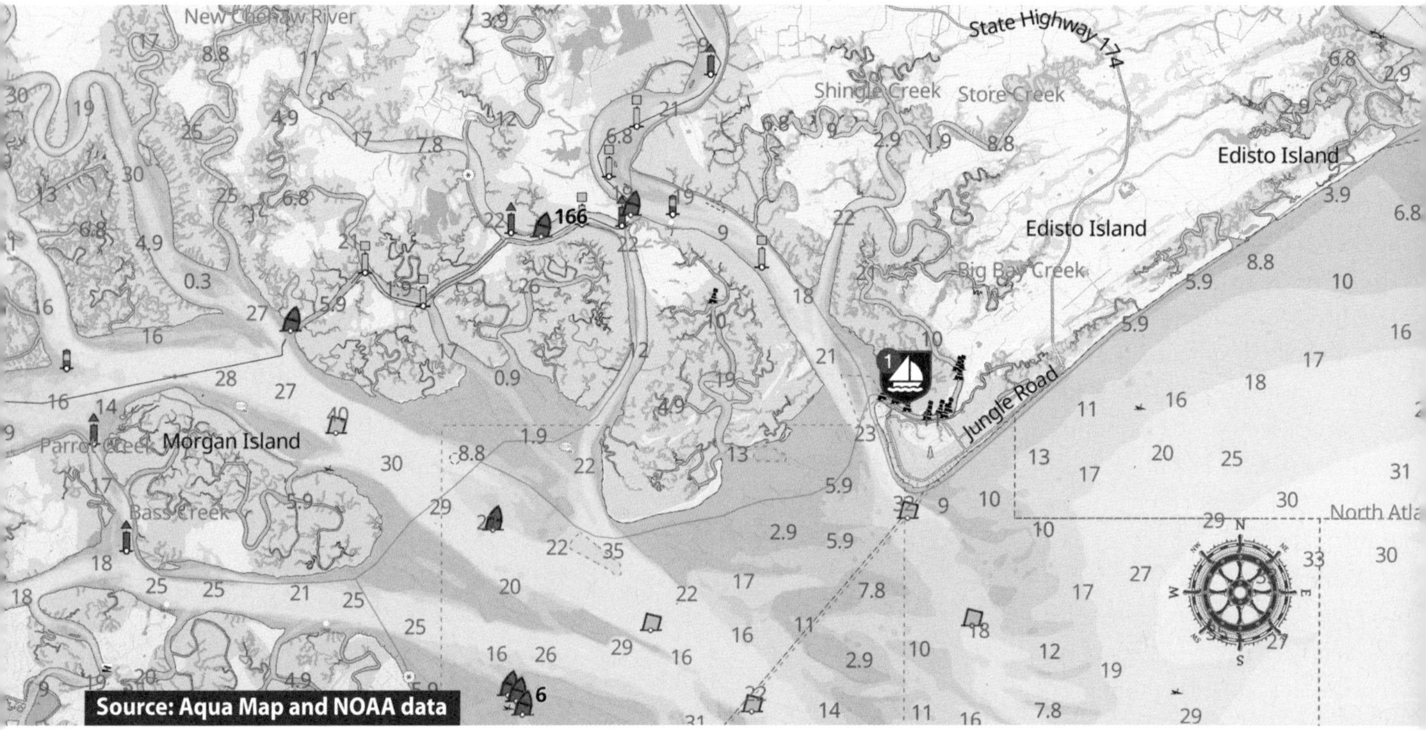

Source: Aqua Map and NOAA data

some highway noise and it can be buggy; nevertheless, this is one of the best anchorages along this section of the ICW. As in all anchorages be sure to use your anchor light at night.

South Edisto River to Ashepoo River–ICW Mile 504 to Mile 511

The main destination along the South Edisto River is Edisto Island overlooking the Atlantic Ocean. Edisto Island is home of the community of Edisto Beach and offers deep-sea fishing opportunities. The town has beautiful, well-preserved Colonial homes, a popular residential resort with golf course, an oceanfront state park and good stores and boutiques. You will find a slower pace that harks back to the 1950s; there are no high-rise motels or typical carnival-type boardwalk activities here.

NAVIGATION: Use NOAA Charts 11521. The South Edisto River is easy to follow. Remember, however, that you are in a strong tidal zone so do not cut too close to the markers or the bends in the channels. At Mile 510 Range "C" marks the ICW course along the South Edisto River between Watts Cut and Fenwick Cut. These ranges keep boaters off the river's wide shoals and projecting points. Note that green daybeacon "161B," shown on some older charts, no longer exists.

At Mile 511 the ICW heads southwest along the Ashepoo River, while the South Edisto River meanders in a southeasterly direction toward the Atlantic Ocean. Despite recent dredging, shoals continually build at both the north and south entrances to Fenwick Cut and along its entire length.

Dockage: The Marina at Edisto Beach is located behind Edisto Island on Big Bay Creek, 4.5 miles south from the ICW. This sportfishing-oriented facility has transient slips. Nature and fishing charters leave from here daily. Be sure to call the marina well in advance for slip availability.

Anchorage: The South Edisto River provides a good fair-weather anchorage at Mile 504.2 (Sampson Island). When southbound out of Watts Cut, bear off to starboard into the South Edisto River. Anchor in the middle about 1 mile from Watts Cut where the chart shows 10- and 11-foot MLW depths with a soft, mud bottom. This is a wide open, relatively quiet spot with good holding, although we advise against anchoring here in any strong wind. There is considerable current (1 to 2 knots) just as with all the rivers in this area of the ICW, and conditions can become uncomfortable with opposing wind and current. Continuing around the next bend is an option. This is a good spot to wait if you are going north and want to time the tide through Dawho River.

Just past the lower end of Alligator Creek at Mile 509.4 and opposite green daybeacon "157" is an anchorage for settled weather with good protection from the northwest. Be cautious when entering this creek as it has been reported to have a shallow entrance. Once you are in sound your way toward the shore to avoid trap markers and anchor in 8 to 11 feet MLW, well off the channel. The current may reach 1.5 knots so vessels may lay to the current rather than the wind.

There is an anchorage up the St. Pierre Creek south of the ICW (east side) with good holding in mud and 9- to 17-foot MLW depths.

Ashepoo River & Ashepoo Coosaw Cutoff–ICW Mile 511 to Mile 518

The ICW route continues to the southwest leading from the South Edisto River through Fenwick Cut and into a short section of the Ashepoo River.

NAVIGATION: Use NOAA Chart 11518. Once you have transited the Ashepoo River the ICW enters the first part of the Ashepoo Coosaw Cutoff. The Ashepoo Coosaw Cutoff soon jags in a northwesterly direction entering Rock Creek at Mile 515 before it continues as a narrow land cut toward the wide Coosaw River.

> Shoaling has been observed in both Fenwick Cut at Mile 511 (to 7.8 feet MLW and the southern part of the Ashepoo Coosaw Cutoff at Mile 516.5 (to 5.6 feet MLW). The best path is no longer the visual center of the dredged channel. See suggested track on Waterway Explorer (www.waterwayguide.com). Proceed with care.

Given the proximity of Port Royal Sound, Charleston and North Edisto Inlets, St. Helena Inlet should be skipped.

Dockage: B & B Seafood House Marina is 1.8 miles off the Ashepoo River on Mosquito Creek. This is a seafood wholesale/retail outlet that can accommodate two vessels up to 50 feet but it is not a traditional marina. Power is available (30 amp) but you'll need a long cord to reach it. There are restrooms but no showers. The

Ashepoo River, SC

MOSQUITO CREEK		Largest Vessel	VHF	Total Slips	Approach/ Dockside Depth	Floating Docks	Gas/ Diesel	Repairs/ Haulout	Min/Max Amps	Pump-Out Station
1. B & B Seafood House Marina 1.8 mi. N of MM 513.5	(843) 844-2322	50	68	2	10.0 / 10.0	F	GD			

Wireless Internet Access   onSpot Dockside WiFi Facility
Visit www.waterwayguide.com for current rates, fuel prices, website addresses and other up-to-the-minute information.
(Information in the table is provided by the facilities.)

Scan here for more details:

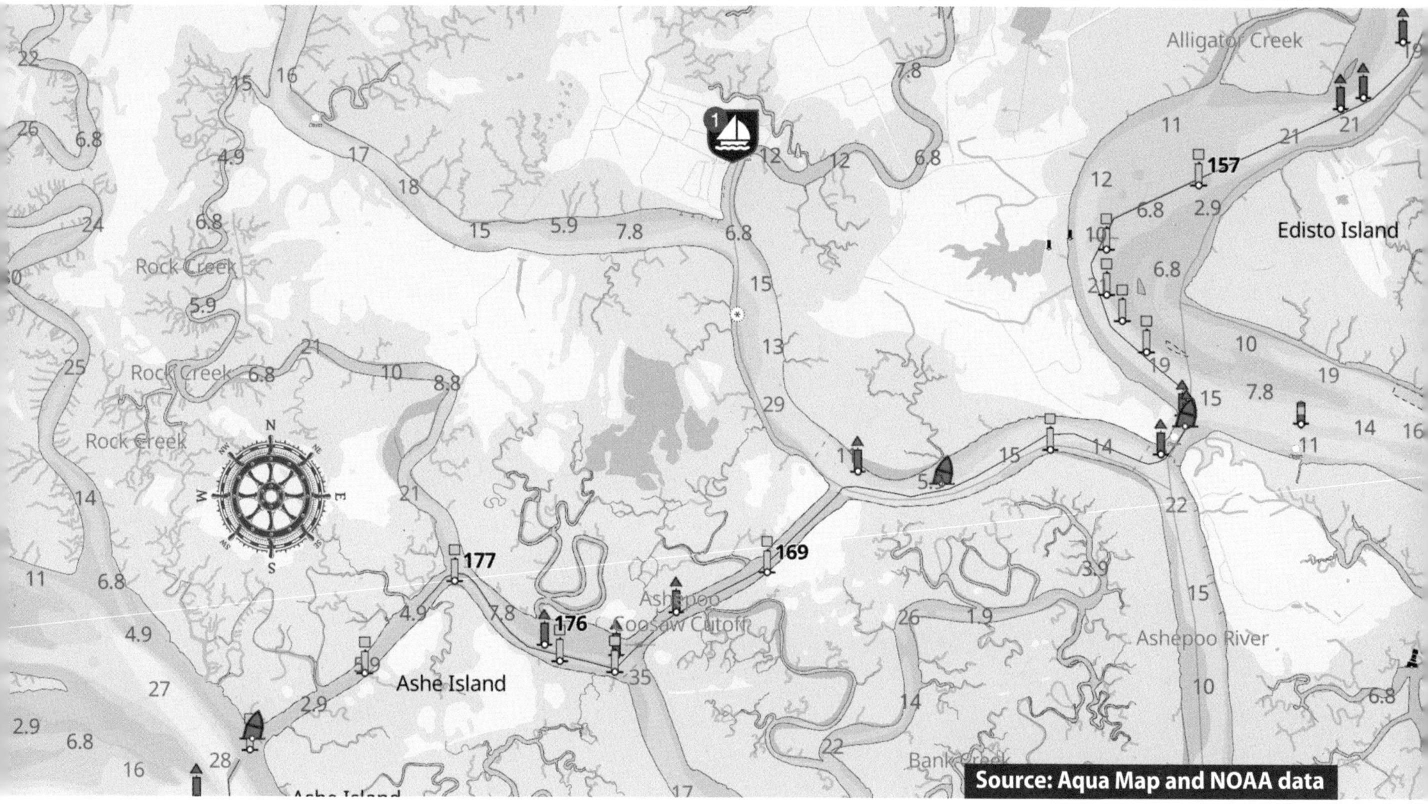

oysters and shrimp are fresh off the boat (in season) and very economical.

Anchorage: Just past B & B Seafood House Marina is an anchorage on Mosquito Creek with at least 7 feet MLW with a mud bottom.

Most anchorages along the Ashepoo River are open but pleasant with good holding. There are two anchoring possibilities at Fenwick Island. The one north of the cut on the ICW is at Mile 511.6 and is fairly open with a strong current, making anchoring challenging. At Fenwick Island south of the ICW, there is an anchorage with at least 11 feet MLW.

The headwaters of Rock Creek at Mile 516 provide a narrow but well-protected anchorage with minimum 8-foot MLW depths to the second bend. Use the depth sounder to avoid the shoals on the inside of the turns in the creek; however, deep-drafted boats swinging on the current have also frequently grounded in this anchorage.

Coosaw River–ICW Mile 518 to Mile 529

While the Coosaw River is wide and unobstructed, it is always best to keep to the channel and run at least a rough compass course to help you spot the markers, which are spaced fairly far apart.

NAVIGATION: Use NOAA Chart 11518. The Bull River at Mile 521.5 and the Combahee River at Mile 518.5 flow off the north side of the Coosaw River. Approximately 2 miles south of red daybeacon "186" Parrot Creek leads south off the Coosaw River to a marina at Morgan River and an anchorage at Lucy Point Creek. Depths exceed 10-foot MLW depths for the entire approach to Parrot Creek from the ICW.

Dockage: Dataw Island Marina is 3 miles south of ICW Mile 521 by following Parrot Creek and rounding the south side of Coosaw Island on the Morgan River. The marina is located inside a gated golf and tennis

Coosaw River, SC

DATAW ISLAND		Largest Vessel	VHF	Total Slips	Approach/ Dockside Depth	Floating Docks	Gas/ Diesel	Repairs/ Haulout	Min/Max Amps	Pump-Out Station
1. Dataw Island Marina 3.0 mi. S of MM 521.0	(843) 838-8410	50	16	22	15.0 / 8.0	F	GD	RH	30 / 50	

WiFi Wireless Internet Access onSpot Dockside WiFi Facility
Visit www.waterwayguide.com for current rates, fuel prices, website addresses and other up-to-the-minute information.
(Information in the table is provided by the facilities.)

Scan here for more details:

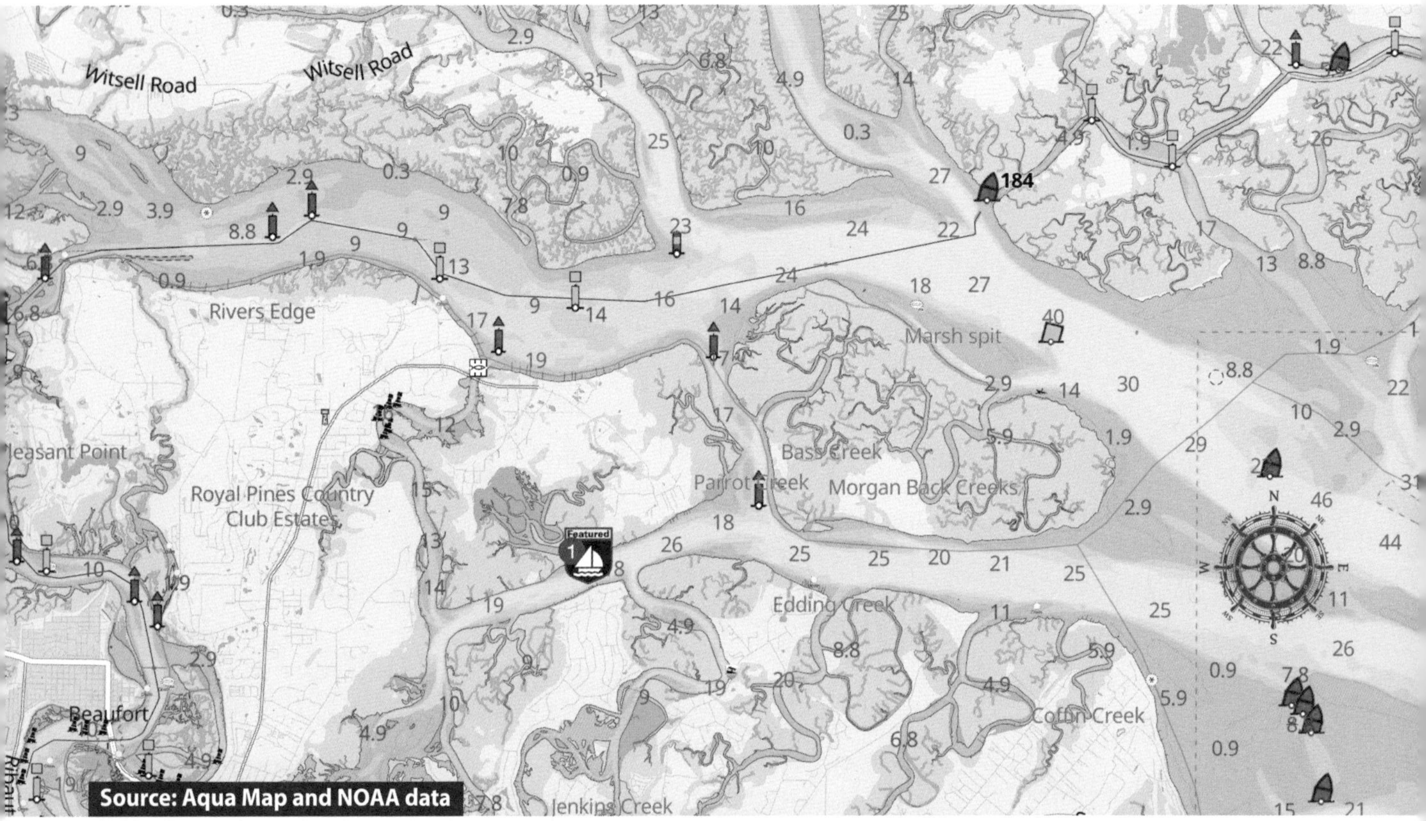

Source: Aqua Map and NOAA data

Dataw Area

community also featuring pickleball, croquet and bocce (available to transient boaters with advance coordination). This marina offers wet slips, transient dockage, dock and dine and dry stack storage. On site you'll find the full-service Marine Tech boat yard (www.marinetechhhi.com) with maintenance and repair services. Morgan River Grill (www.morganrivergrill.com) is a local favorite for fun fare in a casual atmosphere for lunch and dinner, as is the Outpost for snacks and sundries.

Anchorage: Many spots in this area are suitable for anchoring. At Mile 521.5 you can anchor inside Wimbee Creek off the Bull River just north of the ICW. Watch for the shoal below Summerhouse Point and leave the island to starboard. Holding is good here in 11 to 18 feet MLW, although the bottom also is hard with shells in some areas.

South of the ICW (Mile 521.5) there are anchoring possibilities east and south of Coosaw Island accessed by Parrot Creek. Bass Creek has 13 to 16 feet MLW and wave (but not wind) protection. Continuing south you can anchor past Dataw Island Marina at Lucy Point Creek. Even though there is an entrance to Lucy Point Creek directly off the ICW, the fixed 14-foot vertical clearance SC 802 Bridge at the mouth necessitates the "back door" approach.

Brickyard Creek to Beaufort–ICW Mile 529 to Mile 536

The ICW leaves the Coosaw River at Mile 529, where you will find a well-marked entrance range heading into Brickyard Creek. Military aircraft might buzz you you travel south on Brickyard Creek. While the noise from the military aircraft in this area can disrupt a peaceful anchoring experience, the U.S. Marine Corps Air Station here–along with the nearby famous Parris Island Recruit Depot–is a major contributor to the local economy.

Beaufort Area, SC

LADYS ISLAND		Largest Vessel	VHF	Total Slips	Approach/ Dockside Depth	Floating Docks	Gas/ Diesel	Repairs/ Haulout	Min/Max Amps	Pump-Out Station
1. Marsh Harbor Boat Works (WiFi) MM 534.4	(843) 521-1500	70	16	16	6.0 / 6.0	F		RH	30 / 50	
2. Lady's Island Marina (WiFi) 0.8 mi. S of MM 536.0	(843) 522-0430	210	16	75	7.0 / 14.0	F			30 / 50	P
BEAUFORT										
3. Safe Harbor Beaufort (WiFi) MM 536.2	(843) 524-4422	150	16	100	20.0 / 15.0	F	GD		30 / 50	P

(WiFi) Wireless Internet Access onSpot Dockside WiFi Facility

Visit www.waterwayguide.com for current rates, fuel prices, website addresses and other up-to-the-minute information.

(Information in the table is provided by the facilities.)

Scan here for more details:

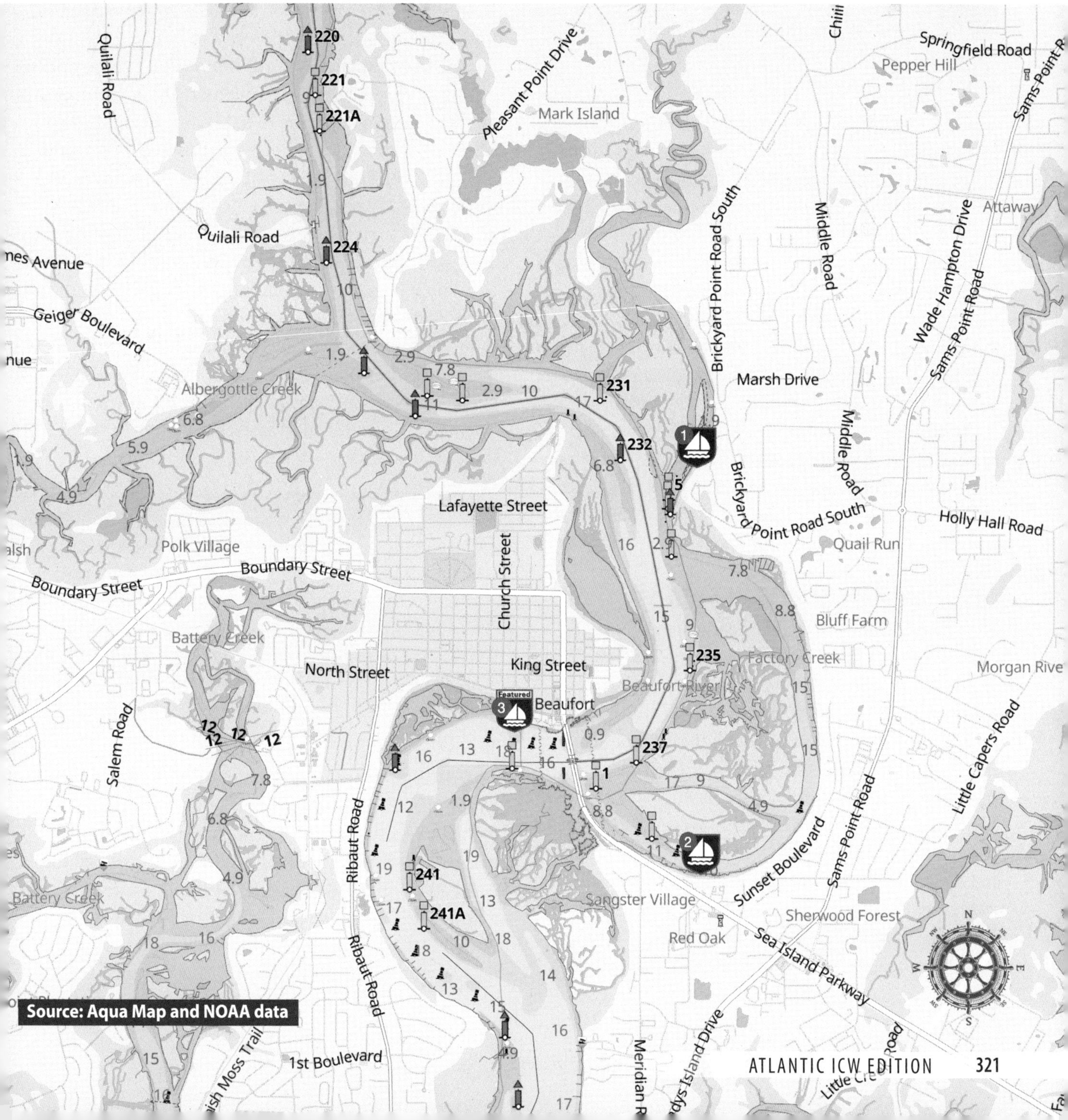

NAVIGATION: Use NOAA Chart 11518. Stay to mid-channel where the ICW begins its 4-mile run along Brickyard Creek (the headwaters of the Beaufort River). There are flats along both sides of the channel, particularly where the Coosaw River enters Brickyard Creek.

Between green daybeacon "209" at Brickyard Point and flashing red "210," travel outside the channel on the green side by 50 feet for 10 feet MLW. Pass flashing red "210" by 100 feet off to avoid a 1-foot MLW shoal.

Slow boats should note that the current between Brickyard Creek and Beaufort changes at about flashing red daybeacon "224" (Mile 532). If you catch the end of the flood or the slack, you can usually ride the current to Beaufort.

Dockage: At Mile 533 just north of green daybeacon "233" a marked channel leads into the well-regarded Marsh Harbor Boat Works on Ladys Island. Marsh Harbor is a small but efficient boat yard specializing in repair and painting. They generally do not take transients but make be able to make room for you in a pinch. Call ahead.

Anchorage: Brickyard Creek at Mile 530.4 has 5 to 9 feet MLW with a mud bottom and all-around protection. The deep-water channel is very narrow and residential docks extend far out from the shore so we recommend exercising caution when anchoring here.

City of Beaufort, SC–ICW Mile 536

The City of Beaufort appears to starboard at about the point where Brickyard Creek becomes the Beaufort River. Beaufort's attractions include an entire downtown on the National Register of Historic Places, a multi-purpose park along the waterfront, an amphitheater, markets and a bandstand, all within sight of bed and breakfasts, attractive shops and meticulously restored historic houses. The homes in Beaufort are typically West Indies-style in a T-shaped floor plan with a raised first floor, high ceilings and double porches. Over time Beaufort has spread gently southward along the western bank of the river toward Port Royal. See more on Beaufort at "Goin' Ashore: Beaufort, SC" in this chapter.

Beaufort is pronounced "Bew'-fort" not "Boe'-fort" as when referring to Beaufort, NC. If you are new to cruising the ICW in the Carolinas, do take an extra moment to get the pronunciation of the two straight or you can just wait to be corrected by the locals.

NAVIGATION: Use NOAA Chart 11518. Heading south along the ICW Brickyard Creek reaches Beaufort and the Lady's Island (Woods Memorial) Bridge at Mile 536 (closed vertical clearance of 30 feet). While there is ample maneuvering room both above and below the bridge, the strong side-current is tricky; adequate power and careful boat handling are required.

The **Lady's Island (Woods Memorial) Bridge** opens on signal, except Monday through Friday, from 6:30 a.m. to 9:00 a.m. and 3:00 p.m. to 6:00 p.m., when the draw need not open to navigation. Also, between 9:00 a.m. to 3:00 p.m., the draw need open only on the hour. During the months of April, May, October and November from Monday through Friday (except federal holidays), the draw will open on signal except from 7:00 a.m. to 9:00 a.m. and 4:00 p.m. to 6 p.m., when the draw need not open to navigation. Between 9:00 a.m. to 4:00 p.m., the draw need open only on the hour and half-hour. The Lady's Island (Woods Memorial) Bridge is slow and cumbersome to open and is frequently under repair. There may be lengthy delays so check ahead to see if there are any issues.

NO WAKE ZONE

A strictly enforced No-Wake Zone extends nearly all the way from the Lady's Island (Woods Memorial) Bridge to the fixed **McTeer Memorial Twin Bridges** (65-foot fixed vertical clearance) over the Beaufort River at Port Royal (Mile 539.7). Signs on both bridges warn that violators of the No-Wake Zone will pay a fine of $1,025 or spend 30 days in a South Carolina jail cell.

Dockage/Moorings: To port (south) just above Lady's Island (Woods Memorial) Bridge is Factory Creek with ample water depth and Lady's Island Marina. The marina has transient space at floating docks with all the usual amenities plus an on-site yoga studio, canvas shop, massage therapist and restaurant, Lady's Island Dockside (843-379-3288). Historic downtown Beaufort is one mile away, a scenic 15-minute walk (or take a courtesy

Discover life with
the Lowcountry tides.
From convenient marinas and stunning natural beauty to authentic culture and cuisine, refuel in more ways than one in historic Beaufort, SC. Experience the transformative beauty of a place that has turned countless overnight anchorages into week-long retreats—and lifelong cruisers into locals.
inner coastal
VISIT
BEAUFORT
PORT ROYAL SEA ISLANDS

GOIN' ASHORE

BEAUFORT, SC

Beaufort is a thriving city surrounded by rivers and waterways with cool breezes and lush gardens under oak tree canopies that enchant the most seasoned visitor. It is a gracious place that is true to its Southern heritage. Lazy summer days are spent casting a shrimp net, walking on an undeveloped island beach or kayaking down the river. People come for the Lowcountry seafood, tomato stands and the Sea Islands.

SERVICES

1. **Beaufort Post Office**
   501 Charles St. (843-525-9085)

2. **Downtown Beaufort Library**
   311 Scott St. (843-255-6456)

3. **Veterinary Wellness Care**
   1609 North St. (843-524-5972)

4. **Visitor Information/Beaufort History Museum**
   The Beaufort Visitor Center is housed in the Arsenal at 713 Craven St. (843-525-8500), which was built in 1798 to house the Beaufort Volunteer Artillery after it fought with the Continental Army during the Revolutionary War. The Beaufort History Museum is here as well, featuring exhibits on the town's history and culture. Open daily except Sunday from 10:00 a.m. to 4:00 p.m.

SERVICES

5. **Harry C. Chambers Waterfront Park**
   Riverfront park with landscaped green space, a playground and a performance stage. If all that is just too exhausting, grab one of the 20 bench swings and enjoy the water views, people watch or read a good book.

6. **John Mark Verdier House Museum**
   The Federal-style mansion was built around 1790 and was the headquarters for the Union forces in the area during the Civil War. It also hosted the aged Marquis de Lafayette upon his return to the country after the Revolutionary War. It currently houses a museum and is open for tours at 801 Bay St. (843-379-6335).

7. **Santa Elena History Center**
   Learn the story of Santa Elena, which was settled in 1566 on Parris Island. Their history encompasses religion, geopolitics, cultural clashes, war and struggles to survive. The area even served as the Spanish capital of Florida from 1569 to 1587.

You may have noticed that the Lady's Island Swing Bridge is referred to on some charts as "Ladies Island." To further complicate matters, the official bridge name has nothing to do with ladies or lady's; it's the Richard V. Woods Memorial Bridge.

8. St. Helena's Episcopal Church
Erected in 1724, the church at 507 Newcastle St. (843-522-1712) is surrounded by a wall built of bricks arriving from England as ship ballast. The church has an ancient graveyard where tombstones served as operating tables for wounded soldiers during the Civil War.

SHOPPING

9. Lowcountry Produce Market and Café
This cafe and market offers small plates and quick bites plus "grab & go" provisions at 302 Carteret St. (843-322-1900). This is just a few blocks from the marina and is popular with the boating crowd.

10. McIntosh Book Shoppe
This is one of those rambling book stores where you can easily get lost (mentally and physically) in the stacks. Located at 917 Bay St. (843-524-1119).

MARINA

11. Safe Harbor Beaufort
1006 Bay St. (843-524-4422)

Port Royal Area, SC

PORT ROYAL	Largest Vessel	VHF	Total Slips	Approach/ Dockside Depth	Floating Docks	Gas/ Diesel	Repairs/ Haulout	Min/Max Amps	Pump-Out Station
1. Safe Harbor Port Royal (WiFi) MM 539.0 (843) 525-6664	120	16	140	20.0 / 15.0	F	GD		30 / 50	P

(WiFi) Wireless Internet Access onSpot Dockside WiFi Facility
Visit www.waterwayguide.com for current rates, fuel prices, website addresses and other up-to-the-minute information.
(Information in the table is provided by the facilities.)

Scan here for more details:

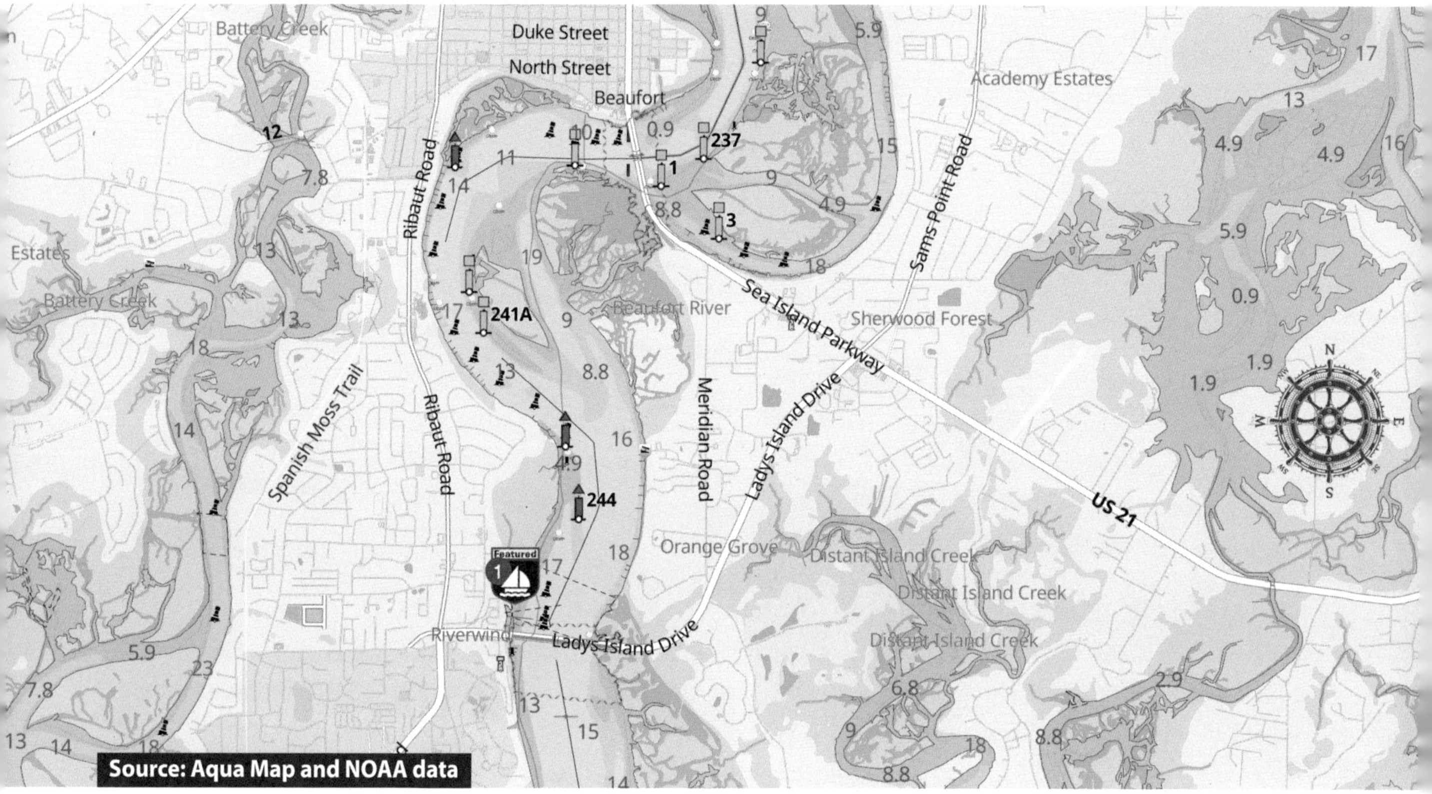

Source: Aqua Map and NOAA data

bike from the marina) across the Lady's Island (Woods Memorial) Bridge.

The Beaufort River and ICW lead to Safe Harbor Beaufort, which overlooks the Henry C. Chambers Waterfront Park. Restaurants, inns and charming shops open to the waterfront and the historic business district. The marina offers ample dockage and some marine services. Currents are very strong here with 7- to 9-foot tides so use considerable caution in docking. Call ahead to the marina for dockage availability and assistance. Floating docks on the T-head accommodate transient cruisers; even so, set ample fenders on approach. A large portion of the anchorage area has been converted to a mooring field that is managed by Safe Harbor Beaufor. There are 30 moorings. The fee includes the use of showers and the dinghy dock.

Smaller boats may tie up along the seawall at the Waterfront Park, which is also managed by Safe Harbor Beaufort. These docks are only useful for short tie-ups during periods of high or slack tide due to the strong currents, large tidal range (7 feet) and plethora of oyster shells on the seawall. Dock dinghies on the inside of this dock. The Beaufort Day Dock (a 140-foot-long floating dock south of the marina) is owned by the city, which does not allow overnight docking. Depths at the courtesy dock are 8 feet at the west end and 5 feet at the east end.

Three miles south of downtown Beaufort immediately north of the McTeer Memorial Twin Bridges is Safe Harbor Port Royal with full amenities, an easy-access floating face dock with gas and diesel fuel, a fully stocked Ship Store and a courtesy car. It is less than one-mile drive to a supermarket, liquor store, drug store, ATM and West Marine. Be sure to phone ahead for reservations or hail the marina on VHF Channel 16 before you approach to check for dockage availability and directions to a berth on its floating docks.

Anchorage: A protected anchorage is available in Factory Creek, which opens just north of and parallel to the Lady's Island (Woods Memorial) Bridge (at Mile 536). This anchorage is somewhat narrow for larger vessels. Enter as if heading to the Lady's Island Marina, favoring the red side of the channel as there is only 6 feet MLW near green daybeacon "1." Then anchor in a minimum of 7-foot MLW depths past the marina. Anchored boats can pay a fee to dock dinghies at Lady's Island Marina or can anchor closer to the public boat ramp before the marina and dinghy ashore there. The current is less intense here than on the ICW and you will not be rolled by nighttime traffic.

It is possible to anchor west of Safe Harbor Beaufort if you keep well clear of ICW traffic and anticipate the effects of strong southerlies, substantial tidal-current swings and lots of boat traffic. The 30 moorings here are closely spaced (with more to come) making it difficult to anchor. It is best to anchor near the turn in the river. The depths are generally 10 to 20 feet MLW with a mud bottom with good holding. The staff at Safe Harbor Beaufort asks that vessels anchor at least 200 feet away from their facility. This is part of a city ordinance of which even some locals are not aware. And, as always, use a light when anchored. You can dock your dinghy behind Beaufort Day Dock next to Safe Harbor Beaufort.

You can drop the hook at Mile 538.6 in the eastern fork of the Beaufort River just before the McTeer Memorial Twin Bridges. Enter from the south near flashing red "242" (at Mile 538.6) off Spanish Point. Proceed east and then turn north between the marsh island to the west and the marshes to the east. Set your hook in 15 to 20 feet MLW over a sandy bottom. Do not try to re-enter the Beaufort River proper (to the north) due to severe shoaling.

TO HILTON HEAD ISLAND, SC

Port Royal to Hilton Head Island–ICW Mile 542 to Mile 553

The Beaufort River runs broad and deep and its well-marked main channel is easy to follow past Port Royal, Parris Island (the Marine Corps Recruit Depot) to the Port Royal Sound Entrance. There is plenty of commercial fishing traffic in the channel and much to see ashore as the river arcs along between Parris Island and St. Helena Island.

NAVIGATION: Use NOAA Charts 11507, 11516 and 11518. Battery Creek joins the Beaufort River from the west. On Battery Creek's north shore is Port Royal, the deepwater commercial shipping center for the Beaufort area. If headed up Battery Creek, keep red daybeacon "42" to starboard and follow the channel to Port Royal. Farther upstream is the fixed **U.S. 21 Bridge** (45-foot vertical clearance). The creek carries 12-foot MLW depths or more for 4 miles upstream and is charted (NOAA Chart 11516) but no markers are present.

If northbound on the ICW, be sure to make the turn to the north on the Beaufort River between red nun "40" and quick flashing green "41," beyond which you will pick up the ICW markers again, rather than continuing straight westerly into Battery Creek and Port Royal. Both routes have bridges visible ahead and this mistake has been known to dismast sailboats.

At the junction of Battery Creek and the Beaufort River the familiar ICW marker system reverses: Keep red to port for the next 6.5 miles.

The ICW returns near Parris Island Spit as you make the turn to cross Port Royal Sound towards Hilton Head Island. Stay clear of the Spit and the shoaling in that area. To do so, when leaving the Beaufort River channel for the 5-mile crossing of port Royal Sound lay a course from ICW flashing red daybeacon "246" off Parris Island Spit to red nun buoy "2" and then to flashing green daybeacon "3" just past Dolphin Head. It can be bumpy if wind and tide oppose. At Mile 553 you enter Skull Creek between Hilton Head Island and Pinckney Island (a wildlife refuge).

Anchorage: There is an anchorage at Port Royal on Battery Creek with 8 to 20 feet MLW and a sand bottom. It is protected from all directions except southeast. There have been reports of debris on the bottom so make sure your anchor is well set.

If you really want to get off the beaten path, explore the upper reaches of Cowen Creek off the ICW at Mile 544.5. You will find deep water throughout the creek. On Distant Island Creek tuck into the deep water slot behind the unnamed island between Distant Island and the marsh for complete solitude in at least 12 feet MLW.

Port Royal Sound Entrance–ICW Mile 550

NAVIGATION: Use NOAA Chart 11518. Port Royal Sound Entrance is a big ship inlet and is wide, deep and very long. If you are headed south offshore, this is not the best option as a point of entry as you will backtrack some distance to re-enter the ocean. However, it is a great exit to use to make an overnight run south to St. Marys. When a cold front passes through the area expect breaking ocean swells throughout the channel until rounding Bay Point. Under these conditions the going will be tedious but still negotiable for well-found vessels. More difficult is the combination of a stiff onshore breeze against an ebb tide (driven here by local tides of 9 feet); this is a situation best avoided.

Hilton Head Island–ICW Mile 553 to Mile 565

A bustling but beautiful year-round resort, Hilton Head Island, is probably the best known of South Carolina's Sea Islands. As one of the largest barrier islands on the Atlantic Coast, it is amply endowed by nature and history and offers something nearly year-round for everyone including a choice of excellent marina resorts. The ICW amenities offered on Hilton Head range from the ultra-luxurious to comfortable casual. Read more in "Goin' Ashore: Hilton Head, SC" in this chapter.

NO WAKE ZONE

As you progress through Skull Creek you will notice many commercial and private docks along the way. Note the No-Wake Zones around Hilton Head Island; proceed at slow speed in these areas, especially in Broad Creek and Skull Creek. Local marine patrols are frequently in this area and will stop boaters throwing a wake into the marinas.

The numerous ferry boats plying the waters of Calibogue Sound between Hilton Head and Daufuskie

Island can leave large wakes. The ferries usually slow down to "no-wake speed" when passing recreational boats. **Wilton J. Graves (US 278) Twin Highway Bridges** (65-foot fixed vertical clearance) at Mile 557.6 provide the only automobile access to and from Hilton Head Island.

Just opposite the spot where the ICW leaves Calibogue Sound for the Cooper River (Mile 565) is beautiful Broad Creek. To the north handsome houses, many with their own docks, line the creek at Shelter Cove. Oyster beds line the banks, crab pot markers dot the marsh flats and fishing drops are at the entrance to tidal streams along the way.

NAVIGATION: Use NOAA Chart 11507. Markers lead past oyster beds until Mile 555 where the first of Hilton Head Island's several marinas shows to port. (Note that several markers were reported missing at press time in 2021.) At Safe Harbor Skull Creek Marina, slack tide is 2 hours after slack tide at the south end of Skull Creek. Watch for the shoal just in front of the marina to the north.

The proper entrance to Broad Creek and more dockage options is at green daybeacon "1." Give the marker a rather wide berth at low tide and enter between it and red daybeacon "2" on the opposite side. The shoal extends northeast of green daybeacon "1" so use caution. Once you are inside Broad Creek runs deep to its banks all the way to the marinas well upstream. Be aware that ferries to Daufuskie and other destinations use this creek.

The break between Brams Point and Buck Island at green daybeacon "29A" is too tricky for strangers. Do not attempt to use this secondary entrance to Broad Creek without local knowledge.

Dockage: Safe Harbor Skull Creek Marina offers slips on modern concrete floating docks and can accommodate vessels to 200 feet. They also offer repairs. There is a restaurant a short walk from the docks. Other services will require transportation. At Mile 555.6 is The Boathouse Hilton Head, which is a boat storage and brokerage facility. They do not have transient dockage but sells all fuels.

At Mile 557, Hilton Head Harbor Marina has an easily accessed fuel dock right on the ICW. The independently owned marina offers dockage in an enclosed basin and is also a luxury RV resort with resort amenities. They are also pet friendly. Car rentals

Hilton Head Area, SC

SKULL CREEK		Largest Vessel	VHF	Total Slips	Approach/ Dockside Depth	Floating Docks	Gas/ Diesel	Repairs/ Haulout	Min/Max Amps	Pump-Out Station
1. Safe Harbor Skull Creek WiFi MM 555.0	(843) 681-8436	200	16	179	12.0 / 10.0	F	GD		30 / 100	P
2. The Boathouse Hilton Head MM 555.6	(843) 681-2628	35	69		6.0 / 6.0	F	GD	RH		
3. Hilton Head Harbor Marina WiFi MM 557.0	(843) 681-3256	100	16	101	30.0 / 20.0	F	GD		30 / 50	
4. Windmill Harbour Marina WiFi onSpot MM 558.3	(843) 681-9235	70	14	258	5.0 / 8.0		GD	R	30 / 50	P

WiFi Wireless Internet Access onSpot Dockside WiFi Facility
Visit www.waterwayguide.com for current rates, fuel prices, website addresses and other up-to-the-minute information.
(Information in the table is provided by the facilities.)

Scan here for more details:

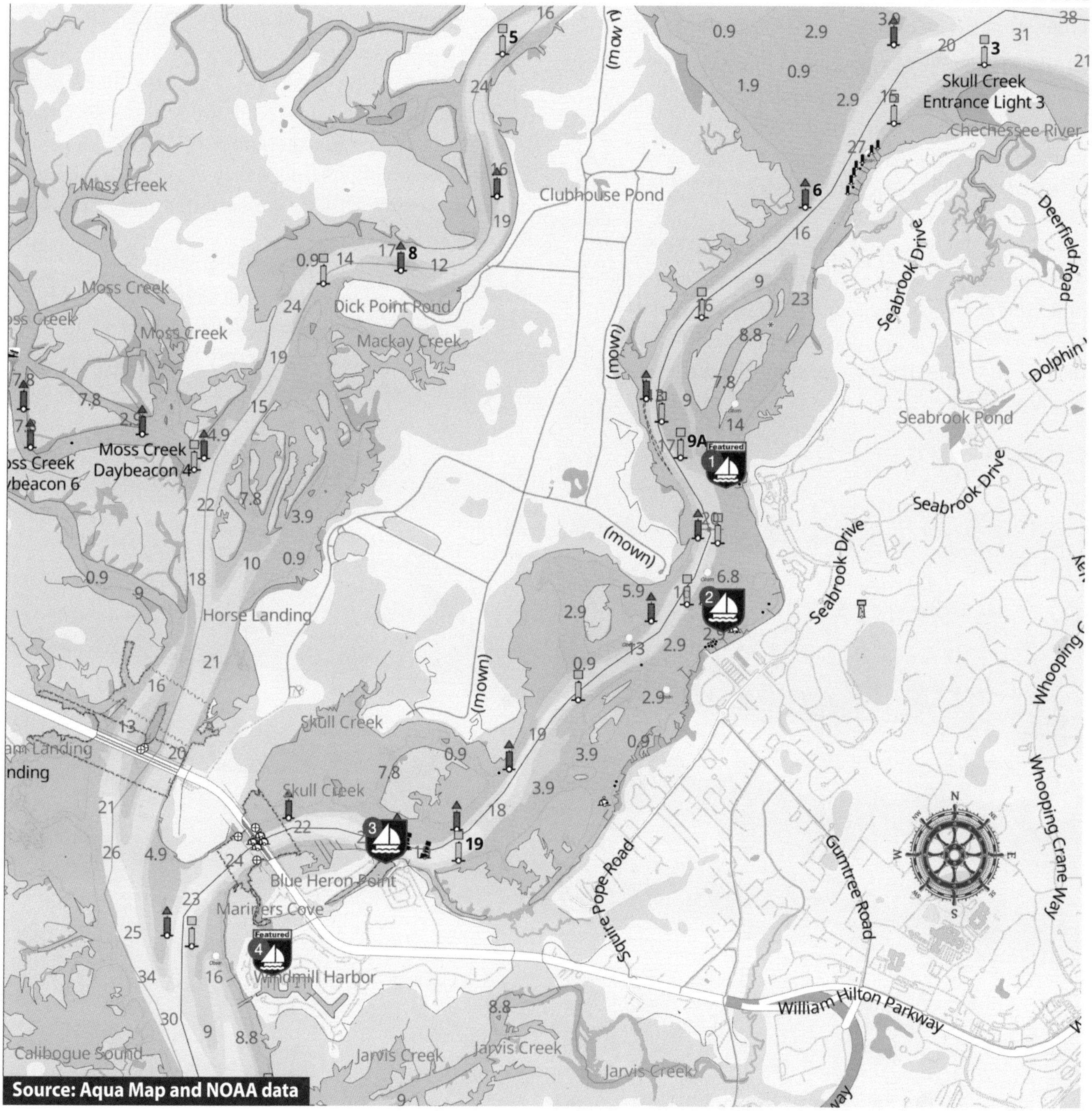

Source: Aqua Map and NOAA data

Safe Harbor Port Royal

GOIN' ASHORE

HILTON HEAD, SC

Most people know Hilton Head Island for its red and white striped lighthouse and fine golf courses, but it is also a great family getaway with long beaches, and walking and bicycling trails through its well-preserved natural areas. Shopping centers, more than 250 restaurants and golf courses have proliferated on the island. There are several large grocery stores for provisioning and shopping areas at Coligny Plaza at Forest Beach, Shelter Cove Harbour at Palmetto Dunes, The Village at Wexford and along William Hilton Parkway (Hwy. 278).

SERVICES

1. Heritage Animal Hospital
130 Arrow Rd. #101 (843-842-8331)

2. Hilton Head Island Visitor & Convention Bureau
1 Chamber of Commerce Dr. (843-785-3673)

2. Hilton Head Post Office
10 Bow Circle (843-785-7002)

4. Sea Pines Circle Immediate Care
2 Greenwood Dr. (843-341-2700)

ATTRACTIONS

5. Aerial Adventure Hilton Head
If you feel adventurous, try the 50 in-the-tree challenges on 6 ability courses at this playground in the sky located next to Broad Creek Marina (33 Broad Creek Marina Way). Or see the world from heights of up to 75 feet in the salty air as eight interconnected ziplines take you from a tree platform to a suspended bridge to an aerial staircase ("don't look down") to a 75-foot tower tour. Harnesses and helmets provided. Call 843-682-6000 for fees and hours.

6. Coastal Discovery Museum
This learning center offers a wide range of activities including guided tours (walking and by boat or kayak) of 68 coastal acres of the Honey Horn property. There are trails, gardens, horses and a butterfly enclosure at 70 Honey Horn Dr. Open daily. Call ahead for exact hours (843-689-6767).

7. Harbour Town Lighthouse
The landmark red and white striped lighthouse rises 90 feet above Calibogue Sound. "Climb through time" allows you to learn about a different period in SC history on each of the 10 floors. Open daily from 10:00 a.m. to sundown.

MARINAS

8. Broad Creek Marina
18 Simmons Rd. (843-681-3625)

9. Harbour Town Yacht Basin
149 Lighthouse Rd. (843-363-8335)

10. Palmetto Bay Yacht Center
86 Helmsman Way (843-785-5000)

11. Shelter Cove Harbour & Marina
1 Shelter Cove Ln. (843-593-9116)

Hilton Head Area, SC

BROAD CREEK		Largest Vessel	VHF	Total Slips	Approach/ Dockside Depth	Floating Docks	Gas/ Diesel	Repairs/ Haulout	Min/Max Amps	Pump-Out Station
1. Harbour Town Yacht Basin WiFi onSpot MM 565.0	(843) 363-8335	135	16	85	7.0 / 7.0	F	GD		15 / 100	P
COOPER RIVER										
2. Freeport Marina WiFi MM 568.0	(843) 342-8687	100		50	20.0 / 12.0	F	GD	H		

WiFi Wireless Internet Access onSpot Dockside WiFi Facility
Visit www.waterwayguide.com for current rates, fuel prices, website addresses and other up-to-the-minute information.
(Information in the table is provided by the facilities.)

Scan here for more details:

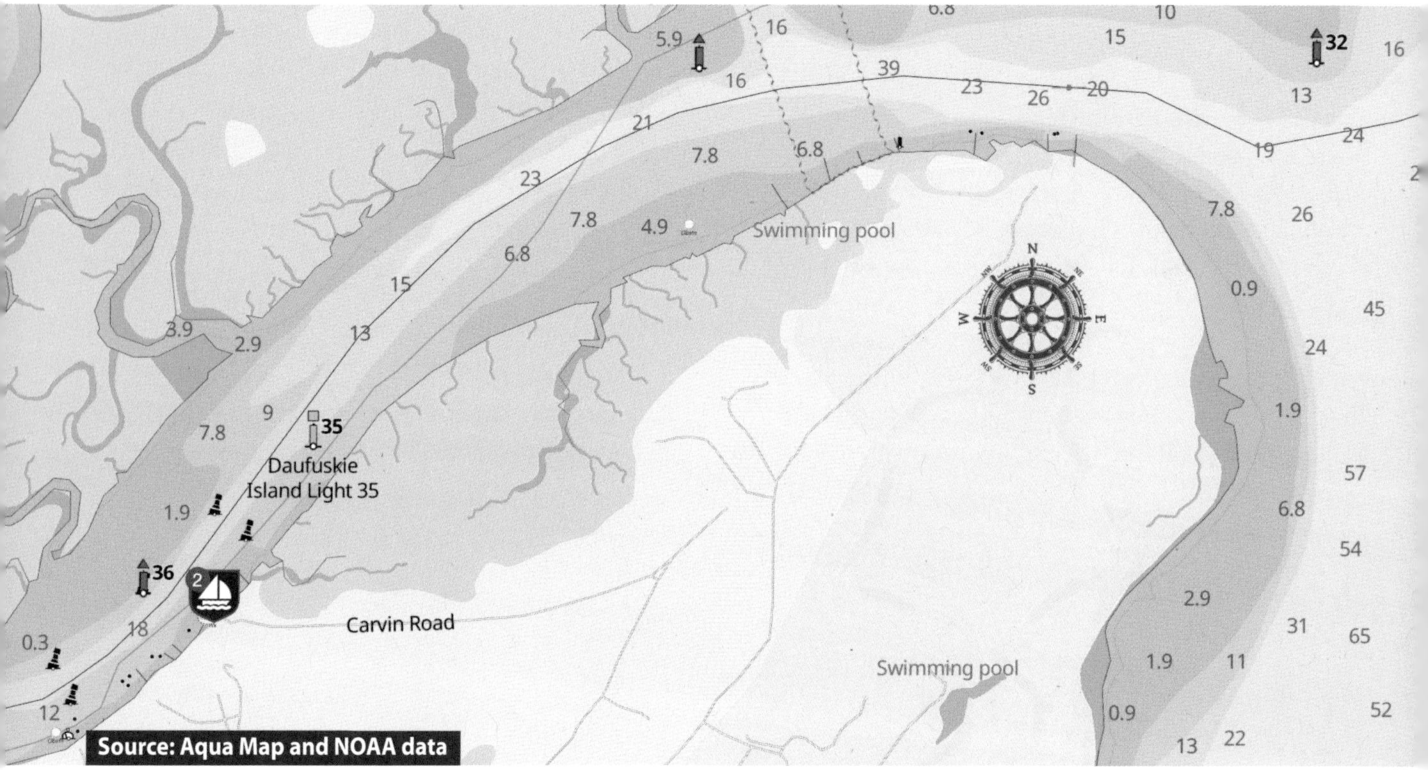

Source: Aqua Map and NOAA data

and shuttle service are available upon request. Note the direction and velocity of the current carefully as you approach the marina. When approaching from the north favor flashing green daybeacon "19" and give red daybeacon "20" just below the entrance channel a fair berth. A bar extends well up from the daybeacon.

In Calibogue Sound on the port side (to the east) before Jarvis Creek a pier marks the entrance to the lock leading into Windmill Harbour Marina, which lies in one of two secure, tide-free, lock-controlled harbors along the ICW. (The other is at the private Wexford Plantation, also on Hilton Head.) The harbormaster monitors the lock and stands by on VHF Channels 14 and 16. This harbor is home to the South Carolina Yacht Club and is surrounded by the well-maintained grounds of a gated residential community with a pool, restaurant and bar. Be aware that this is a sizable harbor (over 15 acres) and depending on where you are docked, it may be a hike to the bathhouse or to the club's dining room.

Perhaps one of the best-known features along this stretch of the ICW is the red and white striped 90-foot-tall lighthouse located east of Mile 564 and south of the entrance to Broad Creek. This marks Harbour Town Yacht Basin and the entrance to the original residential development on Hilton Head Island, Sea Pines Plantation. Enter between two jetties (the one to port is an observation pier) into Harbour Town's circular basin with its floating concrete docks. Condominiums, shops and multiple restaurants rim the circular basin. This is a full-service marina with many amenities plus beach access and a pool as well as fitness center access.

Near red daybeacon "36" on the Cooper River is Freeport Marina, which offers slips. This is a great place to get off the boat and rent a cottage (with a golf cart) and visit the nearby Old Daufuskie Crab Co. Restaurant (843-785-6652). Dockage at the marina is free during the day when you dine at the restaurant. This is a popular restaurant for boats in transit to stop for a quick lunch. (Daufuskie is detailed in the next section.)

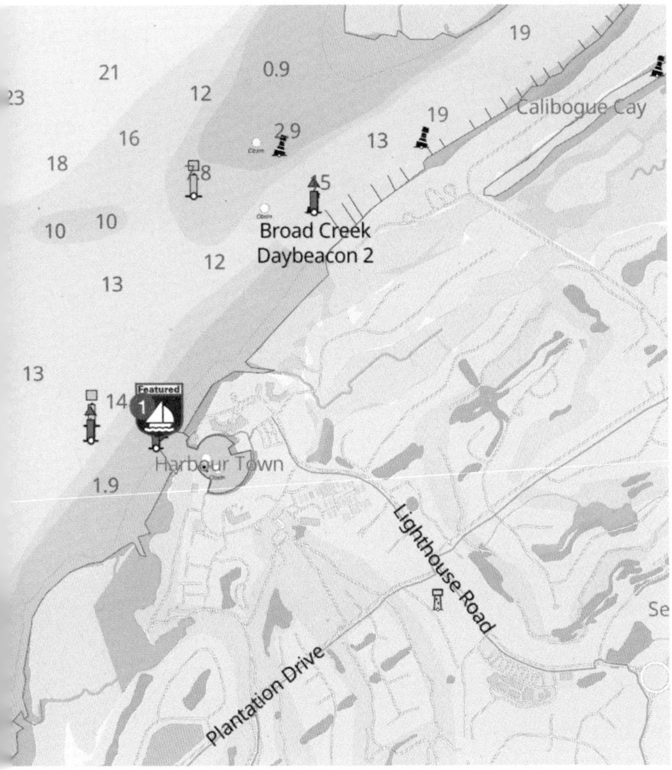

Palmetto Bay Marina is before the Cross Island Parkway (US 278) Bridge (65-foot fixed vertical clearance) in Broad Creek. The marina has 400 feet of transient dock space (new in 2020), yacht services and three restaurants, among other amenities. Palmetto Bay Yacht Center is nearby offering repairs and services.

On the starboard side of Broad Creek beyond the bridge is the private Wexford Plantation. You must be a member of a reciprocal yacht club to stay here. Broad Creek Marina on the port side offers wet slips and dry storage plus both a mechanical shop and body shop. They also have a popular on-site restaurant, Up the Creek Pub & Grill (843-681-3625).

Shelter Cove Harbour & Marina across from Palmetto Dunes Oceanfront Resort is an oasis for waterfront shopping, dining, water activities and tours and has spectacular water views. The marina offers resort amenities for vessels to 160 feet and a full-service marina store with boating gear, the latest coastal merchandise, snacks, convenience items, bait, tackle and more.

Broad Creek is a designated No-Discharge Zone. No onboard sewage–even that which has been treated–may be pumped overboard here. Y-valves and seacocks for overboard discharge must be wire-tied shut; simply closing them will not do. Fines will be levied if you are boarded and inspected, which can happen in this area.

Anchorage: It is possible to anchor outside the channel in Broad Creek at Buck Island in at least 19 feet MLW. You may want to set two anchors because the area outside the channel is narrow and the current reverses strongly. The holding in Broad Creek is excellent in thick mud. At the head of Broad Creek you can anchor behind Opposum Point. To reach this protected anchorage leave the ICW and round green daybeacon "1" into Broad Creek. Follow Broad Creek for about 3 miles to just above Opossum Point. Anchor near the south shore below Palmetto Bay Marina. There is a public landing and boat ramp under the Cross Island Parkway (US 278) Bridge.

You can also drop the hook in the channel near green daybeacon "19" in Broad Creek. Holding is good in clay with 10-foot MLW depths in the middle of the creek. There is also an anchorage at green daybeacon "13" in at least 15 feet MLW. Access to Hilton Head is easy from either of these.

COME ASHORE TO THE BEST OF HILTON HEAD ISLAND

Enjoy Harbour Town Yacht Basin and the unparalleled amenities of The Sea Pines Resort

Be surprised and captivated by The Sea Pines Resort and a luxury experience unmatched by any coastal resort destination. Experience miles of beautiful beaches, world-class dining, tennis and golf, including Harbour Town Golf Links, host to the PGA TOUR's RBC Heritage Presented by Boeing. For accommodations off the boat, stay at the stunning Inn & Club at Harbour Town, Hilton Head Island's only AAA Four-Diamond, Forbes Four-Star hotel, just steps from the Harbour Town Yacht Basin.

Harbour Town Yacht Basin features:

- LOA up to 150-foot vessels
- MLW 7 feet
- Daily/weekly/monthly dockage rates
- Electric: 30/50/100A, some 3-phase 100A
- VHF 16/68
- Fuel: High-speed gas and diesel; ValvTect fuels
- Complimentary pump-out
- Restrooms/showers/private laundry
- Complimentary Wi-Fi internet
- Complimentary access to The Sea Pines Resort Fitness Center equipment
- Complimentary access to the Harbour Town Pool
- Beach access
- Access to the Harbour Town Clubhouse, Sea Pines Beach Club and Plantation Golf Club
- Resort Guest Amenity Card offering valuable benefits and room-charging privileges

Inn & Club Guest Room

Harbour Town Golf Links

Links, an American Grill

Sea Pines Beach Club

EXPERIENCE HARBOUR TOWN

Shopping, dining, watersports and much more

Shopping

Enjoy unique boutique shopping, a variety of premier dining options featuring views of the harbour and Calibogue Sound, and exciting watersports, recreation and attractions, including the famous Harbour Town Lighthouse. It all combines to create a Hilton Head Island vacation experience you'll never forget.

- *Over 20 unique shops*
- *A total of 10 fabulous dining options*
- *Live entertainment*
- *Kayaks, WaveRunners, parasailing, stand-up paddleboards and more*
- *Fishing charters and kids' adventures*

Dining

Request dockage at
harbourtownyachtbasin.com
or call (843) 363-8335.

Watersports

THE SEA PINES RESORT

HARBOUR TOWN
YACHT BASIN

32° 08' 20" N / 80° 48' 40" W - St. Mile 564 | HILTON HEAD ISLAND, SC | (843) 363-8335 | harbourtownyachtbasin.com

Hilton Head Area, SC

BROAD CREEK		Largest Vessel	VHF	Total Slips	Approach/ Dockside Depth	Floating Docks	Gas/ Diesel	Repairs/ Haulout	Min/Max Amps	Pump-Out Station
1. Palmetto Bay Marina (WiFi) 3.5 mi. E of MM 563.8	(843) 785-5000	150	16	65	20.0 / 20.0	F	GD	RH	30 / 100	P
2. Palmetto Bay Yacht Center (WiFi) 3.5 mi. E of MM 563.8	(843) 686-5989	70			20.0 / 20.0	F	GD	RH	30 / 50	P
3. Wexford Plantation-PRIVATE (WiFi)	(843) 686-8813	70	16	280	7.0 / 7.0	F			30 / 50	P
4. Broad Creek Marina (WiFi) 4.5 mi. E of MM 563.8	(843) 681-3625	100	16	55	23.0 / 16.0	F	GD	R		P
5. Shelter Cove Harbour & Marina (WiFi) onSpot	**(844) 238-3237**	**160**	**16**	**178**	**9.0 / 9.0**	**F**	**GD**	**R**	**30 / 100**	**P**

(WiFi) Wireless Internet Access **onSpot** Dockside WiFi Facility
Visit www.waterwayguide.com for current rates, fuel prices, website addresses and other up-to-the-minute information.
(Information in the table is provided by the facilities.)

Scan here for more details:

Side Trip: Bluffton, May River

NAVIGATION: Use NOAA Chart 11516. The May River, which comes into the ICW at Mile 560, offers an interesting side trip to the small town of Bluffton. Flood tide at the head of Calibogue Sound begins 1 hour and 23 minutes before the flood tide at the Savannah River entrance and ebbs 54 minutes before. The May River offers good anchorage almost anywhere past the bar at the mouth of its tributary stream, Bass Creek. The anchorage at Bluffton offers all-around protection in 10 to 20 feet MLW with a mud bottom.

Calibogue Sound Entrance

NAVIGATION: Use NOAA Chart 11516. Many boats use the ocean entrance to Calibogue Sound Entrance in fair weather and seas. It is a shortcut to reach the ICW from the ocean and is much shorter than the Savannah River approach. The markers, however, are widely spaced and sometimes difficult to locate. It is approached from the Jones Island Range area of Tybee Roads. Note that if using this route to the Tybee Roads channel the shoal to the east of quick flashing green buoy "3" has built to the west to within about 200 feet of that buoy.

Anchorage: Across Calibogue Sound and the ICW at Mile 563 is well-protected Bryan Creek. When entering take care to clear the 2-foot MLW bar extending from the north. Once inside favor the west shore. Anchor in 8- to 11-foot MLW depths with a sandy bottom. This anchorage is pretty tight and can get buggy in warmer weather.

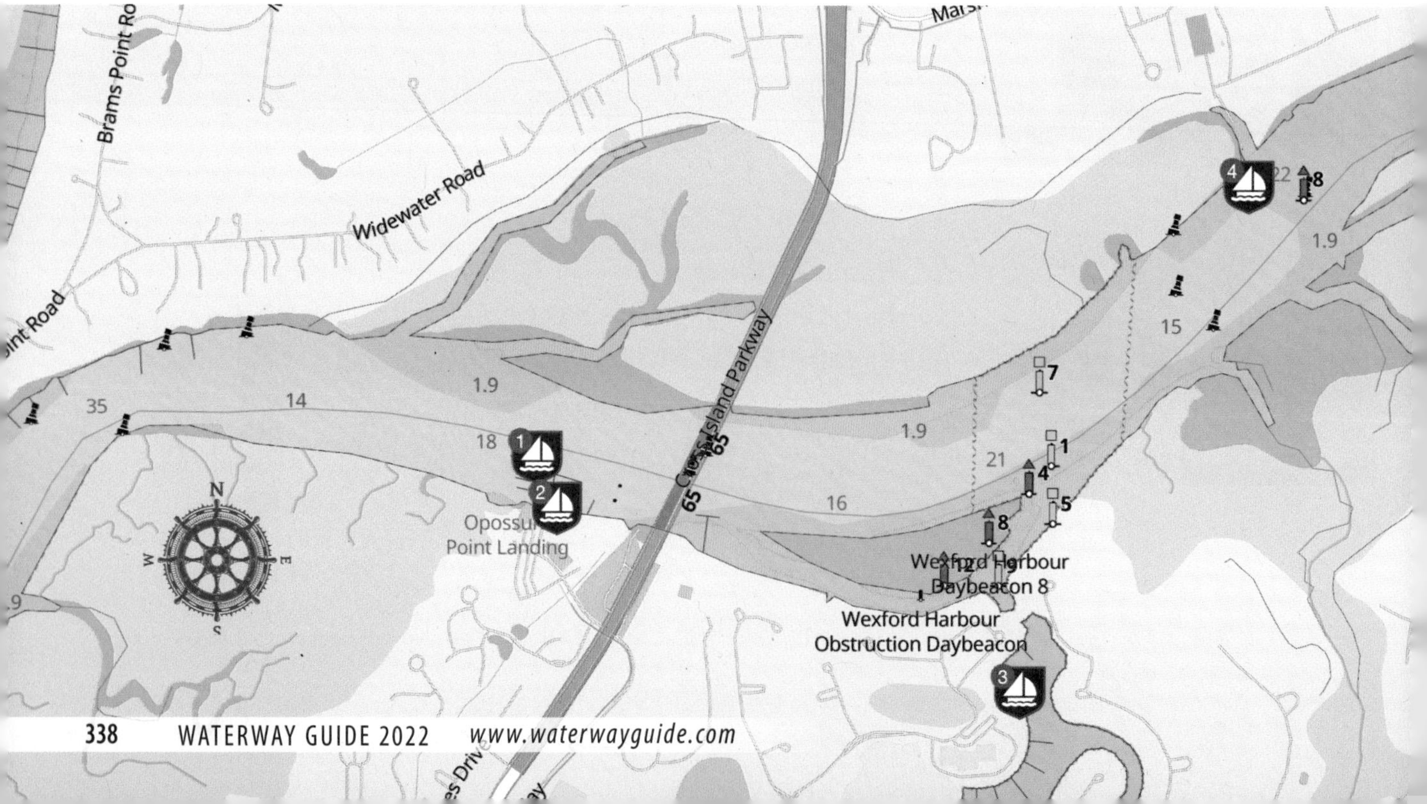

TO ST. CATHERINES SOUND

Daufuskie Island–ICW Mile 565 to Mile 571

Heading south on the ICW Daufuskie Island awaits at the confluence of Calibogue Sound and the Cooper River. (The ICW continues to run past Daufuskie Island as the channel goes south along the Cooper River, Ramshorn Creek and the New River.) With no bridge linking Daufuskie Island to the mainland the small native population (direct descendants of slaves brought from Africa) once lived an isolated life having little contact with the outside world. Nowadays, inspired by Hilton Head Island's development, Daufuskie Island continues to undergo extensive development of its own, with resorts and residential areas springing up each year. There is still, however, no vehicular access to the island.

NAVIGATION: Use NOAA Chart 11507. The old lighthouse on Daufuskie Island at Haig Point serves as a landmark for spotting the lighted buoy at the entrance to the Cooper River. When passing Daufuskie Landing on the Cooper River follow the dredged channel of narrow Ramshorn Creek into the New River, favoring the green side of the channel between flashing green daybeacon "39" and red flashing buoy "40" for 7.4 feet MLW. The tidal current reverses every 2 or 3 miles along this stretch and depths vary widely from year to year.

Slow down! Over the years, the wakes of passing vessels have damaged locally berthed craft at the floating dock and boat ramp at Daufuskie Landing.

Dockage: You can tie up at Daufuskie Landing at green daybeacon "39" during the day. Be sure to stop in at the "not so general" General Store located just off the ferry docks for groceries and gifts or at the tiny and historic Silver Dew Winery, located in a building that dates all the way back to 1883. The building was originally constructed as a "wick house" for the nearby Bloody Point Lighthouse. Open daily for tours. (Call 843-342-8687 for details.)

Anchorage: Bull Creek just past Mile 565 is a favorite anchorage and rafting site for local boats and ICW travelers alike. Just inside the entrance is good holding with sufficient depths but the currents are strong and there is no place to go ashore. The best spot to anchor on Bull Creek is past the little creek to the west because shrimp boats use the lower part of the creek.

You can anchor in 8 to 15 feet MLW with excellent holding in mud on the northern branch of the Cooper River, which leaves the ICW before green daybeacon "37." South of flashing green "39" at Mile 570 the New River anchorage has 8- to 20-feet MLW depths with excellent holding in mud. Enter from the south side of the river, watch your depth gauge and avoid the shallow water to the northwest.

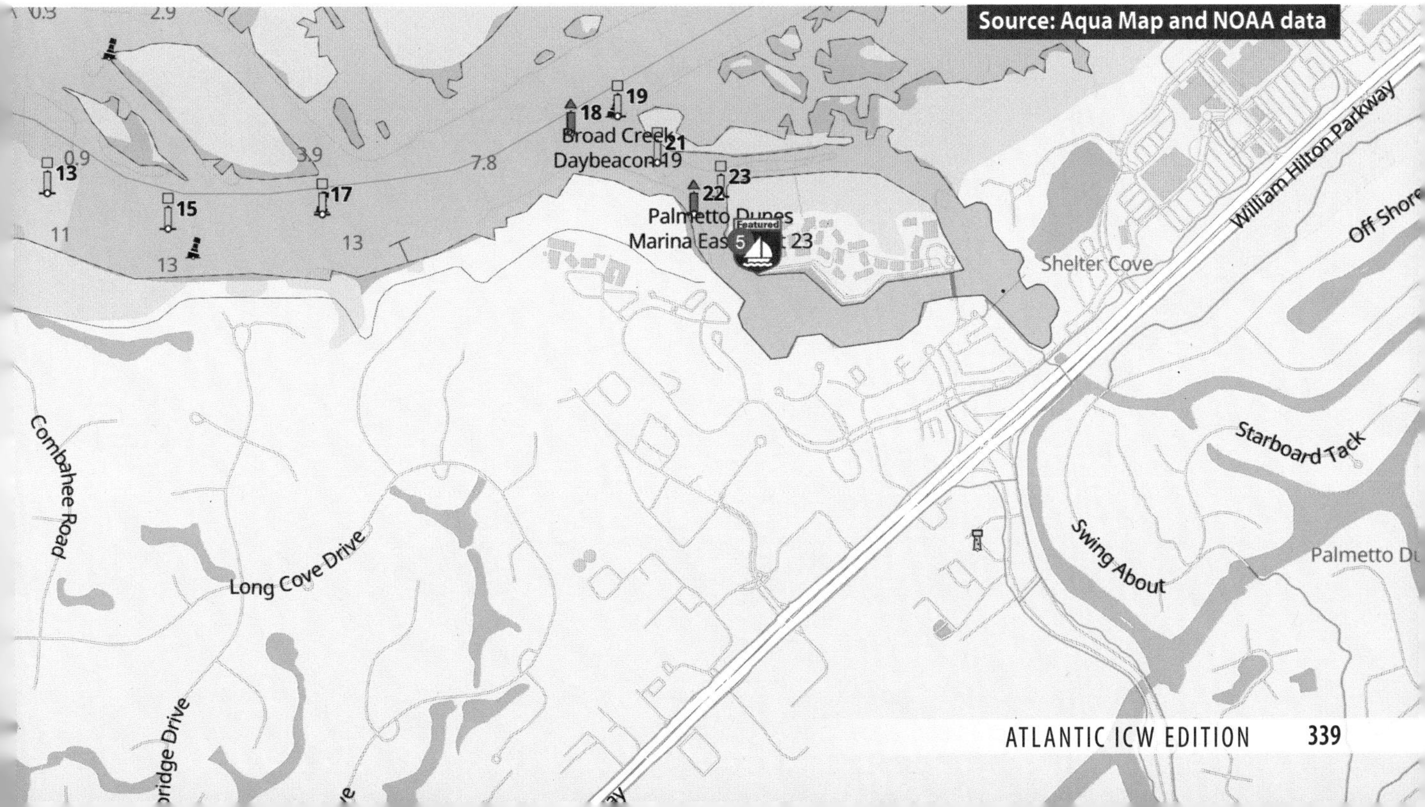

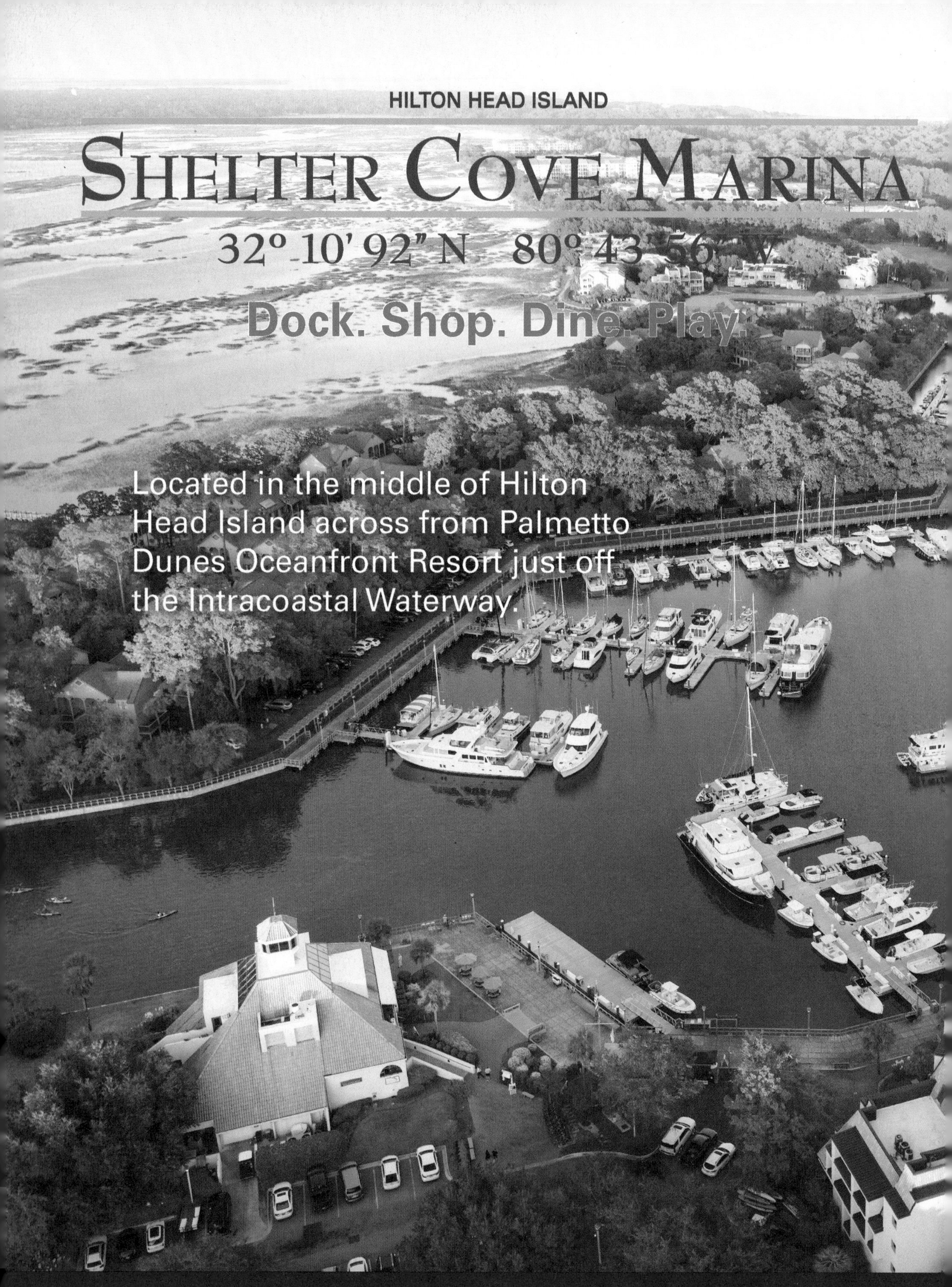

1 Shelter Cove Ln, Hilton Head Island, SC 29928

Shelter Cove Harbour & Marina offers easy access to great shopping and restaurants plus activities at Palmetto Dunes with access to golf, tennis, pickleball, bikes & the beach.

The Ship's Store offers a large selection of apparel, accessories, convenience items & fishing tackle.

- **Floating docks / vessels up to 150 feet**
- **Electrical: 30, 50, 100 amp**
- **9' MLW, well marked channel**
- **Pump-out boat**
- **Monitor channels 16/71**
- **Restrooms, showers, laundry**
- **Grocery store nearby**
- **Full service yacht maintenance**
- **Wi-Fi internet access and cable available**
- **Seasonal resort shuttle**

844-238-3237 • ShelterCoveHiltonHead.com

Fields Cut/Walls Cuts–ICW Mile 571 to Mile 576

NAVIGATION: Use NOAA Chart 11507. Leaving South Carolina you will pass through several shallow land cuts before reaching the Savannah River at the end of Fields Cut. This has typically been an area of concern due to constant shoaling. Fields Cut and Walls Cut were dredged in summer 2019 and depths are holding except for the spots indicated below. The tidal range here is 8 to 9 feet so most boats will have no trouble at mid to high tide.

At Walls Cut (Mile 572), keep in the middle of the channel following the deeper water as shown on your chart for 8.6 MLW by flashing red "42." At Field Cut (Mile 575) pass flashing green "47" within 10 feet and aim to pass red daybeacon "48A" by 100 feet off. Do not hug the daybeacon! Continue on the same heading for 200 feet before turning to starboard and the center of the channel. If you turn too soon, you will see shoal water. Stay in the center of the channel and favor the outside of the turns. At the southern exit favor the red side and pass the range tower by 100 feet off and flashing red "50" by 200 feet off.

Be advised that when approaching red daybeacon "50" you will be entering the Savannah River. This river carries very heavy large shipping traffic that can create large swells. Keep your radio on and lookout for these large ships. They are visible above the marsh grass. You might have to wait to cross the river and it is definitely advisable to do so.

Anchorage: In calm weather cruisers will sometimes anchor south of the ICW and Walls Cut in the Wright River at Mile 572.2 near Turtle Island. There is 10 to 15 feet MLW here and a mud bottom. This is a convenient spot to stop north of the Georgia border with good holding and wave/wake protection. It is pretty anchorage but has little wind protection and no amenities.

Savannah River

As you cross the Savannah River betwen Fields Cut and Elba Island Cut you leave South Carolina and enter Georgia. From here until the sheltered waters of Florida pay close attention to currents and depths as well as markers and ranges.

Study your charts before beginning this passage since the next 140 miles down the ICW are visually interesting and also physically demanding. You will use your GPS, compass, depth sounder and binoculars as you wind along serpentine rivers and cross open sounds that can be choppy and downright nasty when the wind kicks up. The route winds past Georgia's barrier islands and then becomes an entirely different kind of ICW when you cross into Florida.

It is especially important to stay in the channel, use the charted magenta ICW line as a guide (except where noted in the text), make use of the numerous navigational ranges and give markers–especially those at turns in natural rivers–a wide berth. Plan ahead in timing your arrival at the known trouble spots. If it is low tide when you arrive, drop the hook for a while to wait for higher water; it doesn't take long for the tide to come up a foot or two. "Mid-tide and rising" is always preferable in these areas. Remember that strong winds and the lunar cycle affect tidal range. Conditions change so check the latest *Local Notice to Mariners* (www.navcen.uscg.gov) before you go.

The Bonaventure Cemetery, made famous in the book "Midnight in the Garden of Good and Evil," is visible from the ICW along the Wilmington River between flashing red daybeacon "30" and flashing green daybeacon "31" (past Mile 580) on the west side of the route.

You have to make a decision when you reach the Savannah River:

1. Turn east to head to the Tybee Roads Entrance and out to sea;
2. Head west up the river to the beautiful city of Savannah; or
3. Continue on the ICW through the Elba Island Cut to the Wilmington River.

Option 1: To Savannah River Entrance

NAVIGATION: Use NOAA Chart 11507. Sixteen miles down the Savannah River from Savannah is the Savannah River Entrance (also called the Tybee Roads Entrance). This is a big ship entrance offering entry to Savannah via the ICW and Savannah River. Slower boats bound for the Savannah River on this route should try to enter Tybee Roads with a favorable current, if possible, as the effects of the current start many miles offshore in the Atlantic.

Dockage: The entrance to the Savannah River near Tybee Island, Savannah's primary beach area, makes

WATERWAY GUIDE
THE CRUISING AUTHORITY
Subscription
Subscribe to Explorer and open the world of boating adventure
waterwayguide.com
Guide Content
Inlet - Sapelo Sound Entrance
Sign in to Waterway Guide
Sapelo Sound Entrance, GA
Sea buoy: Red and white can buoy "S" located at N 31° 31.210'/W 81° 03.890'.
Overview: Used by fishermen and shrimpers, not to mention legendary pirate Edward Teach ("Blackbeard"). (You will pass just north of Blackbeard Island and Blackbeard Creek while transiting this inlet.) Southbound cruisers hoping to avoid the Georgia ICW rarely use the inlet, preferring to jump offshore through the big ship channels at Charleston, Port Royal or Savannah.
Navigation: Current and trustworthy local knowledge required. From the sea buoy, proceed first to red nun buoy "2" and then head slightly south of west to green can buoy "3." Depths will drop from more than 20 feet down to 12 feet MLW along the way. If you see 10-foot MLW depths, you are in trouble and need to reverse course. At green can buoy "5," you will see 20-plus-foot MLW depths return, and it is a simple matter of following the red buoys in until you meet up with the ICW past red nun buoy "10."
Cautions and hazards: Not the best inlet in rougher weather, due to extensive shoals to the north and south of the inlet. Sound is quite wide and the aids to navigation are unlighted, making it unfavorable for nighttime passage except by the well experienced. Depths between green can buoy "3" and green can buoy "5" drop to 12 feet MLW in places, and there are breaking shoals to the north of the channel; otherwise, depths typically run to over 20 feet MLW. Do not be tempted to cut corners. Once in the sound, be aware of the shoal by green daybeacon "143" and stay at least 100 feet off.
Depth: See interactive charts on Waterway Explorer at waterwayguide.com.
ICW connection: Junction of Sapelo Sound and ICW is at Mile 632.
Nearest recommended inlet: Northbound, you should bypass St. Catherines Sound (9.5 nm) and continue to Wassaw Sound (22 nm) if conditions are calm or, best yet, go on to Tybee Roads to the Savannah River (31 nm). Southbound, the ship channel at St. Simons Sound is 29.5 nm away.
INLETS: NORFOLK, VA TO ST. MARYS, GA
SAPELO SOUND
Experiment Shoal
Use Chart 11509
78 WATERWAY GUIDE 2020
Not a member? Join
Learn More
Join
Plan
Go
waterwayguide.com/learn-more

GOIN' ASHORE

SAVANNAH, GA

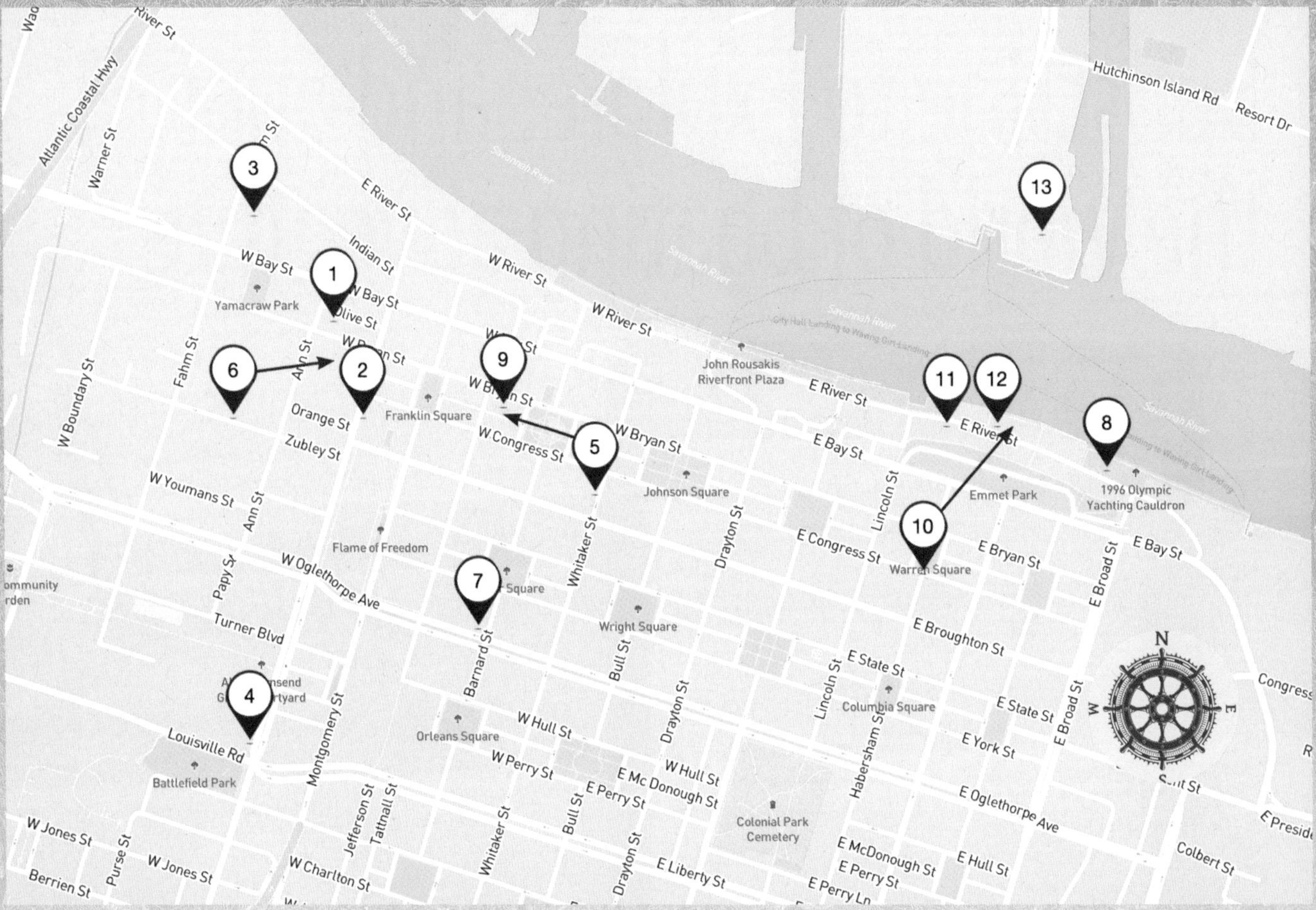

Savannah sits serenely on a bluff 40 feet above the banks of the Savannah River, where General James Oglethorpe and 120 passengers landed in 1733 to found Britain's last American colony. General Oglethorpe laid out the city in a series of 24 squares, 22 of which remain as lovely parks surrounded by a mix of architectural styles, including Federal, Georgian, Victorian and Italianate. Walking and driving tours, carriage tours, audio tours and guided bus tours highlighting the historic homes built around Savannah's squares are all available. The easiest way to move around downtown is aboard the Express Shuttle, which operates daily, with 24 stops around the Historic District.

SERVICES

1. Savannah Animal Care
510 W. Bryan St. (915-335-1200)

2. Savannah Emergency Care
210 Fahm St. (912-662-8645)

3. Savannah Post Office
2 N. Fahm St. (912-235-4666)

4. Savannah Visitor Center
1 W. River St. (912-651-6662)

ATTRACTIONS

5. American Prohibition Museum
Artifacts and displays about the ban of alcohol from 1920-1933 at 209 W. St. Julian St. At night (Wednesday through Saturday) a retro speakeasy opens upstairs serving classsic cocktails and offering cocktail classes (912-220-1249).

6. Ships of the Sea Maritime Museum
Founded in 1966, this museum features nine galleries of ship models, plus maritime paintings and artifacts from the 18th and 19th centuries. The Museum's Collection is housed in the elegant home built in 1819 for William Scarbrough, one of the principal owners of the Steamship Savannah and president of the Savannah Steamship Company at 41 Martin Luther King Jr. Blvd. (912-232-1511).

7. Telfair Museums
Includes three museums: Jepson Center, Telfair Academy and Owens-Thomas House and Slave Quarters. Telfair Academy is one of the south's first public museums and was built as a mansion in 1812. The 1938 bronze Bird Girl statue, made famous on the cover of John Berendt's novel "Midnight in the Garden of Good and Evil," is on display at Telfair Academy at 121 Barnarrd St. (912-790-8800).

8. Waving Girl
This statue commemorates Florence Martus (1868-1943), unofficial greeter of all passing ships on the Savannah River at 2 E. Broad St. Legend has it she waved a handkerchief by day and a lantern by night and never missed a ship in her 44 years on watch.

SHOPPING

9. City Market
In the heart of the Historic District four blocks of warehouses have been renovated to represent the 18th century marketplace. Features artists working in their lofts and exhibits of works for sale, as well as open-air cafes and shops offering crafts, accessories and gifts (219 W. Bryan St., 912-232-4903).

10. River Street Market Place
Housed in one-time cotton warehouses, there are more than 75 boutiques, galleries, artists' studios, restaurants and pubs on the river at 502 E. River St. (912-441-2664).

MARINAS

11. River Street LLC
318 E. River St. (912-232-4252)

12. River Street Market Place Dock
502 E. River St. (912-398-6038)

13. The Westin Savannah Harbor Golf Resort & Spa
1 Resort St. (912-201-2000)

Savannah River, GA

TYBEE ISLAND		Largest Vessel	VHF	Total Slips	Approach/ Dockside Depth	Floating Docks	Gas/ Diesel	Repairs/ Haulout	Min/Max Amps	Pump-Out Station
1. Tybee Island Marina (WiFi)	(912) 786-5554		16	54	18.0 / 16.0	F	GD	RH	30 / 50	P

(WiFi) Wireless Internet Access onSpot Dockside WiFi Facility
Visit www.waterwayguide.com for current rates, fuel prices, website addresses and other up-to-the-minute information.
(Information in the table is provided by the facilities.)

Scan here for more details:

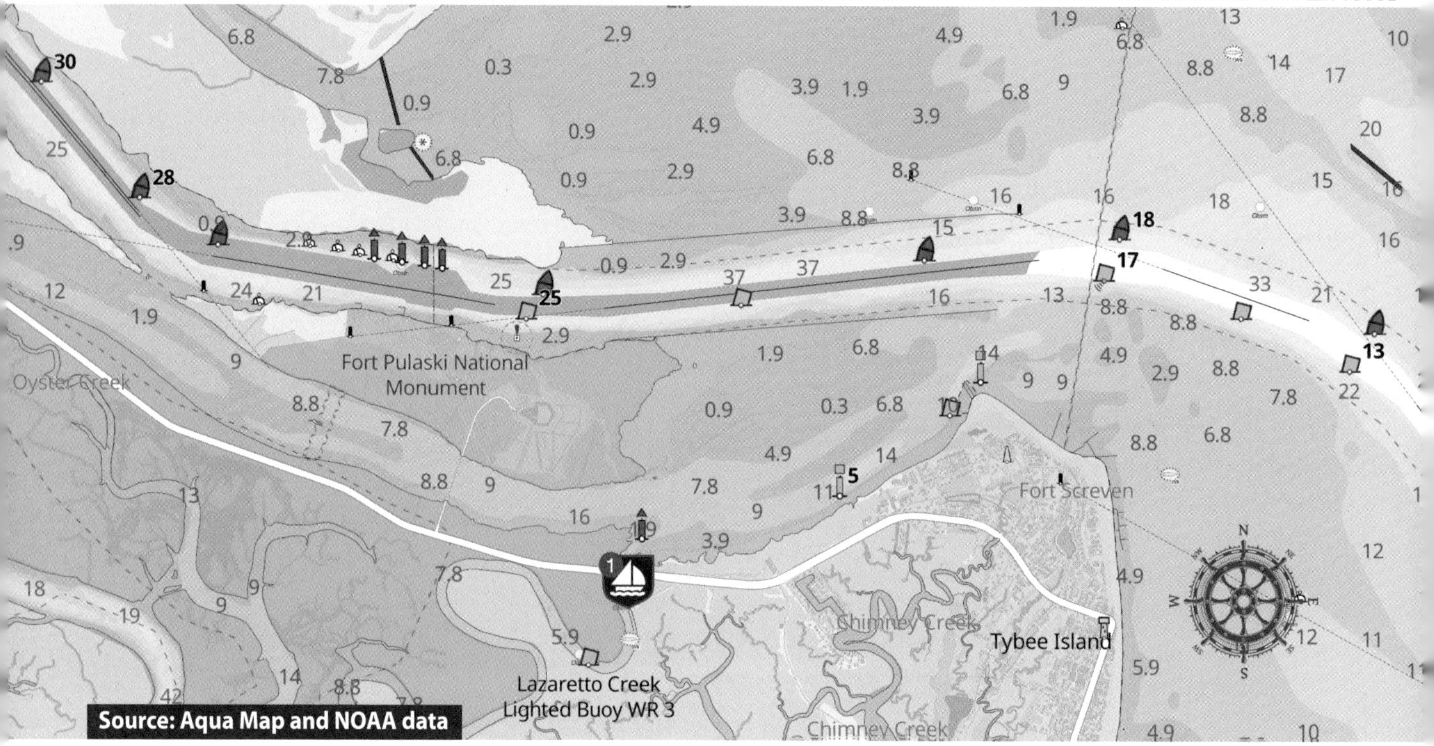

Source: Aqua Map and NOAA data

a good fuel stop for powerboaters going south on the outside run down the Atlantic. Tybee Island Marina offers boat storage, fishing charters, a boat launch and a restaurant. The marina is on the south side of the Savannah River's mouth but the 35-foot fixed vertical clearance **U.S. 80-GA 26 Bridge** over the marina's access channel restricts usage by sailboats.

Option 2: Upriver to Savannah

NAVIGATION: Use NOAA Chart 11507. Savannah is about 8 miles up the Savannah River from ICW Mile 576. (See "Goin' Ashore: Savannah, GA" in this chapter for details). Expect strong currents, a 9-foot tide and heavy commercial traffic on the way. Those with low-powered boats should check the tide tables and plan arrivals and departures accordingly. Following the Savannah River another 170 miles will bring you to Augusta, home of the Professional Golf Association's annual Masters Championship.

When returning to the ICW you can do so via the south channel (below Elba Island), assuming you can navigate under the 35-foot fixed vertical clearance **Elba Island Road Bridge**.

Dockage: The Westin Savannah Harbor Golf Resort & Spa on Hutchinson Island is directly across from River Street in Savannah with slips on floating docks. Their deep-water slips can accommodate vessels to 300 feet and they offer resort-style amenities. Be sure to call well in advance for reservations. Water ferry service is available to reach the other side of the harbor.

Across the channel River Street Market Place Dock offers concrete floating dockage with direct access to downtown. They can accommodate megayachts up to 250 feet with full amenities. The River Street Market features re-creations of the sheds that stood on River Street in the mid 1800s. The open-air market has more numerous shops representing countries from all over the world.

The nearby Savannah River Dock is limited to 3-hour tie-ups and offers no water or electrical services.

Option 3: ICW to Thunderbolt–ICW Mile 576 to Mile 585

Thunderbolt is an important seafood-packing center with good marinas and restaurants. The shore is lined with shrimp boats, often rafted two abreast. Bus service is available with stops about close to Thunderbolt's marinas. (A taxi is better for the trip to Savannah.)

NAVIGATION: Use NOAA Chart 11507. The ICW passage is not straight across the Savannah River but diagonal. When you cross the Savannah River allow for the strong river current. Slow boats may have to correct course several times. Watch for big ships, which will announce their presence on VHF Channels 13 and 16. They approach fast from both directions and port pilots have had many close encounters with pleasure boats in the river where the ships have no room to maneuver in the narrow, swiftly running channel.

Heading south on the ICW you can pick up the beginning of the flood current and carry a fair (flood) current all the way through Walls Cut (Mile 572) and Fields Cut to just south of Thunderbolt (Mile 585). (An ebb current gives the same advantage to northbound vessels.)

A rock jetty at Elba Island Cut's confluence with the Savannah River (on the southeast side of the river) is submerged at high tide but marked with a white danger beacon. Because of the shoal on the west side in Elba Cut, flashing red daybeacon "2" and flashing red daybeacon "4" have been moved eastward and appear to be in the middle of the channel. Pass by 120 feet off–do not hug the markers–and gradually return to the center of the channel south of red "4."

Depths are well maintained here but since the tidal range is between 8 and 9 feet MLW be sure to stay in the channel. From Elba Island Cut the ICW heads briefly westward along St. Augustine Creek. It then enters the winding upper reaches of the Wilmington River, which is not nearly as intricate as it appears on the chart and then approaches the town of Thunderbolt. Multiple sets of ranges guide you through this area.

Causton Bluff (Sam Varnedoe, SR 26) Bridge at Mile 579.9 has a closed vertical clearance of 21 feet and is the only opening bridge in Georgia for southbound vessels.

Welcome to Georgia!

After passing through Fields Cut, you will encounter the Savannah River and the State of Georgia. Islands, estuaries, creeks and bars dominate the Georgia coast. If South Carolina is the Lowcountry then Georgia is the Backcountry, with miles of salt marsh, rushing tides, plentiful anchorages and mosquitoes (bring bug spray).

The channels are narrow here with wind-driven tides and sizable mud banks. It is best to travel on a high tide, especially through the challenging Hells Gate channel south of Savannah, the Sapelo River (ICW Mile 635) and Cumberland Dividings into Cumberland Sound. The charts may not represent the most recent placement of navigation aids, which are frequently moved by the Army Corps of Engineers to mark the shifting channels. (As always, listen on VHF Channel 13 for dredging operations and give them a wide berth.) Refer to the Waterway Explorer at www.waterwayguide.com for navigational alerts and updates.

You often hear about skippers choosing to run offshore to avoid Georgia but with good planning and prudent navigation, this isn't necessary. While you can easily jump outside at Tybee Roads or St. Simons Sound, you would miss the natural beauty of these pristine waters and endless sky.

Savannah River, GA

SAVANNAH AREA		Largest Vessel	VHF	Total Slips	Approach/ Dockside Depth	Floating Docks	Gas/ Diesel	Repairs/ Haulout	Min/Max Amps	Pump-Out Station
1. The Westin Savannah Harbor Golf Resort & Spa WiFi	(912) 201-2021	300		25	27.0 / 16.0	F			30 / 200+	
2. River Street Market Place Dock WiFi 8.0 mi. W of MM 576	(912) 398-6038	250			24.0 / 18.0	F			30 / 100	

WiFi Wireless Internet Access onSpot Dockside WiFi Facility
Visit www.waterwayguide.com for current rates, fuel prices, website addresses and other up-to-the-minute information.
(Information in the table is provided by the facilities.)

Scan here for more details:

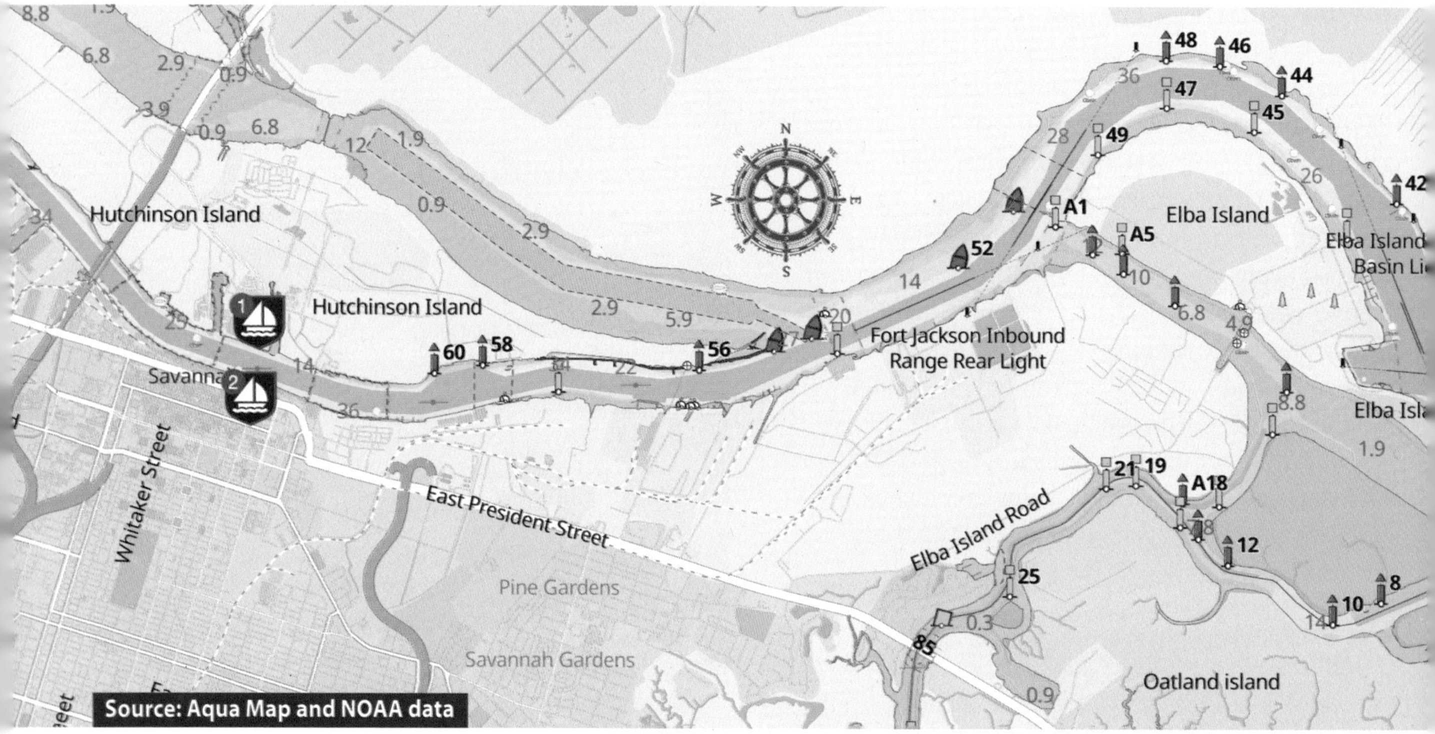

Source: Aqua Map and NOAA data

Georgia bridges monitor VHF Channel 09, as they do in South Carolina and Florida. The bridgetender will often request that boats bunch together for openings, which are restricted year-round. The draw will open on signal, Monday through Friday (except federal holidays), except from 6:30 a.m. to 9:00 a.m. and from 4:30 p.m. to 6:30 p.m., when the draw will only open for waiting traffic at 7:00 a.m., 8:00 a.m. and 5:30 p.m.

A bridge replacement project is underway to replace the existing Causton Bluff (Sam Varnedoe, SR 26) Bridge with a dual- span, high-level (65-foot fixed vertical clearance) bridge. The project is estimated to be completed by November 2021. Mariners are requested to use caution when transiting the area. For additional waterway information, contact Coast Guard Marine Safety Unit Savannah at 912-652-4353.

The tidal current reverses between the Causton Bluff (Sam Varnedoe, SR 26) Bridge and the high-rise **State Of Georgia Memorial (U.S. 80) Bridge** (65-foot fixed vertical clearance) at Mile 582.8. (The bridge is known locally as the Thunderbolt Bridge.)

Note that both sides of the bridge are No-Wake Zones.

Shoaling has been observed between green daybeacon "29" and flashing red "30." Favor the green side of the channel for 7.2 MLW. Then pass flashing red "30" by 150 feet off for the deepest water (19 MLW). Stay on the green edge of the channel, visually splitting the marker and the shore.

At Thunderbolt and farther down the ICW at Isle of Hope (Mile 590) the current and direction of flow must be considered when docking. Marina personnel are generally knowledgeable and when assigning berths, they try to put the less maneuverable, single-screw boats in slips that are easy to enter and leave in this area of high tides and swift currents. If no attendant is around, it is best to put in at the fuel dock to size up the situation and then locate someone who can give directions or lend a hand. All marinas at Thunderbolt have floating docks.

When heading south from Thunderbolt take flashing green daybeacon "37" a little wide and then favor flashing green daybeacon "37A" avoiding the shoal near red daybeacon "38."

Southeast of Mile 585 you will find additional dockage and anchorage opportunities on Turner Creek off the Wilmington River. Beware of the charted 4-foot MLW area soon after the first bend.

Dockage: Hinckley Yacht Services Savannah located to starboard just northwest of the State Of Georgia Memorial (U.S. 80) Bridge is a premiere yacht care and service facility. They have just eight transient slips so call ahead. Across the ICW at Mile 582 is Savannah Bend Marina with four reserved transient slips.

At Mile 582, Safe Harbor Bahia Bleu on the south side of the State Of Georgia Memorial (U.S. 80) Bridge is convenient to the ICW and to Thunderbolt's restaurants and shops. They can accommodate vessels up to 200 feet at their deep-water docks. They also have a well-stocked Ship Store and offer boat detailing and storage.

Thunderbolt Marine is at Mile 583 with transient dockage close to town and full-service repairs. Their lifts are capable of hauling the smallest to the largest of yachts. They also have spacious laundry facilities and pump-out facilities. A long-standing tradition of fresh Krispy Kreme doughnuts delivered to your vessel each morning makes this a favorite stop. Restaurants and a bus stop are within walking distance.

The private Savannah Yacht Club is about 2 miles past Thunderbolt to port. The yacht club has limited space and its reciprocation policy varies so be sure to contact the club before you arrive.

There are two options on Turner Creek: Sail Harbor Marina & Boatyard and Hogans' Marina. Sail Harbor Marina & Boatyard is a family-owned marina and boatyard with five reserved transient slips to 50 feet. They have contract diesel mechanics as well as painting and canvas service. Hogans' Marina offers wet and dry storage and is a charter fishing base. Farther south on the Wilmington River is Landings Harbor Marina with dry rack storage (to 30 feet), wet storage (to 40 feet) in length. Call ahead for slip availability.

Anchorage: A mile or so below Thunderbolt the Wilmington River widens and the channel begins to straighten out. The popular Herb River anchorage is located at Mile 584.5. Most skippers anchor along the east bank before the first turn. The river bottom is a bit irregular and very deep at the bend but holding is better than in the lower stretch of the river where there is an oyster bank. Local boat traffic is minimal and the tidal currents moderate. Depths are good at 13 to 15 feet MLW with a mud bottom but be sure to set the anchor well and, as always, show an anchor light.

It is possible to anchor before or after the fixed **Spence Grayson Bridge** (35-foot vertical clearance) on Turner Creek and dinghy into Hogans' Marina. Remember to get permission to leave the dinghy should you decide to shop. Several boats on private mooring balls leave room for only one or two boats to anchor.

Wilmington River, GA

THUNDERBOLT AREA		Largest Vessel	VHF	Total Slips	Approach/ Dockside Depth	Floating Docks	Gas/ Diesel	Repairs/ Haulout	Min/Max Amps	Pump-Out Station
1. Hinckley Yacht Services Savannah WiFi onSpot MM 582.4	(912) 629-2400	100	16	30	12.0 / 12.0	F		RH	30 / 50	P
2. Savannah Bend Marina WiFi MM 582.3	(912) 897-3625	100	16	28	12.0 / 10.0	F	GD	RH	30 / 50	
3. Safe Harbor Bahia Bleu WiFi MM 582.6	(912) 354-2283	100	16	45	26.0 / 20.0	F	GD	RH	30 / 50	P
4. Thunderbolt Marine WiFi MM 583	(912) 356-3875	200	16	45	20.0 / 20.0	F	GD	RH	30 / 100	P

WiFi Wireless Internet Access onSpot Dockside WiFi Facility
Visit www.waterwayguide.com for current rates, fuel prices, website addresses and other up-to-the-minute information.
(Information in the table is provided by the facilities.)

Scan here for more details:

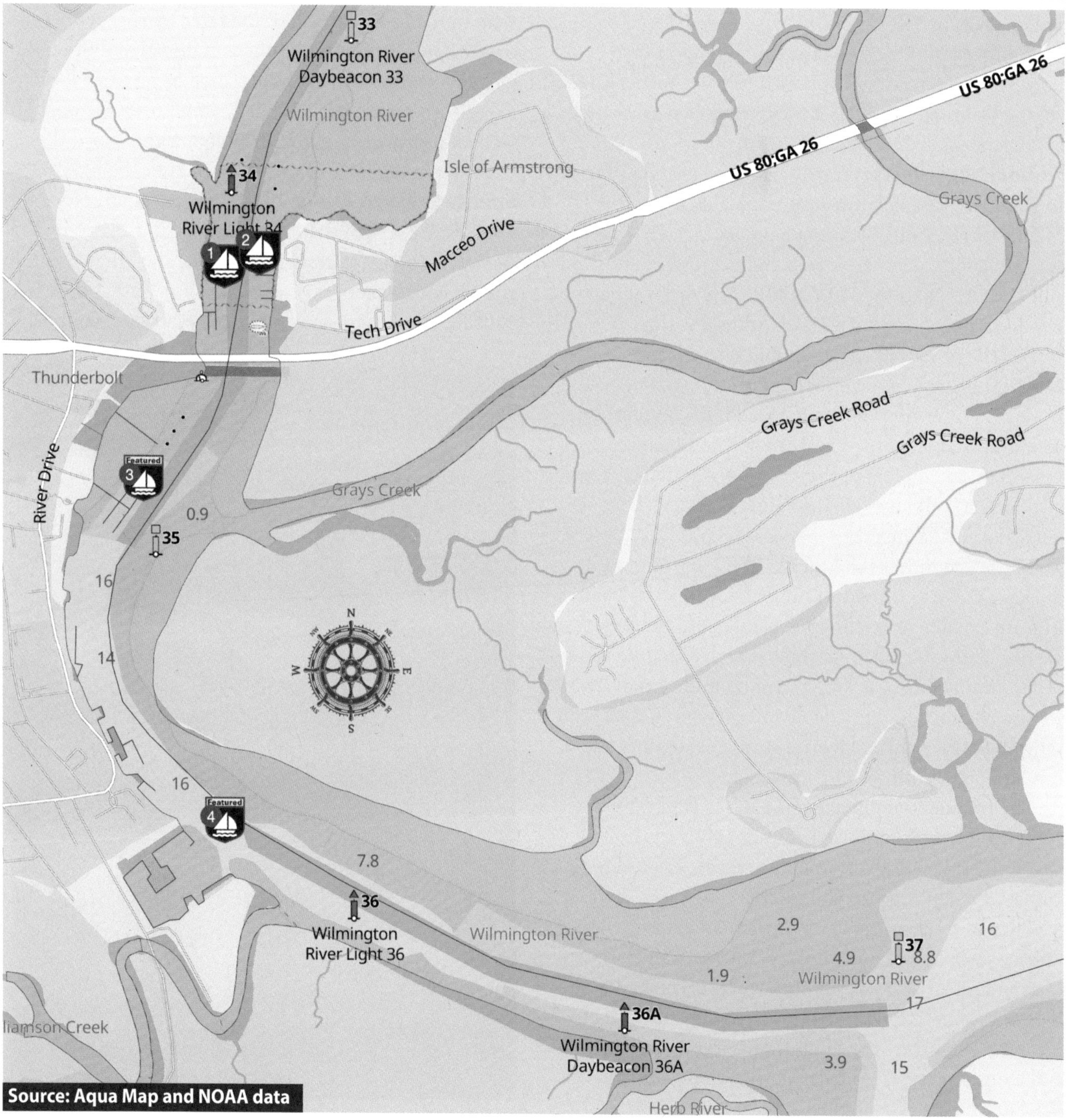

Source: Aqua Map and NOAA data

Wilmington River, GA

WHITE MARSH ISLAND AREA		Largest Vessel	VHF	Total Slips	Approach/ Dockside Depth	Floating Docks	Gas/ Diesel	Repairs/ Haulout	Min/Max Amps	Pump-Out Station
1. Savannah Yacht Club-PRIVATE	(912) 644-4100	45		60	20.0 / 20.0	F	GD		30	
TURNER CREEK										
2. Sail Harbor Marina & Boatyard WiFi SE of MM 585.4	(912) 897-2896	50	16	45	7.0 / 10.0	F		RH	30 / 50	P
3. Hogans' Marina MM 585.4	(912) 897-3474				8.0 / 8.0	F	G	RH	30	P

WiFi Wireless Internet Access onSpot Dockside WiFi Facility
Visit www.waterwayguide.com for current rates, fuel prices, website addresses and other up-to-the-minute information.
(Information in the table is provided by the facilities.)

Scan here for more details:

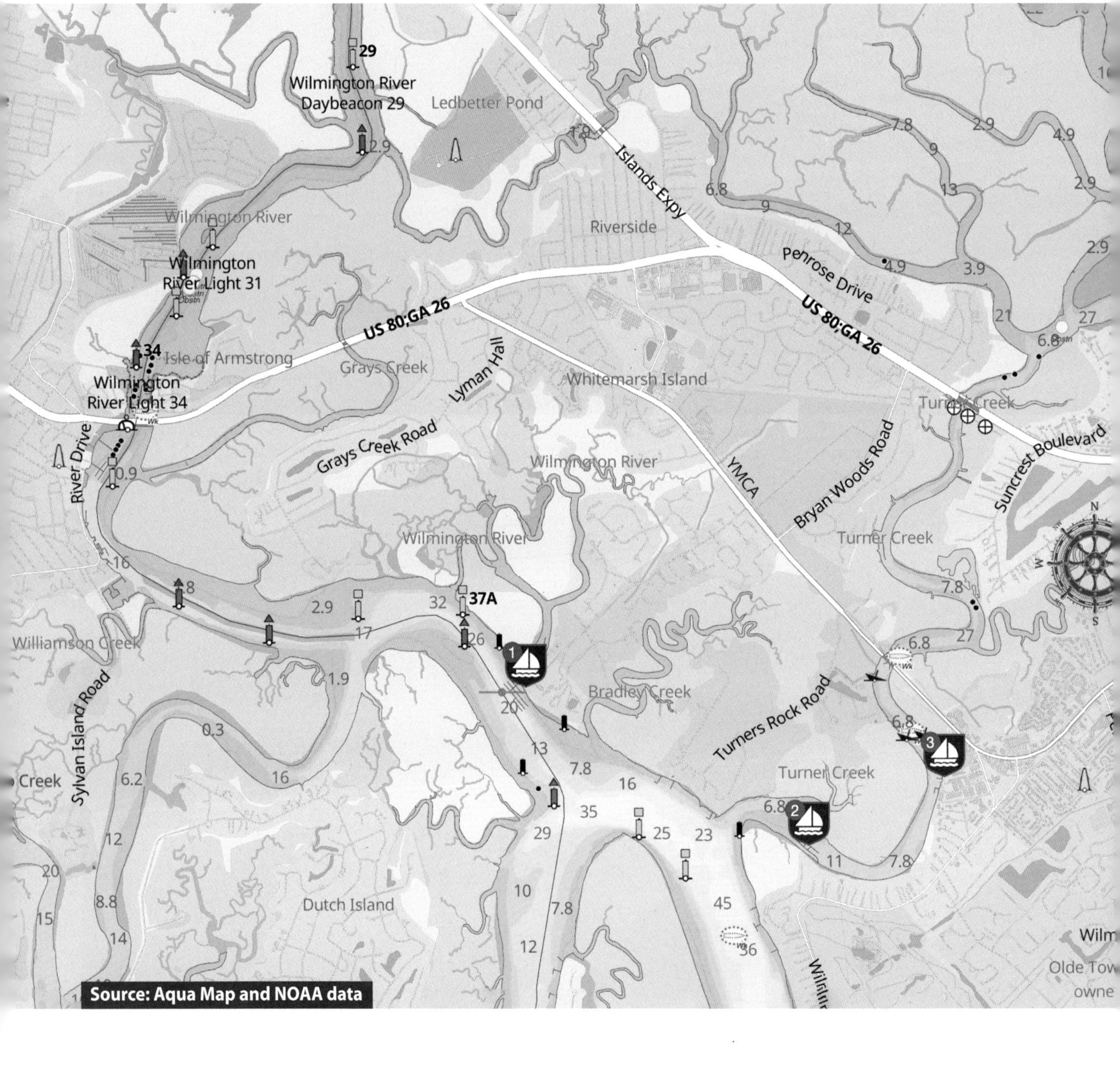

Source: Aqua Map and NOAA data

Wilmington River, GA

WILMINGTON RIVER		Largest Vessel	VHF	Total Slips	Approach/ Dockside Depth	Floating Docks	Gas/ Diesel	Repairs/ Haulout	Min/Max Amps	Pump-Out Station
1. Landings Harbor Marina (WiFi)	(912) 598-1901	40	16	29	20.0 / 8.0	F	GD	RH	30 / 50	P

(WiFi) Wireless Internet Access onSpot Dockside WiFi Facility
Visit www.waterwayguide.com for current rates, fuel prices, website addresses and other up-to-the-minute information.
(Information in the table is provided by the facilities.)

Scan here for more details:

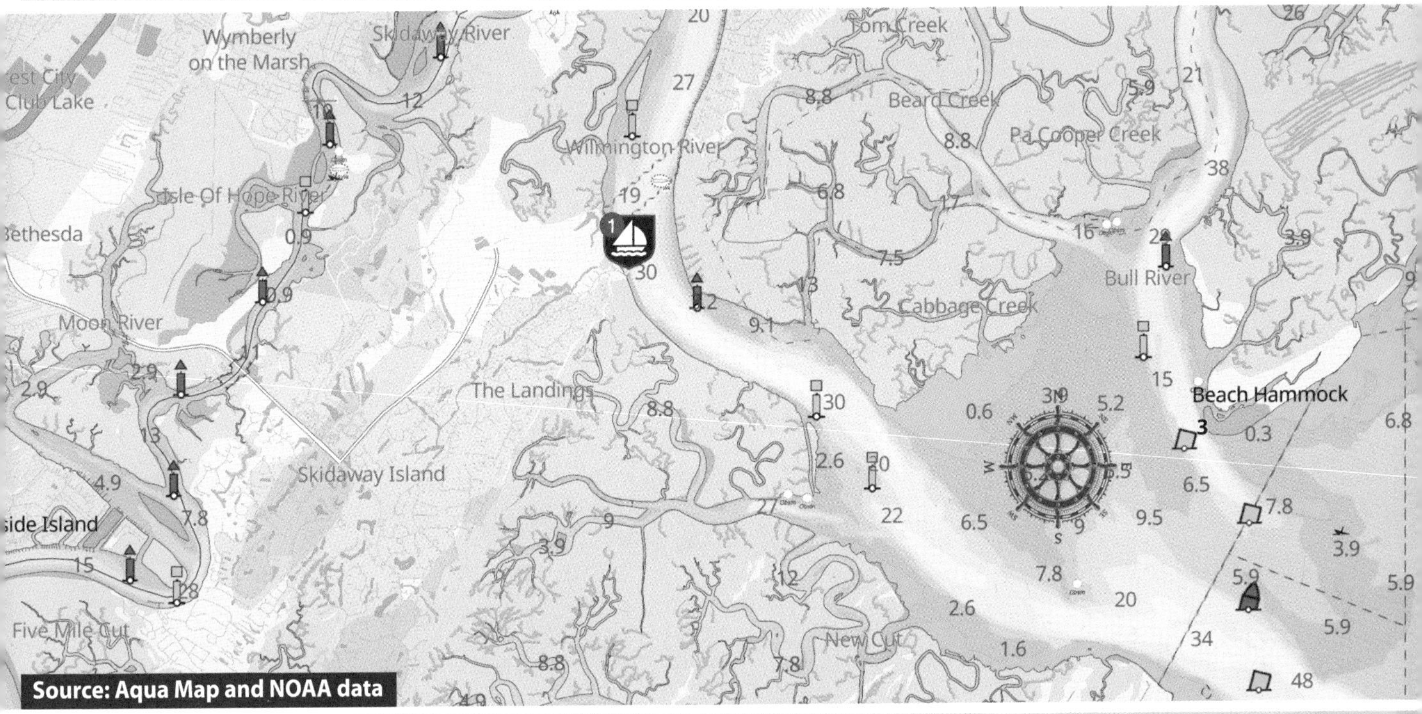

Source: Aqua Map and NOAA data

Wilmington Island

Wilmington River, GA

BULL RIVER		Largest Vessel	VHF	Total Slips	Approach/ Dockside Depth	Floating Docks	Gas/ Diesel	Repairs/ Haulout	Min/Max Amps	Pump-Out Station
1. Bull River Marina WiFi 4 mi. NE of MM 586	(912) 897-7300	110	16	70	25.0 / 18.0	F	GD	R	30 / 100	P

WiFi Wireless Internet Access onSpot Dockside WiFi Facility
Visit www.waterwayguide.com for current rates, fuel prices, website addresses and other up-to-the-minute information.
(Information in the table is provided by the facilities.)

Scan here for more details:

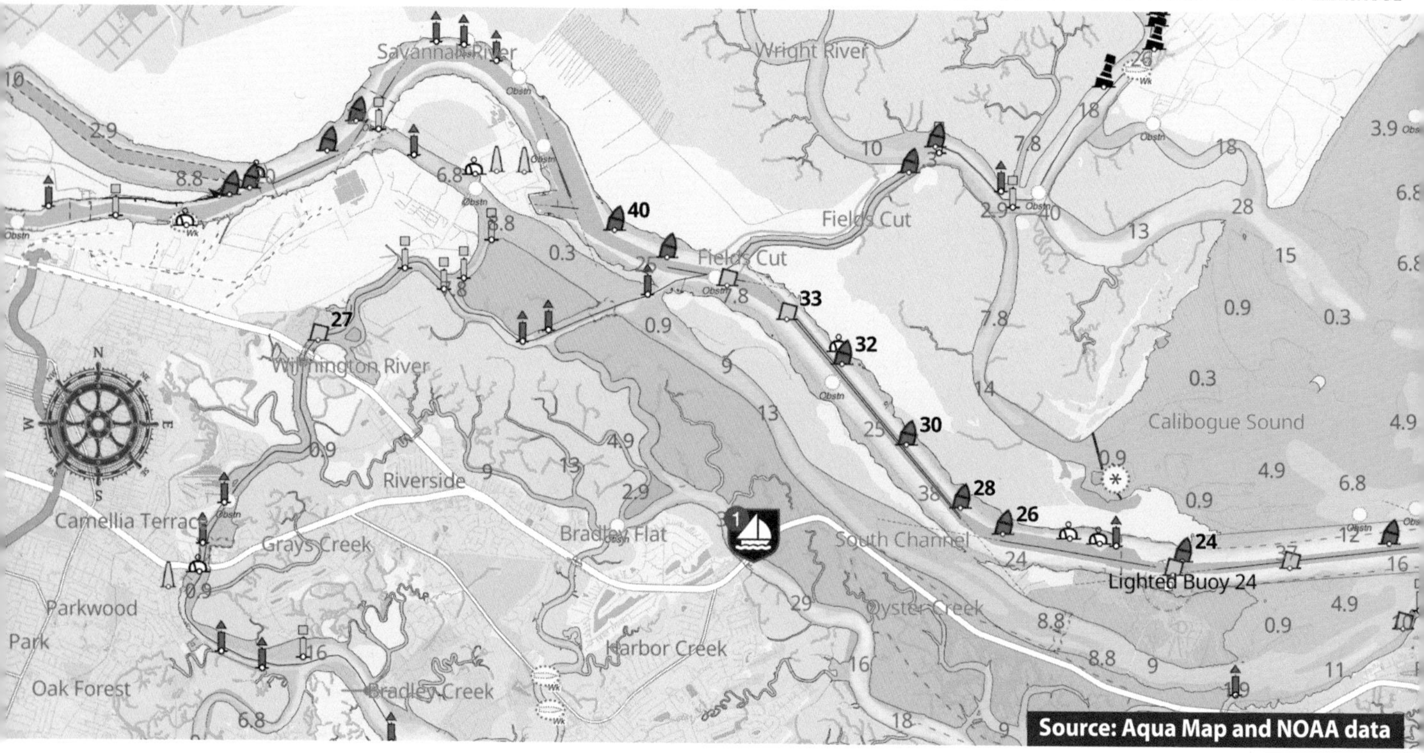

Wassaw Sound Entrance

NAVIGATION: Use NOAA Chart 11512. Wassaw Sound Entrance provides quick access to the Savannah area from the Atlantic Ocean. A fair amount of local traffic regularly uses this inlet but we do not recommend it except with up-to-date local knowledge, excellent visibility, calm seas and at mid-tide. This is not an inlet for dark and stormy arrivals as it is poorly marked and surrounded by shoals nearly 5 nm out from the entrance. This is the Atlantic inlet sometimes used by vessels bound for Thunderbolt Marine and unable to clear the 65-foot State Of Georgia Memorial (U.S. 80) Bridge over the Wilmington River at Mile 582.8.

Local boats anchor off a beautiful sandy beach at a spit on the northeast corner of Wassaw Island for day outings. Wassaw Sound and the Wilmington River carry about 25-foot MLW depths between flashing red buoy "10" in the Atlantic Ocean to flashing green daybeacon "29" at Skidaway River (Mile 585.5).

Dockage: Bull River Marina is accessible from Wassaw Sound with no bridges or other height restrictions but with a shallow bar (6- to 7-foot MLW spots charted) across its entrance channel. It is located 4 miles from ICW Mile 586 on the Bull River before the 20-foot fixed vertical clearance US 80 (Bull River) Bridge. The marina is home to boat rentals, fishing charters, excursions and the Daufuskie water taxi. They can accommodate vessels up to 110 feet.

Anchorage: Parts of Wassaw Sound and the Tybee River are subject to anchoring restrictions. Be sure to check GA DNR online before dropping the hook. "Anchoring Permits" are required if you plan to anchor in one place for more than 14 days in a year. ("One place" is defined by a circle of 1 mile radius.) "Anchoring Restriction Areas" apply to overnight anchoring in these areas: within 300 feet of a marina, within 150 feet of a marine structure (such as a private dock) or within 500 feet of an approved shellfish area.

Wilmington River, GA

SKIDAWAY RIVER		Largest Vessel	VHF	Total Slips	Approach/ Dockside Depth	Floating Docks	Gas/ Diesel	Repairs/ Haulout	Min/Max Amps	Pump-Out Station
1. Isle of Hope Marina WiFi MM 590.0	(912) 354-8187	220	16	125	12.0 / 15.0	F	GD		30 / 100	P

WiFi Wireless Internet Access onSpot Dockside WiFi Facility
Visit www.waterwayguide.com for current rates, fuel prices, website addresses and other up-to-the-minute information.
(Information in the table is provided by the facilities.)

Scan here for more details:

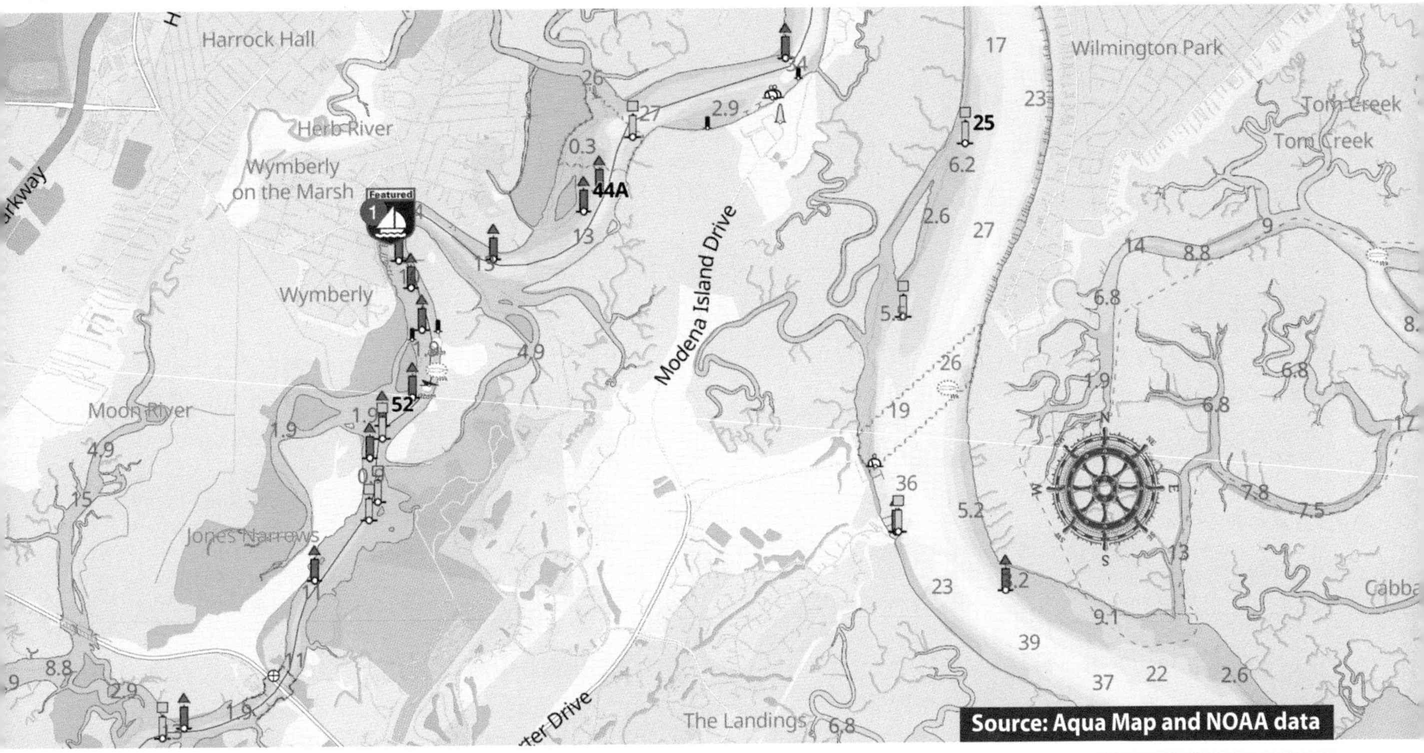

Source: Aqua Map and NOAA data

Skidaway River & Narrows–ICW Mile 585 to Mile 596

Isle of Hope at Mile 590 is a charming village of winding roads and old houses scattered among the tall pines and oaks located on the shore of the Skidaway River. It is 7 miles by water down the twisting ICW from Thunderbolt but only half that by road. The town stands on a bend high above the river and is listed on the National Register of Historic Places. Signs politely request that you slow down as you pass and keep your wake to a minimum; better yet, tie up here to enjoy a walk among the antebellum homes.

> About 1 mile from the Isle of Hope Marina is the Wormsloe Historic Site (912-353-3023) with a museum, ruins of a fortified house and a nature walk. Wild deer and pigs leave their tracks and sometimes appear on the grounds. The on-site Wormsloe Mansion is not open to the public because it is a private residence still occupied by the descendants of Noble Jones, one of the earliest Georgia settlers and the original owner of the property. You can visit the site on foot, bike or by tour bus from Savannah.

NAVIGATION: Use NOAA Chart 11507. Turn southwest into the Skidaway River at Mile 585 for a meandering 5-mile cruise to Isle of Hope. Skidaway Narrows, immediately below Isle of Hope, is a twisting stretch of the ICW that weaves erratically back and forth around curves and bends. Take your time, cut your speed as necessary, watch your course and enjoy this winding creek with its fringes of salt marsh extending back to distant woods.

> Skidaway Narrows is the preferred swimming hole of the local river otter population.

The pretty Vernon View at Mile 596 is a Savannah suburb overlooking the Burnside River portion of the ICW. This begins at Skidaway Narrows' southern end about 6 miles below Isle of Hope. Private docks line the shore (and are well charted) but there is no public marina. Remember that you are responsible for your wake here.

Slow boats should note that high slack water at Mile 592 (Skidaway Narrows) occurs 49 minutes before

Ossabaw Sound, GA

DELEGAL CREEK		Largest Vessel	VHF	Total Slips	Approach/ Dockside Depth	Floating Docks	Gas/ Diesel	Repairs/ Haulout	Min/Max Amps	Pump-Out Station
1. Delegal Creek Marina WiFi 1.0 mi. E of MM 601	(912) 224-3885	150	16	58	3.0 / 15.0	F	GD		30 / 50	P

WiFi Wireless Internet Access onSpot Dockside WiFi Facility
Visit www.waterwayguide.com for current rates, fuel prices, website addresses and other up-to-the-minute information.
(Information in the table is provided by the facilities.)

Scan here for more details:

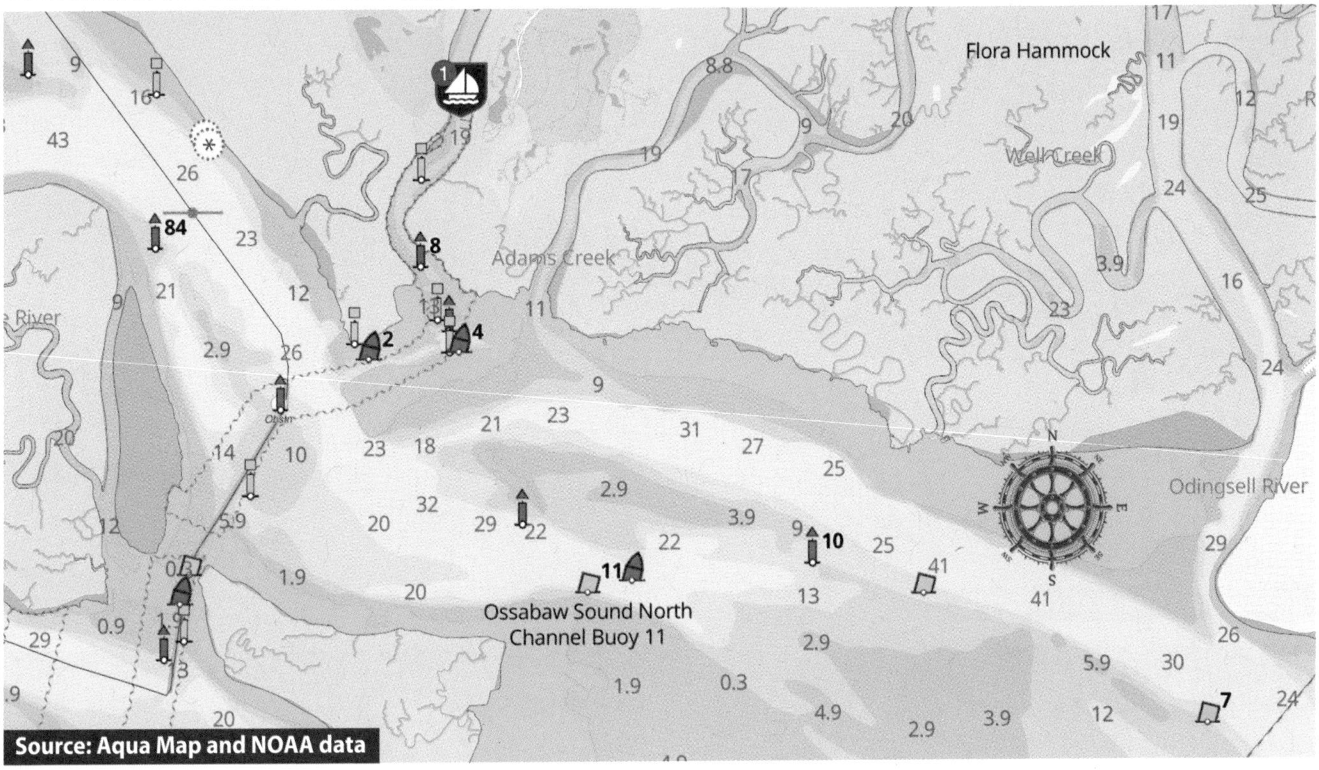

Source: Aqua Map and NOAA data

the Savannah River Entrance. This is good to keep in mind as arriving at Skidaway Narrows at slack water provides the most favorable currents from Mile 585 to Mile 603. Tidal currents reverse in the vicinity of the fixed 65-foot vertical clearance **Diamond Causeway (Skidaway) Bridge**.

The channel narrows from red daybeacon "46A" (Mile 592.9) to the bridge. Favor the eastern bank until red daybeacon "50." A boat ramp just below the bridge creates considerable small-boat traffic so keep alert. There is also a buoyed-off swimming area. Note the Slow Speed signs here.

On the Burnside River (Mile 596) favor the north side of the channel between red daybeacon "76" and flashing green daybeacon "79," which marks the turn into the Vernon River. A shoal is building out along the southeast side of the Burnside River so don't cut flashing green daybeacon "79" too closely and watch for shoaling to flashing green daybeacon "81."

Dockage: Located in one of the most beautiful settings on the entire ICW, the convenient Isle of Hope Marina provides large slips at concrete floating docks with full amenities including laundry facilities and a pool. This is the logical jumping-off point for the long run south and the first landing near Savannah when you are headed north with bus service to the city. The marina also offers a courtesy car and bicycles. Note that this is the last fuel stop on the ICW (southbound) for 90 miles. There are food markets, a West Marine, Walmart and restaurants within courtesy car range.

Anchorage: Anchor just north of the Diamond Causeway (Skidaway) Bridge on the eastern shore just before slight bend at Mile 592.9. This area shoals up quickly (depth of 15 feet MLW and tide of 7 feet) but is protected and offers small beaches for dog walking. Beware of your swing and don't anchor in the middle of the channel.

Ossabaw Sound, GA

OGEECHEE RIVER		Largest Vessel	VHF	Total Slips	Approach/ Dockside Depth	Floating Docks	Gas/ Diesel	Repairs/ Haulout	Min/Max Amps	Pump-Out Station
1. Ft. McAllister Marina (WiFi) 6.0 mi. W of MM 605.5	(912) 727-2632	80	16	60	15.0 / 20.0	F	GD	H	30 / 50	P

(WiFi) Wireless Internet Access onSpot Dockside WiFi Facility
Visit www.waterwayguide.com for current rates, fuel prices, website addresses and other up-to-the-minute information.
(Information in the table is provided by the facilities.)

Scan here for more details:

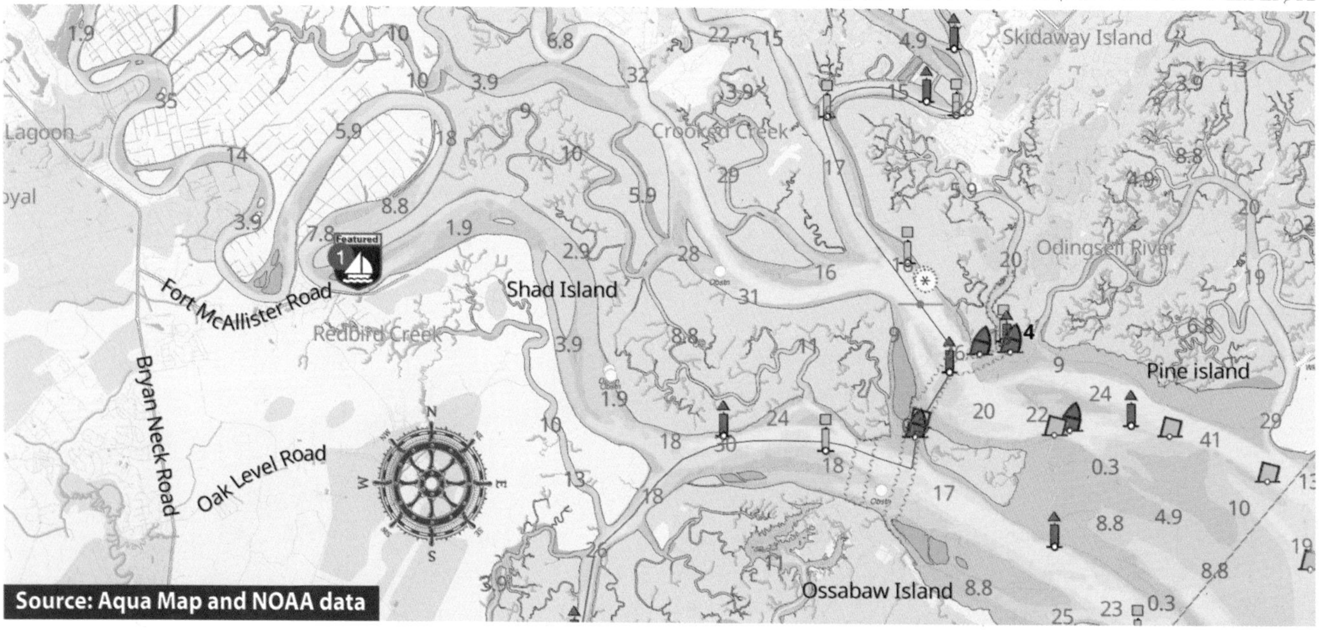

Source: Aqua Map and NOAA data

Richmond Hill, Fort McAllister

Moon River, made famous by songwriter Johnny Mercer, is just short of Mile 595. Boaters have reported shoaling to around 4-foot MLW depths at the entrance although depths are still charted at 8 feet MLW with shoaling indicated. Anchor behind Marsh Island and remember that in periods of strong and prolonged westerly wind and during the new and full moon phases tides can be much lower than normal charted depths. Stay clear of flashing red daybeacon "74" and the shoaling before heading northwest up the river.

If you give the long shoal off Possum Point a wide berth, you can turn northward up the Vernon River well off the ICW to drop the hook south of the village of Montgomery. Currents can be strong here and you should allow for an 8-foot tidal range. You will probably share this anchorage with a shrimp boat or two during the season. They usually anchor on one long stretchy nylon rode and keep their arms down so give them plenty of space to swing. This is a pleasant anchorage in more than 14-foot MLW depths. Anchor before the charted 1-foot MLW bar, which extends out to the middle of the river.

Vernon River to St. Catherines Sound– ICW Mile 596 to Mile 618

NAVIGATION: Use NOAA Charts 11507, 11509 and 11511. The Vernon River runs wide and deep until you reach Hell Gate, a land cut leading from the Vernon River to the Okeechobee River. If strong northeast winds kick up, you might see swells breaking up the long fetch of both the Vernon and Ogeechee Rivers. The Ogeechee River is Georgia coast's second largest river and has a particularly strong ebb current. From here the ICW channel leads south through the Florida Passage, which flows into the Bear River, running the length of Ossabaw Island. One of Georgia's eight major Sea Islands, Ossabaw Island is pierced by a number of narrow but deep creeks fanning out from the Bear River.

The Ossabaw Inlet to the ocean is used by small local craft but is not suitable for use by cruising vessels other than in very calm weather and with local knowledge.

Hell Gate is one of the most notorious sections of the ICW for shoaling but it was dredged to 12 feet MLW in 2019 so it should be stable for awhile. For now, just go down the middle but favor the green side of the channel by the southern exit. Go slow and watch the depthsounder. Mid-tide and rising is the safest time to go through these questionable areas of the ICW and stay in the center of the channel. There are strong side-sweeping currents at Hell Gate, especially on the ebb when entering from the north (Vernon River) so keep track of your progress by looking both ahead and astern. Leaving Hell Gate run beyond flashing green daybeacon "91" and round quick flashing red daybeacon "92" to make the turn for the 3-mile run up the Ogeechee River.

There is a 9.8 MLW spot at the southern exit of Hell Gate halfway between flashing green "91" and flashing red "92" that was not dredged due to a buried electrical cable.

Pay particular attention to the markers at the passage through Middle Marsh. Carefully follow the markers, changing course as indicated to pass safely between Middle Marsh to the south (which is obscured at high tide) and the shoal north of red daybeacon "94" off Charles Creek's entrance.

Ossabaw Sound, GA

LITTLE OGEECHEE RIVER		Largest Vessel	VHF	Total Slips	Approach/ Dockside Depth	Floating Docks	Gas/ Diesel	Repairs/ Haulout	Min/Max Amps	Pump-Out Station
1. Coffee Bluff Marina	(912) 231-3628	200		20	25.0 /	F	GD	H	30 / 50	P

WiFi Wireless Internet Access onSpot Dockside WiFi Facility
Visit www.waterwayguide.com for current rates, fuel prices, website addresses and other up-to-the-minute information.
(Information in the table is provided by the facilities.)

Scan here for more details:

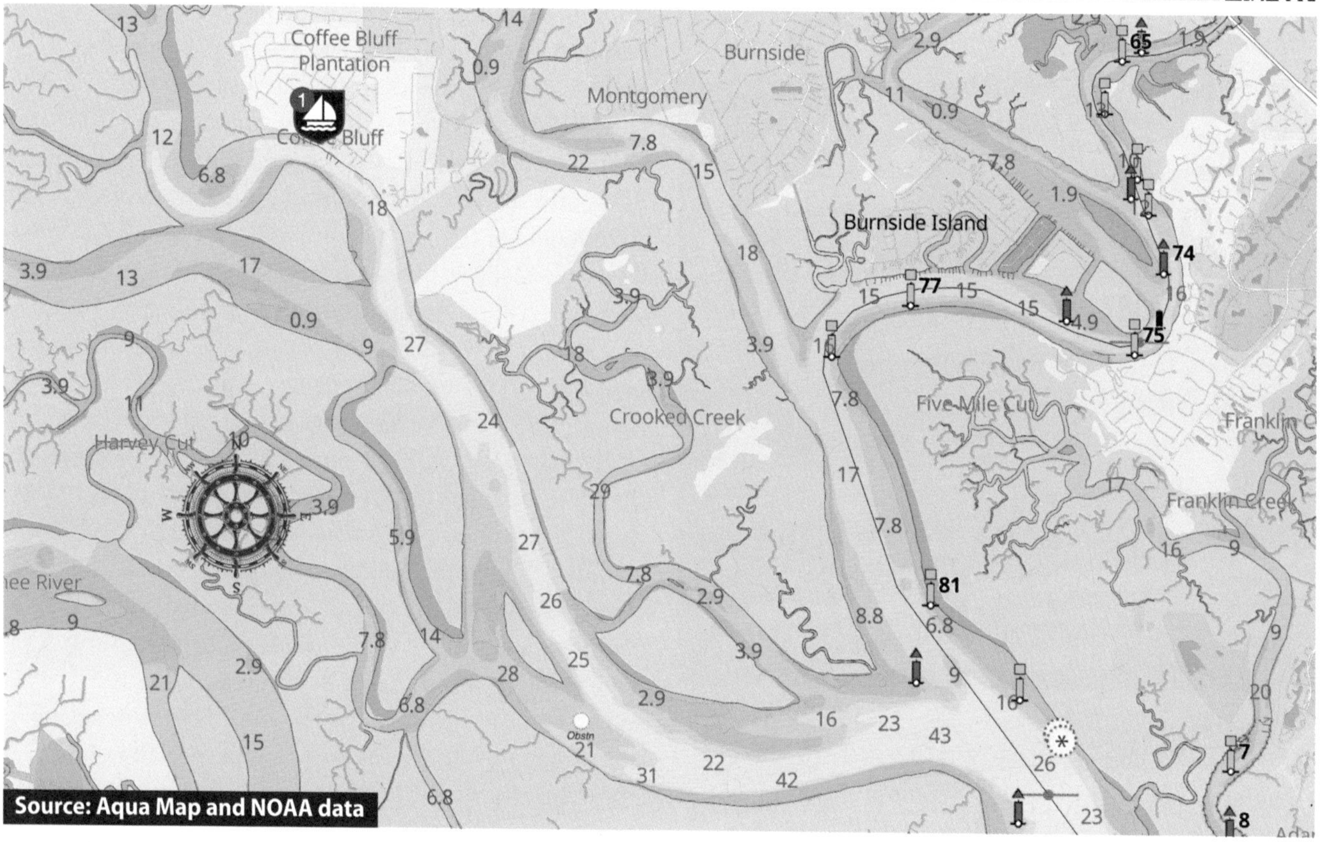

Dockage: Delegal Creek makes off to the north at Mile 601 just above Hell Gate across the Vernon River. The marked channel leads to the well-regarded Delegal Creek Marina, a 70-slip marina in a beautiful setting. Marina guests enjoy Delegal's convenience and amenities, as well as dining, tennis, pool and golf privileges offered by The Landings Club during their stay. This is a well-known stopping point for transient boaters and the facility welcomes boats up to 125 feet. Call ahead on VHF Channels 16 or 68 to check depths and get directions for entering the marked channel prior to docking.

Five miles up the Ogeechee River from flashing red daybeacon "98" (Florida Passage intersection) is Ft. McAllister Marina. This river requires you to cross from the north to the south side after Shad Island. The dockmaster can see vessels approaching up river and may contact you to offer guidance. If not, you should call the marina for directions on your approach. It is easy to fetch up on the sand bar without proper directions. There are signs here that some have found to be confusing. The channel in this rapidly flowing estuary is constantly shifting and even current charts may not be wholly accurate. Study NOAA Charts 11507, 11509 and 11511 before heading upriver and absolutely call for local knowledge before attempting passage.

Ft. McAllister Marina is a friendly marina with 15 acres of boat/RV storage (covered and open storage). They offer repairs in addition to slips to 80 feet on floating docks. The on-site Fish Tales Restaurant (912-727-3473) is a lively waterfront eatery with a Caribbean flair at reasonable prices. They have live music most weekends. North on the Little Ogeechee River is Coffee Bluff Marina, which caters to sportfishing vessels and has limited transient space. Call ahead.

Ossabaw Sound, GA

KILKENNY CREEK		Largest Vessel	VHF	Total Slips	Approach/ Dockside Depth	Floating Docks	Gas/ Diesel	Repairs/ Haulout	Min/Max Amps	Pump-Out Station
1. Kilkenny Marina WiFi MM 614.0	(912) 727-2215	100	16	10	8.0 / 6.0	F	GD	H	30 / 50	

WiFi Wireless Internet Access onSpot Dockside WiFi Facility
Visit www.waterwayguide.com for current rates, fuel prices, website addresses and other up-to-the-minute information.
(Information in the table is provided by the facilities.)

Scan here for more details:

At Mile 614 on the Bear River you can turn westward into Kilkenny Creek at ICW green daybeacon "107. The Texaco sign at the entrance is a good landmark. About 1.5 miles up from the marker is rural Kilkenny Marina, which welcomes transients. The marina reports that its entrance channel carries 10 feet MLW if you stay 30 feet north of the center of the creek.

Anchorage: Parts of the St. Catherines Sound area (Bear and Medway River) are subject to anchoring restrictions. Be sure to check Georgia DNR online before dropping the hook. "Anchoring Permits" are required if you plan to anchor in one place for more than 14 days in a year. ("One place" is defined by a circle of 1 mile radius.) "Anchoring Restriction Areas" apply to overnight anchoring in these areas:

- Within 300 feet of a marina
- Within 150 feet of a marine structure (such as a private dock)
- Within 500 feet of an approved shellfish area

There is a fine selection of anchorages in Redbird Creek north off the Florida Passage at Mile 606.8. Here you will find 6- to 18-foot MLW depths and good holding in mud. The current is very strong here so be sure to set your anchor well. Queen Bess Creek is directly across the Florida Passage with at least 4 feet MLW.

At Mile 608.5 stay on the range until you are well past red daybeacon "102" then turn eastward up the Bear River to Cane Patch Creek or Buckhead Creek, then pick a spot with suitable depths and set the anchor well. Depths vary from 10 to 30 feet here and the current is exceptionally strong.

At Mile 612 you can turn north into Birthday Creek and anchor in 9- to 14-foot MLW depths with good holding in mud. Nearby Big Tom Creek at Mile 612.5 is a popular overnight anchorage. Anchor either near its entrance or around the first bend in 9-foot MLW depths.

Kilkenny Creek provides a popular but peaceful spot to drop the hook with 15-foot MLW depths and

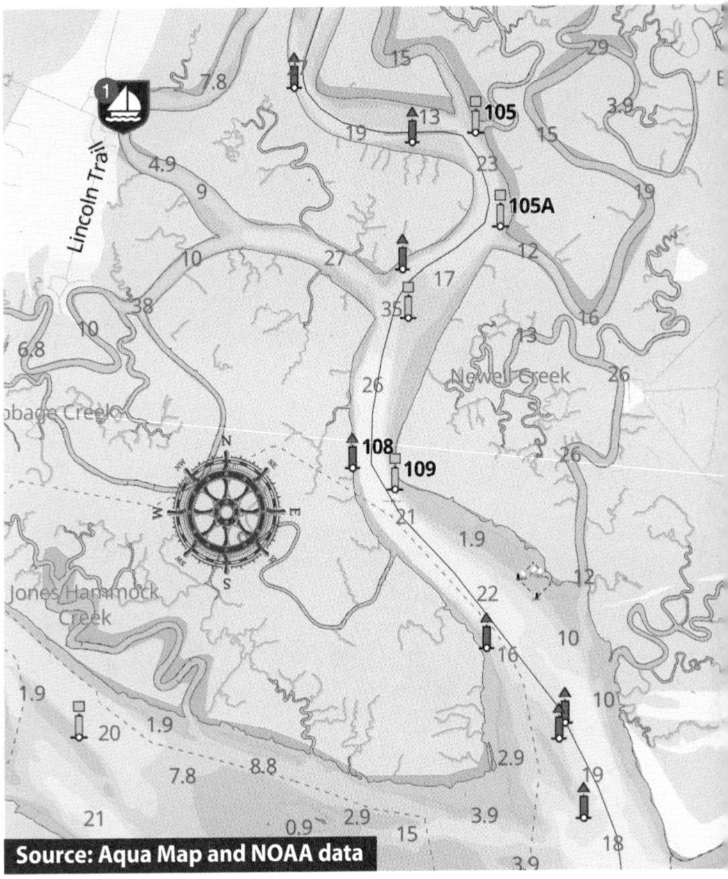

Source: Aqua Map and NOAA data

a mud bottom. This anchorage borders the marsh, making insect screens and repellent essential. There is considerable nighttime traffic from shrimp boats in Kilkenny Creek during the harvesting season so be sure your anchor light is working properly.

NEXT STOP

The next chapter takes you to the first of many large sounds. You will pass through St. Catherines Sound on the way to St. Marys, GA, passing the stop-worthy St. Simons Island, Brunswick and Jekyll Island on the way. The open sounds will be a welcome change from the twisty rivers and straight land cuts to the north.

America's Waterway Guide Since 1947
WATERWAY GUIDE
Southern
Florida, the Keys and the Gulf Coast to Bay St. Louis
Chesapeake Bay
Cape May, NJ to Norfolk, VA including Delaware Bay
Great Lakes Vol. 1
Great Lakes Vol. 2
Atlantic ICW
Intracoastal Waterway from Norfolk, VA to St. Marys River, GA
Northern
Cape May, NJ to Eastport, ME Including the Hudson River
Bahamas
Florida Keys
From Fort Lauderdale to the Dry Tortugas
Western Gulf Coast
Lake Pontchartrain & New Orleans to South Padre Island, TX
Cuba
With Departure Points from the Florida Keys
Skipper Bob Publications
Cruising Comfortably on a Budget
Bahamas Bound
Anchorages Along the Intracoastal Waterway
Cruising the New York Canal System
SKIPPER BOB Publications
Cruising the Gulf Coast
Cruising America's Great Loop
Cruising the Rideau & Richelieu Canals
Marinas Along the Intracoastal Waterway
Cruising the Trent-Severn Waterway, Georgian Bay and North Channel
Cruising from Chicago to Mobile
The iOS App from Waterway Guide
To St. Augustine
The beach regions running south from Jacksonville are collectively referred to as the "First Coast" because this is the location of Florida's first European settlements. It vigorously competes with the Gold Coast, the Sun Coast and the Treasure Coast for developer and tourist dollars. The area begins a parade of shoreside communities
WATERWAY EXPLORER
Waterway Explorer Magazine
The Explorer web app
waterwayguide.com
WATERWAY GUIDE MEDIA
No Signal? No Problem!
DOWNLOAD CONTENT
Download on the App Store

ICW Mile 618-Mile 714

■ TO JEKYLL ISLAND, GA

The ICW follows the Bear River as it empties into St. Catherines Sound at Mile 618. This is the first in a series of sounds connected by rivers that you will pass through as you transit the Georgia portion of the ICW. Other sounds along this stretch include Sapelo Sound, Doboy Sound, Altamaha Sound, Buttermilk Sound, St. Simons Sound, Jekyll Sound and St. Andrews Sound. Some of these sounds are large and exposed enough to get rough, but they also provide a nice change of pace from the rivers and land cuts to the north. It is always advisable to keep a close eye on the weather. You do not want opposing wind and tide anywhere on these sounds.

When the sounds are open for shrimping keep an eye on all shrimp boats in your vicinity. They move fast when heading to and from their shrimping grounds. When they are working their movements will be erratic and they will be occupied with their trailing nets so you will be the one to take evasive action. They often travel with their long "arms" extended so even if you are under sail, do not expect shrimp boats to alter course or raise their booms. They have been known to go under bridges with their "arms" partially or fully down, leaving no room for other boats. Stand well clear of them and keep your horn handy; five blasts is the danger signal.

St. Catherines Sound to Sapelo Sound–Mile 615 to Mile 634

NAVIGATION: Use NOAA Chart 11507, 11509, 11511. Expect low slack water at Mile 618 to be 39 minutes earlier than at the Savannah River Entrance. For slow-moving north or southbound boats the best time to arrive at St. Catherines Sound is at low slack water when the sea is calmest and the currents are most favorable. Tidal range is 7 to 8 feet. Watch your course between Miles 615 and 617 and take care that wind and current do not set your vessel too far to the west.

The shoal reported on the charts does indeed exist near red daybeacon "110A." Give flashing red "112," "114" and "114A" a wide berth and keep to the charted ICW magenta line.

St. Catherines Sound Entrance has a wide, uncomplicated entrance with good depths within. As with other smaller inlets in Georgia, channel markers are widely placed and it can be difficult to visually pick them out, even though the offshore sea buoys are in their charted position and easy to locate with GPS. Some of the smaller markers are frequently moved to locate better water.

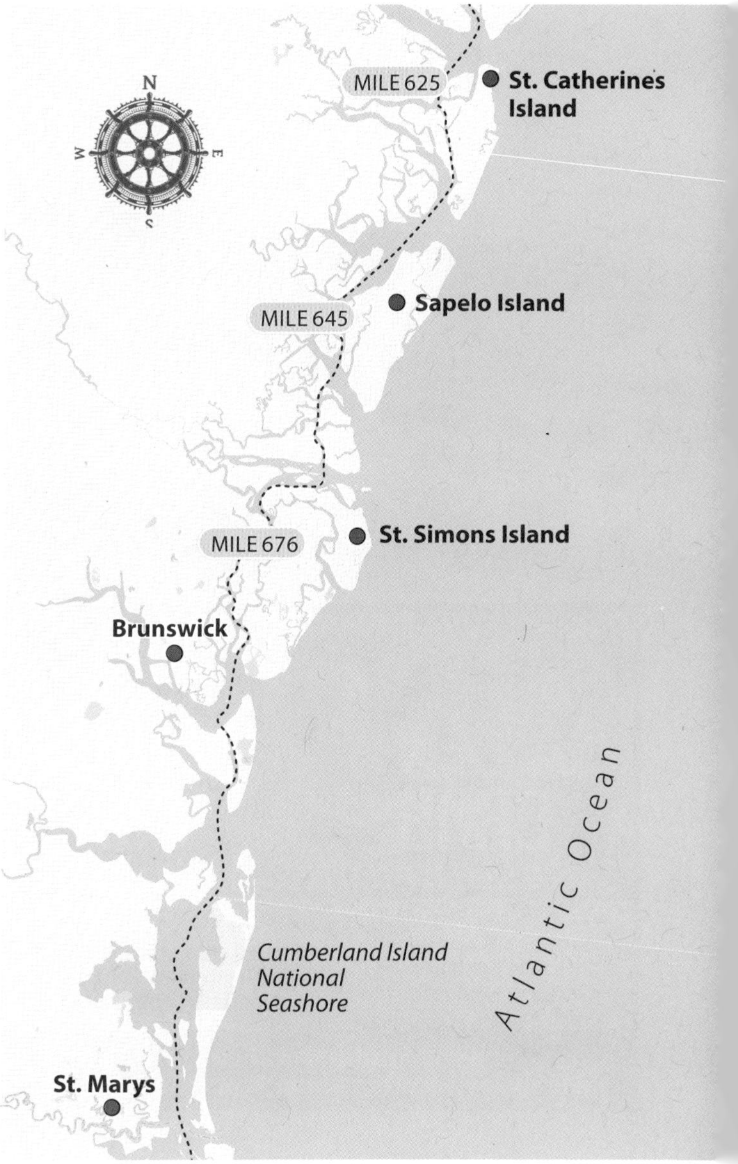

St. Catherines Sound, GA

MEDWAY RIVER		Largest Vessel	VHF	Total Slips	Approach/ Dockside Depth	Floating Docks	Gas/ Diesel	Repairs/ Haulout	Min/Max Amps	Pump-Out Station
1. Sunbury Crab Co. Restaurant & Marina WiFi MM 618.0	(912) 884-8640	125		28	/ 23.0	F	GD		30 / 100	

WiFi Wireless Internet Access onSpot Dockside WiFi Facility
Visit www.waterwayguide.com for current rates, fuel prices, website addresses and other up-to-the-minute information.
(Information in the table is provided by the facilities.)

Scan here for more details:

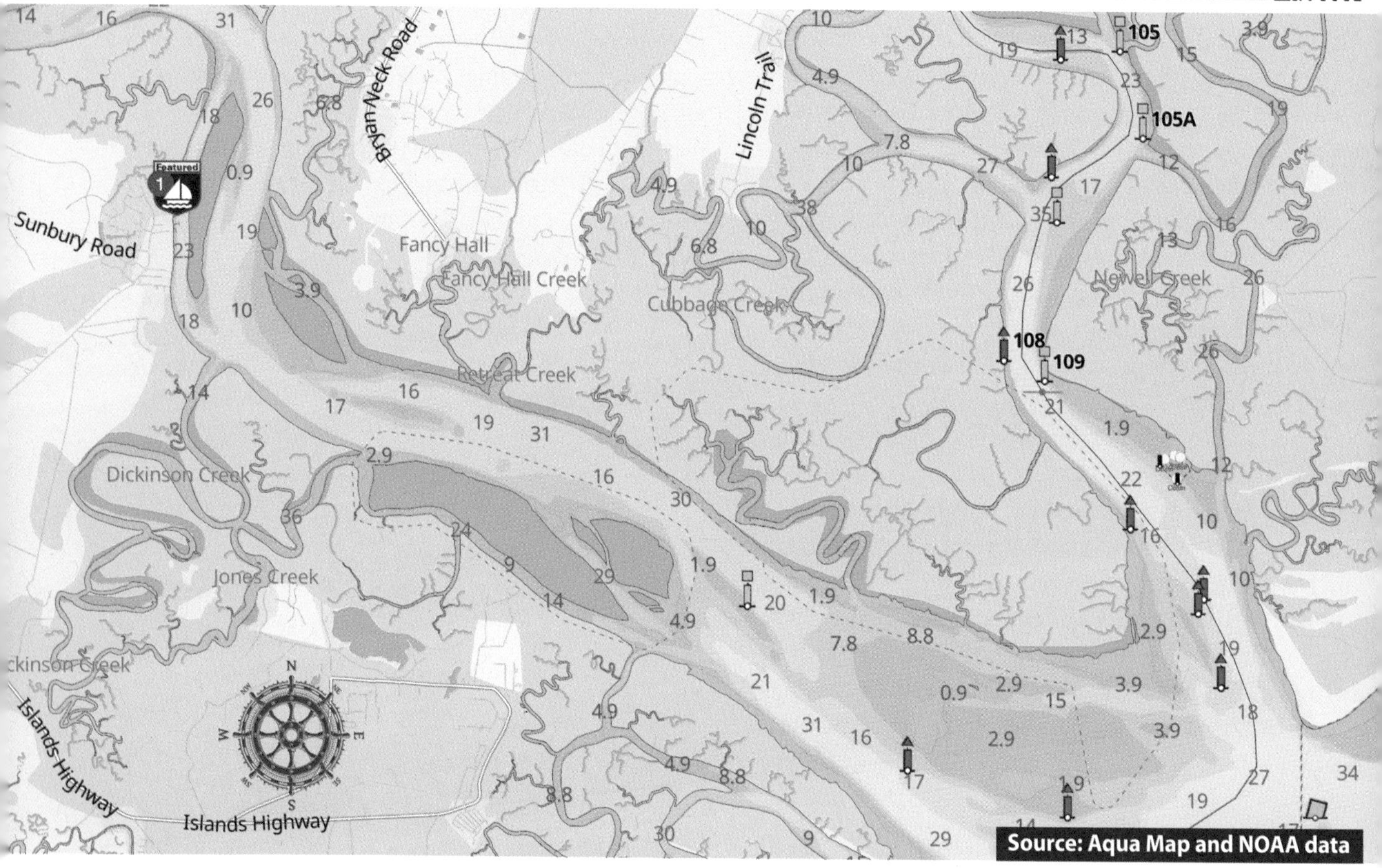

A protected but seldom-used alternate to the ICW route along the exposed North Newport River is the charted Walburg Creeks channel, which flows past the western shore of St. Catherines Island to join with the ICW route at Mile 622.5. Green can buoy "7," which marks the end of the shoal at Middle Ground in St. Catherines Sound off Walburg Creek, needs to be honored if you intend to enter and anchor in Walburg Creek. Although the northern entrance to Walburg Creek (from St. Catherines Sound) is straightforward, the southern passage back into the North Newport River is tricky with depths of 4 to 5 feet MLW.

Beyond Mile 620 the ICW enters the mouth of the North Newport River and follows along that river to about Mile 623, where the North Newport River bears off to the

St. Catherines Sound, GA

THE HALFMOON		Largest Vessel	VHF	Total Slips	Approach/ Dockside Depth	Floating Docks	Gas/ Diesel	Repairs/ Haulout	Min/Max Amps	Pump-Out Station
1. Halfmoon Marina WiFi 6.0 mi. W of MM 622.5	(912) 884-5819	100	16	10	15.0 / 30.0	F	GD		15 / 50	

WiFi Wireless Internet Access onSpot Dockside WiFi Facility
Visit www.waterwayguide.com for current rates, fuel prices, website addresses and other up-to-the-minute information.
(Information in the table is provided by the facilities.)

Scan here for more details:

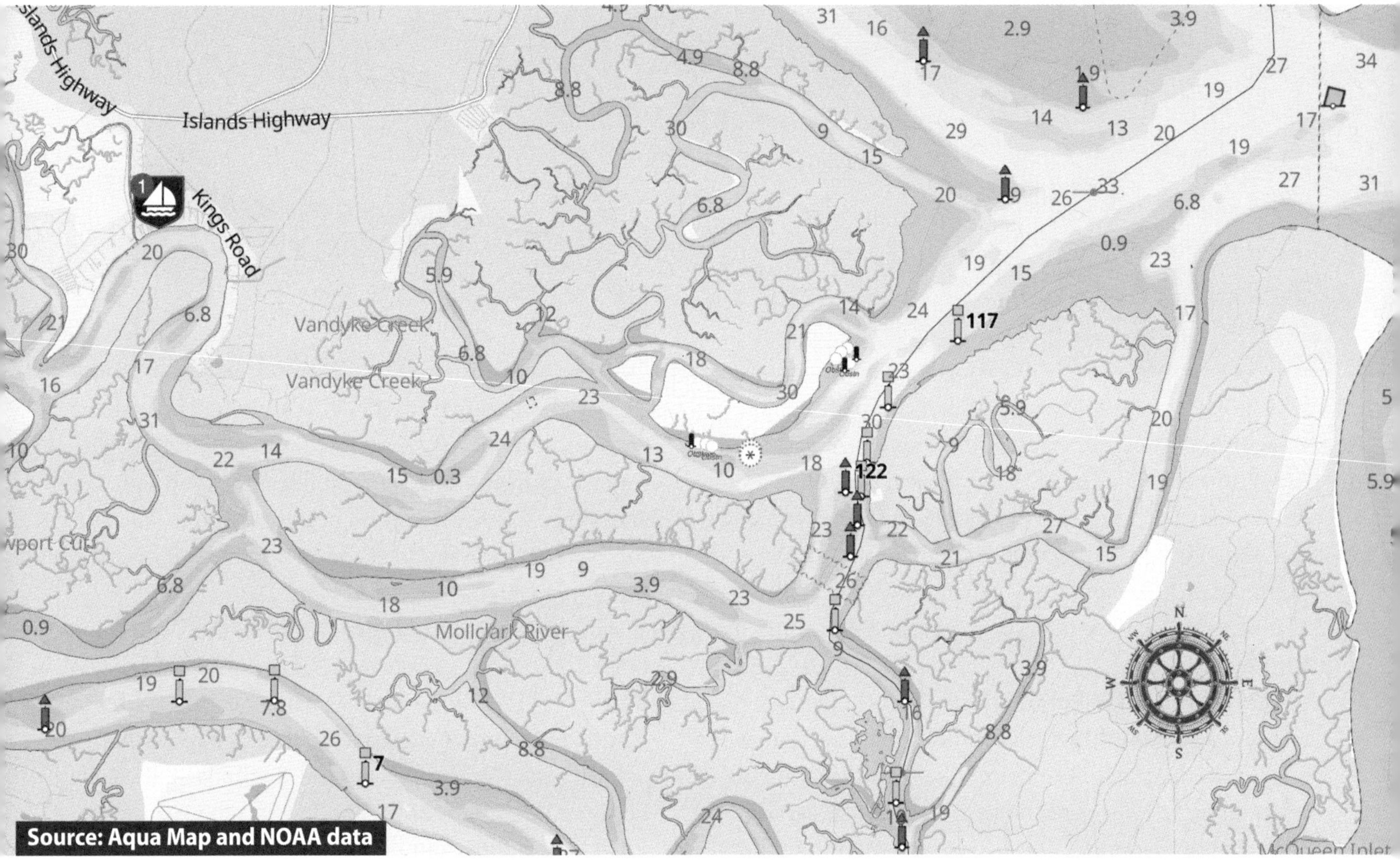

Source: Aqua Map and NOAA data

west. The ICW channel continues south along Johnson Creek. Heading south along the ICW you will exit Johnson Creek for a short run along the South Newport River to its mouth. The ICW route heads up Sapelo Sound to the Sapelo River, running past Sapelo Island.

At Mile 627 on Johnson Creek favor the red side of the channel for 18 feet MLW by keeping 120 feet off green "131A" where less than 5 feet MLW has been observed.

Dockage: About 6 miles northwest of St. Catherines Sound (from ICW Mile 618) on the Medway River is the popular Sunbury Crab Co. Restaurant & Marina. To reach Sunbury pass between red flashing "114A" and "116" upriver and follow the chart. Cross to the west side of the river at Fancy Hall Creek (to starboard). There are no markers, just watch your depth sounder. As you approach Sunbury, hug the western shore and enter the Sunbury channel between the unnamed island and the shore. Sunbury Crab Co. Restaurant & Marina will be the next to last docks on your left. (Look for signs.)

Sunbury Crab Co. Restaurant & Marina is one of those fun, off-the-beaten-path places that is worth the few extra miles to go visit. The staff is friendly, they offer transient dockage to 125 feet and the restaurant offers large portions at reasonable prices in a relaxed, laid-back atmosphere. This place is funky, eclectic and fun.

From flashing green daybeacons "119" and "121" (Mile 623.7) turn to the west and cruise 7 miles up the North Newport River to the small Halfmoon Marina,

Sapelo Sound

which offers space for transients at a competitive rate. You can also get there via the Timmons River a couple miles further down the ICW. Be advised that there are no markers on either side of these rivers in this area. Call the marina for directions and follow your chart plotter and depth sounder very carefully. The Halfmoon Marina is the last marina near the ICW southbound for the next 40 miles.

Anchorage: Walburg Creek provides splendid anchorages. Go northwest 1.2 miles from Mile 630 and anchor by the stand of trees on the north shore. If you go as far as the 90-degree bend to the west be careful of the shoal on the north side as it is encroaching farther into the channel. You can drop the hook in 15- to 20-foot MLW depths with good sand holding. Shrimp boats often use this anchorage too so be sure that your anchor light is working properly. Avoid anchoring in the bend of the creek off the southern tip of Walburg Island, where the water is deep and currents run swiftly. A dinghy ride to the north end of St. Catherines Island reveals a desolate but beautiful sandy barrier island beach. Note that the St. Catherines Island Foundation owns the island and limits visitation.

Cattle Pen Creek, south of Johnson Creek at Mile 625.5, provides a fine overnight anchorage for boats up to about 40 feet in length but may be too narrow for larger boats that need more swinging room. While the charted depths inside Cattle Pen Creek are good expect entrance depths to be only 7 feet MLW rather than the 14 feet MLW shown on the NOAA chart. The marsh does not provide much protection from wind but the water is narrow enough that it does not get rough in the anchorage. It provides good holding in mud. The current can be strong but if you set your anchor well, there should not be a problem.

Southbound out of Johnson Creek, the Wahoo River makes off the South Newport River portion of the ICW at Mile 630. The Wahoo River is a fine overnight anchorage if you are willing to backtrack about 2 miles. When entering the river be wary of the shoal that is located between the mouth of the Wahoo and the Newport River. Go slightly past the mouth of the Wahoo River and turn back to avoid the shallow, well-marked shoal. Go northwest 1.2 miles and anchor by the stand of trees on the north shore. If you go as far as the 90-degree bend to the west be careful of the shoal on the north side as it is encroaching farther into the channel. The depth range throughout this area is 10 to 15 feet MLW in mud.

Sapelo Sound to Doboy Sound–ICW 634 to Mile 650

NAVIGATION: Use NOAA Chart 11501 and 11507. On Sapelo Sound, as well as other large sounds, give both lighted aids and daybeacons a wider berth than usual, especially around low tide. Keep track of your markers, running a compass course between distant ones. Many boats have erroneously run for an outlying sea buoy instead of a marker leading into a nearby tributary.

Sapelo Sound Entrance at Mile 632 is a favorite of area fishermen and shrimpers, not to mention legendary pirate Edward Teach (Blackbeard). You will pass just north of Blackbeard Island and Blackbeard Creek while transiting this inlet.

If coming from the ocean, note that there is a sand bar west of red nun "6." Depths of 7 to 10 feet MLW have been observed despite the 19 feet marked on the chart.

Southbound cruisers hoping to avoid the Georgia ICW rarely use this inlet, preferring to jump offshore through the big ship channels at Charleston or Port Royal, SC, or Savannah, GA. This is not the best inlet in rougher weather due to extensive shoals to the north and south of the inlet. Note that low slack water on Sapelo Sound Entrance occurs 30 minutes before it occurs at the Savannah River Entrance.

Mind the markers at the western end of Sapelo Sound where the ICW route enters the Sapelo River. At low tide approach the whole stretch with caution. Specific areas of concern are detailed below.

Despite recent dredging (2019) two shoals have been observed in Sapelo Sound. The first is by green daybeacon "143." Stay off the marker by 500 feet for 39 feet MLW. There is also extensive shoaling by red daybeacon "150" so pass it about 600 feet off for 16 feet MLW.

Continuing south the ICW route leaves the Sapelo River and enters the Front River. The Front River is narrow but deep in mid-channel. Many of the hammocks of land west of the channel show piles of ballast stone, which is all that remains of a once-prosperous riverside community. The ICW route continues south along the Front River before heading into Creighton Narrows at Mile 642.

Along the stretch through Creighton Narrows a succession of daybeacons and lights mark the channel; observe them carefully. When leaving Creighton Narrows and entering the Crescent River run straight past red daybeacon "156" until passing flashing green daybeacon "157" to avoid shallow depths to the west. The marked channel leads you into Old Teakettle Creek, which widens as it reaches Doboy Sound at Mile 649.

On Old Teakettle Creek at At Mile 643.6 there is a shoal between red daybeacon "158A" and "160." Follow the outside of the bend passing red "160" by at least 170 off for 24 feet MLW.

Arriving at Doboy Sound at low slack water will speed up your run from Mile 644 to Mile 654. (Trying to hit low slack water at either Sapelo Sound or Buttermilk Sound is not quite as critical, as both of these sounds provide more open waters and easier currents to navigate.)

Doboy Sound Entrance with 7-foot controlling depths is not our first choice in bad weather. On the other hand, if you have to get in it is uncomplicated and the breakwaters may give you some protection from south-setting waves once behind them. The preferred St. Simons Sound Entrance is 18 nm to the south.

Shoaling has been observed at Doboy Sound by flashing red "178" at Mile 649.5. Pass 300 feet off, favoring the green side for 12.5 feet MLW.

Anchorage: Parts of the Sapelo Sound area including the Mud River are subject to anchoring restrictions. Be sure to check Georgia DNR onsite before dropping the hook. "Anchoring Permits" are required if you plan to anchor in one place for more than 14 days in a year. ("One place" is defined by a circle of 1 mile radius.) "Anchoring Restriction Areas" apply to overnight anchoring in these areas:

- Within 300 feet of a marina
- Within 150 feet of a marine structure (such as a private dock)
- Within 500 feet of an approved shellfish area

It is important to note that shrimp boats came and go at all hours and often have their outriggers down increasing their beam up to 120 feet, which consumes the narrow channel.

Some boats anchor to the west of where Creighton Narrows empties into the Crescent River at Mile 644. One of the main attractions is the sandy beach for pet relief by red daybeacon "156," which is dry during an

8-foot low tide. You can also drop the hook farther upriver in the Crescent River in 12- to 16-foot MLW depths. Nearby Cedar Creek is another option.

The most popular anchorage between Sapelo Sound and Doboy Sound is New Teakettle Creek at Mile 646.5. The charted depths are good (15 to 20 feet MLW) and the best protection lies around the first bend to starboard. Be careful to avoid the charted 2-foot MLW lump in New Teakettle Creek just past Mary Creek.

Another attractive anchorage is up the Duplin River at Mile 649. Go past the very busy ferry dock at Marsh Landing 1 mile or so to the high ground of Little Sapelo Island and anchor in 15 to 16 feet MLW. Note the overhead power cable upstream on the Duplin River with a 38-foot vertical clearance. The holding here is very good and you will have plenty of swinging room as it is wide and deep to its banks. The current is swift but this is a good spot to spend the night. A lot of boats anchor here in order to stage for a favorable tide to transit the Little Mud River. Dinghy to the ferry dock and take a hike on the island. There are restrooms at the ferry dock.

Doboy Sound to Altamaha Sound–ICW Mile 650 to Mile 656

NAVIGATION: Use NOAA Chart 11502.

Caution: Low slack water at Mile 655 occurs 38 minutes before it occurs at the Savannah River Entrance. At Mile 660, only 5 miles away, low slack water occurs two hours and 6 minutes before it does at Savannah. NOAA provides up-to-date tide tables online at www.tidesandcurrents.noaa.gov.

The ICW continues down Doboy Sound to flashing red daybeacon "178" at the mouth of the North River (Mile 649.5). Follow the channel carefully here and in the dredged areas past the Darien, Rockdedundy and South Rivers. The range markers for this area that are shown on older NOAA charts have been removed. Mariners are advised to use extreme caution while transiting the area.

The ICW follows a dredged channel down Little Mud River to the Altamaha Sound and into Buttermilk Sound. Although the Little Mud River is one of the shallowest areas on the entire ICW, this area is not on the list of areas to be dredged due to environmental restrictions. There is no deep water path and shoals to 2 to 3 feet MLW on either side of the channel. If you choose to attempt the passage without the aid of a track, then be sure to pass with a half or full tide. Do not hug any of the markers.

Darien River

A PLACE WHERE INTRACOASTAL
TRAVELERS
HAVE COUNTLESS REASONS TO STOP
Experience the Exceptional
Nestled graciously between ancient live oaks and the historic riverfront bluff of Darien–Georgia's second-oldest city–elegant amenities, rich history, engaging activities and breathtaking views await your arrival at Oaks on the River Luxury Boutique Resort.
Escape to the quiet retreat of elegant suites, gourmet dining at The Oaks Club Restaurant, poolside refreshments at The Mimosa Bar & Bistro, and a massage treatment at our luxury spa. Then launch your Golden Isles adventure from this centrally-located haven with golf packages, kayak and paddle boarding adventures, historic bike tours and more.
Driven by a commitment to excellence and attention to detail, the team at Oaks is devoted to providing exceptional personalized service for the ultimate Golden Isles guest experience. Come coast with us.
205 Fort King George Dr., Darien, GA 833-550-OAKS (6257)
OAKS ON THE RIVER
LUXURY BOUTIQUE RESORT
OaksOnTheRiverResort.com

Darien River, GA

DARIEN RIVER		Largest Vessel	VHF	Total Slips	Approach/ Dockside Depth	Floating Docks	Gas/ Diesel	Repairs/ Haulout	Min/Max Amps	Pump-Out Station
1. Darien River Waterfront Park & Docks 6.0 mi. W of MM 655	(912) 437-6659		11	12	25.0 / 25.0	F			30	

Wireless Internet Access onSpot Dockside WiFi Facility
Visit www.waterwayguide.com for current rates, fuel prices, website addresses and other up-to-the-minute information.
(Information in the table is provided by the facilities.)

Scan here for more details:

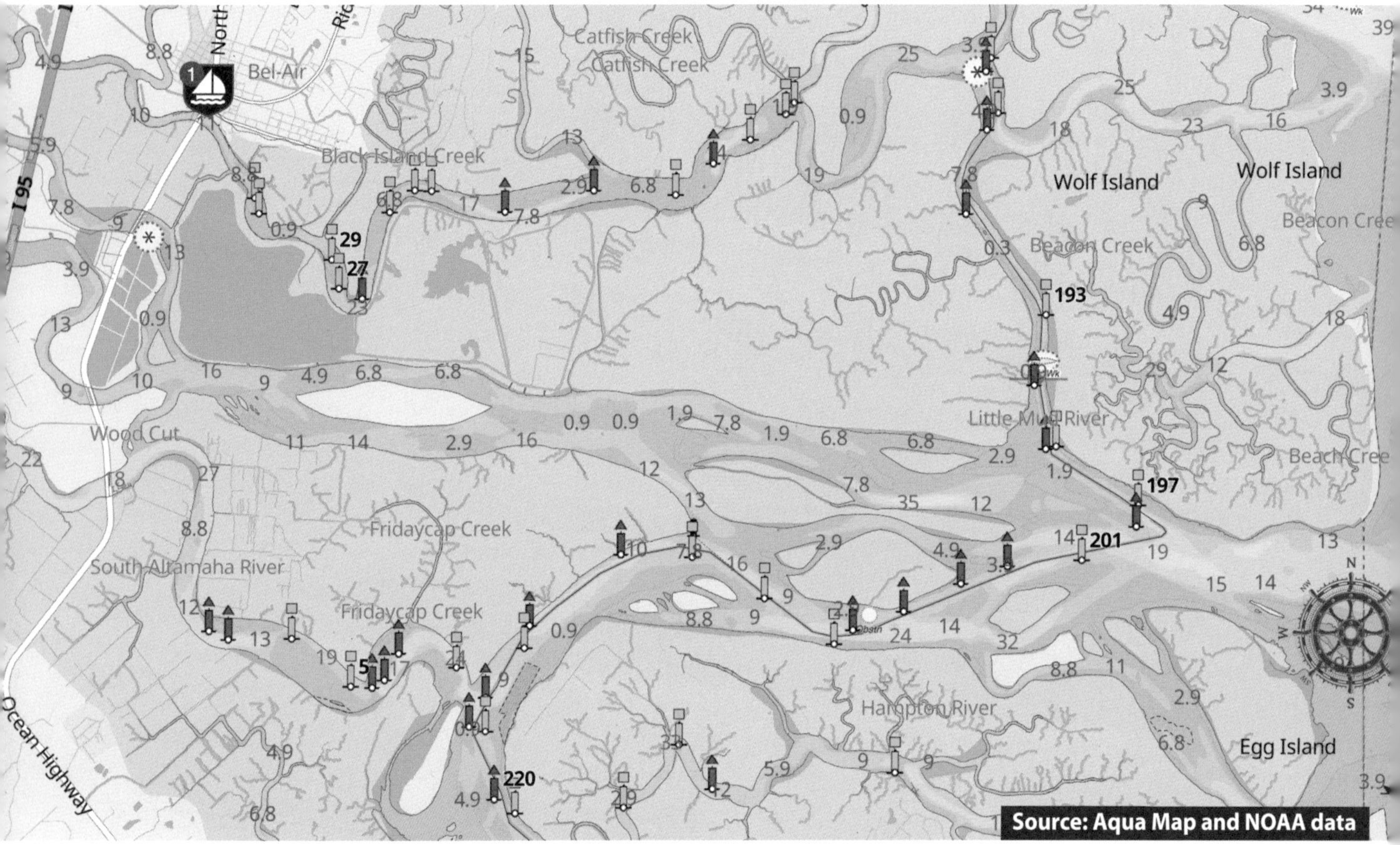

Extreme shoaling has been observed between red daybeacon "188" and green daybeacon "195" on the Little Mud River. Favor the green side, staying at least 280 feet off red daybeacon "192," 150 feet off green daybeacon "193," 200 feet off red daybeacon "194" and 50 feet off flashing green "195." See detailed route suggestions at Waterway Explorer (www.waterwayguide.com).

Boaters consistently report shallower depths than the NOAA charts/surveys show in this area. It is best to plan this transit for a rising two-thirds tide. Crosscurrents can quickly push slow vessels out of the channel when exiting narrow stretches like the Little Mud River to enter open water like Altamaha Sound.

Anchorage: If you know that the tide will be too low when you reach one of the well-known shallow areas like the Little Mud River, anchor for a while and let the tide rise before you enter. There is an anchorage on the Back River at Mile 651.3 in 8 to 11 feet MLW with good holding in sand. It provides protection from all except westerly winds. The Little Mud River at red daybeacon "182" is also a great anchorage. There is plenty of swing room and you can drop your anchor in 12 to 18 feet MLW with good holding. The current is moderate in this entire area. Local fishing boats will come by but that usually dies down around dinner time.

At Mile 653.7 the South River carries 10 to 14 feet MLW with excellent holding in mud. Across the sound you can anchor behind Dolbow Island at Mile 659 where there is 13 to 20 feet MLW and fair holding in soft mud.

Side Trip: Darien River–ICW Mile 651.6

NAVIGATION: Use NOAA Chart 11510. The Coast Guard has placed channel markers all the way to Darien, located 7 miles up the Darien River, which shrimp boats use heavily. Plan your passage for mid-tide and rising going off the ICW up the river.

Shoaling to 3-foot MLW depth has been reported between red daybeacon "12" and "14" at the intersection with Rockdedundy River and further shoaling on the west side between green daybeacons "27" and "29" of the Darien River.

Some southbound cruisers have been tempted to return to the ICW from Darien via the slightly shorter route on the Rockdedundy River. We do not recommend this route. There are no markers of any kind on the Rockdedundy River and 3-foot MLW shoaling has been observed at the bends in the river as shown on the most recent NOAA chart.

Dockage: Cruising boats making the trip up the Darien River can find dockage at Darien River Waterfront Park & Docks. Be aware that there is an 8- to 9-foot tide and a ripping current. Dockage is strictly first-come, first-served and is not free but is cheap. There is a dockmaster available most times of the day.

On the north side of the fixed **N. Walton Street Bridge** (31-foot vertical clearance) is the free dock with a 6-hour limit of use. This dock is unattended and does not offer water or electricity. The town is very welcoming to cruisers and there are amenities and restaurants within walking distance. Nearby Skipper's Fish Camp may have transient dockage (no shore power). This dock is also on a "first-come, first-served" basis. Call 912-437-3474. There is a 48-hour time limit here.

Anchorage: Overnight anchorage for boats up to about 40 feet in length can be found near green daybeacon "1" in the Darien River at Mile 651.6. There is 12 feet MLW but this anchorage may be too narrow for larger boats that need more swinging room.

Altamaha Sound to St. Simons Sound–ICW Mile 665 to Mile 676

NAVIGATION: Use NOAA Chart 11506, 11507 and 11508. The Coast Guard has removed all markers from the Altamaha Sound entrance channel to and from the Atlantic Ocean (not part of the ICW) due to shoaling. Do not attempt to use this inlet to or from the ocean. Watch for bare-land areas near the ICW channel in Altamaha Sound during extreme low tides, particularly in areas where the NOAA chart shows less than 3 feet MLW.

Specific areas of concerns begin around Mile 658 and include the following.

- Stay well off the reds from red daybeacon "204" to "206" for a minimum of 7.5 MLW.
- Stay off red daybeacon "208" by 360 feet. Many boats run aground here.
- Do not follow the Range C markers as there is shoaling at green daybeacon "211" and just to the south. Go outside the channel to the red side.

Heading south from Buttermilk Sound several sets of ranges guide you over the flats to the headwaters of the southward-flowing Mackay River. Dredging to 12 feet MLW took place in summer 2019 between from green daybeacon "217" to flashing green "223" in Buttermilk Sound and the Mackay River.

You may encounter high-speed, outboard-powered boats manned by uniformed personnel in the Althama River. You will find almost a dozen of these docked at Two Way Fish Camp, located 5 miles west of the ICW at Mile 662. They are operated by the nearby Federal Law Enforcement Training Center. This is where Customs and Border Patrol, marine patrols and other federal agents receive their boat training.

The South Althama River intercepts the ICW at Mile 662 (west side), while the Hampton River branches to the east at Mile 664. There are docking facilities up each of these rivers.

Flashing green "237" marks shallow water on the east bank. Keep red daybeacon "238" to starboard and continue along the Mackay River. The ICW turns to the west and continues down the Mackay River until it intersects with the lower end of the Frederica River and enters St. Simons Sound. Current NOAA charts show this correctly but some skippers still attempt to take the wrong

Altamaha River, GA

SOUTH ALTAMAHA RIVER		Largest Vessel	VHF	Total Slips	Approach/ Dockside Depth	Floating Docks	Gas/ Diesel	Repairs/ Haulout	Min/Max Amps	Pump-Out Station
1. Two Way Fish Camp WiFi 5.0 mi. W of MM 664.0	(912) 265-0410	70	16	110	10.0 / 15.0	F	GD	RH	30 / 50	

WiFi Wireless Internet Access onSpot Dockside WiFi Facility
Visit www.waterwayguide.com for current rates, fuel prices, website addresses and other up-to-the-minute information.
(Information in the table is provided by the facilities.)

Scan here for more details:

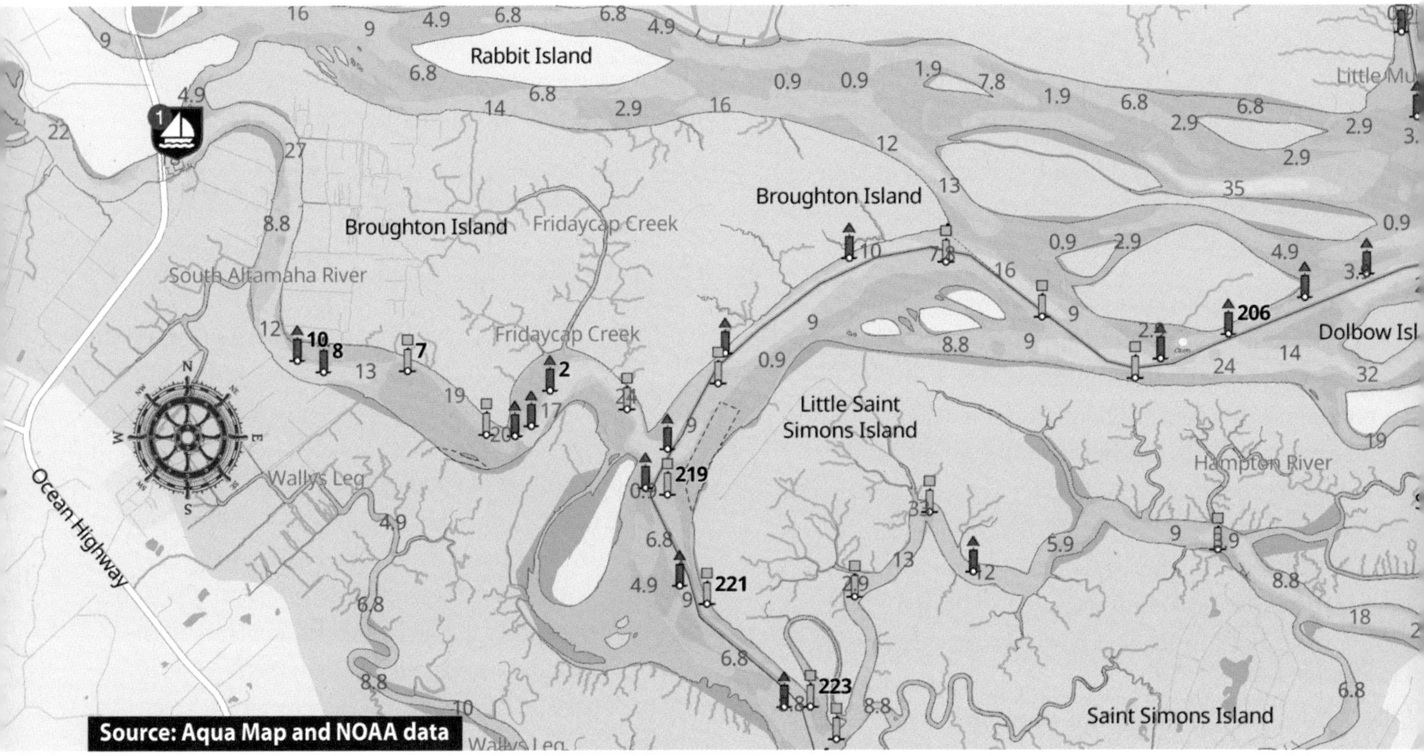

route around the eastern side of Lanier Island only to be stopped by the 9-foot fixed vertical clearance bridge over the Frederica River.

The fixed **F.J. Torras Causeway Bridge** (65-foot vertical clearance) spans the Mackay River portion of the ICW at Mile 674.5. The current under this bridge is very strong. The 5-mile stretch from Mile 673 to Mile 678 is straightforward. The only problem area is the shoal south of Lanier Island. Leave flashing green "245A" and "247" well to port when passing. Flashing green daybeacon "249" has been moved and appears to be far to the east of the ICW channel. Leave this to port as well.

Dockage: The full-service Two Way Fish Camp, located 5 miles west of the ICW at Mile 662 on the South Althama River, usually has transient space in a natural setting with friendly people. Bait, tackle and sundries are available in the Ship Store. Mudcat Charlie's Restaurant (912-261-0055) is on site offering good food at reasonable prices. The current here can be fierce. If approaching the fuel dock during times of maximum current flow, stand by until the current slackens before you approach the dock. Contact the fuel dock for instructions.

About 3 miles up the marked channel of the Hampton River at Mile 664, you will find the Hampton River Marina set amidst the naturally beautiful marsh. To reach the marina follow the Hampton River abruptly back to port at Mile 664 between flashing green "223" and "223A." Note that shoaling extends into the channel from both riverbanks up to green daybeacon "27." Proceed slowly and watch the depth sounder. Daybeacons farther downstream mark some of the shoals so pass wide of the markers. At green daybeacon "21" the chart shows a slot of 4 foot MLW but there are reports of the water being substantially deeper.

Hampton River Marina welcomes transients if space is available but caters mainly to local boaters (with slips to 40 feet). This 6-acre operation includes are wet slips, dry stack and trailer storage, boat maintenance, a Ship Store

Hampton River, GA

LITTLE ST. SIMON ISLAND	Largest Vessel	VHF	Total Slips	Approach/ Dockside Depth	Floating Docks	Gas/ Diesel	Repairs/ Haulout	Min/Max Amps	Pump-Out Station
1. Hampton River Marina WiFi 3.5 mi. E of MM 664.0 (912) 638-1210		16	20	12.0 / 14.0	F	GD	R	30 / 50	

WiFi Wireless Internet Access onSpot Dockside WiFi Facility
Visit www.waterwayguide.com for current rates, fuel prices, website addresses and other up-to-the-minute information.
(Information in the table is provided by the facilities.)
Scan here for more details:

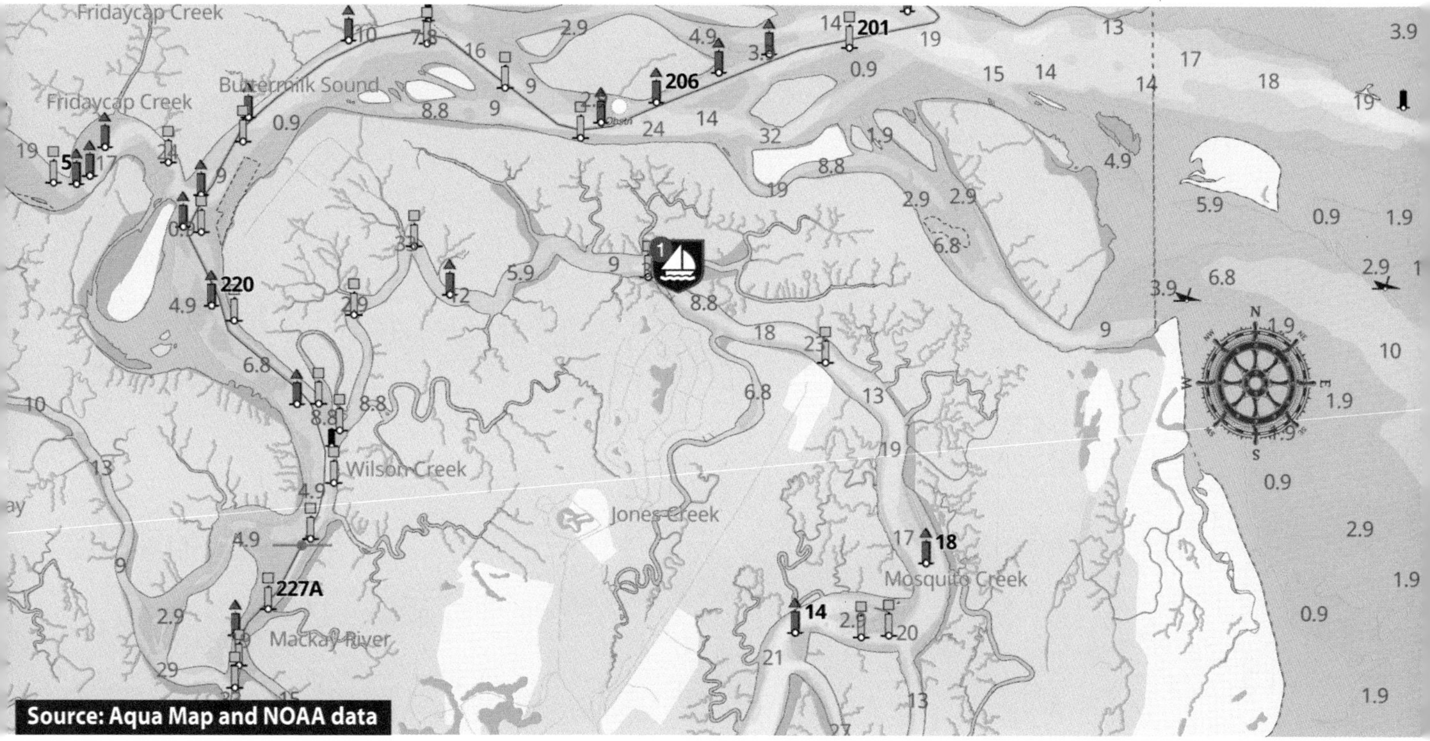

Source: Aqua Map and NOAA data

and bait. Call before making plans to stop here.

Hidden Harbor Yacht Club on Troup Creek (north of ICW Mile 670.5) has slips to 100 feet on their floating docks. Call ahead.

Anchorage: The South Altamaha River at Mile 662 is deep and well marked with a 7-foot MLW bar at the entrance near red daybeacon "218." Holding is good in 7 to 20 feet MLW with a mud bottom and is protected from all but the southeast. The anchorage is large but the current tears through it so we recommend using two anchors. A sandy beach and pine tree-covered bank is accessible by tender where the river enters the waterway.

At Mile 666.5 west off the main ICW route Wallys Leg, opens up to the west into a good anchorage but only in fair weather. Wind from the east can be annoying but if out of the west, it will blow your socks off! Enter mid-stream opposite flashing green "231" and then favor the north shore; go in slowly and use the depth sounder. Anchor in 10- to 12-foot MLW depths off the clump of trees to the north. Holding is good but the current is strong so know the state of the tide and set your anchor well. This anchorage can get crowded in season but there is room for several boats.

Alternate Route: Frederica River–ICW Mile 666

Fort Frederica National Monument preserves the archaeological remnants of a fort and town built by James Oglethorpe between 1736 and 1748 to protect the southern boundary of the British colony of Georgia from Spanish raids. About 630 British troops were stationed at the fort. A Visitor Center (with a bookstore and restrooms), a 23-minute informational movie and ranger programs make this worth a visit (912-638-3630).

NAVIGATION: Use NOAA Chart 11506. At Mile 666 and flashing green "229" the Frederica River heads off the ICW to the east. This makes for a fun side trip as you wend your way north or south along the ICW. Slightly more scenic than the ICW in this area, the Frederica River flows past St. Simons Island, rejoins the ICW farther down the Mackay River at approximately Mile 674 and then

Mackay River, GA

TROUP CREEK		Largest Vessel	VHF	Total Slips	Approach/ Dockside Depth	Floating Docks	Gas/ Diesel	Repairs/ Haulout	Min/Max Amps	Pump-Out Station
1. Hidden Harbor Yacht Club WiFi MM 670.5	(912) 261-1049	100	16	20	15.0 / 15.0	F		R	20 / 50	P

WiFi Wireless Internet Access onSpot Dockside WiFi Facility
Visit www.waterwayguide.com for current rates, fuel prices, website addresses and other up-to-the-minute information.
(Information in the table is provided by the facilities.)

Scan here for more details:

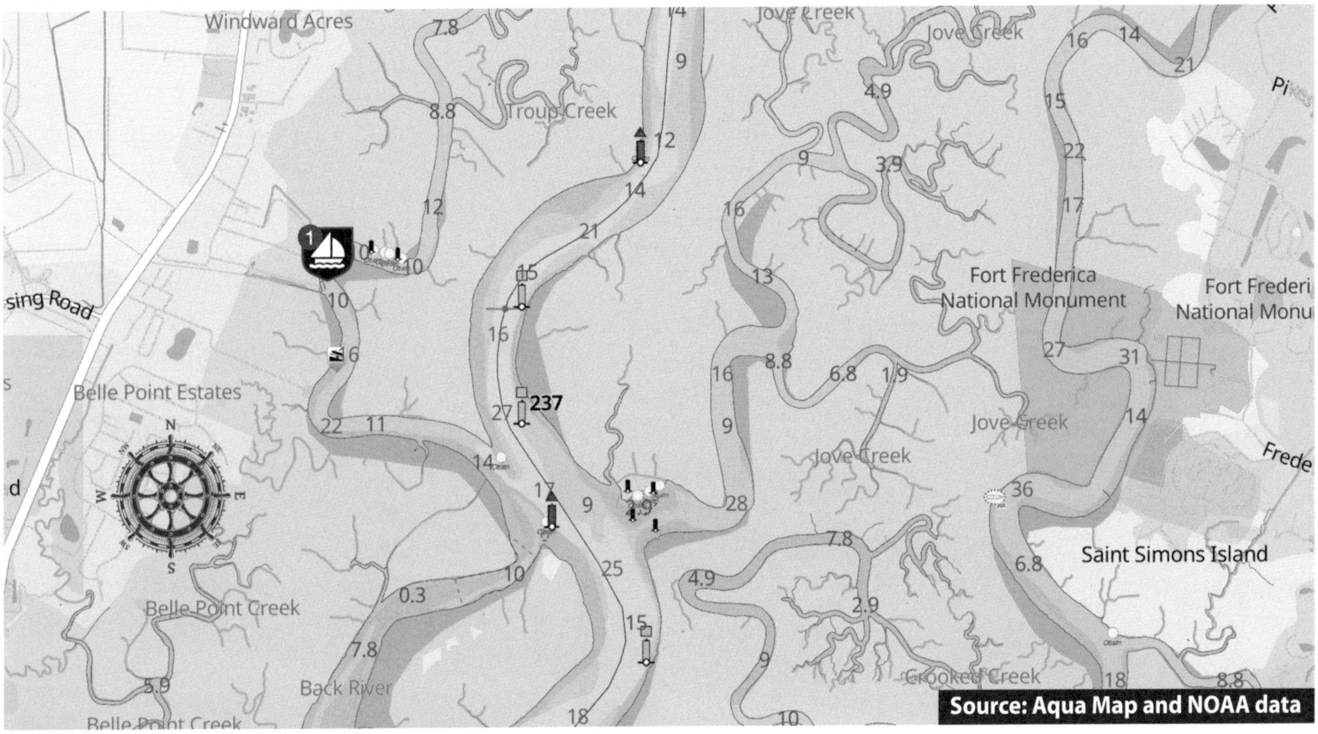

Source: Aqua Map and NOAA data

continues under the 65-foot fixed F.J. Torras Causeway Bridge (Mile 674.5).

Take care if you are entering the Frederica River with the current. A bar protrudes from below flashing green daybeacon "229" and the current seems to split here. Keep well to the north side at the entrance and don't hesitate. Do not confuse flashing green "229" (flashing every 2.5 seconds) with flashing green daybeacon "231" (flashing every 4 seconds) at the entrance to Wallys Leg. Though winding and unmarked, this slightly longer side route runs deep to the shore except at the mouth of the lower end at Manhead Sound where the water depth is 5 feet MLW midway between the two banks.

Anchorage: Many cruisers like to anchor in the Frederica River (North) off the Fort Frederica National Monument in 9 to 20 feet MLW. Visits ashore are possible at some states of the tide but be mindful that the tide can sometimes rise and fall 2 feet in an hour during the middle of the cycle. During a low tide dinghies can be left high and dry making re-entry into the water difficult, if not impossible.

St. Simons Sound to St. Andrew Sound– ICW Mile 676 to Mile 685

The "Golden Isles" area includes St. Simon Island, Sea Island, Jekyll Island, Little St. Simon Island and Brunswick. The largest of its sea islands, St. Simon Island is a draw for history buffs, golf and tennis players, nature lovers and, of course, boaters. On the island's ocean side exclusive Sea Island is home to the fashionable 5-star Cloister Hotel and beautifully landscaped residences. Golf courses are plentiful on the islands and one near the Cloister hosts a yearly PGA tournament.

The downtown district in Brunswick (on the Brunswick River) features a growing mix of antique shops, specialty shops, art galleries, theaters and restaurants. With daily shrimping excursions heading in and out of Brunswick's harbor, there is plenty of fresh, local seafood to be had at Brunswick restaurants.

Finally, Jekyll Island is a staff favorite at Waterway Guide because of its historical significance and the natural beauty of the island. It is home to one of the Rockerfeller's favorite vacation homes, the Jekyll Island Club, which to this day has an air of wealth and sophistication.

NAVIGATION: Use NOAA Chart 11506 and 11504. St. Simons Sound Entrance is the big ship entrance to Brunswick and is an all-weather inlet; nevertheless, it can be rough when the wind and current are opposed. Extra care should be taken and be sure to study the weather before venturing into the sound. Heading north you can arrive at Mile 678 at low slack water and ride the flood current up the Mackay River.

When heading up the Brunswick River in the vicinity of red flashing "20A" and "22" note that the charted sandbar to the north is a spoils island created with dredge material from a deepening of the entrance to St. Simons Sound. A rock bulkhead surrounds the island, which is highly visible in daylight; however, if you are traveling at night or in other conditions of poor visibility be sure to stay in the marked channel as the warning beacons around this island are not lit or currently charted.

This route leads in a westerly direction before turning north at flashing green "1" and heading to downtown Brunswick. Crossing the shipping channel is the **Sidney Lanier Bridge**, which carries SR 17. The suspension bridge has more than 185 feet of clearance, is visible for several miles and is one of the more scenic bridges on the ICW. The town of Brunswick is located just north of the bridge.

Heading south from St. Simons Island the ICW crosses St. Simons Sound and runs 3 miles up the Brunswick River to the mouth of Jekyll Creek (Mile 681), which flows between Jekyll Island and marshland. From there the ICW proper continues south down Jekyll Creek, which eventually flows into Jekyll Sound located farther south.

The much-needed dredging of Jekyll Creek was completed in summer 2019 from green daybeacon "3" through red flashing "20." For now passage through Jekyll Creek should not be a problem; however, this is a constantly changing area so be alert. The dredged channel is only 75 feet wide and has been moved farther east than the old channel.

The tidal range is 7 to 9 feet and the creek is greatly affected by wind tides. An east wind of 15 knots or greater will add 1 foot to the depths, while a west wind will lessen the depths by 1 foot. The channel is also affected by the tugs that pass through. Conditions are going to be variable so plan to traverse the area near high tide or at least on a rising tide.

The charted Jekyll Island Range you will use to approach Jekyll Creek has unusual characteristics. The dayboard for green daybeacon "1," located on the front structure of this set of range markers, is difficult to see northbound and confusing to line up with when southbound. A range (labeled "Jetty Range" on the chart) leads past a single stone jetty on the red side between the red daybeacons at the entrance to the creek, which is submerged at high tide. Be aware that this jetty extends from the shore all the way out to flashing red "4." Because the current sets strongly to the side be sure to follow the range until past this jetty.

Continuing south, start your turn by flashing red-green "19" about 160 feet before reaching it and pass 80 feet off. Pass flashing red "20" by 180 feet off and flashing red "20A" by 185 feet off. The channel is farther east than you might think if you just looked at the buoys. When approaching flashing green "25" at the mouth of the creek be aware that it is a short daybeacon (about 10 feet) and is difficult to see at high tide. **Jekyll Island (SR 520) Bridge** crosses the ICW at 684.4.

GOIN' ASHORE

BRUNSWICK, GA

Known as the "Gateway to the Golden Isles," the "Land of Five Flags" and the birthplace of the original Brunswick stew, Brunswick now boasts a revitalized commercial and residential historic district. The British gave the town its name from Braunsweig, Germany, the ancestral home of King George III; however, five nations have claimed this area of Georgia as t own. First, explorer Hernando de Soto raised the Spanish flag in 1540; followed by Frenchman Jean Ribault in 1562; ther the Spanish expelled the French in 1565 and ruled again until 1736, when the British flag flew until the Revolutionary W The American flag was lowered during the Civil War, replaced by the stars and bars of the Confederate flag until 1865, w the United States flag was raised once again. All these flags can be found flying at the marina.

SERVICES

1. Alnighty Urgent Care
208 Gloucester St.
(678-704-3919)

2. Brunswick-Glen County Library
208 Gloucester St.
(912-279-3740)

3. Brunswick-Golden Isles Chamber of Commerce
1505 Richmond St. (2nd Floor)
(912-265-0620)

4. Brunswick Post Office
208 Gloucester St.
(912-280-1250)

5. Golden Isles Animal Hospital
1965 Glynn Ave. #200
(912-267-6002)

SERVICES

6. Historic Ritz Theater
Built in 1899 as the Grand Opera House, the three-story ornate Victorian building at 1530 Newcastle St. is a year-round cultural center that features films (including summer classics), live theater, concerts and more. There's not a bad seat in the house (912-262-6934).

7. Lover's Oak
The old oak (said to date back to the 12th century) is located at the intersection of Albany and Prince Streets. According to local legend, Native American lovers met under the majestic spreading limbs of this enormous oak. The tree's trunk is about 13 feet in diameter and it branches into 10 limbs measuring 12 to 30 inches in diameter.

8. Mary Ross Waterfront Park
Brunswick has been a port city since the 1700s and in addition to the cargo and shrimp traffic, the J.A. Jones Company built 99 Liberty Ships in three years during World War II. The shipyard set an unbroken record in December 1944 by constructing seven ships in one month. See a scale model of the ship at 209 Gloucester St. (912-267-2600).

SHOPPING

9. Adams Meat Market
Independent market that sells produce and other groceries in addition to a full line of fresh meat and a large selection of Hispanic food (1700 Norwich St., 912-574-7506).

10. Central Hardware
Full-service independent hardware store at 1730 Norwich St. (912-265-3510).

MARINA

11. Brunswick Landing Marina
1 Torras Landing (912-262-9264)

Mary Ross Waterfront Park

St. Simons Sound Area, GA

ST. SIMONS ISLAND		Largest Vessel	VHF	Total Slips	Approach/ Dockside Depth	Floating Docks	Gas/ Diesel	Repairs/ Haulout	Min/Max Amps	Pump-Out Station
1. Morningstar Marinas Golden Isles WiFi onSpot N of MM 677.0	(912) 434-4751	200	16	137	10.0 / 18.0	F	GD	R	30 / 100	P

WiFi Wireless Internet Access onSpot Dockside WiFi Facility
Visit www.waterwayguide.com for current rates, fuel prices, website addresses and other up-to-the-minute information.
(Information in the table is provided by the facilities.)

Scan here for more details:

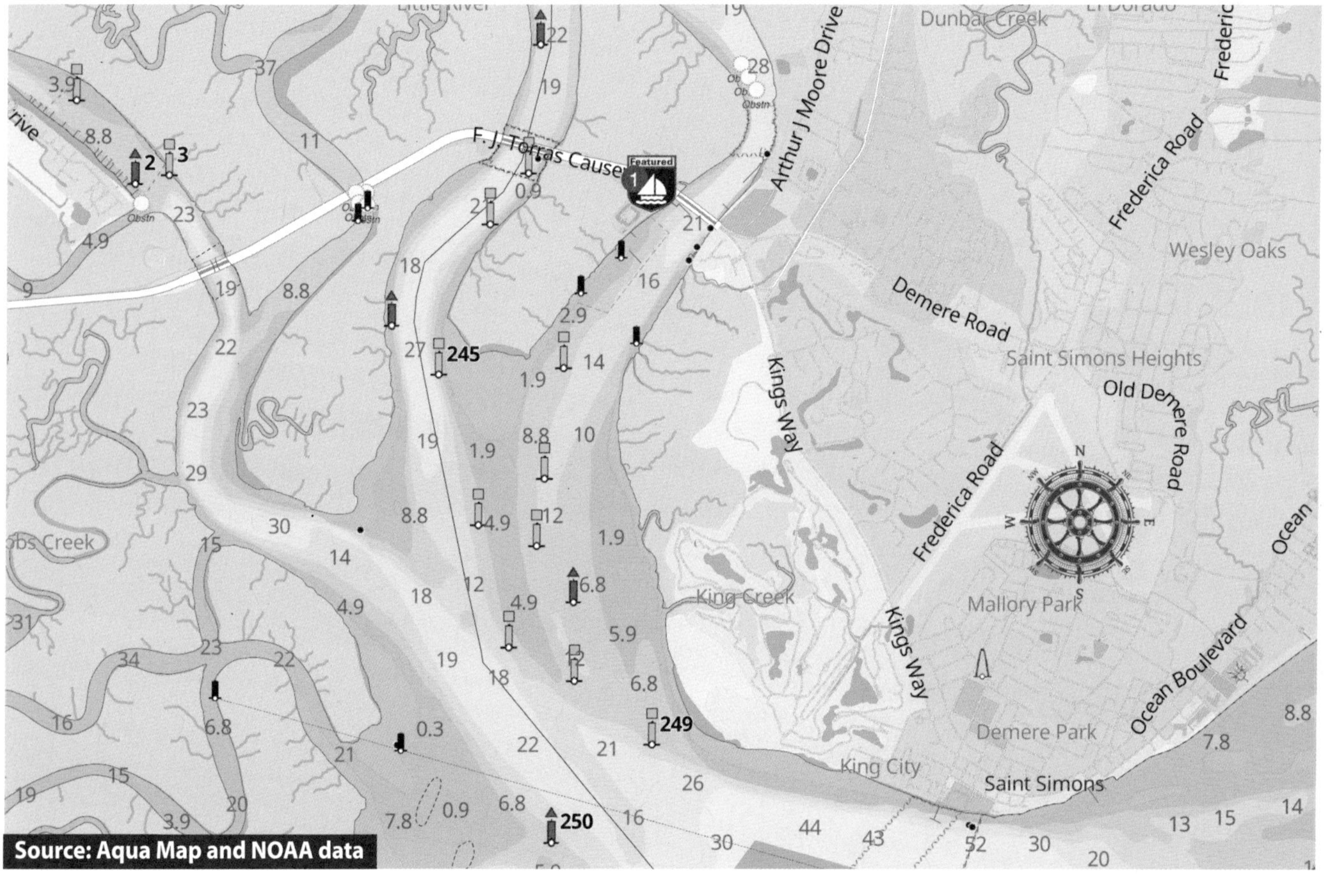

Source: Aqua Map and NOAA data

Dockage: Morningstar Marinas Golden Isles is 2 miles north of Mile 676 on the east side of Lanier Island. This facility is south of the low bridge (9-foot vertical clearance) across the Frederica River connecting Lanier Island with St. Simons Island so it must be approached from the south. When entering and exiting the marked channel to Morningstar Marinas Golden Isles, follow the chart carefully and do not confuse these channel markers with the ICW markers nearby. The markers have recently been reconfigured and may differ from what is shown on your NOAA chart.

Morningstar Marinas Golden Isles offers ample amenities including a courtesy car, pool, laundry facilities, fully-stocked Ship Store and concierge service. They also offer complimentary breakfast pastries and newspapers. On site are charter fishing, a dive shop, boat brokers and a restaurant. The marina provides immediate access to historic St. Simons Island located just over the bridge. The configuration of the docks eases current issues, although there is still a strong current running parallel to the docks so be sure you have fenders rigged before you come alongside.

In a hurricane hole off the Brunswick River, the 20-acre Brunswick Landing Marina, Inc. is in the center of Brunswick's Historic District. Head north at flashing green "1" then follow the Brunswick Harbor range markers to the marina just beyond the shrimp boat docks. This marina is protected from all directions and has little current making maneuvering easy. The marina's boatyard and lift are north of the transient facilities.

ICW
Morningstar Marinas
Golden Isles
Lanier Island
Frederica River

St. Simons Sound Area, GA

BRUNSWICK		Largest Vessel	VHF	Total Slips	Approach/ Dockside Depth	Floating Docks	Gas/ Diesel	Repairs/ Haulout	Min/Max Amps	Pump-Out Station
1. Brunswick Landing Marina, Inc. WiFi onSpot NW of MM 680.0	(912) 262-9264	250	16	347	36.0 / 12.0	F	GD	RH	30 / 100	P

WiFi Wireless Internet Access onSpot Dockside WiFi Facility
Visit www.waterwayguide.com for current rates, fuel prices, website addresses and other up-to-the-minute information.
(Information in the table is provided by the facilities.)

Scan here for more details:

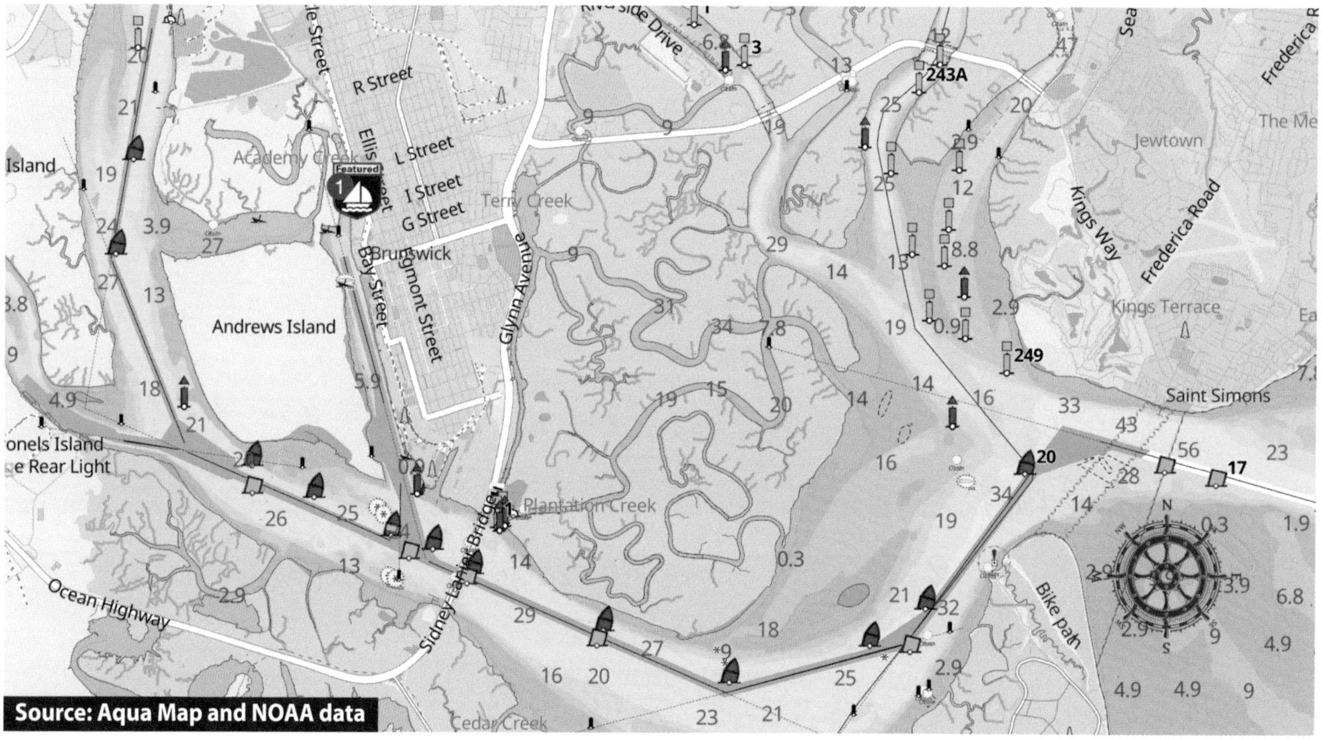

Jekyll Harbor Marina is on the south side of the high-rise Jekyll Island (SR 520) Bridge. This is the last marina before St. Marys so be sure to fuel up and provision if necessary. Fuel will not be available again until Fernandina Beach at about Mile 716. This service-oriented facility has slips for vessels to 120 feet and offers loaner bikes and golf carts. A grocery, package store, bank, Post Office and such are a 20-minute bike ride. The historic district is 10 minutes away.

Anchorage: Just slightly below Morningstar Marinas Golden Isles, south of the 9-foot fixed vertical clearance bridge, the Coast Guard has established a special anchorage area in 10 to 14 feet MLW at Lanier Island. Yachts measuring 65 feet or less are not required to show anchor lights in the area but it is a good idea to do so anyway. The bottom is hard in some places and it is difficult to get the anchor set. Pick a spot clear of the few (private) moorings and be mindful of the current. Wakes can be a problem at the outer end of the anchorage near green daybeacon "7." Morningstar Marinas Golden Isles provides dinghy dockage for a modest fee.

Southwest of Jekyll Harbor Marina, drop your anchor for at least 7 feet MLW north of red daybeacon "24." You can land the dinghy at the marina for a daily fee and have access to their many amenities. This is perfect for taking your dog to shore or just for getting out and stretching your legs.

Parts of the Jekyll Sound area are subject to anchoring restrictions. Be sure to check Georgia DNR online before dropping the hook. "Anchoring Permits" are required if you plan to anchor in one place for more than 14 days in a year. ("One place" is defined by a circle of 1 mile radius.) "Anchoring Restriction Areas" apply to overnight anchoring in these areas:

- Within 300 feet of a marina
- Within 150 feet of a marine structure (such as a private dock)
- Within 500 feet of an approved shellfish area

BRUNSWICK
LANDING MARINA
A TORRAS COMPANY
No Liveaboard Fees
Hurricane Hole
Large Cruiser Community
Daily Activities
Downtown Location
Cheap Fuel
CALL US TO
RESERVE YOUR SLIP!
Brunswick Landing Marina, Inc.
(912) 262 9264
info@brunswicklandingmarina.com

Brunswick

St. Simons Sound Area, GA

JEKYLL ISLAND		Largest Vessel	VHF	Total Slips	Approach/ Dockside Depth	Floating Docks	Gas/ Diesel	Repairs/ Haulout	Min/Max Amps	Pump-Out Station
1. Jekyll Harbor Marina (WiFi) MM 684.5	(912) 635-3137	120	16	49	12.0 / 10.0	F	GD		30 / 100	P

(WiFi) Wireless Internet Access onSpot Dockside WiFi Facility
Visit www.waterwayguide.com for current rates, fuel prices, website addresses and other up-to-the-minute information.
(Information in the table is provided by the facilities.)

Scan here for more details:

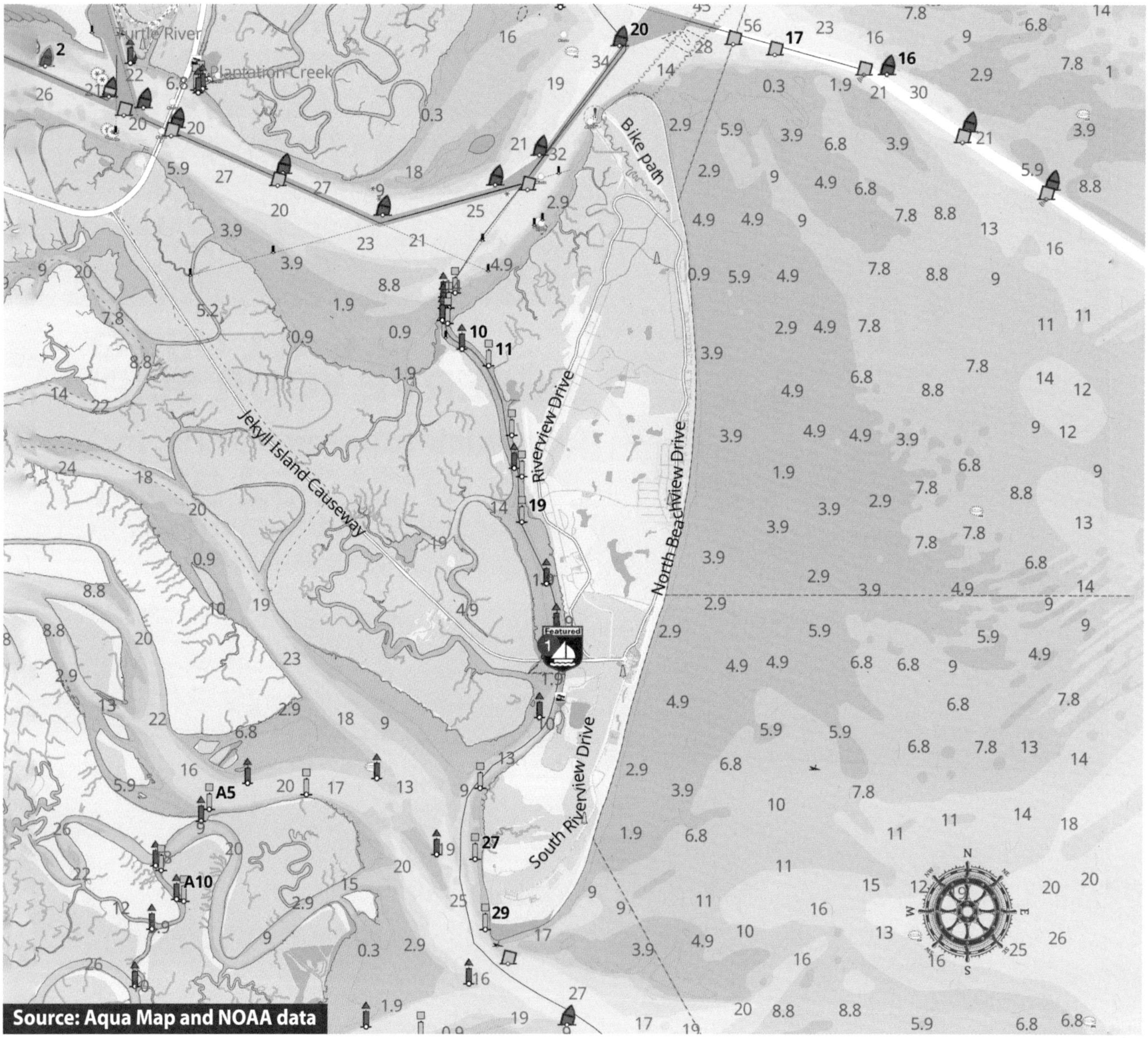

Source: Aqua Map and NOAA data

■ TO ST. MARYS, GA

St. Andrew Sound to Cumberland Sound–ICW Mile 685 to Mile 705

The ICW route at the mouth of St. Andrew Sound just north of Cumberland Island marks the closest spot to the ocean on the ICW south of Norfolk, VA. Look to the northwest and you will be looking back at the ocean side of Jekyll Island.

NAVIGATION: Use NOAA Chart 11503 and 11504. The ICW route becomes progressively more complicated as it approaches the Cumberland Dividings Channel and Cumberland Sound. This whole route is subject to shoaling (including St. Andre Sound inlet), which is why many cruisers opt to jump outside at the preferred St. Simons Sound Entrance, just a few miles to the north.

Exercise extreme caution in this area. Study the NOAA charts for this area carefully before transiting this area. Markers in the sound can be hard to spot from a distance and may be off station.

The ICW passage crosses St. Andrew Sound south of Jekyll Island. A stiff onshore wind running against the current can make the short passage across very wet and uncomfortable. As always, the seas will be calmest when the wind and current are in the same direction.

After transiting Jekyll Creek, give a wide berth to Jekyll Point. Green can "29A" marks the end of a shoal in the seaward part of St. Andrew Sound; this point continues to build out. You can see the remains of a sunken shrimp boat at low tide close inshore of flashing green "29." Set your course for flashing red "32," the more easterly of two red lighted buoys far out in the sound. If timed correctly, you will have a fair current on the ICW from about Mile 685 to a little past Mile 700. Otherwise, the current will be going with you in one direction and against you when you make the turn at red flashing buoy "32" (Mile 689) with seas behaving accordingly.

Flashing green "31" marks the breakers to the northwest of flashing red "32." This area of shallow water and breakers is marked by the two green floating aids,("31" and "31A") but is slowly building southward and the strip of deep water marked by flashing red "32" has narrowed. Inside the flashing red "30" and "32" the bottom not only shoals but also shelters the sunken remains of old wrecks. A shoal has built out approximately 150 feet east of red buoy "32."

Once you round flashing red buoy "32" you can safely head into the wide entrance of the Cumberland River and southward down the ICW. Heading south into the Cumberland River you will pass two markers at the northern tip of Little Cumberland Island: flashing green "33" on the northern tip and green daybeacon "33A" just beyond.

Even though there is a large house visible on the St. Andrew Sound shore of Little Cumberland Island, a sign on the island warn against any landings as this is a wildlife sanctuary.

Favor the green side of the channel for 10 feet MLW and proceed with extreme caution from green daybeacon "59A" to just south of flashing red daybeacon "60A." Stay at least 200 feet off the reds. Boats go aground here by getting too close to flashing red daybeacons "60" and "60A."

At Mile 703 the deep but unmarked Brickhill River joins the ICW route above Cumberland Sound at flashing red "60A." Note that markers are frequently missing in this area and the entire area is subject to shoaling. Enter the Brickhill River slowly and watch the depth sounder.

Anchorage: There are many options for anchoring along this route. On the Cumberland River in the bight just east of flashing green "37" at Mile 693 you will find a fair-weather anchorage protected only from east and southeast winds. Avoid the shoal marked by flashing green daybeacon "37" and drop the hook in about 10 feet MLW. This anchorage is away from the Cumberland River traffic but gets uncomfortable with wind from any direction except east.

On the Brickhill River, 1.5 miles northeast of the ICW, you can anchor in 9 to 20 feet MLW just north of the Plum Orchard Plantation dock on Cumberland Island. Plum Orchard Plantation (Cumberland Island), one of the Carnegie family estates, was built in 1898. Dinghy ashore and you will be rewarded with a walk among huge live oaks draped with Spanish moss and a view of the well-preserved mansion. If you are fortunate, you may encounter a family of wild horses grazing on the

GOIN' ASHORE

JEKYLL ISLAND, GA

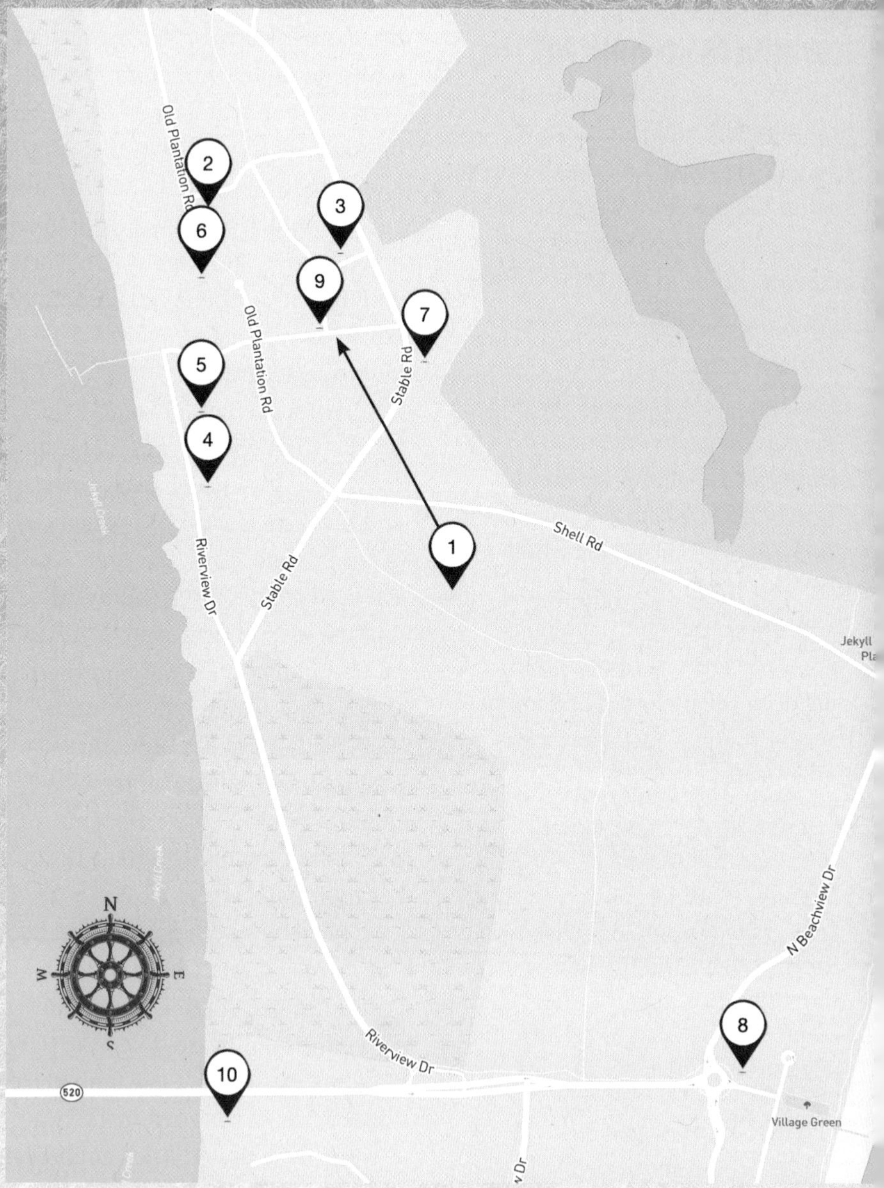

From early settlers to America's social elite to today's young explorers, the story of this Georgia barrier island has captured imaginations for generations. Strolling along the wide, cabbage palm and oak-lined streets is a pleasant way to check out the Colonial, antebellum and Victorian homes, several of which are now inns. The best way to explore Jekyll Island is by bicycle, electric car or trolley. Well-marked paths lead to majestic forests, saltwater marshes, wide-open beaches, historic ruins and opulent cottages.

SERVICES

1. Jekyll Island Post Office
17 Pier Rd. (912-635-2625)

ATTRACTIONS

2. Faith Chapel
The charming circa 1904 church at 375 Riverview Dr. features whimsical animal carvings, terra cotta gargoyles, and Tiffany and Armstrong stained glass windows. Open daily, 8:00 a.m. to 10:00 a.m. for contemplation or take a tour (included with purchase of museum tour or tickets sold separately) daily from 10:00 a.m. to 4:00 p.m.

3. Georgia Sea Turtle Center
Located at 214 Stable Rd. this educational center serves as a hospital for ill and injured sea turtles with interactive exhibits and experiences. Open daily from 9:00 a.m. to 5:00 p.m. Call ahead for admission fee (912-635-4444).

4. Goodyear Cottage
This white stucco home (circa 1906) on Riverview Dr. is now used as a Center for Creative Arts, housing both the Jekyll Island Art Association and the Jekyll Island Pottery Guild. Exhibits change monthly.

5. Indian Mound Cottage
William and Almira Rockefeller's spacious vacation home is named for the on-site Indian burial mound on Riverview Dr. Daily tours are offered of the house and historic artifacts on the hour (10:00 a.m. to 4:00 p.m.).

6. Jekyll Island Club Resort
Established as a retreat for wealthy families in 1888, the castle-like resort includes five buildings at 371 Riverview Dr. (888-445-3179).

7. Jekyll Island Museum
Housed in a former stable, guests will find exhibits, a gift shop and tour opportunities at 100 Stable Rd. (912-635-4036). Open daily from 9:00 a.m. to 5:00 p.m.

SHOPPING

8. Jekyll Market
Gourmet grocery store with fresh meats and produce, a large selection of beer and wine, plus a coffee shop and bakery, a sweet shop, a deli and a gift shop at 11 Main St. (912-635-2253).

9. Pier Road Shops/The Commissary
The Pier Road Shops include gift, art and clothing shops, including the Commissary (24 Pier Rd., 912-635-2878), a treasure trove of Georgia food products–jams, jellies, sauces and Georgia peach and Vidalia onion items–plus regional cookbooks.

MARINA

10. Jekyll Harbor Marina
1 Harbor Rd. (912-635-3137)

Jekyll Island Club Resort

lawn or alligators swimming in the anchorage. (No swimming!)

South of the Brickhill River you can anchor in the Crooked River west of the ICW with charted depths of 8 to 13 feet MLW at Mile 703.8. Here you will find soft mud so anchor accordingly. Another option is nearby Delaroche Creek at Mile 702.

Side Trip: Cumberland Island

Cumberland Island, behind which the ICW winds for more than 20 miles, was once the center of controversy over development plans. It achieved its protected status as a National Seashore decades ago, ensuring that most of the island will remain in its primitive state. No road or causeway from the mainland will ever be constructed. Public land acquisition continues today and the federal government owns approximately 85 percent of the island. Most visitors arrive via ferry service from St. Marys, a 45-minute trip. However you arrive, you will find is 50 miles of maritime forest trails, undeveloped beaches, wide marshes and more than 150 wild horses that have survived here in the wild since the Spanish originally set them free. Dungeness, ruins of the Carnegie family mansion, is a good spot for viewing some of the horses roaming freely.

> You will need insect repellent on Cumberland Island in the spring, summer and fall.

Dockage: Limited daytime dockage is available at the National Park Service's Sea Camp Dock and Visitor Center. Head east near Mile 711 in the vicinity of flashing red "34" and then proceed north along the shore of Cumberland Island following the eastern branch

Dungeness Ruins on Cumberland Island

of Cumberland Sound about 1.25 miles to the Sea Camp Dock and Visitor Center. The ferry from St. Marys occupies the major portion of the dock and the National Park Service boats take most of the inside section. That leaves room for dinghies on the outside docking area aft of the ferry. There is more space after hours. There are no power or water hookups but this is an excellent base from which to explore the island.

It is an easy 0.50-mile hike east to the beach and a little more than 1 mile south to the ruins of Dungeness. (Private boats may not dock at the National Park Service's Dungeness dock.) The privately-owned Greyfield Inn may have limited dockage available for its overnight guests (904-261-6408). The circa 1900 estate is now an upscale all-inclusive inn. It is mostly accessed by a private ferry from Fernandina Beach.

Anchorage: You can anchor near the Sea Camp Dock and Visitor Center where holding is good in 10 to 22 feet MLW. Mind the 7- to 9-foot tides and consider the effects of reversing current in the narrow channel. There is a long southwest exposure here and this Cumberland Island anchorage can become uncomfortable in wind-against-tide situations. The anchorage is often very crowded during warm weekends and during spring and fall transient seasons. You can dinghy into the Sea Camp Dock and go ashore while waiting for weather to make passage from the St. Marys River Entrance.

Parts of the Cumberland River and its tributaries are subject to anchoring restrictions. Be sure to check Georgia DNR online before dropping the hook. "Anchoring Permits" are required if you plan to anchor in one place for more than 14 days in a year. ("One place" is defined by a circle of 1 mile radius.) "Anchoring Restriction Areas" apply to overnight anchoring in these areas:

- Within 300 feet of a marina
- Within 150 feet of a marine structure (such as a private dock)
- Within 500 feet of an approved shellfish area

Alternate Route: Umbrella, Dover and Floyd Creeks–ICW Mile 685 to Mile 705

NAVIGATION: Use NOAA Chart 11489. If you want to avoid St. Andrew Sound and the Cumberland River, a 15-mile-long alternate, foul-weather route avoids the direct crossing. This shallow route, via Umbrella, Dover and Floyd Creeks, is charted and reasonably easy to run. It will add approximately 5 miles to the ICW route and there are some very shallow spots. Shallow-draft vessels may attempt this route but only on a rising tide.

A set of markers leads across Jekyll Sound at Mile 685 and into the Little Satilla River, where you can enter Umbrella Creek via the land cut at flashing green "A5." Enter Umbrella Cut dead on its centerline instead of trying to line up with the two markers. During strong northeast winds, high water makes it more difficult to navigate by obscuring much of the marsh grass along the shores of Umbrella Creek.

Depths of less than 1 foot MLW have been reported in Umbrella Creek between red daybeacon "A8" and flashing red "A11" to Dover Cut. The tidal range here is 8 feet MLW or better. Run this route on a rising tide or high tide.

A second area that deserves extra attention is Dover Cut, connecting Umbrella Creek with Dover Creek. The cut is narrow and winding with 8-foot MLW charted depths. Continuing along this alternate route a straight land cut connects Dover Creek to the Satilla River, which is easily followed for 1.75 miles to the entrance of Floyd Creek, the next section of the alternate route. The next shoal area to watch for is at the junction of Floyd Creek and Floyd Basin from green daybeacon "A21" to just past green daybeacon "A31" with a charted controlling depth of 8.5 feet MLW. From here on it is smooth sailing out to red daybeacon "40" in the center of the Cumberland River and back on the ICW at Mile 696.

Anchorage: Umbrella Creek offers 10 to 15 feet MLW and protection from all but northeast winds. Floyd Creek to the south is deep (17-plus feet MLW) but nighttime commercial shrimp boat traffic makes it a less desirable anchorage.

Cumberland Sound to St. Marys River–ICW Mile 705 to Mile 716

The ferry that takes visitors to Cumberland Island leaves from St. Marys. You can buy tickets at the Cumberland Island Visitor Center (912-882-4336). The ferry makes several trips a day from the waterfront and runs daily March through November. December through February finds a reduced schedule of Thursday through Monday. See more in "Goin' Ashore: St. Marys, GA" in this chapter.

St. Marys is a "cruiser friendly" location. There is even a "Cruisers Net" at 8:00 a.m. daily on VHF Channel 68. During the net you can get information about town activities and announcements along with help, if needed, and also make arrangements for transportation.

NAVIGATION: Use NOAA Charts 11503. (Be sure to use the latest edition of NOAA Chart 11503, as many marks have been renumbered.) The Cumberland Sound Range starts at Mile 705. Take time here to sort out the mosaic of lights, markers and ranges now serving the huge government installation on Kings Bay at Mile 708. This stretch is well marked and sufficiently deep but watch the depth sounder. Shoaling also exists near the range markers northwest of Drum Point Island.

Here, the green markers will be left to starboard southbound out of Cumberland Sound to the Florida line until you pick up quick-flashing green buoy "1" in the Amelia River near Mile 715.

When passing from Cumberland Dividings into Cumberland Sound, there is a tricky spot in the ICW channel just south of green daybeacon "75" (Mile 707.8 just east of Kings Bay). Heading south, alter course westward to favor red daybeacon "76," leaving it close to starboard and then continue south in the channel, avoiding the charted 4- to 5-foot-deep shoal to starboard. Be sure to leave green daybeacon "79" well to port heading south.

GOIN' ASHORE

ST. MARYS, GA

St. Marys is one of the oldest cities in the United States. It sits aside the St. Marys River, looking the part of a fishing village with a dash of charm–lovely Victorian homes, inns, restaurants and shops. The "Gateway to Cumberland Island" is quickly growing, in large part because of nearby Kings Bay Submarine Base. Strolling along the wide, cabbage palm and oak-lined streets is a pleasant way to check out the Colonial, antebellum and Victorian homes, several of which are now inns.

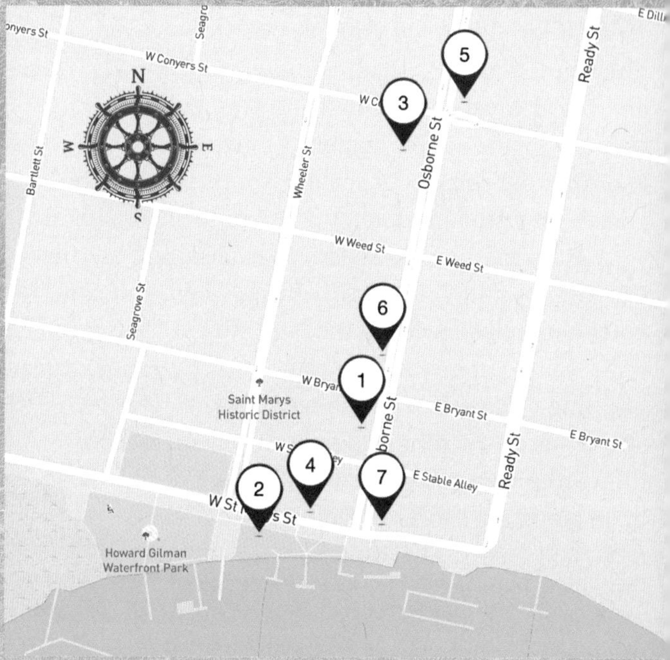

ATTRACTIONS

1. **Cumberland Island National Seashore Museum**
Opened in 2001 to house a collection of artifacts at 129 Osborne St. (912-882-4335). Exhibits include a Native American Indian canoe, pottery and arrowheads, as well as old black-and-white photos of people who lived on the island in the late 1800s and early 1900s.

2. **Cumberland Island Visitor Center**
Departure point for the ferry to Cumberland Island (113 St. Marys St., 912-882-4336). The ferry makes several trips a day from the waterfront daily March through November. You can explore the ruins of Dungeness, the old Carnegie Estate, where you may see wild horses roaming the grounds.

3. **Orange Hall House Museum**
The circa 1830-38 house is an architectural showcase of Greek Revival style. It was named for a large sour-orange grove behind the house at 311 Osborne St. (912-576-3644).

4. **St. Marys Submarine Museum**
Learn everything you ever wanted to know about submarines and check out a working periscope at 102 W. St. Marys St. (912-882-2782).

5. **St. Marys Welcome Center**
Located at 400 Osborne St. (800-868-8687). Also home to the Georgia Radio Museum (free admission).

SHOPPING

6. **Once Upon a Bookseller**
Bookstore with all types of books, gifts and nautical charts (207 Osborne St., 912-882-7350).

7. **The Market on the Square**
This old-fashioned general store at 100 Osborne St. (912-882-2215) sells sundries and souvenirs plus gift baskets and sweets. Pick up a sack lunch for trips to Cumberland Island or the nearby waterfront park.

St. Marys River, GA

NORTH RIVER		Largest Vessel	VHF	Total Slips	Approach/ Dockside Depth	Floating Docks	Gas/ Diesel	Repairs/ Haulout	Min/Max Amps	Pump-Out Station
1. St. Marys Boat Services WiFi	(904) 219-2869	65			5.0 / 5.0			RH	30	

WiFi Wireless Internet Access onSpot Dockside WiFi Facility
Visit www.waterwayguide.com for current rates, fuel prices, website addresses and other up-to-the-minute information.
(Information in the table is provided by the facilities.)

Scan here for more details:

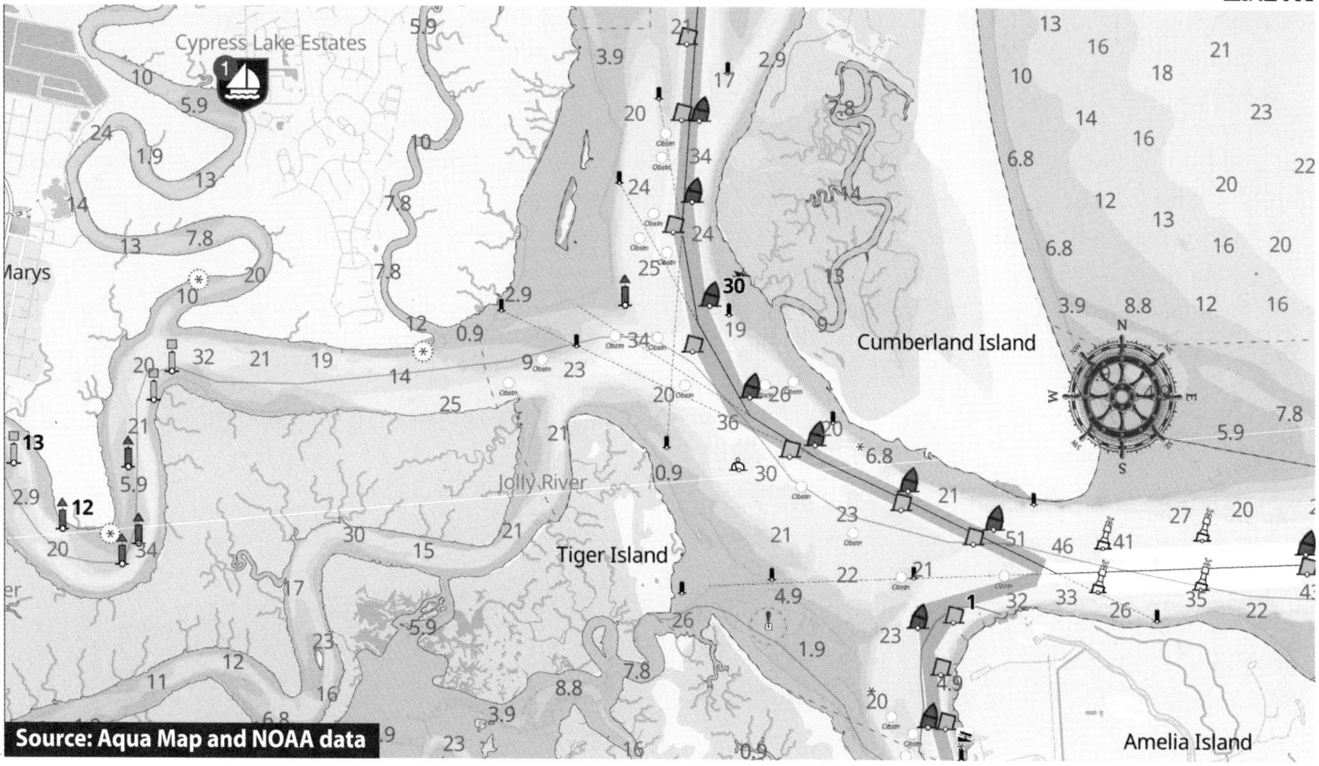

The ICW fronts the Kings Bay Naval Submarine Base near Mile 708 and Navy security patrols carefully monitor traffic from both directions, especially when submarines are passing through Cumberland Sound and the St. Marys River Entrance. Kings Bay and the area west of the ICW channel here are strictly off limits to cruising skippers. No-Wake Zones have been established in this vicinity and are strictly enforced. The patrol boats will ask you to move outside of the ICW channel if a submarine is in the vicinity and there is plenty of water off of the main channel. Patrol boats respond on VHF Channel 16. The submarines travel at high speeds in open water creating very large wakes.

The active Kings Bay Naval Submarine Base continues to be the reason for the frequent dredging and renumbering of buoys, beginning where the ICW joins the head of Cumberland Sound and continuing to the ocean inlet. Older charts may not show this change. Remember, the ICW daybeacons all have a yellow square or yellow triangle to designate them as ICW markers.

St. Marys River Entrance at Mile 714 is a relatively easy entry and exit point conveniently located just off the ICW. The inlet is deep, wide and jettied but exercise caution when going through as there are some shoal sections to the north of the channel inside the jetties. The St. Marys River Entrance channel buoys offshore of the entrance were eliminated several years ago. The current in this inlet is very strong and dictates appropriate boat handling to compensate. Slower boats are well advised to time their passages for slack water or a favorable tide.

The charted and well marked St. Marys River enters Cumberland Sound from the west. Favor the center of the river and take flashing green "3" wide to starboard. Follow the markers to avoid extensive shoaling of the west bank from red daybeacon "6" to flashing red "10." An unmarked red nun buoy is between red daybeacons "6" and "8" to mark the shoal encroaching the channel from the west bank. Temporary (uncharted) red nun buoy "6A" has been added to assist with navigation.

If you are on a northerly leg to St. Simons Island, you can cut out the meandering shallows found in Cumberland Sound and Jekyll Creek. Both the St. Johns Entrance Channel and the St. Simons Inlet involve long entry channels and strong currents to return to the ICW so be careful and try to plan exits and entries with a slack current or fair tide.

Dockage: St. Marys Day Dock has been completely rebuilt after being closed for several years due to hurricane damage. The east floating docks are ADA accessible and can be used for loading and unloading equipment and the west floating docks will accommodate a few 35-foot vessels for a 6-hour period. Overnight dockage is not allowed. The docks accommodate a wet and dry kayak launch protected from the current.

The full-service St. Marys Boat Services on the North River offers boat repairs of all kinds. They allow DIY repairs or can provide contract professionals to assist you. They report 5-foot approach and dockside depths. Call ahead.

Anchorage: There is a substantial anchorage area in front of St. Marys with 8- to 13-foot MLW depths. Tidal currents run swiftly here so keep that in mind when dropping anchor and be sure to set your anchor well.

NEXT STOP

The short 20-nm offshore jump from here to the St. Johns River at Mayport (near Jacksonville) or to the inlet at St. Augustine bypasses the sometimes shallow, shifting channels at Nassau Sound. If you do this, however, you will miss Fernandina Beach at Mile 716.5, the next town to the south on the ICW.

Waterway Guide's Southern edition will get you from Fernandina Beach to the Florida Keys, where you can set off for the islands (and switch to the Bahamas edition of the Waterway Guide), or continue on to Tampa and then the Big Bend to Mobile, AL, on the Gulf Coast (covered in Waterway Guide's Western Gulf edition).

Marina/Sponsor Index

Sponsors are listed in **BOLD**

J

L

M

N

O

P

V

W

Y

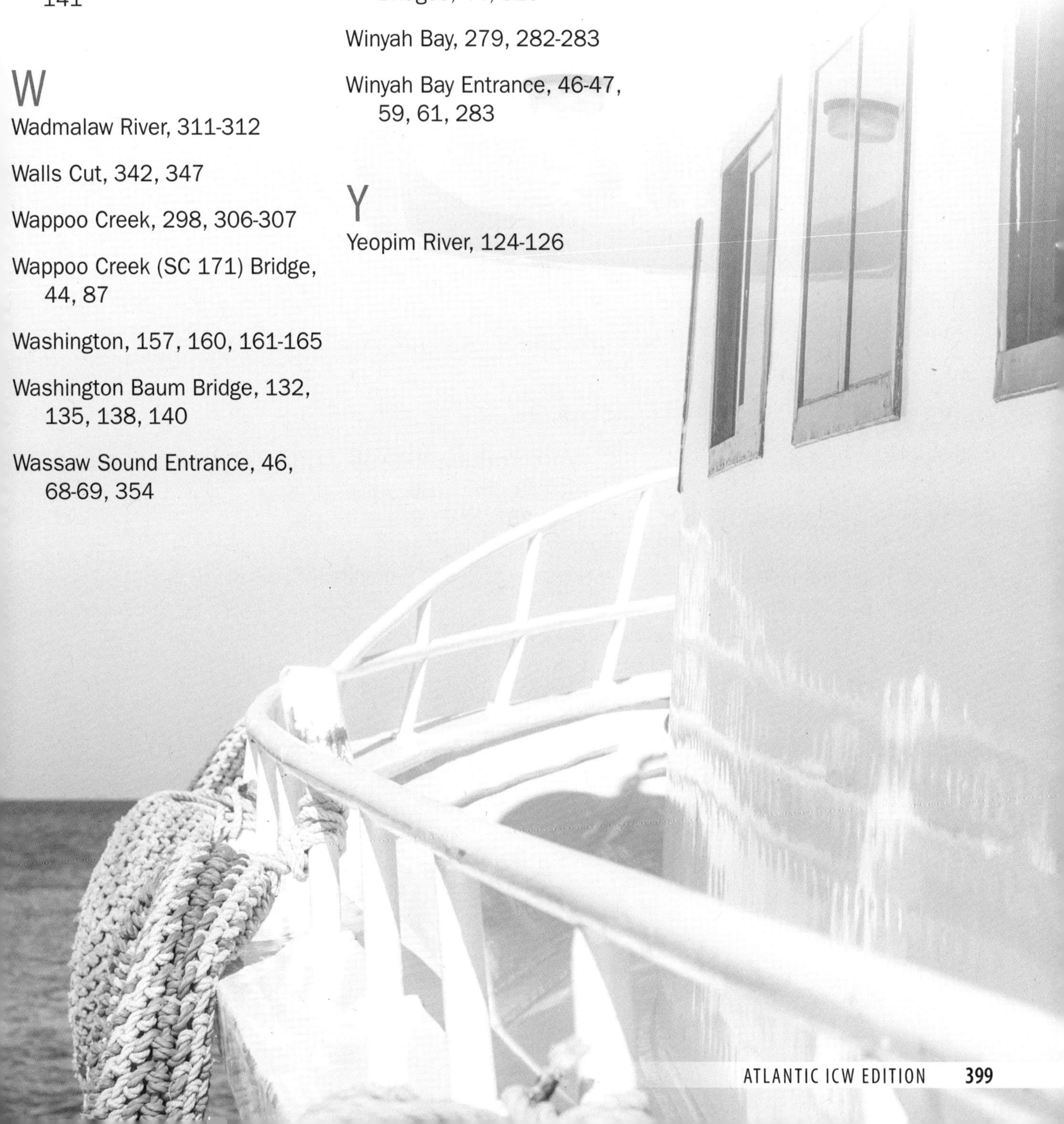

Goin' Ashore Index

Inlets Index